Nation and Society

Readings in Post-Confederation Canadian History

Margaret Conrad
University of New Brunswick

Alvin Finkel
Athabasca University

PEARSON
Longman
Toronto

National Library of Canada Cataloguing in Publication

Nation and society : readings in post-confederation Canadian history / Margaret Conrad, Alvin Finkel, [editors].

Includes bibliographical references and index.
ISBN 0-201-74379-5

1. Canada—History—1867– I. Conrad, Margaret II. Finkel, Alvin, 1949–

FC500.N38 2004   971.05   C2003-901396-0
F1033.N38 2004

ISBN 0-201-74379-5

Vice President, Editorial Director: Michael J. Young
Acquisitions Editor: Christine Cozens
Marketing Manager: Ryan St. Peters
Developmental Editor: Adrienne Shiffman
Production Editor: Richard di Santo
Copy Editor: David Handelsman
Proofreader: Emmanuelle Dauplay
Production Coordinator: Patricia Ciardullo
Page Layout: Heidi Palfrey
Literary Research: Lisa Brant
Photo Research: Amanda McCormick
Art Director: Mary Opper
Cover Design and Interior Design: Michelle Bellemare
Cover Images: Top-left: Office of Elijah Harper; top-centre-left: Glenbow Archives, ND-3-6850b; top-centre: Provincial Archives of Alberta, A-010688; middle-left: National Archives of Canada/PA142540; bottom-left: Black Cultural Centre for Nova Scotia; background: National Archives of Canada/MIKAN 99947

7 8 9 DPC 11 10 09

Printed and bound in Canada.

PEARSON
Longman

Contents

PART V   Post-Modern Canada   453

Index   517

List of Sources

PART I

Peter G. Goheen, "Order of Procession, D'Arcy McGee Funeral, 1868," *Historical Atlas of Canada*, Volume II (Toronto: University of Toronto Press, 1987), Plate 58. 1 page.

D.N. Sprague, "Dispossession vs. Accommodation in Plaintiff vs. Defendant Accounts of Métis Dispersal from Manitoba, 1870–1881," *Prairie Forum* 16, 2 (Fall 1991): 137–56.

Sarah Carter, "Categories and Terrains of Exclusion: Constructing the 'Indian Woman' in the Early Settlement Era in Western Canada," *Great Plains Quarterly* 13 (Summer 1993): 147–161.

Gordon T. Stewart, "Political Patronage Under Macdonald and Laurier, 1878–1911," *American Review of Canadian Studies* X, 1 (Spring 1980): 3–26.

Michael Bliss, "Canadianizing American Business: The Roots of the Branch Plant," in Ian Lumsden, ed., *Close the 49th Parallel, etc.: The Americanization of Canada* (Toronto: University of Toronto Press, 1970), 26–42.

William R. Morrison, "Eldorado," in *True North: The Yukon and the Northwest Territories* (Toronto: Oxford University Press, 1998), 78–104.

PART II

Bill Parenteau, "'Care, Control and Supervision': Native People in the Canadian Atlantic Salmon Fishery, 1867–1900," *Canadian Historical Review* 79, 1 (March 1998): 1–35.

Gillian Creese, "Exclusion or Solidarity? Vancouver Workers Confront the 'Oriental Problem,'" *BC Studies* 80 (Winter 1998–9): 24–51.

Sarah-Jane (Saje) Mathieu, "North of the Colour Line: Sleeping Car Porters and the Battle Against Jim Crow on Canadian Rails, 1880–1920," *Labour/Le Travail* 47 (Spring 2001): 9–42.

Margaret E. McCallum, "Prairie Women and the Struggle for a Dower Law, 1905–1920," *Prairie Forum* 18, 1 (1993): 19–34.

Veronica Strong-Boag, "'A Red Girl's Reasoning': E. Pauline Johnson Constructs the New Nation," in Veronica Strong-Boag, ed., *Painting the Maple: Essays on Race, Gender and the Construction of Canada* (Vancouver: UBC Press, 1998), 130–154.

Ramsay Cook, "The Roots of Modernism: Darwinism and the Higher Critics," in *The Regenerators: Social Criticism in Late Victorian English Canada* (Toronto: University of Toronto Press, 1985), 7–25.

George Grant, Chapter 5 of *Lament for a Nation: The Defeat of Canadian Nationalism* (Ottawa: Carleton University Press, 1997).

Neil Earle, "Hockey as Canadian Popular Culture: Team Canada 1972, Television and the Canadian Identity," *Journal of Canadian Studies* 30, 2 (Summer 1995): 107–123.

PART V

Gerald Friesen, "Defining the Prairies: or, Why the Prairies Don't Exist," in Robert Wardhaugh, ed., *Toward Defining the Prairies: Region, Culture, and History* (Winnipeg: University of Manitoba Press, 2001), 13–28.

Canadian Charter of Rights and Freedoms, Part I of the Constitution Act, 1982, being Schedule B to the Canada Act 1982 (U.K.), 1982, c. 11.

Tania Das Gupta, "Political Economy of Gender, Race and Class: Looking at South Asian Immigrant Women in Canada," *Canadian Ethnic Studies* 26, 1 (1994): 59–73.

Jim Stanford, "The Economics of Debt and the Remaking of Canada," *Studies in Political Economy*, 48 (Autumn 1995): 113–135.

Jane Jenson, "Family Policy, Child Care and Social Solidarity: The Case of Quebec," in Susan Prentice, ed., *Changing Child Care: Five Decades of Child Care Advocacy and Policy in Canada* (Halifax: Fernwood Publishing, 2001), 39–62.

Preface

Nation and Society: Readings in Post-Confederation Canadian History offers students a sample of some of the best scholarship on the history of Canada since Confederation. Although designed to accompany our two-volume *History of the Canadian Peoples* and our one-volume synthesis, *Canada: A National History*, this book can supplement any survey of Canadian history or serve as a stand-alone text. The readings are grouped in a combination of time periods and themes that are commonly used in studying the post-Confederation period: Inventing Canada, 1867–1914; Economy and Society in the Industrial Age, 1867–1918; Transitional Years: Canada, 1919–1945; Reinventing Canada, 1945–1975; and Post-Modern Canada.

Our main goal in selecting articles to publish was to ensure a balance of social, political and economic topics as well as a balanced coverage of Canadian regions. Given the size of Canada and the explosion of historical research in recent years, this proved to be a difficult task. We also wanted to make the selections as accessible to the general reader as possible. To best achieve our several goals, we have abridged some of the articles published here. Notes documenting where the article was originally published will enable students to consult the full version should they wish to do so.

The scholarly articles in this text are what historians call *secondary* documents. They offer an historian's interpretation of events in the past. To enable students to experience some of the excitement of coming face-to-face with the raw material of historical inquiry, we have also included in this reader a few *primary* documents. We hope that such documents as the Order of Procession at D'Arcy McGee's funeral and the Canadian Charter of Rights and Freedoms will whet the reader's appetite for more original sources. Students who find that they enjoy working with primary documents are encouraged to consult Jeff Keshen and Suzanne Morton's *Material Memory: Documents in Post-Confederation History* (Toronto: Pearson Education Canada, 1998).

Several of the articles published here demonstrate how Canadians in various periods have viewed their past. These articles make a contribution to *historiography*, the study of how history has been written and its changing interpretations over time. Jonathan Vance's article about inter-war commemorations of the First World War, for example, is less concerned with determining what Canadians really did during the war than with dissecting the ways in which they tried to make sense of the war effort in the years that followed. By contrast, Esther Delisle focuses on what French-Canadian intellectuals were saying during the Second World War as a way of challenging the claims they would make after the war about their attitudes to fascism. In recent years, the lines between history—what happened in the past—and historiography—the study of how historians have written about the past—have blurred somewhat. Most professional historians recognize that their interpretations, like those of their predecessors, are shaped by present biases and interests. As a result, they are more modest in their claims to objectivity and, instead, strive to examine their own motivations and explore a variety of perspectives on the topics they analyze.

The bias of this reader is toward articles in social history, a field of study that came into its own in the 1960s. As a result, many of the readings in this text deal with issues of class, culture, gender and region—the mantra of social historians—categories of analysis that have changed the way Canadian history has been written. Articles such as the one by Sarah Carter on Native women in Western Canada in the late-nineteenth century and Sarah-Jane Mathieu on African Canadian railway porters have benefited greatly from the work of social historians, who have developed new avenues of inquiry. Social history has also changed the way older fields, such as intellectual history, have been understood. For instance, feminist approaches to the past have enabled Mona Gleason, in her article published here, to explore how gendered understandings of social roles shaped the conclusions of psychologists as they searched for ways to ensure "normalcy" in post-war Canada. Even political history has been transformed by social history approaches, as the article by Gary Kinsman on loyalty tests in the civil service in the 1950s attests.

In approaching secondary historical sources, students will need to apply their own critical reading skills. Some readings are more accessible than others, and a few can be downright challenging, even to the experienced professional historian. Whatever the style of historical writing, students must engage the material. It is often best to read quickly, jotting down arguments and themes that seem most apparent. In particular, it is important to establish the thesis, or the controlling argument, of the reading. Ideally, the thesis will be stated in a sentence or two. In a well-written essay, the thesis is usually clearly stated at the beginning and elaborated upon throughout the rest of the piece.

Once the arguments and themes have been determined, it is important to evaluate them. Are the arguments sound and well supported? One way of making such an assessment is to check the endnotes to see if the author has consulted primary and secondary sources relevant to the topic. Evaluating sources is a fundamental exercise for students of history. Another approach is to check for additional publications on the topic to see if they corroborate the author's claims or at least do not contradict them.

It is also important to evaluate the author's point of view, which often has an impact on how source materials are selected and interpreted. All of the articles in this reader have been written by either trained historians or social scientists with historical interests. So it can be assumed that they know the nuts and bolts of their craft. Nevertheless, we must also remember that they write in a context that may slant their interpretations. For example, a historian may be eager to prove that a political policy has been damaging to a particular group and offer only evidence to support such a claim, ignoring all counter-evidence. Students often have not read broadly enough to detect such bias, but there are shortcuts to help them in their efforts. By finding out what else the author has published, it may be possible to discover that the article has been written by someone who has produced one or more books on the topic that have been reviewed by other scholars. These reviews usually highlight the positive and negative aspects of the author's approach.

The tone of the article also reveals something about the author. While some historians strive for a detached, impersonal style, others bring passion and political commitment to the work; still others may be ironic or even sarcastic. History is written by people with their own special character traits and it is useful to reflect on how these find expression in their publications.

While it is often easier to detect bias in primary sources than in secondary ones, the same basic rules of assessment apply to both. It is important when reading primary sources to establish the credibility of the author(s) of the document and the context in which it was written. In addition, consider how assumptions, based on conditions at the beginning of the twenty-first century, shape our judgment of the sources. So, for example, Cynthia Comacchio's sympathetic presentation of youth in the inter-war period and her correspondingly unsympathetic view of their detractors reflect today's increasingly majoritarian view that the pursuit of individual freedom has greater merit than the pursuit of eternal salvation by following the decisions of the churches.

We hope that students will find these readings both challenging and enlightening. By helping students understand that the past as represented in textbooks is constructed from sources such as the ones published here, we hope to open a window not only on developments in Canada's past but also on the discipline of history, which is ever evolving.

We would like to thank the following people who were instrumental in the production of this volume: Adrienne Shiffman, Christine Cozens and Richard di Santo from Pearson Education Canada; our copy editor, David Handelsman; and Michael Dale (Conestoga College), Robert A. Campbell (Capilano College) and Ruth Compton Brouwer (King's College), who reviewed this project during development.

CONFEDERATION!

THE MUCH-FATHERED YOUNGSTER.

Inventing Canada

1867–1914

Under the British North America Act of 1867, four British North American colonies—New Brunswick, Nova Scotia, Ontario, and Quebec—united to form the Dominion of Canada. Over the next half century, Canada expanded to the Pacific and the Arctic, its population more than doubled to 8 million, and the economy was transformed by industrial development. The second largest nation in the world, Canada was still part of the British Empire when it entered the First World War in 1914. The war experience helped to speed Canadians along the road to greater national autonomy.

Canadian society at the time of Confederation was no more homogeneous than it is today. Divided along lines of class, culture, ethnicity, gender, and religion, immigrants to Canada often brought their grudges with them and developed new ones in their adopted homeland. The largest immigrant group in 1867 were the Irish, many of whom had experienced oppression at home and played out their frustrations in Canada. The first reading in this text is a document listing the individuals and groups represented at the procession associated with the funeral of D'Arcy McGee in Montreal. A keen supporter of Confederation, McGee had earlier been an ardent Irish nationalist but had transferred his nationalist enthusiasm to his adopted homeland. He was assassinated on 7 April 1868 by a militant Irish Roman Catholic who apparently felt betrayed by what he believed to be McGee's willingness to accommodate British imperial interests. For historians, orders of procession in ceremonies such as this one provide clear documentary evidence of the class and cultural identities that characterized Canada's premier city in the 1860s.

The role of the state emerged as a major force in nation-building after Confederation. Under the guiding hand of Conservative Prime Minister John A. Macdonald (1867–1873; 1878–1891), railway construction, immigration, western settlement, and industrial growth stimulated by high tariff walls against imports became the four pillars on which Canada's early national policy was built. A sluggish global economy in the first three decades after Confederation meant that the new national policy was slow to bear fruit. When prosperity returned in the late 1890s, Liberal Prime Minister Wilfrid Laurier (1896–1911) reaped the benefits of staying the course with Macdonald's national policy. New railways were built, immigrants flocked to the West and to Canada's bustling industrial cities, and the economy boomed.

While many Canadians benefited from the new industrial order, others were not so fortunate. Those who seemed to stand in the way of "progress" were summarily shunted aside. This was especially the case with the Métis and First Nations peoples who, in the mid-nineteenth century, still constituted the vast majority of those who lived on the Prairies, in British Columbia, and in the North. A people identified by their mixed Native and French heritage, the Métis of the Prairies were overwhelmed by forces they could not control. D.N. Sprague charts the fate of the Métis who were dispersed following the two uprisings associated with Louis Riel in 1869–1870 and 1885. Sprague argues that the federal government violated the agreement that ended the Red River Resistance in 1870 by failing to provide the Métis with a land base that would allow them to continue to farm in the region. Sprague's charge that the Métis were dispossessed is controversial, with the federal government, backed by some scholars, claiming that many Métis left Manitoba because they wanted to continue hunting the buffalo rather than because they were not allowed to farm there.

Under the British North America Act, policy with respect to First Nations peoples was the responsibility of the federal government. The Indian Act of 1876 marked the beginning of a sad chapter in Canadian history that saw First Nations peoples restricted in their mobility and stripped of defining features of their culture. As Sarah Carter demonstrates, Native women were destined to bear the brunt of racial discrimination, stereotyped in ways that would ensure their second-class status in a West that was increasingly defined by immigrant norms. Federal policies and authorities stereotyped Aboriginal women as alcoholic whores and indifferent mothers and wives, and blamed them for poor housing conditions and the spread of fatal diseases. The settlers who benefited from Natives being dispossessed from their lands happily accepted such explanations of Native poverty. Regrettably, their unfavourable views of Natives became entrenched for generations in Prairie culture.

Creating a nation from the diverse peoples who lived in the territory called Canada was no easy task in the early years of Confederation. As a result of national policies relating to the Metis and separate schools, Quebec became increasingly disaffected with John A. Macdonald's Conservative Party. The Maritime provinces, never powerful enough to ensure that their agenda would be pursued in Ottawa, resorted to threats of secession in the late 1860s and again in the 1880s. Even British Columbia, which joined Canada under terms that seemed generous to the original provinces in Confederation, grumbled when it appeared that the Pacific railway would not materialize in the time frame agreed to. When religious and cultural differences were piled upon regional differences and provincial rights claims, the bonds uniting the country often seemed too weak to hold.

Gordon Stewart argues that political parties and the patronage they dispensed played a major role in legitimizing Confederation. Successful politicians such as Macdonald and Laurier governed by policy when they could and through well-placed patronage, when necessary, to remain in office. Serving as brokers for powerful individuals, groups, and regions, the Conservative and Liberal parties emerged as genuine national institutions in the first half century after Confederation, but patronage, Stewart maintains,

ensured that Canadian political culture remained localized. Conservative Party leader Robert Borden came to power in 1911 determined to run a less corrupt regime by establishing a civil service based on merit and creating boards of experts that would handle such patronage-ridden issues as the tariff.

The national policy also encouraged another long-standing trend in Canada: the American branch plant. Established as a means of escaping the high tariff wall erected after 1879, branch plants became a source of considerable criticism in the middle of the twentieth century. According to their detractors, they remitted hefty profits to head offices in the United States, spent little on research in Canada, reduced Canada's control over its own resources, and even threatened Canadian autonomy. Michael Bliss's article, published in 1970 at the height of the debate over the Americanization of the Canadian economy, demonstrates that branch plant investment was a goal of John A. Macdonald's "national" policy, not the result, as some critics claimed, of a sellout by subsequent prime ministers.

Although the North was largely ignored in the early plans for economic development, it became the focus of intense interest when gold was discovered in the Klondike in the summer of 1896. Gold seekers from all over the world flocked to the area and by 1898 Dawson had become the second largest city in the West. Determined to establish its jurisdiction, the federal government moved quickly, carving the Yukon Territory out of the old Northwest in 1898, building railway access to the coast, and dispatching the North-West Mounted Police to maintain law and order and to collect royalties on the gold being extracted. As the reading by William Morrison shows, gold fever died down as quickly as it began, and had little impact on the First Nations in the area, but it marked the beginning of developments that would transform Canada's northern regions.

Order of Procession, D'Arcy McGee Funeral, 1868

The City Police

The Fire Brigade

The Officers of the Corporation

The Members of the Corporation

The City Treasurer

The City Clerk

The Recorder of Montreal

Marshal—The Mayor—Marshal

The Committee of Management

The Mayor

Members of the House of Assembly

Legislative Councillors

Members of the Local Governments

Members of the House of Commons

Senators

Foreign Consuls

Officers of Militia in Uniform

Militia Commandant and Staff

Adjutant-General and Staff

Officers of the Army

Major-General Russell and Staff

Marshal—Mounted Orderlies—Marshal

Officers of the Courts of Law

Magistrates

Judges

Members of the Privy Council

Representative of the Lieutenant Governor
of Ontario

Representative of the Lieutenant Governor
of Quebec

Representative of the Governor-General

Sir Charles Wyndham, KCB, and Staff

Horticultural Society

THE BODY

Chief Mourners

Supporters of the Chief Mourners

Funeral Carriages

Clergy

Bar

The Notaries

Medical Profession

Universities

Professors, University of McGill College

Students of Law, Medicine

Students in Arts, McGill

St. Jean Baptiste Society

St. Patrick's Society

Irish Protestant Benevolent Society

St. Patrick's Benevolent Society

St. Patrick's Temperance Society

Marshal—St. George's Society—Marshal

English Workingmen's Benefit Society

St. Andrew's Society

The St. Andrew's Society of Ottawa

Caledonian Society

Thistle Society

Peter G. Goheen, "Order of Procession: D'Arcy McGee Funeral, 1868," *Historical Atlas of Canada*, Volume II (Toronto: University of Toronto Press, 1987), Plate 58. 1p. Reprinted by permission of the publisher.

Other National Societies

German Society

The New England Society

Literary Societies

Marshal—The Literary Club—Marshal

Board of Arts and Manufactures

Benevolent Society (not being National Societies)

St. Ann's Catholic Young Men's Society

Catholic Young Men's Society

Temperance Societies

Howard Division No 1, Sons of Temperance

St. Ann's Temperance Society

Montreal Temperance Society

Workingmen's Societies (not being National Societies)

Montreal Typographical Union

Montreal Workingmen's Benefit Society

United Protestant Workingmen's Benefit Society

Canada Sugar Refinery Benefit Society

Citizens

Government—Police

Chief Marshal

Dispossession vs. Accommodation in Plaintiff vs. Defendant Accounts of Métis Dispersal from Manitoba, 1870–1881

D.N. Sprague

According to well-established Métis oral tradition, the Red River Resistance of 1869–1870 was more than Canada could bear. Riel was driven from power, his people lost their land; and the Red River Métis were forced to ever more remote parts of their own homeland by hostile invaders. They were classic victims. Such is the stuff of oral tradition—it simplifies and deifies, but reduces complex reality to the nub of some usable memory, not necessarily false.[1] An oral tradition is an inherited approximation, a collective editing of fact. For people without written history or archives, the importance of maintaining such touch with the past is perhaps most well developed.

For academic historians, oral traditions are useful for formulating questions in documentary investigation. From the 1930s George Stanley, for example, was alert to evidence of victimization and confirmed the injustice done Riel.[2] At the same time, he reiterated the legend of the wholesale swindle of the general population, but without elaborate documentation of the process, nor did Stanley impugn the essential good faith of Canada's negotiators of the Manitoba Act, or of the administration of the land-promise provisions of the statute by the Department of the Interior. Nor did W.L. Morton or the other academic historians touching upon the subject in the 1950s and 1960s. The novelty of the dispossession-preceding-migration explanation of the turnover of population in Manitoba in academic history appearing in the 1980s was the suggestion that Métis dispersal was fostered by "government lawlessness," processes of legislative amendment and administration that unfolded more or less without regard to legal propriety.[3]

The reckless amendment aspect of "government lawlessness" was found in the evisceration of the land-promise provisions of the Manitoba Act by amending statutes and orders in council (as if the law were any ordinary statute, rather than an integral part of the constitution of Canada). The other aspect of "lawlessness" appeared in the records of the Department of the Interior showing its discriminatory administration of land claims. Since the two patterns of evidence together are the basis for allegations in a lawsuit still pending,[4] the "government lawlessness" version of the story is fairly characterized as the plaintiff account of Métis dispersal.

D.N. Sprague, "Dispossession vs. Accommodation in Plaintiff vs. Defendant Accounts of Métis Dispersal from Manitoba, 1870–1881," *Prairie Forum* 16, 2 (Fall 1991): 137–156. Reprinted courtesy of the Canadian Plains Research Center.

Historians Gerhard Ens and Thomas Flanagan have been retained by the Canadian Department of Justice since 1986 to defend Canada from the plaintiff's claims. Both have published what they consider a better view of the same evidence.[5] As the defendants' defenders they argue that the dispersal of the Red River Métis after 1870 was simply an acceleration or accentuation of disintegration evident for at least a decade before the transfer of Rupert's Land to Canada. In 1870 (continuing to about 1872) many conflicts are admitted to have occurred between old settlers and newcomers, especially between the French-Catholic Métis and Ontario-origin Protestants. Such conflict (said to be completely beyond the control of Canada) is regarded by Flanagan and Ens as tipping the balance in the minds of many Métis who were already tempted by the pull factors that are supposed to have become almost irresistible by the 1860s. The assertion Ens and Flanagan stress is that virtually all persons who wanted to remain on the land they occupied in 1870 had merely to corroborate their claims to occupancy with the testimony of neighbours, and their titles would eventually be confirmed as free grants by Canada. So powerful was the temptation to sell, however, particularly in the context of escalating land values during the boom of 1880 to 1882, even many confirmed landowners sold out and moved on. At the same time, of course, they liquidated other assets. Flanagan argues that the prices received reflected fair current values. On that account, if descendants of the original settlers in poor circumstances today identify the root of their problems with the imaginary dispossession of their ancestors in the last century, they dream a "morally destructive"[6] nightmare in Flanagan's characterization. According to Ens and Flanagan, Canada fulfilled and overfulfilled the land promise provisions of the Manitoba Act. Some small mistakes were made, but as errors in good faith; the assertion of an overall pattern of

deliberate discouragement conflicts with what Flanagan calls "overwhelming" evidence proving nearly the exact opposite was the case.[7]

What follows is a comparison of the evidence of the two sides on the issues for which a central claim and counter-claim have emerged to date.

Migration History

Did the pattern of the 1870s represent a dramatic accentuation? or abrupt departure from previous trends?

The position taken by Ens on migration, 1870–1881, is basically a continuity thesis. Table 1 exhibits some figures reported by Ens in support of his argument. A quick glance at the population trends in St. Andrew's and St. François Xavier (SFX) shows that both parishes sustained phenomenal growth rates even with considerable out-migration for his first period of observation, 1835 to 1849. The population of the Protestant-Métis parish increased 195 per cent in that fourteen-year period. The Catholic-Métis example grew slightly less rapidly in the same interval (180 per cent) because SFX sustained a higher rate of outmigration. Still, the base period was one of unsurpassed *rates* of growth for both areas of the Red River settlement.

The new pattern, allegedly extending into the 1870s, is supposed to be evident from the 1850s and 1860s. According to Ens, there was a steady increase in out-migration in response to a dramatic change in the economy, a shift away from summer-autumn pemmican production (with people maintaining a home-base claim to their river-front properties at Red River) towards winter harvest of buffalo for their hide and fur when the coat of the beasts was thickest. With more people chasing fewer animals at a different time of year, the result was expansion of the trade at the expense of the population of

TABLE 1 | POPULATION TRENDS, WHOLE SETTLEMENT VS. SELECT AREAS

	St. Andrew's		SFX		Whole Settlement	
	Observed	Expected	Observed	Expected	Observed	Expected
1835	547	—	506	—	3646	—
1849	1068	—	911	—	5391	—
1856	1207	—	1101	—	8691	—
1863	—	2082	—	1640	—	7979
1870	1456	—	1857	—	11960	—
1877	—	4060	967	2952	—	11809
1881	947	—	743	—	—	—

Explanation: "Expected" figures are based on the rate of increase for each area observed in the interval between 1835 and 1849 (195 per cent in 14 years for St. Andrew's, 180 per cent in 14 years for St. François Xavier, and 148 per cent in 14 years for the whole settlement).

Sources: The St. Andrew's and SFX "Observed" values are in Ens, "Dispossession or Adaptation," 128, 136, and 138 (footnote 62); Whole Settlement "Observed" values are the totals from the Red River Census of 1835 and 1849 in the Hudson's Bay Company Archives, Provincial Archives of Manitoba and the tabulation of the 1870 census of Manitoba reported in the Canadian Sessional Papers, No. 20 (1871).

the Red River settlement. Ens argues that "scrip records" of the Department of the Interior, 1885–1921, show an ever-increasing exodus which began in the 1850s.[8]

The most serious difficulty with the attempt to locate the beginning of the great dispersal before 1870 is that the argument relies on population trends in two parishes taken in isolation from the rest of the settlement. When the focus shifts to the larger picture, the "Whole Settlement" column of Table 1, the obvious conclusion is that the older parishes began to exhibit declining rates of increase in the 1850s and 1860s as they became crowded and more and more people moved to well-timbered vacant land in nearby satellite parishes. As a result, the rate of increase in the older areas began to level off, but population increase for the settlement as a whole (projected as a figure from the overall rate of growth observed for the

1835–1849 period) continued unabated. Indeed, the whole-settlement population expected for 1863 and 1877 (on the sustained rate calculation projecting the 1835–1849 rate to 1877) was in fact exceeded by the observed figures for 1856 and 1870. In other words, while the rate of increase in the over-populated parishes slowed, that of the newer areas in Red River accelerated because the population surplus from the old spilled over to vacant land in the new. The hypothesis of an increasing *rate* of outmigration to distant destinations is not sustained by the undiminished growth of the community taken as the old parishes and their nearby satellites. Net migration plus natural increase sustained the same rate of growth for that entity from 1850 to 1870, as from 1835 to 1849. Table 1 shows that the dramatic change from the pattern—the real break in continuity—dated from the 1870s, not the 1860s.

Persistence to 1875

Large or small?

While the population data show that the great dispersal began sometime before 1877, the same figures do not show the precise timing and, of course, the reasons for migration between 1870 and 1877. Ens and Flanagan admit that certain push factors were present in August 1870. They deny that the pushes—formal or informal—were as powerful as the lure of the new fur trade dating from the earlier period. They agree that a "reign of terror"[9] began with the arrival of Canada's peacekeepers and continued until 1872;[10] they do not hold Canada responsible for the lawlessness. Nor do they see delays of Métis land claims during the terror period (along with encouragement of newcomers to take up land wherever they found apparently vacant locations)[11] as part of an unstated policy of deliberate discouragement to original settlers. Ens and Flanagan insist that the outcome was an inadvertent rather than an intended result. From that standpoint, it is important to show that large scale migration began before a single claimant was disappointed in his land claim.

Late in 1873 Canada finally opened the door to wholesale consideration of Métis claims to river lots and more than two thousand applications for letters patent confirming ownership came forward over the next twelve months. The surveyor general reported in December 1874 that "2059 applications under section 32, and subsequent amendment[s] of the Manitoba Act, have been received and filed, of which, 614 have been examined and recommended for patent."[12] Over the next several years Canada completed the examination of several hundred more claims. Table 2 shows that by the end of 1877 approximately 850 river lot claims had passed through the process of application, consideration, and confirmation. The same tabulation also makes clear that roughly one-third (282 of 855) represented cases of purported buyers claiming the land of occupants who may have sold out *before* 1875. According to Ens, "This early glut of river-lot sales would seem to contradict Mailhot and Sprague's assertion that 90 per cent of those Métis found in the 1870 census were still in the settlement in 1875."[13] In fact, the record of the "early glut of river-lot sales" exhibited in Table 2 is evidence of something completely separate from the issue of the persistence of an increasingly discouraged Métis population.

The data supporting Mailhot and Sprague's "assertion" of large-scale persistence are census returns reported in 1875 permitting comparison with the pattern of 1870. The 1870 figures, printed in the *Sessional Papers* of 1871,[14] indicate that the Métis population then was 9,800 people (9,778 according to the enumeration of the whole province by "English" enumerators, 9,840 according to the "French"). The comparison number for 1875 is found in the returns of commissioners who took affidavits from Métis and descendants of "original white settlers" to enrol both for Canada's revised concept of the benefit of section 31 of the Manitoba Act and its amendments. Their lists of diverse categories of claimants have survived for nearly every parish.[15] Table 3 shows that Commissioners Machar and Ryan accounted for more than 9,000 of the persons enrolled in the 1870 census. However, Machar found about 500 "half breeds" in the 1870 enumeration of the Protestant parishes ineligible for Canada's concept of benefits under section 31 in 1875 (mainly because they had "taken treaty" since 1871 and become "Indians," or because they were absent at the time of the transfer on 15 July but present for enrolment in the census in October, or because they were children whose birth dates fell between the date of the transfer and time of the census, between July and October 1870). Ryan's list of claims "disallowed" in the French Catholic parishes has not been found. But assuming a rate of disallowance in the Catholic parishes that was at least half as much as the Protestant (because French "half breeds" were

TABLE 2 | MANITOBA ACT GRANTS OF RIVER LOTS BY PARISH AND YEAR

| | French Parishes | | | | English Parishes | | | | |
| | Old | | New | | Old | | New | | |
	Owner	Buyer	Owner	Buyer	Owner	Buyer	Owner	Buyer	Totals
April–June 1875	57	10	2	—	102	11	28	—	210
June 1876–									
March 1877	78	46	9	15	124	34	29	20	355
March–Nov.1877	44	52	24	45	41	33	35	16	290
Totals	179	108	35	60	267	78	92	36	855

Explanation: "Old" parishes are the areas included in the HBC survey in the 1830s. "Old French" are St. Boniface, St. Charles, St. Vital, St. Norbert, and SFX. "New French" are Ste. Anne, St. Laurent, Ste. Agathe, and Baie St. Paul. "Old English" includes St. Johns, Kildonan, Headingly, St. Pauls, St. Andrew's, and St. Clements. "New English" are Portage la Prairie, Poplar Point, High Bluff and Westburne.

Until 1878, special forms were used for different kinds of Dominion Lands grants. "D.L. Grant (33. Vic.)" distinguished Manitoba Act grants from all others. Each such patent described the land, named the owner in 1870 as well as the patentee.

Source: Government copies of the Manitoba Act grant patents are in the National Archives of Canada, microfilm reel C-3992, C-3994, and C-3996. The confirmation that the three cited locations embrace every "D.L. Grant (33 Vic.)" is the Alphabetical Index, Parish Land, Manitoba (1875–1883), also in the NAC, microfilm reel M-1640.

less likely to have "taken treaty"), the number of disallowed claims for the Catholic parishes by reason of absence from Manitoba on the date of the transfer and disqualifying birth date was probably no less than 250 persons, making an overall total of 9,334—"half breeds" and "original white settlers"—in 1875. Since 714 of the claimants were in the "original white settler" category, the persistent Métis component would appear to be 8,620 persons, or 88 percent of the 1870 figure.

The situation of many persisting families with unresolved claims puts in question migration estimates based on purported sales of land by "landowners" where a landowner population is still indeterminate. The census of 1875 provides a more appropriate statement of the facts regarding persistence to that time. There were approximately 2,000 Métis families in the Red River settlement in 1870 and approximately 1,800 were enumerated again in 1875. River lot

claims establish that 2,059 persons represented themselves as "landowners" by 1874 but 1,200 were still unconfirmed as late as December 1877. Since the beginning of the great exodus would appear to fall between 1875 and 1877, Canada's delays and denials might account for far more migration than Ens and Flanagan are willing to concede.

Canada's Confirmation of Titles to River Lots

Every occupant seeking accommodation? or systematic denial of the customary rights guaranteed by the Manitoba Act?

Ens's analysis of land occupancy and sale presupposes a system of formal survey and documentary evidence establishing a chain of title from date of survey to most recent recorded owner. No

TABLE 3 | ENROLMENT OF MANITOBA "HALF BREEDS" AND "ORIGINAL WHITE SETTLERS" BY COMMISSIONERS MACHAR AND RYAN, MAY-DECEMBER 1875[15]

	Categories of Claimants				
	"Half breed"	Whites	Totals	"heads"	"children" disallowed
Protestant Parishes					
St. Peters	35	61	270	—	366
St. Clements	132	251	3	—	420
St. Andrew's	392	798	116	29	1335
Kildonan	23	58	5	369	455
St. Johns	44	106	27	38	215
St. Pauls	66	133	11	27	237
St. James	87	157	6	21	271
Headingly	56	156	11	45	268
High Bluff/Pop. Pt.	160	360	27	22	569
Portage/White Mud	78	178	33	24	313
Catholic Parishes					
St. Boniface	283	526	—	19	828
St. Vital	72	171	—	44	287
St. Norbert	252	562	—	19	833
Ste. Agathe	135	240	—	—	375
Ste. Anne	81	226	—	32	339
St. Charles	97	190	—	3	290
SFX/Baie St. Paul	495	897	—	22	1414
St. Laurent/Oak Pt.	80	189	—	—	269
Totals	**2568**	**5259**	**543**	**714**	**9084**

Note: Machar canvassed the Protestant parishes, Ryan the Catholic.

survey, no land description or record of ownership. No record of ownership, no owner. Sprague's discussion of Métis land tenure assumes a system of customary demarcation of boundaries and descent of rights by community consent. People allotted what they needed. They owned what they used. The obvious point of potential conflict between the two historians was also the point of disagreement between the Métis and Canada in 1869. Métis leaders recognized that the transfer of Rupert's Land to the new Dominion would bring a transition from the customary to the formal system of land tenures, and there was no assurance when Canada's surveyors started their work even before the transfer that the existing population would not be "driven back from the rivers and their land given to others."[16] What made the potential for conflict all the more ominous was that the Red River settlement already had a system of land survey and registry that covered enough of the population that some future authority might be tempted to assert that everyone who deserved protection was already registered.

The system of survey and registry that was partially in effect dated from the mid-1830s. Always eager for a new way to turn a shilling, the Hudson's Bay Company (HBC) had authorized subdivision of the settlement almost as soon as the company clarified the matter of overall title with the heirs of Lord Selkirk. The surveyor hired for the task of confirming the boundaries of the lots occupied by Selkirk settlers (to receive free land), other settlers (expected to pay), and room to grow (lot by lot, as succeeding generations of established settlers and newcomers bought land from the HBC) was George Taylor. He laid out 1528 river lots of approximately 100 acres each by 1838 and the HBC capped the project with the opening of a land registry that most settlers cheerfully ignored.[17] In effect, the settlement developed on a dual-track basis—customary as well as formal, especially as the population expanded beyond the limits of the Taylor survey in the 1850s.

By 1860 the HBC abandoned any pretense of enforcing payment for lands. That year, the local Council of Assiniboia adopted a homestead ordinance affirming the legitimacy of the customary, unrecorded system, but required a survey and registration of ownership (in the territory beyond the Taylor survey) where disputes arose. To be sure, settlers with some knowledge of the paper mysteries surrounding formal land tenure did order such surveys in advance of their occupation of vacant land. R.A. Ruttan, the commissioner of Dominion Lands in Winnipeg in the late 1880s, explained the practice to Archer Martin, a jurist-historian trying to make sense of Red River land tenures in the mid-1890s:

> The Council of Assiniboia authorized two surveyors [probably the only ones in the settlement] Goulet and Sabine, to make surveys for parties desiring to take up land *outside the H.B. surveys*. A survey made by one of those gentlemen defined the land which you or I might hold: gave us a facility for recording too. There was no limit other than that imposed by custom to the river frontage (the country distant from the rivers wasn't considered of any value in those days) which might be taken, excepting the Minute of Council which prescribed 12 chains as the limit in cases of dispute which practically enabled one to take possession of part of the property if anyone were trying to hold more than 12 chains.
>
> I cannot learn that there ever was a dispute before 'the transfer.'[18]

Unfortunately for the Métis, Canada took the formalities of ownership more seriously than the pattern of residency. Mailhot and Sprague were careful to point out that "the land surveyors were not part of a conspiracy to overlook most Métis while recording a few."[19] They do suggest, however, that the surveyors were more interested in running the boundaries of lots than mapping the locations of persons in the haste to complete everything quickly.[20] The result was many families included in the 1870 census are not found in the surveyor's field notes[21] even though most such persons enrolled in 1870 were enumerated as residents again in 1875 by the "Half breed commission." Subsequently, any such resident faced two obstacles in establishing his claim by occupancy under the amendments of the Manitoba Act. The first was proving his residency notwithstanding the surveyor's returns to the contrary. Ens and Flanagan correctly point out that supporting affidavits from nearest neighbours were sometimes sufficient to establish occupation overlooked by the surveyor. They conclude too readily, however, that officials at the first level of consideration (Dominion Lands Office, Winnipeg) were willing to accept claims without evidence of "really valuable improvements." No amount of neighbourly corroboration could establish a Métis claim in the mid-1870s if the level of improvements was considered insufficient proof of "occupation."[22] And no level of improvements by "squatters" could establish their title if a non-resident "owner" produced documentation of a chain of title predating the tenure of the actual resident.[23] Table 4 exhibits the scope of vulnerability. What makes the tabulation especially interesting is that the labelling and numbers (except for the "Whole Settlement" column) are Ens's own words and data.

The key issue pertains to the half of the population that Ens and Flanagan consider justifiably outside the claims process. The observation that Canada eventually accorded direct or indirect recognition of everyone except the half of the population in Ens's "squatter" category begs the question of the accommodation or denial of "squatter" rights. A better view of the data in Table 4 (in comparison with Table 2) is that almost half of the entire population of the

Red River settlement were excluded from the outset. Such a suggestion is supported by testimonial evidence as well.

Joseph Royal, member of Parliament representing the French parishes of Manitoba, wrote numerous letters to officials in Ottawa from the mid-1870s through the early 1880s seeking "more liberal" treatment of "squatters" claims. In the spring of 1880 his appeal took the form of a concise history intended to persuade the prime minister that the administration of such cases since 1870 had been anything but accommodating. Royal asserted that "hundreds of claims are disallowed, *not having this or that*, which was never required by the Act of Manitoba." The especially difficult cases involved settlement without survey, and occupancy with little "improvement":

> We easily understand the difficulty for officials to recognize the condition of things [before the transfer] which admitted of nothing official, and it was in fact with a foresight of that difficulty that the people of Red River dreaded a loss of their property. They knew perfectly well that their right to the portion of the Settlement Belt regularly surveyed and occupied could not be disputed, but they apprehended that the

TABLE 4 | RECOGNITION OF 1870 OCCUPANTS BY CANADA

Occupancy Status	St. Andrew's		SFX		Whole Settlement	
	Number	(%)	Number	(%)	Number	(%)
"Owned or wererecognized as being in possession"	161	56	174	52	959	53
"Residing on lots ownedby other members of the extended family... or squatting on others'land"	126	44	160	48	849	47
Total	287	100	334	100	1808	100

Sources: The Occupancy Status labels and data for St. Andrew's and SFX are from Ens, "Dispossession or Adaptation," 136 (footnote 50) and 128 (Table 1); Whole Settlement data are from Mailhot and Sprague, "Persistent Settlers," 11 (Table 1).

same right to the land they possessed outside of the surveyed Settlement Belt might be contested: consequently that they would be, more or less, at the mercy of the New Government that might refuse to accept or understand the former condition of this country.[24]

Royal was not alone in making the same complaint. The principal spokesman for Métis interests in the negotiations for the Manitoba Act, Noel Ritchot (parish priest of St. Norbert), also appealed to Macdonald, in Ritchot's case as one negotiator of the Manitoba Act to another. Ritchot reminded the prime minister that they both knew that the law was

> not intended to say that all persons having a good written title and duly registered, etc etc that he shall have continually resided and cultivated so many acres of land yearly and for so many years before the Transfer to Canada, and that he shall cultivate and continually reside during the period of ten years after the Transfer to Canada, so many acres etc etc to be entitled to letters Patent for lands so cultivated and inhabited, [but]...this is what is required today by the Government through their employees.[25]

Both quotations from credible sources confirm a pattern of discouragement by delay and denial. As early as 1876, large numbers of such discouraged "squatters" were liquidating their assets and moving on. Speculators purchased rights to their claims evidently confident that additional documentation from them would assure eventual confirmation of even the most "doubtful" cases.

Scrip and Children's Allotments

Valuable asset disposed of at fair market prices? or ephemeral benefit sold for derisory return?

The most plausible interpretation of the Métis people's understanding of the land promises they won in the Manitoba Act, was that they had an assurance from Canada for continuity where they were already established and additional scope to expand freely for at least one more generation onto the unoccupied terrain along the rivers and creeks of the new province. One part of the Manitoba "treaty" (section 32) protected the tenure of land already occupied. Another part (section 31) assured heads of families that they might select vacant land for their children. Such a view was not inconsistent with the assurances outside the "treaty" given in writing by Cartier in the name of Canada to Ritchot in May 1870 and by Lieutenant Governor Archibald to Métis leaders when he invited them to designate areas from which families might select their land in 1871.[26] A great deal of claim-staking followed accordingly. Commissioner Ruttan joked about the proceedings in his correspondence with Martin:

> They moved with wonderful alacrity and unanimity. Since '62 or about that time the [French Métis] had been in the habit of wintering stock along the Seine, Rat and La Salle Rivers. These lands naturally offered the favourite playground for the staker who in short order had the entire riverfront neatly staked off. A man didn't confine himself to 1 claim. He frequently had 2 or 3. Sometimes for children, present and in expectancy, he would have the riverside dizzy with 'blazes' and 'stakes.'
>
> Venne, whose first name was most pertinently Solomon, must have staked 15 claims and, being of uncommon ambition, laid them down along the Red River.[27]

Notwithstanding Archibald's encouragement, the Dominion government refused to recognize any such arrangement as an appropriate administration of section 31 of the Manitoba Act.

In 1875 Canada launched its substitute. In the new arrangement, married adults—with or without recognized claims to river lots—were to receive a special monetary gratuity called "scrip," redeemable for 160 acres of Dominion Lands open for homestead. The population of unmarried persons (not "heads of families" therefore "children" regardless of their age) were to have access to a lottery for drawing 240-acre rectangles of open prairie, no closer than two or four miles to the "settlement belt" along the rivers. Neither benefit was of great value to the Métis, especially as the proposed method for distributing the 1.4 million acres was random selection by lottery. Flanagan observes that "the partition of reserve land into 240-acre parcels made it difficult to resettle there as a group; it would only be by chance if a group of relatives happened to get allotments near each other." The value of both "children's" allotments and "heads of family scrip" was, therefore, as liquidated assets, in Flanagan's characterization, "to finance a departure from Manitoba."[28] From that perspective, the Métis would have been more justly served (and at considerably less trouble to the bureaucracy) if Canada had simply handed each head of family $160 and each "child" $240 and ordered them to move. Instead, the government called the residents of all of the parishes to meet with commissioners in the summer of 1875 to swear to their residency in Manitoba on 15 July 1870. Each person whose claim was corroborated by at least two neighbours was assured future consideration. In the meantime, on-the-spot speculators were willing to pay $30 or $40 instant gratification to secure power of attorney to collect whatever reward should arrive in the future.[29] The government then offered deliberate or inadvertent protection to such speculators by requiring every claimant "not known personally to the Dominion Lands Agent" to hire an intermediary who was known to the man behind the counter to do the actual collecting of the land or scrip.[30] The holder of the power of

attorney thus had the edge over the claimant. Still, an important element of risk remained for "attorneys" because individual "half breeds" were said to have sold their claims more than once. Consequently, when the first scrip arrived in Winnipeg in June 1876, there was a great rush on the land office by the speculators to claim their property. They had to rush because Canada distributed the paper to the first "attorney" in line for the claim. Later arrivals were simply denied their reward (Canada did not wish to investigate frauds).[31]

The process of separating recipients of the 240-acre allotments from their land was somewhat more orderly. Moreover, since allotments were of land rather than a specialty currency, their distribution had the fuller cover of documentation that necessarily surrounds all transactions in real estate. More documents mean more room for conventional historical debate as well.

Flanagan does not question the propriety of Canada's substitution of scrip and bald prairie for the benefit the Métis preferred but he does state the facts of enrolment and allotment clearly and correctly: by the end of 1875 more than 5,000 "children" were enrolled, drawings began in 1876, continued in 1877, then became stalled in 1878, according to Flanagan, "for reasons that are not fully understood."[32] Table 5 shows the pattern—Protestant parishes first, the large French-Métis parishes last. The sequence has considerable analytical significance because the timing meant that the allotments for SFX, for example, were not available until that parish had begun wholesale dispersal of its 1870 population (compare Table 5 with Tables 1 and 2).

Still, the migration of recipients was no impediment to the sale of their land. Table 6 shows that in a random sample of 289 allottees whose parentage and sale history has been traced, French-Métis children with landless parents (probably the first to migrate) were also the most likely to become separated from their land within one year of allotment. Nor was age a bar-

TABLE 5 | TIMING OF GRANTS BY PARISH, OCTOBER 1876– FEBRUARY 1880

Parishes*	1876	1877	1878	1879	1880	Totals
Portage la Prairie	183					183
Kildonan	55	11	11			77
Ste. Anne	163	58				221
St. Peters		68				68
St. Clements		264				264
St. Andrew's		840				840
St. Pauls		133				133
St. Johns		113				113
Headingly		163				163
High Bluff		359				359
St. Laurent		194				194
St. James			179			179
Ste. Agathe			279			279
St. Charles			186			186
St. Boniface			768	24		792
St. Norbert					631	631
St. François Xavier					1319	1319
Totals	401	2203	1423	24	1950	6001

*Poplar Point probably included with High Bluff, St. Vital with St. Boniface and St. Norbert, and Baie St. Paul with SFX.

Source: National Archives of Canada, "Register of Grants to Half-Breed Children," RG 15, volume 1476.

rier, almost 60 per cent of a larger random sample of "vendors" were under the legal age of 21 (the age of majority in general application). Flanagan's sample of fifty-nine cases shows that a smaller proportion of land recipients were under age when they became separated from their allotments,[33] in part because Flanagan uses age 18 as the appropriate threshold, and partly because his sample is too small to test the relationship between age and date of sale. Table 7 shows that the ages of the overall population are so skewed beyond 21 years by the time most allotments occurred, a much larger sample than Flanagan's is needed to draw a population of minors large enough for meaningful statistical generalization.

Given customary preferences as to location and patterns of occupancy, the issue of sale versus retention was settled as soon as Canada devised the lottery scheme from section land on open prairie. No better system for encouraging immediate sale could have been invented. The more open question concerns value received. Table 8 exhibits data from sales records supporting Flanagan's contention that the proceeds to Métis vendors were more than reasonable, an overall average exceeding $1 per acre (approximately the

TABLE 6 | TENURE OF CHILDREN'S ALLOTMENTS BY LAND STATUS OF PARENTS

Parents' Status	Children's Tenure (in years)			
	less than 1	1 to 5	5 or more	Totals
Landless French Métis	72	5	4	81
Landless English Métis	27	9	11	47
French Métis patentees	63	7	9	79
English Métis patentees	35	30	17	82
Totals	197	51	41	289

Sources: Every tenth grant starting with grant 10 drawn from the Grants Register (NAC RG 15, vol. 1476) yielded a sample of 626 cases. Linkage with a separate register of "Manitoba Half Breed Children" (NAC RG 15, vol. 1505) yielded information on parentage enabling linkage with the land tenure data compiled from the "Census of Manitoba, 1870" (MG2 B3) and land patent data cited in Table 2. Information on tenure of the children's allotments was taken from the Abstract Books in the Winnipeg and Morden Land Titles Offices.

same value obtained by sellers of other unimproved lands distant from the rivers).

On closer scrutiny, however, a surprising anomaly becomes readily apparent. It is known that the exodus from the French-Métis parishes such as SFX was well on its way by 1877, and nearly complete by the time of the allotment of that parish in 1880. There is also reason to suggest that almost three-quarters of the "children" in the French parishes could neither read nor write to the extent of signing their own names on the sales documents. Notwithstanding the two disabilities of absenteeism and illiteracy, the anomaly is that they appear to have received the very best prices for their land—almost $400 per 240-acre allotment.

One possible explanation is the rapidly rising land values after 1879, but the other anomaly is that the recipients of land in the English parishes in 1876 and 1877 who held on to their allotments waiting for just such a speculative return fared remarkably more poorly than the illiterate, absentee recipients of land in the French parishes purportedly selling in the same period after 1879. Is it possible that the docu-

ments filed at the Land Registry and Dominion Lands Office were fictional covers for much less respectable— or even nonexistent—sales?

According to the sworn testimony of the chief justice of the Manitoba Court of Queen's Bench before a provincial commission inquiring into the sales of "half breed lands" in 1881, actual prices were $40 to $80 per 240-acre claim.[34] The reason for the discrepancy with the documentary evidence, in Justice Wood's testimony (and he was in an excellent position to know because he and three of his sons played important roles in claim running), is that almost anything was possible in the construction of the paper trail from allottee to the land office:

> All sorts of conveyances were resorted to. Deeds were executed beforehand in blank. A power of attorney was taken to fill them up, or they were filled up without it. And so soon as the allotment came up, there was such a race to the Registry Office with the conveyances to get registered first that horses enough could not be found in the City of Winnipeg for that purpose. In some cases, a man would be at the Registry

Ages	Sale Periods				Totals
	1876–78	1879–81	1882–84	1885 and later	
8	1				1
9	1				1
10	3	4			7
11	2	4			6
12		14	1		15
13	1	12	4		17
14	2	7	1		10
15	1	4	4	1	10
16	1	9	3		13
17	1	7	4	1	13
18	4	23	19	23	69
19	2	16	9	11	38
20	6	15	2	12	35
21	8	16	1	13	38
22+	40	51	15	26	132
Totals	73	182	63	87	405

Sources: Grant registers and Abstract Books cited under Table 6.

Office with his deed, and they [his accomplices] would telegraph him the number of the section [as soon as it was posted in the parish outside Winnipeg], when he would fill it in, and thus be enabled to put in his deed first—five or ten minutes perhaps before half a dozen others would come rushing into the office with deeds for the same lands. The Halfbreed lost all moral rectitude and would sell to every man as fast as they possibly could—all the contest was as to registering the papers first.[35]

While Wood blamed the allottees for multiple "sales" of the same property, the absence of hundreds if not thousands of "vendors" from the province at the time of the purported transactions would suggest many instances of "sales" with no involvement of the owner at all. Either way, however, the risks to buyers were great and would predict low prices for Métis lands. Quite simply—why would a claim runner pay "retail" prices for land he was acquiring "wholesale," especially considering that the "wholesale"

TABLE 8 | AVERAGE RECORDED SALE PRICES OF CHILDREN'S GRANTS BY CHRONOLOGICAL PERIOD OF SALE AND ETHNICITY OF "VENDOR"

| | Chronological Period | | |
Ethnicity	1876–78	1879 and later	Overall Averages (Totals)
"French" vendors	$213	$394	$374
(74 percent illiterate)	(N = 31)	(N = 245)	(N = 276)
"English" vendors	$126	$317	$242
(44 percent illiterate)	(N = 76)	(N = 119)	(N = 195)
Overall Averages	$151	$369	$310
(Totals)	(N = 107)	(N = 364)	(N = 471)

Sources: Literacy information taken from Powers of Attorney in NAC, RG 15, volumes 1421–1423. Ethnicity and sales price data are from grant registers and Abstract Books cited under Table 6.

buyer had little assurance that his paper was going to be the first conveyance registered? Flanagan concedes that such purchases were risky, and his selective quotation of testimony from the record of the provincial commission of inquiry impugning the veracity of all such documents suggests deep skepticism is warranted.[36] Inexplicably, however, Flanagan concludes that the sales contracts all "appear normal."[37] The conclusion strains his credibility to say the least.

Conclusions

Undisputed statistical data impugn the hypothesis of accommodation on four central points. *The Red River settlement sustained the phenomenal growth of the 1830s to 1870.*

Crowding of population was a problem in the older parishes, but the pull of migration before the transfer was mainly to nearby river frontage rather than to the smaller settlements in the distant west and north. Red River remained the central location of the Métis "nation." To be sure, profound internal divisions developed along lines of religion and economic interest. Even so, the shared fear of disruption by colonization from Canada united Red River in one effective community, the provisional government of 1869–1870. The success of negotiating the "Manitoba treaty" with Canada in April appeared to guarantee continuing political autonomy and adequate land to assure continuity for the Red River settlement as a province of Canada after 1870. *Almost 90 per cent of the Métis population enumerated in the autumn of 1870 persisted to 1875, evidently waiting for the terms of the "Manitoba treaty" to come into effect.*

Flanagan concedes that Métis patience was bound to be disappointed, however, because Canada had "no intention of establishing a Metis enclave,"[38] no intention of administering the Manitoba Act as understood by the Métis leadership. Nor did Canada sustain Lieutenant Governor Archibald in his similar understanding of the law and its appropriate administration. The Government of Canada regarded the Métis as a "semi-barbarian," "insurgent" population in need of rule by a "strong hand until...swamped by the influx of settlers."[39] For two years the population was terrorized by a Canadian "peace-keeping" force. For four years, not one Métis claim to a river lot was confirmed in accordance with section 32, not one Métis reserve was established "for the benefit of the families of the half-breed residents" in accordance with section 31. *Once Canada did devise a process for administering claims through the Department of the Interior in 1873, the Lands Branch received 2,059 applications for titles to river lots by the end of 1874, but confirmed less than 42 per cent as late as 1878, moving especially slowly on the claims to river lots in the parishes that had developed without general survey before 1870.*

Registered owners of lands surveyed under the authority of the HBC were most likely to obtain their patents within one or two years from date of application. A "squatter" improving vacant land registered in the name of another person had to disprove the competing title to establish his own; a "squatter" on vacant Crown land with improvements overlooked by surveyors faced enormous frustration proving occupation contrary to surveyors' returns. Anyone discouraged by the process (for whatever reason) became increasingly tempted to sell his land (at discounted value) to the growing army of land sharks willing to pay at least some pittance for a claim, no matter how "doubtful." Then, after submission of appropriate supplementary documentation a patent would eventually issue to the speculator. As more and more lots passed from original occupants to apparent newcomers, Canada relaxed its criteria concerning the kind of improvements needed to establish a "squatter's" claim. Virtually any type of land use that had routinely disqualified a Métis claim in the mid-1870s was allowed purported buyers of such lands pressing their claims in the 1880s. By that time, the dispersal of the original population was so advanced that there was no longer any threat of a significant Métis enclave remaining. By that time, Flanagan agrees, much of the "agitation carried on in the name of Métis rights had little to do with the

actual interests of the Métis."[40] By the same admission, of course, most of the patents conceded after 1878, had little to do with accommodating the Métis and their claims. On that account, the observation that Canada eventually patented 1,562 river lots in the old surveyed part of the Red River settlement, and 580 in the newer, outer parishes[41] does not prove that the Métis migration was "not caused by any inability to obtain Manitoba Act patents"[42] nearly so much as the statistic documents Canada's willingness to reward the informal agents of Métis dispersal. Flanagan's interpretation mistakes long term results (river lots were eventually patented) for what should have occurred many years earlier (when the lands were still occupied by Métis claimants). *Discouraged by harassment and unreasonable delays, most Métis people dispersed from their river lot locations in the 1870s before the 1.4 million acres of reserve lands were distributed.*

The value of the 1.4 million acres went to claim runners who collected patents at the Dominion Lands Office as "attorneys" of the allottees. Many nominal recipients may have known of their grants and intended to sell, some may have realized substantial considerations. The sales documents were certainly intended to create such an impression. However, the testimony of knowledgeable claim runners, lawyers, and jurists concerning transactions in Métis lands in November 1881 suggests a different reality. The sworn testimony of several witnesses impugned the veracity of the documentation generated routinely by most rapacious speculators. Since the same small population of claim runners were at the forefront of transactions in the transfer of claims to river lots as well, a cloud of suspicion must remain over all of the evidence generated by claim runners. In sum, it would seem that the "cascade of benefits"[43] concerning Métis lands in Manitoba fell upon land sharks and their cronies with connections in the bureaucratic apparatus created by Canada more than upon the people who rallied to the provisional government in 1869, and cheered the triumph of their collective resistance in 1870. By 1877 most of that population had become "desperate under the repeated delays"[44] and began selling out to finance retreat west and north. Interpreting the exodus as a reasonable adaptive response states the obvious; asserting that the migration had nothing to do with the frustration of land claims in Manitoba before 1877 is completely contrary to fact. In the case of the dispersal of the Red River Métis, justice delayed was quite literally justice denied.

Notes

1   See Jan Vansina, "Oral Tradition and Historical Methodology," in D.K. Dunaway and W.K. Baum, eds., *Oral History: An Interdisciplinary Anthology* (Nashville: American Association for State and Local History, 1984), 102–6.

2   See Stanley's account of his work in "Last Word on Louis Riel—The Man of Several Faces," in F. Laurie Barron and James B. Waldram, eds., *1885 and After: Native Society in Transition* (Regina: Canadian Plains Research Center, 1986), 3–22.

3   D.N. Sprague, "The Manitoba Land Question, 1870–1882," *Journal of Canadian Studies* 15 (1980): 74–84; Sprague, "Government Lawlessness in the Administration of Manitoba Land Claims, 1870–1887," *Manitoba Law Journal* 10 (1980): 415–41; Sprague, *Canada and the Métis, 1869–1885* (Waterloo: Wilfrid Laurier University Press, 1988); and P.R. Mailhot and D.N. Sprague, "Persistent Settlers: The Dispersal and Resettlement of the Red River Métis, 1870–1885," *Canadian Ethnic Studies* 2 (1985): 1–31.

4   In *Dumont, et al.* vs. *A.G. Canada and A.G. Manitoba,* Canada's initial defense was a motion for dismissal on grounds that the outcome of the case was so "plain and obvious" the question was "beyond-doubt." In March, 1990 the Supreme Court held that the constitutionality of the legislation enacted in the course of administration of the Manitoba Act was "justiciable" and in the event that judgement went in favour of the plaintiffs, "declaratory relief...in the discretion of the court" was an appropriate remedy. New procedural motions have now been brought by Canada. Rejected in the Manitoba Court of Queen's Bench, Canada has appealed to the Manitoba Court of Appeal.

5   Gerhard Ens, "Dispossession or Adaptation? Migration and Persistence of the Red River Métis, 1835–1890," *Canadian Historical Association, Papers* (1988): 120–44. Thomas Flanagan, "The Market for Métis Lands in Manitoba: An Exploratory Study," *Prairie Forum* 16, no. 1 (Spring 1991): 1–20; and *Metis Lands in Manitoba* (Calgary: University of Calgary Press, 1991).

6   Flanagan, *Metis Lands,* 232.

7   Ibid., 189.

8   Only the general reference appears in Ens, "Dispossession or Adaptation," 131. There is no citation of a particular series.

9   Ens uses the "reign of terror" phrase in "Dispossession or Adaptation," 137; Flanagan prefers less colourful language. The evidence of assault, rape, and murder inflicted on the Métis people by Canada's troops becomes merely a "push of English-Protestant immigrants" in Flanagan's latest characterization of the process, "Market," 17.

10 Fred J. Shore, "The Canadians and the Metis: The Re-Creation of Manitoba, 1858–1872" (Ph.D. dissertation, University of Manitoba, 1991).

11 See Sprague, *Canada and the Métis,* 94–95.

12 Canada, *Sessional Papers,* 1875, no. 8.

13 Ens, "Dispossession or Adaptation," 138.

14 Canada, *Sessional Papers,* 1871, no. 20, 90–93.

15 The missing returns are Machar's list of "Half breed heads of families" for the parish of St. Johns; the supplementary heads of families list prepared by Ryan in January 1876; and Ryan's claims disallowed in the Catholic parishes. The first deficiency is remedied by the figure of forty cases for St. Johns appearing in the preliminary tabulation published as Appendix 4 in the "Report of the Surveyor General, 31 October 1875," in Canada, *Sessional Papers,* 1876, no. 9. The second can be estimated from the supplementary children's claims on the assumption that there would be two heads of family per family of claimant minors. Even if such an assumption is somehow defective, the resulting bias is trivial: 30 cases in the Protestant parishes, 76 in the Catholic, for a total of 96 in a universe of 9,000. Thus Table 3 is primarily a tabulation of the "Returns of Half Breed Commissioners" exactly as

found on the lists in National Archives of Canada (NAC), RG 15, vols. 1574–1607. Two aspects of aggregation are that heirs are reduced to single decedents and claimants disallowed by reason of double enumeration are not included in the tabulation.

16 NAC, MG 26A, Macdonald Papers, Incoming Correspondence, 40752, William McDougall to Macdonald, 31 October 1869.

17 D.N. Sprague and R. Frye, "Manitoba's Red River Settlement: Manuscript Sources for Economic and Demographic History," *Archivaria* 9 (1978–80): 179–93.

18 Provincial Archives of British Columbia, Archer Martin Papers, Add Mss 630, box 1, file 5, Ruttan to Martin (11 July 1894).

19 Mailhot and Sprague, "Persistent Settlers," 5.

20 One of the surviving diaries, that of M. McFadden, surveyor of Baie St. Paul from 29 July to 7 September 1871, shows that the survey of that parish occupied him for a total of thirty-one working days. Only two days, 4 and 11 August, were noteworthy for "a good deal of time taken up with the claimants in getting their claims properly defined." PAM, RG 17-C1, Survey Diary and Report, No. 274: 8–14.

21 McFadden's "Field Notes" recording the names, locations and readily apparent improvements of occupants in Baie St. Paul are in ibid., Field Notebook, No. 533: 3–9.

22 Flanagan does not admit that the level of improvements demanded by officials was fluid and more stringent in the 1870s than in the mid-1880s. The kind of case Flanagan cites as typical of Canada's generosity was dated 1883, but all such claims were consistently rejected in the 1870s. Compare evidence cited in Flanagan, *Metis Lands*, 164, with Sprague, *Canada and the Métis*, 115–20.

23 A particularly instructive example affected the family of Alexis Vivier, in occupation of unsurveyed land in Baie St. Paul between Baptiste Robillard and James Cameron since 1863. One of the first difficulties was Canada's surveyor divided the Vivier claim into four different lots, with only one showing significant improvements. Still, the Viviers regarded the entire tract as their land, and claimed more cultivation, housing, and outbuildings than that recorded in the survey. A new problem arose in 1878 when documentation purportedly proving the sale of part of the tract by the now absent Robillard to one Isaac Cowie brought Vivier into a conflict with Cowie over title. Cowie's claim prevailed. See

documentation in PAM, Parish Files, Baie St. Paul, lots 126–130.

24 NAC, RG 15, vol. 245, file 22638, Royal to Macdonald, 8 March 1880.

25 NAC, MG 26A, Macdonald Papers, Incoming Correspondence, 141514–141526, Ritchot to Macdonald, 15 January 1881.

26 See Sprague, *Canada and the Métis*, 94–95.

27 Provincial Archives of British Columbia, Archer Martin Papers, Add Mss 630, box 1, file 5, Ruttan to Martin, 11 July 1894.

28 Flanagan, "Market," 10.

29 Ibid., 11–12.

30 Order in Council of Canada (23 March 1876) stipulated that recipients with "proper identification to the satisfaction of the Dominion Lands Agent" might collect their scrip in person, otherwise, they would be required to hire an agent with power of attorney. In practice, however, the route was as stated above. See the form letter from Donald Codd, Dominion Lands Agent, Winnipeg, to Mrs. E.L. Barber (10 May 1879) in Provincial Archives of Manitoba, Barber Papers (MG 14 C66), item 2954.

31 Sprague, *Canada and the Métis*, 124–25.

32 Flanagan, "Market," 4.

33 Ibid., 5–6.

34 Provincial Archives of Manitoba, RG7 B1, Commission to Investigate Administration of Justice in the Province of Manitoba, Transcript of Testimony, 207–208.

35 Ibid., 210–11.

36 Compare Flanagan's quotation in "Market," 8, with the fuller text of Wood's testimony cited above. See also Flanagan's admission of "artificially high" prices evident by comparing certain sales instruments and figures in the Abstract Books ("Market," 18, footnote 11).

37 Flanagan, *Metis Lands*, 231.

38 Ibid., 229.

39 Sir John A. Macdonald quoted in Sprague, *Canada and the Métis*, 89.

40 Flanagan, *Metis Lands*, 179.

41 Ibid., 186–88.

42 Ibid., 190.

43 Flanagan's ill-chosen phrase, *Metis Lands*, 227.

44 Report in *Manitoba Free Press* quoted in ibid., 147.

Categories and Terrains of Exclusion

Constructing the "Indian Woman" in the Early Settlement Era in Western Canada*

Sarah Carter

In 1884 Mary E. Inderwick wrote to her Ontario family from the ranch near Pincher Creek, Alberta, where she had lived with her new husband for six months.[1] The letter provides a perspective on the stratifications of race, gender, and class that were forming as the Euro-Canadian enclave grew in the district of Alberta. Mary Inderwick lamented that it was a lonely life, as she was twenty-two miles from any other women, and she even offered to help some of the men near them to "get their shacks done up if only they will go east and marry some really nice girls." She did not consider the companionship of women such as "the squaw who is the nominal wife of a white man near us," and she had dismissed her maid, who had become discontented with her position as a servant. Inderwick had disapproved of a ball at the North-West Mounted Police (NWMP) barracks at Fort Macleod, despite the fact that it was "the first Ball to which the squaws were not allowed to go, but there were several half breeds." Commenting on the Aboriginal population that still greatly outnumbered the new arrivals, Inderwick wrote that they should have been "isolated in the mountains," rather than settled on nearby reserves, and that the sooner they became extinct the better for themselves and the country.

At the time of Mary Inderwick's arrival in the West, the consolidation of Canada's rule was not yet secure. The Metis resistance of 1885 fed fears of a larger uprising, and an uncertain economic climate threatened the promise of a prosperous West. There was a sharpening of racial boundaries and categories in the 1880s and an intensification of discrimination in the Canadian West. The arrival of women immigrants like Mary Inderwick after the Canadian Pacific Railway was completed through Alberta in 1883 coincided with other developments such as the railway itself, the treaties, and the development of ranching and farming that were to stabilize the new order and allow the recreation of Euro-Canadian institutions and society. The women did not introduce notions of spatial and social segregation, but their presence helped to justify policies already in motion that segregated the new community from indigenous contacts.[2] The Canadian state adopted increasingly segregationist policies toward the Aboriginal people of the West, and central to these policies were images of Aboriginal women as dissolute, dangerous, and sinister.

Sarah Carter, "Categories and Terrains of Exclusion: Constructing the 'Indian Woman' in the Early Settlement Era in Western Canada," *Great Plains Quarterly* 13 (Summer 1993): 147–161.

*The author thanks Hugh Dempsey for sharing his research with her and for his valuable suggestions as to other sources.

From the earliest years that people were settled on reserves in western Canada, Canadian government administrators and statesmen, as well as the national press, promoted a cluster of negative images of Aboriginal women. Those in power used these images to explain conditions of poverty and ill-health on reserves. The failure of agriculture on reserves was attributed to the incapacity of Aboriginal men to become other than hunters, warriors, and nomads.[3] Responsibility for a host of other problems, including the deplorable state of housing on reserves, the lack of clothing and footwear, and the high mortality rate, was placed upon the supposed cultural traits and temperament of Aboriginal women. The depiction of these women as lewd and licentious, particularly after 1885, was used to deflect criticism from the behavior of government officials and the NWMP and to legitimize the constraints placed on the activities and movements of Aboriginal women in the world off the reserve. These negative images became deeply embedded in the consciousness of the most powerful socio-economic groups on the Prairies and have resisted revision.

The images were neither new nor unique to the Canadian West. In "The Pocahontas Perplex" Rayna Green explored the complex, many-faceted dimensions of the image of the Indian woman in American folklore and literature. The beautiful "Indian Princess" who saved or aided white men while remaining aloof and virtuous in a woodland paradise was the positive side of the image. Her opposite, the squalid and immoral "Squaw," lived in a shack at the edge of town, and her "physical removal or destruction can be understood as necessary to the progress of civilization."[4] The "Squaw" was pressed into service and her image predominated in the Canadian West in the late nineteenth century, as boundaries were clarified and social and geographic space marked out. The either/or binary left newcomers little room to consider the diversity of the Aboriginal people of the West or the complex identities and roles of Aboriginal women. Not all Euro-Canadians shared in these sentiments and perceptions. Methodist missionary John McDougall, for example, in 1895 chastised a fellow missionary author for his use of the term "squaw": "In the name of decency and civilization and Christianity, why call one person a woman and another a squaw?"[5] While it would be a mistake to assume a unified mentality among all Euro-Canadians, or, for example, among all members of the NWMP, it is nonetheless clear that the negative stereotype not only prevailed but was deliberately propagated by officials of the state.

Euro-Canadian Settlement of the West

Following the transfer of the Hudson's Bay Company territories to the Dominion of Canada in 1870, the policy of the federal government was to clear the land of the Aboriginal inhabitants and open the West to Euro-Canadian agricultural settlement. To regulate settlement the North-West Mounted Police (later Royal North-West and then Royal Canadian Mounted Police) was created and three hundred of them were dispatched west in 1874. A "free" homestead system was modeled on the American example, and a transcontinental railway was completed in 1885. To open up the West to "actual settlers," seven treaties with the Aboriginal people were negotiated from 1871 to 1877, and through these the government of Canada acquired legal control of most of the land of the West. In exchange the people received land reserves, annuities, and, as a result of hard bargaining by Aboriginal spokesmen, commitments to assist them to take up agriculture as their buffalo-based economy collapsed. A Department of Indian Affairs with headquarters in Ottawa was established in 1880, and in the field an ever-expanding team of Indian agents, farm instructors, and inspectors were assigned to implement the reserve system and to enforce the Indian Act of 1876. The people who had entered into treaties were wards of the government who did not have the privileges of full citizenship and were subject to a wide variety of controls and regulations that governed many aspects of life.

Much to the disappointment of the federal government, the West did not begin rapid development until the later 1890s. There were small pockets of Euro-Canadian settlement, but in 1885 in the district of Alberta, for example, the Aboriginal and Metis population was more than 9500 while the recent arrivals numbered only 4900.[6] All seemed hopeless, especially by the mid-1880s when immigration was at a near standstill. Years of drought and frost and problems finding suitable techniques for farming the northern Plains account in part for the reluctance of settlers, and the 1885 resistance of the Metis in present-day Saskatchewan did little to enhance the image the government wished to project of the West as a suitable and safe home.

Resistance to Settlement

The Metis were people of mixed Aboriginal and European ancestry who regarded the Red River settlement (Winnipeg) as the heartland of their nation. It was here in 1869–70, under the leadership of Louis Riel, that the Metis first resisted Canadian imperialism, effectively blocking Ottawa's takeover of the West until they had been guaranteed their land rights, their French language, and their Roman Catholic religion. But the victory negotiated into the Manitoba Act of 1870 soon proved hollow as the Canadian government adopted a variety of strategies to ensure that the Metis did not receive the lands promised them, and many moved further West.[7] In their new territories the Metis again demanded land guarantees but

when the Canadian government largely ignored their requests, they asked Louis Riel to lead another protest in 1884. The Canadian government dispatched troops west and defeated the Metis at Batoche in May 1885. Riel was found guilty of treason and was hanged, as were eight Aboriginal men convicted of murder.

Despite desperate economic circumstances and deep resentment over government mistreatment, few of the treaty people of the West joined the Metis resistance, although at a settlement called Frog Lake, in present-day Alberta, some young Cree men killed an Indian agent, a farm instructor, and seven others, and in the Battleford district two farm instructors were killed. This limited participation became a rationale for the increasingly authoritarian regime that governed the lives of the treaty people. Anxious to see western development succeed in the face of all of the setbacks of the 1880s, the Canadian government restricted the Aboriginal population in order to protect and enrich recent and prospective immigrants.

Development of Stereotypes

Particularly irksome to many of the recently-arrived "actual settlers" was Aboriginal competition they faced in the hay, grain, and vegetable markets. Despite obstacles, many Aboriginal farmers had produced a surplus for sale. Settlers' particularly vocal and strident complaints led the government to curtail farming on reserves. To explain why underused reserves had become pockets of rural poverty, Indian Affairs officials claimed that Aboriginal culture and temperament rendered the men unwilling and unable to farm.

Plains women were also responsible: according to government pronouncements they were idle and gossipy, preferring tents to proper housing because tents required less work to maintain and could be clustered in groups that allowed visiting and gossip. Reports of the Superintendent General of Indian Affairs claimed that Indians raised dust with their dancing and the women's failure to clean it up spread diseases such as tuberculosis. Administrators blamed the high infant mortality rate upon the indifferent care of the mothers. The neglected children of these mothers grew up "rebellious, sullen, disobedient and unthankful."[8] While men were blamed for the failure of agriculture, women were portrayed as resisting, resenting, and preventing any progress toward modernization. As an inspector of Indian agencies lamented in 1908, "The women, here, as on nearly every reserve, are a hindrance to the advancement of the men. No sooner do the men earn some money than the women want to go and visit their relations on some other reserve, or else give a feast or dance to their friends.... The majority of [the women] are discontented, dirty, lazy and slovenly."[9]

The unofficial and unpublished reports of reserve life show that officials recognized that problems with reserve housing and health had little to do with the preferences, temperament, or poor housekeeping abilities of women. Because of their poverty the people were confined in large numbers in winter to what were little better than one-room and one-story huts or shacks that were poorly ventilated and impossible to keep clean, as they had dirt floors and were plastered with mud and hay. Tents and tipis might well have been more sanitary and more comfortable. One inspector of agencies noted in 1891 that women had neither soap, towels, wash basins, nor wash pails, and no means with which to acquire these.[10] Officials frequently noted that women were short of basic clothing but had no textiles or yarn to work with. Yet in official public statements, the tendency was to ascribe blame to the women rather than to draw attention to conditions that would injure the reputation of government administrators.

"Licentiousness" and Government Officials

Officials propagated an image of Aboriginal women as dissolute, as the bearers of sinister influences, to deflect criticism from government agents and policies. This image was evoked with particular strength in the wake of an 1886 controversy that focused upon the alleged "brutal, heartless and ostentatious licentiousness" of government officials resident in Western Canada.[11] The remarks of Samuel Trivett, a Church of England missionary on the Blood reserve in present-day southern Alberta, became the focus of the controversy. To a special correspondent for *The Mail* of Toronto, Trivett said that Indian women were being bought and sold by white men who lived with them without legally marrying them and then abandoned the offspring to life on the reserve.[12]

Trivett strongly hinted that some government agents were involved in licentious behavior, an accusation seized upon by critics of the administration of Indian affairs in western Canada. In the aftermath of the Metis resistance of 1885, opponents of John A. Macdonald's Conservatives amassed evidence of neglect, injustice, and incompetence and were delighted to add immorality to this list. In the House of Commons in April of 1886, Malcolm Cameron, Liberal Member of Parliament, delivered a lengthy indictment of Indian affairs in the West, focusing upon the unprincipled and unscrupulous behavior of officials of the Indian department. Cameron quoted Trivett and further charged that agents of the government, sent to elevate and educate, had instead acted to "humiliate, to lower, to degrade and debase the virgin daughters of the wards of the nation." He knew of one young Indian agent from England, unfit to do anything there, who was living on a reserve in "open adultery with two young squaws...revelling in the sensual enjoyments of a western harem, plentifully supplied with select cullings from the western prairie flowers."[13]

Cameron implicated members of the NWMP in this behavior, wondering why it was that over 45 per cent of them were reported to have been under medical treatment for venereal disease. Cameron was not the first to raise the matter of police propriety in the House. Concern about possible improper relations between the police and Aboriginal women long predated the Trivett scandal and was one aspect of a larger debate in the press and in the House in the late 1870s over charges of inefficiency, lack of discipline, high desertion rates, and low morale in the force. Lieutenant-Governor of the North-West Territories David Laird alerted NWMP Commissioner James Macleod in 1878 that reports about immoral conduct were in circulation: "I fear from what reports are brought me, that some of your officers at Fort Walsh are making rather free with the women around there. It is to be hoped that the good name of the Force will not be hurt through too open indulgence of that kind. And I sincerely hope that Indian women will not be treated in a way that hereafter may give trouble."[14]

Although Macleod and Assistant Commissioner A.G. Irvine denied that there was "anything like 'a regular brothel'" about the police posts, such reports persisted. In the House of Commons in 1880 Joseph Royal, a Manitoba Member of Parliament, claimed that the NWMP was accused of "disgraceful immorality" all over the West. Royal had evidence that at one of the police posts that winter there had been "an open quarrel between an officer and one of the constables for the possession of a squaw..." and that one officer slapped another "in the face on account of a squaw." Royal had been informed that "many members of the force were living in concubinage with Indian women, whom they had purchased from their parents and friends."[15] In 1886 public attention was once again drawn to police behav-

ior. *The Mail* informed its readers that between 1874 and 1881 the police had "lived openly with Indian girls purchased from their parents" and only the arrival of settlers had compelled them to abandon or at least be "more discreet in the pursuit of their profligacy."[16]

There is little doubt that Trivett and other critics based their accusations of both the police and government officials on some foundation, but remaining evidence is scanty and scattered. Missionaries depended to a large extent on the goodwill of government and were rarely as outspoken as Trivett or John McLean, a Methodist missionary on the Blood reserve near Fort Macleod, who in 1885 characterized many reserve employees as utterly incompetent and urged the government to employ only married men, "of sterling Christian character."[17] But missionaries were instructed in 1886 by Edgar Dewdney, lieutenant-governor of the North-West Territories, not to voice their accusations to the newspapers "even if allegations against public officials were true," as this would do more harm than good, would affect mission work, and could be used to stir up political strife.[18] Government officials generally investigated reports of government misconduct themselves and this functioned to cover up or to mitigate such allegations. Similarly members of the NWMP themselves looked into any complaints about the force's behavior.

Marriages of Aboriginal Women and NWMP Members

There were members of the NWMP, especially among the earliest recruits of the 1870s and early 1880s, who formed relationships with Aboriginal and Metis women, as did a great many other male immigrants of these years. Some of these were marriages of long-standing, sanctioned by Christian ceremony or customary law. Lakota author/historian John O'Kute-sica noted that six "Red Coats" of the Wood Mountain Detachment in the early 1880s married Lakota women from Sitting Bull's band, and most of the couples, such as Mary Blackmoon and Thomas Aspdin, lived together to old age and death. One couple, Archie LeCaine and Emma Loves War, separated because she did not wish to move to Eastern Canada.[19]

Other relationships were of a more temporary nature. Of course there were children. Cecil Denny for example, while a sub-inspector at Fort Macleod, had a daughter with Victoria Mckay, a part-Piegan woman who was the wife of another policeman, constable Percy Robinson.[20] Denny was forced to resign from the force in 1881 as a result of his involvement in a series of court cases that Robinson brought against him for "having induced his wife to desert him and also having criminal connections with her."[21] The child was raised by her mother on the American Blackfoot reservation. Assistant Surgeon Henry Dodd of the NWMP had a daughter who lived on one of the Crooked Lake reserves in the Qu'Appelle Valley. There is a record of this in the police files only because Dodd was granted leave to attend to her when she was very ill in 1889.[22]

D. J. Grier, who served three years with the NWMP beginning in 1877 at Fort Macleod, married Molly Tailfeathers, a Piegan woman, and together they had three children.[23] By 1887, however, Grier had remarried a white woman. For a short time the children from his first marriage lived with their mother on the Piegan reserve, but the two eldest were taken from her and placed in the care of Grier's parents, who had also settled in Fort Macleod. Grier was one of the most prominent men of the West. Renowned as the first commercial wheat grower in Alberta, he also served as mayor of Macleod for twelve years from 1901 to 1913.

Abuse of Aboriginal Women

John O'Kute-sica wrote at length about one unsuccessful Wood Mountain customary marriage, that of his aunt Iteskawin and Superintendent William D. Jarvis, an Englishman with the original contingent who was dismissed from the force in 1881. According to O'Kute-sica his aunt consented to marry Jarvis because he promised that her brothers and sisters would have something to eat twice a day, and all of her people were in want and suffering. After only a few weeks of marriage, Jarvis, in a jealous rage, publicly assaulted Iteskawin at a Lakota "Night Dance," an incident that strained relations between the two communities, and she immediately left him.[24] On most of the few occasions that Aboriginal women laid charges against policemen for assault or rape, their claims were hastily dismissed as defamation or blackmail.[25]

Some government employees resident on reserves clearly abused their positions of authority. In 1882, for example, Blackfoot Chief Crowfoot and his wife complained that the farm instructor on their reserve demanded sexual favors from a young girl in return for rations, and when an investigation proved this to be the case the man was dismissed.[26] Both the documentary and oral records suggest that several of the government employees that the Crees killed at Frog Lake and Battleford in the spring of 1885 were resented intensely because of their callous and at times brutal treatment of Aboriginal women. The farm instructor on the Mosquoito reserve near Battleford, James Payne, was known for his violent temper—he once beat a young woman and threw her out of his house when he found her visiting his young Aboriginal wife. The terrified and shaken woman, who was found by her father, died soon after, and her grieving father blamed Payne, whom he killed in 1885.[27] Farm instructor John Delaney, who was killed at Frog Lake in 1885, laid charges against a man by the name of Sand Fly in 1881 so he could cohabit with Sand Fly's wife. Delaney first claimed that Sand Fly had struck him with a whip, and when this charge did not result in the desired jail sentence, Delaney claimed that the man had beaten his wife. The farm instructor then lived with Sand Fly's wife, and the general feeling in the district, shared by the local NWMP, was that "Mr. Delaney had the man arrested in order to accomplish his designs."[28] As a Touchwood Hills farm instructor told a visiting newspaper correspondent in 1885, the charges of immorality among farm instructors on reserves were in many instances too true, as "the greatest facilities are afforded the Indian instructor for the seduction of Indian girls. The instructor holds the grub. The agent gives him the supplies and he issues them to the Indians. Now you have a good idea of what semi-starvation is...."[29]

Blaming Aboriginal Women

The most vocal response to the accusations of Trivett and other critics was not to deny that there had been "immorality" in the West but to exonerate the men and blame the Aboriginal women, who were claimed to have behaved in an abandoned and wanton manner and were supposedly accustomed to being treated with contempt, to being bought and sold as commodities, within their own society. In defending the NWMP in 1880, the Toronto *Globe* emphasized that Aboriginal women had "loose morals" that were "notorious the world over" and that "no men in the world are so good as to teach them better, or to try to reform them in this respect." These sentiments were echoed again and again in the wake of the 1886 controversy. The editor of the Fort *Macleod Gazette*, a former

NWMP, argued that whatever immorality there might have been came from the women themselves and from the customs of their society. They were prostitutes before they went to live with white men, who did not encourage this behavior but were simply "taking advantage of an Indian's offer." *The Mail* told readers that Aboriginal males had sold their wives and children in the thousands to soldiers and settlers since the time of the French fur trade in exchange for alcohol, and that with the arrival of the police a great deal had been done to end this situation.[30]

The *Gazette* stressed, incorrectly, that there was no marriage in plains societies, simply a little lively bartering with the father and a woman could be purchased for a horse or two. The argument that Aboriginal women were virtual slaves, first to their fathers, and then to their husbands, was called upon by all who wished to deflect criticism from government officials and the NWMP. In the House of Commons in April 1886 Sir Hector Langevin defended the record of the government against Cameron's charges of immorality. Langevin claimed that to Indians marriage was simply a bargain and a sale and that immorality among them long predated the arrival of government agents in the North-West.[31]

The government published its official response to the criticisms of Indian affairs in the North-West in an 1886 pamphlet entitled "The Facts Respecting Indian Administration in the North-West." A government official had again inquired into accusations about the misconduct of employees of the Indian department and, predictably, had found no evidence. The investigator, Hayter Reed, assistant commissioner of Indian affairs, was one of those unmarried officials who had been accused of having Aboriginal "mistresses" as well as a child from one of these relationships.[32] The pamphlet boldly asserted that Trivett was unable to come up with a shred of actual evidence, although the missionary vehemently denied this.[33] The pamphlet writer admitted that some men had acquired their wives by purchase, but claimed that this was the Indian custom, and that "no father ever dreams of letting his daughter leave his wigwam till he has received a valuable consideration for her." If the government stopped this custom, there would be loud protests, over and above the Indians' "chronic habit of grumbling." "The Facts" insisted that it was not fair to criticize the behavior of the dead, such as Delaney and Payne, who had "passed from the bar of human judgment."[34]

Endangered White Women

The real danger was not to Indian women but to white women, who might again be dragged into horrible captivity if critics encouraged Indians in their exaggerated, misled notions. Two white women, Theresa Delaney and Theresa Gowanlock, had been taken hostage by Big Bear's band following the events at Frog Lake. There were a great number of Metis and Aboriginal women (and men) hostages as well, but outrage and indignation did not focus upon them. Although Delaney and Gowanlock were fed and housed as well as their captors, and released unharmed, the government publication played up the perils, hazards, and threat to the safety of these women and others who might move west. The women's account of their two months of captivity stressed the "savagery" of their captors, and the ever-present danger of "the fate worse than death."[35]

Following the period of heightened tensions within the Euro-Canadian community after the events of 1885, there was an increased emphasis upon the supposed vulnerability of white women in the West. Rumors circulated through the press that one of Big Bear's wives was a white woman being held against her will.[36] After a girl of about nine with fair hair and blue eyes was spotted on the Blackfoot reserve by an English artist accompanying Canada's governor general on a tour across the continent, in 1889, the story of a "captive" white child attracted international attention and calls for a rescue mission. Indignant outrage was expressed, especially in the Fort Macleod newspaper, which called for prompt action to rescue the girl from "the horrible fate that is surely in store for her." The NWMP and Indian affairs officials assigned to look into the case knew all along that the child was not a captive at all but resided with her mother on the reserve. The captivity story functioned, however, to reaffirm the vulnerability of white women in the West and to provide a rationale for those who wished to secure greater control over the Aboriginal population.[37]

The Image of the "Squaw Man"

The use of the term "squaw man" to denote men of the lowest social class became increasingly frequent during the later 1880s. There was disdain for those within the community who did not conform to the new demands to clarify boundaries. Police reports blamed "squaw men" for many crimes such as liquor offenses or the killing of cattle. S.B. Steele of the NWMP wrote from the Fort Macleod district in 1890 that the wives of these men "readily act as agents, and speaking the language, and being closely connected with the various tribes, their houses soon become a rendez-vous for idle and dissolute Indians and half breeds, and being themselves in that debatable land between savagery and civilization possibly do not realize the heinousness and danger to the community...."[38] The *Moosomin Courier* of March 1890 blamed the "squaw-men" for stirring up trouble with the Indians in 1885 and prejudicing them against policies that were for their own good.[39]

Lives of Aboriginal Women

The overwhelming image that emerged from the 1886 "immorality" controversy was that of dissolute Aboriginal women. They, and the traditions of the society from which they came, were identified as the cause of vice and corruption in the new settlements of the prairie West. This was not an image shared or accepted by all Euro-Canadians in the West at all times, nor did the image bear resemblance to the lives of the vast majority of Aboriginal women. Women were not commodities that were bought, sold, or exchanged at will by men. Plains marriage practices entailed mutual obligations between the families of the couple and an on-going exchange of marriage-validating gifts.

Aboriginal oral and documentary sources suggest that in the early reserve years, particularly in the aftermath of the events of 1885, women provided essential security and stability in communities that had experienced great upheaval. In these years of low resources and shattered morale, the work of women in their own new settlements was vital, materially as well as spiritually. Cree author Joe Dion wrote that when spirits and resources were low on his reserve in the late 1880s "much of the inspiration for the Crees came from the old ladies, for they set to work with a will that impressed everybody."[40] Aboriginal women also provided considerable assistance to new immigrants, particularly women. They were important as midwives to some early immigrants and they helped instruct newcomers in the use of edible prairie plants and other native materials.[41] Aboriginal women formed what was described as a "protective society" around the women and children hostages in Big Bear's camp in 1885, keeping them out of harm's way, but this aspect of the drama was absent from the headlines of the day.[42]

Constraints on Aboriginal Women

It was the image of Aboriginal women as immoral and corrupting influences that predominated in the non-Aboriginal society that was taking shape. Authorities used this characterization to define and treat Aboriginal women, increasingly narrowing their options and opportunities. Both informal and formal constraints served to keep Aboriginal people from the towns and settled areas of the prairies and their presence there became more and more marginal. While they may not have wished to live in the towns, their land-use patterns for a time intersected with the new order and they might have taken advantage of markets and other economic opportunities, but townspeople believed that Aboriginal people did not belong within the new settlements that were replacing and expelling "savagery."[43] Their presence was seen as incongruous, corrupting, and demoralizing. Classified as prostitutes, Aboriginal women were seen as particular threats to morality and health. An 1886 pamphlet of advice for emigrants entitled "What Women Say of the Canadian Northwest" was quick to reassure newcomers that Aboriginal people were seldom seen. The 320 women who responded to the question "Do you experience any dread of the Indians?" overwhelmingly replied that they rarely saw any. Mrs. S. Lumsden, for example, thought they were "hundreds of miles away with sufficient force to keep them quiet."[44]

Following the events of 1885, government officials as well as the NWMP made strenuous efforts to keep people on their reserves. A pass system required all who wished to leave to acquire a pass from the farm instructor or agent declaring the length of and reason for absence. A central rationale for the pass system was to keep away from the towns and villages Aboriginal women "of abandoned character who were there for the worst purposes."[45] There is evidence that some Aboriginal women did work as prostitutes.[46] Cree chiefs of the Edmonton district complained to the prime minister in 1883 that their young women were reduced by starvation to prostitution, something unheard of among their people before.[47] Officials attributed prostitution not to economic conditions but to what they insisted was the personal disposition or inherent immorality of Aboriginal women.[48] Classified as prostitutes, Aboriginal women could be restricted by a new disciplinary regime. Separate legislation under the Indian Act, and, after 1892, under the Criminal Code governed Aboriginal prostitution, making it easier to convict Aboriginal women than other women. As legal historian Constance Backhouse has observed, this separate criminal legislation, "with its attendant emphasis on the activities of Indians rather than whites, revealed that racial discrimination ran deep through the veins of nineteenth century Canadian society."[49]

The pass system was also used to bar Aboriginal women from the towns for what were invariably seen as "immoral purposes." Women who were found by the NWMP to be without passes and without means of support were arrested and ordered back to their reserves.[50] In March of 1886 the Battleford police dealt with one woman who refused to leave the town by taking her to the barracks and cutting off locks of her hair. Two years later the Battleford paper reported that

> during the early part of the week the Mounted Police ordered out of town a number of squaws who had come in from time to time and settled here. The promise to take them to the barracks and cut off their hair had a wonderful effect in hastening their movements.[51]

Accustomed to a high degree of mobility about the landscape, Aboriginal women found that the pass system not only restricted their traditional subsistence strategies but also hampered their pursuit of new jobs and resources. Government officials further limited the women's employment and marketing opportunities by advice such as that given by one Indian agent, who urged the citizens of Calgary in 1885 not to purchase anything from or hire Aboriginal people, so as to keep them out of the town.[52] The periodic sale of produce, art, and craftwork in urban or tourist areas could have provided income to women and their families, as did such sales for Aboriginal women in eastern Canada. Studies of rural women in western Canada suggest that in the prairie boom and bust cycle the numerous strategies of women, including the marketing of country provisions and farm products, provided the buffer against farm failure.[53] Aboriginal women were not allowed the same opportunities to market these resources.

The mechanisms and attitudes that excluded Aboriginal women from the new settlements also hampered their access to some of the services these offered. Jane Livingston, the Metis wife of one of the earliest farmers in the Calgary district, found that whenever there was a new policeman in Calgary, he would ask her and her children for passes and make trouble because of their appearance. On one occasion when a child was sick and she needed medicines from downtown Calgary, she rubbed flour into her face and "hoped I looked like a white Calgary housewife" so that the new police constable would not bother her about a pass.[54]

Murders of Aboriginal Women

Community reactions to the poisoning of one Aboriginal woman and the brutal murder of another in the late 1880s in southern Alberta reflect the racial prejudices of many of the recent immigrants. In 1888 Constable Alfred Symonds of the NWMP detachment of Stand Off was accused of feloniously killing and slaying a Blood woman by the name of Mrs. Only Kill by giving her a fatal dose of iodine. The woman had swallowed the contents of a bottle given to her by Symonds that apparently held iodine and had died the next morning. The same day she had also eaten a quantity of beans that had turned sour in the heat. Although Only Kill died on Wednesday morning, the matter was not reported to the coroner until late on Friday night. The coroner claimed that by this time the body was too decomposed for post mortem examination, and the coroner's jury decided that the deceased had come to her death either from eating sour beans or from drinking the fluid given to her by Symonds, who was committed to trial and charged with having administered the poison.[55] Constable Symonds was a popular and jocular cricketer and boxer, the son of a professor from Galt, Ontario.[56] In his report on the case, Superintendent P. R. Neale of the NWMP wrote to his superior, "I do not think any Western jury will convict him." Symonds appeared before Judge James F. Macleod, former commissioner of the NWMP, in August of 1888 but the crown prosecutor made application for "Nolle Prosequi," which was granted, and the prisoner was released.[57]

During the 1889 trials of the murderer of a Cree woman identified only as "Rosalie," who had been working as a prostitute, it became clear that there were many in Calgary who felt "Rosalie was only a squaw and that her death did not matter much."[58] Instead the murderer gained the sympathy and support of much of the town. The murder was a particularly brutal one, and the accused, William "Jumbo" Fisk, had confessed and given himself up to authorities, yet there were problems finding any citizens willing to serve on a jury that might convict a white man for such a crime. The crown prosecutor stated that he regretted having to conduct the case, as he had known the accused for several years as a "genial accommodating and upright young man."[59] Fisk was a popular veteran of 1885, and he was from a well-established eastern Canadian family. At the end of the first of the Rosalie trials the jury astoundingly found the accused "Not Guilty." Judge Charles Rouleau refused to accept this verdict and he ordered a re-trial at the end of which Rouleau told the jury to "forget the woman's race and to consider only the evidence at hand," that "it made no difference whether Rosalie was white or black, an Indian or a negro. In the eyes of the law, every British subject is equal."[60] It was only after the second trial that Fisk was convicted of manslaughter and sent to prison for fourteen years at hard labor. The judge intended to sentence him for life, but letters written by members of parliament and other influential persons who had made representations to the court as to his good character, combined with a petition from the most respectable people of Calgary, persuaded him to impose the lesser sentence.

The people of Calgary tried to show that they were not callous and indifferent toward Rosalie by giving her "as respectable a burial as if she had been a white woman," although several months later the town council squabbled with the Indian Department over the costs incurred, as the department did not think it necessary to go beyond the costs of a pauper's funeral. As a final indignity Rosalie was not allowed burial by the priests in the mission graveyard, although she had been baptized into the Roman Catholic Church, because they regarded her as a prostitute who had died in sin. The lesson to be learned from the tragedy, according to a Calgary newspaper, was "keep the Indians out of town."[61]

Aboriginal Women and Anglo-Saxon Moral Reformers

There was an intensification of racial discrimination and a stiffening of boundaries between Aboriginal and newcomer in the late 1880s in western Canada. In part this may have been because the immigrants exemplified the increasingly racist ideas and assumptions of the British toward "primitive" peoples.[62] Like the Jamaica Revolt and the India Mutiny, the events of 1885 in western Canada sanctioned perceptions of Aboriginal people as dangerous and ungrateful and justified increased control and segregation.[63] Aboriginal women presented particular perils and hazards. The Metis of the Canadian West had fomented two "rebellions" in western Canada, so authorities wanted to discourage such miscegenation, which could potentially produce great numbers of "malcontents" who might demand that their rights and interests be recognized.[64]

A fervor for moral reform in Protestant English Canada also began to take shape in the later 1880s. Sexual immorality was a main target and racial purity a goal of the reformers.[65] There were fears that Anglo-Saxons might well be overrun by more fertile, darker, and lower people who were believed not to be in control of their sexual desires. Attitudes of the moral reformers toward the inhabitants of the cities' slums were similar to categorizations of "savages" as improvident, filthy, impure, and morally depraved. The 1886 accusations of Malcolm Cameron about the extent of venereal disease among the NWMP had led to an internal investigation of the matter, and although this proved that Cameron's claims were exaggerated, they were not entirely incorrect.[66] The concerns of the moral reformers, however, justified policies segregating Aboriginal and newcomer communities.

The Invalidation of Mixed Marriages

Also at issue in the West at this time was the question of who was to control property and capital, who was to have privilege and respectability, and who was not. The possibility that the progeny of interracial marriages might be recognized as legitimate heirs to the sometimes considerable wealth of their fathers posed problems and acted as a powerful incentive for the immigrants to view Aboriginal women as immoral and accustomed to a great number of partners. With the arrival of Euro-Canadian women, Aboriginal wives became fewer, and there is evidence, just as Trivett had suggested, that in the 1880s husbands and fathers were leaving their Aboriginal wives and children for non-Aboriginal wives. D. W. Davis, for example, began his career in Alberta as a whiskey trader at the infamous Fort Whoop-Up, but by 1887 was elected as the first Member of Parliament for the Alberta district. He had a family of four children with a Blood woman by the name of Revenge Walker, but in 1887 he married an Ontario woman, Lillie Grier (sister of D. J. Grier), with whom he had a second family. Although Davis, like Grier, acknowledged the children of the earlier marriage and provided for their education, they were excluded from the economic and social elite in the non-Aboriginal community.[67]

While the validity of mixed marriages according to "the custom of the country" had been upheld in Canadian courts earlier in the nineteenth century, this changed with the influential 1886 ruling in *Jones v. Fraser.* The judge ruled that the court would not accept that "the cohabitation of a civilized man and a savage woman, even for a long period of time, gives rise to the presumption that they consented to be married in our sense of marriage."[68] In 1899 the

Supreme Court for the North-West Territories decided that the two sons of Mary Brown, a Piegan woman, and Nicholas Sheran, a founder of a lucrative coal mine near Lethbridge, were not entitled, as next of kin, to a share of their father's estate, as the judge found that Sheran could have but did not legally marry Brown while they lived together from 1878 until Sheran's death in 1882.[69]

Haunted by an Image

Negative images of Aboriginal women proved extraordinarily persistent. Their morality was questioned in a number of sections of the Indian Act. If a woman was not of "good moral character" for example, she lost her one-third interest in her husband's estate, and a male government official was the sole and final judge of moral character. As late as 1921 the House of Commons debated a Criminal Code amendment that would have made it an offense for any white man to have "illicit connection" with an Indian woman. Part of the rationale advanced was that "the Indian women are, perhaps, not as alive as women of other races in the country to the importance of maintaining their chastity." The amendment was not passed, as it was argued that this could make unsuspecting white men the "victims" of Indian women who would blackmail them.[70] By contrast, any critical reflections upon the behavior of early government officials and the police in western Canada did not survive beyond the controversy of the 1880s. Ideological constraints, combined with more formal mechanisms of control such as the pass system, succeeded in marginalizing Aboriginal women and in limiting the alternatives and opportunities available to them.

Local histories of the prairies suggest that by the turn of the century many of the settlements of the West had their "local Indian" who was tolerated on the margins or fringes of society and whose behavior and appearance was the subject of local anecdotes. "Old Dewdney" for example, an ancient, often flamboyantly dressed man, was a familiar sight in Fort Macleod. Local people exchanged stories about the exotic past of the old man and of their generosity and kindness toward him.[71] "Nikamoos" or the Singer camped each summer by herself on the trail to the Onion Lake reserve agency in Saskatchewan. Among the white community it was reputed that as a girl Nikamoos had run away with a policeman but that he had been compelled to leave her. The child she bore died and Nikamoos went insane.[72]

A solitary Indian woman known only as Liza camped on the outskirts of Virden, Manitoba, for many years until her disappearance sometime in the 1940s. By then Liza was thought to have been well over one hundred years old. She lived winter and summer in an unheated tent by the railroad tracks although she spent the long winter days huddled in the livery stable and also at times crept into the Nu-Art Beauty Parlour, where she sat on the floor in front of the window, warming herself in the sun. Liza smoked a corncob pipe as she shuffled about the streets and lanes of Virden, rummaging in garbage tins. She bathed under the overflow pipe at the water tower, sometimes clothed and sometimes not, and dried off by standing over the huge heat register in Scales and Rothnie's General Store. To an extent she was tolerated and even assisted; town employees shoveled out a path for her when she was buried under snow, and it was thought that the town fathers supplied her with food from time to time. Children were half fascinated and half frightened by this ancient woman. Old-timers believed that Liza was there well before the first settlers, that she was among the Sioux who had escaped the pursuing American army in 1876, that she received regular checks from the United States, and that she was capable of fine handwriting, where learned, no one knew.[73]

The presence of Liza, and the stories told about her, served to sharpen the boundaries of community membership and to articulate what was and what was not considered acceptable and respectable.[74] Liza was the object of both fascination and repugnance as she violated norms of conventional behavior, dress, and cleanliness, representing the antithesis of "civilized" prairie society. Although economically and socially marginal, Liza was symbolically important. Her role attests to the recurrent pattern through which the new society of the West gained in strength and identity and sought to legitimate its own authority by defining itself against the people who were there before them. Liza was a real person, but what she represented was a Euro-Canadian artifact, created by the settlement. The narratives circulated about Liza were not those she might have told herself—of the disasters that had stripped her of family and community, or perhaps of her strategies in adopting the character role—and this folklore reflected less about Liza than about the community itself. Her solitary life was unique and in contrast to the lives of Aboriginal women; Liza was not representative of a Lakota woman within Lakota society. Yet, her presence on the margins of the settlement was tolerated and encouraged in the way these women were not, as she appeared to fit into the well-established category of the "squaw" that still served to confirm the Euro-Canadian newcomers in their belief that their cultural and moral superiority entitled them to the land that had become their home.

Notes

1   Mary E. Inderwick, "A Lady and Her Ranch," *The Best From Alberta History*, ed. Hugh Dempsey (Saskatoon: Western Producer Prairie Books, 1981), 65–77. In 1882 the North-West Territories were divided into four provisional districts named Assiniboia, Saskatchewan, Alberta, and Athabasca.

2   For an examination and critique of the argument that European women introduced segregation, see Margaret Strobel, *European Women and the Second British Empire*, (Bloomington: Indiana University Press, 1991). See also essays by Ann Laura Stoler, "Carnal Knowledge and Imperial Power: Gender, Race and Morality in Colonial Asia," in *Gender at the Crossroads of Knowledge: Feminist Anthropology in the Postmodern Era*, ed. Micaela di Leonardo (Berkeley: University of California Press, 1991), 51–101, and Stoler, "Rethinking Colonial Categories: European Communities and the Boundaries of Rule," in *Colonialism and Culture*, ed. Nicholas B. Dirks, (Ann Arbor: University of Michigan Press, 1992), 319–52.

3   See Sarah Carter, *Lost Harvests: Prairie Indian Reserve Farmers and Government Policy* (Montreal: McGill-Queen's University Press, 1990).

4   Rayna Green, "The Pocahontas Perplex: The Image of Indian Women in American Culture," in *Unequal Sisters: A Multicultural Reader in U.S.* *Women's History*, ed. Ellen Carol DuBois and Vicki L. Ruiz (New York: Routledge, 1990), 15–21.

5   John McDougall, "A Criticism of 'Indian Wigwams and Northern Camp-Fires'" (n.p.: 1895), 12–13.

6   P.B. Waite, *Canada, 1874–1896: Arduous Destiny* (Toronto: McClelland and Stewart Ltd., 1971), 149.

7   D.N. Sprague, *Canada and the Métis, 1869–1885*, (Waterloo: Wilfrid Laurier Press, 1988).

8   Canada. *Sessional Papers*, Annual Report of the Superintendent General of Indian Affairs for the year ending 30 June 1898, xix, for the year ending 31 December 1899, xxiii, xxviii, 166; *The* [Toronto] *Mail*, 2 March 1889; Pamela Margaret White, "Restructuring the Domestic Sphere—Prairie Indian Women on Reserves: Image, Ideology and State Policy, 1880–1930" (Ph.D. diss, McGill University, 1987); W.H. Withrow, *Native Races of North American* (Toronto: Methodist Mission Rooms, 1895), 114 (quoted).

9   Canada. *Sessional Papers*, Annual Report of the Superintendent General of Indian Affairs for the year ending March 1908, 110.

10 Inspector Alex McGibbon's report on Onion Lake, October 1891, National Archives of Canada (NA), Record Group 10 (RG 10), records relating to Indian Affairs, Black Series, vol. 3860, file 82, 319-6.

11 *The* [Toronto] *Globe,* 1 February 1886.

12 *The* [Toronto] *Mail,* 23 January 1886.

13 Canada. House of Commons *Debates.* Malcolm Cameron, Session 1886, vol. 1, 720–21.

14 E.C. Morgan, "The North-West Mounted Police: Internal Problems and Public Criticism, 1874–1883," *Saskatchewan History* 26 no. 2 (Spring 1973): 56–59, Laird quoted 56.

15 Canada. House of Commons *Debates,* 21 April 1880, Joseph Royal, Fourth Parliament, Second Session, 1638.

16 *The Mail,* 2 February 1886.

17 John Maclean, "The Half-breed and Indian Insurrection," *Canadian Methodist Magazine* 22 no. 1 (July 1885): 173–74.

18 Edgar Dewdney to the Bishop of Saskatchewan, 31 May 1886, NA, RG 10, vol. 3753, file 30613.

19 John O'Kute-sica Correspondence, collection no. R-834, File 17(b), 15, Saskatchewan Archives Board (SAB).

20 *Blackfeet Heritage: 1907–08* (Browning: Blackfeet Heritage Program, n.d.), 171.

21 A.B. McCullough, "Papers Relating to the North West Mounted Police and Fort Walsh," Manuscript Report Series no. 213 (Ottawa: Parks Canada, Department of Indian and Northern Affairs, 1977), 132–33.

22 L. Herchmer to Comptroller, 23 May 1889, NA, RG 18, vol. 35, file 499-1889.

23 Personal interview with Kirsten Grier, great-grand-daughter of D. J. Grier, Calgary, 19 May, 1993. See also *Fort Macleod—Our Colourful Past: A History of the Town of Fort Macleod from 1874 to 1924* (Fort Macleod: Fort Macleod History Committee, 1977), 268–69.

24 O'Kute-sica Correspondence, (note 19 above) 3.

25 See, for example, S.B. Steele to Commissioner, Fort Macleod, 20 July 1895, NA, RG 18, vol. 2182, file RCMP 1895 pt. 2, and Gilbert E. Sanders Diaries, 20 October 1885, Edward Sanders Family Papers, M1093, File 38, Glenbow Archives.

26 F. Laurie Barron, "Indian Agents and the North-West Rebellion," in *1885 and After: Native Society in Transition,* ed., F. Laurie Barron and James B. Waldram (Regina: Canadian Plains Research Center, 1986), 36.

27 Norma Sluman and Jean Goodwill, *John Tootoosis: A Biography of a Cree Leader* (Ottawa: Golden Dog Press, 1982), 37.

28 Hugh A. Dempsey, *Big Bear: The End of Freedom* (Vancouver: Douglas and McIntyre, 1984), 117. See also *The [Battleford] Saskatchewan Herald,* 14 and 28 February 1881.

29 Newspaper clipping, "Through the Saskatchewan," n.p., n.d, NA, William Henry Cotton Collection.

30 *The Globe,* 4 June 1880; [Fort Macleod] *Macleod Gazette,* 23 March 1886; *The Mail,* 2 February 1886.

31 Canada. House of Commons *Debates.* Session 1886, vol. 1, 730.

32 William Donovan to L. Vankoughnet, 31 October 1886, NA, RG 10, vol. 3772, file 34983.

33 *The Globe,* 4 June 1886.

34 *The Facts Respecting Indian Administration in the North-West* (Ottawa: 1886), quoted 9, 12.

35 Theresa Gowanlock and Theresa Delaney, *Two Months in the Camp of Big Bear* (Parkdale: Parkdale Times, 1885).

36 *[Winnipeg] Manitoba Sun,* 7 December 1886.

37 Sarah Carter, " 'A Fate Worse Than Death': Indian Captivity Stories Thrilled Victorian Readers: But Were They True?" *The Beaver* 68 (no. 2, April/May 1988): 21–28, *Macleod Gazette* quoted 22.

38 Canada. *Sessional Papers.* Annual Report of the Commissioner of the North West Mounted Police for 1890. vol. 24, no. 19, 62.

39 *Moosomin Courier,* 13 March 1890.

40 Joe Dion, *My Tribe the Crees* (Calgary: Glenbow-Alberta Institute, 1979), 114.

41 See Sarah Carter, "Relations Between Native and Non-Native Women in the Prairie West, 1870–1920," paper presented to the Women and History Association of Manitoba, Winnipeg, February 1992.

42 Elizabeth M. McLean, "Prisoners of the Indians," *The Beaver,* Outfit 278 (June 1947): 15–16.

43 David Hamer, *New Towns in the New World: Images and Perceptions of the Nineteenth Century Urban Frontier* (New York: Columbia University Press, 1990), 17, 213.

44 "What Canadian Women Say of the Canadian North-West" (Montreal: *Montreal Herald,* 1886), 42–45, quoted 44.

45 L. Vankoughnet to John A. Macdonald, 15 November 1883, NA, RG 10, vol. 1009, file 628, no. 596-635.

46 S.W. Horrall, "The (Royal) North-West Mounted Police and Prostitution on the Canadian Prairies," *Prairie Forum* 10 no. 1 (Spring 1985): 105–27.

47 Clipping from the [Edmonton] *Bulletin,* 7 January 1883, NA, RG 10, vol. 3673, file 10,986.

48 Canada. *Sessional Papers.* Annual Report of the Superintendent General of Indian affairs for the year ending 1906, 82.

49 Constance B. Backhouse, "Nineteenth-Century Canadian Prostitution Law: Reflection of a Discriminatory Society," *Histoire sociale/Social History* 18 (no. 36, November 1985): 420–22, quoted 422.

50 Canada. *Sessional Papers.* Annual Report of the Commissioner of the North-West Mounted Police Force for the year 1889, reprinted in *The New West,* (Toronto: Coles Publishing Company, 1973), 101.

51 [Battleford] *Saskatchewan Herald,* 15 March 1886, 13 March 1888 (quoted).

52 *Calgary Herald,* 5 March 1885.

53 See for example Carolina Antoinetta J. A. Van de Vorst, "A History of Farm Women's Work in Manitoba" (M.A. thesis, University of Manitoba, 1988).

54 Lyn Hancock with Marion Dowler, *Tell Me Grandmother* (Toronto: McClelland and Stewart Ltd., 1985), 139.

55 *Macleod Gazette,* 18 July 1888.

56 John D. Higinbotham, *When the West Was Young: Historical Reminiscences of the Early Canadian West* (Toronto: Ryerson Press, 1933), 260–61.

57 R.C. Macleod, *The North-West Mounted Police and Law Enforcement, 1873–1905* (Toronto: University of Toronto Press, 1976), 145. See also NA, RG 18, vol. 24, file 667-1888.

58 Donald Smith, "Bloody Murder Almost Became Miscarriage of Justice," *Herald Sunday Magazine,* 23 July 1989, 13. Thanks to Donald Smith, Department of History, University of Calgary for allowing me to draw upon his sources on this case.

59 James Gray, *Talk To My Lawyer: Great Stories of Southern Alberta's Bar and Bench* (Edmonton: Hurtig Publishers Ltd., 1987), 7.

60 Rouleau quoted in Smith, "Bloody Murder" (note 58 above), 15.

61 *Calgary Herald,* 24 July, 10 September (quoted), 27 February, and 8 March (quoted) 1889.

62 See Christine Bolt, *Victorian Attitudes to Race* (Toronto: University of Toronto Press, 1971); Philip D. Curtin, *The Image of Africa: British Ideas and Action, 1780–1850* (Madison: University of Wisconsin Press, 1964); V.G. Kiernan, *The Lords of Human Kind: European Attitudes Toward the Outside World in the Imperial* Age (Middlesex: Penguin Books, 1972); Douglas A. Lorimer, *Colour, Class and the Victorians* (Leicester University Press, Holmes and Meier Publishers, 1978); and Philip Mason, *Patterns of Dominance* (London: Oxford University Press, 1971).

63 Walter Hildebrandt, "Official Images of 1885," *Prairie Fire* 6 no. 4 (1985): 31–40.

64 This is suggested by Backhouse, "Nineteenth-Century Canadian Prostitution Law" (note 49 above), 422.

65 Mariana Valverde, *The Age of Light, Soap, and Water: Moral Reform in English Canada, 1885–1925* (Toronto: McClelland and Stewart Inc., 1991).

66 NA, RG 18, vol. 1039, file 87-1886, pt. 1.

67 Beverley A. Stacey, "D.W. Davis: Whiskey Trader to Politician," *Alberta History* 38 (no. 3, Summer 1990): 1–11.

68 Sylvia Van Kirk, *"Many Tender Ties": Women in Fur Trade Society, 1670–1870* (Winnipeg: Watson and Dwyer Publishing Ltd., 1980), 241, and Constance Backhouse, *Petticoats and Prejudice: Women and the Law in Nineteenth-Century Canada* (Toronto: Osgoode Society, 1991), Chapter 1; judge quoted in Van Kirk, 241.

69 Brian Slattery and Linda Charlton, ed., *Canadian Native Law Cases* 3, 1891–1910 (Saskatoon: Native Law Centre, 1985): 636–44.

70 Canada. House of Commons *Debates,* Session 1921, vol. 4, 26 May 1921, 3908.

71 *Fort Macleod* (note 23 above), 217–18.

72 Ruth Matheson Buck, "Wives and Daughters," *Folklore* 9 (no. 4, Autumn 1988): 14–15.

73 "Talk About Stories," *Anecdotes and Updates: Virden Centennial, 1982* (Virden: Empire Publishing Company, 1982), 57–59.

74 Diane Tye, "Local Character Anecdotes: A Nova Scotia Case Study," *Western Folklore* 48 (July 1989): 196.

Political Patronage Under Macdonald and Laurier, 1878–1911

Gordon T. Stewart

[...]

I

A useful and informative starting point for examining the mechanics of the patronage system is to look at John A. Macdonald's own constituency of Kingston. The picture that emerges from the Kingston patronage evidence shows that patronage was distributed by the party on a bureaucratic-like basis. Appointments and contracts were not distributed hurriedly but invariably followed discussion between local party leaders in Kingston and the Member of Parliament (in this case Macdonald) in Ottawa. Those party activists seeking posts in the public service or public contracts made application, usually in writing, to the executive committee of the local Conservative Association. The committee considered all the applications, weighed the contributions of each applicant to the party's electoral campaigns and then passed on a recommendation to Macdonald who in turn would pass on the name to the appropriate cabinet minister for formal action. In no case in the correspondence was consideration given to the applicants' qualifications—the sole criterion was service to the party.[1]

Within the executive committee there was formal discussion over each piece of patronage.

The local party, through its executive committee, functioned almost as an employment agency for party workers. In 1889, for example, Edward Smythe, a barrister and president of the Liberal-Conservative Association, discussed with Macdonald various jobs in the Kingston Post Office. Smythe informed Macdonald that the committee had now filled all but one of the current vacancies. "That will leave," he noted, "a vacancy among the letter carriers that we will subsequently fill up."[2] Two months earlier Macdonald had written to the executive committee to inform the local party leaders of changes in the Kingston post office that would open up new jobs. These developments, Smythe replied, "received the hearty recommendation of our Executive Committee."[3] When the committee discussed the distribution of such posts, the merits of the candidates were discussed exclusively in terms of their work in the local party organization. Writing in January 1891 in connection with the application of William A. Newlands for a clerkship in the post office, J. A. Metcalfe explained that "his [New-lands'] father and brother are active workers in the Conservative interest and William A. is a good Conservative." Metcalfe added that Newlands had followed the proper procedure, having "applied through the Executive Committee."[4] Once Macdonald received the rec-

Adapted from Gordon Stewart, "Political Patronage Under Macdonald and Laurier, 1878–1911," *American Review of Canadian Studies* X, 1 (Spring 1980): 3–26. Reprinted with permission.

ommendation from the committee, he passed it on to the cabinet minister in charge of the appropriate department. In response to one such recommendation to the Customs Department, the minister, Mackenzie Bowell, sent a note to Macdonald explaining he had signed the necessary papers implementing the requested appointments. Mackenzie Bowell pointed out that neither of the two individuals recommended had "passed the 'qualifying' examinations" and therefore could not be employed as landing-waiters or clerks. But they still received posts in the customs service.[5] Local party considerations took precedence over questions of qualifications.

Because party considerations were paramount it was essential for any applicant to show a solid record of work in local electoral campaigns. An example of these values occurred over the position of second engineer at the federal dry dock facility in Kingston. Thomas McGuire, a local party notable, had been told "the Conservative Association have recommended" Joseph Levitt for the post. McGuire wrote in support of Levitt and warned Macdonald about two other aspirants for the job who should be rejected because they had made contract with the Liberal "enemy." Those other two, wrote McGuire, "are Heretics while Levitt is one of the Faithful as that term is understood by the archbishop."[6] In another case the importance of long, faithful and uncontaminated party service was emphasized. In this instance the record of the family as a whole was considered. A "claim of patronage has been brought before the Executive Committee," wrote J. H. Metcalfe to Macdonald. "I do not admire the tone of the letter yet as the old man and his sons have never gone grit I feel kindly disposed toward them."[7] During the winter of 1890–91 similar considerations dominated discussion of a vacancy for a staff officer in the militia. In December 1890 S. M. Conger, president of the Prince Edward County Liberal-Conservative Association, pressed the claims of his candidate, Colonel Graveley. Conger wrote

of Graveley that he was not only "a most efficient military officer...he is more...he is a staunch Conservative and has made many sacrifices for the party."[8] Another endorsement of Graveley came from R. R. Pringle of Cobourg who reminded Macdonald that "as far as this riding is concerned he [Graveley] has always worked well and he certainly sacrificed himself when he ran for the local [elections] when nothing but defeat stared him in the face."[9] Writing from Port Hope another correspondent addressed himself to the essential point—Graveley deserved the appointment because of "his service to the party."[10]

The fact that service to the party was the most important element in appointments did not make Macdonald's or the committee's task any easier for in many cases there were several suitable party workers seeking a post. In such cases it was difficult to make a recommendation without causing dissent and factionalism in the local organization. In other cases local party notables might either try to dominate the executive committee or try to by-pass the committee and deal directly with Macdonald on patronage issues. All these factors appeared over the appointments of a landing-waiter in the customs service at Kingston, a case that well illustrates some of the local complexities involved in distribution of patronage. In this instance John Gaskill of the Montreal Transport Company and a prominent local Conservative had ignored the work of the executive committee and had pressed his own candidate on Macdonald. On January 8, 1891 Macdonald was warned by George Fitzpatrick of the consequent trouble— "Gaskill is raising a row and I hear that the Executive Committee had a real lively time yesterday. The Kilkenny Election was nothing to it."[11] Fitzpatrick sent a telegram to Macdonald asking that the appointment be held up until a local solution to the conflict was found. The situation was more tangled because Gaskill's candidate had been "insulting" to the executive committee. The committee's viewpoint was put by John McIntyre who explained to the Prime Minister that "we are all anxious to do what we can for the party...but I know the majority of the Committee will feel greatly humiliated if Gaskill is allowed to reverse every recommendation that is made."[12]

The Kingston patronage letters also reveal that Macdonald and local party leaders did not deal simply with appointments but also were actively involved in promotions within the public service and even in the creation of new posts to satisfy the patronage demands within the party. In September 1889, for example, John Haggart, Postmaster General in Ottawa, replied to the Prime Minister concerning the promotion of a clerk within the postal service. Macdonald himself had requested the promotion after hearing from the executive committee and Haggart was willing to comply except there was no vacancy to which the clerk could be promoted. Haggart, however, went on to suggest a solution. He could do what Macdonald requested by "providing in the Estimates for the coming year a first-class clerkship in the Inspectors office at Kingston."[13] There was no discussion about the necessity of a clerkship; it was simply to be created in the interests of the local party.

From this Kingston evidence we begin to get an idea of the workings of patronage, particularly the relationship between Ottawa and the localities. The Member of Parliament, in this case Macdonald, made the formal and final decision about appointments from the Kingston area as he passed on names to other cabinet ministers. Usually the MP received the nomination from the local executive committee. It was assumed that the local party organization, by its executive committee, was the normal channel through which patronage business flowed. When acting on patronage matters the committee did so in a formal way, receiving and reviewing applications, weighing credentials, passing resolutions and forwarding the recommendation to the MP at Ottawa. One final point to emerge is that the structure of the patronage system, as revealed in the Kingston evidence, excluded outsiders from sharing in contracts and appointments. The patronage was given only to local figures who could prove their loyalty to the local party organization.

II

The Kingston evidence while informative may not be typical because of Macdonald's position as Prime Minister. This may have led him to leave much of the daily patronage business in the hands of the local leaders. It is therefore essential to examine other evidence to assess whether this pattern was representative.

One report during the period revealed a good deal about the day-to-day workings of the patronage system. This was the investigation in 1909 by Judge Cassels into the Department of Marine and Fisheries. A basic point made in the report was that since 1867 the department had been used by both the Conservatives and Liberals, when they were in power, for partisan purposes. Positions and contracts were given to reward party activists. Regular "patronage lists" drawn up by the MP and local party leaders were kept on file so business could be directed to party faithful. "The system," noted the report,

> seems to have been handed down from one administration to another since Confederation.... It is apparently based on the old maxim of 'to the victor belong the spoils' utterly ignoring the fact that the money to be disbursed is mainly contributed by the people generally and not the money of the political followers of the party at the time being in power.[14]

During the course of the investigation the activities of the department's office in Halifax provided detailed evidence on how the system worked. In the case of Halifax the MPs were active in the regular distribution of jobs and contracts. The report explained that

> patronage in Halifax extended beyond the mere naming of the merchants and others who should comprise the patronage list. It extended to the nomination by the Members of Parliament representing the constituency of individuals or an individual to whom orders were to be given.[15]

The questioning of witnesses showed the way things were managed. When work needed to be done or supplies furnished "then the members would recommend...that the orders should be given to A, B, C, or D as the case may be." Mr. Jonathan Parsons, the Department's chief agent in Halifax, explained that this was done "under the rules of patronage." He further explained that these rules applied "from year to year and from month to month every year." On every occasion a contract was to be placed the MPs "would designate...which merchant or manufacturer or dealer particular orders should be given to." The questioning concluded:

Q: That has been the cause?

A: Yes.

Q: Each time?

A: Yes.

Q: So it is not your independent judgment that was exercised from time to time as to where the work should be done or by whom material should be furnished; that was done upon the recommendations?

A: By the member of parliament having the patronage.[16]

The evidence also showed that aside from this regular management of patronage the MPs authorized "taking on an employee" because they "had the patronage."[17]

The 1909 Report on the Department of Marine and Fisheries confirmed the assessment made the previous year by a civil service inquiry that the organization of the department, comprehensively influenced by patronage, had "few redeeming features." The Commission of 1908 had made a broad investigation of the public service outside the home departments in Ottawa and had concluded that the outside agencies were entirely at the disposal of the party in power. "As a rule," the commissioners explained,

> in the outside service...politics enter into every appointment and politicians on the spot interest themselves not only in the appointments but in the subsequent promotion of the officers...in the outside service the politics of the party is of greater importance in making appointments and promotions than the public interests of the Dominion.[18]

In each locality the MP and the party leaders regarded appointments and contracts as their exclusive right to be used to reward local party workers. "In practically no case," the commissioners discovered, "is it possible to fill a vacancy in one locality by a transfer from another."[19] In the Inland Revenue Department, for example, "political appointments, as in other branches of the public service, prevail and as a rule the officers in one district are confined to that one district." In Montreal all the appointments in the customs service were made "at the insistence of the members of parliament for the district." Indeed throughout the entire customs service the commissioners concluded that each riding was "looked upon as local patronage" and that posts were awarded to local people only.[20] In his evidence Dr. Barrett, inspector of Inland Revenue at Winnipeg, explained the active role MPs took in preserving local patronage exclusively for local party use. Barrett described how when a post became available "the member for the constituency says, 'No, I will not allow any one outside my constituency to go in there.'" In Winnipeg as in Kingston, the names for appointments were "generally given by the Liberal Association of Winnipeg." Barrett emphasized that "when the Conservatives were in power they did the same thing."[21] In their general observations on this kind of evidence, the commissioners concluded that "each locality was separately guarded."[22] Even the national party leader could not interfere with this local exclusivity. Writing to a party worker who had asked for a position outside his own constituency, Wilfrid Laurier pointed out how hard this would be to arrange. "I need not tell you," wrote the Prime Minister, "that it is always difficult to bring an outsider into a locality."[23]

It is important to note that this type of patronage distribution exclusively to party activists was not confined to minor posts in the customs or postal services and other such branches of the federal bureaucracy but operated at all levels. This can be demonstrated by looking at Macdonald's policies in making appointments to the bench and the bar. County judgeships and the earning of the title of Queens Counsel (QC) were sought-after plums in the legal profession and were at the disposal of the party in power. As with the customs service workers and post office employees, the positions in the judiciary were given by the party in power primarily on the basis of the candidate's service to the party. An example of the essential relationship between party service and advancement in the legal profession is contained in correspondence from 1887 between John Small and John A. Macdonald. Small wrote a confidential memorandum to the Prime Minister with a list of barristers eligible for a QC and set out against each name the reasons for his recommendation:

Michael Murphy: defeated candidate 1882... attended meetings in recent elections.... Roman Catholic; Daniel Defoe: strong supporter,

always took a prominent part in political movements; James Reeve: did good work in the last election; James Fullerton: takes the platform in the interests of the party; George Blackstock: has contested elections; Emerson Coalsworth: rising young barrister, pillar of the Methodist Church, a strong Temperance advocate, President of the Liberal Conservative Association for his ward, was my agent in the last election.[24]

These candidates for QC had varied characteristics—some Roman Catholic, others Methodist, some with long legal experience, others just beginning to become noted in the profession—yet each shared one necessary qualification without which any other would be useless. In one way or another all had worked for their local Conservative parties either by running as candidates, being speakers or canvassers, or drawing up and scrutinizing the voters lists. It was this kind of information on good hard party work that Macdonald looked for when creating a new batch of QC's. And these criteria were well understood throughout the party. In October 1889 Robert Birmingham, the Secretary-Treasurer of the Liberal Conservative Union of Ontario, sent Macdonald "the names of a few legal friends who rendered us special service in the recent campaign in the hope that you might be able to repay them with the much sought after QC."[25]

The next step up beyond QC were county judgeships and these too were distributed with the party's interest in mind. The context in which the awarding of judgeship was discussed can be seen from a case involving the Prime Minister, Frank Smith, the Senator who was the most important Ontario Catholic in the party, and B. L. Doyle, a party worker seeking a promotion to the bench. Doyle set forth his qualifications which rested on the premise that his "services to the party for the last 18 years entitled me to something." He then proceeded to recount the details of this party work, emphasizing that he had "stood by the party in the darkest hours of its severest trials [and] fought for it when it was down and persevered in the desperate struggle on behalf of our principle till the victory again crowned our efforts." Doyle then went on to describe the election campaigns, particularly the one of 1878, in which he had done a great deal to get out the Catholic vote. He concluded his letter with the blunt request—"I want a County Judgeship."[26] This request was endorsed by Senator Frank Smith, who confirmed that Doyle had indeed done all the party work he claimed to have done over the years. Smith wrote of Doyle that he was "a plucky, active man whom I know to have worked hard for his party." Therefore, concluded the Senator, "he deserves to get what he asks."[27] Macdonald was unable to satisfy Doyle immediately because of some rival candidates but he did promise to do what he could and in January 1880 Doyle was appointed junior judge of Huron county.[28]

Other evidence from the Macdonald papers confirms this pattern of judicial appointments being related to partisan activity. In November 1883 Robert Smith QC was recommended for a vacant judgeship in Huron. He was considered deserving of such honor because he was "ever willing to go where duty to his party called him." In April 1885 H. C. Gwyn applied to the Prime Minister for a vacant judgeship on the grounds that he had been:

actively identified with the party...and up to a year ago and for seven or eight years previously [was] the Secretary of the Liberal-Conservative Association of North Wentworth....[29]

In May 1884 a Conservative MP recommended J. M. Hamilton of Sault Ste. Marie for a judgeship, explaining that Hamilton was "very much esteemed throughout Algoma and it is of some political importance that he should

be appointed."[30] About a year later another conservative MP, N. C. Wallace, in recommending Edward Morgan, a barrister for a junior county judgeship in York, explained that Morgan had "fought, bled and almost died for the Party and has very much stronger claims than anyone else that has been promised for the position."[31] In the summer of 1887 A. M. Boswell, a party leader in Toronto, after reporting to Macdonald about party fund raising, turned to judicial patronage and recommended N. C. Stewart for a junior judgeship in that city. Stewart, explained Boswell, was "an out and out Conservative and as steady as a rock. At one time he was not a cold water man but now he is all right."[32]

This evidence concerning the legal profession confirms that at all levels of public employment, from judgeships down to landing-waiters in the customs service, the party in power distributed patronage only to those who had worked for the party. It was not enough simply to be a contributor to party funds or an occasional canvasser but necessary to prove a long period of active, dedicated work in the ridings. The immutability of this standard was well illustrated by a case from London, Ontario, that developed in that spring of 1900. It concerned the family of John A. Donegan who had volunteered to fight in the Canadian contingent in the Boer War. Donegan had been killed in South Africa, leaving a widow and two sons in London. There were some efforts to find jobs for the two boys to help support the family and James Sutherland, a Liberal MP, had written to local party leaders in London asking their views of the proposal to find posts for the Donegan boys. It might be expected that in this part of Ontario the sons of war-dead in South Africa would receive sympathetic treatment but the local party balked and refused to consider them for any posts. In response to Sutherland's inquiries, George Reid, a local party leader, explained that as for making a position for either of the Donegans in this locality, it would be very unpopular, they have never been Friends of ours in any particular and [it] would never do to appoint any one who has not been identified with the work of the party.... To appoint him for any position purely [and] simply because his father was killed in Africa would be to my mind very absurd.[33]

Reid also pointed out that the man who was doing most to find jobs for the Donegans was not a party supporter. If he had been, that might have been a reason to give the Donegans something to reward a party worker but, warned Reid, there was no point in helping the Donegans' backer for "he is a strong supporter of the enemy and of no use to us whatsoever."[34]

A comprehensive example of the normalcy of these expectations is contained in some private correspondence between Laurier and Roy Choquette concerning the Liberal party in the district of Quebec. Following the Liberal victory in 1896 Laurier had asked Choquette to report on the patronage requirements of the local party in the Quebec area. Choquette was to sound out party notables and send Laurier "une liste des nominations...sur lesquels nos amis insistent le plus pour le moment." On September 12 Choquette sent Laurier a detailed list of demands by Quebec Liberals:

> Voici ce qui en est: L'Hon. M. Joly [controller of Inland Revenue] devrait immédiatement remplacer le Dr. Fiset de St. Sauveur par le Dr. Coté, et ce, pour faire plaisir à nos jeunes amis de Québec. M. l'Orateur devrait remercier de ses services M. Fournier, pour satisfaire M. Talbot, et en mème temps le Ministre des Chemins de fer devrait faire l'échange des stations de l'Intercolonial entre Castonguay de St. Charles et M. Roy de St. Moise. M. l'Orateur devrait encore destituer un nommé Gagnon, messager sessional pour donner satisfaction à

M. LaForest, notre candidat contre Costigan. M. Paterson [minister of customs] ou Joly devrait remplacer Philéas Dubé, de Fraserville, officier de Douane, part M. Amédé Gagan de St. Arseire, Comte de Temiscouta....[35]

Choquette then continued, in the same matter-of-fact manner, to list further patronage requirements of other important local Liberals, each of whom, typically enough, had specific rewards in mind for himself and his fellow-workers:

> Pour faire plaisir à l'ami Lemieux, un nommé Baudin, gardien de phare de la Grande Rivière, et qui a voulu le battre à son arrivée à cet endroit, devrait être remerciér de ses services et remplacé par M. William Bisson. L'ami Fisset attend avec impatience, ce qui lui est promis depuis longtemps, la nomination du Dr. Ross de Ste. Flavie, à la place du Dr. Gauvreau, partisan bleu enragé, comme médecin du port à la Pointe au Père; et la nomination du Dr. Boullion, de Matane, à la place du Dr. Pelletier comme médecin du port à cet endroit. L'ami Angers aimerait avoir la réinstallation immédiate de M. Joseph Gaudreau, comme maître de poste à Grands Fonds, Malbaie.[36]

Choquette ended this list of patronage requirements by briskly noting his own demands, "Quant à moi," he wrote, "si l'ami Fisher [minister of Agriculture] pouvait me nommer Desiré Vezina à la place de Zephiron Danceuse comme homme de police à la Grosse Ile, et l'ami Mulock [postmaster-general] me nommer M. Georges Gagné, maître de poste à Ste. Pierre, à la place de madame C. Dienne, j'en serais bien content.[37]

The working of the patronage system as revealed by these examples continued right down to the eve of World War I. The Royal Commission that investigated the civil service in

1911–1912 uncovered the same practices that their predecessors have described in the 1880's and 1890's. One particular interchange between the commissioners and a witness laid out clearly the merchanics of the patronage system. The witness was Robert G. MacPherson, post-master at Vancouver. He was asked how appointments were made to the staff and the following exchange took place:

A: Appointments are made through recommendations by the patronage committee or the members supporting the government.

Q: Do they communicate directly with you when vacancies occur?

A: No. I will apply for one or two men to the department at Ottawa who authorize the appointment of men who shall be recommended by the member of parliament or the patronage committee as the case may be.[38]

From the other side of Canada, on Prince Edward Island, came evidence of how the system worked there. Thomas Mann, agent at Charlottetown for the Department of Marine and Fisheries, explained that appointment and purchasing worked "by patronage." If a position fell vacant, "the members supply a list of men they want put on and if they are suitable I put them on.... In the matter of buying supplies these were purchased "from the patronage people." The questioning continued:

Q: You have a list?

A: It is not a list from the government, just from the local members. They do the same as when the other government was in power. They have their friends to go and so have these.

Q: You have a patronage list?

A: A patronage list of friends to go to, the same as before.[39]

The evidence in this section has provided an overview of the workings of the patronage system in the years between 1878 and 1911. There emerges a remarkable similarity in how the system worked under Macdonald and Laurier and a remarkable stability in a system that had the same structure in 1912 as it did in the 1880's. From Vancouver to Halifax, from London to Quebec, from Winnipeg to Prince Edward Island, Conservative and Liberal administrations of the period used their power in the same way. Federal posts and contracts were given to local party activists in a regular, time-honored manner. Although the actual decisions on patronage were made by the cabinet ministers in Ottawa, the evidence shows that much of the work in terms of identifying applicants and proposing candidates was done by the local party organization, usually working through a committee. It is also clear that the patronage system applied to all levels of the public service from judgeships down to temporary positions in the post office. The system had become so rooted a part of Canadian political culture that it was considered legitimate and normal. It was only late in the period with the Royal Commission of 1911–1912 that serious questions were raised about the impact of so extensive a system of patronage on Canadian governments and their effectiveness in dealing with the needs of society.[40]

III

To understand all the ramifications of the patronage system it is essential to relate it to the structure of Canadian society during this period. The first and most fundamental point to make here is that Canada was a small-town, rural society which was only beginning to be changed by the consequences of industrialization and urbanization. Professor Waite has reminded us of this basic fact in his authoritative study of the period between 1873 and 1896. The rural nature of Canada, he writes, "must be kept continually in mind when considering the character and setting of Canadian life. The conservativeness of the French-Canadian countryside is well known, its resistance to social change is as strong as its political allegiances, but so much of Canada was similar.... Canada was rural."[41] In 1881 the census classified 81 per cent of the population as rural. By 1911 it was down to 56 per cent, still over half the population. But even that figure does not tell the whole story. The census for 1911 shows that out of a total population of 7,206,643 there were 5,507,214 Canadians living in rural areas or in towns with less than 30,000. As late as 1911 about 76 per cent of the Canadian population was living in small-town or rural conditions.[42]

One characteristic related to these conditions is that Canadian society was localistic. Professor Gibson has remarked on this quality of Canadian society, pointing out that "at Confederation and for many years afterwards, the Canadian people, a small and widely dispersed population, formed a simple and individualistic society, exhibiting strong local loyalties."[43] The evidence on patronage cited above shows again and again how social and political leaders in each locality were anxious to keep "outsiders" from moving in to their traditional sphere of influence. An insight into the isolation and localism of Canadian society in this period is provided by the memoirs of the historian A. R. M. Lower. He was born and raised in Barrie, Ontario, and recalled that in 1907 when he was eighteen years old he "had not been more than sixty or seventy miles away from home." Lower wondered whether he was "exceptional" in being thus rooted. "It is remarkable," he then added, "how local everyone was in those days."[44]

Another basically important fact to be borne in mind was that there was limited economic growth during this period and that in contrast to the United States, for example, there was no dramatic advance of industrial capitalism. Even the Laurier "boom years" after 1900 rested on the development of agriculture in the West and well into the first decade of the twentieth century contemporaries still regarded Canada's economy as essentially an agricultural one.[45] In 1896 Byron Walker wrote in the *Monetary Times* that agriculture was "the substratum of our well-being."[46] Two years later D. R. Wilkie, in a speech before the Canadian Bankers Association, explained that Canada "was essentially an agricultural country"[47] and in 1907 this characteristic was again referred to, that "the real backbone of Canada is its agricultural and its dairy and pastoral interests."[48] A 1906 piece in *Industrial Canada* pointed out that "Canada is and always will be a great agricultural country...[the farmer] is the very foundation stone of our social economy."[49]

A natural consequence of this reality was the relative insignificance of the industrial, manufacturing sector of the Canadian economy in moulding the social structure and value system of Canada. Some caution is required in broaching this topic for there is some disagreement among scholars about the nature and performance of the Canadian economy during this period. It used to be a conventional enough statement that there was little economic development between 1867 and 1900, at which point there was a take-off based on the wheat boom in the West. The picture of unrelieved gloom for the pre-1896 years can no longer be sustained, as Professor Waite has recently explained in his assessment of the new evidence.[50] There was steady growth in some manufactures; the GNP rose from $710,000,000 in 1873 to $1,800,000,000 in 1896. Clearly the economy did grow and the transportation and banking structures developed before 1900 proved a solid base from which the more rapid, diversified growth of the twentieth century could develop. Yet, while acknowledging the reality of this economic growth, its limitations must be kept in mind. The manufacturing firms in Canada were small, employed tiny work forces and had a very restricted impact on the social structure.[51] In 1870 the average number of persons employed in each manufacturing establishment was 4.6; in 1890 it had risen to only 5.5.[52] Manufacturing was still small-scale, decentralized and geographically dispersed.

These economic circumstances were important for sustaining such a flourishing patronage system. The key point is that there were limited job opportunities available in the private manufacturing sector and that as a consequence, federal contracts and positions in the federal public service were important areas of career opportunities.[53] In a system in which there was dynamic capitalist growth, as in the United States, employment opportunities at the disposal of the federal government assumed a minor place but in the case of Canada such opportunities were a foremost feature in the job market. The way in which the Donegan family immediately turned to political patronage for jobs is a good example of the role federal posts played in this respect. When it is further remembered that the major capitalist activity of the period—the Canadian Pacific Railroad— was also controlled by the state, it is clear that federal patronage played a dominant role in job distribution in post-Confederation Canada. It is revealing to note that patronage started to decline once the economy began to develop and diversify. There were several reasons for the decline of patronage after the 1914–18 war but one of the basic ones was that the advance of manufacturing reduced the heavy dependence on the federal government (and therefore the federal political parties) for jobs and contracts.[54]

The slow development of industry in Canada had another social consequence that intensified the central significance of the patronage system. Again, in contrast to contemporary United States, where capitalists and businessmen formed the dominant social class, these groups were numerically small and socially insignificant

in Canada. In a society where industrial development was in its infancy and where manufacturing was small-scale, the professional middle-classes flourished.[55] The prestige occupations in Canada lay in this area—barristers, solicitors, clergy, civil servants. In the case of Quebec the pre-eminence of these groups is accepted readily enough. Jean-Charles Falardeau has provided a good summary of the situation in Quebec, pointing out that by the mid-nineteenth century the professional middle-classes had succeeded the traditional elites. "La noblesse professionelle," Falardeau notes, "constitue effectivement, jusqu'à l'époque contemporaine, l'élite Canadienne-Française— c'est cette élite que l'on est tenté d'appeler et que l'on appelle souvent notre bourgeoisie."[56] But while this social phenomenon of a "bourgeois" class composed mostly of professionals rather than businessmen is normally associated with Quebec, it was equally a hallmark of English-Canadian society before the industrialization of the twentieth-century. Because there was no rapid capitalist and industrial development in Canada, there failed to develop a large and powerful middle class whose members could earn a living in ways that were open to trained and educated men in the United States and Britain. Opportunities for upward mobility through business corporations or by selling technical skills were very limited in Canada. This weakened "the development within Canadian society of capitalist, urban middle-class social values and forms of social structure."[57] In these circumstances there was little choice for each generation between 1867 and 1911 but to earn a living and social status by entering the legal profession or gaining a position in the public service.

A nice example of the social prestige a professional man could achieve in this small-town society was given by the Civil Service Commission in their 1908 report. Looking back to the 1880's for an overview of the reasons why public service was so attractive to Canadians the commissioners pointed out the advantages:

Owing to the small mileage of railways and to the lack of communications, most of the necessities of life raised in the different localities were consumed locally. Butter, eggs, meats, foodstuffs and articles entering into daily consumption were produced in the locality in which they were consumed. The same characteristic feature was applicable to domestic servants employed in the households of officials in the public service. A generation ago there was no means by which the farmers' daughters could remove easily from the locality in which they were born, and as the supply of domestic servants was greater than the demand the wages were comparatively small.... The civil servant in these days, although not in receipt of a large income, had his wants satisfied cheaply and without stint.[58]

Not all public employees could afford servants. Nevertheless, it is a valid proposition that for most of the 1867–1911 period, bearing in mind prevailing economic conditions, the public service was the biggest single area of attractive, secure and prestigious employment. Even as late as 1911 employees in the public service still talked in terms of the "dignity" and "respectability" of their position in society.[59] The only way to get one of these jobs was to have some claim on one of the two political parties. It was these basic social and economic realities that enabled the political parties to make the patronage system such a powerful organizing force in Canadian society and politics. [...]

V

In turning to the long-term consequences of the patronage system a paradox appears. On the one hand patronage helped to create and maintain political stability, an essential condition if Confederation were to succeed, but on the other hand it helped to entrench a political culture which because of its nature pushed problems concerning the nature of Confederation to the background. On the positive side the ability of the parties to utilize patronage on so grand a scale over so long a period helped them to attract and retain supporters and thereby establish a solid base in the population. The process of establishing political stability has been analyzed by many scholars studying new nations in the modern world and one conclusion they have come to is that political stability usually requires political parties to have an extensive and influential reach in society. The political parties must be able to show that they can effectively reward supporters and so encourage loyalty to the party. Often some form of patronage or corruption is the means by which a party establishes its position. As Joseph Palombara puts it, "corruption or its functional equivalent may be critically important to a developing nation."[60] For example, in such a new nation, if merit alone were the criterion for appointment to the public service then there would be a growth of bureaucratic power which would push the parties to the sidelines and thus lead to political instability as the parties became unable to attract and reward supporters. In the Canadian case, patronage functioned in this manner. Patronage cemented the support of both federal parties, enabled them to exert extensive influence throughout society, and thus helped create a stable party system.

Such an achievement should not be underestimated in a country as fragmented ethnically and regionally as Canada. But for the achievement of political stability, there was a price to pay. One of the adverse consequences of the patronage system was that it encouraged the persistence of localism in Canadian politics. The way in which patronage was dispersed made every local party organization across Canada jealous of its own territory and suspicious of outsiders. Local exclusivity was sanctioned by the national party leaders. Indeed, this was a deliberate object of policy in order to create strong local organizations to fight election campaigns. This tendency must be kept in perspective. Localism, given the social, economic and geographic setting of Canada at the time, was bound to be a natural characteristic of Canadian politics.[61] The parties were moulded by the type of society in which they functioned. It is therefore a question of degree. Localism was bound to exist and the parties could either simply live with this reality or try to lessen its impact or encourage its persistence. They did the last. The patronage system of the two parties encouraged Canadian political culture to remain localized. From a party viewpoint this was a good thing since it created strong, loyal, hard-working local associations that could be managed by skilled leadership in Ottawa from the center of the patronage web. But it also restricted the vision of those in politics: MPs and local party notables were not encouraged by the system to interest themselves in affairs outside their own areas. The system worked in the direction of local inwardness. Because of this the Canadian House of Commons was in a metaphorical sense "la maison sans fenêtres."[62] The MP's vision was narrowly focussed back into his locality and the windows on national issues were closed or obscured. The long reign of the patronage system contributed to a persistent parochialism in Canadian politics.

The great paradox lying at the center of Canadian political culture in this period was that this emphasis on localism and avoidance of debate on the relationships between the two linguistic groups were the very reasons for the success of the party system in maintaining stability prior to 1911. To explain this paradox it is useful to relate the case advanced in this article to recent work done by Arend Lijphart on elite accommodation and consociational democracy.[63] Lijphart's model seems a fruitful one to apply to Canada. He argues that European countries which have an ethnically segmented population have developed a peculiar form of democracy. In these systems each major ethnic group supports its own political party and the leaders of these parties, the representative elites, negotiate and mediate to form governments and maintain stability without sacrificing the interests of one particular group. Thus, while there may be little communication and even great tension between the various linguistic blocs, the elites of each group compromise in an attempt to reach solutions to national problems. The system then is characterized by elite accommodation. In a stimulating and thoughtful study Kenneth McCrea has applied the consociational democracy model to the Canadian case.[64] McCrea points out that the model can be useful for Canada only if it is modified to account for the fact that the two major ethnics blocs have never been represented by separate political parties at the national level. If accommodation does take place between the elites of each society, it must take place within the parties rather than between ethnically based parties. Having made this adjustment to the model, McCrea analyzed how the system has worked in Canada and concluded that "even by the most charitable interpretation, the political system's capacity to learn and adapt to linguistic-cultural diversity has not been high."[65] The federal parties have not been able to work out solutions to national problems but have instead created a situation of "immobilism and stalemate" in which the federal government seems weak and ineffective. Accommodation within the parties which should have been going on since 1867 has not taken place. On the contrary the gulf between English- and French-Canadians has widened to the point where the continued survival of the nation is in doubt. McCrea concludes that the Canadian political system has a low learning capacity.[66]

This is a complex topic which requires multi-factor analysis. Yet, one of the principal reasons for the apparent ineffectiveness of the federal party system lies in the structure of parties as they developed between 1878 and 1911. The cardinal point here is that both parties relied on patronage so heavily that they reduced the need for any genuine accommodation on such issues, for example, as language in the public service. As Brown and Cook have recently pointed out, communication between the two groups hardly existed except in the realm of politics. In 1902 Lord Minto remarked that he found "the leaders of society of both races unacquainted with each other."[67] In these conditions much depended on the intercourse among the politicians of each group within the two federal parties and they found it easier and more congenial to deal with patronage and localized politics rather than "questions of race."[68]

The impact of patronage limited accommodation in the whole system of appointments and promotions in the public service. As far back as 1877 William Le Sueur drew attention to the fact that in the Canadian public service, no heed was paid to whether or not an employee or candidate was bilingual and no recognition or reward was given to those who happened to be bilingual. Le Sueur pointed out that:

> In a service where two languages are used it is obviously unfair that a man who brings to the Service a knowledge of both, and whose knowledge of both is made use of by the Department in which he serves, should derive no advantage whatever from the fact. Such, however, is the fact. In the Department in which I serve, a man who knows both French and English is made to do work requiring a knowledge of both those languages and to do it for his seniors. A senior clerk may send to a junior clerk that portion of his work which requires knowledge of a second language and the junior gets nothing at all in the way of promotion for this special qualification.[69]

It is important to emphasize that both English- and French-speaking politicians were responsible for this non-recognition of the value of two-language people in the public service—it was not a policy concocted by bigoted Anglo-Canadian politicians. The fact that a contemporary like Le Sueur could put his finger on a fundamental issue like this shows that it is not anachronistic to suggest that more could have been done by the parties to incorporate linguistic duality more securely and formally into the structure of the federal administration. The parties did not do so because it did not occur to them to do so. Whether they came from the Gaspé or western Ontario or Halifax or Vancouver the politicians of the day were interested in the public service from the viewpoint, above all, of patronage. Their interest lay in placing party workers in the service, not trying to make the civil service a setting for reasonable accommodation of French- and English-Canadian interests.[70] In such ways the patronage system, while satisfying the immediate needs of local party associations in Quebec and the rest of Canada, constricted any incipient structural accommodation between the two linguistic blocs.

Canadians of the twentieth century are reaping the harvest of patronage politics during the 1867 to 1911 period. Parties relied heavily on patronage to satisfy ethnic groups within each party and so avoided the need to think about genuine accommodation in terms of the relationship of English- and French-Canadians in Confederation. Patronage was a great strength yet also a great weakness in the Canadian party system. It enabled the parties to flourish and maintain political stability as long as social and economic conditions were fertile ground for patronage and as long as society placed no major demands upon the parties. But once conditions changed, as Canada became an industrialized, urbanized society, as the provinces became more powerful and, above all, as Quebec modernized and began demanding that attention be paid to the basic meaning and structure of Confederation, then the parties which had been successful before 1911 began to become less effective. Their historical development had not prepared them for finding solutions to national problems.[71]

Notes

1 The evidence is taken from the John A. Macdonald Papers, Public Archives of Canada [hereafter P.A.C.], Vol. 14, Kingston Patronage. On the formalities of the process see John McIntyre to John A. Macdonald, October 11, 1891.

2 Edward Smythe to John A. Macdonald, Kingston, November 13, 1889, Private, Macdonald Papers, Vol. 14, P.A.C.

3 Smythe to Macdonald, Kingston, September 17, 1889, Private, Macdonald Papers, Vol. 14, P.A.C.

4 J.A. Metcalfe to John A. Macdonald, Kingston, January 18, 1890, Macdonald Papers, Vol. 14, P.A.C.

5 Mackenzie Bowell to John A. Macdonald, Ottawa, January 8, 1891, Macdonald Papers, Vol. 14, P.A.C.

6 Thomas H. McGuire to John A. Macdonald, Kingston, January 9, 1891, Macdonald Papers, Vol. 14, P.A.C.

7 J.A. Metcalfe to John A. Macdonald, Kingston, November 29, 1890, Private Macdonald Papers, Vol. 14, P.A.C.

8 S.M. Conger to John A. Macdonald, Picton, December 26, 1890, Macdonald Papers, Vol. 14, P.A.C. The militia appointment involved the interests of several ridings in south-east Ontario.

9 R.R. Pringle to John A. Macdonald, Cobourg, December 28, 1890, Macdonald Papers, Vol. 14, P.A.C.

10 H. Ward to John A. Macdonald, Port Hope, December 23, 1890, Private. On the relationship of this piece of patronage to local party "strength" see also Sam Hughes to Charles Tupper, Jr., Lindsay, Ontario, December 25, 1890, Macdonald Papers, Vol. 14, P.A.C.

11 George Fitzpatrick to John A. Macdonald, Kingston, January 8, 1891, Private, Macdonald Papers, Vol. 14, P.A.C.

12 John McIntyre to John A. Macdonald, January 10, 1891, Private.

13 John Haggart to John A. Macdonald, Ottawa, September 19, 1889. In another case Edward Smythe discussed with the Prime Minister the plight of "our old friend B. McConville," a party activist who had been given a contract for carrying the mail and now wished the amount to be increased. See Smythe to Macdonald, Kingston, September 17, 1889. Private, Macdonald Papers, Vol. 14, P.A.C.

14 Report of Investigation into Department of Marine and Fisheries (1909), 10.

15 Ibid., 41.

16 Ibid., 44.

17 Ibid., 42–43.

18 Report of the Civil Service Commission (1907–08), 37, 27.

19 Ibid., 28.

20 Ibid., 89–90.

21 Ibid., 7, 28, 440–443.

22 Ibid., 28.

23 Hugh Falconer to Wilfrid Laurier, Shelbourne, Ontario, January 13, 1908; Laurier to Falconer, Ottawa, January 15, 1908, Private Laurier Papers, P.A.C. Vol. 950.

24 John Small to John A. Macdonald, Toronto, April 5, 1887, Confidential, Macdonald Papers, P.A.C., Vol. 24.

25 Robert Birmingham to John A. Macdonald, Toronto, October 10, 1889, Macdonald Papers, P.A.C., Vol. 24. Macdonald kept a list of all the barristers in Toronto and noted opposite each name the party affiliation. He also estimated the composition of the Ontario bar as a whole according to party membership. The Toronto bar had 150 barristers eligible for the QC—95 were Conservatives, 55 were "Reformers." See List of in Toronto, Macdonald Papers, P.A.C., Vol. 24.

26 B.L. Doyle to Frank Smith, Goderich, November 28, 1879, Private, Macdonald Papers, P.A.C., Vol. 25 II.

27 Frank Smith to John A. Macdonald, [?], December 1, 1879, Macdonald Papers, P.A.C., Vol. 25 II.

28 N.O. Cote, *Political Appointments, Parliaments and the Judicial Bench in Canada 1890–1903* (Ottawa, 1903), 571–72.

29 H.C. Gwyn to John A. Macdonald, Dundas, April 22, 1885, Macdonald Papers, P.A.C., Vol. 26.

30 S. Dawson to John A. Macdonald, Ottawa, May 13, 1884, Macdonald Papers, P.A.C., Vol. 26.

31 N.C. Wallace to John A. Macdonald, Ottawa, July 15, 1895, Private, Macdonald Papers, P.A.C., Vol. 26.

32 A.M. Boswell to John A. Macdonald, Toronto, July 7, 1887, Macdonald Papers, P.A.C., Vol. 27 II.

33 George Reid to James Sutherland, London, May 4, 1900, Laurier Papers, P.A.C., Vol. 873.

34 Ibid.

35 Roy Choquette to Wilfrid Laurier, Ottawa, September 12, 1896, Personelle, Laurier Papers, P.A.C., Vol. 833.

36 Ibid.

37 Ibid. Laurier himself would act on these patronage requests even down to the most minor, by notifying (as Macdonald had done) the appropriate minister of the appointments. For example, in response to one request for Liberal appointees to the International railroad Laurier made out a memorandum naming those employees to be dismissed and indicating their replacements. See H.G. Carroll to Wilfrid Laurier, Quebec, December 29, 1896; Memorandum by Laurier in Reply, n.d., Laurier Papers, P.A.C., Vol. 833.

38 Royal Commission on the Public Service (1911–12), 1292. Macpherson's evidence was given on July 30 and 31, 1912.

39 Ibid., 1416–1417.

40 With the changes wrought by industrialization and urbanization the Canadian government was forced to acknowledge that the patronage-ridden public service system was inefficient and ineffective in the new conditions. This was a basic factor pushing for change. Public opinion was also increasingly critical of patronage after 1900, and an increasing sense of professionalism within the service were additional factors. Public employees in the western provinces were particularly critical in their appearance and representation to the Royal Commission of 1911–12. See R.C. Brown and R. Cook, *Canada 1896–1921. A Nation Transformed* (Toronto, 1974), 192–194, 321; Norman Ward, *The Canadian House of Commons* (Toronto, 1950), 275–281; Royal Commission on the Public Service (1911–1912), 16–20, 337–338; Civil Service Commission (1908-09), 13. The latter report noted that "it was the universal feeling amongst the officials who gave evidence...that this patronage evil was the curse of the public service."

41 P.B. White, *Canada 1873–1896* (Toronto, 1971), 8–9.

42 M.C. Urquhart and K.A.H. Buckley, eds., *Historical Statistics of Canada* (Toronto, 1965), 5, 14–15, Series A 15–19 and A 20–24. On pp. 5–7 Urquhart and Buckley discuss the problems of "urban" and "rural" classification in this period.

43 F. Gibson, ed., *Cabinet Formation and Bicultural Relations* (Ottawa, 1970), 171.

44 A.R.M. Lower, *My First Seventy-five Years* (Toronto, 1967), 33. Some examples of suspicion of "outsiders" appear in this article. The patronage papers of both Macdonald and Laurier are full of other instances. For example a lawyer looking for work in London, Ontario was regarded with deep antipathy because he had no roots in the area. Another individual who was not known locally was described as an "unscrupulous professional man"—i.e., with no base in the local church or community, simply interested in pursuing a career wherever he could get a job. See John Barwick to John A. Macdonald, Woodstock, February 10, 1879, Macdonald Papers, P.A.C., Vol. 251; A. McKean to John A. Macdonald, Bothwell, Ontario, September 19, 1887, Macdonald Papers, P.A.C., Vol. 271. Also see note 30 above for an example in the Laurier Papers.

45 Michael Bliss, "A Living Profit: Studies in the Social History of Canadian Business 1883–1911," Ph.D. Thesis, University of Toronto, 331.

46 *Monetary Times,* June 21, 1896, quoted in Bliss, "A Living Profit," 331.

47 *Journal of Commerce,* November 4, 1898, 634–635; Byron Walker to G.F. Little, October 10, 1907, both quoted in Bliss, "A Living Profit," 331.

48 Byron Walker to G.F. Little, October 10, 1907, quoted in Bliss, "A Living Profit," 331.

49 *Industrial Canada,* March 1906, 484, quoted in Bliss, "A Living Profit," 332.

50 Waite, *Canada 1893–1896,* 74–78.

51 S. D. Clark, "The Canadian Manufacturers Association," *Canadian Journal of Economics and Political Science,* Vol. IV (1938), pp. 506–508. R. T. Naylor, *The History of Canadian Business 1867–1914,* 2 Vols. (Toronto, 1975), Vol. 2, 276–284 argues Canadian industrial development was stultified during these decades.

52 Urquhart and Buckley, eds., *Canadian Historical Statistics,* 463, Series Q 1–11.

53 Naylor, *History of Canadian Business 1867–1914,* Vol. 2, 276–284. Contemporaries talked of the very recent growth of industrial capitalism in Canada and referred to the fact that there was not as yet a class of entrepreneurs who could sit back and enjoy their profits. W. T. R. Preston in *My Generation of Politics* (Toronto, 1927), 204, 487 described the 1880's and 1890's as "the twenty years [which witnessed] the creation and establishment of a capitalist system." Robert Laird Borden in his *Memoirs* (Toronto, 1938), 151, pointed out that "we have no men of leisure or of means." Goldwin Smith in his

Reminiscences (New York, 1910) 456–457, 487 remarked that "Toronto wealth is not munificent. It certainly is not compared with the United States." All these points reflect the fact that Canadian industry was as yet only a struggling part of the social and economic structure.

54 The Report of the Civil Service Commission (1907–08), 14, 17, pointed out that public service positions while still sought after were becoming less attractive as opportunities expanded in the economy. They pointed to the significance of the fact that the lower levels of the public service were being increasingly filled by women. Norman Ward in his study of Canadian MPs emphasizes that many of them went on to important patronage positions. "The evidence is fairly strong," he writes, "that politics in Canada is by no means the precarious occupation it is often assumed to be. Until very recently, only a small number of private businesses were in a position to provide positions for 30% of their employees." See Ward, *House of Commons*, 98–101, 103, 146.

55 Bliss, "A Living Profit," 1, 321, 341; S. D. Clark, *The Developing Canadian Community* (Toronto, 1968), 227, 234. Clark argued that "in a way scarcely true of any other Western nation, the middle class in Canada has been the Establishment."

56 J. C. Falardeau. "Evolution des structures sociales et des élites au Canada français (Quebec, 1960), 10–11.

57 Clark, *The Developing Canadian Community*, 243–252.

58 Report of the Civil Service Commission (1907–08), 14–17.

59 Royal Commission on the Public Service (1911–12), 1213.

60 Joseph Palombara, ed., *Bureaucracy and Political Development* (Princeton, 1963), 11; Hodgetts, et al., *Biography of an Institution*, 14–16.

61 Gibson, ed., *Cabinet Formation*, 171. See note 51.

62 Daalder, "Parties, Elites and Political Development," op. cit., 64–65.

63 Arend Lijphart, *The Politics of Accommodation. Pluralism and Democracy in the Netherlands* (Berkeley, 1968). "Typologies of Democratic Systems," *Comparative Political Studies*, Vol. I (1968), 17–35, "Consociational Democracy," *World Politics*, Vol. 21 (1969), 207–225.

64 Kenneth D. McRae, *Consociational Democracy. Political Accommodation in Segmented Societies* (Toronto, 1974).

65 Ibid., 250, 259–260.

66 Ibid., 254, 261.

67 Brown and Cook, *Canada 1896–1921*, 164–165.

68 In a letter written shortly before his death Macdonald complained, almost in a tone of surprise, that such issues should arise in Canada, that it was "a great pity that these questions of race should arise so frequently." John A. Macdonald to Alphonse Desjardins, Ottawa, January 6, 1891, Alphonse Desjardins Papers, P.A.C., MG 271, E22.

69 Notes on Civil Service Reform by William D. Le Sueur Select Committee on Present Conditions of the Civil Service (1877), 106.

70 McRae's comments are pertinent here. "In retrospect," he writes, "the quest to accommodate linguistic diversity in Canada may be viewed as a series of lost opportunities...and it seems likely that this low capacity of the system to devise effective solutions has helped to increase the intensity of linguistic and cultural cleavage in recent decades." McRae, *Consociational Democracy*, 259.

71 It is necessary not to press this case too far lest the tone become anachronistic. Professor Creighton has warned against placing politicians of post-Confederation Canada in an alien context. They were not eighteenth century politicians interested in ethnic and cultural issues. They were Victorian politicians who were successful in building a viable Canada in arduous circumstances. D. G. Creighton, *Canada's First Century 1867–1967* (Toronto, 1970), 8. These are weighty reminders of the dangers of anachronistic analysis. Yet, as the 1877 evidence of Le Sueur shows, there were alternatives even in the context of the times. Macdonald and Laurier then can be characterized as limited in their responses to the basic problem of Confederation—and these limitations took root and flourished because the patronage system enabled the political leaders to close their minds to structural responses to the "question of race."

Canadianizing American Business: The Roots of the Branch Plant

MICHAEL BLISS

I love my two boys, my only sons, and they are living in a big city of the United States. My heart is aching to have them home again in some Canadian city. I am afraid they will marry American girls and settle down there, almost forgetting their mother…. Isn't it dreadful? Divorces are so common over there. You will say, "What has all this to do with the tariff?" I will tell you just what. I got a letter two weeks ago from one of my boys. They both work in the same factory. The letter said, "What do you think, mother? We may be back in Canada before long. I heard our manager say yesterday…that if the Dominion Government should raise the Canadian tariff as high as the American tariff it would be necessary for our company to start a big branch factory in Canada…. I guess there would be quite a lot of branch factories started in Canada if the tariff should be raised and there would be lots of work for Canadians at home." Now, Mr. Editor, do you see why I am interested in the tariff question? I want my boys to come home, because I think Canada is a purer and better country. They will be better men here. I don't mean that they are not good now. They are both good boys, but I am afraid of the future (From a letter to the Montreal Family Herald and Weekly Star, *1903).*

Was there a Golden Age of Canadian economic nationalism? Did Canadians implement a national economic policy in the era of Sir John A. Macdonald that protected Canada and its resources from the United States? Can those salad days of energetic nation-building before the long Liberal sell-out be held up by modern nationalists, or nationalist-socialists, as an example of what anti-American (or pro-Canadian) economic nationalism should be trying to achieve now?

No.

In the light of present issues, the Canadian National Policy of tariff protection was a very limited form of economic nationalism. Its effect was to resist only certain kinds of potential foreign domination of Canadian economic life, while encouraging exactly those other forms of outside penetration that are now, according to economic nationalists, our most serious economic problem. There was nothing accidental about this apparent contradiction. The old economic nationalism was based on premises about the needs of the Canadian people that transcended the simple black and white attitudes towards Americans familiar to readers of this book. These premises have continued to operate, virtually without regard to the political

---

Bliss, Michael, "Canadianizing American Business: The Roots of the Branch Plant," in Ian Lumsden, ed., *Close the 49th Parallel, etc.: The Americanization of Canada* (Toronto: University of Toronto Press, 1970), 26–42. Reprinted by permission of the University of Toronto Press.

labels of governments in power, as the underlying consensus shaping much of Canadian economic strategy.

The 1911 election seems to have been the apogee of classic Canadian economic nationalism. Laurier's relatively innocuous reciprocity agreement with the United States roused Canadian protectionists to one last spirited defence of the old National Policy. Once again, as in the 1891 campaign, the issue of Canada's commercial relations with the United States was transfigured into a plebiscite on the future of the Canadian nationality. Reciprocity, it was argued, would subvert the economic foundations of Canada (an industrialized central Canada servicing a dynamic agrarian West through a developed east-west communications network), leading inevitably first to economic integration and then to political integration with the United States. More important, the Canadian attempt to preserve a distinctive identity in the northern half of the continent would be abandoned. Imperialists and nationalists—who were never very distinguishable—agreed that continued tariff protection for Canadian industries equalled Canadian patriotism and *vice versa*. This compelling equation split the Liberal party as its protectionist wing rallied round the flag, drove protectionist business organizations like the Canadian Manufacturers' Association into active politics in the comfortable role of national guardians, and doomed Laurier's desperate gamble for one final mandate for his crumbling regime. The election campaign was characterized by anti-Americanism ranging from the rational to the paranoid. John Diefenbaker tried but failed to resurrect its spirit in 1963; one wing of the NDP keeps trying.

But one of the minor themes of the Conservative-protectionist argument in 1911 illustrates the paradox of the "nationalism" of the National Policy. By 1911 there were already enough American branch plants in Canada to arouse concern when Canadians considered tar-

iff policy. That concern, though, was not to limit what had already been called an American "invasion" of Canada,[1] but rather to sustain and encourage the branch-plant phenomenon. Branch plants were obviously a creation of the tariff, and it was equally obvious that tariff reductions under reciprocity might lead to an American withdrawal back across the border. According to the *Financial Post,* the possibility of such an *undesirable* situation developing was already worrying the Laurier government in 1910:

> Now our ministers at Ottawa have not the slightest desire to do anything, or to agree to anything, that will have any tendency whatever to check the movement of United States manufacturers to establish large plants in this country. These American establishments operate importantly to build our population and trade, and to build up a good market for the produce of our farms. And it seems that the existence of our moderate tariff against United States manufactured goods has been instrumental in many cases in bringing us these industries. Hence a strong argument exists for not meddling overmuch with the duties.[2]

When the government none the less pushed on with an agreement that raised the prospect of lower duties on manufactures, Canadian nationalist-protectionists made the branch-plant issue a minor but significant part of their campaign. In his landmark speech to the House of Commons, when he finally broke with the Liberal party, Clifford Sifton specifically pointed to the good effects the Quaker Oats Company was having on the economy of Peterborough, cited an interview in which its president had announced the company's intention to return to the United States under reciprocity, and worried that reciprocity would put an end generally to the beneficial development of American branch plants in Canada.[3] Lloyd Harris, another renegade Liberal, read to the House of Commons letters from American manufacturers threatening to withdraw from Canada and/or refusing to expand. Harris spelled out the branch-plant creating effect of the tariff, and concluded: "That is exactly what I want the Canadian policy to do. I want the American manufacturers to be forced to establish plants on this side of the line and provide work for our Canadian workmen if they want to have the advantage of supplying our home markets."[4]

Still another defecting Liberal MP, William German of Welland, was moved by exactly the same consideration. He pointed out that the tariff had caused seven or eight million dollars of American capital to be invested in branch plants in his constituency, had given employment to thousands of workers, and had created a home market for agricultural products. Reciprocity likely would destroy all of this and ruin the economy of the Welland area.[5] German supported the National Policy because it fostered American economic expansion into his constituency.

Canada's leading protectionist publications similarly were worried about the inhibiting effects of reciprocity on the branch-plant movement. The *Montreal Star* compiled lists of the American branch plants in Canada, and the Toronto *News* asked, "Why ratify a reciprocity agreement that will largely remove this necessity for American industries to establish branch factories in this country? Why do anything that may stop the influx of United States capital for industrial enterprises in Canada?"[6] The *Monetary Times* headlined an anti-reciprocity article, "Americans Will Not Establish Branches."[7] *Industrial Canada,* the organ of the Canadian Manufacturers' Association, worried about branch plants in every issue during the campaign; once, its cartoonist depicted an American manufacturer standing on the Canadian side of the tariff barrier meditating, "I'd build a factory here if I was sure they wouldn't destroy the dam."[8]

All the while, of course, protectionists were branding Americans as monopolistic marauders lusting to exploit Canada's resources and ravish her political nationality. But it was only American Americans to whom these phrases applied. Let an American move across the border and locate his business in Canada and he immediately became a useful economic citizen whose presence should be appreciated and encouraged. Geography, it seemed, had marvellous pacifying qualities.

The branch-plant-creating effect of the protective tariff was not new in 1911, only a bit more obvious. The 1858 tariff on agricultural implements had caused at least one implement firm to pole-vault into Canada. This was noticed and used in 1875 as an argument for further protection.[9] Although Macdonald did not rely on the investment-creating argument in his speeches defending the National Policy, his supporters were quite conscious of it (one Conservative in 1879 claimed the protective tariff "would bring capital into the country, that that was one of its chief attributes").[10] As early as 1880, in fact, MPs were read a communication from the manager of a branch-plant-child of the tariff: "Tell the members of the House of Commons that the St. Catharines Cotton Batting Company would not be in Canada today had it not been for the National Policy, and if the duty is taken off they will take the machinery back to the other side, as we can get cotton cheaper and save freight, which is quite a consideration.... We sell more cotton batting in this part of Canada than all the factories combined. We would ask for a further increase in duty."[11]

Throughout the 1880s and 1890s the establishment of branch plants was noticed in the Canadian press and hailed as one of the finest achievements of the National Policy. From 1882 to 1896, for example, various issues of the *Canadian Manufacturer* (the first organ of the Canadian Manufacturers' Association) contain sixty-nine references to branch plants being considered by Americans, negotiations being carried on towards the establishment of branch plants, branch plants being established, and the benefits of branch plants. Invariably the phenomenon is explained as a result of the protective tariff; the notices often end with comments like "Score another for the N.P.," "the N.P. does it," "more fruit from the N.P. tree," and "another monument to the glory and success of our National Policy." The need to protect American branch plants was used as an argument against unrestricted reciprocity in the 1880s; and the fear that Americans would withdraw from Canada was used as an argument in favour of the Conservative National Policy in both the 1891 and 1896 elections.[12] By the early 1900s it was common knowledge that Canada's protective tariff had encouraged such major American companies as Singer Sewing Machine, Edison Electric, American Tobacco, Westinghouse, Gillette, and International Harvester to establish Canadian subsidiaries. By 1913 it was estimated that 450 off-shoots of American companies were operating in Canada with a total investment of $135,000,000; the triumph of the National Policy in 1911 had greatly encouraged the branch-plant movement.[13] But as early as 1887 a federal royal commission had been told by the secretary of the CMA that there was scarcely a town of importance in Ontario that did not contain at least one branch of some American business.[14]

As economists have long recognized and historians long ignored, the roots of the branch-plant economic structure in North America must clearly be traced to the operations of the National Policy of tariff protection. The situation could hardly have been otherwise; for in an integrated continentalist economy, a branch-plant structure designed for anything but regional economies would have been inefficient and superfluous. The economic nationalism of the late nineteenth century, then, operated and

was known to operate to induce Americans to enter Canada and participate directly in the Canadian economy. Accordingly, the National Policy sowed many of the seeds of our present problem with foreign ownership. Possibly it caused more American manufacturing penetration than completely continentalist or free trade policies would have encouraged. From the perspective of the late 1960s it now appears to have been a peculiarly self-defeating kind of economic nationalism. The funny thing about our tariff walls was that we always wanted the enemy to jump over them. Some walls!

The paradox dissolves once the real nature of traditional Canadian economic nationalism is clarified. The impulse behind the National Policy and the whole complex of policies comprising our strategy for national development was not simply or even basically anti-American. It was rather a kind of neo-mercantilism designed above all to secure the maximum utilization in Canada of a maximum of Canadian resources. The nationality of foreigners competing to manufacture Canadian resources in their own countries or to supply Canadians with foreign resources was quite irrelevant. In the early years our tariffs shut out foreign products without regard to their national origin. They probably had a much more negative impact on trade with England than on trade with the United States, and the economic nationalism of Canadian producing classes supplied much of the resistance to any serious system of imperial preferences in the twentieth century.

Similarly, massive inputs of foreign capital were seen to be absolutely central for this concept of national economic development. Outside money was wooed without regard for either nationality or modern distinctions between direct and portfolio investment. Few people, in the half-century after Confederation, questioned Canada's absolute reliance on foreign capital. Aside from worrying now and then about our ever being able to pay off our debts, no one was seriously upset about the ultimate consequences of a high percentage of foreign ownership—either British or American—of our resources. Least of all were they worried about the flow of interest and profits to foreign countries. As *Industrial Canada* commented in 1908, "That a portion of the profits made on the development of our latent resources has to be paid out in interest is no hardship, since without the capital there would have been no profits at all."[15]

If the Canadian tariff policy was consciously designed to attract foreign capital to Canada in whatever form it chose to come, there were other more precise policies to encourage the same migration. The applications of export duties on saw-logs in the 1890s and then again on pulpwood in the early 1900s were deliberate and successful attempts to force American lumber and pulp manufacturers across the border to set up their mills in Canada.[16] Intermittently throughout the 1890s and early 1900s both the Dominion and the Ontario governments blustered, cajoled, and legislated in an unsuccessful attempt to force the International Nickel Company to move its main refinery to Canada.[17] And the most important of all of these efforts to induce direct foreign investment has been the least noticed: every Canadian province, every Canadian city, every Canadian hamlet pursued its own "national policy" of offering all possible incentives to capitalists and developers to come into its territory and establish manufacturing enterprises. The practice of granting bonuses to industries in the form of free sites, free utilities, tax concessions, loans, and outright cash grants was universal and persistent, despite the vehement objections of established capitalists. It was responsible for the attraction of countless American branch plants to specific cities as well as for the occasional municipal bankruptcy.[18] The federal government led the way in "bonusing" with its subsidies to the CPR and the general subsidy to manufacturing industries inherent in the tariff. On an even grander scale it conducted an astonishing alienation of public resources by "bonusing" every farmer who came to the Canadian West, regardless of his nationality, with 160 acres of free land. Many American farmers came; and there was more concern about their effect on Canadian national life in the early twentieth century than about all the branch plants combined (in a way every American-owned homestead that had family connections to the United States was a little branch plant).[†]

The basic assumption underlying all of this activity was the conviction that foreign capital and business enterprise should be Canadianized, that is, that they should be put to work inside Canada on Canadian resources and thereby produce the maximum benefit for the Canadian people and the Canadian nation. This explains precisely why Americans in the United States were competitors and economic enemies, but were invaluable allies once they had crossed the border with their money and skills. The bare fact of their crossing the border Canadianized them. In this sense the Canadianization of foreign business was one of the basic themes of economic nationalism, at least until the First World War.

Vague dreams of a "Big Canada," of population growth, wealth, status, and power undoubtedly all motivated Canadian National Policy-makers.[19] But there was one significant specific variation of these themes that deserves

[†] In a paper read at the 1969 meeting of the Canadian Historical Association, "The Decline and Fall of the Empire of the St. Lawrence," Donald Creighton argues that the chief subversion of the National Policy came only after the rise to prominence of provincially controlled resources in the 1920s. He implies that the federal government shepherded resources under its control more responsibly, or at least more nationalistically, than the provinces did. My argument may suggest a reconsideration of Creighton's thesis.

more attention. After defence and public order, the most important function of government in nineteenth century Canada was the provision of more and better jobs. Hamlets, towns, cities, provinces, and the nation all assumed that they had a duty to promote jobs for their citizens and for incoming future citizens. They rightly knew that jobless citizens left depressed communities and that such emigration was a sign of communal failure in the most basic way. Particularly in bad times this explains the desire on the part of every political unit to promote industrial development (in good times the "bigness" theme became predominant). The argument of development to create employment was especially important on the national level in the depression of the 1870s. Macdonald's concern for the emigrating unemployed echoes (with only a touch of hyperbole) through his great 1878 speech demanding a National Policy:

> We have no manufactures here. We have no work-people; our work people have gone off to the United States. They are to be found employed in the Western States, in Pittsburg, and, in fact, in every place where manufactures are going on. These Canadian artizans are adding to the strength, to the power, and to the wealth of a foreign nation instead of adding to ours. Our work-people in this country, on the other hand, are suffering for want of employment. Have not their cries risen to Heaven? Has not the Hon. the Premier been surrounded and besieged, even in his own Department, and on his way to his daily duties, by suffering artizans who keep crying out: "We are not beggars, we only want an opportunity of helping to support ourselves and our families"? Is not such the case also in Montreal and in Quebec? In fact, is not that the state of things which exists in every part of Canada...? ...if these men cannot find an opportunity in their own country to develop the skill and genius with which God has gifted

them, they will go to a country where their abilities can be employed, as they have gone from Canada to the United States.... The hon. gentleman opposite sneered at the statement that thousands of our people had left this country to seek for employment in the United States. Why, the fact is notorious that the Government of the Province of Quebec have been taking steps to bring back their people.... If Canada had had a judicious system of taxation [a protective tariff] they would be toiling and doing well in their own country.[20]

By fostering home industries, protection would give these artisans the jobs they were going to the States to find. It was only a small step to the realization that protection would also draw American manufacturers across the border to provide even more jobs for Canadian artisans. And once this was realized, good nationalists—nationalists concerned with protecting the Canadian community from emigration through unemployment—could only encourage the process. Whether or not this whole argument made or makes sense theoretically is irrelevant; it was the economic theory that Canadians acted upon.

French Canadians faced the same problem even more dramatically. The greatest threat to the French-Canadian nationality in the late nineteenth century was emigration to the textile mills of New England. Quebec governments had to create jobs to preserve the national identity of their overpopulated community. The colonization programmes that were begun in the 1840s were serious attempts to create employment in agriculture—far more serious and sophisticated than historians have credited them with being. But there were also significant French-Canadian attempts to encourage industrial development of all kinds in the province of Quebec from at least the 1880s. Thanks to William F. Ryan's *The Clergy and Economic Growth in Quebec (1896–1914)*, we now know that French Canadians at many levels of society understood the potential benefits of industrialism to their community and deliberately encouraged manufacturing and resource-development as job-creating alternatives to emigration. Anglophones, usually Americans, were entirely welcome in Quebec because of the ultimate value they had for preserving the French-Canadian nationality. Ryan's discussion of the role of Laurentide Pulp in the community of Grand-Mère summarizes volumes of French-Canadian social and economic history: "Jamais de memoire d'homme on n'avait vu tant d'argent dans la région et dans la paroisse," comments a native about the early years of the pulp mill; "Owing to the new prosperity the curé of Sainte-Flore was able to complete his new church in 1897," remarks Ryan; and a succeeding curé tells the American manager of Laurentide, "Mr. Chahood, you and I are partners—I look after the spiritual welfare of my people while you are responsible for their bodily well-being."[21]

Extreme dependence on capitalists—often foreigners—for initiating crucial economic development with its accompanying employment explains much of the respect for "captains of industry" before the great depression. Capitalists created jobs; they spent money; they enabled curés to build churches. Even when they behaved badly, as the capitalists of the International Nickel Company did before the First World War, the jobs they provided were so critical that neither Ontario nor Canada wanted to stand up to them.[22] The leaders of the province of Quebec often had to genuflect to capitalists by urging deference and docility upon the working class for fear that a militant labour movement would discourage investment in Quebec and thereby create even more desperate poverty leading to emigration and denationalization.

The nineteenth century economy created the role of the capitalist as hero, as nation-builder.‡

When the foreign capitalist's work led to the development of Canadian resources he too qualified as a builder of the Canadian nation, whether or not he repatriated his profits. Van Horne of the CPR is the most famous Canadianized American (C. D. Howe seems to have won more notoriety than fame, although his contributions to Canada vastly exceeded Van Horne's); but perhaps the most exciting in his day was Frank Clergue, a semi-respectable American promoter who in the late 1890s created the multi-million dollar industrial complex at Sault Ste. Marie. Clergue's remarkable ability to turn the wasteland of northern Ontario into a seeming El Dorado amazed, delighted, and shamed Canadians who marvelled at a man with more faith in their country than they had themselves. For a time, in fact, Clergue became a stronger Canadian nationalist than the Canadians, urging them to have confidence in their own country and its resources and campaigning at all levels of government for extensions of Canadian mercantilism (which would, of course, benefit his industries). Clergue's activities aroused concern about the participation of Americans in Canadian development, but only in the form of exhortations to native Canadians to be as enterprising and dynamic as this American and his Philadelphia backers.[23] Here was a fully Canadianized American businessman, right down to the refurbished Hudson's Bay Company blockhouse he lived in, communing with the spirits of the builders of the empire of the St. Lawrence. Despite the spectacular bankruptcy in 1903 that effectively ended his Canadian career, Clergue has been the only "Canadian" businessman to live on in our fiction, the subject of our most prolonged hymn to capitalist enterprise.[24]

---

‡ This is recognized in our historiography in the popularity of the "Laurentian thesis" and in the interpretation of the construction of the CPR as a national epic. Frank Underhill has been the only major historian to promote a "robber baron" approach to nineteenth century Canadian businessmen.

In a 1901 speech to the citizens of Sault Ste. Marie, Clergue spelled out the ultimate arguments for the American economic penetration of Canada:

Let me summarize the conditions which the captious critic would discover here. He would find in the different lines of industry we had expended here in the neighbourhood of nine millions of dollars, cash, all of which has been foreign money injected into the circulating medium of Canada, to remain forever to the everlasting blessing of thousands of its inhabitants; that the completion and successful operation of our undertaking will require the expenditure of a sum nearly as large; that several thousands of inhabitants had found new employment in these undertakings at a higher scale of wages than had ever before prevailed in Canada...that our works sent over $300,000 in cash to Georgian Bay ports last year for purchases; that we sent nearly as much to Hamilton, and nearly as much to Toronto; that the machinery and electrical supplies that we have purchased from Peterborough have amounted to over $100,000; that Brantford, Galt, Dundas and every other Ontario town engaged in mechanical manufactures had received from twenty-five thousand to two hundred thousand dollars of patronage from us; that our requirements had advanced the price of horses and nearly all the farm products in that part of Ontario tributary to Sault Ste. Marie.... Looking over our office staff he would find scientific and classical graduates from every college in Canada, clerks from nearly every bank in Canada and accountants from almost every city in Ontario. Among the artisans, mechanics and laborers he will find nearly every town and city in Ontario represented, and all of these people have assembled here because they found the rewards of labor greater here than elsewhere.[25]

To Canadians of the day these were unanswerable arguments. The citizens of Sault Ste. Marie had literally danced at the opening of Clergue's works.

Could things have happened differently in the two or three generations after Confederation? Could a more foresighted and active Canadian government or a more dynamic entrepreneurial class have perceived the ultimate American threat to Canadian society and thwarted it before serious inroads were made? Even if Canadians had recognized an American threat—unlikely inasmuch as Canadianizing American business was integral to Canadian nationalism—there would have been no acceptable alternative to reliance on foreign capital and capitalists for national development. Mel Watkins has suggested that a more thoroughgoing state capitalism, including a national investment bank, would have obviated dependence on outsiders.[26] In the context of the late nineteenth century this is utopian: Canadian governments were barely competent to run a post office efficiently or anything honestly, let alone be entrusted with hundreds of millions of dollars for national development; the Canadian people fiercely resisted all forms of public appropriation of their incomes; the safety-valve of emigration to the United States put firm limits on the extent to which Canadian development policies could diverge from American, or the Canadian standard of living could fall below that of the United States. Recently Watkins has also argued that a weak and timid entrepreneurial class abdicated from its crucial role as moulder of a natively Canadian economic policy.[27] Such a Schumpeterian or proto-Marxist approach to economic development is probably inadequate in theory. It is at least unproven in fact, for we know virtually nothing about the actual entrepreneurial activities of native Canadians in the formative years of industrialism. My suspicion is that Canadian businessmen did meet ordinary standards of entrepreneurial prowess and that in areas like industrial education they were frustrated by the conservatism and élitism of the cultural establishment, notably professors of the humanities.

This argument has no more implications for present policy than any historical study. It does, I hope, do something to save the past record from the distortions of the present-minded. The economic nationalism of the National Policy was clearly inadequate as a defence against American penetration of the Canadian economy. On the contrary, it encouraged the commencement of American penetration in the form that most worries modern nationalists, and it did this with a fair measure of purposefulness. The great "sell-out" did not begin with Mackenzie King in the 1920s or with C. D. Howe in the 1940s. If anything it was a consistent policy about which there was an extraordinarily broad consensus. If King and Howe are to be criticized for not perceiving that Americans were the "real" threat to Canadian independence, surely Macdonald also must be censured either for not perceiving the future course of North American economic development or for wilfully promulgating a policy that encouraged American economic migration to this country. In all three cases it is much more fruitful to emphasize the force of their desire to create a community of prosperous and happy Canadians (largely happy because prosperous) and their willingness to import outside resources to that end.

Discussions of the role of élites in Canadian history have so far had little to do with historical reality. If élite theory must be used to explain Canadian economic development, some of the points raised in this essay should lead to a reconsideration of the interaction of élites in the late nineteenth century. In so far as industrial employment depended on the existence of capitalists, the industrial worker had a profound common interest with his employer—in the preservation of his job. The benefits of tariff protection in sustaining and encouraging manufacturing, including branch plants, were distributed to the industrial working class in much the same proportion as to the industrial employing class. Instead of a working class being oppressed by a capitalist élite, there was, at least on issues of high commercial policy, a single "industrial élite" which perceived itself as the beneficiary of the National Policy and all its consequences. By the 1890s a few union leaders had developed a working-class consciousness that led them away from paternalism and conventional Canadian economic wisdom. The mass of Canadian industrial workers, though, were still protectionist. The tariff, they thought, protected their jobs and created new jobs in industrial production. After all, the working class supplied the Canadian content of the American branch plants.

Some of the problems and attitudes reviewed here are still directly relevant. The Canadianization of Texas Gulf Sulphur takes another step forward as the Robarts government is egged on by the NDP to force it to transfer its refinery to Canada—creating jobs in Timmins by sacrificing the possibility of native Canadians some day building their own refinery. Joey Smallwood offers to deal with the devil if he has the capital to produce jobs for Newfoundlanders through industrial development (and what are a few Erco-poisoned fish compared to the wages that ex-fishermen can get in factories?); his alternative is the depopulation of the island. Anglophone control of the Quebec economy is despised, but its withdrawal threatens to destroy the economic base of the French-Canadian nationality. In Manitoba Ed Schreyer finds out as the head of an NDP provincial government that he must take capital where he finds it whatever his theoretical doubts about the extent of American investment in Canada. On the whole Canadians continue to believe—wisely, I think—that a limited but prosperous national existence is preferable to a pure, poor nationality.

In 1909 the Canadian Manufacturers' Association launched another crusade for the support of Canadian home industries. One of the first companies proudly advertising its product as "Made in Canada" was Coca-Cola. Things went better....

Notes

1 *Financial Post,* June 11, 1910.

2 Ibid., June 4, 1910.

3 *House of Commons Debates,* Feb. 28, 1911, 4394–6.

4 Ibid., March 8, 1911, 4905.

5 Ibid., March 2, 1911, 4486–7.

6 Reprinted in *Industrial Canada,* XI, 10 (May 1911), 1072.

7 March 4, 1911, 918.

8 XI, 7 (Feb. 1911), 729. For the issue of branch plants and reciprocity in the United States, see Ronald Radosh, "American Manufacturers, Canadian Reciprocity, and the Origins of the Branch Factory System," *C.A.A.S. Bulletin,* III, 1 (Spring/Summer 1967).

9 William Dewart, "Fallacies of Reciprocity," *Canadian Illustrated News,* Feb. 13, 1875.

10 *House of Commons Debates,* March 28, 1879, 791. Mr. John Weiler brought this and the letter cited in the next footnote to my attention.

11 Ibid., March 23, 1880, 836–7.

12 See *Canadian Manufacturer,* May 6, 1887, 263; April 17, 1891, 198; June 5, 1896, 468.

13 Fred W. Field, *Capital Investments in Canada* (Toronto, 1914), 25. For another account of early American investments see Herbert Marshall *et al., Canadian-American Industry* (Toronto, 1936), chap. 1.

14 Royal Commission on the Relations of Capital and Labor in Canada, *Evidence—Ontario* (Ottawa, 1889), 179.

15 VIII, 10 (May 1908), 763.

16 H.G.J. Aitken, ed., *The American Economic Impact on Canada* (Durham, NC, 1959), chap. 1; Aitken, "Defensive Expansionism: The State and Economic Growth in Canada," in W.T. Easterbrook and M.H. Watkins, eds., *Approaches to Canadian Economic History* (Toronto, 1967). It is significant that the federal government, not the provinces, first began the use of export duties on saw-logs as a means of inducing manufacture in Canada.

17 O.W. Main, *The Canadian Nickel Industry* (Toronto, 1955), chap. 4.

18 For "bonusing" see any Canadian business periodical for any year between Confederation and 1914, but especially the note beginning "Belleville...has organized a little National Policy of its own," *Canadian Manufacturer,* May 17, 1889, 329; also ibid., July 19, 1895, 69, "American firms of every description...have only to make public their designs and be inundated by letters from Canadian municipal authorities."

19 R. Craig Brown, "The Nationalism of the National Policy," and John Dales, "Protection, Immigration and Canadian Nationalism," both in Peter Russell, ed., *Nationalism in Canada* (Toronto, 1966).

20 *House of Commons Debates,* March 7, 1878, 857, 859.

21 Ryan, *The Clergy and Economic Growth in Quebec (1896–1914)* (Quebec City, 1966), 62, 64, 67.

22 Main, *The Canadian Nickel Industry,* chap. 4.

23 For Clergue's career, see Margaret Van Every, "Francis Hector Clergue and the Rise of Sault Ste. Marie as an Industrial Centre," *Ontario History,* LVI, 3 (Sept. 1964); for his exhortations to Canadians, see Francis H. Clergue, *An Instance of Industrial Evolution in Northern Ontario, Dominion of Canada; Address Delivered to the Toronto Board of Trade, April 2nd, 1900* (Toronto, 1900); for reaction to Clergue see *Monetary Times,* April 6, 1900, 1323; Feb. 1, 1901, 987; March 8, 1901, 1160.

24 Allan Sullivan, *The Rapids* (Toronto, 1922).

25 *Address by Francis H. Clergue at a Banquet Given in His Honor by the Citizens of Sault Ste. Marie, Ont. Feb. 15, 1901* (n.p.), 29–30.

26 "The 'American System' and Canada's National Policy," *C.A.A.S. Bulletin,* III, 2 (Winter 1967).

27 "A New National Policy," in Trevor Lloyd and Jack McLeod, eds., *Agenda 1970; Proposals for a Creative Politics* (Toronto, 1968).

Eldorado

William R. Morrison

In the last years of the nineteenth century, an event occurred that once again riveted the attention of the world on the Canadian North. The discovery of gold near what is now Dawson City in the summer of 1896 led to the Klondike gold rush of 1897–99, and eventually made the most westerly region of the North a part of the modern world.

The Klondike gold rush is one of the most melodramatic episodes in Canadian history—a history that is notably lacking in the kind of freewheeling, dramatic action associated with the history of the American West. In fact many people, then and now, confused by the geography of the far northwest and the theatrical nature of the story, think that the Klondike cannot be Canadian; the Dawson City post office still receives mail addressed to "Dawson, Alaska." It was the quintessential frontier episode in the history of the Canadian North. No Klondiker ever "emigrated" to the Yukon, or even "moved" there—both terms imply a permanence that no gold-seeker ever intended; they simply went there, fully intending to leave once their fortune was made.

The world was surprised when gold was discovered in the Yukon, but it should not have been: the great discovery was really no more than the last of the great finds in the mountains of western North America, of which the California gold rush of 1849 had been the first. After that first discovery, miners had been scouring the Rocky Mountains for decades on the reasonable assumption that the California

lode could not be the only one. They were right, and after 1849 further great discoveries were made, notably in south-central British Columbia in 1858, in 1860 in the Cariboo country, in 1861 on the Stikine River, and ten years later in the Cassiar district of northern British Columbia. It was gold, in fact, that led to the initial settlement of the BC interior. The bright trail of gold had been drawing miners northward for twenty years before the strike on Bonanza Creek.

Among those miners were three men who arrived in the Yukon in 1872. Leroy Napoleon McQuesten, a young man from a New England farm who much preferred to be called by his nickname, "Jack," was a likeable fellow who later came to be known as the "Father of the Yukon." Arthur Harper had emigrated from northern Ireland in 1832 and had been looking for gold in various places in North America since the 1850s. Arthur Mayo was a former circus acrobat from Kentucky. The three men worked part-time looking for gold, and part-time as traders. In 1874 they built a post, Fort Reliance, near an Indian village six miles downstream from the present site of Dawson City. The trade prospered, and although they did not come across any large gold deposits, they did find enough to keep them looking. Other miners trickled into the Yukon Valley, and by 1882 approximately fifty men were searching for gold and finding small but promising amounts. By the early 1890s they had grown to nearly a thousand, centred around the community of

William R. Morrison, "Eldorado," in *True North: The Yukon and the Northwest Territories* (Toronto: Oxford University Press, 1998), 78–104. Copyright © Oxford University Press Canada, 1998. Reprinted by permission of Oxford University Press Canada.

Fortymile, located where the river of the same name empties into the Yukon. These were the men who worked out the technique of extracting gold from the frozen gravel (by burning and thawing) upon which the later gold industry would initially be based.

Fortymile, which reached its zenith in 1894, was one of the most isolated communities in North America. It depended for supplies on merchants in San Francisco, 8,000 kilometres away, who shipped their goods north on two small trading steamers belonging to the Alaska Commercial Company. Because there were no government officials in the region, the residents of Fortymile lived in a society of their own making, a "community of hermits whose one common bond was their mutual isolation," as Pierre Berton put it.[1] It was mostly a male society, though some men brought their wives and children north with them, in which miners came and went as they pleased, subject only to the regulations of the "miners' meeting," the governing body of the community.

The miners' meeting, which regulated social as well as mining issues, was an assembly of all the miners who lived in the region, and could be convened by anyone who had a grievance. The meeting would listen to all sides in a dispute, and then deliver a verdict by majority vote. The punishment was often banishment from the community. So long as the community remained a small group of people all engaged in the same pursuit, the miners' meeting functioned quite well. An example of how it worked was the case of Frank Leslie, a confidence man who, in 1886, had persuaded four experienced miners in Seattle that he knew where a rich strike of gold could be made on the Stewart River. The miners put up money and supplies, and the party travelled into the Yukon. But the story proved false, and as the men spent the winter on the Stewart River, the four miners discussed lynching Leslie. Fearing for his life, Leslie waited until it was his turn to cook, then dosed the food with arsenic kept on hand to poison wolves. But he used too little, and only made his victims sick. He then tried to shoot them, but was overpowered and brought before a miners' meeting. He claimed that he had acted in good faith in telling his story, and had acted in self-defence. The meeting decided that he was

an undesirable citizen, and after much discussion it was decided to banish him, so he was furnished with a sled, provisions enough to get out if he could, was ordered to move up-river at least one hundred and fifty miles from that camp, and assured that if ever he was seen within that distance of it, any one then present would be justified in shooting him on sight. He left to make his way unaided up the Yukon.... It was thought he richly deserved punishment, but as they had no prison in which to confine him, nor any way to detain him for any length of time, all they could do was hang him or banish him. His death they did not want to be directly responsible for, though many of them felt they were condemning him to death in agreeing to the sentence imposed.[2]

Leslie was successful in reaching tidewater, however, and he survived. The miners' meeting as an institution did not; when a party of twenty Mounted Policemen arrived in the Yukon in the summer of 1895, one of their first acts was to ban it.

What made the Klondike rush so notable was its timing, not so much for Canada as for the rest of the world, and particularly for the United States. The 1890s was the decade of the "closing" of the American frontier, when the US census revealed that although there was still much free land available for settlement in what are now the "lower 48" states, for the first time since the founding of Virginia and Massachusetts, some 250 years earlier, there was no longer a continuous line of steadily advancing settlement. There was a sense that America had reached its limits, and the Klondike drew many men and women who were looking less for gold than for a new frontier with new possibilities.

The other factor that made the Klondike rush so timely was the great economic depression that gripped the industrialized world, and especially the United States, during the 1890s. Second in severity only to the depression of the 1930s, it led to, among other things, a tremendous political battle over whether the American currency should be backed by gold or could be inflated. This complex and difficult question was the main issue of the American election of 1896, with the result that gold was on everybody's mind. When huge quantities were discovered in the far northwest, the effect in the south was electric.

Had the Klondike gold been found locked in quartz and other rocks, as it is in northern Ontario and around Yellowknife, the rush would have been very different, for individual miners are not capable of extracting gold of that kind. What is needed is heavy machinery for moving and crushing large quantities of rock, each tonne of which contains only small quantities of gold. Apart from the original prospectors, individuals cannot make money from such gold unless they have large amounts of capital to invest in machinery. But the Klondike gold did not have to be extracted with hardrock mining techniques; it was placer gold, and with luck even children could easily fill their pockets with it.

Placer, or alluvial, gold was once locked in rock. But over the millennia it was eroded out of the base rock as grains and small pebbles, along with grains and pebbles of ordinary rock. These were washed into creeks and rivers, but the fragments of gold, being much heavier than rock and silt, sank quickly to the bottom of creeks and were covered with muck and debris. Over the years these creeks shifted their courses; some of the gold ended up covered by many feet of overburden, while some remained right at the surface, or was uncovered by later creeks. The

Klondike district appears on the map as a number of creeks running in all directions down from a prominent hill. Many of the creeks were gold-bearing, and it is thought that the original source of the gold was in this hill, from which it had washed out in all directions. There is, therefore, no longer a mother lode in the Klondike: all the gold was long ago deposited in the creeks.

The technique was simple, though it could be arduous. The prospectors looked for gold by "panning" the gravel in the beds of streams. This technique—which tourists visiting the Dawson City suburb of Guggieville can practise today—involves taking a quantity of gravel in a pie shaped pan about two feet in diameter, filling it half-full of water, holding it away from your body at a slight downward angle, and swirling the mixture around in such a way that the gravel will spill out of the pan in small quantities; because the gold is heavier than the gravel, it will remain when the lighter material is washed out. This technique is easily learned and works even with "colours," or very small flakes of gold, as tourists find to their delight: every one seems to find a few small flakes, though the proprietors of this attraction swear that the gravel is not salted.

If panning showed that the area looked promising, prospectors would stake a claim and then dig down. This was where the hard work began. Because the Klondike is in the region of permafrost, the creek beds are frozen a few centimetres below the surface, even in midsummer. Hence prospectors had to thaw the ground by building fires before they could scrape up the loose gravel. This process was repeated until either gold was struck or a shaft was thawed down to bedrock. If gold was found, the prospectors would start digging horizontally at that level, following the vein and thawing as they went; this was generally done in the winter, since the shafts and tunnels were likely to collapse if warm summer air weakened them. The gravel was piled on the surface to wait for the creeks to thaw in the spring.

When warm weather came, the pile of gravel thawed in the sun and was then run through a sluice-box. This was a wooden trough roughly two metres long, placed at a slight angle. Small strips of wood, called "riffles," were placed across the bottom of the sluice-box, then gravel was shovelled into the upper end of the box and water was diverted into it. As the water washed the gravel down the length of the box, the gold fell to the bottom, where it was caught by the riffles. Periodically the water was stopped and the gold was scraped off the upper edge of the riffles. The whole process, from thawing to sluicing, was simple and cheap, and could be managed by one or two men. However, it was profitable only where the gold was plentiful, as inevitably a considerable amount escaped the sluice box. Quite soon this method was replaced by more capital-intensive methods.

The great discovery of August 1896 was made by three men: two Tagish brothers from the southern Yukon and one veteran miner. George Carmack, born in California, had been prospecting in the Yukon and Alaska for more than ten years. His partners were Skookum Jim and Dawson Charlie (also known as Tagish Charlie). Carmack did not share the prejudice against Indians that was common among miners. In fact, he was married to his partners' sister Kate, and his friendship with the Indians had earned him the nickname "Siwash George." This was a pejorative term; "siwash" was the regional equivalent of "kaffir" or "darkie." Later, though, when he became rich, Carmack also sought to be respectable, and then he deserted Kate.

In mid-August 1896 the three men were panning on Rabbit Creek, which flows into the Klondike River a few kilometres east of Dawson City. On the 16th of the month one of them found a good-sized nugget lying near a rock. Turning over the rocks, they found gold lying in the cracks, "thick between the flaky slabs, like cheese sandwiches," as Carmack later recalled.[3] The men shouted for joy, panned some more

gold, and staked their claims, each of which, under the rules adopted by the miners' meeting, ran 500 feet (152 metres) along the creek, and from "rim-rock to rim-rock" of the narrow valley where the creek lay. The two brothers each staked a single claim, and Carmack, as discoverer, took one more. Later, when he had deserted his wife and fallen out with her brothers, they claimed that it was Skookum Jim who had made the discovery, and that they had agreed to let Carmack take credit for it because he was white and would thus stand a better chance of having his claim recognized. It was Carmack who renamed the creek "Bonanza," a name that was soon to become world-famous.

The three men then travelled down the Yukon River to Fortymile to register their claims, and within a few days the settlement was all but deserted as virtually every miner in the region descended on Bonanza Creek. By the end of month the whole creek and several of its neighbours had been staked, a rich harvest of gold was being gathered, and a small settlement was springing up a few kilometres away, at the confluence of the Klondike and Yukon Rivers. Joe Ladue, a trader as well as a prospector, staked not a creek but the tract of flat land where the Native people dried their salmon, in anticipation of the trade that would follow a great rush. He paid some earlier prospectors $10 an acre for their rights to the land, bought some cabins from the Indians, and named his town Dawson City, after George M. Dawson, the director of the Geological Survey of Canada, who had explored the region nine years earlier. He was soon selling building lots for $1,000 each.

An irony of the Klondike gold rush was that, with a few spectacular exceptions, most of the good claims were staked by men who were already in the North. Although rumours travelled quickly, solid proof of the strike did not reach the south until the spring of 1897, and by the time southern gold-seekers got to the Klondike, no earlier than the fall of that year and in most cases not until the spring of 1898, there were no claims left to be staked. In August 1896 Bonanza Creek was staked, and two weeks later another discovery was made on a small "pup" or tributary creek named Eldorado. About fifty claims were staked on this short creek, reputedly yielding an average of half a million dollars each (about $30 million altogether), and this with the inefficient sluicing method. Gold is now worth about twenty times as much as in 1896, when it sold for US$20 per ounce, so the gold from this one creek would be worth roughly $600 million US dollars today, or $800 million Canadian.

The news of the great discovery soon spread to the other settlements of the Yukon River Valley, downstream in Alaska, and to the towns of the Alaska panhandle. Hundreds of men and women already in the north rushed to Dawson City—if not to stake a claim, then to "mine the miners" as saloon-keepers, laundresses, hotel-keepers, barbers, or prostitutes. On 14 July 1897 the *Excelsior,* a steamer owned by the Alaska Commercial Company, reached San Francisco with $500,000 in gold, and on the 17th the *Portland* docked at Seattle with over $1 million's worth. Men staggered down the gangplank, grimy but smiling, bent under the weight of suitcases filled with gold. At 1897 prices the *Portland's* cargo alone—literally a tonne of gold—represented an incredible fortune; in an era when the average industrial wage in the United States was $460 a year, an ounce of gold was worth more than two weeks' wages. Some of the early strikes on Bonanza and Eldorado creeks had yielded ten or more ounces per pan—half a year's wages for a factory worker, pulled out of a Yukon stream in ten minutes. This fact—or, as it was for most, this fantasy—of easy riches helps to explain the furore surrounding the Klondike gold rush.

As the news from the Pacific coast ports went out over the cables, the steamship companies were swamped with inquiries, not only from the United States and Canada but from Western Europe and as far away as Australia. Within weeks, thousands were looking in atlases to find out where the Klondike was, and the merchants of Seattle, Victoria, San Francisco, and Vancouver were laying their plans to profit from the craze.

The gold-seekers—or Klondikers, as they came to be called—were not only poor folk hoping to strike it rich. A good number of well-to-do people made the trip simply because the spirit of the late Victorian period made it almost obligatory for a man with "pluck" to pursue the opportunities available in the "colonies."

There were many ways to get to Dawson City. The easiest, and the most costly, was to buy a ticket on a steamship travelling by sea to the mouth of the Yukon, then up that long river to Dawson City. The trip from Seattle or Victoria could be made in three weeks, but space was very limited, since the few steamers that plied that route carried mostly freight; the trip included a stretch over open ocean that could be unpleasant; and the tickets were very expensive—well over $1,000 at the height of the rush. A much cheaper route was the traditional one over the Chilkoot or the White Pass, and this was the one that the majority of Klondikers took. There were other routes as well: the merchants of Edmonton, a small town at the end of the railroad in northern Alberta, touted an "all-Canadian" route running from their community north to Lake Athabasca, thence to Great Slave Lake, down the Mackenzie to Fort McPherson, then to Alaska by way of the Rat, Bell, and Porcupine Rivers, and finally back up the Yukon River to Dawson City. A glance at a map should have discouraged anyone from trying it, yet over 1,600 people did, of whom roughly half succeeded in reaching Dawson, though not until the spring of 1898. Several, including the police chief of Hamilton, Ontario, died en route of starvation and scurvy, trapped in the mountains between the

Mackenzie Valley and Dawson City. It was this episode of misery and death that provided the inspiration for "Klondike Days," Edmonton's annual summer festival.

Other routes were even less practical. Of the hundred Americans who tried to reach the Klondike by travelling across the Malaspina Glacier at the head of Yakutat Bay, nearly half died. The North-West Mounted Police tried an overland route from British Columbia to the Yukon by way of Fort Nelson, in the province's northeastern corner; it took them fourteen months. Others, including a party of Canadian soldiers sent to help the police preserve order in the Yukon, travelled through central British Columbia along the old telegraph trail to Teslin Lake and eventually the Klondike. Whatever the route, it was not an easy journey, except for the few who could afford ship passage up the Yukon River.

The great majority of Klondikers used the old route over one or other of the passes at the head of the Lynn Canal, where two towns a few kilometres apart, Skagway (serving the White Pass route) and Dyea (serving the more popular Chilkoot Pass route), had sprung up to serve them. They landed at Skagway, by 1898 a city of 10,000 and a roaring frontier town in the lawless tradition of the American West. It was ruled by a gangster named Soapy Smith, whose agents robbed the "cheechakos," as the greenhorns were called, or fleeced them in gambling dens. It is about 30 kilometres from tidewater to the Canadian border at the summit of the two passes, but it was a gauntlet that had to be run. Sam Steele, who commanded the Mounted Police in the Yukon at the height of the gold rush, described Skagway as it was when he saw the town early in 1898:

> Robbery and murder were daily occurrences.... Shots were exchanged on the streets in broad daylight.... At night the crash of bands, shouts of "Murder!" cries for help, mingled with the cracked voices of the singers in the variety halls; and the wily "box rushers" [variety actresses] cheated the tenderfeet.... In the White Pass and above the town the shell game expert plied his trade, and occasionally some poor fellow was found lying lifeless on his sled where he had sat down to rest, the powder marks on his back, and his pockets inside out.[4]

In the summer of 1898, Soapy Smith met his fate in the great western tradition, shot dead by a vigilante, and Skagway settled down. The town was given a new lease on life when the White Pass and Yukon Railway linking it to Whitehorse was completed in 1900, and it now survives, with a population of 750, as a destination for tens of thousands of tourists who come on summer cruise ships to see the spectacular coastline of British Columbia and Alaska.

On the map the Chilkoot Pass route looks easy enough. By a fluke of geography, the headwaters of the Yukon River lie at Lake Lindeman, less than 50 kilometres from the ocean at Dyea. From that lake it is possible to float or sail all the way to Dawson City, and past it roughly 1,500 kilometres to the Bering Strait, with only two impediments to navigation: the White Horse rapids and Miles Canyon, both near present-day Whitehorse. The hard part was getting to that lake. First the Klondikers walked from Skagway around a point of land to the smaller but equally corrupt town of Dyea. Nothing now remains of this community apart from a graveyard and a few rotting cabins, but it was lively enough in 1898. Here the Chilkoot trail started as an easy walk through spruce woods. Within two or three kilometres it began to steepen, however, and the small streams that crossed it, together with the scores of horses and people that used it, turned it to clinging mud.

In 25 kilometres a Klondiker would have climbed 300 metres and arrived at the community of Sheep Camp, a crude tent community where meals could be bought and packers hired to help carry goods over the pass. Now the trail became steeper still, and over the next 3 kilometres it climbed to 600 metres to reach "the Scales," at the bottom of the pass itself. Here was the really difficult part, for the final stretch to the summit of the pass reached almost 1000 metres in a short distance, and the last few hundred metres rose at an angle of nearly forty degrees.

Yet it was not the pass that made the experience such torture—it is used today by hikers, and is perhaps easier in winter, when most Klondikers went over it, than in summer, when large boulders uncovered by snow make walking more treacherous. What made the experience so grim was the number of times the pass had to be climbed. The Mounted Police, who guarded the Canadian border at the summit of the pass, decreed that no one would be permitted to cross it without enough money or supplies to last six months, which meant bringing perhaps a tonne of goods over the pass. If a man carried 45 kilograms—a heavy burden up a forty-degree slope—he would have to make the trip twenty times. The alternative was to hire Chilkat packers, who charged as much as two dollars a kilo, or use the aerial tramway that an ingenious entrepreneur had strung from the Scales to the summit; but this was also expensive. The famous images of men bent under massive packs, their heavy wool cold-weather gear wet with snow and sweat, climbing in lockstep up the slope—afraid to drop out lest they be forced to wait hours to get back in the queue—are all the more dramatic when one realizes that each one of them had to make the journey over and over again. It is no wonder that many Klondikers looked at the pass, sold their goods, at a loss, on the spot, and took the next ship home.

But thousands more did make the journey, and not all of them were men. Legend has it that the women who went to the Klondike were typically prostitutes, but this was not the case: like the miners, some were seeking wealth and some simply adventure. One of the best-known of this last group was Martha Black. Born in 1866, in Chicago, to a wealthy family, at the age of nineteen she married a railway executive. After a decade the two had become bored with middle-class life, and when they heard of the tonne of gold in Seattle, they decided to become Klondikers. But her husband had second thoughts about the Yukon and decided to go to Hawaii instead, so Martha left him and travelled north with only her brother as companion. She crossed the Chilkoot Pass in July 1898 and left a vivid account of the journey in her memoirs:

> In my memory it will ever remain a hideous nightmare. The trail led through a scrub pine forest where we tripped over bare roots of trees that curled over and around rocks and boulders like great devilfishes. Rocks! Rocks! Rocks! Tearing boots to pieces. Hands bleeding with scratches. I can bear it no longer. In my agony, I beg the men to leave me—to let me lie in my tracks.[5]

Of course they didn't leave her, and eventually she made it to Dawson City where she went into the lumber business, raised a son alone, and eventually married a local lawyer who had the luck and the political connections to become first the Territorial Commissioner and later the Yukon's member of Parliament. She served in Parliament herself while her husband was ill, becoming in 1935, at the age of 70, only the second woman elected to the House of Commons. She lived to be 91, and at her death in 1957 she was the undoubted doyenne of the Yukon. Her feelings about the Chilkoot Pass, like those of many others, were decidedly mixed. In her memoirs, first published in 1938 as *My Seventy Years,* she asked herself if she would do it again: "Not for all the gold in the Klondyke" was the reply; "And yet, knowing now what it meant, would I miss it?... No, never!... Not even for all the gold in the world!"

The alternative to the Chilkoot route was the White Pass, which was not so steep, cresting at just under 900 metres. It was, however, not only some 24 kilometres longer, but wetter and hence muddier. For considerable periods it was nearly impassable. But pack horses could be used along the entire trail, and hundreds of them broke their legs on it, or fell over cliffs, or died straining to the summit. A stretch of the trail named Dead Horse Gulch became infamous, and the American novelist Jack London wrote a horrifying description of the place:

> The horses died like mosquitoes in the first frost and from Skagway to Bennett they rotted in heaps. They died at the rocks, they were poisoned at the summit, and they starved at the lakes; they fell off the trail, what there was of it, and they went through it; in the river they drowned under their loads or were smashed to pieces against the boulders; they snapped their legs in the crevices and broke their backs falling backwards with their packs; in the sloughs they sank from fright or smothered in the slime; and they were disembowelled in the bogs where the corduroy logs turned end up in the mud; men shot them, worked them to death and when they were gone, went back to the beach and bought more.[6]

It was the gentler grade of the White Pass that would lead the railroad builders to choose it over the Chilkoot, and thus to ensure the survival of Skagway.

Both the Chilkoot and the White Pass routes led to the same pair of joined lakes, Lindeman and Bennett. Here the Klondikers pitched camp and built boats from scratch by cutting trees and sawing the green lumber in saw-pits. These were platforms of rough logs with enough space between them to fit the tree to be sawn and a long straight saw with a handle at both ends. One man stood on the ground and another on the platform, the first pulling on the saw and the second pushing. It was brutally hard work, and a fair division of labour was almost impossible. Many friendships and partnerships foundered before the boat was half-built. When, on 29 May 1898, the ice broke up on the lakes, 7,000 boats and rafts left for Dawson City. Five men were drowned in Miles Canyon before the Mounted Police began inspecting the vessels and forcing those judged unsafe to portage around the canyon—an entrepreneur built a crude tramway with logs for rails. But for most the trip to Dawson City was a pleasant one that involved no effort but steering.

By the time the first Klondikers reached Dawson City in the early summer of 1898, nearly two years after the discovery on Bonanza Creek, all the gold-bearing creeks had been staked and there were no more bonanzas to be found. Their choices were to turn around and go home—if they could afford to—or to find some sort of wage labour, either on someone else's claim or in Dawson City. By the end of that year the population of the Yukon had reached a number estimated at between thirty and forty thousand—nearly ten thousand more than it is today.

Dawson City at the height of the gold rush was a turbulent town, where gambling and prostitution were, if not legal, at least openly tolerated by the authorities. Saloons and dance-halls ran twenty-four hours a day, but, significantly, not seven days a week: they shut down at midnight on Saturday and remained closed until midnight on Sunday. This fact illustrates what in some ways was the most remarkable feature of the Yukon during the gold rush—the power of the police to enforce a nominal orderliness on a community of considerable turbulence. However, theft and other property crimes were endemic.

The Yukon, made a District of the North-West Territories in July 1895 and a Territory in June 1898, was firmly under the control of the North-West Mounted Police. Local government consisted of the Territorial Commissioner and a small Council, all appointed by Ottawa rather than elected locally, and the council's meetings were at first closed to the public. The federal government was determined to have no hint of local self-government in the Yukon, so the laws were made and enforced by people who were in no way answerable to the population of the territory. These men—among them Sam Steele of the NWMP, who was also a member of the Council—had as their first priority the maintenance of public order. Although no proper census was taken in the Yukon until 1901, after the rush was over, there is no doubt that the population was overwhelmingly American. For this reason, the authorities were all the more determined that Dawson City would not become a wild-west town on the Skagway model, a development that might have cast doubt on Canadian sovereignty in the region.

Thus the government rushed police reinforcements to the Yukon. There had been 20 officers in the region when gold was discovered in 1896. By February 1898 they numbered 196, eventually reaching more than 300, and were backed up by the Yukon Field Force, a unit of 200 men drawn from the Canadian Army (nearly a quarter of the entire army!), who served in the Yukon from 1898 until 1900. The presence of 500 police and soldiers in a population of at most 40,000 was one reason that Dawson was so free of violent crime. The other reason was that the Mounted Police were tireless in asserting their authority. They vigorously enforced the law against carrying weapons in Dawson City, and as a result there were very few murders in the Yukon during the rush, and none at all in the saloons—a notable contrast to the situation in Skagway. They enforced the peace in Dawson City partly by handing out stiff sentences—hard labour on the woodpile at the police barracks was the usual punishment for minor crimes—and since the commander of the police also served as magistrate, convictions were not difficult to obtain. The police made a habit of ordering bad characters to leave the Yukon, sometimes even when no real crime had been committed; this policy was very much in the tradition of the miners' meetings that the police had supplanted.

Of course, as the police themselves noted, the Yukon was not a good country for criminals. Not only was it hard to escape from the region unless one had highly developed survival skills, which most criminals did not, but there were only three common routes out, and the police guarded them all closely to make sure that the royalty on gold was paid. The fact that anyone who tried to leave the Yukon overland took a serious risk of starving in the wilderness helped to curb violent impulses. The popular image of the Yukon, epitomized in Robert Service's famous poem "The Shooting of Dan McGrew," is a product not of fact but of the idea that all frontiers must be violent, and of the popular confusion between the Yukon and the Alaskan mining communities, which did conform to the frontier stereotype.

Robert Service (1874–1958) was an Englishman who came to Canada at the age of 24 and, as an employee of the Canadian Bank of Commerce, was stationed for several years at Whitehorse and Dawson City. It was at Whitehorse, far from the events he recounted, that he wrote and published his first book of poems, *Songs of a Sourdough* (1907), which included "Dan McGrew." The first stanza sets the scene; its rough, forceful style shows why in his time he was called "the Canadian Kipling":

A bunch of the boys were whooping it up in the Malamute saloon,

The kid that handles the music-box was hitting a jag-time tune;

Back of the bar, in a solo game, sat Dangerous Dan McGrew

And watching his luck was his light-o'love, the lady that's known as Lou.

As far as it goes, this is a reasonably accurate picture of saloon life in the gold-rush period. But then Service reaches for a dramatic climax:

Then I ducked my head, and the lights went out, and two guns blazed in the dark;

And a woman screamed, and the lights went up, and two men lay stiff and stark;

Pitched on his head, and pumped full of lead, was Dangerous Dan McGrew,

While the man from the creeks lay clutched to the breast of the lady that's known as Lou.

What is wrong with this picture is that there was not a single murder in a Dawson City saloon during the entire gold-rush period. The police did not permit men to carry firearms in town, and the law was strictly enforced. Since Service was writing eight years after the height of the rush, he may have been influenced by the tall tales told him by veterans. Or perhaps he just wanted to tell an exciting story. Of course this is popular verse, not a legal record of events. But Service was world-famous; he probably made more money from his work than any other poet writing in Canada, and there are still people who will declaim his verse at length unless forcibly prevented. For many, Service's work represents the truth of the gold rush, and it is a pity that he bent his material to fit preconceived ideas of what a "frontier" society ought to be like. Presumably, though, a poem in which the climax consisted of an arrest for disorderly conduct, and the denouement of a sentence to two weeks' work cutting stove wood, would not have had the same success.

The gold rush pushed the Canadian north onto the national and the world stage in a number of ways. The arrival of thirty to forty thousand people focused attention on the region, and public interest was heightened by the dispatches of the newspaper reporters who covered the story. The rush also forged important links between north and south. In order to improve the dismal communication links between the Territory and the outside, the federal government built a telegraph line to Dawson City. More impressive still was the construction, by a British consortium, of the White Pass and Yukon Railway, a narrow-gauge line built from Skagway through the White Pass to Whitehorse between 1898 and 1900, a distance of 166 kilometres. This was a remarkable feat of engineering, since the railroad had to climb from sea level to nearly 900 metres in just 33 kilometres. Even more remarkable was the fact that the line was built without a cent of government subsidy; few North American railroads can make the same claim. Profitable from the beginning, the line operated for eighty years, and closed only when a downturn in the Yukon economy, and competition from a highway, put it out of business. The section from Skagway to the Canadian border later reopened as a tourist attraction, however, and today provides a truly spectacular trip for the thousands who visit Skagway on cruise ships. For a few years the Yukon even had a second railway: in 1906 the Klondike Mines Railway was built from Dawson City to the creeks, using rolling stock shipped to the town by steamboat. But it never showed a profit, and closed in 1914.

The construction of the White Pass and Yukon Railway spurred the growth of the Yukon's second community, one that in time would supersede its rival to the north. The White Horse rapids marked the head of steamboat navigation on the Yukon River, and it was for that reason that the small settlement there was chosen as the terminus for the railroad. The town of Whitehorse flourished in summer as a transfer point between the trains and the boats, and in winter, on a much reduced scale, it handled passengers and mail transferring between the trains and the overland sled service to Dawson City.

The gold rush ended abruptly in the summer of 1899 when gold was discovered on the beaches of Nome, Alaska, and the more volatile elements of the population—those with the stamina to follow another rush—left the Yukon. The territory's population began a slow decline that was not reversed for forty years. The mining industry did not disappear, but its technology changed, and fewer people were needed in any case to extract the precious metal. If the rush itself had ended, however, the mines would remain profitable for several decades to come. In 1897 gold worth $2.5 million was taken from the creeks; in 1898 the value was $10 million; and in 1900, the year of greatest production, over $22 million. Total production up to 1911 amounted to $140 million—about $3.5 billion in modern Canadian dollars.

The Klondike gold rush was the first "modern" event to occur in the Canadian North, in the sense that it brought to the region for the first time a large non-Native population, along with modern technology, urbanization, and all the other paraphernalia of the twentieth century. Though it left the NWT virtually untouched, it transformed the Yukon, or at least part of it; the Aboriginal people stood aside—or were excluded—from the events of the gold-rush period. The legacy of the 1890s for the Yukon was an infrastructure that, modern for its day, proceeded to decay over the next forty years; an economy dependent on world mineral prices; and a white population that shrank in twenty years from 40,000 to 2,500 and did not begin to grow again until the Second World War. The wealth of the North had always left the North, extracted by outsiders, and this was as true of the gold of the Yukon as it was of the furs and whales of the NWT.

The effect of the gold rush on the First Nations people of the North was not great. Although they were discriminated against by the mine owners, who would not hire them, it is not clear that many sought such work. Some did take seasonal wage employment cutting wood or in other similar occupations, but most continued doing what their people had done since the arrival of the Hudson's Bay Company sixty years earlier: supplementing their traditional economy with the small cash income provided by trapping for furs. The gold rush transformed part of the Yukon, but the part that was still the preserve of the Native people was to remain largely unaltered for another half-century.

Notes

1 Pierre Berton, *Klondike: The Last Great Gold Rush* (Toronto: McClelland and Stewart, 1972), 17. First published in 1958, this is still the best account of the episode. Berton's *Klondike Quest: A Photographic Essay 1897–1899* (Toronto: McClelland and Stewart, 1983) contains excellent reproductions of some of the best photographs taken of the gold rush.

2 William Ogilvie, *Early Days on the Yukon & The Story of Its Gold Finds* (Ottawa: Thorburn and Abbott, 1913). The miners' meetings have been analysed by Thomas Stone in three articles: "The Mounties as Vigilantes: Perceptions of Community and the Transformation of the Law in the Yukon, 1885–1897," *Law and Society Review* 14, 1 (Fall 1979); "Atomistic Order and Frontier Violence: Miners and Whalemen in the Nineteenth Century Yukon," *Ethnology* 22 (October 1983); "Flux and Authority in a Subarctic Society: The Yukon Miners in the Nineteenth Century," *Ethnohistory* 30, 4 (1983).

3 Quoted in K. S. Coates and W. R. Morrison, *Land of the Midnight Sun: A History of the Yukon* (Edmonton: Hurtig, 1988), 80.

4 S. B. Steele, *Forty Years in Canada* (London: Jenkins, 1915), 296.

5 Martha Black, *My Ninety Years* (Anchorage: Alaska Northwest Publishing, 1976), 30. For a more detailed account of her early life, see Martha Black, *My Seventy Years* (London: Thomas Nelson, 1938).

6 Quoted in Berton, *Klondike*, 143–4.

PART II

Economy and Society in the Industrial Age

1867–1918

As the industrial age gathered steam in the second half of the nineteenth century, Canadians experienced a transformation in the ways they made a living and the values they embraced. People flocked to cities in growing numbers to take up wage-paying jobs and found their activities increasingly regulated by the clock more than by the seasons. In rapidly expanding urban centres, individuals and families faced new challenges that sometimes proved overwhelming. Poverty and misery became the lot of many people who lived in the slums that quickly developed in industrial centres. Rural areas, meanwhile, faced rapid adjustment to both new commercial values and extensive out-migration. With time-honoured religious beliefs coming under the double assault of scientific scepticism and secular values, many people felt that they were being left behind in a world that they no longer understood.

Native peoples, in particular, were on the losing end of the competition for power and control in the new industrial order. As Bill Parenteau reveals in his study of the East Coast salmon fishery in the late nineteenth century, Mi'kmaq and Maliseet lost easy access to one of their major sources of food and income when governments, influenced by sporting elites, began imposing rules on how and what time of the year salmon could be caught. Ironically, Natives lost access to the land and its natural resources at the very time that they were being idealized in intellectual circles as a "race" closely identified with nature and its spiritual potential.

Like Native peoples, immigrants whose skin was not white faced discrimination from the dominant society when they attempted to settle in Canada. People from Asia were the object of periodic anti-Asian sentiment in British Columbia, where they were relegated to the permanent category of "foreigner." They nevertheless often played a significant role in building the new nation. Chinese labourers, for example, were hired by the thousands to perform the dangerous work of laying the rails of the Canadian Pacific Railway in the early 1880s. As Gillian Creese demonstrates in her article, anti-Asian sentiment in Vancouver labour circles was built on a mix of racism and competition for jobs.

Blacks, too, experienced the cold shoulder of prejudice from both employers and white-dominated labour unions. Although African American, West Indian, and African Canadians were hired to work on railways, the only jobs available to them on the trains were as porters in the sleeping and dining cars. When the Canadian Brotherhood of Railway Employees and Other Transport Workers was established in 1908, black porters were excluded from membership. Sarah-Jane Mathieu describes how the railway porters eventually used their segregated work as a base for forming their own union, the Order of Sleeping Car Porters, in 1917, the first black railway union in North America. In addition to fighting for better wages and working conditions for its members, the OSCP also led the struggle to end the so-called Jim Crow practices that encouraged racial segregation.

Women in industrializing Canada also faced discriminatory practices that they struggled to overcome. Margaret McCallum examines the homestead laws that denied married women on the Prairies their dower right—that is, a widow's right to a life interest in one-third of the property owned by her husband at any time during the marriage. In jurisdictions that recognized dower rights, including the Maritimes, Ontario, and British Columbia, a husband needed his wife's consent to mortgage, sell, or give away his property. Married women on the Prairies, in contrast, could find that their homestead was literally sold out from under them. As McCallum shows, this legal innovation, introduced to expedite the transfer of property, stirred up a storm of protest that helped to invigorate the female suffrage movement on the Prairies.

Although legal reform and female suffrage were important vehicles for improving the status of women in the new industrial order, they were not the only avenues in which women's achievements can be charted. Women excelled in creative writing and several Canadian women, including Sara Jeanette Duncan, L.M. Montgomery, Nellie McClung, and Margaret Marshall Saunders, attracted international audiences for their work. So, too, did E. Pauline Johnson, the daughter of a Mohawk father and English mother who addressed issues of racism and sexism in her poetry and prose. Veronica Strong-Boag argues that Johnson's hybrid ancestry formed the context for her emphasis on inclusiveness and partnership as the best course for the new nation. During her lifetime, Johnson's argument was largely lost on Canada's leaders, who operated on a model of domination in their policies toward both Native peoples and women.

Ideas such as those expressed by Johnson were part of a whole cluster of new thought that is often summarized under the term "modern." In his article on the roots of modernism in Canada, Ramsay Cook focuses on the impact that Charles Darwin's scientific ideas had on the intellectual climate of the late nineteenth century and in particular on religious beliefs. Darwin's *On the Origin of Species,* published in 1859, called into question the biblical interpretation of Creation, touching off a debate about the origins of human life that shook the foundations of religious orthodoxy and helped to blur the lines between the sacred and the secular that had governed western values for nearly two millennia. This debate, the drift toward secular values, and the challenges faced by the poor in Canada's industrial cities, helped to inspire many leaders of Canadian churches to see social reform in Canada and around the world as part of their earthly mission.

The modern age also encouraged new ideas about the natural environment. While early European settlers viewed the North American landscape as a hostile wilderness that needed to be domesticated or a resource frontier ripe for exploitation, Canadians in the late nineteenth century began to romanticize nature. George Altmeyer in his article explores the new attitudes that inspired an environmental movement and the founding of a host of organizations designed to enable Canadians to communicate with "Mother Nature."

The final reading in this section also focuses on ideas. By tracing the process by which Canadians came to terms with their involvement in the First World War, Jonathan Vance reveals how historical memory is created around important events in the past. The First World War sacrificed a generation of young men on the battlefield, exaggerated societal divisions based on class, gender, language, race, and region, and swept away ways of thinking that historians often describe as "Victorian," in reference to the British Queen whose reign (1837–1901) dominated much of the nineteenth century. In their commemorations and retrospective comments, Canadians tended to emphasize the noble character of the young men who participated in a "just war" to preserve British and Canadian values. Any lingering notions that the war was fought because of less exalted ideals were conveniently forgotten.

"Care, Control and Supervision"

Native People in the Canadian Atlantic Salmon Fishery, 1867–1900[*]

BILL PARENTEAU

It was June 1886 and "the ladies" had come to Camp Harmony a few weeks into the season to join the gentlemen of this Restigouche River Fishing Club in the annual rite of salmon angling and communing with nature. On this occasion, club member Dean Sage recalled in a published account, the men had prepared a special treat; the ladies were to witness a bloodless simulation of the "primeval" Mi'kmaq custom of spearing salmon by torchlight. The "Indians entered heartily into the idea," Sage explained, and set about binding the birchbark *flambeaux,* all the time "chanting...a recital of an old chief's former prowess with the spear."

With darkness approaching, the party and their guides took to the canoes, in anticipation of experiencing the mysteries of nature. The *flambeaux* were lit and stuck crossways in the canoes, which were formed in a line across the river. As the guides poled the canoes upriver, the line between water and atmosphere vanished. "Every pebble on the bottom was as distinct as if nothing but air lay between us and it, the canoes seemed to be floating on air and the small fish, trout, suckers and parr looked like

flying machines, so perfect was the delusion." The illusion became even more mesmerizing as the party passed over the salmon pools and large fish, up to forty pounds in weight, began "in a dazed way" to dart under and follow the canoes.

The spell was broken only "when the Indians began to get excited." They became "half-crazed," the sportsman-naturalist remembered, "by the likeness of this to their old expeditions when the river was free to them." Even the trusted head guide Jacques had shed the trappings of civilization. "Ef we spearin' now we git couple dis time, den pole back, an run over 'em again, an' git couple more meebe," Jacques was said to have suggested, as he stood up in the bow of the canoe, poised to bludgeon the passing salmon with his blunt pole. "[O]nly by a strong effort and my repeated warnings," Sage proudly recalled, did Jacques "restrain himself from driving at each fish that crossed his path." "Alexis Vicaire, a cousin of Jacques, in another canoe, couldn't control his natural instincts, and at last, with a wild yell, struck at a passing salmon, fortunately missing him." This most unsporting display, and the prospect of similar

Bill Parenteau, "'Care, Control and Supervision': Native People in the Canadian Atlantic Salmon Fishery, 1867–1900," *Canadian Historical Review* 79, 1 (March 1998): 1–35. Reprinted by permission of the University of Toronto Press.

[*] The research and writing of this article were made possible by a postdoctoral fellowship from the Social Sciences and Humanities Research Council of Canada. The author would like to thank David Frank, Kerry Abel, Delphin Muise, Colin Howell, and the anonymous *CHR* referees for their helpful comments and suggestions.

acts, forced the club members to intervene. "We were obliged to assert our authority very strongly," Sage lamented, "to check the growing desire of the Indians to kill the salmon with their poles, which they easily could have done." The *flambeaux* were extinguished and the party headed back to camp. The "repressed spirits of the Indians," according to the author, were vented in a race back to the camp, at the end of which all members of the party were soaked with river water. Then "the Indians gradually calmed down, under the influence of the hearty meal, which their exertions gave them the excuse for taking."[1]

The story told by Sage makes an excellent starting point for understanding the on-going restructuring of harvesting patterns of Atlantic salmon in Canada as well as the emerging power relationships between sportsmen and other resource users. During the second half of the nineteenth century, Native people in Nova Scotia, New Brunswick, and Quebec were systematically excluded from the Atlantic salmon harvest. The agency primarily responsible for their exclusion was the federal Department of Fisheries, which after 1867 enacted conservation measures banning the modes of harvesting used by Native fishers and instituted an administrative régime for enforcement. The fisheries department was strongly influenced by élite salmon anglers both in constructing its conservation program and in enforcing regulations. The regulations banning spearing and other Native harvesting methods were aggressively pursued by the angling fraternity and, in fact, had grown out of the "code of the sportsman," which viewed these fishing methods as "villainous practices."[2] After 1870, élite sport fishermen solidified their position at the top of the hierarchy of resource users by contributing to the rehabilitation of salmon rivers and paying for surveillance and the prosecution of poachers. Participation in the state conservation and administrative program allowed anglers to

extend their control over salmon rivers and, progressively, to restrict harvesting by other groups of commercial and subsistence resource users.[3] On the watersheds of eastern Canada, the process of eliminating Native salmon fishing was lengthy and often uneven; not surprisingly, it involved a great deal of resistance and accommodation on the part of Native people. The morality play that featured Sage and his fellow sportsmen of Camp Harmony heroically subduing the "natural instincts" of the Mi'kmaq demonstrated how far the process had progressed on many salmon rivers by the 1880s.

The story can also be seen as a metaphor for the transformation of Native people from active resource users to cultural commodities—there to enhance the wilderness experiences of the fly fishermen. If Native people were demonized as destroyers of the salmon fishery, they were also highly valued by the élite angling fraternity. Native men were generally competent fishing guides and, in some instances, the only ones available. The Native guides who accompanied salmon anglers also served an ideological/cultural function. An integral part of the code of the sportsman was that each "true sportsman" should be a naturalist, that he fully understand the habits of his quarry as well as the environment. For the élite angler, Native people were part of the environment. Virtually without exception, the sporting literature of the period 1850–1900 that concerns salmon fishing also contains information on the racial characteristics, living habits, customs, and mythology of Native people. Sportsmen of the Victorian era were fond of comparing their modern existence with the supposed primitive world of Native people. What many élite anglers wanted was not simply someone to help them catch fish, but an authentic "primitive" man to guide them into an imagined world of primeval wonder—someone to legitimize their adventure as a true wilderness experience. Elite anglers paid dearly, sometimes thousands of dollars, to fish for salmon in the rivers of eastern Canada; they also expected for their money the privilege of experiencing such perfect illusions as that enjoyed by the members of Camp Harmony.

[...]

Care, Control and Supervision

Among the earliest initiatives undertaken by the fishery department was prohibiting the spearing of salmon in up-river pools and on spawning beds. As was the case with some colonial legislation, the federal fisheries act passed in 1868 recognized the tradition of Native spear fishing. An exemption was included in the clause prohibiting spear fishing that allowed the minister of fisheries to "appropriate and license or lease certain waters in which certain Indians shall be allowed to catch fish for their own use in and at whatever manner and time are specified in the license or lease, and may permit spearing in certain localities."[4] These privileges were extended by the minister in only a few instances during the late 1860s and early 1870s, although some of the bands in New Brunswick and on the north shore of the St. Lawrence River were allowed to operate or share the proceeds of net-fishing stands on waters that ran through their reserves. The intention of the federal government was to "civilize" the Native people by encouraging them to establish permanent agricultural communities; this initiative formed part of the underlying logic behind prohibiting the spearing of salmon, which was seen by Fishery and Indian Affairs officers as part of the wandering life characterized by indolence and vice.[5] The paternalist attitude of the government was summed up by one Indian agent who, when commenting on the agitation of the band on Burnt Church Reserve (Miramichi River) for the extension of fishing rights, suggested that "the Indians need care, control and supervision."[6] All three of these administrative imperatives were demonstrated by the Department of Fisheries during the late nineteenth century; overwhelmingly, the emphasis was on control and supervision.

The impact of the initiative to remove Native people from the salmon fishery was felt unequally by the bands that resided near the rivers of Nova Scotia, New Brunswick, and Quebec. In Nova Scotia and the Bay of Fundy shore of New Brunswick, obstructions to the salmon run, pollution, and overfishing had so degraded the resource that it was no longer a central component in the Native economy. In the places where salmon did still run—the Saint John and Margaree rivers, for example—competition from white settlers significantly reduced the opportunities for Native people.[7] The impact of the legislation was particularly hard felt on the New Brunswick shore of the Baie des Chaleurs, the Gaspé Peninsula, and the tributaries on the north shore of the St. Lawrence. The new fisheries policies placed the Montagnais bands of the St. Lawrence River "in a very precarious condition," observed Théophile Tétu, captain of the government schooner *La Canadienne*. The solution to the problem, the fishery officer believed, was to increase the annual relief allowance given to the Native people of the north shore and to provide seed and agricultural implements to the bands on the Baie des Chaleurs. "Those people would come to understand that the Government is friendly to them," Tétu concluded, and, within a few years, he predicted, "the increase of fish in our rivers would repay the expense incurred for the attainment of the desired object."[8]

If Tétu understood and sympathized with the plight of Native people on the north shore of the St. Lawrence, he was also duty-bound to participate in the on-going destruction of their hunting and gathering economy. The limits of government friendliness were demonstrated during the cruise of *La Canadienne* in 1868. Tétu received orders from the fisheries department to investigate reports of Native people netting and spearing salmon on the Mingan River (which empties into the St. Lawrence to the north of the western tip of Anticosti Island) in open defiance of the local fishery officer. Bands of Montagnais had long been in the habit of visiting the small rivers in the region; the Mingan was a favoured fishing locale and the site of a Roman Catholic mission and Hudson's Bay Company trading post. When *La Canadienne* reached Mingan, Tétu was informed by the local fishery officer that three Montagnais— Pierre Hamel, Jerome Jeromish, and P. Musquarro—had netted and speared a large quantity of salmon over the period of two weeks. This offence was by no means the only illegal salmon fishing on the river during the season. When the two fishery officers inspected the river they found "quite a number *of flambeaux* along the banks," and at the falls "pulled down some sort of scaffolding probably erected by the Indians to reach a salmon-resting pool below the falls."[9] Nevertheless, in keeping with the developing strategy of the department, this flagrant and openly defiant transgression was treated to an example of the power of the new federal administration.

Upon investigation, Tétu determined that Hamel was "the leader," but he could not be found and brought to justice. The captain of the *La Canadienne* therefore settled for apprehending and interrogating Jeromish. This incident bears close examination, as it reveals a common tactic used by the department, as well as the impact of the new regulations:

> Jerome was very much frightened; we had some difficulty in apprehending him, and could not prevent his wife and daughters from accompanying him on board, as they would have starved during his absence. He admitted having set a net and caught salmon on the Mingan River, but pleaded as an excuse (and I have no hesitation in believing him) that he

did so to prevent himself from starving, and that he could get nothing from the Hudson's Bay Company—that he would never have violated the law, had he any food for his family... I therefore condemned him to pay a fine of $10 or 15 days in gaol, and for some time made him believe I should take him with me; at last however, I took pity on him and seeing that his family would starve if he were really sent to gaol, I let him go with the solemn promise that he would neither spear nor net salmon again. This arrest, I am led to believe, will have a good effect with the other Indians, for the sight of the armed sailors of La Canadienne arresting Jerome, gave them quite a fright.[10]

The arrest of Jeromish may well have had the temporary effect of curbing the open resistance of the Mingan Montagnais to the new régime. However, with the situation of the Montagnais on the coastline of the Gulf of St. Lawrence becoming increasingly desperate, prohibiting spearing became more complicated than simply staging a few acts of intimidation.

By the 1870s, the Montagnais were facing destitution. Growing competition from white hunters and settlers resulted in marked resource depletion, particularly with regard to seals and migratory birds. The waning of the fur trade, and subsequent policies of the Hudson's Bay Company to reduce or eliminate advances to hunters, also had a devastating impact on the Native economy. The summer of 1878, when the Hudson's Bay Company completely cut off advances along a 100-miles stretch of the coast, was particularly desperate. As "there was in July no birds or seals to be caught or killed on the coast," a fishery officer remarked in 1878, "the Indians from Mingan to St. Augustine are really left in a state of starvation.... They are scattered all along the coast asking for food from all comers and unable to reach the winter hunting grounds for want of provisions." The officer grimly predicted that without government relief, "it is certain that death will make a sweep among them before the middle of winter."[11]

Adding considerably to the desperation during this period was the elimination of the spring and summer salmon harvest, previously a time of abundance after the long winter hunt. The cautionary statement made by a field officer to the minister of fisheries in 1875 demonstrated quite graphically the direct impact that the fishery regulations could have on the Native peoples on the north shore of the St. Lawrence. In regard to the prospects for protecting the salmon fishery in the spring of 1875, he noted, "it will be difficult to make a complete submission to the fishery laws from these Indians next summer, should they be exposed to the same privations as this year and left to compare their utter state of destitution with the luxurious mode of living of the fastidious Lord [leaseholder Sir George Gore] who fed his dogs on food which would have kept them alive." An incident between the leaseholder and the Montagnais band on the Mingan River in 1878 further underscored the extent to which the new salmon fishing régime contributed to the difficulties faced by the Native people of this region. It was not a particularly good season for fly fishing; salmon "were very plentiful in the pools but would not take the fly," the local fishery overseer noted, which resulted in the leaseholder on the Mingan River taking only thirty fish. To make matters worse, "the Indians went up and speared in the presence of Mr. Molson and the guardian," taking thirty-six salmon. On being issued a stern warning, the band informed the overseer that "they were starving and could not get anything to eat and that they asked Mr. Molson to give them something and he would not. Mr. Scott [the local HBC agent] corroborated what they said"; the officer further reported, "that they were actually starving and that his orders from the Hudson's Bay Company were not to give them anything."[12] Finally, in December, the Department of Indian Affairs intervened and ordered the Mingan agent of the Hudson's Bay Company to provide relief "to such Indians as he is quite sure cannot procure subsistence for themselves."[13]

In an attempt to provide compensation for the loss of their salmon fishery, the Department of Fisheries, on occasion in the decade after Confederation, licensed net-fishing stations to Montagnais bands on the tributaries of the St. Lawrence. It was not equal or even adequate compensation. One net-fishing station could not yield the quantity of fish speared over the course of a spring and summer, even if it was favourably located, which was usually not the case with stations licensed to Native people. Increasingly after 1870, it became the policy of the department to authorize white settlers to operate netting stands on behalf of a particular band; the feeling of the department was that Native people could not efficiently operate a fishing station or be trusted to maintain the nets from season to season. The surrogate fishermen were paid in shares of up to one-half of the catch, further diminishing the value of the opportunity. Quickly, under this system, a program that started as a means of compensation came to be viewed as charity within the fisheries department, the idea being that Native people benefited unduly from the salmon harvest without doing any work.[14]

The modern licensing and leasing system taking shape in the decade after Confederation also made it difficult for Native bands to secure netting licences. In the early 1880s Indian agents requested the issuing of licences to several bands as part of a policy to end the chronic misery of the Montagnais of the north shore.[15] In some instances, the requests were turned down because the rivers were leased to anglers; in others, the rivers were already being netted by white settlers.[16] For example, in 1880 the fisheries department agreed to give a local band a separate licence to fish on the Grand Romaine, a small stream on which an aged settler, George Metiver, operated a net station. Because the local Indian agent believed that the settler would drive the Montagnais away, another request for exclusive Native rights to the stream was made. This request led to a clash in policy between the Indian Affairs and the Fisheries departments. W.F. Whitcher, the deputy minister of marine and fisheries who was dealing with similar issues across Canada, flatly denied the request, and, without a hint of irony, suggested that, "it would be a cruelty toward him [Metiver] wholly unexcused by any real necessity on the part of the local Indians were the department to take away his license." Whitcher went on to describe for his counterpart in the Department of Indian Affairs how Native practices of spearing fish "at all times and all places" had ruined the salmon fishery on other rivers, and he explained that the fishery regulations were enacted "quite as much for the benefit of the Indians themselves as for other subjects of the realm."[17] The Department of Indian Affairs offered some resistance but, ultimately, the station was not licensed. Such incidents revealed the extent to which sympathy for Native salmon fishers and notions of compensating them for the loss their traditional fishery had expired in the decade and a half of federal fisheries administration.

A similar pattern of weaning Native people away from their long dependence on the Atlantic salmon was evident in the treatment of the Mi'kmaq band at Mission Point. The home of between 300 and 400 Mi'kmaq, Mission Point was located across from Campbellton on the Quebec side of the estuary limit of the Restigouche River. For generations, bands of Mi'kmaq had come together at this spot each spring to go up-river and exploit the salmon-rich pools and spawning beds of the Restigouche and its tributaries. In the years from 1867 to 1871, recognizing that a total prohibition would cause great misery, the department allowed the band to spear fish in designated areas on certain nights each week.

The boundaries set out by the fisheries wardens were almost wholly ignored, and the Restigouche River became a meeting place for even larger groups of Mi'kmaq. "As spearing was prohibited on all other rivers," the local fishery officer John Mowat recalled, "Indians from Bathurst, New Richmond, Gaspé and Miramichi made a business of coming here, in fact were invited by the Mission Indians to come here and partake and, to my astonishment, in 1872 I found double the number of canoes spearing." As Mowat and others in the department believed that "one of the principal causes of the increasing scarcity of salmon was the pertinacity with which the few fish which escape the tidal nets are followed to the head waters by the Indians," spearing privileges were no longer granted after 1872. In preventing further spearing, the local fisheries officers were aided by the white settlers along the river, who sometimes "threatened to seize their fish," but settled for "compel[ling] them to sell for half price."[18]

In compensation for the loss of their salmon-spearing privileges, the fisheries department granted the Mission Point band a net-fishing station on the waters running through the reserve in 1872.[19] Not surprisingly, the planned transition was greeted less than enthusiastically when it was introduced to the band. "They seemed much astonished to learn that a privilege which they claimed to have been granted to them by treaties, was withdrawn, and they appeared to accept this change in their habits with very little relish indeed," fisheries officer Napoleon Lavoie noted. "I did my best to make them understand that the present system would be more advantageous to them, as it would enable them to derive more profit with less work and hardship, that it would give them more time for the farming of their lands, securing thereby peace of mind and support for old age, and concluded by telling them that they could no longer be considered as spoiled children." Lavoie further observed: "This passion for spearing, born with them and still further developed with age, is so deeply rooted in these Indians that several of them were almost disheartened in learning that in the future they would be deprived of such a pleasure."[20]

The preference for spearing was abundantly evident in the resistance to the netting station in 1873. With funds obtained from the Department of Indian Affairs, John Mowat set about in the spring of 1873 obtaining equipment and hiring an experienced fisherman to instruct the Mi'kmaq. He and the resident missionary on the reserve also spent time counselling the band on the benefits of the fishing station in preparation for the first run of salmon. When the salmon did come, the "men of the tribe broke out in open rebellion."[21] "So soon as the first salmon appeared," it was reported, "they were attacked with the spear, whilst others in the band were engaged in destroying the nets supplied by the Indian Department, or pulling the stakes out which had been procured at great cost. Fishery officers were openly defied, and things had a very threatening aspect for a while."[22] Eventually, the government schooner *La Canadienne* was called in to restore order. Commander Napoleon Lavoie promptly arrested, convicted, and imprisoned four men rumoured to be the "ringleaders," an action that "had a most beneficial effect." "In a meeting which took place afterwards," he reported, "I succeeded in having them fully understand the folly of their course, and pointed out to them that their true interests consisted in acting harmoniously with the government's desires. They understood this, and the Chief signed a pledge on their behalf."[23]

The raid of the *La Canadienne* ended the open defiance of the Mission Point Mi'kmaq to the fisheries regulations. It also set off a political crisis in the band, when the chiefship of Polycarp Martin, who made the written agreement with fishery officers, was challenged by a group of more militant men.[24] After 1873, spear fishing became a covert activity, practised when the opportunity arose, but progressively more prone to detection with the leasing of the Restigouche and its tributaries to anglers. The net-fishing station on the reserve was never fully accepted by the band. Because of a division of opinion within the band in 1874, the nets were not set until Lavoie came again and authorized a local white fisherman to fish the station on their behalf. This arrangement was continued for a number years, with the Mi'kmaq being granted one-half of the proceeds from the catch, the feeling of the fishery officers being that the band was "not capable of being trusted with the expensive plant."[25] In 1882 the stand was leased for five years for the flat rate of $75 per year. Finally, in 1888 the fisheries department appropriated the stand for the purpose of obtaining parent fish for the Restigouche hatchery, thus ending the legal participation of the Mission Point Mi'kmaq in the salmon fishery.[26]

The prohibition on spear fishing eliminated a central part of the economy of the Mission Point Mi'kmaq. Even under the limited spearing privileges granted in 1872, Mowat estimated the legal catch of the Mission Point band at 10,000 to 16,000 pounds of salmon, which would have netted between $600 and $900 at market prices.[27] By all accounts, the fishing station never generated more than $150 in income for the band in any one season. Undoubtedly, this condition contributed to the continuing inability (which some fishery officers found perplexing) of band members to understand the great benefits to be derived from net fishing. The failure of the station, which Lavoie wrongly considered "one of the best and most coveted salmon stations" on the river, was confirmed when the fisheries department abandoned it after two years, because it would not yield the few hundred salmon necessary to run the hatchery.[28]

The proceedings at Mingan and Mission Point illustrate a larger pattern whereby Native people, over the course of two decades, were alienated from the salmon harvest. They allow for reconstruction in narrative form because of the bias in the historical record of state regulation towards those events where people show open and collective defiance of regulations and cause officials to fear for the integrity of a particular administrative régime. Beneath these dramatic, visible incidents were a great number of individual acts of petty defiance and less overt transgressions of the fishery laws perpetrated by Native people which escape documentation, or which appear only as thin fragments in the historical record.[29] The primary recourse of people around the world who fail to recognize the legitimacy of state regulations that infringe on traditional patterns of hunting and fishing is, of course, "poaching." Not surprisingly, the annual reports of local fishery officers and the published narratives of sportsmen in the late nineteenth century abound with references to poaching by Native people. Most Native people were certainly not restrained by moral considerations, as the salmon fishing laws were widely held to be unjust, and the practice of fishing at night lent itself to engaging in such furtive activities. However, the extent of Native poaching may have been exaggerated. White settlers throughout the region, particularly in New Brunswick, were equally ill-disposed towards the federal salmon fishing regulations and fished illegally in large numbers.[30] It is likely that Native people sometimes became the scapegoats for other poachers, particularly when *flambeaux* and other signs of spearing were in evidence. The attitude of riverine residents of European descent was suggested by Sage: "The white settler on the Restigouche and its tributaries 'drifts' for salmon with great persistence and success. He is, however, dreadfully shocked at the idea of an Indian taking a salmon with a spear."[31] In addition, many stories of Native poaching in sporting narratives were embellished to serve as morality plays for promoting sportsmanship and reaffirming the intellectual/racial superiority of Europeans. In reality, Native people, when on the reserves at least, were more closely watched and monitored than settlers. The successful Native poacher had to contend not only with fishery officers but also with Indian agents and resident missionaries, who routinely invaded their privacy in search of alcohol or other illicit products.

Patterns of poaching were diverse and were influenced, among other factors, by the level of surveillance on a particular river and by the needs and proclivities of Native residents. Poaching activities ranged from the individual who speared a single fish when afforded the opportunity, to well organized groups of Native fishermen filling several canoes with salmon. The observations of Napoleon Comeau, who served as guardian for the leaseholders of the renowned Godbout River from late 1860s until after 1900, are instructive for understanding patterns of illegal salmon fishing. He divided poachers into two groups, the first being "professionals," who needed a considerable outfit (canoes, nets, etc.) and connections with a merchant who would buy the illegal fish and protect their anonymity. The second group he classified as the "poacher through necessity," who could not cause "any serious damage" but was difficult to control and "sometimes very annoying." "Their outfit is very light," he noted, "and may consist of only a landing net, spear, gaff, or snare, easily hid on the person, and frequently thrown away, when danger is scented. They also have the sympathy of the community and no evidence can be had against them."[32] This statement about community support was a near-universal condition that stood as one of the primary barriers to the eradication of poaching throughout the Atlantic salmon fishery. As Comeau and other fishery wardens reported, it was commonplace for their movements to be closely monitored by Native people and white settlers alike.[33] Overall, with the leasing of an ever-increasing number of salmon rivers after 1875, poaching became more difficult for both Native people and white settlers. From just a few prized salmon waters being leased at Confederation, the number of rivers in New Brunswick and Quebec on which anglers held exclusive fishing rights increased to more than sixty by the early 1890s.[34] Poaching was certainly not eliminated, but the addition of hundreds of private guardians to protect the rivers on behalf of anglers had a marked restrictive impact.

The removal of Native bands in Nova Scotia, New Brunswick, and Quebec from the salmon harvest hastened their entry into the sport-fishing industry as guides. This transition was looked upon with favour and was even pro- moted by fishery officers, as it meant, from their perspective, that the segment of the Native pop- ulation most likely to spear salmon would be under the supervision of people who understood the importance of conservation.[35] The economic "benefit" of guiding over fishing was neatly stat- ed by a local officer in 1895, when the Mission Point band began to demand that it be compen- sated for the removal of its fishing station: "While the absorption of the Mission Point Station by the Department may be made to appear to be a great loss to the Indians financially, it is really a benefit, because the rental paid for the net, even had it judiciously been distributed would have only amounted to $0.50 per annum to each fam- ily, while the removal of the net from a critical position at the entrance to the north channel on the middle ground of the river was a great bene- fit to the upper waters, and anglers, consequent- ly a great advantage to the Indians as the better the angling the greater the amount to employ- ment at $3.00 per day."[36] It was an unequivocal admission that the fishing station was never an adequate replacement for spear fishing. The offi- cer also failed to mention that one successful night of spearing would have easily netted more income than a few weeks of poling a canoe for 10 or 12 hours per day, watching some "sport" strug- gle with the delicate art of fly fishing.

Guiding in the Ideal World of the Sportsman

By virtue of their skills with the birchbark canoe and their knowledge of rivers and forests, Native people served as guides from the earliest days of recreational sporting in the North American colonies. As the sport-hunting and sport-fishing industries expanded after 1870, Native men from Nova Scotia, New Brunswick, and Quebec entered the guiding profession in increasing numbers. Exact figures for the number of Native men employed as guides are not part of the historical record; however, it is clear from the records of the Department of Indian Affairs that men from nearly every band in the three provinces were engaged in this work. Frequent statements by Indian agents to the effect that "the greater portion of the male population dur- ing the summer season hire themselves as guides to sportsmen" suggest that, for a considerable number of bands, guiding was a vital economic activity.[37] With regard to the salmon fishery, hundreds of Native men served as guides, and they were both pushed in this direction by fish- ery policies and pulled in by economic incen- tives. Compared with the other wage-labour opportunities open to Native people—woods work and farm labour, for example—the pay for guiding was high. Salmon guides were particu- larly well paid, earning as much as three dollars per day in the 1890s, while wages for common labourers were rarely more than one dollar.[38]

Although there were often long stretches of time during the day, particularly on hot after- noons in mid-summer, when guides could lounge in their quarters adjacent to the angling lodge, salmon guiding generally involved long hours of work and could be physically demand- ing. Guides attached to salmon fishing lodges, which were common on the best rivers, such as the Restigouche and the Casapedia, were at the disposal of anglers at any time during daylight hours and occasionally for moonlight cruises. Those who worked for travelling fishing parties were saddled with the additional duties of hauling gear, making camp, and preparing meals. From a physical standpoint, the most difficult part of the job was poling up-river. The sporting narratives of the period frequently comment on the amount of skill needed for poling and the stamina of their Native guides:

> It is a very difficult accomplishment to pole a canoe at all, and still more difficult to do it well. There is a certain kind of swing that has to be learned in order to make the pole leave and enter the water correctly, and the centre of gravity must be maintained on the very small base afforded at the narrow end of the canoe so exactly, that the frequent slipping of the pole from the round stones at the bottom shall not effect it, nor the unexpected twists and dodges of the light bark as it encounters some sudden turn in the current or puff of wind. The skillful poler meets all of these emergencies successfully as if by instinct, and without apparent effort.[39]

Poling was only one of many skills, both physical and social, needed to be a competent salmon guide. Guides, naturally, needed to know the spots where a fly cast would have the greatest chance of meeting with success and how to approach the easily spooked salmon. These requirements of the job were vital in serving the inexperienced salmon angler, but less important with club members who fished the same pools year after year. With the exception of some small rivers, anglers generally hooked salmon while in the canoe, at which time they were paddled or poled to a convenient and safe landing place. The contest between angler and salmon could go on for up to two hours, depending on the size of the fish and the strength of the rod and line used; lengthy battles often demanded that the angler get in and out of the canoe two or more times, as the salmon emptied the reel of line and the

party was forced to give chase. In such situations, the angler had to be guided in and out of the canoe quickly, smoothly, and safely, so that he might give all his attention to keeping the salmon on the line. The guides also needed to keep track of the location of the fish, so as not to get the canoe in an unfavourable position or allow the salmon to break the line by wrapping it around a rock or sunken tree. At the end of the contest the salmon needed to be gaffed, which, if not performed with a steady hand, could jar the fish off the hook and set it free. Many fishing stories ended sadly with the loss of a salmon at this critical juncture.[40] As anglers often travelled hundreds of miles and spent considerable sums for the privilege of salmon fishing, it was important for guides to avoid even the appearance of responsibility for losing a fish.

From the perspective of the salmon angler, a good salmon guide was a companion who gave assistance and shared in the thrill of the catch, without being intrusive or too pointedly giving directions. Personality traits, such as stoicism, a sense of humour, and the ability to recount Native folk legends, could enhance the reputation of a guide and bring further opportunities.[41] In addition to being relatively well paid, salmon guides also had a more stable clientele than other Native guides. In contrast to canoeing guides attached to the so-called watering places, where the relationship with a group of tourists was most often a one-time affair, individuals and crews of guides frequently returned to service the same salmon fishing lodges each year. Here, guides could establish a reputation for good work and, within fairly rigid boundaries defined by class and race, forge more intimate relationships with their clients. A good guide was akin to a trusted domestic servant—reliable, competent, and able to understand his place. It was a relationship with which a great many salmon fishermen were familiar in their domestic lives.[42]

Understanding the systematic exclusion of Native peoples as active resource users in the salmon fishery is a fairly straightforward proposition, compared with examining the relationship to the anglers who set up sporting enterprises near their reserves. The historical record of salmon guiding in the late nineteenth century consists mainly of scattered, passing references in government documents and the published narratives of sportsmen. Native people left few, if any, unadulterated accounts of their experiences as guides; therefore, any assumptions about how they perceived the job or their interactions with anglers must be filtered through the thick lens of these narratives. Ultimately, any discussion of guiding that uses sporting narratives must be as much about élite anglers as it is about Native salmon guides.[43]

Overall, the pursuit of sporting activities in Canada became more inclusive in the decades after Confederation, but salmon fishing remained an exception. Virtually all the major salmon rivers in New Brunswick and Quebec were colonized by the wealthy and politically connected by 1890. Secure access to good salmon fishing required buying waterfront property and/or leasing a stretch of river from the New Brunswick or Quebec government. Groups of élite angling enthusiasts quickly formed into clubs and took control of the best salmon waters in the fifteen years after Confederation. The exclusivity of these clubs was epitomized by the "wealthy and aristocratic" Restigouche Salmon Club, which was dominated by well-heeled members of the New York financial community and, by 1890, had an initial membership fee of $7500. Beyond this initial fee, the average cost for a twenty-day fly-fishing trip on the Restigouche in 1890 was estimated to be $450, not counting rods and other personal gear.[44] Although not all salmon clubs were as exclusive, there were precious few opportunities for good salmon fishing open to even the middle-level executive.[45]

One of the by-products of the wealth of salmon anglers and of their closer, more pro-

tracted contact with Native people was that Native guides and their bands were more often than others favoured by the *noblesse oblige* of sportsmen. Starting in the mid-1870s, the salmon clubs on the Restigouche River began making periodic grants to the Mission Point Reserve, which contained the largest single contingent of salmon guides, for specific projects, or when the conditions on the reserve appeared particularly bad.[46] More often, charity came in the form of salmon. While some anglers salted or pickled the salmon that could not be consumed while at camp, many others routinely gave a portion of the catch to Native people. It was also the practice of some camps to donate perishable food items to the guides at the end of the season. On a practical level, Native people needed and even came to depend on the charity of salmon anglers.

On a cultural level, such acts were a way of reaffirming the power relations between the anglers and the local Native people and of distinguishing salmon angling as a sportsmanlike endeavour. In examining big-game hunting in India and Africa within the context of British imperialism, J.M. MacKenzie and others have suggested that when élites reverted from industrial modernity and brought their sentimental version of the hunting phase of social development to other places, they also projected social relations on the host people.[47] With its wealthy patrons buying and leasing riparian rights and building luxurious lodges, the salmon angling industry certainly had the same imperialist profile as big-game hunting. Salmon fishing was also similarly ritualized and guided by a chivalric code. Giving away a portion of the catch was a way of legitimizing the sometimes enormous catches of the anglers, separating the true sportsman from the "game hog," who turned the noble arts of hunting and fishing into a crass and uncivilized quest for meat. The ideological underpinnings of such acts were well represented in the statement of the poet Charles G.D.

Roberts about a fishing trip on the Tobique River in New Brunswick: "We imagined the mahogany youngsters at Tobique mouth reveling in the fruits of our prowess; and we imagined them so vividly that the artist forthwith made a sketch of our imaginings. And thus we felt no scruples on the abundance of our catch."[48] Thus, in part, salmon anglers participated in the sometimes brutal exclusion of Native people from the resource, paid extraordinary amounts of money to catch salmon, and then gave a portion of the catch away, "to make class and race divisions, and hierarchical rule, seem immemorial."[49]

As the preceding statements suggest, the code of the sportsman, increasingly adopted in North America after 1850, played an important role in determining the relationship between anglers and guides. The core of the sportsmen's code was a set of rules about proper methods of taking fish and game, and the appropriate seasons for killing each species. These aristocratic notions, which could be traced back to the seventeenth-century writings of Izaak Walton, the patron saint of anglers, had a profound effect on harvesting patterns in the Atlantic salmon fishery. However, the code was more than a guide to sporting etiquette. To be fully accepted as a member of the sporting fraternity, the individual hunter or angler had to be a naturalist, knowledgeable of the habits of fish and game as well as the habitats in which they thrived. For many salmon anglers this meant an intimate knowledge of "woodcraft," an integral part of which was the customs, language, technology, and hunting and fishing methods of Native people.[50]

The sportsmen's interest in Native culture was related to and stimulated by the growing wilderness cult of the late nineteenth century. In Europe the search for the unadulterated character of man through an examination of supposed primitive cultures dated back to at least the late Middle Ages; modern notions of the "wild man" or "noble savage" began to take form in the mid-eighteenth century with the writings of Rousseau and the Romantics. With the closing of the American frontier, the acceleration of urbanization, and the passing of Native people as a perceived threat, eastern North Americans also began to reassess the long-held negative images of wilderness and indigenous peoples. Wilderness, in the North American mind, was slowly transformed, in the nineteenth century, from being a barrier to civilization to being a positive influence—a foundation of national character.[51] In addition to being represented as a symbol of savagery, the wild man—in this case the Native peoples of North America—became also a symbol of freedom, nobility, and vitality, as increasingly oppressive urban environmental conditions forced a reassessment of the process of "civilization."[52] In ever larger numbers in the last decades of the nineteenth century, middle- and upper-class North Americans began to seek out rather than avoid wilderness experiences and contact with Native people.

It was this "antimodern" impulse that fuelled the sporting tourism industry, creating guiding opportunities and transforming Native culture into a commodity to be consumed by curious visitors.[53] Already by the 1870s, provincial governments, railroads, and the popular press began to cater to the search for authentic wilderness experiences, advertising Native culture as a tourist attraction, with emphasis on the primitive qualities most cherished by the traveller. The feelings of sporting and travel writer C.H. Farnham, as he first entered the Montagnais village on the Betsiamits River in the mid-1880s, was indicative of the manner in which these agencies catered to the growing numbers longing to be "released from the iron cage of modernity into a world re-enchanted by history, nature and the mysterious."[54] "As I walk through an Indian village I am startled by seeing my aboriginal self," Farnham informed the readers of *Harper's Magazine:*

We rarely meet our prehistoric ancestors, but here I sit down on the earth with my disconnected forefathers; I talk with men and women who still are absolutely a part of nature. Here I see how far we have come since my family left the woods.... I met yesterday on the beach an Indian coming from a seclusion of two years in the heart of the continent. He lived without any of what we call the necessities of civilization, and yet he was quite like other men in flesh and limb. The shyness and quietness of his nature were upon him so strongly that I would not break into his reserve, nor dissipate the awe I felt in his presence. He had a very different feeling for me; he knew a hundred men, even a whole tribe, far more skillful at getting a living out of the wilderness, so he had no wonder to waste on an inferior.[55]

As in other places, the organization of what scholars have referred as the "tourist gaze" had political, economic, and cultural implications.[56]

The transforming capacity of the tourist gaze was exemplified by broad changes in the native economy of eastern Canada after 1860. Thousands of Native people abandoned other economic pursuits to produce handicrafts for the tourist market. By 1890 there were so many Native people making seasonal visits to tourist venues to sell moccasins, necklaces, baskets, and other "Indian curiosities" that the market had become glutted and it was no longer a viable means of subsistence.[57] Native men also entered the guiding industry during the same period. Tourism promoters naturally ignored any negative consequences of the transformation in the lives of Native people, as the tourist gaze did not allow for such complications. Thus, even the Montagnais, who suffered and died of starvation as a result of fishery policies that promoted recreational fishing, could be reconstructed and packaged as a simple, happy people, willing to assist the sporting tourist. "In addition to the magnificent sport afforded to salmon fishermen

by many of the streams upon the north shore of the Lower St. Lawrence," a government pamphlet noted, "there is the added attraction of the romance and glamour that connect themselves with the peculiar folk-lore of the aboriginal inhabitants of the country through which they flow—, the dusky Montagnais who make such splendid guides and canoe men for the anglers who fish these waters."[58]

Sportsmen, even more than other wilderness tourists, were fascinated by all aspects of Native culture. Their closer contacts with Native people, and the pretensions of many sportsmen that they were experts on the increasingly popular subject of natural history, prompted them to speak as authorities on the Native *mentalité*. Many salmon anglers truly believed that their wilderness experiences and contacts with Native culture were more authentic than those of mere tourists; they used sporting narratives as a means of establishing their credentials as sportsmen and legitimizing their experiences as true wilderness adventures. Sporting narratives frequently used Mi'kmaq, Maliseet, or Montagnais words to describe commonly used camp items and translated the names of rivers, mountains, and other places from their Native language into English. When Native guides were given speaking parts in salmon-fishing stories, it was common for the authors to attempt to reproduce their broken English. Words such as "um," "em," and "mebbe" appear over and over again as representations of Native use of the English language.[59] Even more common in sporting narratives was the assignment of particular personality and character traits to all Native people. Native guides were often portrayed in salmon fishing narratives as physically imposing, capable of great feats of stamina and of enduring weather, heat, the wrath of insects, and other hardships without complaint. "The strength and endurance of these guides are marvelous," one sportsman commented. "I have known them to carry over 300 pounds of baggage each over a portage."[60] Accounts of the virtues of individual guides were not infrequently accompanied by sketches and pictures. The mythologized Native guide was a man of instinct, "lazy and generally worthless at any regular labor," but "indefatigable in avocations containing an element of sport."[61] Normally taciturn and retiring, the Native guide of sporting narratives was animated by the thrill of the chase.

Sporting writers paid especially close attention to what they perceived as the naïveté of guides, their ignorance of social graces and their clumsiness when stepping out of the natural environment. "They have a charming disrespect for persons and personages," Sage explained, as he told the story of "old Larry Vicaire" who, "annoyed" by the refusal of "Princess Louise" to listen to her husband and sit down in the canoe, "placed his hands on the royal shoulders, and forced their owner into a sitting position, with some allusion to the wishes of the 'ole man.'"[62] Roberts, in a similar vein, delighted in telling the story of his Maliseet guide's misadventure in attempting to fish with a fly rod.[63] Informed by Victorian notions of race and class, stories that revolved around the naïveté of guides constituted the principal form of humour in salmon fishing narratives. They served to reconfirm for élite sportsmen that Native men, while they might possess attractive masculine character traits and assert a measure of authority on the river, were impotent when confronted with civilization and best confined to their proscribed role as domestic servants of the wilderness.

There were intellectual contradictions to sport tourism, beyond the realities that sporting tourists were simultaneously idealizing traditional Native culture and aggressively participating in its destruction. Principal among these contradictions was that the glorification of Native woodcraft ran counter to the code of the sportsmen with respect to methods of taking fish and game. While sporting tourists wished to be in communion with Native people, they also desired membership in the fraternity of sportsmen who adhered to the code, which, in its condemnation of such Native practices as snaring, baiting, and spearing, separated the civilized gentleman from the base pot hunter or poacher. The fixation of sporting writers with spearing illustrated the contradictory tensions between the code of the sportsman and the cult of wilderness.

Native poachers using the traditional *negog* were used in some salmon fishing narratives as a foil for demonstrating the moral superiority of recreational modes of fishing and the ingenuity and intelligence of the civilized angler. One such morality play featured prominent American sporting writer Charles Hallock and the degenerate "half-breed" Indian Joe, matching wits on a river in Nova Scotia. When the indiscretion was detected, Joe was hiding in the bushes. He was lured out with the promise of "a little whiskey" and goaded into revealing the location of his illegally caught fish by the suggestion that a member of the angling party wished to purchase a salmon. The story ended with Joe being shown mercy (he was let off with stern warning) and the obligatory diatribe against barbarous fishing practices.[64] In another probably fictional scenario, two teenage boys, who were taken to a noted salmon river on the Gaspé Peninsula as part of a wilderness "summer school," stumbled upon the notorious "half-breed" poacher Pete Labouisse night fishing with spear and *flambeaux*.[65] The two adolescents chased Pete until his canoe was shattered in a set of rapids; Pete, who couldn't swim and had broken his leg, was thrown into the churning water. Jumping into the water, one of the boys made a daring rescue. In returning to camp with the injured prisoner, the two boys further demonstrated their humanity by insisting that Pete not be imprisoned.[66] In this instance, showing a revulsion to destructive fishing practices and a willingness to take action is represented as an initiation to the élite sporting fraternity. Indeed, the triumph of the civilized boys over primitive Pete is held up as a rite of manhood.

While spearing was vilified as the most destructive of all forms of salmon fishing, it was also idealized as a grand spectacle of Native culture, an event that brought into full view the glories of primitive masculinity. J.E. Alexander, for example, who bitterly condemned the practice, could still admire spearing as a ritual that stirred what he and so many other sporting tourists saw as the natural instincts of the Native hunter. "The native love of excitement in the chase has something to do with their pertinacious pursuit of salmon by spears and flambeaux.... Nothing can exceed the wild excitement with which these men pursue it.... The flame and the shadow, swayed by ripples, conceals the spearers' forms, and bewilder the doomed salmon. Their silvery sides and amber coloured eye-balls glisten through the rippling water. The dilated eyes, the expanded nostrils, and the compressed lips of the swarthy canoe men, fitly picture their eager and excited mood. A quick, deadly aim, a violent swirl, and some momentary convulsive struggles all tell the rest."[67] The identical language used in describing the physical attributes of the salmon and the fishermen, in this and other sporting narratives, underscored the supposed primitiveness of Native people and the extent to which their actions were instinctual rather than conscious and considered. It followed that these instincts needed to be controlled.

Contextualized within the cultural politics that surrounded representations of the traditional Native practice of spearing salmon, the significance of the "staged authenticity" of the ritual undertaken by the members of Camp Harmony in 1886 comes into full view.[68] Underneath the frequent professions of admiration and brotherhood, the relationship between salmon anglers and Native guides was about power and control. Perhaps even more than other sporting tourists, salmon anglers sought to reconstruct the "contact zones" between the two groups—to produce a wilderness environment that included Native people but was relatively free from the inherent conflicts that characterized the history of Native-white relations over natural resources.[69] Sporting tourists wanted to consume Native culture at a comfortable level and at a safe distance. The mock spearing party was essentially a cultural experiment, containing just the ideal amount of primitive danger and excitement deemed appropriate for "the ladies" but never beyond control of the so-called civilized sportsmen. It demonstrated the extent to which salmon anglers, by the late 1880s, were controlling both the salmon harvest and the content of the Native culture to which they were exposed. Sage and his fellow club members had found, or, rather, created a satisfactory resolution to the contradictions between the code of the sportsman and the cult of wilderness.

Conclusion

The removal of Native people from the Atlantic salmon harvest was part of a larger process of economic, political, and social change in the last decades of the nineteenth century. Resource depletion from growing competition with white settlers, sport hunters, and commercial interests hastened the destruction of a hunting and gathering economy that had long been in decline. Central to the acceleration of this process was the advent of more comprehensive state administration, in the form of changes in fish and game laws that favoured recreational over subsistence and commercial exploitation. Also vitally important, but beyond the scope of this study, were the policies of the Department of Indian Affairs, which were founded on idealized notions of "civilizing" Native people and consolidating them into communities of independent yeoman farmers, oftentimes in areas where environmental conditions made this goal unrealistic. Policies prohibiting salmon fishing for subsistence and, especially, commercial purposes were in direct contradiction to the developing policy of forcing Native people to become more self-sufficient and individualistic; they served to underline the duplicitous nature of the administrative initiatives undertaken by the Department of Marine and Fisheries and the Department of Indian Affairs in the late nineteenth century. It is important to recognize that in an era when Native people were, for the most part, prevented from mounting legal challenges, state policy could have devastating consequences. In particular, the alienation of the Montagnais on the north shore of the St. Lawrence River from the salmon harvest contributed to severe deprivation and even starvation in the region during the 1870s and 1880s. The threat of starvation was not uncommon among the bands on the Godbout, Saint John, and Mingan rivers, for example, where thirteen salmon anglers caught slightly over 16,000 pounds of salmon in 1871.[70] In hindsight, at least, the true sportsmen of the nineteenth century were less civilized than they appeared in the self-congratulatory sporting literature of the time.

The exclusion of Native people as active resource users coincided with their entry into the guiding profession in larger numbers in the second half of the nineteenth century. Native men possessed the requisite skills, and salmon guiding provided relatively high wages, at a time when other opportunities were diminishing. The transition was also stimulated by cultural forces, namely the growing cult of wilderness and the anti-modern impulse sweeping through North America during the second half of the nineteenth century. Whether they were sightseers or "sports," what the wilderness tourists of the nineteenth century wanted was to journey into the past, in the hope that gazing upon "primitive culture" would help them cope with and understand their own increasingly complex and divisive society. After 1850 this demand was increasingly met by an organized tourist industry, complete with its own literature, which advertised and sold Native culture as part of the wilderness experience and was predicated on the economic dependence of Native people. Necessity and imagination created a class of Native seasonal workers who served both as conduits, to lead élite anglers into the spiritual realm of the wilderness, and as domestic servants, to provide comforts in the temporal world.

Notes

1   Dean Sage, *The Restigouche and Its Salmon Fishing, with a Chapter on Angling Literature* (Edinburgh: D. Douglas 1888), 216–23.

2   This phrase was used by renowned American sportsman Charles Lanman in his *Adventures in the Wilds of the United States and British North America* (Philadelphia: J.W. Moore 1856). On the code of the sportsman, see John Reiger, *American Sportsmen and the Origins of Conservation* (Norman and London: University of Oklahoma Press 1977); James A. Tober, *Who Owns the Wildlife? The Political Economy of Conservation in Nineteenth Century America* (Westport, Conn.: Greenwood Press 1981); and Richard P. Manning, "Recreating Man: Hunting and Angling in Victorian Canada" (MA thesis, Carleton University 1994).

3   It should be recognized that Native people were by no means the only resource users affected by this process. The Atlantic salmon fishery had a significant commercial net-fishing sector; and thousands of farmers, settlers, and other residents along the rivers of eastern Canada also used the resource, fishing for salmon by various means, including the spear. Efforts by the sport fishing industry and the government to control the harvesting activities of these groups resulted in local political struggles and numerous incidents of social violence, which are beyond the scope of this study. For an elaboration of the larger

picture see Bill Parenteau, "Creating a Sportsman's Paradise: Salmon Fishing Regulation and Social Conflict in New Brunswick, 1867–1900," paper presented at the biennial conference of the American Society for Environmental History, Las Vegas, Nevada, March 1995. For a case study of the conflicts between non-Native resource users, see Neil S. Forkey, "Anglers, Fishers and the St. Croix River: Conflict in a Canadian-American Borderland, 1867–1900," *Forest and Conservation History* 37, 4 (1993): 160–6.

4   Canada, *Statutes of Canada*, 31 Vict., 1868, c. 60, 183.

5   For a good statement of this notion, see *Sessional Papers*, 1872, no. 5, Annual Reports of the Department of Marine and Fisheries, Napoleon Lavoie, "Report of the Cruise of the Government Schooner *La Canadienne* in the River and Gulf of St. Lawrence," appendix, 23–4.

6   NA, Records of the Department of Marine and Fisheries, RG 23, vol. 298, file 2331, R. Mitchell to L.H. Davis, minister of marine and fisheries, "Report on Burnt Church Indian Fishing," 31 May 1897.

7   *Sessional Papers*, 1867, no. 43, "Reports of the Fisheries of the Dominion, 1867," "Mr. Venning's Report."

8   Ibid., "Reports of the Fisheries of the Dominion, 1867," and Théophile Tétu, "Some Remarks on Our Sea and River Fisheries," appendix, 27–8.

9   *Sessional Papers*, 1869, no. 12, Annual Reports of the Department of Marine and Fisheries, "Report of Théophile Tétu, Esq., of the Cruise of *La Canadienne* in the River and Gulf of St. Lawrence, for the Season of 1868," appendix 4, 44–5.

10   Ibid., 45.

11   NA, Records of the Department of Indian Affairs, RG 10, vol. 2066, file 10, 300, "Extract of Mr. Lavoie's Report of Progress, 11 August 1878." On the changing policies of the Hudson's Bay Company during this period, see Arthur J. Ray, *The Canadian Fur Trade in the Industrial Age* (Toronto: University of Toronto Press 1990).

12   NA, Records of the Department of Indian Affairs, RG 10, vol. 2066, file 10, 300, "Extract of the Annual Report of B. McGee, Fishery Overseer for the Mingan Division, 1878."

13   Ibid., L. Vankoughnet, deputy superintendent of Indian Affairs, to James Bissett, Hudson's Bay Company, Montreal, 18 Dec. 1878; Bissett to Vankoughnet, 19 Dec. 1878.

14   There was general agreement within the upper level of the department with the opinion of Napoleon

Lavoie, captain of *La Canadienne*, who implemented the policy in the early 1870s. As he said about a netting station that was given to the Mingan band in 1875: "I think it will be better to have this stand fished by other parties than the Indians, as is done on the Restigouche because they do not care about the stand now that they have got it, and I am sure that there will not be an Indian to set the stand another season. But as they are big children we must think for them and attend to their interests." NA, Records of the Department of Indian Affairs, RG 10, vol. 1991, file 6653, "Report of Napoleon Lavoie on the Mingan Indians, 30 June 1876."

15   This policy was plainly stated in the department's 1881 Annual Report. In recognizing the lack of opportunity to engage in farming, the deputy superintendent promised that "no effort will be spared to secure for the Montagnais a fair share of the fisheries of the Lower St. Lawrence." He also conceded, however, "that the monopoly by white men over the most important salmon streams will prove a most serious barrier to the policy of the department being attended with the success one would wish"; and, he added, "nor are the Indians by any means indifferent to the alienation of fishing rights which they had learned to regard as exclusively their own from time immemorial." *Sessional Papers*, 1881, no. 14, Annual Report of the Department of Indian Affairs, 5.

16   See the requests made by L.F. Boucher, Indian agent, in 1880. NA, Records of the Department of Indian Affairs, RG 10, vol. 2126, files 24, 222, and 24, 227.

17   Ibid., file 24, 224, L.F. Boucher, Indian agent, to L. Vankoughnet, deputy superintendent of Indian affairs, 4 Dec. 1880; Vankoughnet to W.F. Whitcher, deputy minister of marine and fisheries, 27 Dec. 1880; Whitcher to Vankoughnet, 8 Jan. 1881; Vankoughnet to Boucher, 15 Jan. 1881; Boucher to Vankoughnet, 1 Feb. 1881; Vankoughnet to Whitcher, 3 Dec. 1881; Whitcher to Vankoughnet, 7 Dec. 1881 (quoted); Vankoughnet to Whitcher, 15 Dec. 1881; Whitcher to Vankoughnet, 22 Dec. 1881.

18   Ibid., vol. 1978, file 5967, John Mowat to minister of marine and fisheries, 4 March 1876. On the increased prosecution of the Native fishers, see *Sessional Papers*, 1872, no. 5, Annual Reports of the Department of Marine and Fisheries, Napoleon Lavoie, "Report of the Cruise of the Government Schooner *La Canadienne* in the River and Gulf of St. Lawrence," appendix, 24. On similar conflict in other places, see J. Michael Thoms, "Illegal

Conservation: Two Case Studies of Conflict between Indigenous and State Natural Resource Paradigms" (MA thesis, Trent University 1995); Dianne Newell, *Tangled Webs of History: Indians and the Law in the Pacific Coast Fisheries* (Toronto: University of Toronto Press 1993).

19 Because this grant was made too late to allow the band to set up its station, spearing was allowed during the 1872 season, with a stern warning that thereafter "no more spearing will be tolerated in the Restigouche." *Sessional Papers*, 1873, no. 8, Annual Reports of the Department of Marine and Fisheries, "Report of John Mowat, Overseer, Restigouche and Matapedia Division," in "Synopsis of Overseers and Guardians Reports in the Province of Quebec, for the Season of 1872," appendix, 87–8.

20 Ibid., 1872, no. 5, Annual Reports of the Department of Marine and Fisheries, Napoleon Lavoie, "Report of the Cruise of the Government Schooner *La Canadienne* in the River and Gulf of St. Lawrence," appendix, 23–4.

21 NA, Records of the Department of Indian Affairs, RG 10, vol. 1978, file 5967, John Mowat to minister of marine and fisheries, 4 March 1876.

22 *Sessional Papers*, 1874, no. 4, Annual Reports of the Department of Marine and Fisheries, Napoleon Lavoie, "Report of the Cruise of the Government Schooner *La Canadienne* in the River and Gulf of St. Lawrence," appendix, 20.

23 Ibid., 21.

24 NA, Records of the Department of Indian Affairs, RG 10, vol. 1978, file no. 5967, Petition of John Barnaby and Alex Marchand to the Department of Marine and Fisheries, 4 Jan. 1876; John Mowat to minister of marine and fisheries, 4 March 1876.

25 Ibid., John Mowat to minister of marine and fisheries, 4 March 1876.

26 Ibid., vol. 2171, file 930, Rev. A. Drapeau to deputy superintendent of Indian affairs, 1 Feb. 1882; memorandum of agreement between Richard Parker and the Mission Point Band, 21 Feb. 1882.

27 *Sessional Papers*, 1873, no. 8, Annual Reports of the Department of Marine and Fisheries, "Report of John Mowat, Overseer, Restigouche and Matapedia Division," in "Synopsis of Overseers and Guardians Reports in the Province of Quebec, for the Season of 1872," appendix, 87–8.

28 NA, Records of the Department of Marine and Fisheries, RG 10, vol. 298, file 2331, Alexander Mowat to E.E. Prince, commissioner of fisheries, 16 Nov. 1895.

29 There were also many petty acts of intimidation and coercion on the part of fishery officers and Indian agents, such as threatening to withhold annual grants unless the fishing regulations were respected, that are similarly elusive.

30 Parenteau, "Creating a Sportsmen's Paradise," 42–55

31 Sage, *The Restigouche and Its Salmon Fishing*, 22.

32 Napoleon Comeau, *Life and Sport on the Lower St. Lawrence and Gulf*, 2nd ed. (Quebec: Telegraph Printing Company 1923), 108–10.

33 The cat-and-mouse games played between Comeau and the residents of a nearby reserve are recounted in his *Life and Sport on the Lower St. Lawrence and Gulf*, 110–13. On the monitoring of fish and game wardens, see the North American Fish and Game Protective Association, *Minutes of the Proceedings of the First Meeting* (Montreal 1900), 23–4.

34 For a listing of the leased rivers in the early 1890s, see Charles G.D. Roberts, *The Canadian Guide Book: The Tourist's and Sportsman's Guide to Eastern Canada and Newfoundland* (New York: D. Appleton 1891, 264–7.

35 On this logic, see, for example, "Editorial," *Rod and Gun in Canada* 3, (1901): 10.

36 NA, Records of the Department of Marine and Fisheries, RG 10, vol. 298, file 2331, Alexander Mowat to E.E. Prince, commissioner of fisheries, 16 Nov. 1895.

37 *Sessional Papers*, 1893, no. 26, 14. Annual Report of the Department of Indian Affairs, "Report of V.I.A. Venner, Indian agent," 30.

38 NA, Records of the Department of Marine and Fisheries, RG 23, vol. 298, file 2331, Alexander Mowat to E.E. Prince, commissioner of fisheries, 16 Nov. 1895. Information on wages in the late nineteenth century can be found in various volumes of the *Report on the Royal Commission on the Relations of Capital and Labour in Canada* (Ottawa 1889). On the opportunities for guides to earn additional money by providing other services or goods, see Thoms, "Illegal Conservation."

39 Sage, *Salmon Fishing on the Restigouche*, 20.

40 For a particularly good account of a lengthy struggle with a salmon and the importance of an expert guide, see Henry P. Wells, *The American Salmon Fisherman* (London: S. Low, Marston, Searle and Rivington 1886), 155–62. See also T.R. Pattillo, *Moose Hunting, Salmon Fishing and Other Sketches of Sport, Being a Record of Personal Experiences of Hunting Wild Game in Canada* (London: S. Low, Marston 1902), 24–57.

41 See, for example, the character study of "Pierre Joseph" in *Rod and Gun in Canada* 2, 6 (1900): 364; Roberts, *The Canadian Guide Book*, 165–6; Sage, *Salmon Fishing on the Restigouche*, 22–32; E.T.D. Chambers, "Among the Northern Lakes," *Rod and Gun in Canada* 2, 5 (1900).

42 The attributes of a particular guide could be known to a surprisingly wide circle of sportsmen. Even the early modern sporting/travel guides recommended specific guides to their readers. See Robert Barnwell Roosevelt, *Game Fish of the Northern United States and British Provinces* (New York: Carleton 1869); Charles Hallock, *The Fishing Tourist: Angler's Guide and Reference Book* (New York: Harper 1873).

43 The topic of Native guides in eastern Canada has not been studied to any great extent. On the methodological and conceptual problems of examining the relationship between sportsmen and guides, see Patricia Jasen, "Who's the Boss: Native Guides and White Tourists in the Canadian Wilderness, 1850–1914," unpublished paper, presented at the Annual Meeting of the Canadian Historical Association, Ottawa, June 1993; Jasen, *Wild Things: Nature, Culture and Tourism in Ontario, 1790–1914* (Toronto: University of Toronto Press 1995), 133–5.

44 *Sessional Papers*, 1891, no. 24, 8a, Annual Report of the Department of Marine and Fisheries, "Report of Salmon Fisheries on the Bay des Chaleurs," appendix, 30–1. On the exclusivity of clubs in Quebec, see L.Z. Joncas, *The Sportsmen's Companion, Showing the Haunts of Moose, Caribou and Deer, also of the Salmon, Ouananiche and Trout of the Province of Quebec* (Quebec 1899), 101–2.

45 An exception to the general pattern could be seen in Nova Scotia, where the rivers were more open to local people and the occasional fishing tourist of modest means. However, the fishing was much less consistent and usually not as good as in places like the Gaspé and the North Shore of New Brunswick. Salmon fishing in Nova Scotia could also be a contentious affair, with rival parties in dispute over the best pools. See Pattillo, *Moose Hunting, Salmon Fishing and Other Sketches of Sport*; Richard Lewes Dashwood, *Chiploquorgan, or Life by the Camp Fire* (London: Simpkin, Marshall 1872).

46 NA, Records of the Department of Indian Affairs, RG 10, vol. 1991, file 6653, "Report of Napoleon Lavoie, Progress of the Mission Point Indians, 1876"; *Sessional Papers*, 1884, no. 16, 4, Annual Report of the Department of Indian Affairs, "Report of Octave Drapeau, Mission Point Reserve," 31.

47 See John M. MacKenzie, *The Empire of Nature* (Manchester: Manchester University Press 1987); MacKenzie, "The Imperial Pioneer and Hunter and the British Masculine Stereotype in Late Victorian and Edwardian Times," in J.A. Mangan and James Walvin, eds., *Manliness and Morality: Middle Class Masculinity in Britain and America* (Manchester: Manchester University Press 1987), 176–98; Dennison Nash, "Tourism as a Form of Imperialism," in V.L. Smith, ed., *Hosts and Guests: The Anthropology of Tourism* (Philadelphia: University of Pennsylvania Press 1977), 37–52; Martin Green, *The Adventurous Male: Chapters in the History of the White Male Mind* (University Park, PA: Pennsylvania State University Press 1993).

48 Roberts, *The Canadian Guide Book*, 177.

49 Green, *The Adventurous Male*, 68.

50 On adoption of the code of the sportsman in North America, see Reiger, *American Sportsmen and the Origins of Conservation*; Richard Manning, "Recreating Man: Hunting and Angling in Victorian Canada"; Tober, *Who Owns the Wildlife?*

51 The classic statement on this subject is Roderick Nash, "The Wilderness Cult," in his *Wilderness and the American Mind*, 3rd ed. (New Haven: Yale University Press 1982). An excellent discussion of these issues can be found in Jasen, *Wild Things*, 13–20; see also Nelson H.H. Grayburn, "Tourism: The Sacred Journey," in Smith, *Hosts and Guests*, 21–35.

52 Jasen, *Wild Things*, 17–19. On representations of Native people in Canada, see Daniel Francis, *The Imaginary Indian: The Image of the Indian in Canadian Culture* (Vancouver: Arsenal Pulp Press 1992); Terry Goldman, *Fear and Temptation: The Image of the Indigene in Canadian, Australian and New Zealand Literature* (Montreal and Kingston: McGill-Queen's University Press 1989); Leslie Monkman, *A Native Heritage: Images of Indians in English-Canadian Literature* (Toronto: University of Toronto Press 1981).

53 The classic statement on antimodernism is T. Jackson Lears, *No Place of Grace: Antimodernism and the Transformation of American Culture, 1880–1920* (New York: Pantheon 1981); see also Ian McKay, *The Quest of the Folk: Antimodernism and Cultural Selection in Twentieth Century Nova Scotia* (Montreal and Kingston: McGill-Queen's University Press 1994).

54 McKay, *The Quest of the Folk*, xv.

55 C.H. Farnham, "The Montagnais," *Harper's Magazine*, Aug. 1888, 379–80; for another excel-

lent comparison between "primitive" and "civilized" man, see Edward A. Samuels, *With Rod and Gun in New England and the Maritime Provinces* (Boston: Samuels and Kimball 1897), 23–6.

56 John Urry, *The Tourist Gaze: Leisure and Travel in Contemporary Societies* (London: Sage 1990); McKay, *The Quest of the Folk*; Dean MacCannell, *The Tourist: A New Theory of the Leisure Class*, 2nd ed. (New York: Shocken 1989).

57 Abundant evidence of the pervasive trade in Native handicrafts and the eventual saturation of the market can be found in the synoptic reports of Indian agents in the annual reports of the Department of Indian Affairs. On the decline of the trade see, for example, *Sessional Papers*, 1892, no. 14, Annual Report of the Department of Indian Affairs, 28, 35, 37, and 39.

58 Joncas, *The Sportsman's Companion*, 105.

59 Dashwood, *Chiploquorgan, or Life by the Camp Fire*; Wells, *The American Salmon Fisherman*; Hallock, *The Fishing Tourist*; Sage, *Salmon Fishing on the Restigouche*.

60 E.T.D. Chambers, "The Ouananiche and Its Canadian Environment," *Harper's Magazine*, vol. XCIII (June 1896), 119; on the physical attributes of guides see also Charles G.D. Roberts, *The Canadian Guide Book:* "Pierre Joseph," *Rod and Gun in Canada*, vol. 2, 6 (November, 1900); St. Croix, "Second Sight and the Indian," *Rod and Gun in Canada* 4, 3 (August, 1902), 103–4; Heber Bishop, *Guide Book to the Megantic, Spider and Upper Dead River Regions of the Province of Quebec and the State of Maine* (Boston: Megantic Fish and Game Club 1897).

61 Sage, *Salmon Fishing on the Restigouche*, 23.

62 Sage, *Salmon Fishing on the Restigouche*, 23–4.

63 Charles G.D. Roberts, *The Canadian Guide Book*, 98.

64 Hallock, *The Fishing Tourist*, 36–8.

65 The fact that both Indian Joe and Pete Labouisse were "half breeds" was by no means a coincidence. Like other Victorians, sporting writers were fixated with issues of racial purity. The assignment of mixed-race lineage to poachers was, in some respects, a way of maintaining idealized, romantic notions of the character of "primitive man" (ie, racially pure Native people). On the importance of racial purity to nineteenth-century tourists, see Jasen, *Wild Things*, 107–12.

66 Robert Grant, *Jack in the Bush, or a Summer on Salmon River* (New York: Charles Scribner's Sons 1893), 297–331.

67 Alexander, "Fishing in New Brunswick and etc.," 330.

68 The concept of "staged authenticity" is elaborated in MacCannell, *The Tourist*, 98–100.

69 Mary Louise Pratt defines "contact zones" as "the space of colonial encounters, the space in which peoples geographically and historically separated come into contact with each other and establish ongoing relations, usually involving conditions of coercion, radical inequality, and intractable conflict." Pratt, *Imperial Eyes: Travel Writing and Transculturation* (London: Routledge 1992), 5.

70 Complete statistics are available for the year 1871. The average for the three rivers combined was probably closer to 10,000 pounds per year. Still, it does not seem unreasonable to suggest that five tons of salmon may have been put to good use by the Montagnais. *Statements of Salmon Fishing on the River Godbout, from 1859–1875* (Ottawa: A.S. Woodburn 1876), 10; Comeau, *Life and Sport on the Lower St. Lawrence*, 368, 375, 386.

Exclusion or Solidarity? Vancouver Workers Confront the "Oriental Problem"*

GILLIAN CREESE

Vancouver, from its very beginning it may be stated, has always been thoroughly anti-Chinese in its sentiments.[1]

The Chinese question was then constantly before the [Vancouver Trades and Labour] Council and many motions were made on the various phases of the question.[2]

The history of labour politics in early twentieth-century British Columbia was marked by periods of intense anti-Asian agitation.[3] Although the labour movement is commonly seen as an indication of developing working-class consciousness, white workers' consciousness of a common working-class interest in British Columbia did not extend to Asian workers.[4] This leads us to question why the white labour movement followed a strategy of excluding rather than including Asian workers in attempts to collectively improve their lives in British Columbia.

Those who have attempted to answer this question have focused on two different factors: social psychology and economic competition. W. Peter Ward is the strongest proponent of the

psychological approach, suggesting that the "Oriental problem" was fundamentally a product of "the social psychology of race relations."[5] "At the bottom of west coast radicalism lay the frustrated vision of a 'white' British Columbia."[6] Ward sees ideas as historically free-floating and therefore sufficient explanation for social action. This argument is premised on the sociologically untenable assumption that social structures are primarily the outcome of the conscious creation of the human mind. The relationship between human agency, social structures, and ideas is a reflexive social process in which people are both the products and the producers of their social environment.[7] Ideological factors are important for understanding racism, but it is necessary to consider the social context in which ideas have efficacy in specific historical times and places.

The more common explanations for racial exclusion by white workers focus on economic factors, either alone or in combination with psychological or cultural differences. For Paul Phillips, Thomas Loosmore, Ross McCormack, Rennie Warburton, and Robert Wynne, economic competition between high-wage white workers and low-wage Asian workers explains

Gillian Creese, "Exclusion or Solidarity? Vancouver Workers Confront the 'Oriental Problem,'" *BC Studies* 80 (Winter 1998–9): 24–51.

* Research for this paper was supported by fellowships from the Social Sciences and Humanities Research Council of Canada and the Ontario Ministry of Colleges and Universities. I would like to thank Bob McDonald and an anonymous *BC Studies* reviewer for helpful comments on an earlier draft of this paper.

racial exclusion by white workers.[8] These authors agree that labour competition was the central feature of ethnic divisions in the working class, and that exclusion was the only viable strategy under those circumstances. Exclusion was the only viable strategy because Asians were, they suggest, unorganizable. As McCormack argues, Asians were "unassimilated and, therefore, impossible to organize."[9] Two factors make this explanation weak: white workers did not try to organize Asians and then exclude the latter when organization failed; and Asian workers showed greater involvement in labour militancy than conventional wisdom allows, suggesting that solidarity with Asians was a possible alternative to exclusionary practices. The exclusion of Asian workers was not, then, the automatic outcome of competition in the labour market; other factors, such as the denial of political rights to Asians and their status as permanent "foreigners," were important considerations that shaped the practices of white workers.

Other authors have attempted to combine economic and ideological explanations. Patricia Roy and Carlos Schwantes both argue that racism had two distinct loci: economic competition and the ideology of racism, or, in Roy's words, fear for the future of a "white" British Columbia.[10] Neither considers the relationship between economic and ideological factors, however, so an integrated analysis is undeveloped. David Bercuson and H. Clare Pentland consider cultural differences as emigrants from different ethnic origins compete with one another. Pentland argues that large numbers of low-status immigrants led to lack of solidarity, while few low-status immigrants facilitated labour radicalism.[11] British Columbia is placed in the latter category, ignoring the coexistence of radicalism and anti-Asian exclusion. Bercuson suggests that the key to intra-working-class conflict was immigrants' different expectations before arriving in Canada. Asians

were cheap and docile because they faced worse conditions in their countries of origin and expected nothing better than they found in Canada; while European, especially British, immigrants expected better conditions and were radicalized.[12] Bercuson does not explain why radicalized white workers excluded rather than included Asians as a solution to cheap labour competition. He also seems to assume that Asian docility gave white workers no choice but exclusion.

What follows is a case study of patterns of racial exclusion and solidarity among one group of workers in an attempt to analyze the circumstances that shaped such actions. Practices of Asian exclusion and inclusion within the Vancouver labour movement are explored in the period prior to the Second World War. Racial divisions within the working class reflected the importance of race in defining workers' lives, not only in the workplace, but also in the political sphere, in civil society, and in prevailing ideologies through which people understood their lives. Race appeared more or less salient in workers' understanding of their lives and problems under different circumstances. As the following analysis will attempt to show, white workers' treatment of Asian workers varied with economic conditions, adherence to radical political ideologies, and the participation of Asian workers in labour conflicts. The white labour movement often pursued anti-Asian activities in the period before the Second World War. Yet racial solidarity grew during periods of heightened labour radicalism and Asian labour militancy, especially during the Great Depression, even though competition for jobs was at its most intense. At such times white workers no longer distinguished Asians as "foreigners" whose exclusion would advance the situation of "real" (white) workers; they were seen as members of the Vancouver working class with interests similar to other workers.

Cheap Labour/Foreign Workers

Patricia Roy, W. Peter Ward, Edgar Wickberg, Tien-Fang Cheng, Peter Li, Ken Adachi, and others have documented the pervasiveness of racism against Asians during the early twentieth century.[13] Racism was expressed both through dominant ideologies about the inferiority of non-Europeans and through discriminatory practices in the labour market, in the political system, and in most areas of daily life. Asians were not equal to whites in the province during the first half of this century, either in popular consciousness or in the social institutions of the society.

Racial inequality was firmly linked to, and much acrimony rested upon, the role of Asians as cheap wage labourers in the economy. The push and pull of Asian immigration was tied to their status as wage labourers. The first large-scale migration of Chinese recruited by the Canadian Pacific Railway was precipitated by the demand for cheap labour, and Chinese, Japanese, and East Indian migrants actively sought entry into Canada in pursuit of wage-labour opportunities. With a small indigenous population, immigration filled economic development needs, and the motivations for emigration were little different for European or Asian immigrants.[14] Immigrants of all kinds sought better economic opportunities, and the vast majority would find those opportunities labouring for someone else. Capitalism was, and remains, a central organizing feature of Canadian society, and immigration patterns were, and are, closely linked to the demands of capitalist economic development.

What differentiated Asian migrants from Europeans was not only the precise role that the former played in the labour market, as an underclass of cheap labourers, but also their being denied political rights by the Canadian state. The mostly male Asian workers were largely confined to the least desirable unskilled labour and concentrated in the primary and service sectors of the economy; earned from one-half to three-quarters of the wages of unskilled white men in the same industries; and were typically hired under labour contractors rather than as individuals, a system that added to their lower standard of living and segregation from the white labour force.[15] Low wages and restricted employment opportunities were directly related to the second-class political status accorded Asians in Canada. Unlike other immigrants, Asians were denied the rights of political citizenship, restricted in areas of employment, regulated, taxed, and even prohibited from immigration to Canada.[16] In its policies the Canadian government clearly distinguished between desirable white settlers and Asian migrants who would be encouraged to work but not to settle in Canada.[17] Asians were considered unassimilable permanent "foreigners," irrespective of naturalization or place of birth.

The different treatment Asian and European immigrants received from employers and the Canadian state created a racially stratified society.[18] Asian subordination was an integral part of social relations in British Columbia. As a result, class relations were shaped by practices of white domination and Asian subordination.

Class relations of power and domination derived from the rights of private property and the pursuit of profit central to a capitalist economy, and were a part of the daily life (if not always daily consciousness) of all who laboured in the province.[19] Although class inequality was common to all wage labourers, practices attributed to the race and the gender of the worker shaped the nature of the subordination. To a considerable extent racial and gender characteristics defined the type of work available, the wages received for work, the ability to acquire various kinds of skills, and even conditions in the workplace.[20] White men monopolized the skilled trades, and received higher wages than other workers in unskilled labour. Some work was clearly classified as "women's work" and other work as "coolie labour," sometimes with overlapping boundaries.[21] Workers in British Columbia were not, then, neutral units of labour power: they were hired as white *or* Asian workers, male *or* female workers, and were treated differently by employers. In a society where racial and gender characteristics defined the nature of citizenship and political rights, women and Asian workers were socially defined as more exploitable than white male workers.[22] It should not be surprising, then, that both race and gender affected the development of the labour movement in British Columbia, a movement dominated by white men, the strongest segment of the working class.

The Politics of Exclusion in the Vancouver Labour Movement

The Vancouver Trades and Labour Council (VTLC), founded in November of 1889, was the centre of the Vancouver labour movement and the centre of working class anti-Asian activity. The "Oriental problem" was constantly before council during its early years, as a review of its first year of operation shows. In February the VTLC supported an agreement between the City of Vancouver and Rogers Sugar Refinery granting the latter tax concessions in exchange for an all-white hiring policy.[23] In September 1890 the VTLC pursued a boycott of Chinese laundries and enforcement of Sunday closing bylaws against Chinese businesses.[24] In October VTLC delegates attended the Trades and Labour Congress convention in Ottawa to express their views on the dangers of Chinese immigration, and met with Prime Minister John A. Macdonald to demand an increase in the Chinese head tax from $50 to $500.[25] In November the VTLC

formed a committee to investigate and compile statistics on Chinese labour to be used in its agitation for stricter immigration laws.[26] And in April of the following year the VTLC adopted a resolution calling for the total prohibition of Chinese immigration to Canada.[27]

Individual unions within the Labour Council regularly complained of cheap Chinese, and later Japanese and East Indian, competition undermining union workers. In a single council meeting on 4 June 1908, for example, three different unions identified Asian competition as the cause of poor labour conditions for the union concerned.[28] The Tailors' Union reported:

> Trade dull; Chinese competition displacing membership. Delegates urged the demand for their label, the only guarantee that their clothes were made outside Asiatic sweat-shops and non-union premises.

The Cooks and Waiters' Union reported:

> Asiatic competition was a continual menace to their organization. Complaint that white cooks could not be secured was due to higher wages demanded.... Many members out of employment; trade very dull.

The Typographical Union reported on the existence of Chinese and Japanese print shops "doing work for 'patriotic' local businessmen" that were putting union members out of work. Two motions were passed at the meeting concerning Asian competition. One motion was directed to the provincial Attorney-General to find out

> why the Asiatic population is not compelled to comply with the civic Health by-laws the same as others...[and] urged that prompt measures be taken to see that the Chinese disease-breeding sweat-shops be at least cleaned up and made to comply with the law.

And the VTLC executive was directed to inquire why Japanese establishments were granted liquor licences. Although all VTLC meetings were not as preoccupied with the "Oriental problem" as this meeting in June 1908, Asian competition was a recurring concern for the Council.

The VTLC and its union affiliates engaged in numerous forms of anti-Asian activities. Exclusionary labour practices included boycotts against Asian businesses, campaigns to replace Asian labour with white labour, to disallow the employment of white women alongside Asian men, to restrict areas of Asian employment, areas of Asian residence and the hours that Asians could work, to prohibit further Asian immigration, and to prohibit Asian membership in trade unions. The labour movement tended to equate non-union labour with Asian labour, even though only a minority of white workers were unionized.[29] And while cheaper Asian labour was criticized for undermining union workers, Asian workers were explicitly excluded from membership in trade unions.

Concern with cheap Asian labour competition was pressed most strongly by unions faced with direct Asian competition, especially tailors, garment workers, laundry workers, and restaurant workers. The skilled craft unions, which made up the bulk of VTLC membership, were not often in direct competition with Asian workers, although skilled unions perceived potential Asian competition in their industries as a threat. For the unskilled unions, Asian labour competition was often a preoccupation, especially during periods of high unemployment. The minutes of the Hotel and Restaurant Employees' Union, for example, record persistent denunciations of union men patronizing "unfair" restaurants, referring to restaurants and hotels employing Chinese cooks, waiters, or bus boys rather than non-union establishments employing whites. Chinese waiters and cooks were identified as the major impediment to more successful union organizing in the culi-

nary industry. The Hotel and Restaurant Employees' Union actively supported the Asiatic Exclusion League and tried repeatedly to persuade City Hall to tie licences to white-only hiring clauses and to disallow the employment of white women in Chinese restaurants. The union also directly lobbied hotels and restaurants to replace Chinese employees with whites in return for union patronage of their establishments. The Hotel and Restaurant Employees' Union did not try to include Chinese restaurant workers as a solution to cheap labour competition until 1938, when a Chinese union organizer was hired.[30]

The labour movement's rationale for excluding Asians was based not only on cheap labour competition but also included explicitly racist ideas. Asians were considered inferior social beings: "Japs," "Chinks," "Coolies," Hindoos," "insidious Orientals." Just as the Canadian state distinguished between Asian immigrants without political rights and whites who would become "real" Canadians with political rights, so too did the labour movement define Asian workers as "foreigners" and whites as the "real" working class in Canada. Critiques of the oppression of workers were often linked to demands to hire "citizens" of one's own "race." In 1907 a petition was circulated among upper class women to repeal the $500 Chinese head tax because it contributed to a scarcity of servants in the city. In the VTLC's response to this petition, the importance of race is central to the definition of the working class:

> Thus we urge the present Government to disregard the petition of those ladies of British Columbia, who want Chinese servants. The women of the working class do their own work and when they need help, they employ their own race. Let these ladies who now waste their time...[in] useless functions emulate the example of their poorer sisters and do a little of their own domestic work. If, however, they claim

immunity from work, let them pay the price, or modify the conditions of service in such a manner as will secure for them girls of their own race. It is, we think, absurd that the working class of Canada should run the risk of having its standard of living degraded to the level of a Chinese coolie merely to gratify the whim of an aristocratic lady for a Chinese servant.[31]

For the labour movement, the essential factor defining membership in the Vancouver working class was not, apparently, union membership, length of residence, or Canadian versus foreign birth; it was race. Asians were considered nonassimilable "foreigners" who were undermining the living standards of real (white) workers in British Columbia. The problem was not immigration per se, but the type of immigration into British Columbia:

The demand for Asiatic Exclusion cannot be answered by a counter-demand for the exclusion of all immigration, upon the ground of equal treatment to the peoples of all nations. Admitting that European immigration, as it has recently developed, constitutes a problem demanding immediate attention, it is after all a problem of quantity, whereas Asiatic immigration is distinctly a problem of quality.[32]

The prevalence of racist attitudes about the inferiority of Asian workers in British Columbia was grounded in the social organization of Asians as cheap wage labourers at the bottom of the class structure, and the state's denial of citizenship rights. Racism was part of the dominant ideology of the period, a legacy of British colonialism, which found salience in the conditions of workers' lives since employment practices were explicitly race-conscious. White workers' experiences included witnessing the expansion of cheaper Asian labour in the primary and service sectors of the economy as employers sought to drive down the price of labour and under-

mine union organization. As an article in *The British Columbia Federationist* suggested, white workers feared that the long-term effect of this competition threatened to undermine their already inadequate living standards:

It has been proved, time and time again, that when the Oriental once gets a foothold in a certain line, the standard of wage in that field at once drops because of his basing his wage demands according to his standard of living. It is not a case of possibly raising the Oriental to the white standard, it is a case of the certain lowering of the standard of the whites.[33]

In the context of a racially segregated labour market, the strongest segment of the working class, white (male) workers, organized to exclude, rather than include, cheaper and politically weaker workers who were already defined as "foreigners" within Canadian civil society. In order to overcome racial exclusion, white workers had to begin to define Asian workers as part of the working class rather than as "foreigners" who were the cause of the former's insecurity.

During two brief periods between the First and Second World Wars, when many organized white workers pursued greater solidaristic practices with Asian workers, the labour movement did begin to redefine Asians as part of the Vancouver working class. At the end of the First World War (1917–1921) and during the Great Depression, the two most militant periods of Vancouver labour history, some white labour organizations actively set out to organize with Asians rather than against them. It was also during these periods that Asian workers were most actively involved in labour militancy.

Asian workers were always in a weaker position than white workers in Vancouver. They were less likely to engage in labour militancy and more vulnerable when they did so. This is not surprising. Asian workers lacked political and citizenship rights, possessed fewer economic resources than white workers, lacked well-developed trade union and socialist traditions, faced the resistance of the ethnic community élites, dominated by Asian employers, and were the object of exclusionary practices by white trade unions. Nevertheless, the image of Asians as strikebreakers but never labour activists during the early years of the labour movement is exaggerated. Although much less active in labour conflicts than white workers, there was a thread of Asian labour activism in Vancouver throughout the early twentieth century.[34]

In the Greater Vancouver area, Chinese, Japanese, and East Indian workers took part in no fewer than fifty separate strikes between 1900 and 1939 (see Appendix A).[35] Seventy percent of these strikes involved the joint action of Asian and white workers, mostly in the lumber industry and the fisheries. Two-thirds of the strikes involving Asians were concentrated in two periods: Asian workers struck twelve times at the end of the First World War (1917–1921) and twenty times during the Great Depression (1921–1937). In contrast, Asians engaged in only thirteen strikes during the first sixteen years of this century and in only six strikes between 1922 and 1930.

It is not coincidental that higher levels of Asian labour militancy occurred simultaneously with greater solidaristic practices by white workers. The position of Asian workers was strengthened considerably by common action with white workers, thereby encouraging Asian labour militancy. And the more militant Asians were in the workplace, the more likely that white workers would recognize their common interests and attempt to unite with Asian co-workers. For all workers, the state of the economy shaped labour activism: the labour shortage at the end of the First World War strengthened the position of all workers, while the depth of the economic crisis during the 1930s had a general radicalizing effect. These three interrelated factors—economic conditions, the growth of radical labour politics, and increased Asian militancy—resulted in greater racial solidarity at the end of the First World War and during the Great Depression.

There were, of course, instances of Asian-white co-operation during strikes in the period prior to the First World War, especially, but not exclusively, in the salmon fishery.[36] Whatever co-operation occurred, however, was short-lived, lasting only during a particular labour conflict, and never involved organizational inclusion. Lack of organizational unity weakened joint strike activity, and employers often found it possible to break strikes by forcing weaker Asians back to work. White workers gave little consideration to the weaker economic and political position of Asian workers, and simply branded the latter as strikebreakers. In the fisheries, for example, the areas where Japanese fishermen could fish were restricted, while white and Native fishermen could fish throughout the coast. This had a profound effect on labour conflicts in that industry. As one Japanese fisherman remembered, Japanese fishermen could not strike for long because if they lost the season in their area they could not go elsewhere to recoup as could other fishermen. This made Japanese fishermen "the weak link in the chain" in spite of their commitment to improving fish prices and frequent involvement in fisheries strikes. When economic necessity forced the Japanese back to work, white and Native fishermen simply branded the Japanese as strikebreakers, even though the whites and Natives were instrumental in enforcing restrictive regulations against Japanese fishermen in the first place.[37]

On rare occasions some white labour organizations advocated organizing Asian workers as a solution to cheap labour competition. In 1903 The Western Federation of Miners suggested organizing Chinese coal miners to forestall strikebreaking during the Canadian Pacific Railway strike, but nothing came of it.[38] The

WFM's successor, the International Workers of the World, also, on occasion, suggested organizing Chinese workers, but apparently never acted on the idea.[39] Apart from these two industrial unions, no other unions even considered Asian organization a possibility.

Exclusionary politics were much less prevalent in the more radical industrial unions and in the socialist political parties in the province than in the mainstream labour movement, even before the First World War. The dominant socialist organization in British Columbia during the first two decades of this century was the Socialist Party of Canada (SPC). Like other labour representatives, SPC members of the Legislative Assembly supported legislation discriminating against Asians in the workplace and restricting further Asian immigration.[40] But while endorsing the labour movement's call for the abolition of Asian immigration, socialists also cautioned that this would not solve the labour problem; only the abolition of capitalism would accomplish that end. As the *Western Clarion* suggested:

> Organized workers are even now making loud complaints against what they term the "Sikh invasion." They are calling upon the powers that be to put a stop to it. They overlook the fact that the powers to whom they appeal, and the property interests which profit by the influx of this cheap and docile labor are identical. Their appeal thus of necessity must fall upon deaf ears. If the workers of this or any other country desire the exclusion of people from other lands they must first take possession of the reins of government in order to effect their purpose and enforce their will.[41] This race question is being agitated by the master class in order to delude the workers into participating in a trade war for their masters' benefit.... The longer that the hope of betterment by emigration is before the workers, the longer they will be in discovering that their one common hope of betterment lies in the overthrow of the wage system.[42]

By the beginning of the First World War the Socialist Party's position on Asian workers had become clearly defined in the context of the international solidarity of all workers, and the politics of exclusion was rejected:

> What does it greatly matter who our masters import or exclude? We are slaves here. We are slaves in China or Japan; so our condition can be changed but slightly while the capitalist system lasts. We are not of any nationality; we are not white or black; but one thing suffices to make us all common; we are forced to sell labour power to another class in order to live.[43]

For those who embraced radical socialism there could be little rationalization for excluding some workers, whether socially defined as foreigners or not, from the collective working class when the abolition of the exploitation of all workers was the goal. Socialism more clearly defined the "enemy" as capitalist employers, not other workers.[44] But as Robert McDonald has recently pointed out, the labour movement in Vancouver was not dominated by socialists, it was dominated by "moderate labourism."[45] For the most part, Vancouver workers sought reform, not the abolition of capitalism; and one area where reform was pursued was the exclusion of "foreign" Asian workers from immigration to Canada and from more desirable jobs in the economy.

While the *Western Clarion* was calling on workers to recognize that all workers were the victims of capitalism, the VTLC continued to pass motions seeking the "abolition of Oriental labour in mines, lumbering, fishing and railways"; to legislate "white labour clauses" on public works projects and for the renewal of hotel and restaurant licences; and even to enforce "segregated areas" for Asian residence in Vancouver.[46] However, the shortage of labour and high rates of inflation created by the First World War fostered labour militancy, among

Asian as well as white workers, and when combined with the growth of radical socialism after the war, produced increased solidaristic practices within the Vancouver labour movement for a brief period of time.[47]

The First World War marked a watershed in white-Asian solidarity. The post-war period was marked by general strikes in Vancouver in 1918 and 1919, the rapid growth of support for the One Big Union (OBU), massive organization in the largely unorganized lumber industry, and labour confrontations throughout the province. Asian workers participated in militant labour conflicts, including the 1919 general strike; played dominant roles in some strikes, particularly in the lumber industry; and, for the first time, were admitted into some white labour unions. Chinese and Japanese workers also organized their own trade unions within the lumber industry.[48]

The first confrontation in which Asian workers played a dominant role during the war was the shingle weavers' strike in the summer of 1917. Approximately 800 men, three-quarters of whom were Chinese, struck in dozens of shingle mills in the lower mainland for an eight-hour day with ten hours' pay.[49] White workers were organized, separately, under the Shingle Weavers' Union, and Chinese workers were organized under the Chinese Canadian Labour Union, formed the previous year. According to *The Chinese Times,* the white union distributed leaflets in Chinese urging the Chinese to organize for shorter hours.[50] Once the strike began, however, Chinese workers were the main motivating force. As the *British Columbia Federationist* commented:

> Officials of the Shingle Weavers' Union assert that if they were as sure of some of the married white workers as they are of the Chinese, there would be no difficulty in enforcing union conditions throughout the jurisdiction.... Chinese employees are asking for two cents more per

thousand than the whites. However, it is possible that the whites may be able to get the Chinese to come to a more "reasonable" frame of mind. But at that, it's a sight for the gods.[51]

The strike was not successful, but it marked the beginning of large-scale organization among Asian workers in the lumber industry, and greater co-operation with whites.

In March 1919 Asian shingle weavers again launched a major strike in the industry. Approximately 1,200 Asian workers, mostly Chinese, struck up to fifty shingle mills in the lower mainland and on the coast to resist a 10 percent wage reduction. The strike lasted one month, with the old wage scale restored in April. In May, the Chinese Shingle Workers' Union, formed during the strike, demanded and won a further wage increase.[52] Incidents of this kind of Asian labour militancy led to calls for white workers to unite with Asians to improve the situation of all workers.

By 1919 *The British Columbia Federationist,* formerly affiliated with the VTLC, had adopted an explicitly socialist politics and would encourage the growth of the One Big Union. The paper both reflected and further encouraged greater Asian-white solidarity:

> Yes fellow workers, Asiatic workers should be encouraged as joining [sic] white unions for it is a class problem, and not a race problem that confronts the white mill-worker of B.C.[53] It is time that all workers in Canada realised that the "Chink" is as much a part of this country as the Scotchman [sic]; that the "Bohunk" is as necessary as the Englishman; that all of us are exploited by a master-class who cares not what nationality we are so long as we remain willing slaves.[54]

Asian workers, especially those in the shingle and saw mills, took an active part in the 1919 general strikes in Vancouver and New

Westminster.[55] According to *The Chinese Times*, the VTLC "promised to treat the Chinese workers well after the strike was over...[and] help the Chinese to fight against discriminatory laws."[56] Asian workers also played an active role in many OBU-organized strikes for the eight-hour day in the lumber industry during 1919 and 1920. In some instances Asian workers were members of the Lumber Workers Industrial Union (OBU), although more commonly joint labour agitation occurred with Asians organized separately in the Chinese Shingle Workers' Union and the Japanese Workers Union.[57]

There were many instances of solidarity unparalleled in the past. In April 1920, for example, Chinese workers, at least some of whom were members of the OBU, struck Fraser Mills in Maillardville when a wage increase was refused. White workers quit work in solidarity with the Chinese, and a joint committee was formed that successfully negotiated a wage increase. *The British Columbia Federationist* commented that such incidents should help to educate white mill workers who mistakenly believed that "the reason they are so poorly paid is because they have to compete with Oriental labour." In this and other cases, the "splendid solidarity evidenced in the way in which the white workers, Japs and Chinese stood together" was recognized as an important factor in the gains being made in the lumber industry.[58]

Labour gains did not last long. By 1921 the post-war recession was producing an onslaught of wage reductions and the One Big Union, and radical socialist politics, dwindled almost as quickly as it had grown. The "moderate labourism" of the VTLC dominated Vancouver labour politics again and, with unemployment high and circumstances no longer advantageous for labour militancy among Asians or whites, Asian exclusion became a central focus of organized labour once again.[59] In May 1921 the VTLC launched a "Made in B.C. by citizens of Canada" campaign, suggesting that

the time has arrived when the citizens must draw the line more closely between our own nationals, and the aliens from other countries and particularly those from Asiatic countries with a lower standard of living, by replacing these men [with] returned men and citizens generally, with special regard for those who are suffering from handicaps incurred in the war.[60]

Two weeks later the Council struck an "Asiatic Committee" to gather data on Asian employment. In July the committee reported that Asian immigration "constitutes the most serious social menace facing the citizens of B.C." and demanded that Asian immigration be prohibited.[61] In August the VTLC, seven trade unions, five veterans' associations, and the Retail Merchants' Association formed the Asiatic Exclusion League at a meeting at the Labour Hall. The mandate of the Asiatic Exclusion League was threefold:

1. To educate the white population to the terrible menace of the Oriental immigration.

2. To pledge every candidate who is running for Dominion offices at the next election to give a stated policy for the exclusion of Orientals.

3. To press for immediate registration of all Orientals in British Columbia under the auspices of the government.[62]

Once the exclusion movement had succeeded with the passage of the Chinese Immigration Act in 1923 and the reduction of Japanese labourers to 150 per year, the Council concentrated on replacing Asian workers with whites and boycotting Asian businesses.[63]

In 1921 the Japanese Workers' Union applied for affiliation with the VTLC but was turned down. Six years later, and now the Japanese Camp and Mill Workers' Union, the first Asian union became a member of the

Vancouver Trades and Labour Council. This time only five of the twenty-five unions that voted in the referendum on Japanese union affiliation objected to the latter's inclusion.[64] Japanese affiliation indicated a greater degree of racial tolerance within the VTLC, but it did not end exclusionary practices. The Hotel and Restaurant Employees' Union, the Bakers' Union, the Domestic Workers' Union, and the Shingle Weavers' Union all undertook campaigns, endorsed by the VTLC, to replace Asian labour with white labour.[65] And when the Canadian Labour Party endorsed the enfranchisement of Asians in the spring of 1928, the VTLC withdrew its affiliation after thirty-two of thirty-six unions voted against the motion in a referendum.[66]

Class conflict within the Japanese community was the main outcome of Japanese union affiliation with the VTLC. The Japanese Merchants' Association condemned Japanese involvement in the trade union movement and mounted a campaign to weaken the Japanese Camp and Mill Workers' Union. Japanese employers fired members belonging to the union. Merchants withdrew all advertising from the union's newspaper, *The Daily People,* objecting to the paper's message that Japanese workers should unite against their employers. In response, the Japanese Camp and Mill Workers' Union organized a boycott of Japanese businesses and a food co-operative to supply their members' needs.[67] Anti-union resistance by Asian employers, who were powerful members of the Asian communities, probably mitigated greater Asian labour organization. In any event, Asian workers were involved in few strikes during the rest of the 1920s and still faced considerable anti-Asian activity among white workers. Although the Camp and Mill Workers' Union was a member of the VTLC, Asians were still not welcome in the white unions. As one Japanese labour activist commented, "without the cooperation of the white unions we could achieve nothing."[68]

As the economic crisis deepened and unemployment escalated during the early 1930s, labour militancy, among whites and Asians, and radical socialist politics grew. The social dislocation was so severe during the 1930s that for many workers capitalism was clearly identified as the "enemy," and solidarity between white and Asian workers was actively pursued. By the end of 1930 there were more unemployed in Vancouver than there were union members.[69] The depth of unemployment generated two different forums for labour activism: the organization of the unemployed and its increasing demands for state action; and the organization of the unorganized, especially in the lumber industry again, under the Workers' Unity League (WUL). Both the organization of the unemployed and the WUL occurred under the auspices of the Communist Party of Canada.

The VTLC became increasingly irrelevant to labour activism during the depression. Maintaining its stance of "moderate labourism," the VTLC continued to pursue strategies to increase the security and standard of living of its employed members and remained separate from the unemployed organizations and from the "dual unions" that it condemned.[70] The issue of unemployment did dominate Council concerns, but until the late 1930s one of its major solutions was to demand the exclusion of Asian workers in preference for the employment of whites. As the VTLC's newspaper *The Labor Statesman* often proclaimed, Asians should not be employed when thousands of "Canadian boys" were out of work.[71] Moreover, it was up to the government to ensure the preferential hiring of whites:

> ...the Provincial Government should also require that goods or materials needed for public works should not be purchased from firms employing Oriental labour.[72]

In spite of the persistence of the view in the mainstream labour movement that Asians were "foreigners" and not "real" Canadian workers (so the lives of the latter could be improved if the former were eliminated), the 1930s witnessed the breakdown of racial divisions in a more profound way than the brief post-war radicalism had. In the unions of the Workers' Unity League and in the National Unemployed Workers' Association, the umbrella organization for various unemployed groups, Asians were not only accepted as members, they were actively recruited as equals, and issues specific to Asian workers were placed on the labour agenda during conflicts.

The National Unemployed Workers' Association called for the solidarity of all unemployed workers:

> The unemployed do not recognize any difference of race or color.... Among the many thousands of unemployed workers organized in the NUWA, there are many Oriental workers who are among the most highly respected in the organization.[73]

The situation faced by unemployed workers varied by marital status, race, and sex. Chinese workers, for example, were ineligible for city relief because almost all were single men (unlike the Japanese) and only married men qualified for city relief in the early years of the depression. Unemployed Chinese workers were also ineligible for the Relief Camps for single men because these only accepted white men. Thus, Chinese workers found unemployment particularly difficult and, as the resources within the Chinese community were stretched beyond their limits, formed the Chinese Unemployed Workers' Protective Association (CUWPA). CUWPA fought for relief for the unemployed along with the Single Unemployed Protective Association, which organized single white men in Vancouver, and the Neighbourhood Councils and Block Committees of the National Unemployed Workers' Association, which

organized married families (including Asian, mostly Japanese, families). These organizations successfully pressed for city relief for destitute Japanese (and in at least one instance Chinese) families. They fought for equal relief rates for Asian and white families after the City of Vancouver deemed the former to require 20 per cent less than the latter to live. They also lobbied for relief for single Chinese men and demanded, though unsuccessfully, improved conditions in a mission soup kitchen that was contracted to feed unemployed Chinese in 1933 but was so inadequate that over 100 Chinese men died of starvation by 1935. These organizations also demonstrated from time to time to reinstate Chinese men who were cut off further assistance.[74]

Solidaristic practices were not confined to issues of unemployment. Between 1931 and 1939 Asian workers were involved in at least twenty strikes in the lower mainland area, three-quarters of which were in saw mills and shingle mills (see Appendix A). Nearly half of these strikes took place in a single year, 1932, when Asian workers took part in eight strikes in local lumber mills. Most of these strikes were co-ordinated by the Lumber Workers Industrial Union, affiliated with the Workers' Unity League. During some of these labour conflicts, new demands for racial equality emerged.

In September 1931, 600 white, Chinese, Japanese, and East Indian workers struck Fraser Mills in Maillardville over a reduction in wages. Organized under the WUL, the strikers demanded a 10 per cent wage increase, "equal pay for equal work," union recognition, the "abolition of the contract labour system for Oriental workers," and the immediate dismissal of the Japanese labour contractor.[75] The demands in this strike illustrate the extent to which Asian workers were integrated as fuller members of the union and strike committee, especially the demands for equal pay and the abolition of the contract labour system.[76] In

August 1932 fifty white and Japanese workers struck at Sterling Shingle Mills in Vancouver for a 10 per cent wage increase and the reinstatement of workers discharged for union organizing, most of whom were Japanese. According to *The Lumber Worker* (a WUL newspaper), this was the first strike where white workers went out in order to protect the jobs of Asian workers.[77] In September 1933, 1,200 white and Japanese men and women, organized under the WUL, struck a Fraser Valley hop farm demanding a wage increase and better living conditions, especially improvements in the Japanese living quarters. The strike committee included Japanese and white representatives, with the Japanese initially demanding higher wages than the white strikers.[78] Asian representation on WUL strike committees was common; in fact, it was an intentional strategy of the union and often resulted in placing demands specific to Asian workers on the strike agenda.

The most notable feature of Asian labour militancy during the 1930s was the degree to which Asians were included as equal members of (at least part of) the labour movement in comparison to previous periods.[79] At the end of the 1930s, after the WUL unions had merged into the international labour movement, even some of the most vocal anti-Asian unions in Vancouver began to include Asian workers within their ranks. The Hotel and Restaurant Employees' Union, for example, hired a Chinese labour organizer to help unionize Chinese cooks in 1938.[80] Asian workers were by no means fully integrated into the Vancouver labour movement during the 1930s, but the shift toward the acceptance of Asians as equal workers and citizens (rather than as "foreigners") was well underway within sections of the organized working class during the depression. The events of the Second World War demonstrate that racial equality had not yet been accomplished. As the depression ended with the Second World War, Japanese Canadians were again defined as the "foreign" enemy, not only by the Canadian state but also by the white labour movement in British Columbia.[81]

Conclusions

The politics of the Vancouver working class reflect the heterogeneity of the conditions experienced by workers. The labour movement in Vancouver, as in all capitalist societies, emerged out of the struggle over control in the workplace and the political sphere; but employment practices were neither colour blind nor sex blind. Male, female, white, and Asian workers did not receive equal treatment in the labour market, by the state, or in civil society. The material realities of working-class life included relations of white domination and Asian subordination (and male domination and female subordination) that, to a large extent, defined conditions of work and wages, and the nature of citizenship rights within civil society. It is little wonder, then, that working-class politics were structured by ethnic (and gender) relations of inequality.

Labour competition was indeed central to racial divisions within the Vancouver working class, but labour competition is not sufficient to explain these divisions. Common assumptions that Asian exclusion was the only possible outcome of labour competition while labour solidarity was impossible are challenged by the foregoing analysis. The extent of Asian labour militancy before the Second World War shows that assumptions about docile and "unorganizable" Asians are, at the very least, exaggerated. Moreover, it should be recognized that the actions of white workers thwarted greater Asian labour organization in the first place. It is reasonable to assume that Asians would have been even more active in labour struggles if white workers had been more open to co-operation with Asians. Furthermore, if labour competition was a sufficient explanation for exclusionary practices we would expect such practices to be heightened during the depression of the 1930s, when labour competition was most intense. Instead, racial solidarity was strongest during this period. A fuller explanation for racial divisions, and the process of overcoming these cleavages, must include attention to the subordinate status of Asians within civil society, patterns of Asian labour militancy, and changes in the political/ideological orientation of white workers, since socialists and labour reformists pursued different strategies toward Asian workers.

Asian workers formed a pool of cheap labour whose social status within civil society, established through state immigration policies and the denial of political rights, was as permanent "foreigners." For white workers, whose own precarious existence was further threatened by cheaper Asian labour, the "foreigner" status of Asians led, at least for the majority who embraced labour reformism, to strategies of exclusion; as "foreign" workers, Asians were not considered part of the "real" (white) working class whose common interests organized labour sought to represent. A pattern of ethnic divisions developed in Vancouver whereby economically and politically stronger white workers sought to improve their lives by excluding Asian workers from better jobs and, preferably, from the country. Racist labour practices in turn reinforced the subordination of Asian workers in the labour market and in civil society, and ensured their persistence as cheap labour.

Asian labour militancy was hampered by lack of economic and political resources, the racist practices of organized white workers, and class conflict within the ethnic communities. Yet, contrary to much of the literature on British Columbia labour history, there was a thread of Asian labour militancy throughout this century. At the end of the First World War, increased Asian labour activism was facilitated by the war-induced labour shortage and inflation, greater militancy among white workers, and the strengthening of socialist politics advocating solidarity with Asians. The severity of the depression of the 1930s fostered even greater Asian labour activism, much of it organized by the Communist-led Workers' Unity League and the organizations of the unemployed. During the 1930s, Asian workers began to place their own issues on the political agenda, an indication of their inclusion as more equal members of the labour movement compared to earlier periods of co-operation.

A necessary condition for bridging ethnic divisions among Vancouver workers was the redefinition of Asians as workers, like others in Canada, rather than as "foreigners." The adoption of socialist politics, with its sharper focus on class divisions and solidarity among all workers, and evidence of common class interests shown through Asian labour activism, helped to break down ethnic divisions within working-class politics even though differential racist treatment by employers and the Canadian state, and labour competition between white and Asian men, persisted.

APPENDIX A | STRIKES INVOLVING ASIAN WORKERS IN THE GREATER VANCOUVER AREA, 1900–1939

Date	Industry	Ethnic Composition
July 1900	salmon fishery	Japanese/White/Native
July 1901	salmon fishery	Japanese/White/Native
Aug. 1901	salmon cannery	Chinese
Jan. 1903	sawmill	Japanese/White
May 1903	sawmill	Japanese
June 1903	factory woodworkers	*Asian/White
July 1903	salmon fishery	Japanese/White/Native
Jan. 1905	sawmill	Japanese
Nov. 1906	laundry	Chinese
Feb. 1909	sawmill	East Indian
Aug. 1913	salmon fishery	Japanese/White/Native
Aug. 1913	salmon cannery	Japanese/Native
May 1916	sawmill	Japanese/Native
July 1917	shingle mills	Chinese/White
Nov. 1917	factory	Chinese
April 1918	sawmill	Chinese/Japanese
March 1919	shingle mills	Chinese/E. Indian/Japanese
June 1919	General Strike (Van.)	*Asian/White
June 1919	General Strike (N.W.)	*Asian/White
Oct. 1919	shingle mill	Chinese
Nov. 1919	vegetable hawkers	Chinese
April 1920	shingle mill	Chinese/White
May 1920	seamen	Chinese/Japanese/White
April 1921	sawmill	Japanese
Sept. 1921	shingle mills	Chinese/White
May 1925	salmon fishery	Japanese/White/Native
June 1925	seamen	Chinese
Sept. 1925	salmon fishery	Japanese/White
July 1926	vegetable cannery	Japanese/White
Sept. 1927	salmon fishery	Japanese/White
Oct. 1929	shingle mill	Chinese
Sept. 1931	sawmill	Chinese/Japanese/E. Indian/White

Date	Industry	Ethnic Composition
Sept. 1931	sawmill	*Asian/White
March 1932	bowling alley	Japanese
July 1932	shingle mill	Chinese/Japanese/White
July 1932	shingle mill	Chinese/White
Aug. 1932	shingle mill	Chinese/White
Aug. 1932	sawmill	Japanese/White
Aug. 1932	sawmill	Chinese/White
Sept. 1932	shingle mill	Japanese/E. Indian/White
Sept. 1932	shingle mill	Chinese/White
Nov. 1932	sawmill	Japanese/E. Indian/White
Aug. 1933	shingle mill	*Asian/White
Sept. 1933	hop pickers	Japanese/White
Feb. 1935	shingle mill	Chinese/White
March 1935	shingle mill	East Indian
June 1935	salmon fishery	Japanese/White/Native
Aug. 1935	shingle mill	Chinese/White
Sept. 1935	hop pickers	Japanese/White
June 1936	salmon fishery	Japanese/White
Dec. 1937	shingle mill	Chinese

*Composition of Asian strikers unknown.

Sources: Canada, Department of Labour Strikes and Lockout Files, 1907–1939 (PAC RG 27); Labour Gazette, 1900–1939; The Western Clarion, 1903–1920; The B.C. Trades Unionist, 1908–1909; The Western Wage Earner, 1909–1911; The British Columbia Federationist, 1911–1925; The British Columbia Labor News, 1911–1922; The Labor Statesman, 1924–1934; The Unemployed Worker, 1931–1934; The B.C. Worker's News, 1935–1937; The People's Advocate, 1937–1939; The Chinese Times, 1914–1939; The Lumber Worker, 1932; Gladstone and Jamieson, 1950; and Conley, 1988.

Notes

1 *The British Columbia Federationist*, 18 November 1911, 4.

2 *The B.C. Trades Unionist and Union Label Bulletin*, September 1908, 1.

3 See Thomas Loosmore, "The British Columbia Labour Movement and Political Action, 1879–1906" (unpublished M.A. thesis, University of British Columbia, 1954); A. Ross McCormack, *Reformers, Rebels and Revolutionaries: The Western Canadian Radical Movement, 1899–1919* (Toronto: University of Toronto Press, 1977); Paul Phillips, *No Power Greater: A Century of Labour in British Columbia* (Vancouver: B.C. Federation of Labour Boag Foundation, 1967); Carlos Schwantes, *Radical Heritage: Labor, Socialism, and Reform in Washington and British Columbia, 1885–1917* (Seattle: University of Washington Press, 1979); Robert Wynne, *Reactions to the Chinese in the Pacific Northwest and British Columbia* (New York: Arno Press, 1978).

4 There is a rich body of literature in Marxian theory on the relationship between class structures and class consciousness as well as a plethora of historical studies of working-class conflict in industrial-capitalist societies. Collective action dedicated to

advancing the interests of workers in opposition to employers is commonly seen as an indication of some degree of consciousness of class divisions, although there is much disagreement about the "degree" of consciousness and its links to revolutionary social movements. See, for example, Adam Przeworski, "Proletariat into a class: the process of class formation from Karl Kautsky's *The Class Struggle* to recent controversies," *Politics and Society* 7 (1977): 343–401; and Nicolas Abercrombie and John Urry, *Capital, Labour and the Middle Class* (London: George Allen & Unwin, 1983).

5   W. Peter Ward, *White Canada Forever: Popular Attitudes and Public Policy Toward Orientals in British Columbia* (Montreal: McGill-Queen's Press, 1978), ix.

6   Ibid., 22; and W. Peter Ward, "Class and Race in the Social Structure of British Columbia, 1870–1939," *BC Studies* 45 (Spring 1980): 17–36.

7   Anthony Giddens refers to this process as "structuration." People are the (material and ideological) products of the social structures into which they are born and live, but the structures only exist as the outcome of human actions. So we are, at the same time, structured by pre-existing social arrangements, and reproduce and change those social structures and cultural and ideological forms through human agency (Giddens, *Central Problems in Social Theory* [Berkeley: University of California Press, 1979]). Similarly, Marx observed that "men make their own history, but they do not make it just as they please; they do not make it under circumstances chosen by themselves, but under circumstances directly encountered, given and transmitted from the past" (Karl Marx, *The 18th Brumaire of Louis Bonaparte* [New York: International Publishers, 1963], 15). "New" social history, in an attempt to pursue Marx's historical method, is in essence the study of the structuration of classes, the interplay between the social relations that produce the working class and the social relations that the workers produce and reproduce through their actions. This seems a particularly fruitful approach to the study of ethnic divisions within the British Columbia working class.

8   Phillips, *No Power Greater;* Loosmore, "The British Columbia Labour Movement"; McCormack, *Reformers, Rebels and Revolutionaries;* Wynne, *Reactions to the Chinese;* Rennie Warburton, "Race and Class in British Columbia: a Comment," *BC Studies* 49 (Spring 1981): 79–85.

9   McCormack, *Reformers, Rebels and Revolutionaries,* 10.

10   Schwantes, *Radical Heritage;* Patricia Roy, "The Oriental 'Menace' in British Columbia," in J. Friesen and H. K. Ralston (eds.), *Historical Essays on British Columbia* (Toronto: McClelland and Stewart, 1976), 243–55; and "British Columbia's Fear of Asians, 1900–1950," *Histoire Social/Social History* 13(25) (1980): 161–72.

11   H. Clare Pentland, "The Western Canadian Labour Movement, 1897–1919," *Canadian Journal of Political and Social Theory* 3(2) (1979): 53–78.

12   David Bercuson, "Labour Radicalism and the Western Industrial Frontier: 1897–1919," *Canadian Historical Review* 58(2) (1977): 154–75.

13   Roy, "The Oriental 'Menace'"; "British Columbia's Fear of Asians"; "The Illusion of Tolerance: White Opinion of Asians in British Columbia, 1929–37," in K. Victor Ujimoto and Gordon Hirabayashi (eds.), *Visible Minorities and Multiculturalism: Asians in Canada* (Toronto: Butterworths, 1980), 81–91; and "Citizens Without Votes: East Asians in British Columbia," in Jorgen Dahlie and Tissa Fernando (eds.), *Ethnicity, Power and Politics* (Toronto: Methuen, 1981), 151–71; Ward, *White Canada Forever;* Edgar Wickberg (ed.), *From China to Canada: A History of Chinese Communities in Canada* (Toronto: McClelland and Stewart, 1982); Tien-Fang Cheng, *Oriental Immigration in Canada* (Shanghai: The Commercial Press, 1931); Peter Li, *The Chinese in Canada* (Toronto: Oxford University Press, 1988); Ken Adachi, *The Enemy That Never Was: A History of the Japanese Canadians* (Toronto: McClelland and Stewart, 1976).

14   The context of emigration was not identical for all Europeans or all Asians: conditions inducing emigration from the home country varied enormously; some had stronger ties and obligations to kin left behind; no doubt some were "sojourners" without intentions of settling permanently in British Columbia; some had skills that were in demand while others did not. Yet the common thread inducing emigration was the desire to improve one's life's chances. For a discussion of the concept of the sojourner in Chinese Canadian history, and questions about its efficacy, see Anthony Chan, "The Myth of the Chinese Sojourner in Canada," in *Visible Minorities and Multiculturalism;* and Jin Tan, "Chinese Labour and the Reconstituted Social Order of British Columbia," *Canadian Ethnic Studies* 19(3) (1987); 68–88.

15   Cheng, *Oriental Immigration,* 163–97; Ward, *White Canada Forever,* 17; Gillian Creese, "Working Class Politics, Racism and Sexism: The Making of a Politically Divided Working Class in Vancouver,

1900–1939" (unpublished Ph.D. thesis, Carleton University, 1986), 71–81; Li, *The Chinese in Canada*, 43–55; Canada, *Report of the Royal Commission on Chinese Immigration* (Sessional Papers, no. 54a, 1885); Canada, *Report of the Royal Commission on Chinese and Japanese Immigration* (Sessional Papers, no. 54, 1902).

16 Cheng, *Oriental Immigration*, 38–162; Roy, "Citizens Without Votes," 151–71, "The Oriental 'Menace,'" 243–44, and "British Columbia's Fear of Asians," 168–69; Ward, *White Canada Forever*, 33–38; Peter Li, "A Historical Approach to Ethnic Stratification: The Case of the Chinese in Canada," *Canadian Review of Sociology and Anthropology* 16(3) (1979): 320–32, and *The Chinese in Canada*, 27–33.

17 See, for example, the conclusions in the 1902 *Royal Commission on Chinese and Japanese Immigration*, 272–79 and 397.

18 An explanation for the origins of this differential treatment must begin with the history of uneven capitalist development and colonialism conquest. Racial theories about the inferiority of non-Europeans emerged out of colonial conquest, a product of unequal power relations, European ethnocentrism, and justification for colonial domination. With the colonial settlement of Canada, British racial ideologies formed an integral part of civil society and structured immigration policies, thus shaping the treatment that immigrants from different origins experienced in Canada.

19 There is no direct relationship between objective class structures and subjective class consciousness. Przeworski has pointed out that classes are not simply derived from their objective position in the economy; classes, as social actors, are "the effects of struggles" structured by economic, political, and ideological relations. Rather than a unilinear progression of class consciousness, "classes are continually organized, disorganized, and reorganized." This suggests that economistic notions of the unilinear progression of working-class consciousness are too simplistic. See Przeworski, "Proletariat into a Class," 367–70.

20 For discussions of women's paid labour in early twentieth century British Columbia and the differential treatment that men and women received in the labour market, see Josie Bannerman, Kathy Chopik, and Ann Zurbrigg, "Cheap at Half the Price: The History of the Fight for Equal Pay in BC," in Barbara Latham and Roberta Pazdro (eds.), *Not Just Pin Money: Selected Essays on the History of Women's Work in British Columbia* (Victoria: Camosun College, 1984), 297–313; Marie Campbell, "Sexism in British Columbia Trade Unions, 1900–1920," in Barbara Latham and Cathy Kerr (eds.), *In Her Own Right: Selected Essays on Women's History in B.C.* (Victoria: Camosun College, 1980), 167–86; Gillian Creese, "The Politics of Dependence: Women, Work, and Unemployment in the Vancouver Labour Movement Before World War II," *Canadian Journal of Sociology* 13(1–2) (1988): 121–42; Star Rosenthal, "Union Maids: Organized Women Workers in Vancouver, 1900–1915," *BC Studies* 41 (Spring 1979): 36–55.

21 Muszynski has pointed out that during the late nineteenth century Chinese male labour was in demand, not only to fill the "rough" unskilled male jobs in resource extraction and railway construction, but also to fill typically women's jobs in service occupations due to a shortage of women in the province. See Alicja Muszynski, "The Creation and Organization of Cheap Wage Labour in the British Columbia Fishing Industry" (unpublished Ph.D. thesis, University of British Columbia, 1986), 161–74.

22 Lacking the same political and civil rights as white men, both Asian men and all women were in a weaker bargaining position in any attempts to attain better wages in the labour market. The second-class citizenship status of women and Asians was also reflected in justifications for why white male labour was worth more than Asian (male) labour (because the latter had an innately lower standard of living) or (white) female labour (because women were dependants of male fathers/husbands). Thus women and Asian workers were cheap labour by definition. See Creese, *Working Class Politics*, 277–82.

23 Vancouver Trades and Labour Council Minutes, 14 February 1890.

24 Ibid., 30 September 1890.

25 Ibid., 30 October 1890.

26 Ibid., 14 November 1890.

27 Ibid., 24 April 1891.

28 Ibid., 4 June 1908.

29 In 1916 only 6.3% of the non-agricultural labour force in British Columbia was unionized, rising to 21.8% in 1919, dropping to 9.1% in 1921, 9.2% in 1931, and rising to 12.7% by 1939 (Paul Phillips, "The British Columbia Labour Movement in the Inter-War Period: A Study of Its Social and Political Aspects" [unpublished Ph.D. thesis, University of London, 1967], 388). In Vancouver, union membership reached its pre-war peak with 15% in 1912 (Robert A. J. McDonald, "Working Class Vancouver, 1886–1914: Urbanism and Class in

British Columbia," *BC Studies* 69–70 [Spring/Summer 1986]: 45). In 1931, 7.2% of the Vancouver labour force was unionized (calculated from the number of unionized workers as a percentage of the total Vancouver labour force in 1931). See Phillips, *The British Columbia Labour Movement,* 389; and *Census of Canada,* 1931, vol. 3, 756–63.

30 Hotel, Restaurant, and Culinary Employees' Union, Local 28 Minute Books, 1910–1939.

31 VTLC Minutes, 21 March 1907.

32 *B.C. Trades Unionist,* April 1908, 6.

33 *British Columbia Federationist,* 24, March 1916, 1.

34 In his recent study of the New Westminster labour movement, Allen Seager also points out that Asian workers were much more involved in labour conflicts than is generally supposed. See "Workers, Class and Industrial Conflict in New Westminster, 1900–1930," in Rennie Warburton and David Coburn (eds.), *Workers, Capital, and the State in British Columbia* (Vancouver: University of British Columbia Press, 1988), 117–40.

35 The fifty-one strikes listed in Appendix A are labour conflicts where the involvement of Asian workers could be documented, and probably under-represents Asian labour activism. For a more detailed discussion of Asian labour activism in Vancouver prior to the Second World War see Creese, *Working Class Politics,* 98–172; and "Organizing Against Racism in the Workplace: Chinese Workers in Vancouver Before the Second World War," *Canadian Ethnic Studies* 19(3) (1987): 35–46.

36 Percy Gladstone and Stuart Jamieson, "Unionism in the Fishing Industry of British Columbia," in *Canadian Journal of Economics and Political Science* 16 (1950): 1–11; James Conley, "Relations of Production and Collective Action in the Salmon Fishery, 1900–1925," in *Workers, Capital, and the State,* 86–116.

37 Public Archives of British Columbia, Reynoldson Research Project, Oral History Tape 1462.

38 William Bennett, *Builders of British Columbia* (Vancouver: Broadway Printers, 1937), 115–20; Phillips, *No Power Greater,* 37–41.

39 Bennett, *Builders of British Columbia,* 40–42.

40 *The Western Clarion,* 1903–1914; Phillips, *The British Columbia Labour Movement,* 129–31.

41 *Western Clarion,* 1 September 1906, 1.

42 Ibid., 12 September 1908, 2.

43 Ibid., 14 May 1913, 4.

44 Paul Phillips has suggested that the weakness of the labour movement is often a result of the failure to correctly "identify the enemy," leading to internal divisiveness. (See "Identifying the Enemy: Racism, Regionalism, and Segmentation in the B.C. Labour Movement," unpublished paper, 1981.)

45 McDonald, "Working Class Vancouver," 33–69. Seager argues that the New Westminster Trades and Labour Council was also dominated by moderates. See "Workers, Class, and Industrial Conflict," 125.

46 VTLC Minutes, 21 April 1910, 20 April 1911, 15 April 1915, and 18 June 1914.

47 The growth of radical socialism occurred throughout much of the western world at the end of World War I, as the common problem of economic and social dislocation was widespread. Compared to countries like Italy, Germany, and Hungary, the growth of radical socialism in Canada was weak. See, for example, Charles Bertrand, *Revolutionary Situations in Europe, 1917–1922: Germany, Italy, Austria-Hungary* (Montreal: Interuniversity Centre for European Studies, 1976).

48 In 1916 the Chinese Canadian Labour Union, later called the Chinese Workers' Union, was formed. In 1919 the Chinese Shingle Workers' Union was formed. In 1920 the Japanese Labour Union, later called the Japanese Camp and Mill Workers' Union, was founded. All three unions were involved in strikes in the lumber industry during the post-war period.

49 PAC, Department of Labour, RG 27, Strikes and Lockouts File, Vol. 306, Strike 43; *British Columbia Federationist,* 27 July 1917, 1; *The Chinese Times* (translations in UBCSC), 18 July 1917, and 24 July 1917.

50 *Chinese Times,* 18 July 1917, and 24 July 1917.

51 *British Columbia Federationist,* 27 July 1917, 1.

52 PAC, Department of Labour, RG 27, Strikes and Lockouts File, Vol. 310, Strike 27; *Chinese Times,* 7 March 1919, 9 April 1919, and 27 May 1919.

53 *British Columbia Federationist,* 17 September 1920, 7.

54 Ibid., 10 September 1920, 4.

55 PAC, Department of Labour, RG 27, Strikes and Lockouts File, Vol. 314, Strike 190; Vol. 315, Strike 221.

56 *Chinese Times,* 10 June 1919.

57 Accepting Asian members into OBU unions reflected a greater degree of racial solidarity than limited joint action during a labour conflict. It is probably unlikely, however, that large numbers of Asian work-

ers actually joined OBU affiliates, especially since Chinese and Japanese workers organized their own unions in the lumber industry during this period.

58 *British Columbia Federationist,* 16 April 1920, 1, 8; 21 May 1920, 1.

59 The One Big Union movement had split the labour movement in Vancouver. The craft unions withdrew from the VTLC, controlled by the OBU, in August 1919 and established the VTLC (International). As the OBU rapidly declined after 1920, the international unions again dominated the Vancouver labour movement and a single VTLC reigned by the mid-1920s. All references to the VTLC in the early 1920s refer to the International Council. See VTLC Minutes, 7 August 1919–4 September 1919. Phillips, *The British Columbia Labour Movement,* 196, 389; David Bercuson, *Fools and Wise Men: The Rise and Fall of the One Big Union* (Toronto: McGraw-Hill, 1978), 155–70.

60 VTLC Minutes, 5 May 1921.

61 Ibid., 19 May 1921, and 21 July 1921.

62 *The British Columbia Labor News,* 19 August 1921, 1.

63 Restrictions against Chinese immigration had been in effect since 1885, when a $50 head tax was imposed. The tax was raised to $100 in 1902, to $500 in 1904, and in 1923 the Chinese Immigration Act was passed prohibiting the further immigration of all Chinese to Canada, excepting students, diplomats, and some merchants. The number of Japanese labourers eligible to immigrate to Canada each year was set, by agreement between the Canadian and Japanese governments, at 400 in 1908, and reduced to 150 in 1923; in 1928 "picture brides" were prohibited, ending further female Japanese immigration. East Indian immigration was halted by "continuous journey" legislation in 1908, which stipulated that immigrants must arrive in Canada by continuous journey from their country of origin. There were no direct shipping routes between Canada and India. By 1923, therefore, Asian immigration to Canada had all but ceased. See Adachi, *The Enemy That Never Was,* 81–92; Cheng, *Oriental Immigration,* 60, 66, 71, 92, 126, 136, and 145.

64 VTLC Minutes, 4 August 1921, 19 July 1927, and 2 August 1927.

65 Ibid., 1927–1939; *The Labor Statesman,* 1927–1934.

66 *Labor Statesman,* 6 April 1928, 1, 4; 4 May 1928, 1, 2; and 8 June 1928, 1.

67 VTLC Minutes, February 1929–April 1929; Rolf Knight and Maya Koizumi, *A Man of Our Times:*

The Life History of a Japanese-Canadian Fisherman (Vancouver: New Star Books, 1976), 38–57.

68 Ryuichi Yoshida, quoted in Knight and Koizumi, *A Man of Our Times,* 54.

69 Phillips, *The British Columbia Labour Movement,* 271–74.

70 Since the split with the OBU, the VTLC railed against the problem of "dual unions." During the early 1930s the Workers' Unity League and unemployed organizations (especially the National Unemployed Workers' Association) affiliated with the Communist Party repeatedly applied to speak at VTLC meetings and undertake joint actions, but were always turned down (VTLC Minutes, 1930–1936). Not until the WUL was disbanded to merge into the international unions in 1936 did closer relations between moderates and socialists in Vancouver become possible.

71 *Labor Statesman,* 1 May 1931, 4; and 1930–1934.

72 Ibid., June 1932, 1.

73 *The Unemployed Worker,* 26 September 1931, 5.

74 Ibid., 1931–1934; *The B.C. Workers' News,* 1935–1937; *The People's Advocate,* 1937–1939; Creese, *Working Class Politics,* 146–51, and "Organizing Against Racism," 43–44; Wickberg, *From China to Canada,* 181–85.

75 *Unemployed Worker,* 19 September 1931, 1, 2, and 4; 26 September 1931, 4; and 3 October 1931, 2; *The Labour Gazette,* October 1931, 1071–72; and December 1931, 1302–03. For a detailed analysis of the Fraser Mills strike, see Jeanne Myers, "Class and Community in the Fraser Mills Strike, 1931," in *Workers, Capital, and the State,* 141–60.

76 The union strategy of equal pay was a response to differential wages based on marital status and race. The average hourly wage was 31 cents for married (white) men, 27 cents for single (white) men, and 20 cents for Asian men (Myers, "Class and Community," 146). Strategies of equal pay ran counter to continuing traditions of differential pay for whites and Asians, even when performing the same work. In mainstream trade unions these differentials were included within union agreements in the late 1930s, after the WUL unions had merged into the international unions and Asians were eligible for membership in the latter. For example, in a contract with the International Brotherhood of Papermakers in 1938 "the basic rate for Occidental workers was 51 cents per hour and for Oriental workers 41 cents per hour; from January 1, 1938, these basic rates were raised to 54 and 44 cents per

hour respectively" (*Labour Gazette,* December 1938, 1405). Some union contracts even distinguished racial wage scales for each job classification, as a contract in Ocean Falls shows:

> ...logging (summer)—boommen 68 cents; sawmill—boommen (Oriental) 53 cents, pickers (Oriental) 44 cents, millwrights 68 and 82 cents, bargemen (Oriental) 44 and 58 cents....
> (*Labour Gazette,* December 1938, 1406)

77 *Lumber Worker,* September 1932, 10; PAC, Department of Labour, RG 27, Strikes and Lockouts File, Vol. 353, Strike 140.

78 *Unemployed Worker,* 13 September 1933, 7; VTLC Minutes, 19 September 1933; PAC, Department of Labour, RG 27, Strikes and Lockouts File, Vol. 356, Strike 102.

79 From the perspective of Asian workers, the solidaristic practices of working-class organizations espousing radical socialist views was double-edged. According to some Japanese workers, the socialist orientation of these groups probably deterred many Asians from more active participation in labour struggles. As one Japanese worker remembered, this was because Japanese workers recognized that the socialist movement was deemed illegitimate in the dominant society, and was even less acceptable to leaders of the ethnic community than the mainstream labour movement. This suggests that Asian labour militancy might have been enhanced considerably had the mainstream labour movement, rather than only its socialist wing, adopted solidaristic labour practices. See Public Archives of British Columbia, Reynoldson Research Project, Oral History Tapes 1462 and 1465.

80 Hotel, Restaurant, and Culinary Employees' Union, Local 28, Minute Books, 23 March 1938–17 July 1938.

81 As Werner Cohn has shown, even the CCF and the Communist Party in British Columbia supported the internment of Japanese-Canadians during the Second World War. See "The Persecution of Japanese Canadians and the Political Left in British Columbia, December 1941–March 1942," *BC Studies* 68 (Winter 1985): 3–22.

North of the Colour Line

Sleeping Car Porters and the Battle Against Jim Crow on Canadian Rails, 1880–1920

SARAH-JANE (SAJE) MATHIEU

In April 1854, the Great Western Railway declared that it urgently needed eight hundred workers to guard its tracks against stray cattle and hog crossings. Its advertisement, strategically placed in Canada's most important black newspaper of the day, the *Provincial Freeman,* sought African Canadians for the task.[1] Before the turn of the century, African Canadian men laid down tracks for the transcontinental railroad and worked as cooks and dining car attendants for the Grand Trunk Railway.[2] Black railroaders became more prominent figures on Canadian rails by the 1870s when the Pullman Palace Car Company introduced sleeping car porters to Canada.[3] George Pullman advertised his porters much in the same way he did his opulent sleeping cars: both, he promised, would provide comfort, luxury, and great service.[4]

Canadian railway companies experienced rapid growth between the 1880s and World War I. They spent the period bemoaning persistent labour shortages, blaming restrictive immigration and labour laws for their troubles. William Van Horne, general manager of the Canadian Pacific Railway, fumed over Prime Minister Wilfrid Laurier's opposition to foreign industrial workers, insisting that Canadian prosperity depended on unencumbered immigration. Van Horne, who normally remained tight lipped on federal matters, denounced Canada's restrictive immigration policy, claiming that "[w]hat we want is population. Labour is required... throughout North and South America." He stressed that the "governments of other lands are not such idiots as we are in the matter of restricting immigration."[5]

Annoyed with chronic workforce shortages, Canadian railway companies experimented with Canadian and foreign-born black labour. They initially envisioned black workers for treacherous work—like hauling hog and cattle road kill from railway tracks—believing that workers of African descent were well suited for those positions. Because demand for workers soared when able hands were few, African Canadian railwaymen eventually enjoyed a wider range of employment options during the early days of railroading. For instance, the Intercolonial Railways tapped into existing black communities in the Maritimes and Québec, finding a ready-made pool of experienced transportation workers. In later years, the CPR turned a gleaming eye to Southern African Americans and West Indians as an under-explored source of cheap labour. As of the 1890s, company managers culled African American workers from the Deep South, exporting them to Canada as needed. By the turn of the century, Canadian industrialists also positioned black workers as a useful weapon against white workers clamouring for unionization.

Sarah-Jane (Saje) Mathieu, "North of the Colour Line: Sleeping Car Porters and the Battle Against Jim Crow on Canadian Rails, 1880–1920," *Labour/Le Travail* 47 (Spring 2001): 9–42. Copyright © Canadian Committee on Labour History. Reprinted from *Labour/Le Travail* with the permission of CCLH.

White workers recognized management's heavy-handed tactics and protested the introduction of black workers in Canadian industries as demeaning to their manhood. Black labourers were, in their minds, scabs imported for the sole purpose of undermining unionization. The Canadian Brotherhood of Railway Employees (CBRE), the most powerful railway union of its time, codified its contempt for black railwaymen at its inaugural meeting in 1908 by extending membership to white men only. Locked out of meaningful partnership with white railwaymen by constitutional decree, black railroaders witnessed white supremacy as an integral part of Canadian trade unionism.

Though excluded from white unions, black workers viewed the rails as a viable career path, defending their right to work and newly-found place in Canadian industry. They understood that companies saw them as a disposable workforce, easily dismissed during economic recession. Black railroaders protested their displacement and capitalized on the national press and House of Commons when making their grievances known. Though often migrant workers, they affirmed their right to a livelihood as well. Unable to gain the respect of their white co-workers, they formed a union of their own in 1917, the Order of Sleeping Car Porters—the first black railway union in North America. John Arthur Robinson, who emerged as the chief defender of black workers during this era, cut his young union's teeth fighting Jim Crow trade unionism and segregationist employment policies on Canadian rails. He and other sleeping car porters used existing labour law and publicized the discrimination they faced in the Canadian workforce. By World War I, these politically savvy actors forced a place for themselves in the Canadian House of Labour and unmasked white supremacy in every aspect of their lives as working men and Canadian citizens.

The rapid growth in Canadian railway industries, the emergence of trade unionism, and

institutionalization of segregation across North America gave way to Jim Crow employment practices on Canadian rails between the 1880s and 1914. White supremacy, institutionalized in separate and unequal practices governing both black and white workers, dictated labour-management relations as well as railway trade unionism. Both white workers and railway managers acted out their frustrations on black workers. Canadian companies imported black workers, even considering for a time the annexation of a Caribbean island as a source of cheap labour, because they viewed black men as a malleable class of workers, softened by Southern Jim Crow and colonial rule. Railway executives exploited racialized divisions in their workforce by pitting railroaders against each other and displacing white union men with illegally imported black labour.

White railway workers created, fostered, and capitalized from a racially stratified workforce. By 1915, white railwaymen demanded and won a colour line on Canadian rails. Separate and unequal guidelines prescribed the roles and privileges of black railroaders, hindering their career options in the process. They fought against the introduction of black workers on the rails, targeting them as the sole reason for their failed union efforts. Yet if Canadian industrialists and white trade unionists held conflicting positions on black labour, both conceded to a racialized division of the workforce. Consequently, the period from 1880 to World War I saw Jim Crow institutionalized as an ideal rationale for labour-management relations in the Canadian railway industry.

Canadian railways experienced unprecedented growth after the completion of the CPR transcontinental line in 1885. The Grand Trunk Railways (GTR), in conjunction with the Intercolonial Railway (ICR) and Canadian Northern Railway (CNRY), completed another transcontinental line and joined the rapacious competition for passenger traffic.[6] Steam railway revenues soared at the turn of the century, thanks to William Van Horne's and Charles M. Hays' enterprising expansion of railway service, especially in sleeping, dining, and parlour car departments.[7] A four hundred-pound bonvivant, Van Horne decided that he would make Canadian sleeping cars the most palatial liners in North America. The ambitious president tripled investments in the CPR's parlour and sleeping car department between 1885 and 1895.[8] He commissioned artists and interior designers who improved on Pullman's designs: they broadened berths to accommodate Van Horne's girth, installed bathrooms on first-class sleepers, and served generous portions in dining cars.[9]

Van Horne's tactics proved most lucrative. The Canadian Pacific Annual Shareholders reports boasted that revenue from the parlour and sleeping car department swelled from $24,071 in 1884 to $721,006 in 1904, with a profit margin for the latter year of over a half million dollars.[10] Even smaller lines like the Canada Atlantic Railway (CAR) joined the excitement over sleeping cars. In November 1898, the CAR ordered four new cars from the Pullman Palace Car Company at a total cost of $31,740: two first-class sleeping cars with mahogany interiors and two second-class sleepers "finished in oak with double thick glass... [and] seats of leather."[11] That same year, the Intercolonial Railway spent $159,526.40 on eight sleeping cars built by Pullman's chief competitor, the Wagner Palace Car Company of New York.[12]

Corporate enthusiasm over sleeping car service produced a prodigious demand for other symbols of Pullman's signature service—black railway workers. Soon after the Civil War, George Pullman singled out newly emancipated African American men for his service, regarding them as seasoned service workers. Historian Brailsford Brazeal contends that Pullman also solicited black porters because they were a "plentiful source of labor [and] societal caste distinctions between Negro and white people

created a 'social distance' which had become an accepted fact in the mores of American society."[13] Canadian railway companies avidly sought black railroaders for their sleeping car service because the image of broad smiling, white-gloved, crisply uniformed black men proved a moneymaking triumph with Canada's wealthy white railway clientele. Initially, the CPR, GTR, and ICR culled early black railwaymen from Canadian cities with sizable African Canadian populations, namely Halifax, Montreal, and Toronto.[14] In later years, Canadian railway companies turned to the Southern United States and West Indies for other black railroaders.

The Intercolonial Railway found a ready supply of black transportation workers in Africville, Halifax's historically black neighbourhood. Bordered by railway tracks and Halifax Harbour, Africville became a black neighbourhood during the 18th century when thousands of African American Loyalists and West Indians migrated to Halifax.[15] A vibrant port city and the railway capital of the Maritimes, Halifax teemed with black transportation workers.[16]

Black Haligonians' lives were steeped in Maritime culture. Hundreds of African American and West Indian seafarers docked in Halifax on their transatlantic steamship routes, with many establishing permanent residence in the city after careers at sea. Already accustomed to transnational lifestyles, mariners were well suited to life on the rails. Many seafarers welcomed railway work as relief from long, dangerous sojourns at sea. Charles Pinheiro, a Barbadian steward on the SS Acadia, joined the ICR sleeping car department in 1888 and remained in its employ until his retirement.[17] Other black mariners wedded railroading with seafaring in order to insure full employment, offset boredom, and shield themselves from seasonal layoffs. In some cases, mariners retired their sealegs for work on the rails after marrying into Halifax families. Demararan seaman James Knight married Annie Joseph, a Halifax mariner's daughter, in 1880; thereafter, he worked intermittently for the ICR and sailed on the *Orion*.[18]

Black Haligonians enthusiastically joined the rails during the ICR's heyday. The railroad promised steady employment and a respectable wage for those fortunate enough to land full-time employment, such as W. H. Blair, John Collins, Thomas Corbett, Joseph H. Daley, P. Driscoll, and P. Grannan, each of whom portered over 340 days during 1898.[19] In fact, black railroaders readily found work across Canada. Many African Canadians migrated westward for promotions or better opportunities with the Pullman Palace Car Company, the Canadian Pacific Railway, and the Grand Trunk Railways headquartered in Montreal. Payroll rosters indicate that forty-nine men in Montreal, one hundred in Toronto, and thirty-nine in London portered for the GTR in 1902.[20] Full-time porters drew monthly salaries ranging from $20–35 per month to $300–450 a year.[21] Experienced porters were rewarded with higher-waged runs on private government cars. David Hawes and John B. Cameron, who manned the sleepers *Cumberland, Montreal,* and *Ottawa* exclusively reserved for prominent members of Parliament, earned annual salaries of $420.[22] Even Winnipeg offered work for men willing to bear its harsh winters and long runs to the Pacific coast. Canadian Northern Railway payrolls show that seventy-six men portered out of Winnipeg during the summer of 1909, with wages varying from $1.75 per day to $50 per month for seasoned railroaders like E. Naperton.[23]

Black railroaders in Canada enjoyed a broad range of employment options not available to black railwaymen in the United States at the turn of the century, where Jim Crow and the Big Four brotherhoods limited their occupational choices. Variable wages, uncertain demand, and exclusion from white unions taught these black railroaders the importance of diversifying their experience on the rails, as evidenced by employ-

ment patterns on the Intercolonial Railway. R. J. Murray was a brakeman for $51\frac{3}{4}$ days, worked as a baggagemaster for 2 days, and portered for $12\frac{3}{4}$ days, while L. Scothorn worked as a brakeman for 67 days, then as a shunter for 14 days, and finally portered for 5 days.[24] B. Dickie, R. Elliott, J. R. Fraser, J. P. Gough, and B. F. McKinnon supplemented their portering wages with work as brakemen, car-checkers, shunters, and baggagemasters.[25]

Working the rails in any capacity meant flirting with danger. Brakemen had the death-defying task of running on top of moving railway cars, made icy during winter months, and turning the brake wheel while also maintaining their balance. Those who failed met with sudden death along the tracks. The shunter's work proved no less perilous. Switchmen, as they were also known, dropped a levy to stop the cars and switched often poorly lit tracks so that trains going in the opposite direction could gain safe passage. Less hazardous, though equally rare, were black nightwatchmen who moonlighted when on leave from the sleeping car service.[26] Other black railroaders like Peter Bushenpin and David Jones worked as coopers for the ICR after years of portering.[27] Black men worked as waiters and cooks on the ICR, GTR, and CPR, higher paying positions otherwise solely reserved for white men working for other North American railway companies.[28]

Black railwaymen in Canada held a virtual monopoly over sleeping car service as early as the 1880s. Caring for passengers in first class sleeping cars remained the porter's primary function, though the company also expected that he render various other services without compensation. The porter was responsible for all aspects of the sleeping car ride, except for collecting tickets, which the conductor performed. Railway companies required that porters report to their cars two hours prior to a scheduled run in order to prepare their sleepers. Once assigned to a car, they insured that it was clean and fully equipped;

in case it was not, they hurriedly buffed and polished before passengers boarded. Canadian railway companies did not pay porters for this time consuming compulsory dead work.

Wood or coal burning ovens heated early sleepers not yet equipped with central heating at the turn of the century. Before leaving the station on a run, porters had to load their sleepers with enough fuel for the journey. They constantly struggled to keep soot from soiling the car or flying cinders from starting unruly fires. In summer, huge blocks of ice cooled down the sleepers. Loading these slabs was clumsy, dangerous work as it required that porters crawl onto the sleeper's roof and drop the cube down into its cooling mechanism compartment. Controlling the temperature, an on-going annoyance to both passengers and workers, often made early sleeping cars unbearably hot or cold, depending on the season.

Once on the road, the sleeping car porter tended to his passengers' every whim. The porter greeted travelers, stowed luggage, pulled down berths in the evening, and hurriedly converted them back into seats in the morning. Responsible for remembering passengers' schedules, he was severely reprimanded when someone missed their stop. The porter, whom passengers condescendingly called 'George' or 'boy,' served food, mixed drinks, shined shoes, cared for small children, sick passengers, and drunken ones too.[29] Herb Carvery, who portered during the 1950s, remembered "we were babysitters, not only for little kids but for adults.... [S]omeone would get drunk on the train and many times you would have to stay up all night just to watch them so they wouldn't aggravate somebody else." He added that when "someone would get sick, you would have to attend to them."[30] Historians on wheels, passengers expected that the sleeping car porter know the landscape and history of areas along his trek. A confidante and armchair therapist, the porter feigned interest in travelers' tales and told a few of his own.

Sleeping car porters tended smoggy smoking cars, swept up cigarette and cigar ashes, washed out cuspidors, and inhaled stale, smoky air for hours on end. In the days before automated washrooms, they did their best to maintain sanitary conditions in crudely equipped lavatories. Porters frequently suffered chronic sleep deprivation since the company worked them on seventy-two hour shifts without providing any sleeping quarters. They endured other health hazards on the road as well. Derailments, common in the early days of rail travel, cost many railroaders their lives, particularly when traveling through the Rockies' slippery slopes.[31] Policing gamblers, thieves, and rambunctious passengers also posed a constant danger for black railwaymen.

The consummate diplomat, the porter walked a social tight rope in Pullman's romanticized mobile time capsule. In 1930, journalist Murray Kempton reflected that for many white travelers, porters seemed like "a domestic apparently unaltered by the passage of time or the Emancipation Proclamation." Yet alluding to the film *The Emperor Jones* featuring Paul Robeson, Kempton proposed that "[t]here was a certain thrill to the notion that he might be a Communist or a murderer or even an emperor."[32] Sleeping car porters understood that these racialized fantasies were inseparable from their passengers' other expectations. They enabled white passengers to cling to an Antebellum racial ideal, while black workers understood that their livelihood—and at times their very lives—depended on acting out the part of this offensively racialized construction. Challenges to the charade and perceived social transgressions, especially against white women, carried heavy penalties: a porter could be fired or subjected to a worse fate—lynching. Required to smile and act submissively, they did so hiding their thoughts, their dreams, and sometimes their rage.[33]

Though the work was certainly taxing, black Canadians embraced railway employment since other industrial jobs presented a different set of hazards without the reward of lasting employment. Likewise, working for Canadian railway companies afforded enterprising black transportation workers the freedom to pursue other professional interests. African Australian John D. Curl portered for a time before opening a cigar shop in Halifax.[34] B. A. Husbands operated a West Indian import goods store with money obtained from seafaring and portering, while Jamaican-born Rufus Rockhead financed his famous Montreal jazz club with income earned on the rails.[35]

Thus it seemed that by the end of the 19th century, Canadian railway companies and African Canadians had struck a mutually beneficial covenant. The railroads needed workers just as African Canadians needed stable employment. Canadian railway companies found an untapped pool of ready black workers among African Canadians who spoke English and adapted easily to railroading because of their experience in other transportation sectors. Best of all, black railroaders did not belong to any unions. For African Canadians, the rails fulfilled the wanderlust of men accustomed to lives on the move and promised dependable work during a period of industrial transition.

African Canadian railroaders hoped for a secure place on the rails but they did not find it. During periods of high unemployment or economic recession, Canadian railway companies discharged black workers, replacing them with inexperienced white labour. The *Halifax Herald* exposed this practice in the spring of 1898 when it headlined "Colored Porters on the Intercolonial Railway Were All 'Fired' and Without Cause."[36] J. S. Barbee, one of the dismissed ICR porters, told reporters "[o]ur places have been filled by white officials," and accused railway managers with "drawing the color line with a vengeance."[37] William Dixon, another fired ICR sleeping car porter and brother of the celebrated pugilist George Dixon, informed

Halifax journalists that "the action of the government...is a shabby piece of business. Men with families have been turned out without notice or cause, and failing to find work in Halifax, they must leave the city."[38]

All of the fired Intercolonial Railway porters shared similar backgrounds. Experienced transportation workers, many had joined the ICR after careers at sea. A number of the men were West Indians, residing in Africville after marrying white or bi-racial women. All of the porters also belonged to Union Lodge, a black freemasons' temple popular with seafarers, sleeping car porters, and prosperous black Haligonian businessmen. Established in January 1856, Union Lodge members controlled commercial assets in Africville and served as guardians of their community's interests.[39] Hence, the federally-owned Intercolonial Railway's move against sleeping car porters roused black Haligonians who viewed these Union Lodge men as Africville's prominent denizens. Disillusioned, black Haligonians questioned whether the rails were indeed a wise investment in their future when white supremacy—more than industriousness—determined their fate.

"Righteously indignant," black Haligonians gathered to "consider the best means to be taken to remedy a most serious matter."[40] Reverend Doctor J. Francis Robinson, an African American Baptist minister stationed in Halifax, led the charge. Speaking before his predominantly black congregation at the Cornwallis Street Baptist Church only days after the firings, Reverend Robinson did not mince words. "The recent dismissal of the porters from the service of the ICR brings us face to face again with the race, which in the United States and here remains an unsettled question." Robinson urged his congregation and all African Canadians to concede that race "is no longer a sectional question: it is a national question."[41]

Reverend Robinson and other black Haligonian protesters insisted that in addition to race, the ICR's move against black workers underscored citizenship, right to work, and living wage issues of import to all Canadians. "Don't drive the poor white or the poor black man out of your country. Give him work and give him good pay.... [A] policy which would arm the strong and cast down the defenceless is unwise... and one fraught with disastrous consequences." Robinson admonished white supremacist employment practices, reminding the Canadian government that "[p]eace between the races is not to be secured by degrading one race and exalting another; by giving power and employment to one and withholding it from another." Alluding to the United States' strained race relations, Robinson alerted his congregation that "[e]xperience proves that those [who] are most abused can be abused with greatest impunity." He stressed that white Canadians should distinguish themselves from Americans by "maintaining a state of equal justice between the classes."

African Canadians hoped for due process and "equal justice between the classes" but knew that they would only be attained through political mobilization. Peter Evander McKerrow, a West Indian sailor turned powerful black Haligonian businessman, maintained that since Reconstruction African Americans enjoyed certain citizenship rights still denied to blacks in the Maritimes. "The United States with her faults...has done much for the elevation of the colored races. She has given to the race professors in colleges, senators, engineers, doctors, lawyers, mechanics of every description. Sad and sorry are we to say that is more than we can boast of here in Nova Scotia."

For Reverend Robinson, the solution to black railwaymen's problems was a simple one. He insisted that if "the Negro porters and the race [were] as strongly organized into labour protective unions, etc., like their white brothers, the ICR would not have succeeded so well and peaceably in displacing their colored labour and substituting white in their stead."[42] Without unionization, black railwaymen in Canada would never enjoy true job security and would continually be forced into unemployment or positions "at starvation wages," held Robinson.[43] He berated the Canadian government and ICR managers for subjecting black men and their families to a life of poverty and degradation. "For over 250 years, this race served in bondage, suffering the most poignant sensations of shame, immorality, demoralization and degradation. Its men have been victimized, and they are still victimized, proscribed against and imposed upon by the dominant race both in the United States and here in Canada." Reverend Robinson warned against such white supremacist practices as violations of African Canadians' "civil rights [and] the human right to gain an honest livelihood for themselves and their families."[44]

Black Haligonians called immediate attention to Jim Crow in railway employment policy by notifying the national press.[45] "Have No Use For Them—Coloured Men on the Intercolonial Railway All Fired," exclaimed the Tory newspaper *Chatham Planet*. The Ontario newspaper accused the Liberal government of betraying its African Canadian constituents. "Liberal leaders at Ottawa seem to have completely lost their heads.... While Premier Laurier speaks in the most flattering manner of the African race, his officials strike them down in a most brutal way, no complaint, no investigation—just kick them out."[46]

Blacks in the Maritimes also contacted their federal members of Parliament Benjamin Russell and future Prime Minister Sir Robert Borden. Reverend Robinson emphasized that one thousand African Canadian voters in the Maritimes, "a sufficient number to give them the balance of power" would "get organized...so that their voices and vote would be respected."[47] Conservative Parliament members took Robinson's warning to heart and laid the case of "Coloured Intercolonial Porters" before the House of Commons.[48] George Foster, the member from New Brunswick, inquired whether newspaper reports that "all the porters on the Pullman cars had been dismissed from the service of the Intercolonial" were indeed true. If so, Foster demanded that the Minister of Railways and Canals explain "whether they were dismissed for cause or whether the hon. gentleman is drawing the colour line in that service."[49]

Speaking for the Liberal government, Minister Blair rejected any notion that the colour line fueled employment practices on the government-owned ICR. "I am quite sure that the colour line has not been drawn." He assured the House that nothing had "been done in view of discriminating against the colour line in that service." Alphonse La Rivière of Québec was not so easily persuaded, proposing instead "[p]erhaps the gentleman is colour-blind."[50] Ironically, while Blair denied any governmental wrongdoing with respect to ICR porters, the Minister of Railways and Canals never actually disputed the existence of a colour line in Canadian industries. Over the next two weeks, federal legislators debated the application of discriminatory employment policies, worrying less about its existence than its gentlemanly exercise.

Representatives from Ontario and Nova Scotia resuscitated the "colour line" debate again during question period in early April, this time in defence of ICR managers. Ontario member Archibald Campbell motioned that the House retract "unfounded and unwarranted" charges of discrimination against black railroaders.[51] In the end, the House resolved that "[t]he report that the Government would at once draw the colour line and dismiss all the men, ought to have been rejected by...common sense." Mr. Fraser hoped "that hereafter those who publish those statements will understand what the country understands, that there must be a terrific dearth of any ground of attack upon the Government, when they are compelled to fall back upon an attempt to raise the prejudices of the coloured population of Canada."[52]

Campbell's and Fraser's peculiar parade of circular reasoning branded African Canadians the racists for unveiling the specter of Jim Crow in a federal corporation and in Canadian railway policy. Yet African Canadians' swift mobilization of national advocates demonstrated their political sophistication and understanding of local and national institutions. Reverend Robinson and other advocates shrewdly argued for black railwaymen's entitlement to positions in the most powerful industry of the era, likely preventing greater unemployment among black railroaders. They couched their protest in the language of citizenship, suffrage, and civil rights.

The problems faced by black railroaders on the ICR mirrored growing tensions between management and employees. White workers also protested unfair labour practices, with miners and textile workers most vocal about their grievances. To complicate matters, at least in employers' minds, unions mushroomed, particularly in Quebec and Ontario where their numbers doubled between 1899 and 1903. The International Ladies' Garment Workers' Union founded in 1905 brought working women into the fold of early Canadian trade unionism. Even the Industrial Workers of the World, also known as the Wobblies, trickled into Canada, setting up shop in coal mines, railway construction compounds, and lumbering camps throughout Alberta and British Columbia.[53]

[...]

Canadian Pacific Railway executives blamed their insatiate demand for African American and West Indian railroaders on the Great War. With white men ripped from the rails for military service abroad, Canadian companies argued that the war aggravated existing labour shortages, forcing them into "bringing in colored help." Since special troop trains hauled soldiers and implements of war to eastern ports, railway companies maintained that more sleeping and dining car personnel were urgently needed, especially on western lines.

The movement of Canadian armed forces generated enormous passenger traffic revenues for Canadian railway companies. Canadian Pacific Railway Shareholders Reports indicate that earnings from the sleeping and dining car service rose from $13 million in 1913 to over $20 million in 1920.[54] The war promised such prosperity that the Canadian Northern Railway purchased 100 sleepers from the Canadian Car & Foundry Company Limited for $325,000, the sum of which it hoped to make back from moving returning veterans.[55]

Emboldened by the demands of the war, the Canadian Pacific Railway Company became particularly brazen in its dealings with the Canadian Ministry of Immigration and the US Department of Labor. CPR superintendents notified the local commissioner of immigration, who then informed Ottawa, that African American and West Indian railroaders were headed for the Canadian border and bound for Canadian rails. In turn, the Ministry of Immigration petitioned the US Department of Labor for permission to export black railroaders on behalf of Canadian railway companies. A. Caminetti, the Commissioner General of Immigration in Washington, DC, advised the Canadian government that "there will be no objection to the Canadian Pacific Railway's securing in this country the services of twenty or more colored waiters, cooks, etc. citizens of the United States, for dining car service...[and that] these men so engaged will experience no difficulty leaving."[56]

Once again, the Canadian Pacific Railway's aggressive pursuit of black workers outstripped rival corporations' schemes. The CPR's Superintendent of the Dining and Sleeping Car Department at Winnipeg, H.F. Matthews, shamelessly reminded the Ministry of Immigration of his company's longstanding defiance of labour and immigration laws. "You will recollect that for a number of years past, it has been necessary each spring to bring in a large number of porters from south of the line to crew additional cars operated on summer train service."[57] Like the border guards who admitted black immigrant workers armed with CPR business cards, bureaucrats in the Ministry of Immigration abetted Canadian railway companies' traffic in black railway workers, actively undermining federal immigration and labour laws.

If the Ministry of Immigration obliged Canadian railway executives, trade unionists did not. World War I produced great wealth for Canadian railway corporations at great cost to workers. Desperate for peaceful labour relations, in 1918 the Canadian government used the War Measures Act to issue orders-in-council mandating arbitration of disputes and outlawing strikes and lockouts in all Canadian industries for the remainder of the war. The measures effectively gave Canadian employers free reign over their workers. They could, and often did, violate workers' rights with impunity. If railroaders worked long hours before, they were driven to exhaustion during the war. Though railway companies' incomes soared, profits did not trickle down to overworked railroaders. Unable to strike, disgruntled white railway employees protested what they could: rampant inflation, exploitative working conditions, and the increased presence of black railwaymen on Canadian lines.

Canadian railway unionists filed several complaints with the Minister of Immigration and Minister of Labour over the introduction of foreign black railway workers on Canadian lines. In June 1918, tensions between unionized white railwaymen and the CPR landed both parties before Industrial Disputes Investigations Boards of Conciliation. It was the first of many disputes over foreign black railroaders taken to federal court over the next two decades. At issue was the CPR's "alleged dismissal of certain employees who were union members and their replacement by negroes, the number affected being given as 205 directly and 500 indirectly."[58]

The Board, chaired by Justice W.A. Macdonald of Vancouver, heard evidence that "white employees of the Dining Cars, between Vancouver and Calgary, were being discharged by the company and replaced by negroes imported from the United States."[59] White workers claimed that they were "being discriminated against because of their membership in the Canadian Brotherhood of Railway Employees."[60] According to white railwaymen, the CPR added insult to injury by supplanting them with "negroes." George Hepburn of the CBRE averred that "the men wanted better conditions, and they didn't like being replaced by black labor as Canadians and white men."[61]

White CPR employees testified that when they notified company managers of their intention to become "members of a Union" in April 1918, the CPR began ousting them from their runs. Superintendent at Winnipeg, H.F. Matthews, admitted to the Board of Conciliation that "the company did not want any such organization in the Dining Car Department and would discourage it all they could. Similar feelings of opposition to the Union were entertained or openly expressed" by other superintendents in Winnipeg, Moose Jaw, Calgary, and Vancouver.[62] Rather than recognize unionized dining car workers on its western lines, the Canadian Pacific Railway threatened that it would replace the men with "colored or Oriental help or employ women in their stead."[63] CPR vice president Grant Hall confessed that "the employing of women was seriously considered" but the company abandoned its plot "for obvious reasons, namely inability to provide proper sleeping quarters."[64]

If white women needed special provisions for work on the rails, black railwaymen did not, making it easier for CPR executives to follow through on their threat. The Canadian Brotherhood of Railway Employees charged that "[b]efore the company was called upon...to recognize this Union the situation changed and

a large number of colored dining car employees were engaged and brought into Canada." The company's "discouragement" of unionization among its white running tradesmen was easily measurable. African American railroaders "practically took the place of all the white employees" on runs "between Calgary and Vancouver" while "50 per cent" of dining cars running out of Winnipeg were manned by "colored crews."[65]

Canadian Pacific Railway executives presented the Board of Conciliation with an alternative labour scenario on its western lines. Superintendents bemoaned the perennial workforce shortage occasioned by war and explained that "a policy formulated in February 1918" envisioned "introducing colored help" on Canadian rails. Superintendent Matthews, the CPR's advocate at the IDIA proceedings, could not supply any reliable evidence that his company's policy predated the CBRE's April union drive. Instead, Matthews produced a telegram, dated the day after interviewing white union men, proposing that his colleague in Vancouver "secure a satisfactory colored crew or more in Seattle." Matthews insisted that the company did not inform white workers of the new hiring policy until June because "such publicity might cause disruption amongst the dining car employees and...seriously effect, if not completely destroy, the service for a period."[66]

The Board's majority report exposed a dizzying case of circular reasoning. Justice Macdonald argued that "[i]t was not, and could not be contended, that there was any right or agreement on the part of the employees for continuous employment or that the company could not, without notice, discharge any, or all, of such employees at any time." Trade unionists certainly agreed. Lack of job security and due process in dismissals were longstanding union grievances. Justice Macdonald then argued that the CPR was justified in displacing white railroaders since "dining car employees are migratory in their disposition and frequent changes...

militate against efficiency." Macdonald conveniently disregarded that displacement by non-unionized foreign workers had caused white railroaders' recent unemployment; conscription also accounted for their high turnover rates on the rails. Ultimately, the Board was left to decide whether to believe workers' allegations that, faced with a discrimination suit, CPR executives fabricated a four-month old change of employment policy. Alternatively, Justice Macdonald could side with the Canadian Pacific Railway, assuming "honesty of words and acts" on the part of its executives.[67]

Two Board of Conciliation members, Justice Macdonald and E.A. James, ruled in favour of the CPR, citing "[i]t is not likely that persons would act in the reprehensible manner suggested" by the CBRE. "We believe that the presumptive case made by the employees, on whom the burden rested, has been rebuked by the sworn statements of Mr. Matthews." The third Board member, Victor Midgley, submitted a dissenting minority report. He averred that white workers had presented a "prima facie case of discrimination because of their membership in a labour organization, and insisted that white union men be immediately reinstated and foreign dining car workers be deported by the Canadian government."[68]

Midgley admonished the CPR for displacing white war veterans. "[W]hat will be the thoughts of these men when they learn that the jobs formerly held by them have been permanently filled with negroes, while they were shedding their blood and risking their lives in the defence of the Empire of which the Canadian Pacific Railway forms no small part?" He posited that CPR superintendents began their recruitment of African American railroaders in late April, well after learning of white unionization efforts. "If the company had definitely decided in February, 1918 to replace all the white men on the dining cars with coloured before the end of the summer,

why did Messrs. Matthew, Tingley Simpson, Willard, and Fraser go to the trouble of discouraging the organization of these men?"[69] Neither the CPR nor Justice Macdonald could answer Midgley's inquiry.

The CBRE and the Board of Conciliation could not have known the extent of the CPR's duplicity. With a judgement in its favour and presumed support from the Ministry of Labour, CPR agents continued their hunt for more African American railroaders, this time for its sleeping car service. Aaron Mosher of the CBRE contested CPR recruitment of African American would-be porters in Chicago and Minneapolis, notifying the Department of Immigration: "my information is that Mr. Simpson, Superintendent of Sleeping Car Department, C.P.R., Winnipeg... went to St. Paul and had announcements made in the churches of the colored people there to the effect that the C.P.R., required 500 colored men for work in Canada." Mosher advised the Ministry of Immigration that over 100 men were "being fed and housed in C.P.R. cars at Winnipeg terminals." He posited that the black immigrant workers were "not permitted to mingle with the other employees or citizens of Winnipeg."[70] The CBRE concluded that such strict corporate control over African American railroaders could only mean that they "have been imported for the sole purpose of action as strike breakers."[71] Attorneys for the CBRE alleged that the CPR clandestinely imported sleeping car porters from Minneapolis and St. Paul in anticipation of postwar labour unrest in the West. CBRE president Aaron Mosher warned the Commissioner of Immigration that the continued importation of foreign labour—particularly African Americans—would "very possibly...lead to further industrial warfare and increased unrest among organized labour" in Canada.[72]

Though well aware of the CPR's recruitment program, having authorized the entry of African American railwaymen just months before, the Department of Immigration disavowed any knowledge of black labour migration to Canada. Instead, Mosher received a diplomatic denial of any wrong doing from the Department of Immigration. "I assure you that the immigration regulations are being carefully enforced and we are not consenting to the entry of any labour unable to comply with the law, without first ascertaining from the Labour Department that there are no idle men of the particular class wanted, in Canada."[73]

Completely unaware that his letters were falling into the hands of William "Big Bill" Scott, the CPR's greatest facilitator in the Department of Immigration, Aaron Mosher trusted government officials. The Superintendent of Immigration, Scott, single-handedly dictated department policy on black migration.[74] In every case between 1916 and 1945, the CPR obtained speedy approval for the importation of foreign black railwaymen, usually directly from Scott—the same man ordering border guards to reject black would-be homesteaders.[75]

Department of Immigration bureaucrats carefully monitored black immigration during the 1910s, documenting undesirable migrants in files earmarked "Immigration of Negroes from the United States to Western Canada" and "Dominion Immigration Agent...regarding vessels from the West Indies landing negroes."[76] Black workers bound for the rails, however, were tracked to another dossier—"Canadian Pacific Railway Requests Admission of Coloured Porters (Negroes)."[77] On the one hand, the Department of Immigration castigated border inspectors for indulging black immigrants, deploring that more "colored persons are settling in the undesirable sections of our cities and towns."[78] A department circular groused that "[s]ome Inspectors seem to be under the impression that if a colored person is an American citizen, and of money, he must be admitted." The department counseled more exacting defence of its borders: "strict examination, however, will often reveal some statutory

cause for rejection under section 3, (d), (e), (f), (j), or (k).... Under section 33, ss. 13, a cash deposit may be taken from a non-immigrant, and Inspectors are requested to enforce this section."[79] On the other hand, and without ever admitting to his department's compact with Canadian railway companies, Scott reasoned to Mosher that "when people comply with the law we cannot very well shut them out."[80]

Indeed, Scott's irresolute attempt to "shut them out" had completely failed by World War I when more black railwaymen worked on Canadian rails than ever before. By 1920, Canadian railway companies had assembled a class of black railroaders representing a melee of ethnicities, nationalities, and political cultures. Vexed by white men clamouring for unionization, yet worried about African Canadian trade unionism, railway executives gambled that black railroaders harvested from abroad would make for a malleable pool of workers.

If Canadian railway managers actively solicited a compliant immigrant black workforce, it certainly was not what they got. Black railwaymen in Canada recognized that Canadian industrialists and white trade unionists viewed them as gullible pawns. Canadian railway companies upheld an antiquated racialized mirage in their Pullman Car departments, exploiting black sleeping car porters in the process. When conditions deteriorated with white workers, Canadian railway administrators replaced them with African Americans and West Indians herded into Canada by conniving managers. Since the beginning of the war, conditions on the rails worsened for all workers, even if the work itself became more readily available. Fearing greater unemployment and distracted by the rhetoric of war, white workers begrudgingly worked alongside black railroaders, all the while pressuring for a more rigorous racialized division of the Canadian railway workforce. Their nascent unions targeted black labour, Canadian and foreign-born, making them the scapegoats for unemployment, falling wages, and humiliation at the hands of company men.

Inasmuch as white workers and white managers thought little of black railroaders, West Indian, African American, and Canadian-born black railwaymen envisioned their position on the rails quite differently. Black railroaders understood white workers' growing hostility and sensed the nation's agitation over their presence. In the spring of 1917, Winnipeg-based porters John A. Robinson, J.W. Barber, B.F. Jones, and P. White began holding secret meetings. Robinson, who came to Canada from St. Kitts to work on the CPR in 1909, led the charge. If black railwaymen were to survive World War I, he resolved that they needed protection. The men carefully weighed their options. White union men had made clear that they would not accept black workers in their brotherhood. Their white-only membership clause and open animosity affirmed it daily. Though African American sleeping car porters were likely contemplating the value of railway unionization, no such organization existed at the time.[81]

Robinson and his allies discussed the possibility of forming a union for Canadian sleeping car porters. These clandestine deliberations changed the course of railway unionism in Canada. In April 1917, John A. Robinson and his co-workers chartered the Order of Sleeping Car Porters (OSCP)—the first black railway union in North America.[82] Their organization spread politicized trade union radicalism across Canada. Within two years of its inauguration, the OSCP negotiated successful contracts for all sleeping car porters—black as well as white—on the Canadian Northern and Grand Trunk Railways.[83] By the end of the decade, Robinson emerged as the champion of black railway unionism. His two-fisted approach to Jim Crow on Canadian rails fought segregation at work and in Canadian trade unionism simultaneously.

Black railwaymen in the Order of Sleeping Car Porters targeted white trade unionists, holding union leaders to their rhetoric of working-class solidarity. John A. Robinson began his campaign for national trade union recognition with the Trades and Labour Congress of Canada (TLC), a national coalition of trade and craft unions endowed with official collective bargaining recognition.[84] The Order of Sleeping Car Porters applied for a charter with the TLC in 1917, soon after its creation.[85] Though fully aware of the CBRE's white-only membership policy, TLC president Tom Moore denied the OSCP's petition, ruling instead that Canadian sleeping car porters seek auxiliary endorsement in the existing national railway union—the Canadian Brotherhood of Railway Employees. In effect, the Trades and Labour Congress of Canada Jim Crowed black unionists into auxiliary status, a station otherwise exclusively reserved for women workers or trade unionists' wives and daughters.

Unwilling to concede such easy defeat, black railway unionists plotted their next move. The OSCP set its sights on the Canadian Brotherhood of Railway Employees' annual convention meeting in Port Arthur in September 1918. Sleeping car porters from across the country protested the CBRE's white-only membership policy, forcing the issue onto the convention floor. The question of black membership rocked the CBRE's 1918 assembly, developing into a tempestuous debate. White railroaders from Western Canada reminded delegates that throughout the spring of 1918, the "C.P.R. [had] imported a large number of coloured men from the states and promptly put into effect their threat" to replace "all the White cooks and waiters and putting negroes in their places."[86] Black workers, stressed field organizer E. Robson, jeopardized white workers and their families, as evidenced by the fact that "white men are still off and the negroes are on the road."[87]

Black railwaymen then presented their arguments for membership. George A. Fraser, President of Halifax's Canadian Grand Trunk Railways Sleeping Car Porters Association, seconded John A. Robinson's campaign against white supremacy in the Canadian Brotherhood of Railway Employees. Fraser addressed an open letter to CBRE members meeting in Port Arthur and accused the CBRE of undermining national railway unionism with its racist policies: Fraser emphasized "[w]e wish to point out that we are working in the same capacity as all other railway men and in consequence we are asking for admission into the C.B.R.E." The continued exclusion of black railroaders from the CBRE amounted to an egregious breach of African Canadians' citizenship rights, declared Fraser. "We feel that as British subjects and also Loyal Canadians, that there should be no discrimination shown...between different races." Dismantling racism in the CBRE, Fraser avowed, "will not only benefit us, but will greatly strengthen your Division No. 36, the [white] members of which are working hand in hand with us." Fraser requested that members of the Canadian Grand Trunk Railway Porters Association be admitted to the CBRE and hoped that African Canadian railroaders would "receive a square deal."[88]

White delegates meeting in Port Arthur were not moved by Fraser's appeal for a "square deal." Instead, members buried the matter in the Committee on Constitution and Laws, then boarded a specially commissioned bus for the Orpheum Vaudeville Theatre. There, the men feasted on a banquet, cooled their palates with drink, and washed down the day's events with a minstrel show, "The Boys from Memphis," featuring blackface singers Fox and Evans.[89] Whereas CBRE delegates could not fathom a meaningful partnership with black railwaymen, they cheerfully welcomed burlesqued images of black men. They could digest chuckling and jiving black buffoons, if not equal status among

workers as proposed by Fraser, Robinson, and other sleeping car porters.

Although the Order of Sleeping Car Porters lost in Port Arthur, black railroaders' initial bid for CBRE membership forced a debate on racial segregation among workers and unmasked the deep-seated resentments of white railwaymen. As such, they laid bare the hypocrisy of working-class rhetoric by a CBRE leadership wedded more to white supremacy than working-class solidarity. Insofar as sleeping car porters from across Canada joined in the battle against Jim Crow unionization in the CBRE, it demonstrates that the OSCP's following was indeed national. John Robinson's crusade against the largest and most powerful trade union of its time gave bite to his young union, establishing black railroaders as principled and savvy trade unionists who insisted that white supremacy disparaged the cause of labour for all workers.

World War I served as a catalyst for black insurgency, especially among sleeping car porters. Emboldened by their union and with little else to lose having witnessed the slow encroachment of Jim Crow ideology in the federal bureaucracy, employment policy, and trade unionism, sleeping car porters in Canada became the chief political advocates for their communities. Together with the clergy and black press, African Canadian railroaders protested violations of African Canadians' civil rights, particularly when Jim Crow fixed limitations on their citizenship.

The period between 1880 and 1914 thus held great promise for black railroaders in Canada. After setting tracks and feeding work crews, black railwaymen moved from the fields to the freight yards, finally gaining a footing in the industry poised to dominate the new century. They initially enjoyed a range of employment options and utilized railway work to insure full employment, countervail ennui, and pursue other commercial enterprises. Wages were good, if the work itself gritty and always dangerous. Black railroaders in Canada soon learned, however, that their welcome on the rails was conditional.

White trade unionists and railway management, defining their new roles in an age of rapid industrialization, held conflicting positions on black labour. Against the threat of industrial strife, both adopted Jim Crow as a rational model for labour relations. Railway management, burdened by what it construed as uppity white railwaymen, manipulated its workforce by fuelling racial tensions on their lines. When they wanted to appease disgruntled white railway workers, Canadian railway companies conceded to unionists' segregationist demands. White Canadian unionists won Jim Crow as one such compromise by 1915.

At other times, Canadian railway executives circumvented white unions by importing foreign black workers, knowing that their race prevented membership in existing unions. Canadian railway companies creatively ignored immigration and labour laws and successfully engaged accomplices in the Canadian government. Consequently, 20th-century immigration and labour restrictions never meaningfully hampered Canadian railway companies' insatiate appetite for African American and West Indian workers.

The Great War strained labour-management relations on Canadian lines. If the war made Canadian railway companies rich, it also roused trade union activists. Radicalism among white unionized railwaymen intensified and moved west during the 1910s. Railway unionists posited that the introduction of Southern African American and West Indian railroaders demeaned their white manhood, citizenship, and rights as union men. Their resentment, so deep-rooted, thwarted a bid for interracial unionization by sleeping car porters, favouring hollow white supremacy to equal status for all railway workers.

Likewise, black railroaders took notice of the climate on the rails. As president of the OSCP, John A. Robinson intensified his assault on Jim Crow in white Canadian unionism. The Order of Sleeping Car Porters targeted its first offensive on the Canadian Brotherhood of Railway Employees' white-only membership doctrine. Robinson challenged the CBRE's rank and file, arguing that if the CBRE were really the beacon of Canadian trade unionism, it would set new industrial standards by striking racism out of its constitution. The time had come, Robinson contended, for black workers to get a permanent foothold in the Canadian House of Labour.

Notes

1 *Provincial Freeman*, 16 September 1854.

2 National Archives of Canada (NAC), MG28 I215, Records of the Canadian Brotherhood of Railway Trainmen (CBRE), William W. Overton to J.E. McGuire, 11 March 1943.

3 *Canadian Illustrated News*, August 1870.

4 Malinda Chateauvert, *Marching Together: Women of the Brotherhood of Sleeping Car Porters* (Urbana 1998), William H. Harris, *Keeping the Faith: A. Philip Randolph, Milton P. Webster, and the Brotherhood of Sleeping Car Porters, 1925–37* (Urbana 1991), David Perata, *Those Pullman Blues: An Oral History of the African-American Railroad Attendant* (New York 1996).

5 John Cameron, "Legislation Relating to Immigration in Canada Prior to Confederation," MA Thesis, University of Toronto, 1935, 4.

6 Nick and Helma Mika, *An Illustrated History of Canadian Railways* (Belleville, Ont. 1986), 97 and 208.

7 Van Horne and Hays, both American-born, transformed Canadian railways during their tenure as general managers for the CPR and GTR respectively. Hays died on the Titanic in April 1914, never having witnessed the GTR's national service. See "Charles Melville Hays," 1052 and "William Cornelius Van Horne," *The Canadian Encyclopedia* (Toronto 2000), 2437.

8 *Annual Report of the Canadian Pacific Railway Company,* Montreal, April 1896, 28. In 1885, CPR spent $24,098.99 on the Parlour and Sleeping Car Department. *Annual Report,* May 1886, 27.

9 Walter Vaughan, *The Life and Work of Sir William Van Horne* (New York 1920), 50–52 and 141–143.

10 *Annual Report of the Canadian Pacific Railway Company,* Montreal, May 1884, 27 and August 1904, 26.

11 NAC, Records of the Canadian National Railways (CNR), RG30-12619-508, "Canada Atlantic Railway contract with Pullman Palace Car Company," 1898.

12 *Auditor General's Report, 1898–99 (AGR),* "Railways and Canals Department," 63 Victoria A., 1900, R-29.

13 Brailsford R. Brazeal, *The Brotherhood of Sleeping Car Porters: Its Origin and Development* (New York 1946), 1–5.

14 Dominion Bureau of Statistics, *Census of Canada 1911,* 372–3.

15 James Walker, *The Black Loyalists: The Search for a Promised Land in Nova Scotia and Sierra Leone, 1783–1870* 2d ed. (Toronto 1992), and Robin W. Winks, *The Blacks in Canada: A History* (New Haven 1977), 24–95.

16 Judith Fingard, "From Sea to Rail: Black Transportation Workers and Their Families in Halifax, c. 1870–1916," *Acadiensis,* 24 (Spring 1995), 49–64. For a discussion of West Indian mariners, see James Winston, *Holding Aloft the Banner of Ethiopia: Caribbean Radicalism in Early Twentieth-Century America* (London 1998) and Peter Fryer, *Staying Power: The History of Black People in Britain* 6th ed. (London 1992). For additional readings on the development of Africville, see Donald Clairmont, *Africville* (Toronto 1999).

17 Judith Fingard, "Sea to Rail," 52.

18 Fingard, 53.

19 *AGR 1898–99,* R-242.

20 NAC, RG30-2035, CNR, "Grand Trunk Railway Payrolls for 1902."

21 *AGR 1898–99,* R-207-208. Canadian Census reports do not list porters as a classification on the rails before 1921 and probably included their numbers under "labourers" or "other workers."

22 *AGR 1898–99,* R-38.

23 NAC, RG30-7075, CNR, "May 1909 Payroll Records for Canadian Northern Railway, Western Region."

24 *AGR 1900,* R-196-7.

25 Ibid., R-196-8.

26 Ibid., R-195-9.

27 Fingard, 54.

28 NAC, RG76-576-816222, Immigration Branch Records (IBR), H. F. Matthews to Thomas Gelley, 20 April 1920.

29 Jack Santino, "Miles of Smiles, Years of Struggle: The Negotiation of Black Occupational Identity Through Personal Experience Narratives," *Journal of American Folklore,* 96 (1983), 393–412. Also see Stanley Grizzle, *My Name's Not George: The Story of the Brotherhood of Sleeping Car Porters in Canada* (Toronto 1998).

30 "Good Morning with Avril Benoit," CBC Radio interview with Stanley Grizzle, Herb Carvery, and Saje Mathieu, (Toronto), 11 August 1998.

31 Hugh A. Halliday, *Wreck!: Canada's Worst Railway Accidents* (Toronto 1999).

32 Murray Kempton, *Part of Our Time: Some Ruins and Monuments of the Thirties* (New York 1935), 240.

33 James C. Scott, *Domination and the Arts of Resistance: Hidden Transcripts* (New Haven 1990), 17–45.

34 Fingard, 53.

35 Fingard, 54, and John Gilmore, *Swinging in Paradise: The Story of Jazz in Montreal* (Montreal 1989), 163–7 and 193–5.

36 *Herald* (Halifax), 28 March 1898, 2.

37 Ibid.

38 Ibid.

39 Provincial Archives of Nova Scotia (PANS), MG20-2012 and MG20-2218, Union Lodge Records. Pursuant to an agreement with Mr. Robert Northup, Grand Secretary of the Grand Lodge of Nova Scotia, I am unable to release the names of Union Lodge members. Also see Fingard, 49–64.

40 *Herald,* 25 March 1898, 3.

41 *Herald,* 6 April 1898, 2.

42 Ibid. The dismissed porters were eventually rehired by the ICR or accepted positions with the CPR once they were made available. See Fingard, 57–59.

43 Ibid.

44 *Herald,* 6 April 1898, 2.

45 *Globe* (Toronto), 7 April 1898, 4, *Herald,* 25–28 March and 8–15 April 1898. *House of Commons Debates (HCD),* 31 March–14 April 1898.

46 *Planet* (Chatham), as cited in *HCD,* 6 April 1898, 3167.

47 *Herald,* 6 April 1898, 2.

48 *HCD,* 31 March 1898, 2852.

49 Ibid.

50 Ibid.

51 *HCD,* 6 April 1898, 368–9.

52 Ibid.

53 Jack Williams, *The Story of Unions in Canada* (Toronto 1975), 75–82. Also see Robert H. Babcock, *Gompers in Canada: A Study in American Continentalism Before the First World War* (Toronto 1974), Mercedes Steedman, *Angels of the Workplace: Women and the Construction of Gender Relations in Canadian Clothing Industry, 1890–1914* (Toronto 1997), Mark Leier, *Where the Fraser River Flows: The Industrial Workers of the World in British Columbia* (Vancouver 1990), A. Ross McCormick, *Reformers Rebels and Revolutionaries: The Western Canadian Radical Movement, 1899–1919* (Toronto 1977); Bryan D. Palmer, *Working Class Experience: Rethinking the History of Canadian Labour, 1800–1991,* 2d. (Toronto 1992), 135–142, 155–210.

54 *Annual Report of the Canadian Pacific Railway Company,* August 1913, 29 and March 1920, 29.

55 NAC, RG30-9575, CNR, "Contract for Colonist Sleeping Cars, Canadian Foundry Car & Foundry Co. Ltd. and Canadian Northern Rolling Stock Ltd."

56 NAC, RG76-576-816222, IBR, A. Caminetti to W. W. Cory, 11 January 1919.

57 NAC, RG76-576-816222, IBR, H. F. Matthews to Thomas Gelley, 20 April 1920.

58 *LG* (June 1918), 396.

59 *LG* (August 1918), 597–604.

60 Ibid.

61 Testimony of George Hepburn in *LG* (August 1918), 603.

62 Ibid., 597.

63 Testimony of George Hepburn in *LG* (August 1918), 593 and 598. CPR headquarters approved using women on the rails but Winnipeg officials vetoed the plan in favor of African Americans.

64 Grant Hall to E. A. James, 6 July 1918, as quoted in *LG* (August 1918), 602.

65 Ibid.

66 Ibid.

67 Ibid., 597, 600, 603.

68 Ibid., 600, 604.

69 Ibid., 601, 603–4.

70 NAG, RG76-576-816222, IBR, Aaron Mosher to William D. Scott, 28 May 1919.

71 NAC, RG76-576-816222, IBR, Thomas Murray to Assistant Commissioner of Immigration, 4 June 1919.

72 Ibid.

73 NAC, RG76-576-816222, IBR, William Scott to Aaron Mosher, 23 May 1919.

74 Valerie Knowles, *Strangers at Our Gates: Canadian Immigration and Immigration Policy, 1540–1997* (Toronto 1997), 86–90.

75 See William Scott directives in NAC, IBR, RG76-576-816222, IBR, RG76-566-810666, and IBR, RG76-7552-3.

76 Ibid.

77 NAC, IBR, RG76-816222.

78 NAC, IBR, RG76-7552-6, "Circular to All Border Inspectors of Western District," 2 July 1920.

79 Ibid.

80 NAC, IBR, RG76-576-816222, William Scott to Thomas Gelley, 10 June 1919.

81 Brazeal, *The Brotherhood of Sleeping Car Porters,* 6–14. See also F. Boyd's article "Previous Struggles of the Pullman Porters to Organize" in *The Messenger,* September 1926, 283–4. Boyd describes how twenty African American sleeping car porters on runs from Seattle to Chicago began discussing the possibility of forming a black railway union in 1909. No records indicate that these men considered Canadian porters for their union or that Robinson's group knew of their American compatriots' deliberations.

82 NAC, MG28 I215, CBRE, John A. Robinson to J.E. McGuire, 27 March 1941.

83 Ibid.

84 *Canadian Railroad Employee Monthly,* Convention Number 1929, 33.

85 NAC, CBRE, "CBRE Convention Proceedings, 1918," MG28 I215. See also William E. Greening, *Easy,* 59.

86 NAC, CBRE, MG28 I215, "CBRE Convention Proceedings, 1918," Port Arthur, 24 September 1918, 60.

87 Ibid., 61.

88 Ibid., 61.

89 Ibid., 61. Also see *Port Arthur Daily-News Chronicle,* 24 September 1918, 8 and 28 September 1918, 24.

Prairie Women and the Struggle for a Dower Law, 1905–1920

Margaret E. McCallum

In the Laurier years, Canada lured immigrants to the Prairies with the promise of free land for all who were willing to homestead it—all, that is, who met the eligibility requirements. Generally, women did not. Homesteads were available to adult males, but only to those women who, through no fault of their own, were the sole support of one or more dependent children. Women who wanted to farm could buy land, or contribute to the acquisition of a homestead by a husband, brother or other male relative.[1] Yet wives found that their work did not earn them a share in the property, or even the right to be consulted about its disposition by sale, mortgage or gift. In the first two decades of this century, prairie women wanted access to homesteads and rights to property that they had homesteaded with their husbands; to ensure that their demands were taken seriously in the legislature, they fought for female suffrage.

Some historians have adopted the term "maternal feminism" to describe the ideology and goals of the women and men who worked for votes for women in the late nineteenth and early twentieth centuries. Use of this term characterizes the suffrage movement as conservative at its core, demanding votes for women in order to maintain a status quo threatened by a more urban and less ethnically homogeneous popula-

tion. According to maternal feminist rhetoric, women deserved the vote so that they could apply their special mothering and homemaking skills to the problems of a developing industrial society. When children were educated at school, instead of at mother's knee, ate commercially prepared food, wore factory-made clothing, and contracted diseases spread by poor water and lack of sewage systems in congested urban centres, women could not fulfill their maternal role unless they had a voice in lawmaking. These politically expedient arguments, which appealed to nativist sentiment and to a belief in women's moral superiority, avoided the direct challenge to traditional values inherent in appeals for justice or equality. But as Veronica Strong-Boag observes of Nellie McClung, ardent crusader for temperance and votes for women, "[t]he distinction between maternal and egalitarian arguments was not always spelled out in McClung's thinking or in that of many of her contemporaries. For this hard-pressed generation, politics was a pragmatic exercise: the niceties of theory dissolved before the need to win supporters."[2] These supporters, moreover, would have to be found among male legislators and voters, whose power and privileges were threatened by women's reform demands. Women reformers, then, used both maternal feminist and equal

Margaret E. McCallum, "Prairie Women and the Struggle for Dower Law, 1905–1920," *Prairie Forum* 18, 1 (1993): 19–34. Reprinted courtesy of the Canadian Plains Research Center.

rights rhetoric to secure their demands, and, as Gail Cuthbert Brandt argues, neither individuals nor movements are usefully labelled as one or the other.[3] The campaign for dower or homestead legislation in Manitoba, Alberta and Saskatchewan from 1905 to 1920 reveals both women's commitment to justice and equality, and men's resistance to any change in the power imbalance between the sexes. This article examines the dower debate during this period in the pages of the *Grain Growers' Guide (GGG)*, a periodical published monthly and later weekly in Winnipeg.

Dower is the right of a widow to an interest for her life in one-third of the real property owned by her husband at any time during the marriage. Developed in England before the Norman Conquest, dower was a means to provide some economic security for wives in an age when married women did not have the legal capacity to own land, the principal source of wealth, and property owners did not have the legal power to dispose of their property by will. Because the dower right ended with the death of the widow, it was not easily sold, but it had considerable practical value. Anyone who wanted to purchase property from a married man did so subject to the wife's inchoate right to dower, which would attach to the land at the husband's death. To ensure that a purchaser would not have to meet a future dower claim, the vendor's wife had to bar her dower, that is, she had to join in the conveyance to give up her dower claim. Effectively, the wife's dower right meant that a husband had to have his wife's consent to sell, mortgage or give away his property.[4] Dower was abolished in England in 1925. In the 1970s and early 1980s, the Canadian provinces with a common law dower right substituted a requirement of spousal consent for any valid dealing with the title to a house occupied by the couple as their matrimonial home, a provision adopted from legislation passed in the prairie provinces between 1915 and 1920.[5]

If the word dower means anything at all to most people today, it brings to mind either dowries or dowagers, with faint evocations of a plot device in a Jane Austen novel. But in the first two decades of this century, the need for a dower law was very much a real issue in the prairie west. Despite some differences in emphasis, the arguments for and against the legal rights women sought through a dower law are remarkably like the arguments made during more recent debates on family law reform, particularly those ignited by the decision of the Supreme Court of Canada denying Irene Murdoch a share in the ranch property held in her husband's name because her work was considered to be "just about what the ordinary rancher's wife does," and therefore not to be counted as a contribution to the acquisition of property registered in her husband's name.[6]

Dower was part of the law of the Prairies because it was part of the law of England at the effective dates for the reception of English law in each province, i.e., 15 July 1870. In 1833, however, England by legislation had abolished the dower right in land disposed of during the husband's lifetime or by will, and these statutory limitations became part of the law of the new Canadian territory as well.[7] In the West, therefore, the wife's right to dower provided some protection if her husband died intestate, but did not create any need to obtain the wife's consent to the disposition of property. In an attempt to simplify land transfers and to remove possible encumbrances on title, the provincial legislature in Manitoba abolished dower completely in 1885. The federal government followed suit in The Territories Real Property Act, 1886; the system of land titles registration created by this legislation was adopted by Saskatchewan and Alberta when they were created as provinces in 1905.[8]

Women moving to the Prairies from other parts of Canada, particularly from Ontario, usually took for granted that they would have the same dower rights in their husband's new homestead as they had had in the family farm back home. Although women may not have known precisely what dower was, many of them knew or had heard of women who had tried to use their dower right to delay leaving home and friends back east by withholding their consent to the sale of the farm.[9] When wives discovered that, out west, their husband could sell the farm out from under them, or will it away, they began to demand some legislative protection of the wife's property interest in land owned by her husband. Although women asked for a dower law, they did not use this term in its technical legal sense, but as a general term encompassing two different demands: the right of the wife to be consulted on any *inter vivos* disposition of property which the wife had helped to acquire and manage, and the right of a widow to a share in her husband's estate on his death.

By 1920 all three provincial legislatures had passed legislation addressing these demands in response to a public campaign for dower rights supported by women's organizations including the Woman's Christian Temperance Union, the Women's Canadian Club, the National Council of Women of Canada, the Women's University Club, Women's Institutes, the United Farm Women of Alberta, and the Winnipeg-based Women's Labour League.[10] The *GGG* was instrumental in formulating the demand for these rights, bringing them to the attention of the public, and securing letters and petitions supporting the cause. Established in 1908 by the Grain Growers' Grain Company, a marketing cooperative organized to give farmers direct access to the Winnipeg Grain Exchange, the *Guide* was eagerly read on isolated homesteads where women struggled alone with the problems of raising a family and making a home.[11] The *Guide* was addressed primarily to the farmer, who was presumed to be male, but there was a substantial women's page, offering suggestions on everything from what food to prepare for a

threshing crew to what arguments to use to get signatures on a suffrage petition. From 1912 to 1917, the women's section was edited by Frances Marion Beynon, an active campaigner for women's rights. Under her editorship, letters and comments on dower were a regular feature.[12]

The dower question was first raised in the pages of the *GGG* by a man calling himself "A Saskatchewan Farmer." "It may appear ungallant for me to take up the attitude I do on this question now agitating the women of the West. We know they are getting up petitions to the local parliaments and getting their male and female friends to sign same. They are basing their claim to half their husbands' possessions on the ground that they have made half." But, continued "A Saskatchewan Farmer," usually men are already fairly well-fixed financially before they marry, and to pass legislation giving the wife the right to control what her husband did with his assets would deliver all men into the hands of bad or designing women merely to help the one woman in fifty who had a bad husband. "Nearly all farmers treat wifey generously and a husband is likely to be more liberal in disposing of his goods to her than if the law compels him and fixes the terms for him."[13]

"A Saskatchewan Farmer's" arguments against the dower law, based as they were on mistrust of the other sex, were countered by heartrending tales of women left to fend for themselves and their children when their husbands mortgaged or sold the farm to run off with a younger woman, or squander the proceeds on drink. Many women worried that their husbands might lose everything in a bad business deal, or leave them penniless widows, dependent on the charity of their children.[14] A woman who expressed satisfaction with her farm work and her children nonetheless called herself "An Alberta Drudge": "I will milk, bake, churn, feed hogs, raise chickens and hand the money over to buy a quarter section...and [my husband] might take a notion to sell my home and my children's and I haven't got any say."[15] Another woman responded with mock surprise to a letter saying that women should stay at home where they belong: "that is the first I heard of the home belonging to [women]. There is many a man who will sell it without asking his wife's permission."[16]

In the fall of 1914, the *GGG* entertained and instructed its readers with the tale of John Tightwad and Jennie Armstrong. Five illustrations, with captions, showed Jennie's passage from "Courtship" to "Destitution." Despite her substantial contribution to her husband's economic success, she discovered that her legal position was that of an unpaid domestic: the money, the house and the children were all John's. When he sold everything to run off with a pretty widow, however, it was Jennie who had to support herself and her homeless children.[17] The advocates of dower rights acknowledged that John Tightwad was the exception, then appealed to men who treated their wives decently to support a law that would protect less fortunate wives. Dower supporters did not claim that there were no bad women, but, as one woman tartly complained, "that is no reason why they should be dealt unjustly by. If we waited till men were faultless before we allowed them any means, there would be a queer lot of penniless men."[18] Another commented: "Women are not all perfect wives and homemakers, but if they are not, there is no law upholding them in wrongdoing or injustice to their partners, as there is at present upholding the vicious and selfish among men."[19]

Despite references to marriage as a partnership, it is clear that many writers, both male and female, viewed marriage not as a choice freely made and gladly maintained, but as the price one paid for a chance at economic security. The respective contributions each spouse made to the couple's mutual economic security, however, were valued quite differently by supporters and opponents of the dower law. Like "A

Saskatchewan Farmer," many opponents of property rights for women objected to giving the wife any say in the management or disposition of the homestead. Regardless whether the property had been acquired before or after the marriage, it was the husband's. A female opponent of dower rights viewed a dower law as just another obstacle in the way of the poor beleaguered man who wanted to mortgage his land and invest the money in business or in buying more land:

> The combines, railways, banks and corporations grind Mr. Farmer hard.... Now his wife has been stirred up by a few meddlesome women to beg parliament to take from him his rights he had over his property before marriage, which rightly belongs to ownership and to transfer them to his wife.... We are told, ad nauseum, that a dower law will not control a man's property in his life, nor the man who wants to do right. Those statements have deceived quite a few men, but they are not true...a right-doing man will find himself fixed by a dower law if he has a cranky, ignorant or stupid wife. However good schemes a farmer may have ahead of him, if his wife objects he is done. He is no longer master of his land, or his future.[20]

A man opposed a dower law for the same reasons, explaining that at least one of his several sons was likely "to marry a woman who would use the dower law very unjustly, to his disadvantage. Is it right that property I leave him shall be controlled by any crank of a woman he may marry?"[21]

Clearly, opponents of dower rights for women recognized that owning property gave a person some power and independence, and they feared what might follow if women were able to claim a share. One writer to the *GGG* said: "A dower law is likely to bring in as much injustice as it aims to remove...a dower law makes the wife both judge and jury, her judgment and decision overrides the man's.... A dower law certainly puts a man in a humbling and dependent position under his wife."[22] A man, who called himself Chuck, warned women that if they became too independent, they would lose their "chief charm" and "men will not be brave enough to marry them." He said that he would support women's suffrage, because he believed that the women's vote "would help in getting some reforms which we need," except he was "afraid that some day they will want a dower law or something else. I am not in favour of...forcing a man to hand over any portion of his property to his wife. It would be a huge detriment to the best interests of unmarried women of any age. The men would not know if the girls were marrying them for love or the benefits derived from the dower law."[23] Another said, "I have a great respect for the ladies—when they know their place."[24]

Supporters of the dower law argued, however, that women deserved more than respect. Because their work had contributed to the acquisition of the homestead, women had earned the right to some interest in it. "[The] wife helps to make the home and she should have a say in the giving up of it."[25] "Is it fair that a woman work all her life and then perhaps be left without a cent of what she has helped to earn?"[26] Women who had come to homestead in the West had faced the same risks as their husbands, with the additional burdens of running the farm and caring for children on their own, while their husbands were attending to business or working for wages. The work the women did for the family—preparing meals and clothes, maintaining the house, doing a share of the outdoor work, seeing to the needs of hired help—would have to be paid for if done by a stranger. Why was it worth nothing when done by a wife?[27] Another asked: "And pray tell me what incentive a woman has to work longer hours every day than her husband, if she is to have no say in the selling or mortgaging of land her hard work has helped to pay for?"[28] Beynon spoke for

many others when she observed that "[w]here a woman has performed an equal part in the accumulation of property, she should have an equal say in the disposal of it and it should be made impossible for any man to cheat his life partner out of her share of the property just because she happens to be his wife."[29]

Many of those who wanted a dower law objected to the unfairness of leaving the wife dependent on her husband's good will, or the discretion of a judge, in order to get what was hers anyway. They argued that surely the women who had contributed so much to opening up the West had the right to share in the increased land values thereby created, rather than being "left to the fickle fancy of their husbands to use them justly or otherwise."[30] As "Pioneer" protested in response to "A Saskatchewan Farmer":

> Women do not "lay claim" to the half of the husband's property...only to their own share, to their own property, which the husband has appropriated...with the aid of the law, which law the husband made without the consent of the wife.... Would [opponents of a dower law] like to enter a partnership with some other person, each to labour unceasingly throughout his life, living in semi-barbarous seclusion... participating in nothing but actual necessities... and at the close of this considerate partner's life to be the pitiable recipient of such charity as the partner may in his discretionary ill-humour choose to dole out, and the partner to be the sole judge of the worthiness...to receive anything at all?[31]

Another woman explained the difference between having to ask for something and getting it as of right: "I wanted the law to grant [women] our share as well as the man. I felt humbled to take anything off my husband in a way although I knew it was rightly mine. I always felt I wanted the law to make it straight for me."[32]

Because the supporters of a dower law wanted women's claims to be recognized as rights, and not left to the discretion of husband or judge, they were not satisfied with the dependants' relief legislation passed in Alberta and Saskatchewan in 1910. Although women's rights activists such as Henrietta Muir Edwards and Emily Murphy had fought for this legislation, it was of very limited benefit, merely giving a widow the right to ask the court for an allowance to be paid out of her husband's estate if she received less under his will than the one-third share she would have received had he died without a will.[33] In 1911 similar legislation was introduced in the Manitoba legislature, in response to a request presented to Premier R.P. Roblin, for full dower rights. Roblin told the delegation that any attempt to introduce the full dower law would bring one thousand indignant men to the legislature in less than an hour to protest against it—"men who are our best citizens, lawyers, bankers, real estate men, clergymen. In Ontario the dower law has worked untold harm; it has broken up homes and scattered families. Perhaps a woman would not give her consent [to the sale of some property] and the man has smashed the home, broken the furniture, and happiness has been destroyed."[34] As Isobel, the editor of the *GGG's* women's page, later observed, the premier's idea of domestic bliss was a bit odd. Surely the woman married to a man who would smash up all the furniture needed a one-third share in the family property.[35]

When Roblin's alternative legislation was introduced, representatives of the National Council of Women of Canada, the Women's Labour League, the Woman's Christian Temperance Union, and the University Women's Club appeared before the Law Amendments Committee to suggest improvements. One member of the delegation observed that the women who most needed the promised relief would lack the financial resources to apply for it. Critics of the wide discretion given to judges were told to trust the judiciary—"they are good

fellows." Attorney General A.G. Campbell defended the inalienable right and liberty of a man to make a will in his own way. "We must be very careful how far we interfere with marital relationships. A husband is never far wrong and is better capable of judging than anyone else what he should leave his wife. If he leaves her penniless, there is a good reason."[36] The bill subsequently died on the order paper; the following year, perhaps as a substitute, the Manitoba legislature passed "An Act for the Relief of Widows and Children." Despite its name, the legislation protected administrators of estates much more than widows and children. If a farmer died without a will, the legislation gave his administrator the power to permit the widow and children to carry on farming. The legislation protected the administrator from claims by creditors for any ensuing losses and held the widow accountable to the estate for any profits, less a "reasonable allowance" for her services in carrying on the farm and for the cost of maintaining and educating any infant children.[37]

Despite these discouraging results, women and their male supporters kept up the pressure for legislation to recognize women's right to property which they, with their labour, had helped their husbands to acquire. The long campaign first produced results in Alberta, with passage of the Married Woman's Home Protection Act in 1915, permitting a wife to file a caveat on the title to her husband's homestead. Once the caveat was filed, the registrar of Land Titles was prohibited from registering any transfer, mortgage or other document dealing with the title to the land, unless the husband obtained an order from a superior court judge for removal of the caveat from title. Newspaper headlines described this legislation as giving married women an "equal interest in property," but unlike dower at common law, it did not give wives any property rights in their husband's land. Instead, it provided an equivalent to the requirement that a wife join in any dealings with her husband's property in order to release her dower right. The caveat would prevent any sale or mortgage of the family homestead without the wife's consent, providing the wife knew about the legislation and took the necessary steps to register the caveat.[38]

The Married Woman's Home Protection Act was probably most useful in focussing attention on the defects of the existing law, and providing some encouragement for the reform effort. Letters to the *GGG* asking for more information on the new law gave Beynon a chance to comment that the legislation that had been passed was not what had been requested. "The objection has been raised that a husband could sell or mortgage the property without the knowledge of the wife, and before she could get the notice to the registrar. The only remedy for this would be for the wife not to wait for any action on the part of her husband, but to send the notice in at once, if she thought she needed to protect herself."[39] In introducing the 1915 legislation, Attorney General C.W. Cross declared that Alberta women would now have greater privileges and better protection of their rights than anywhere else in the British Empire.[40] Two years later, on the eve of the first provincial election after women had been granted the right to vote, Cross repeated his earlier boast about the legal status of women in Alberta, adding that their only remaining grievance would be removed with the bill he was about to introduce. The new Dower Act, which repealed the 1915 legislation, required the wife's consent to any dealing with the homestead, and gave the widow an interest for her life in the homestead, regardless of who received it under her husband's will. The interest given by the legislation was a life estate in the whole of the homestead, not just the one-third to which a widow was entitled at common law. If the husband's only real property was the homestead, the widow would receive more than she would have received at common law. However, unlike

dower at common law, the rights given by the legislation applied to the homestead only, not to all property owned by a man at any time during the marriage.[41]

The Saskatchewan legislature, in passing its own version of matrimonial property protection legislation in 1915, avoided some of the defects of the Alberta statute passed earlier that year. Saskatchewan's Homestead Act invalidated any future dealings with the title to a homestead, including disposition of it after the homesteader's death, unless the owner obtained his wife's signature to the necessary documents, and the wife acknowledged before a designated official that she understood her rights and had signed them away of her own free will, without any compulsion. In addition, wives were given the right to file a caveat which would give notice to any potential purchasers or mortgagees of the wife's rights. Passed in haste at the end of the session, the legislation was substantially amended the next year, to give judges the power to dispense with the wife's consent, and to protect the creditors of the husband.[42] Both the Saskatchewan and Alberta legislation applied to a homestead, which was defined as the actual home of the husband and his family, including an urban house and lot. To evade the legislation, therefore, some husbands moved the family into rented premises, or onto a small piece of property in which little capital was invested. The 1919 revision of the Saskatchewan legislation and new Alberta legislation in 1917 and 1919 did not remedy this defect. In 1920, however, Saskatchewan amended its legislation to include any property which had been occupied as a homestead within the year prior to the dealing with the land.[43]

Passage of the initial legislation, even with its defects, must have been particularly gratifying for Beynon, who had been using her column in the *Guide* to advertise and arrange for distribution of petitions calling for a dower law. She had also encouraged women to pressure the Grain Growers' Association to pass formal resolutions in support of dower rights for women, and printed reports from local groups which had done so. The results of such grass-roots efforts were apparent at the annual convention of the Saskatchewan Grain Growers' Association in February 1915 when the delegates adopted the following resolution: "Resolved, that it is the opinion of this Association that the wife should have an equal interest in all property, both personal and real, with the husband, and that neither should have power to convey real estate without the signature of the other."[44]

Strong expressions of support for a dower law from farm representatives contributed to the passage of the Alberta and Saskatchewan legislation. In Alberta, Premier A.L. Sifton was trying, ultimately without success, to demonstrate that his Liberal government could respond to farmers' concerns so effectively that there would be no need for the United Farmers of Alberta to begin fielding its own candidates for political office.[45] In Saskatchewan, the Liberal government worked closely with the Saskatchewan Grain Growers' Association on most proposals for new legislation.[46] The provisions for limited recognition of a wife's claim to the homestead were part of a legislative package to implement the recommendations of the Saskatchewan Royal Commission on Farm Machinery which reported in the spring of 1915. Section 8 of the report, recommending legislation to ensure that farmers would not lose their farms through pledging them as security for the purchase of farm machinery, also recommended that no dealing with a homestead should be valid without the wife's consent. Admitting that the latter recommendation was not quite pertinent to their inquiry, the commission observed that existing legislation restricting creditors' rights to recover against a homestead "was passed for the benefit not only of a homesteader but of his family as well.... To give a man and his family a homestead right and then allow the husband to sell or mortgage it without consulting his fami-

ly does not seem just to the family."[47] The premier, Walter Scott, adopted this recommendation, along with the others in the report, despite his earlier views that such a "radical" step reviving dower in the province could only be taken after extensive study.[48]

Alberta's Home Protection Act and Saskatchewan's Homestead Act were passed a year before women obtained the vote. The order was reversed in Manitoba, the first province to grant female suffrage. Indeed, Beynon urged her Manitoba readers to support votes for women in order to remedy the existing law which permitted a man to sell the family homestead without even a word to his wife.[49] Elizabeth B. Mitchell, a Scottish suffragist and urban reformer who visited in western Canada from May 1913 to April 1914, observed that the "special trouble which has turned the prairie women's minds to politics is connected with the land. The woman so obviously shares with her husband in making the 'improved farm'...that it is felt to be an injustice that this product of their joint labour becomes the sole property of the man, and that he *can,* if he chooses, sell it and break up the home without his wife's consent. Cases where this has been done have raised a great deal of feeling among men as well as women."[50] Activist Nellie McClung maintained that women needed the vote "on account of the laws. In Ontario, a woman has some claim on her husband's property, but none here.... They said they had to do away with the wife's claim...on account of the boom in 1882 when property was changing hands so fast. But it won't be set right until women vote."[51] In letters to the *GGG*, women frequently linked the demand for female suffrage with demands for access to homesteads and dower rights;[52] one woman suggested that it would be wiser to get the vote before tackling the dower law, since there were men who supported female suffrage but opposed dower.[53] In 1914, when Manitoba women put on their mock parliament, a highly effective suffrage program in which males petitioned the female legislature for the privilege of the vote, one of the legislators begged her colleagues for a dower law for men, "basing her appeal touchingly on justice and decency and all the finer sentiments."[54]

Participants in the mock parliament had particular fun parodying Roblin, who was contemptuous of women's demands and showed little interest in reform generally. In power since 1900, Roblin was reelected with a narrow majority in 1914. The following year, when the Roblin government was forced to resign amidst allegations of fraud and corruption, the Liberals swept to power with a reform agenda which included women's rights. Early in the legislative session of 1916, the new government, led by T.C. Norris, extended the franchise to women.[55] Legislative action on women's property rights was delayed until 1918, when, after prompting from various reform organizations, the Norris government passed the Dower Act. Despite its name, this legislation did not reinstate the common law right of dower; it provided the wife with alternative rights in her husband's real and personal property, similar to those granted in Alberta's Dower Act of 1917. During the husband's lifetime, the wife's consent was necessary for any disposition of the property identified as the homestead; in any forced sale of the property to pay debts, the wife was entitled to one-half of the surplus, if any. A widow was entitled to a life estate in her husband's homestead. In addition, if he failed to provide for her adequately in his will, a widow could claim one-third of the value of his net real and personal estate. The Manitoba legislation also provided that husbands would have the same rights with respect to property owned by their wives.[56]

Homestead protection and dower rights legislation provoked a flurry of litigation; between 1915 and 1920, there were sixteen reported cases dealing with the legislation that had been enacted in Alberta and Saskatchewan. Reported cases are an unrepresentative sample

of the disputes on any issue, since not all trial decisions are reported, and since the expense, uncertainty and delay of going to court encourages disputants to settle before trial. Analysis of the reasoning and results in the reported cases, however, does suggest that judges, particularly at the lower level of the hierarchy of courts, were sympathetic to the purpose of the new legislation. Given the poor drafting of the statutes in all three provinces, and the judicial tendency to assimilate new statutory rights to common law principles, judges could have interpreted the dower provisions quite narrowly. In most cases, however, they adopted the interpretation most likely to protect the rights which the legislature had created, even though recognition of these rights would make it more difficult to transfer land, or require lenders to take additional steps to secure their loans.[57] In interpreting the definition of homestead, judges limited the wife's rights to the quarter section (160 acres) on which the house was built. Nevertheless, the same judges held that the legislation applied to property that would not have been subject to dower rights at common law, either because the husband had not yet acquired legal title to it, or because he was not the sole owner.[58] Where case law concerning common law dower favoured the wife's claim, however, judges were willing to follow it.[59] In only one of these sixteen cases, an Alberta trial decision, did a judge use common law conceptions of dower to defeat a wife's claim under the legislation; his reasoning was subsequently criticized in a decision of the Alberta Court of Appeal.[60]

In only five cases were husbands permitted to deal with the homestead without the wife's consent. In three of these, the court enforced leasing and sale agreements which lacked the prescribed form with the wife's consent, because, on the facts as found by the court, the wife had actually consented. In one case, the wife's consent was evidenced by her signature on the lease; even so, two of the four judges hearing the matter in the Alberta Court of Appeal would have set the lease aside because it did not comply with the requirements of the Dower Act.[61] In the other two cases in which the wife's claim was denied, the court permitted the registrar of Land Titles to clear a wife's caveat from her husband's title to land. One of these cases, *Russell v. Russell,* went to the Supreme Court of Canada, which overturned, in a three to two decision, a ruling of the trial judge favouring the wife. The narrow legal issue was whether a caveat filed under Alberta's Married Woman's Home Protection Act was invalid unless it was accompanied by the affidavit which the province's Land Titles Act required of people filing caveats against title. The person making this affidavit swore to his belief that he had a good and valid claim to the land, and that the caveat was not being filed to delay or embarrass any person proposing to deal with the land. The trial judge, and the two dissenting judges in the Supreme Court of Canada, recognized that since the purpose of the married woman's caveat was to delay or prevent the sale of the husband's homestead without the wife's consent, the legislators could not have intended that women must swear an affidavit to the contrary in order to file their caveat. The majority of the Supreme Court took refuge in a technical reading of the two statutes in issue to hold that the affidavit was necessary. Chief Justice Fitzpatrick, one of the majority, supported this technical interpretation by invoking the threat of the "unscrupulous adventurer alleging herself to be the wife of a homesteader or even a lawfully married woman moved by some unworthy motive" who might "improperly and without justification seek to embarrass a man in dealing with his property."[62]

In expressing his objections to the Dower Act in this way, the chief justice may have revealed somewhat more misogyny than his fellow judges, but he shared with them the assumption that the subject under discussion was limitations on a man's rights over his property. Supporters of a dower law argued that a wife, through her contribution to the acquisition of the homestead, had earned the right to some say in its disposition, and to some security against losing the property when her husband died. Few of them, however, demanded joint ownership for the wife. As one farmer explained in a letter to the *GGG,* "Only a few of the more militant of the women want a dower law. These ladies want to be like men—own land." This man did not object to a woman having the right to homestead, or to legislation giving a widow a one-third share in her husband's property, if he did not provide for her in his will, but a dower law "will bring strife and discord into homes that are now happy. While it does so little for women, it will fetter the man and place him in a humiliating position, making him so that he is no longer master of his property or destiny."[63]

The home protection and dower laws enacted on the Prairies between 1915 and 1920 must be read against the complex ideology informing the letter quoted above. It is tempting, from our late twentieth-century perspective, to ask why early twentieth-century reformers did not demand more. In part, they asked for what they thought they could get. Since dower was a recognized right in the older provinces, demands for dower protection could not be readily dismissed as radical, extreme, or likely to impede the economic development of the West. In some ways, indeed, advocates of a dower law got more than they had asked for. By 1920, the legislation passed in all three prairie provinces satisfied the demand for protection for wives from having their homes sold out from under them, by requiring married men to obtain their wives' consent to any disposition of the family home, whether it was an urban lot or a rural homestead. In addition, in Alberta and Manitoba, the widow was entitled to a life interest in her husband's homestead, regardless of what other provision he had made for her in his will.

Saying that reformers asked for what they thought they could get, however, merely raises other questions which cannot be answered with the available evidence: on what did the reformers base that assessment of what they could get, and what alternatives did they decide not to pursue? Essentially, despite their appeals to justice and equality, supporters of a dower law were not contesting the predominant role which custom and law gave to men in conducting the business and financial affairs of the family. Nor did they want to destroy existing property relations based on claims to ownership supported by title to the land. They were asking merely that the law set some limits on the absolute power of a man to dispose of his property, in recognition of the rights of his wife and children. Achievement of this limited objective, however, revealed its limitations. Having obtained legal recognition of their claim to the right to share in the homestead they had created with their husbands, women began to demand changes in the legislation to enable them to exercise that right more effectively. Demands for legislation providing for an equal sharing of the homestead during the husband's lifetime, however, were not successful.[64] Such demands posed too great a challenge to the prevailing ideology, which constrained women as well as men. Despite winning the vote and some dower rights, women were still not viewed as full partners with their husbands, as Irene Murdoch found out to her sorrow half a century later.

Notes

1   For an account of one woman who farmed on her own, see Georgina Binnie-Clark, *Wheat and Woman* (1914; Toronto: University of Toronto Press, 1979).

2   Veronica Strong-Boag, " 'Ever A Crusader': Nellie McClung, First-Wave Feminist," in Veronica Strong-Boag and Anita Clair Fellman, eds., *Rethinking Canada: The Promise of Women's History* (Toronto: Copp Clark Pitman, 1986); on maternal feminism, see Wayne Roberts, " 'Rocking the Cradle for the World': The New Woman and Maternal Feminism, Toronto 1877–1914," in Linda Kealey, ed., *A Not Unreasonable Claim* (Toronto: Women's Press, 1979), 15–45; Carol Lee Bacchi, *Liberation Deferred? The Ideas of the English-Canadian Suffragists, 1877–1918* (Toronto: University of Toronto Press, 1983); Veronica Strong-Boag, "Introduction," in Nellie McClung, *In Times Like These* (1915; Toronto: University of Toronto Press, 1972).

3   Gail Cuthbert Brandt, "Postmodern Patchwork: Some Recent Trends in the Writing of Women's History in Canada," *Canadian Historical Review* 72 (December 1991): 466. For a perceptive study of the strategic use of maternal feminist rhetoric, see "Battles in Another War: Edith Archibald and the Halifax Feminist Movement" and "The Ideas of Carol Bacchi and the Suffragists of Halifax," in E.R. Forbes, *Challenging the Regional Stereotype: Essays on the 20th Century Maritimes* (Fredericton: Acadiensis Press, 1989), 67–99.

4   Ontario Law Reform Commission, *Report on Family Law, Part IV, Family Property Law* (Toronto: Ontario Ministry of the Attorney General, 1974), 26–27.

5   A.J. McClean, "Matrimonial Property—Canadian Common Law Style," *University of Toronto Law Journal* 31 (1981): 379.

6   *Murdoch v. Murdoch* (1973), 41 D.L.R. (3d) 367 (S.C.C.).

7   J.E. Cote, "The Reception of English Law," *Alberta Law Review* 15 (1977): 86–92; R. Megarty and H.W.R. Wade, *The Law of Real Property*, 5th ed. (London: Stevens and Sons, 1984).

8   *Statutes of Manitoba*, 1885, c. 28, Real Property Act; *Statutes of Canada*, 1886, c. 26, ss. 8, 9.

9   Alison Prentice et al., *Canadian Women: A History* (Toronto: Harcourt Brace Jovanovich, 1988), 114.

10 Catherine Cavanaugh, "The Women's Movement in Alberta as Seen Through the Campaign for Dower Rights, 1909–1920" (M.A. thesis, University of Alberta, 1986), 30, 46; *Grain Growers' Guide (GGG)*, 19 April 1911.

11 Ian MacPherson, *Each for All: A History of the Co-operative Movement in English Canada, 1900–1945* (Toronto: Macmillan, 1979), 14; the *GGG* began as

a monthly, but beginning in mid-1909, was published every week.

12 Ramsay Cook, "Francis Marion Beynon and the Crisis of Christian Reformism," in Ramsay Cook and Carl Berger, eds., *The West and the Nation* (Toronto: McClelland and Stewart, 1976), 190, 193, 200; on Beynon's peace activism, see Barbara Roberts, "Women Against War, 1914–1918: Francis Beynon and Laura Hughes," in Janice Williamson and Deborah Gorham, eds., *Up and Doing: Canadian Women and Peace* (Toronto: Women's Press, 1989), 48–65.

13 *GGG,* January 1909.

14 Ibid., 15 July 1914; see also *GGG,* 23 March 1910, 8 January 1913, 16 April 1913, 11 June 1913, 7 January 1914.

15 Ibid., 10 September 1913.

16 Ibid., 6 May 1914.

17 Ibid., 14, 21 and 28 October; 4 and 11 November 1914.

18 Ibid., 29 January 1910.

19 Ibid., 21 May 1913; see also *GGG,* 18 September 1909.

20 Ibid., 7 August 1909.

21 Ibid.

22 Ibid., 14 August 1909.

23 Ibid., 8 December 1919.

24 Ibid., 14 August 1909.

25 Ibid., 5 February 1913.

26 Ibid., February 1909.

27 Ibid., 6 July 1910.

28 Ibid., 6 April 1910.

29 Ibid., 26 May 1915.

30 Ibid., 4 June 1913; see also *GGG,* 6 July 1910, 8 January 1913.

31 Ibid., July 1909, 15–16.

32 Quoted in Linda Rasmussen et al., *A Harvest Yet to Reap* (Toronto: Women's Press, 1976).

33 The Married Women's Relief Act, *Statutes of Alberta,* 1910, c. 18; An Act to Amend the Devolution of Estates Act, *Statutes of Saskatchewan,* 1910–11, c. 13. See Strong-Boag, "Ever A Crusader," 183; Anita L. Penner, "Emily Murphy and the Attempt to Alter the Status of Canadian Women, 1910–31" (M.A. thesis, Carleton University, 1979); Cavanaugh, "The Women's Movement in Alberta," 41–44.

34 *GGG,* 19 April 1911.

35 Ibid., 20 September 1911.

36 Ibid., 19 April 1911.

37 *Statutes of Manitoba,* 1912, c. 98.

38 *Statutes of Alberta,* 1915, c. 4; *Edmonton Daily Bulletin,* 30 March 1915, 1.

39 *GGG,* 19 May 1915.

40 *Edmonton Daily Bulletin,* 15 April 1915, 1.

41 *Edmonton Morning Bulletin,* 4 April 1917, 1, 6; *Statutes of Alberta,* 1917, c. 14.

42 *Statutes of Saskatchewan,* 1915, c. 29; ibid., 1916, c. 27; Journals of the Legislative Assembly of Saskatchewan.

43 *GGG,* 9, 30 August 1916; John Williams, "The Homesteads Act: Reflections on Its Purpose and Operation in Saskatchewan," *Saskatchewan Law Review* 4 (1983–84): 65–66; *Statutes of Saskatchewan,* 1916, c. 27; 1919–20, c. 66; *Statutes of Alberta,* 1917, c. 14; 1919, c. 40.

44 *GGG,* 24 February 1915; for references to the petitions, see ibid., 11 June 1913, 4 July, 22 September 1915.

45 L.G. Thomas, *The Liberal Party in Alberta: A History of Politics in the Province of Alberta, 1905–1921* (Toronto: University of Toronto Press, 1959); *Edmonton Daily Bulletin,* 30 March 1915.

46 David E. Smith, *Prairie Liberalism: The Liberal Party in Saskatchewan 1905–71* (Toronto: University of Toronto Press, 1975).

47 Quoted in Williams, "Homesteads Act," 64.

48 Ibid., 63, quoting from Scott's correspondence of 1909.

49 *GGG,* 26 May 1915; see also ibid., 8 September 1915.

50 Elizabeth B. Mitchell, *In Western Canada Before the War* (1915; Saskatoon: Western Producer Prairie Books, 1981), 56; Bacchi, *Liberation Deferred,* 117, notes that farm and suffrage organizations were able to work together on the campaign for a dower law.

51 Quoted in Rasmussen, *A Harvest Yet to Reap,* 154.

52 *GGG,* 10 January 1912; 5 February, 21 May, 18 June 1913; 15 July, 19 August 1914; 6 January 1915; 12 April 1916.

53 Ibid., 20 September 1911.

54 Ibid., 11 February 1914; for a lively description of the event, see Candace Savage, *Our Nell* (Saskatoon: Western Producer Prairie Books, 1979), 88–90.

55 W.L. Morton, *Manitoba: A History* (Toronto: University of Toronto Press, 1967), 336–38, 342–43, 347–50.

56 *GGG,* 13 December 1919; *Statutes of Manitoba,* 1918, c. 21, replaced the following year by *Statutes of Manitoba,* 1919, c. 26, containing the same rights.

57 For comments on the crudity and lack of precision of the legislation, see *Overland v. Himmelford* [1920] 2 W.W.R. 481 at 484 and *Biggs v. Isenberg* [1920] 3 W.W.R. 357 at 363.

58 *Overton v. Gerrity* (1916) 10 W.W.R. 1113: *Re Land Titles Act and Act Respecting Homesteads: Re Wolter* [1917] 3 W.W.R. 573; *Re The Land Titles Act, Graham's Case* [1919] 2 W.W.R. 943; *Biggs et al. v. Isenberg* [1920] 3 W.W.R. 357; *McDougall v. McDougall et al.* [1919] 2 W.W.R. 637. Under Manitoba's Dower Act, the married woman could claim rights in up to 320 acres of land surrounding the residence. See *Statutes of Manitoba,* 1918, c. 21, s. 2(b).

59 *In Re The Homestead Act, C's Case* [1919] 3 W.W.R. 31, which decided that a woman had not lost her rights under the legislation even though she was living apart from her husband because it was not clear that, at common law, she would not be entitled to support from him.

60 *Choma et al. v. Chmelyk* [1918] 2 W.W.R. 382; *Overland et al. v. Himmelford* [1920] 2 W.W.R. 481 per Ives, J. at 491.

61 *Overland et al. v. Himmelford* [1920] 2 W.W.R. 481; *Halldorson et al. v. Holizki* [1919] 3 W.W.R. 87; *Choma et al. v. Chmelyk* [1918] 2 W.W.R. 382.

62 *Russell v. Russell* [1918] 2 W.W.R. 673, quotation at 674; [1917] 3 W.W.R. 549; *Re The Land Titles Act* [1918] 2 W.W.R. 940.

63 *GGG,* 30 March 1910.

64 Cavanaugh, "The Women's Movement in Alberta," 69, 71, 74–75, 77–81, 86–88.

"A Red Girl's Reasoning"
E. Pauline Johnson Constructs the New Nation

VERONICA STRONG-BOAG

In the late nineteenth and early twentieth centuries, Canadians struggled to make sense of a colonial past, the Riel Rebellions, Native protest, feminist agitation, and the looming presence of a southern rival. The artists and writers who matured in these turbulent years offered some answers. Among this Confederation generation, E. Pauline Johnson is a unique example of a Euro-First Nation poet and non-fiction and short story writer. While well known in her own day, Johnson is largely remembered for producing Canada's best-selling book of poetry, *Flint and Feather* and, in particular, for writing "The Song My Paddle Sings," which has been reproduced in a host of texts as a celebration of a northern nation.[1] More significantly, she developed a nationalist narrative in which Indians, Euro-First Nations, and women reject inferiority and claim an equal place. The daughter of a Mohawk-English union, Johnson publicly challenged the exclusionary nationalist narratives of her day.

Pauline Johnson articulates a racialized femininity that embodied and unsettled many of the middle-class conventions of late nineteenth-century Canada. Hers is one version of what Judith Butler has described as "performative accomplishment" (1990, 271; 1993). Like today's performance artists,[2] Johnson "wore" gender, race, and class in ways that could be both transgressive and reinscriptive. As she sought secure footing among the prejudices of her age, her messages seem sometimes ambiguous and ambivalent. In identi-fying her as a performer who highlighted issues of race and gender in her ongoing conversation with European Canada, I do not dismiss these conditions as in any way "unreal" or as less significant because they are constructed in daily discourses. They remain critical sites of power and oppression in the real world. I wish rather to emphasize their construction, whether consciously or unconsciously, by Johnson and her audiences.[3]

In her efforts at communication, Pauline Johnson became one of those writers who, as postcolonial critics like Edward Said have suggested, endeavoured "to rechart and then occupy the place in imperial cultural forms reserved for subordination, to occupy it self-consciously, fighting for it on the very same territory once ruled by the consciousness that assumed the subordination of a designated inferior Other."[4] To be sure, sometimes her arguments seem dispersed, fragmentary, and often undeveloped. As critics Bill Ashcroft, Gareth Griffiths, and Helen Tiffin point out in *The Empire Writes Back,* such limitations are typical of early postcolonial texts, which came "into being within the constraints of a discourse and the institutional practice of a patronage system which limits and undercuts their assertion of a different perspective" (6). A reconsideration of Johnson as social critic and her work as a subversive narrative reveals a "conscious effort to enter into the discourse of Europe and the West, to mix with it, transform it, to make it acknowledge marginalized or suppressed or for-

Veronica Strong-Boag, "'A Red Girl's Reasoning': E. Pauline Johnson Constructs the New Nation," in *Painting the Maple: Essays on Race, Gender, and the Construction of Canada*, ed., Veronica Strong-Boag et al. (Vancouver: UBC Press, 1998), 130–154. Reprinted with the permission of the publisher. All rights reserved by the publisher.

gotten histories" (Said, 216). Unlike some writers of Aboriginal ancestry who have chosen in the first instance to speak to a Native community, Pauline Johnson performed largely for European Canada (Silvera). So far as we can tell, few listeners and readers were Native. Through stage and published work, she tried to translate Aboriginal and Mixed Race experience into public images that settlers could value. In the process, she outlines a hybrid nationalist identity that denounces oppression and incorporates the inheritance of Native peoples and the recognition of women.

The Making of a Canadian Postcolonial Performer

Born in 1861 in southwestern Ontario to an activist Mohawk father, George Henry Martin Johnson, and an English-born woman from an abolitionist family, Susanna Howells, Pauline Johnson was reared in comfort on the Grand River's Six Nations territory. There, a respectable middle-class enthusiasm for canonical Romantic poets like Byron or Shelley mingled with a passionate commitment to protecting Indian people from the assaults of unprincipled Europeans.[5] Such views situated Johnson and her family within the mainstream of the liberal nationalism of her day.[6] Her elite family entertained leading individuals, from the governor general and Iroquois chiefs on down, exposing her to many of the burning questions of the day. Johnson's family, with its biculturalism, its liberal nationalism, and its middle-class privilege, provided a highly unusual vantage point from which to view the volatile mixture of influences that was to become modern Canada. It sharply distinguished her and, ultimately, her writing from the group of nationalist poets— Duncan Campbell Scott, Archibald Lampman, Isabella Valancy Crawford, Bliss Carman, Charles G.D. Roberts, and Wilfred Campbell— with whom she is commonly compared.

The Johnson household prepared its children to straddle the Aboriginal and European worlds, which, through trade and settlement, still remained closely connected for many nineteenth-century Canadians. As an interpreter and forest warden for the Department of Indian Affairs and a translator for the Anglican Church in the mid-decades of the century, Johnson's father[7] moved among different communities. His two sons and two daughters might have hoped to do the same. They were, as Pauline Johnson remembered in her short story, "My Mother," "reared on the strictest lines of both Indian and English principles. They were taught the legends, the traditions, the culture, and the etiquette of both races to which they belonged; but above all, their mother instilled into them from the very cradle that they were of their father's people, not of hers" (1987, 69). Despite such injunctions, status and nationality for the Iroquois are traced through the mother, not the father. Her identity as a Mohawk could not come in the traditional manner but only from the federal Indian Act.

In the nineteenth century, the Grand River Mohawks remained a powerful and proud part of the Six Nations Confederacy, which had established Canada's most populous and prosperous Native community near Brantford in 1847 (Weaver 1994, 182; 1972). The territory itself was multinational, harbouring European-Canadians, blacks, the members of the Iroquois Confederacy, and a number of smaller allied tribes. During the nineteenth century a decisive split emerged between "culturally conservative Longhouse people and the more acculturated Christians" (Weaver 1994, 183). The Longhouse faction championed traditional language, rituals, and governance (Shimony; Weaver 1972). Such views evoked little support among Anglican Mohawks like the Johnsons, who initially felt optimistic about their relations with the dominant society. The flourishing state of the Christian Grand River community in the last decades of the nineteenth century seemed full of promise to Iroquois Christians who hoped to contribute to the emergence of a Native-European union (see Weaver 1994). Such optimism would later dissipate in rancour and despair. However, until the end of her life Pauline Johnson sought to express the positive vision of an inclusive nationality espoused by her family and others like them.

Johnson's access to the Mohawk community was limited by the fact that her English mother was never fully integrated into the Grand River territory. Close ties to her mother's relatives, schooling by a governess and in a city high school, and Pauline's residence throughout her twenties in Brantford's middle-class neighbourhoods, further undermined the influence of George Johnson and his father, John Smoke Johnson, both of whom were well-known Mohawk leaders, and that of her extensive Native family. Pauline Johnson stood on the periphery of even Grand River's Native community and "its well-integrated system of values and morals" (Weaver 1994, 215).

Given her incomplete immersion, Johnson's performances as a Native woman, or "Indian Princess," always encountered problems of authenticity. One solution, as revealed in the deerskin dress she often wore, was to fabricate a synthetic pan-Indian stage presence that necessarily relied as much upon popular European fantasies of the Native as it did upon direct Aboriginal inspiration. Her reference to whites, such as William Lighthall and Charles Mair, for assistance in putting together a realistic stage presence (by whose standards?) captures her problems most poignantly.

Upon George Johnson's death in 1884, his widow and daughters, Pauline and Evelyn, permanently left the Six Nations territory and resettled in Brantford, a bustling industrial market centre.[8] Their shift from prominence in the Mohawk community to a socially inferior position in town mirrored the general decline in the situation of Mixed Race and Native peoples in Canada. The move also reinforced European cultural influences. Pauline attended and performed in theatrical amateur entertainments in Hamilton and Brantford and continued writing. Like many daughters of the middle class, she experimented with verse whose forms and themes often reflected the conventional sentiments of Victorian Canada.

Throughout Johnson's life she claimed the literary traditions of Great Britain to be as much her own as were those of the Six Nations. The result is a cultural hybrid who juggles influences from both sides of her family as she seeks to bridge Canada's racial divide. In a world that typically thinks in terms of dualisms, Mixed Race individuals are troubling. As one contributor to the 1994 volume *Miscegenation Blues: Voices of Mixed Race Women* points out, those of plural ancestry "embody some of the most unresolved contradictions in current human relations" (Green, 291). In their hands, "nationality" can become "unstable, mobile, and heterogeneous—a fluid process of negotiation rather than a rigid imposition of meaning" (Donaldson, 116). In the heyday of Euro-Canadian nation-building Johnson faced an uphill struggle. Neither she nor her audiences could always be sure what she was expected to, or would, perform. Hers was a life-long search for a credible and profitable means of enacting her own and Canada's hybridity.

The difficulty and loneliness of Johnson's position encouraged her to develop a style that made direct application to her listeners and readers. Much like other performance artists, she communicated in ways that are "intensely intimate," with an "emphasis on personal experience and emotional material, not 'acted' or distanced from artist or audience" (Forte, 255). Her efforts at emotionally direct communication, at the establishment of empathy, especially through the use of melodrama and comedy, encouraged a recognition of women's and men's, of Natives' and non-Natives', shared humanity. Once she forged such bonds with her audience, Johnson could hope to create new space for First Nations and women in Canada's settler society.

As her long days at home, from the age of eighteen until she gave a public recital in Toronto in 1892 at age thirty, further reveal, a strong-minded Euro-First Nation spinster faced many handicaps in creating space for herself during the high age of British imperialism and paternalism.[9] While discrimination has always existed, the European-Canadian assessment of Indians had been deteriorating from an earlier emphasis on their "fundamental humanity to one based on the theological and sociological theories which relegated them to the sub-human" (MacDonald, 103). Those of joint Native and European heritage also fared badly. The collapse of the Prairie resistances in 1870 and 1885 doomed the hopes of Louis Riel and others for recognition of the Euro-First Nations community. By the late 1880s, prospects for those claiming Native heritage looked bleak.

Native Canadian writers emerged to address the ongoing crisis of their relationship with the dominant society. Penny Petrone charts evidence of resistance from an Indian and Euro-First Nations elite armed with a formal education and command of English. While protest came from many tribes, the Iroquois, with their long history of alliance with the British Empire, were especially prominent.[10] Not all Aboriginal participants in debates about the future of North America voiced opposition to European encroachment. One commentator has suggested that the handful of Native writers publishing in the United States at the turn of the century were basically assimilationist. "Their characters accept white values and cultural traits, often rejecting the traditional way of life" (Larson, 36). There is also the question of resistance offered by the Aboriginal performers who peopled Wild West shows, burlesque halls, and popular entertainments of every kind in Europe, North America,

and all around the world during these years. Their performances, constructed by themselves and the managers, negotiated complicated terrains of complicity and protest that are difficult to appreciate or evaluate.[11] In whatever fashion they confronted their common vulnerability, Native writers and performers contributed to the growth of pan-Indian sentiments in these years (Larson). In their preoccupation with relations with white society, they provide a critical backdrop for Pauline Johnson, the first Euro-First Nation or Native woman to assume a major public role in Canada.

The mid-nineteenth century also saw the birth of a generation of Canadians deeply influenced by the feminist movement. Johnson matured in a community debating women's roles, especially their right to higher education, paid work, and political power. Brantford and its surroundings produced, along with Native activists, Emily Stowe, Canada's first female school principal and, later, the founder of the country's first suffrage society (Bashevkin, Chapter 1), and a crowd of pioneer female journalists. For a woman of ambition, Ontario in these years appeared full of promise. Johnson's uncertain position, an unmarried daughter in a widow's family, gave her particular reasons to rethink the situation of her sex and to join other women in asking questions of the new nation.

While the recurring racism of turn-of-the-century feminism has been described by scholars, the politics of gender and race are fluid and never uncomplicated (Bacchi; Valverde). A number of American suffragists had a special interest in the history of Native peoples. They were impressed by the presence of powerful women in the Iroquois Confederacy. For some feminists, Indian society appeared to supply "an alternative to American patriarchy," suggesting that male domination was neither inevitable nor omnipresent.[12] Pauline Johnson draws the same comparison in the *London Daily Express* in 1906:

I have heard that the daughters of this vast city cry out for a voice in Parliament of this land. There is no need for an Iroquois woman to clamour for recognition in our councils; she has had it for upwards of four centuries.... From her cradle-board she is taught to judge men and their intellectual qualities, their aptness for public life, and their integrity, so that when he who bears the title leaves his seat in council to join the league-makers in the happy hunting grounds she can use her wisdom and her learning in nominating his fittest successor.... The old and powerful chiefs-in-council never attempt to question her decision.... There are fifty matrons possessing this right in the Iroquois Confederacy. I have not heard of fifty white women even among those of noble birth who may speak and be listened to in the lodge of the law-makers here. (1987, 232)

Other Iroquois activists, desirous of outside, especially feminist, support, also emphasized the authority of their matrons.[13] As such arguments make clear, the politics of race and gender were not always at odds. In an age of multiple and overlapping protest movements, Johnson was well equipped to make critical connections between the politics of race and gender.

The decision to confront prevailing prejudice is far from easy. One Mohawk writer, Beth Brant, has recently reminded us:

To write or not to write is a painful struggle for us. For everything we write can be used against us. *For everything we write will be used against us.* And I'm not talking about bad reviews. I'm talking about the flak we receive from our own communities as well as the smug liberalism from the white 'literacy' enclave. Writing is an act of courage for most. For *us*, it is an act that requires opening up our wounded communities, our families, to eyes and ears that do not love us. Is this madness? In a way it is—the madness of a Louis Riel, a Maria Campbell, a Pauline

Johnson, a Crazy Horse—a revolutionary madness. A love that is greater than fear. A love that is as tender as it is fierce. (17)

It is just such a counter-discourse, essentially feminist and postcolonialist, that Johnson was to articulate on platforms in theatres, schools, and churches across the country after she entered the uncertain world of the paid recitalist in 1892. In these performances, she staged a femininity that was simultaneously and ambiguously raced. In a white ball gown, she offered herself as the epitome of upper-class Victorian womanhood. Minutes later, she would reappear as a passionate Aboriginal woman clad in leather and feathers.

Johnson's Indian ancestry enhanced her marketability, an appeal she capitalized on in her presentation as an archetypal "Indian Princess"—someone, in other words, like Pocahontas in the American story, or Molly Brant in the case of the northern colonies, who acts to redeem European men, saving them from the wilderness and the wilderness for them.[14] Here is both affirmation and repudiation of the middle-class conventions of gender and race. Johnson's ultimate dependence on the patronage of the dominant society required this ambiguity.

For the rest of her life she orchestrated a public career that fed on melodrama, jingoism, and commercialism, together with a commitment to writing verse and stories that would both win the praise of literary critics and address the oppression of Native peoples and women. Her oral skills proved the key to earning a living, while her ability to publish poems and stories nourished her appeal to audiences and her claim to middle-class respectability.[15] While the results were uneven, as she herself painfully acknowledged,[16] Johnson persevered in struggling to translate her views into forms that would be simultaneously acceptable to both a cultural elite and popular audiences. In the process she extended Native American women's long-standing role—first exercised as mistresses, wives, and guides—as "mediators of meaning between the cultures of the two worlds."[17] Over the course of the twentieth century, Canadian audiences would find that Aboriginal performers, such as Grey Owl (in reality the transplanted Britisher, Archibald Belaney) and Buffy Sainte-Marie,[18] served in some measure as critical "symbols in the Canadian-history enterprise" (Emberley 18; Francis). In many ways, the reality faced by Aboriginal peoples is beside the point. Indian performers are often valued inasmuch as they can confirm Canada's particular relationship to the northern landscape and, ultimately, its difference from the United States. In the face of growing racism, however, Native roots jeopardized Johnson's efforts to parlay a talent for public expression and poetry into a living. As a public woman and as an Indian artist, she was to live on society's periphery, able finally neither to marry nor to guarantee her security.[19]

Marginality was further reinforced by Johnson's role as an interpreter and champion of a peripheral culture. Advocates and creators of Canadian literature had to fight hard to find a hearing. Only too often they found themselves on the defensive in the face of British and American aspirations to imperial domination and the colonialism of Canadians themselves. In her life and her work, Johnson had to negotiate many identities in the dominant culture's commercial and aesthetic markets. She had to sell to the very society she critiqued her need for respectability and sympathy juxtaposed with a message that potentially unsettled conventions of race and gender.

Talking Race

Challenging a dominant narrative that held that "to the majority of English speaking people, an Indian is an Indian, an inadequate sort of person possessing a red brown skin, nomadic habits,

and an inability for public affairs" (Johnson 1900, 440) took courage. This boldness was recognized by her contemporaries. According to the nationalist poet, Charles Mair, the effect of Johnson's "racial poetry...upon the reader was as that of something abnormal, something new and strange, and certainly unexampled in Canadian verse. For here was a girl whose blood and sympathies were largely drawn from the greatest tribe of the most advanced nation of Indians of the continent, who spoke out 'loud and bold,' not for it alone but for the whole red race, and sang of its glories and its wrongs in strains of poetic fire" (cited in Foster, 179). As one of a tiny group of North American Native women who challenged racism on stage and in writing, Johnson was a lonely figure.[20]

Her earliest contributions to public life—in 1884 at the reinternment of the Seneca orator, Red Jacket, and, two years later, at Brantford's unveiling of a statue to the Mohawk chief, Joseph Brant—identify heroic liberal figures who match any in the contemporary European nationalist lexicon.[21] Here are Natives of giant stature. Their merits and those of First Nations and Euro-First Nations peoples in general do not, as Johnson argues, meet with deserved respect. The history of Indian-White contact is the history of recurring ignorance and injustice. Pauline Johnson's inaugural recital in Toronto in 1892 electrified listeners with "A Cry from an Indian Wife," a passionate indictment of the crushing of the Prairie tribes in 1885, an encounter still fresh in memory and one that had sharply divided the country. Early 1890s articles, such as "The Iroquois of the Grand River" and "A Glimpse of the Grand River Indians," construct more realistic portraits to counter prejudices that fail to make critical distinctions among the tribes or to recognize their merits (cited in Keller, 111–12).

Johnson regularly pillories the prejudice that consigns all people of Aboriginal background to inferiority. In 1892, her powerful rejoinder to contemporary racism, "A Strong Race Opinion on the Indian Girl in Modern Fiction," catalogues and dismisses racist stereotypes that relegate Indian women to the losing side in war and in love (cited in Keller, 120–1). Poems like "The Cattle Thief" and "Wolverine" likewise reject the dehumanization that accompanies genocide. Audiences are asked to think of the Native characters as individuals with heroic qualities, more than a match for the erstwhile victors, who are, in turn, not in reality "plucky Englishmen" but "demons," "robbers," and "dogs" (Johnson 1972, 10–4, 22–6). In a nice reversal of conventions, the white intruders are reduced to non-humans. Johnson herself is not immune to racist constructions. In ways that are reminiscent of eugenic thinkers but also evoke older Native rivalries, she accords the Iroquois, the Cree, the Sioux, the Haida, and the Squamish superiority over other Aboriginal tribes. Faith in elite Natives armed her in struggles against those who sought to dismiss her and those she represented.

Throughout her life Johnson wrote and performed works that starkly detail the ruin inflicted by newcomers and their governments. One short story, "As It Was in the Beginning," takes residential schools to task. Another, "Her Majesty's Guest," depicts the brutality of liquor-sellers, enemies who had, on three occasions, physically attacked her own father (Johnson 1989). Poems like "Silhouette," "The Corn Husker," and "The Cattle Thief" dramatize the starvation that dogged the tribes in these years (Johnson 1972, 103, 7–9).[22] In face of injustice, cattle rustling is readily justified. As Johnson explains, in a revealing use of the first person, "When *you* pay for the land you live in *we*'ll pay for the meat we eat" (1972, 13 [author's emphasis]). In other passages, the hypocrisy of conquerors who "had come with the Bible in one hand, the bottle in the other" is exposed.[23] Here are hard lessons about complicity and betrayal that audiences were not used to hearing.

In the early poems "Ojistoh" and "As Red Men Die," Johnson attempts to create sympathy with dramatic portraits of idealized Native women and men who are every bit the equal of those found in the Scottish and English ballads with which listeners might be more familiar (1972). In deference to her audiences and no doubt to her need to earn a living, no poem portrays violence directed at newcomers. First Nations men and women are for the most part noble, long-suffering, generous, and open to reasonable overtures. In poems like "Wolverine" and "The Cattle Thief" (1972), and short stories like "Catharine of the Crow's Nest," they, rather than the European intruders, demonstrate humanity (1987). While Johnson sometimes despairs, as when she laments her "dear dead race" in her story "A Red Girl's Reasoning" (1987), she also insists on the "innate refinement so universally possessed by the higher tribes of North American Indians" (1987, 103). She argues further that if you "put a pure-blooded Indian in the drawing room…he will shine with the best of you" (cited in Keller, 112). The Natives' "adaptability to progress" (1987, 104) makes them fully capable of entering the modern world. Her portrait of heroic and thoughtful Native figures stands in stark contrast to the "disappearing race" chronicled in the poems of her more powerful contemporary, Duncan Campbell Scott of the federal Department of Indian Affairs.[24] Johnson's faith in the ultimate competitiveness of non-Europeans also helps explain her enthusiasm, in the poem "The Man in Chrysanthemum Land," for Japan's defeat of Russia in the 1904–5 war (1972, 158–9).[25] Like other liberal and anti-racist critics of her day, she interpreted that conflict as the belated triumph of non-Europeans over their would-be white masters (Martin).

In 1909, Johnson retired to British Columbia, a province that had by then become the centre of Indian protest.[26] Her assistance to Squamish chief Joe Capilano in 1906 when he and other representatives of BC tribes petitioned King Edward, like the long hours they spent together in Vancouver while he narrated the stories of his people and the assistance she gave to his son in public speaking, were in keeping with long-demonstrated sympathies. Johnson's relationships on the west coast also reflected the ties that increasingly connected Native peoples of different communities in the twentieth century.

The Legends of Vancouver (1911), published at the end of her life, reaffirms Johnson's persistent efforts to remap the Euro-Canadian imaginative landscape. As she reminds readers, the twin peaks that rise to the north of the city are not "the lions," so-named by a foreign-born settler with a mind for the exotic or the patriotic but "without the love for them that is in the Indian heart" (1926, 3). The mountains have a far older indigenous history as "the sisters" of Indian legend. Her retelling of Squamish stories unnames the land colonized by Europeans and evokes a powerful human landscape preceding their arrival.[27] The Native inheritance is located at the centre of human history in British Columbia and Canada. In such writing, Johnson suggests, as Edward Said has said of other resistance writers, that indigenous peoples have "a history capable of development, as part of the process of work, growth, and maturity to which only Europeans had seemed entitled" (213).

Speaking of Women

While she tends to locate oppression primarily in racism, and she is most emphatic about its particular ill effects, Johnson remained sensitive to how women are damaged by the convergence of racial and sexual prejudice. She explains her double vision: "I am a Redskin, but I am something else too—I am a woman" (1987, 13). Indeed, as A. LaVonne Ruoff has observed, Pauline Johnson's writing resembles that of

many other female writers in the nineteenth century. In her stories "the heroine encounters mistreatment, unfairness, disadvantage, and powerlessness which result from her status as female and child. The heroine accepts herself as a female while rejecting the evaluation of female with permanent children. In the course of the narrative women are rejected as sexual prey and a pragmatic feminism is embraced" (Johnson 1987, 19). The Mohawk writer Beth Brant has argued further that Pauline Johnson, in "breaking out of the Victorian strictures of her day... drew a map for all women to follow" (60–1). Unlike Euro-Canadian writers, Johnson identifies racism rather than patriarchy as the chief obstacle to the fair treatment of women.

Race could also be significant in empowering women. Johnson frequently roots her commitment to equality in Native traditions. In one story, "The Lost Salmon Run," a Squamish elder outlines this in describing her reception of a granddaughter: "Very good luck to have a girl for first grandchild. Our tribe not like yours; we want girl-children first, we not always wish boy-child born just for fight. Your people, they care only for war-path; our tribe more peaceful.... I tell you why: girl-child may be some time mother herself; very grand thing to be mother" (1926, 37–8). Much the same argument about the value of women is made when Johnson points to the power of Iroquois matrons. These are influential figures who contest and, often, dominate the landscape.

Johnson's female characters, like her performances, are distinguished by passionate feeling. Polite conventions about heterosexual relations, with their common emphasis on female passivity and male initiative, are rare. A series of love poems, particularly those appearing after her own unhappy affairs, evoke female passion. The canoe figures significantly as an expression of, and vehicle for, women's desires for love and mastery. Her early work, "The Song My Paddle Sings," launches this preoccupation with lines like "I wooed you long but my wooing's past; My paddle will lull you into rest" and its reference to the river as a "bed" and its waters as a "breast." Here, the heroine triumphs in the rapids that "roar," "seethe and boil, and bound, and splash," "but never a fear my craft will feel" (1972, 29–31). In a later poem, "The Idlers," she again uses the first person to conjure up a memory of perfect passion. The male object of her erotic gaze is explicit:

Against the thwart, near by,
Inactively you lie,
And all too near my arm your temple bends
Your indolent rude
Abandoned attitude
And again
Your costume, loose and light,
Leaves unconcealed your might
Of muscle, half suspected, half defined;
And falling well aside
Your vesture opens wide,
Above your splendid sunburnt throat that
    pulses unconfined.

(1972, 59–61)

Disappointment eventually quells this optimism. Sleeplessness and despair dominate the poems "Re-voyage," "Wave-Won," and "In the Shadows." Days were now "haunted" and "dreary." Even the speaker's "arm as strong as steel" brings no salvation (1972, 65 and 67).

By the time of Johnson's second volume of poetry, *Canadian Born* (1903), loss provides the major theme in "Thistle-Down," "Through Time and Bitter Distance," and "Your Mirror Frame" (1972, 99, 105–6, 117–8). The author's lack of repentance about her feelings is perhaps, however, best captured in the poem "In Grey Days":

Deep human love for others
Deep as the sea
God-sent unto my neighbour —
But not to me.

Sometime I'll wrest from others
More than all this
I shall demand from Heaven
Far sweeter bliss.

(1972, 131)

Such depiction of women's physical and emotional responses is unusual in the Canada of her day. In talking of passion and in embodying the very results of miscegenation, she was a controversial figure for her audiences. Were her presentations to be taken as proof that women sui generis had sexual desires? Or were they rather an expression of her Native heritage—in other words, a demonstration of inherent primitivism or even degeneracy? Just who was performing what? Such questions had to be negotiated afresh with each new set of listeners and readers.

Passion was not the only strong emotion requiring interpretation. Betrayal, violence, and death recur in Johnson's work. From her early narrative poem, "Ojistoh," in which a Mohawk woman murders a would-be rapist, to the later story "As It Was in the Beginning," again recounted in the first person, in which the Euro-First Nation heroine takes revenge on an unfaithful priest and a still more unfaithful lover (1987), she champions a stern code in which women are neither to be seized nor taken for granted. When Charles McDonald, in the short story, "A Red Girl's Reasoning," refuses to recognize the customary Native marriage between his wife Christie's parents, an issue which bitterly divided real-life Canadians in these years,[28] she responds, "Why should I recognize the rites of your nation when you do not acknowledge the rites of mine?" (1987, 117).

If heterosexual relations spell trouble, Pauline Johnson joined other women writers in crediting her sex with strong maternal feelings. Remarkable mothers stand out in stories such as "Catharine of the Crow's Nest," "The Next Builder," "Mother o' the Men," and "The Tenas Klootchman" (1987). In the first, an Indian woman, Maarda, shows newcomers the meaning of generosity when she rescues a white foundling. In the stories written for an American boys' magazine and published in 1913 as *The Shagganappi,* good women civilize sons, inspiring them to higher levels of honour and achievement. In her account of her own mother's life, Johnson lovingly portrays a woman who devotes herself to her children (1987). Ultimately it is women's maternalism that provides an important point of connection between the races. In "A Cry from an Indian Wife," the narrator describes her own agony at seeing her family and nation going to war. She nevertheless comments:

> Yet stay, my heart is not the only one
> That grieves the loss of husband and of son;
> Think of the mothers o'er the inland seas;
> Think of the pale-faced maiden on her knees;

These reflections, with their direct appeal to the enemy, cast doubt on "the glories of war" and conjure up a common humanity (1972, 18).

Inspired by their capacity for nurture, women in general emerge, as did the Native women who make peace by marrying tribal enemies in poems such as "Dawendine," as the chief promise of a more just and peaceful world (1972, 118–21). In the story "The Envoy Extraordinary," the character "old Billy" sums up these sentiments: "these mother-wimmen don't never thrive where there's rough weather, somehow. They're all fer peace. They're worse than King Edward an' Teddy Roosevelt fer patchin' up rows, an' if they can't do it no other way, they jes' hike along with a baby, sort o' treaty of peace like" (1987, 138). This faith in women's special nature was a commonplace that Johnson, like a host of her feminist contemporaries, used to contest misogynist conventions.[29] Such shared assumptions added to her appeal for the US *Mothers' Magazine,* in which she regularly published.

While Pauline Johnson self-consciously chose to speak as "One of Them"[30]—as the Iroquois and, by extension, as all Native women of Canada—and their lives lay close to the centre of much of her writing, she maintained close friendships with non-Native women. Her first poem, appearing in the American magazine *Gems of Poetry* in 1884 is dedicated "To Jean," a white girlhood friend. During her itinerant career, she relied on women's work and emotional support. The suffragist Nellie McClung met the recitalist in the mid-1890s and her response captures the response of many. In her autobiography she recollects that "at her first word, we felt at home with her...[this] charming, friendly woman" (1945, 35). That initial regard initiated a now lost correspondence of almost twenty years' duration.

The significance of female friendships is described in Johnson's short story, "Mother o' the Men." Here Mrs. Lysle (we never learn her first name) chooses to accompany her North-West Mounted Police husband to the Yukon. "But there are times even in the life of a wife and mother when her soul rebels at cutting herself off from all womenkind, and all that environment of social life among women means, even if the act itself is voluntary on her part." Later on, "during days when the sight of a woman's face would have been a glimpse of paradise to her," she "almost wildly regretted her boy had not been a girl—just a little sweet-voiced girl, a thing of her own sex and kind" (1987, 182, 187). The author of these words had good reason to value her own sex. Her death from cancer in Vancouver in 1913 was made immeasurably easier by the life she had fostered among women. A host of correspondents encouraged her spirits. Efforts by the Women's Canadian Club, the Women's Press Club, and the Imperial Order Daughters of the Empire ensured no financial worries. A female world anchored her to the end.

What all this begs, of course, is the question of Johnson's own feminism. Certainly her maternalism is characteristic of the women's movement of her day. So too is her recognition of female strength and capacity (Prentice et al.). But as a recent reminder explains, "Native women are feminist in a way that women of other culture groups, other religions, rarely understand.... Where differences arise between mainstream feminists and Native women they centre around causes of oppression and particularly racism. Whereas mainstream feminists see the primary cause of their oppression as patriarchal society, Native women are more inclined to see their oppression as arising from racism and colonialism" (Grant, 43). Johnson seems to fit this definition. Her poems and stories draw clear links between the treatment of women and the racism of the dominant society. Oppression rarely appears a simple relationship between sexes or races. Her female characters must first reject racialization to be recognized as fully human.

Creating a New Nation

While endeavouring to chart her course as a Native and as a woman, Pauline Johnson had to locate and define herself as a Canadian at a time when this identity was far from sure. This preoccupation, which is central to her writings, also revealed how far she had moved from the insistence of other Christian Iroquois on their status as allies of Great Britain rather than as citizens of Canada. Nationalisms in various forms competed for adherents and legitimacy (Berger). As the first post-Confederation collection of Canadian verse, *Songs of the Great Dominion* (1889), indicates, poets were among those who sought to capture the essence of what it meant to grow up in the northern half of the continent. A contributor to that influential volume, Pauline Johnson never gave up the effort to articulate a founding tradition of narrative and metaphor in the wider context of British cultural and political imperialism. Her championship

of a cultural and racial "hybridity" rooted in the northern landscape recalls her own family's efforts on the Grand River. Although Johnson has little to say about French Canada, she shifts the question of racial partnership away from the prevailing Eurocentrism to include Natives.

Membership in a family of Mohawk United Empire Loyalists (UELs) gave a special twist to Johnson's preoccupation with the nature of an identity separate from that of the United States and Great Britain. The patronage of British governor generals, literati, and salon hostesses, invaluable in establishing the credentials and the respectability of the Euro-First Nation poet, deepened her appreciation of and dependence on the centre of empire. Her early initiation in the English cultural canon kept her an enthralled captive. Lines in her poem "My English Letter" provide eloquent testimony to this fascination. Referring to England as the "Motherland," and it is indeed the birthplace of her own mother, Johnson writes of exile:

> Although I never knew the blessed favour
> That surely lies in breathing English air.
> Imagination's brush before me fleeing.
> Paints English pictures, though my longing eyes
> Have never known the blessedness of seeing
> The blue that lines the arch of English skies.
>
> (1972, 76)

Such nostalgia seems typical of what Ashcroft, Griffiths, and Tiffin identify as the "second stage of production within the evolving discourse of the post-colonial," or "the literature produced 'under imperial license' by 'Natives' or 'outcasts'"(5).

Like other elite Natives, Johnson has an ambiguous relationship with empire. As the descendant of British allies and the daughter of an English mother, she seeks to claim the culture of the imperial centre without accepting its denigration of the periphery. She rejects the racism while sharing some of the sentiments of imperialist contemporaries. Like the political economist and humorist Stephen Leacock, who thunders in his essay, "Greater Canada: An Appeal," "the Empire is ours too, ours in its history of the past, ours in its safe-guard of the present" (36), Johnson repudiates inferiority for Canada, Britain's legitimate heir. A unique blending of Old World and New World, it, not the "old land," is the "beloved of God" (1972, 172, 79). Unlike Anglo-Canadian imperialists, however, she includes Native peoples as full participants in the imperial project. The hybrid empire she envisions is pluralistic and meritocratic.

Johnson's relationship with the rising power to the south is, in contrast, much less positive. Kinship with William D. Howells, the American man of letters, seems to have been disappointing. His dismissal of her work and apparent slighting of his Aboriginal cousins went hand in hand with the greater difficulty Johnson encountered with US audiences who tended, like some American literary critics at the end of the twentieth century, to appropriate her as a homegrown product.[31] Their relative rudeness, beginning with her 1896–7 tour south of the Great Lakes (it was claimed that they "treated Pauline as if she too were a circus freak, though they were a bit awed by her obvious refinement and talent" [Keller, 234]) enraged her and helped confirm the benefits of the continuing British connection. Johnson also had a front seat on the American Indian wars of the late nineteenth century, and she shared with many Canadians the faith that matters were better north of the 49th.[32] When she envisions Canada's future, she insists that "the Yankee to the south of us must south of us remain" (1972, 80).

For Pauline Johnson, like some contemporaries, British justice provides the critical imperial inheritance (Dean). The rule of law will allow Canada to escape American unrest and corruption. Revealingly, the United States is frequently "othered" or, in a curious way, even orientalized in the accounts of Canadian imperialists like Johnson. A rebellious colony, the US had repudiated its British inheritance and is thus susceptible to racial degeneration and despotism. In contrast, in Canada, the traditions of British law, with their promise of equality to all, supply an essential bulwark against the tyranny of the majority and allow minorities to survive. Johnson sums up her hope for a pluralistic future in a story entitled "The Brotherhood": "The Mohawks and the palefaces are brothers, under one law.... It is Canadian history" (1913, 220). Similar aspirations concerning the rule of law fuelled the continuing appeal by Native peoples to the courts, the Crown, and, eventually, the League of Nations and the United Nations, where they attempted to speak as the allies, not the conquered, of Great Britain (Drees).

Johnson identifies one institution as central to the maintenance of law and order and as symbolic of the significance of fair play among races. As Keith Walden has suggested, the North-West Mounted Police (NWMP) quickly emerged after their creation in 1873 as a major icon of the new nation (4). The NWMP, later the RCMP, provided an essential guarantee and evidence of Canada's regard for law and of its fundamental difference from the US. Johnson's "The Riders of the Plains" typically loomed as larger-than-life figures who, while few in number, were brave enough "to keep the peace of our people and the honour of British law." "Felons," "rebels," and the lawless, all of whom were only too likely to originate south of the border, have no place in the land of the Lion and the Union Jack (1972, 103). Although no disillusionment is found in Johnson's surviving work, Natives, in general, quickly learned, especially after 1885, that the Mounties were at least as much keepers as protectors.

For Johnson, fair dealing by national authorities not only upheld the principles of British justice, it also helped guarantee Canada itself. She insists that the Indian heritage is a key ingredient of national survival. At the dedication of Brant's memorial in 1886, she writes:

So Canada thy plumes were hardly won
Without allegiance from thy Indian son.

Then meet we as one common brotherhood
In peace and love, with purpose understood.

Today the Six Red Nations have their Canada.
(Van Steen, 45–6)

Her tours across the country with their introduction to other First Nations offered her the opportunity to confirm their special relationship to the Dominion. In regard to the Sioux, her heroic hunters of the Plains, she explains: "King Edward of England has no better subjects; and I guess it is all the same to His Majesty whether a good subject dresses in buckskin or broadcloth" (cited in Van Steen, 263). The appeal of Squamish chief Capilano to the same monarch in 1906 is the right of an ally and an equal.

While European newcomers may offer the advantage of British law, First Nations also bring important qualities to a biracial partnership. There is, of course, the courage and loyalty that stood at the core of Johnson's own family history, but there is also, contrary to the racist depictions of Natives as savage, a special proclivity for peacemaking. She employs a youngster in one story to speak for the newcomers in acknowledging "brotherhood with all men.... We palefaces have no such times.... Some of us are always at war. If we are not fighting here, we are fighting beyond the great salt seas. I wish we had more of...your Indian ways. I wish we could link a silver chain around the world; we think we are the ones to teach, but I believe you could teach us much (1913, 213).

The peaceful inclinations credited to the original inhabitants of North America resemble the higher sentiments ascribed to women. Indeed, Indian women in her stories and poems are often the special champions and expressions of intergroup harmony. Whether nature or nur-

ture creates this phenomenon is never clear. Today it seems best explained as part of the idealization of the oppressed that characterizes much resistance writing. The essential moderation of Johnson's appeal is reaffirmed by her associated message of the need for mutual forgiveness. She leaves it to a character to explain: "Forgive the wrongs my children did to you, And we, the red-skins, will forgive you too" (cited in Van Steen, 263).

European settlers are also encouraged to reconsider their bloody history of contact with other peoples. Her poems "Wolverine" and "The Cattle Thief" testify eloquently to ignorance, irrationality, and violence, and their cost in Native lives. In one story, a formerly jingoistic hero reconsiders the Boer War and recants old allegiances. The death of a good friend makes him realize that "the glory had paled and vanished. There was nothing left of this terrible war but the misery, the mourning, the heartbreak of it all" (1913, 211). Such reflections suggest Johnson's affinities with the liberal critics who questioned Britain's attack on the Boers (Schoeman; Koss; Page). The same critique of British morality informs her condemnation of the Christian churches' treatment of Natives. It also explains her contribution to the international condemnation of official France's antisemitism in the Alfred Dreyfus affair. In "Give Us Barrabas," she exposes supposedly civilized Europe as diseased, "leprous," without claim to moral authority (1972, 118–8).[33] In her writings, Native peoples supply Canada with ready sources of indigenous virtue.

The key to Johnson's understanding of the best course for the new nation is inclusiveness and partnership—between Native and British and between female and male. The highly visible women who crowd narratives are ultimately "sisters under the skin." In articulating key values, they are not passive bystanders in history but forces to be reckoned with. Their courage, loyalty, generosity, and persistence will anchor a young nation into the future. Pauline Johnson's Canada, like the "land of the fair deal" proposed by Nellie McClung, charts an important place for women in the creation of civil society.

Superior qualities justify adoption into the Canadian "tribe," but Johnson also hopes that the fact of being "Canadian-born" will itself create shared sympathies and qualities. The title poem of her second volume of verse suggests that offspring of aristocrats and common folk can grow up, like the members of the NWMP, in harmony and equality, the products of an essentially beneficent northern environment. The "glory" of a "clean colonial name," of fresh beginnings, is enough to make "millionaires" of all (cited in Van Steen, 271). In the new Dominion, Euro-First Nations individuals are well equipped to claim citizenship as their "blood heritage" (ibid.). In one story, where a member of the British elite is typically required to draw the appropriate moral, a governor general repudiates the prejudices of lesser men in defending a Euro-First Nation boy: "The blood of old France and the blood of a great aboriginal race [Cree] that is the offshoot of no other race in the world. The Indian blood is a thing of itself, unmixed for thousands of years, a blood that is distinct and exclusive. Few White people can claim such a lineage. Boy, try and remember that as you come of Indian blood, dashed with that of the first great soldiers, settlers and pioneers in this vast Dominion, that you have one of the proudest places and heritages in the world. You are a Canadian in the greatest sense of the great word...you are the real Canadian" (cited in Van Steen, 272–3). As these remarks suggest, the issue of race was important—and dangerous. Race could confer virtue and intermarriage, even among great "races," and it could compromise the purity increasingly valued by the racial theorists of the day. Hybridity might combine the best; it might also bring with it degeneration. In opt-

ing for hope, Johnson denies the prejudices of the age. The hybrid Canada she attempts to will into being is to repudiate the corrupt heritage of European racism.

Johnson's hopes appear especially rooted in the West, where she spent many of the later years of her life. "Booster" poems, such as "The Sleeping Giant" on Thunder Bay; "Calgary of the Plains"; "Brandon"; "Golden of the Selkirks"; and, the most rambunctious of all, "A Toast" (dedicated to Vancouver), celebrate the erasure of past differences (1972, 110, 158–9, 133, 96, 121–2). In the future, individuals and races are to be taken on their own merits. Such cities, like Canada itself, do not care who you have been, only what you may contribute to an emerging identity.

The nation described by Johnson struggles with racism and sexism. The future of Native and Euro-First Nations peoples absorb her, to the exclusion of any examination of how non-British Europeans and others might fit in. Confronted with the vulnerability of First Nations communities in her day, Johnson had no hope of taking back the country, of returning Europeans to their own homelands. However she might celebrate the virtues of Native peoples, she has to deal with the ongoing reality of injustice, of conquest and settlement, with no other explanation than, as one of her characters says, "perhaps the white man's God has willed it so" (1972, 19). Her hopes rest with a renewal of the old partnership that had united the British and the Iroquois in the War of American Independence and with a recognition of women's value. In her attention to the injustices suffered by women and First Nations, Pauline Johnson voices something more than the "sentimental nationalism" some critics have seen (Doyle, 50–8). In her hands, "nationalism" becomes "one of the most powerful weapons for resisting colonialism and for establishing the space of a post-colonial identity" (Donaldson, 8).

A Postcolonial Liberal Inheritance

We know little of how Pauline Johnson's audiences received her views and almost nothing of her reception by First Nations listeners. For the most part, only one part of a conversation has survived. To be sure, there are clues. A veteran of the 1885 Prairie campaign, in near tears upon hearing "A Cry from an Indian Wife," confessed, "When I heard you recite that poem, I never felt so ashamed in my life of the part I took in it" (cited in Keller, 60). A host in a small Manitoba town was heard to say, by way of introduction, "Now, friends, before Miss Johnson's exercises begin, I want you all to remember that Injuns, like us, is folks" (121). The liberalism of the supposed "colour blindness" embodied in these remarks suggests one influential source of support for Johnson. Her appeal to a tolerance and fair-mindedness based on a faith in a universal humanity convinced at least some receptive listeners. A few in her audiences understood some part of the message about First Nations, women, and Canada that she tried to deliver.

It is also clear that part of Johnson's appeal was her apparent lack of threat. Some listeners and readers, like one 1892 reviewer, enjoyed the fact that "speaking through this cultured, gifted, soft-voiced descendant" was the "voice of the nations who once possessed this country, who have wasted away before our civilization" (cited in Francis, 113). Representatives of dead or dying competitors for resources are easy to patronize, especially when they promise the illusion of a stronger national connection with the natural landscape. As Daniel Francis suggests in *The Imaginary Indian,* "Having successfully subdued the Indians, Whites could afford to get sentimental about them" (123). Such scepticism is, however, only part of the story. It does not capture the common ambivalence and the outright opposition of some white Canadians to the abuses of European and male power. Johnson always had sympathizers. Her subversion of traditions that consign women and Natives to subordination and anonymity are significant, nourishing recurring liberal hopes for a more pluralist and egalitarian society. In her own way, like other resistance writers and performers at the turn of the century, Pauline Johnson prepared society to "relinquish or modify" the idea of domination (Said, 200). Today she has literary heirs in Euro-First Nations writers like Beatrice Culleton, Maria Campbell, Beth Brant, and Lee Maracle who, too, name injustice and call for an equal partnership in a reformed nation (Lundgren; Brant).

Notes
ACKNOWLEDGMENTS

My thanks to the "Race and Gender Group," whose discussions have been supported by a SSHRCC Strategic Grant 1992–5. Thanks too for the comments of Gillian Creese, Julie Cruikshank, Margery Fee, Carole Gerson, Nitya Iyer, Jane M. Jacobs, Kathy Mezei, Dorothy Seaton, Donald Smith, Wendy Wickwire, Donald Wilson, and members of the audience at a talk based on this chapter that I gave to Native Studies and Women's Studies at the University of Toronto on 22 April 1996. I would also like to thank Lorraine Snowden for her research assistance.

1   This chapter employs the terms "Indian," "Native," "Aboriginal," and "First Nation" to refer to the original human inhabitants of North America, excluding the Inuit peoples of the North. Turn-of-the-century Canada regularly referred to individuals and populations who are a product of Indian-French unions as Métis and to those who are a product of Indian-British unions as "mixed bloods." "Half-breed" was used to refer to both groups. In order to avoid the racism embodied in such usage, I have used the term Euro-First Nation to refer to such individuals and groups. "European" is used in reference to individuals, Canadian and otherwise, whose families originate in the continent of Europe. So far as I have discovered, Pauline Johnson chose to refer to herself as Iroquois, Mohawk, Indian, and "red" or "redskin."

2   For a fascinating discussion of contemporary women performing artists, see Forte. I would also like to thank Dr. Merlinda Bobis (herself a performance artist) of the Faculty of Creative Arts, University of Wollongong, Australia, for her assistance in making this connection to Johnson.

3   For the limits and opportunities of "performance," see the essays in Diamond, especially the "Introduction" by Diamond and Rebecca Schneider, "After Us the Savage Goddess."

4   Said (210). See also Turner, who provides a useful exploration of selected Canadian texts that attempt to create "new discursive space" for a postcolonial nation. Turner focuses on Euro-Canadian writers, and Johnson is not a concern.

5   Her father, for example, was active, to the point of being assaulted by non-Natives, in efforts to protect Indian timber and Indians from the liquor trade. See Keller and also Barron.

6   The classic feminist figure of this international liberalism was Lady Ishbel Gordon, Countess of Aberdeen, disciple of William Gladstone and founder of the National Council of Women of Canada in 1893. See Saywell and Strong-Boag.

7   On the role of children of Indian/European unions, see Brown (204–11). George M.H. Johnson was the son of Helen Martin (d. 1866), the daughter of the Mohawk George Martin and Catherine Rolleston (a woman of German background who was captured during a raid on Pennsylvania settlements), and John Johnson (1792–1886), hero of the War of 1812 and the speaker of the Council of the Six Nations. See also Smith (1987) for an important account of the efforts of one outstanding Euro-First Nation individual to find accommodation between the Native peoples and European settlers in early nineteenth-century Ontario.

8   On the development of Brantford's middle class, see Burley. Unfortunately, this study makes no mention of Native peoples and pays little attention to the role of women. See Johnston, especially Chapter 10, for greater, although still limited, attention to the Iroquois Confederacy.

9   On British imperialism and patriarchy in these years, see Ramusack and Burton (469–81).

10   See, for example, the writers (Dr. Peter Martin or Oronhyatekha [1841–1907], Frederick Ogilvie Loft [1861–1934], Levi General or Deskeheh [1873–1925], and John Ojijatekha Brant-Sero [1867–1914]—all closely associated with the Grand River reserve) who regularly challenged prejudices. Brant-Sero, for example, campaigned to win recognition of the Iroquois as the first United Empire Loyalists, founders of Canada itself. (See Petrone, Chapters 2, 3, 4.)

11   See, for example, the case of the dancer described in McBride. My thanks to Trudy Nicks of the Royal Ontario Museum for drawing this volume and the issue in general to my attention. See also the related situation of the Australian Aborigines discussed in Poignant. My thanks to Kay Schaffer of the University of Adelaide for giving me a copy of this volume.

12   Landsman (274). See also Wagner. For a critical assessment of women's power in Iroquois society, see Tooker.

13   See Levi General or Deskeheh as cited in Petrone (104).

14   On this myth, see the now classic article by Green (1975, 698–714). See also Larson (Chapter 2, "The Children of Pocahontas").

15   Her efforts to combine European and Native traditions are also seen in the work of contemporary writers like Lee Maracle. See Lundgren (69).

16   See the comments in her letter to a friendly critic, cited in Petrone (82–3).

17   Kidwell (97). On the role of the wilderness and the function of Native guides, see Jasen (especially Chapters 4 and 5).

18   See Smith (1990). Buffy Sainte-Marie is a folksinger and songwriter born at the Piapot Reserve in Saskatchewan in 1941.

19   See Keller on Johnson's failed romances and recurring financial problems.

20   Somewhat later, Iroquois women such as the

American activists Minnie Kellogg (1880–1948) and Alice Lee Jemison (1901–64) would also assume major public roles as critics of European prejudice. Kellogg was born at the Oneida Indian Reservation in Wisconsin and educated at Stanford, Barnard, and Columbia's School of Philanthropy. She married a non-Indian lawyer and became an activist in the Society of American Indians and a powerful writer. She was the author of *Our Democracy and the American Indian* (1920). Alice Lee Jemison was born in New York State, graduated from high school, married a Seneca steelworker, and worked at various jobs while active as an outspoken critic of the American Indian Bureau. See Hauptman (1981, 12 and passim). See also Hauptman (1986, and passim; 1985). At least one powerful speaker from another tribe also appeared somewhat earlier. See Sarah Winnemucca (1844?–1891), the American Northern Paiute woman who produced the autobiography *Life among the Paiutes: Their Wrongs and Claims* (1883). See Canfield. Unfortunately, we do not know whether Pauline Johnson knew of such women.

21 See, for example, her characterization of Red Jacket's thought as "liberal, and strong, / He blessed the little good and passed the wrong / Embodied in the weak" (cited in Van Steen, 47).

22 See Carter and Andrews.

23 "My Mother" (1987, 64–5). See also her poem, "The Derelict" (1972).

24 See Titley. See also the more sympathetic view of Scott's treatment of Indians in Dragland.

25 Death and disappearance are also major themes for contributors to the section, "The Indian," in Lighthall.

26 On British Columbia in these years, see the important studies by Barman and Tennant.

27 On "unnaming," see Ashcroft, Griffiths, and Tiffin (141). On similar efforts by other Native writers, see Petrone (Chapters 2 and 3).

28 See Van Kirk (49–68).

29 See, for example, the arguments in McClung (1915).

30 Her nom de plume (1900, 440–2).

31 See, for example, the otherwise excellent "Introduction" by A. LaVonne Ruoff (Johnson 1987).

32 See Prucha. On Canadian assumptions of superiority, see Owram.

33 On the significance of the Dreyfus affair as a touchstone for the liberalism of the day, see Wilson and Feldman.

Works Cited

Andrews, Isabel. 1975. "Indian Protest Against Starvation: The Yellow Calf Incident of 1884." *Saskatchewan History* 28 (2):41–51.

Ashcroft, Bill, Gareth Griffiths, and Helen Tiffin. 1993. *The Empire Writes Back. Theory and Practice in Post-Colonial Literature.* London and New York: Routledge.

Bacchi, Carol Lee. 1983. *Liberation Deferred? The Ideas of the English-Canadian Suffragists,1877–1918.* Toronto: University of Toronto Press.

Barman, Jean. 1991. *The West Beyond the West. A History of British Columbia.* Toronto: University of Toronto Press.

Barron, F.L. 1983. "Alcoholism, Indians and the Anti-Drink Cause in the Protestant Indian Missions of Upper Canada, 1822–1850." In I.A.L. Getty and A.S. Lussier, eds., *As Long as the Sun Shines and Water Flows: A Reader in Canadian Native Studies,* 191–202. Vancouver: UBC Press.

Bashevkin, Sylvia. 1985. *Toeing the Lines: Women and Party Politics in English Canada.* Toronto: University of Toronto Press.

Berger, Carl. 1971. *The Sense of Power: Studies in Ideas of Canadian Imperialism, 1867–1914.* Toronto: University of Toronto Press.

Brant, Beth. 1994. *Writing as Witness: Essay and Talk.* Toronto: Women's Press.

Brown, Jennifer. 1980. *Strangers in Blood: Fur Trade Company Families in Indian Country.* Vancouver: UBC Press.

Burley, David G. 1993. *A Particular Condition in Life: Self-Employment and Social Mobility in Mid-Victorian Brantford, Ontario.* Toronto: University of Toronto Press.

Butler, Judith. 1990. "Performative Acts and Gender Constitution: An Essay in Phenomenology and Feminist Theory." In Sue-Ellen Case, ed., *Performing Feminism: Feminist Critical Theory and Theatre,* 270–82. Baltimore and London: Johns Hopkins University Press.

———. 1993. *Bodies That Matter: On the Discursive Limits of "Sex."* London: Routledge.

Canfield, Gae Whitney. 1983. *Sara Winnemucca of the Northern Paiutes*. Norman: University of Oklahoma Press.

Carter, Sarah. 1990. *Lost Harvest: Prairie Indian Reserve Farmers and Government Policy*. Montreal and Kingston: McGill-Queen's University Press.

Dean, Misao. 1991. *A Different Point of View: Sara Jeannette Duncan*. Montreal and Kingston: McGill-Queen's University Press.

Diamond, Elin, ed. 1996. *Performance and Cultural Politics*. London and New York: Routledge.

Donaldson, Laura E. 1992. *Decolonizing Feminisms. "Race," Gender, and Empire Building*. Chapel Hill and London: University of North Carolina Press.

Doyle, James. 1994. "Sui Sin Far and Onoto Watanna: Two Early Chinese-Canadian Authors." *Canadian Literature/Literature canadienne* 140 (Spring):50–8.

Dragland, S.L. 1974. *Duncan Campbell Scott: A Book of Criticism*. Ottawa: Tecumseh.

Drees, Laurie Meijer. 1995. "Introduction to Documents One through Five: Nationalism, the League of Nations and the Six Nations of Grand River." *Native Studies Review* 10 (1):75–88.

Emberly, Julia V. 1993. *Thresholds of Difference: Feminist Critique, Native Women's Writings, Post-Colonial Theory*. Toronto: University of Toronto Press.

Feldman, Egal. 1981. *The Dreyfus Affair and the American Conscience, 1895–1906*. Detroit: Wayne State University Press.

Forte, Jeanie. 1990. "Women's Performance Art: Feminism and Postmodernism." In Sue-Ellen Case, ed., *Performing Feminisms: Feminist Critical Theory and Theatre*, 251–69. Baltimore and London: Johns Hopkins University Press.

Foster, W. Garland. 1931. *The Mohawk Princess: Being Some Account of the Life of TEKAFHON-WAKE (E. Pauline Johnson)*. Vancouver: Lions' Gate.

Francis, Daniel. 1993. *The Imaginary Indian: The Image of the Indian in Canadian Culture*. Vancouver: Arsenal Pulp.

Grant, Agnes. 1994. "Reclaiming the Lineage House: Canadian Native Women Writers." *SAIL* 6 (1):43–62.

Green, Heather. 1994. "This Piece Done, I Shall Be Renamed." In Carol Camper, ed., *Miscegenation Blues*, 291–303. Toronto: Sister Vision.

Green, Rayna. 1975. "The Pocahontas Perplex: The Image of Indian Women in American Culture." *Massachusetts Review* 16 (4):698–714.

Hauptman, Lawrence M. 1981. *The Iroquois and the New Deal*. Syracuse: Syracuse University Press.

———. 1985. "Designing Woman: Laura Minnie Cornelius Kellogg, Iroquois Leader." In Raymond Wilson and L.G. Moses, eds., *Indian Lives*, 159–86. Albuquerque: University of New Mexico Press.

———. 1986. *The Iroquois Struggle for Survival: World War II to Red Power*. Syracuse: Syracuse University Press.

Jasen, Patricia. 1995. *Wild Things: Nature, Culture, and Tourism in Ontario 1790–1914*. Toronto: University of Toronto Press.

Johnson, E. Pauline (Tekahionwake). 1900. "One of Them [Pauline Johnson]." "The Iroquois Women of Canada." *Women of Canada. Their Life and Work*. Ottawa: National Council of Women of Canada.

———. 1913. *The Shagganappi*. Toronto: William Briggs.

———. 1926 [1911]. *Legends of Vancouver*. Toronto: McClelland & Stewart.

——— 1972 [1911]. *Flint and Feather. The Complete Poems of E. Pauline Johnson*. Toronto: Paperjacks.

———. 1987 [1913]. *The Moccasin Maker*. Introduction, Annotation, and Bibliography by A. LaVonne Brown Ruoff. Tucson: University of Arizona Press.

Johnston, Charles M. Brant. 1967. *Brant County: A History 1786–1945*. Toronto: Oxford University Press.

Keller, Betty. 1981. *Pauline. A Biography of Pauline Johnson*. Vancouver and Toronto: Douglas and McIntyre.

Kidwell, Clara Sue. 1992. "Indian Women as Cultural Mediators." *Ethnohistory* 39 (2):97–107.

Koss, Stephen. 1973. *The Pro-Boers: The Anatomy of an Anti-War Movement*. Chicago: University of Chicago Press.

Landsman, Gail. 1992. "The 'Other' as Political Symbol: Images of Indians in the Woman Suffrage Movement." *Ethnohistory* 39 (3):247–84.

Larson, Charles R. 1978. *American Indian Fiction*. Albuquerque: University of New Mexico Press.

Leacock, Stephen. 1973. "Greater Canada: An Appeal." In A. Bowker, ed., *The Social Criticism of Stephen Leacock*, 3–11. Toronto: University of Toronto Press.

Lighthall, William D. 1892. *Canadian Songs and Poems: Voices from the Forests and Waters, the Settlements and Cities of Canada*. London: Walter Scott.

Lundgren, Jodi. 1995. "'Being a Half-Breed': Discourses on Race and Cultural Syncreticity in the Works of Three Metis Women Writers." *Canadian Literature* 144 (Spring):62–79.

McBride, Bunny. 1995. *Molly Spotted Elk: A Penobscot in Paris*. Norman and London: University of Oklahoma Press.

McClung, Nellie L. 1915. *In Times Like These*. Toronto: Thomas Allen.

———. 1945. *The Stream Runs Fast*. Toronto: Thomas Allen.

MacDonald, Mary Lu. 1990. "Red & White; Black, White & Grey Hats." In W.H. New, ed., *Native Writers and Canadian Writing*, 92–111. Vancouver: UBC Press.

Martin, Christoper. 1967. *The Russo-Japanese War*. London and New York: Abelard-Schuman.

Owram, Douglas R. 1972. "European Savagery: Some Canadian Reaction to American Indian Policy, 1867–1885." MA thesis, Queen's University, Kingston, Ontario.

Page, Robert. 1987. *The Boer War and Canadian Imperialism*. Ottawa: Canadian Historical Association.

Petrone, Penny. 1990. *Native Literature: From the Oral Tradition to the Present*. Toronto: Oxford University Press.

Poignant, Roslyn. 1993. "Captive Aboriginal Lives: Billy, Jenny, Little Toby and Their Companions." *Captured Lives: Australian Captivity Narratives. Working Papers in Australian Studies*, 85, 86, 87. The Sir Robert Menzies Centre for Australian Studies and the Institute for Commonwealth Studies: University of London.

Prentice, Alison, et al. 1996. *Canadian Women: A History*. 2nd edition. Toronto: Harcourt Brace.

Prucha, Francis P. 1986. *The Great Father: The United States Government and the American Indians*. Lincoln and London: University of Nebraska Press.

Ramusack, Barbara, and Antoinette Burton. 1994. "Feminism, Imperialism and Race: A Dialogue Between India and Britain." *Women's History Review* 3 (4):469–81.

Said, Edward. 1994. *Culture and Imperialism*. New York: Vintage.

Saywell, John T., ed. 1960. *The Canadian Journal of Lady Aberdeen, 1893–1898*. Toronto: Champlain Society.

Shimony, Annemarie Anrod. 1994. *Conservatism among the Iroquois at the Six Nations Reserve*. Syracuse: Syracuse University Press.

Shoeman, Karel. 1992. *Only an Anguish to Live Here: Olive Schreiner and the Anglo Boer War, 1899–1902*. Cape Town: Human and Rousseau.

Silvera, Makeda, ed. 1995. "Maria Campbell Talks to Beth Cuthand: 'It's the Job of the storyteller to Create Chaos.'" In *The Other Woman: Women of Colour in Contemporary Canadian Literature*, 264–70. Toronto: Sister Vision.

Smith, Donald. 1987. *Sacred Feathers: The Reverend Peter Jones (Kahkewaquonaby) and the Mississauga Indian*. Toronto: University of Toronto Press.

———. 1990. *From the Land of Shadows: The Making of Grey Owl*. Saskatoon: Western Producer Prairie Books.

Strong-Boag, Veronica. 1976. *The Parliament of Women: The National Council of Women of Canada*. Ottawa: National Museums of Canada.

Tennant, Paul. 1990. *Aboriginal Peoples and Politics: The Indian Land Question in British Columbia, 1849–1989*. Vancouver: UBC Press.

Titley, E. Brian. 1986. *A Narrow Vision: Duncan Campbell Scott and the Administration of Indian Affairs in Canada*. Vancouver: UBC Press.

Tooker, Elisabeth. 1996. "Women in Iroquois Society." In Wendy Mitchinson et al., eds., *Canadian Women: A Reader*, 19–32. Toronto: Harcourt Brace.

Turner, Margaret E. 1995. *Imagining Culture. New World Narrative and the Writing of Canada*. Montreal and Kingston: McGill-Queen's University Press.

Valverde, Marianna. 1991. *The Age of Light, Soap, and Water: Moral Reform in English Canada, 1885–1925*. Toronto: McClelland & Stewart.

Van Kirk, Sylvia. 1976. "'The Custom of the Country': An Examination of Fur Trade Marriage Practices." In L.H. Thomas, ed., *Essays on Western History*, 49–68. Edmonton: University of Alberta Press.

Van Steen, Marcus. 1965. *Pauline Johnson: Her Life and Work*. Toronto: Musson.

Wagner, Sally Roesch. 1990. "The Root of Oppression Is the Loss of Memory: The Iroquois and the Earliest Feminist Vision." In W.G. Spittal, ed., *Iroquois Women. An Anthology*, 223–8. Ohsweken, ON: Iroqcrafts.

Walden, Keith. 1982. *Visions of Order*. Toronto: Butterworths.

Weaver, Sally M. 1972. *Medicine and Politics among the Grand River Iroquois: A Study of the Non-Conservatives.* Publications in Ethnology, No. 4. Ottawa: National Museums of Canada.

———. 1994. "The Iroquois: The Grand River Reserve in the Late Nineteenth and Early Twentieth Centuries, 1875–1945." In E.S. Rogers and Donald B. Smith, eds., *Aboriginal Ontario: Historical Perspectives on the First Nations,* 213–57. Toronto and Oxford: Dundurn.

Wilson, Stephen. 1982. *Ideology and Experience: Anti-Semitism in France at the Time of the Dreyfus Affair.* London: Associated University Presses.

The Roots of Modernism
Darwinism and the Higher Critics

RAMSAY COOK

Karl Marx, no mere dabbler in theological questions, concluded in 1844 that "the criticism of religion is the presupposition of all criticism." To make his meaning unmistakable, he continued: "The abolition of the *illusory* happiness of the people is the demand for their *real* happiness. The demand to abandon the illusions about their condition is the *demand to give up a condition* that required illusions. Hence criticism of religion is in embryo a *criticism of this vale of tears* whose halo is religion."[1] For Marx the only salvation was to be found in this world, and the road to that predestined classless society followed the path traced by historical materialism. All other religions preached illusory destinies.

That religious belief sanctioned the social order, became something of a commonplace conviction in the nineteenth century, even among non-Marxists. Those who agreed with Marx in wanting to change society attacked religious belief, at least as traditionally taught, for that very reason. If it could be demonstrated that religion was false, or at least misinterpreted and misapplied, then the legitimacy of the established order that religion supported could also be brought into question. For Marx, religious belief, particularly the Christian claim that man's ultimate relief from his sufferings in "this vale of tears" would come in the eternal life hereafter, was nothing more than an opiate, sure evidence of alienation. Only in a world unfettered by such illusions, a secular world, would men and women be free to concentrate on mundane conditions and eventually realize that those conditions could be changed. Secularism then would not only destroy the claims of religion, it would also challenge the legitimacy of the social order.[2]

Though Marx's teachings played only a marginal role in the rise of Canadian social criticism,[3] his point about the role of religion in society was widely accepted both by conservatives and social critics. Indeed, in Canada criticism of society was rooted in criticism of religion. Yet, in contrast to Marx, Canadian critics of religious orthodoxy were rarely advocates of atheism, nor would many of them have admitted that their goal was a thoroughly secular society. Instead, their aim was almost invariably a reinterpretation of Christianity to make it more relevant to the supposed everyday world of Canadians. Virtually every social reformer in late Victorian Canada wanted to stand orthodox Christian teaching on its head. Rather than sanctioning the social order, social critics argued, Christianity properly interpreted should provide the standard against which society should be judged. Implicit, sometimes even explicit, in that contention was the conviction that society so judged would be found sadly wanting.

I

The critique of religious orthodoxy which eventually led to the "social gospel" that formed the

Ramsay Cook, "The Roots of Modernism: Darwinism and the Higher Critics," in *The Regenerators: Social Criticism in Late Victorian English Canada* by Ramsay Cook (Toronto: University of Toronto Press, 1985), 7–25. Reprinted by permission of the publisher.

essence of social criticism in English Canada originated in the religious and theological turmoil of the last third of the nineteenth century. That there was such a turmoil, even what could be accurately called a "crisis of belief," in Protestant Canada that paralleled similar events in Great Britain and the United States, is readily demonstrated.[4] Virtually every issue of the *Canadian Monthly and National Review*, the leading intellectual quarterly of late Victorian Canada, provided illustrations of that crisis. That publication and others regularly carried contributions by Goldwin Smith, Professor John Watson, Agnes Machar, Principal G.M. Grant, Principal William Dawson, and W.D. LeSueur, to name only the most prominent, on topics of science and religion, biblical criticism, positivism, and philosophical idealism. What was true of secular magazines was even more evident in the religious publications—*The Christian Guardian, The Westminster, The Canadian Methodist Quarterly,* and others. Nor were these topics ignored by the popular press. Within the courts and colleges of the Protestant churches and in the minds and consciences of individual ministers and laymen, questions of fundamental religious importance were regularly debated. "The struggle for physical well-being, with which we in this country have hitherto been mainly occupied," Professor John Watson of Queen's University wrote in 1876, "has served as a breakwater to the tide of scepticism which has already swept over Europe; but the roar of its waters is now in our ears and its spray on our faces, and we can only hope to keep all that we most highly value from being torn from the grasp of the more cultured among us, by calmly and manfully facing the emergency."[5]

Watson had only just arrived in Canada, bringing to the department of philosophy at Queen's University a Scottish interpretation of Hegelian idealism that would become a major influence in the development of theological liberalism in Canada. Though he personally laboured manfully in facing the emergency he identified,

his influence in the long run probably contributed in a major way to the triumph of the secular forces he had warned against. But he was certainly not the first to realize that Canadians were far from immune to the currents of religious and philosophical dispute so prominent elsewhere. As early as 1860 the then principal of Queen's University had rung the alarm bells loudly at the opening of the new university term. "The newspaper, the magazine, the novel, teem with theological speculation, put in the most attractive forms," he worried out loud, "...One cannot mingle much in society without finding that a large proportion of the well-educated classes are conversant with the questions which arise from the apparent conflict of faith and reason, and the difficulties started by the progress of science."[6]

From the viewpoint of the leading spokesmen for Protestantism in English Canada, the most dramatic challenge to the traditional Christian understanding of man came from science. "Assaults have been made upon her from various positions and by different engines," Professor Watson, remarking upon the embattled position of theology, wrote in 1876, "but it is probably from the vantage point of science, and by scientific artillery, that she has been exposed to the fiercest and roughest kind of battery."[7] Science in general seemed to raise questions about religious teaching, but what most late nineteenth-century writers meant by "science" was the view put forward in 1859 by Charles Darwin in *On the Origin of Species*. The debate that revolutionary volume set off in Great Britain and the United States had its counterpart in Canada.[8] Most of that controversy, at least in the non-scientific intellectual world, turned less on the validity of the evolution-by-natural-selection hypothesis than on the theological implications which Darwinism appeared to bear for the biblical account of creation and man. It was more a debate about "evolution" than about Darwinism, more about religion than about science.

Nevertheless, the most important contributor to the Darwinian controversy in Canada took serious issue with the new wisdom on both scientific and theological grounds. Sir William Dawson, principal of McGill University, was Canada's most eminent scientist in the nineteenth century. A geologist of international standing, Dawson was also an accomplished university administrator and, not least important, a Presbyterian of unshakeable conviction.[9] As a scientist and a Presbyterian, Dawson belonged to that dominant pre-Darwinian school of geological thought which insisted that "natural history must devote itself to exhibiting evidence of divine design and of material Providence."[10] For Dawson, religion could no more be banished from science than it could be separated from life. He recognized that Darwin's determination to separate science from religion would almost certainly lead to a separation of religion from life. And that separation had implications that went far beyond the scientific laboratory. He therefore took up the defence of natural theology against the claims of scientific naturalism.

Dawson read, reviewed, and rejected—at least in part—On the Origin of Species almost immediately after it came off the press. His first response was temperate but firm. He confessed admiration for the careful empirical work upon which the study was based, but he rejected the Darwinian procedure. Dawson insisted that the Baconian empirical method was the only truly scientific one and that Darwin, by setting out to test a hypothesis, had sinned against orthodox science. (He would later refer to Darwin's rejection of "the Baconian mode" as a "return to the mediaeval plan of setting up dogmas based on authority only.")[11] Nor did he find Darwin's evidence compelling; as Dawson correctly pointed out, the fossil record contained too many gaps to support Darwin's contention that evolution of species rather than fixity of species should be accepted by science.[12] Though

Dawson's first response to Darwin was moderate and based mainly on scientific reservations, he nevertheless shared the conviction expressed by Professor E.J. Chapman, who taught geology and mineralogy at the University of Toronto, and whose review of On the Origin of Species concluded with a reaffirmation of the traditional Paleyite argument for nature's divine design. "Certain facts are given," he wrote, "certain remarkable phenomena are witnessed everywhere around us. We are asked to explain them. We are forced to confess they transcend our explanation. We are asked to explain how the world comes to be peopled by so many very different plants and animals. We reply, by the act of the Creator; these plants and animals being essentially unchanged descendants of species created at the commencement of the existing state of things."[13] Indeed, in the same year that Dawson reviewed On the Origin of Species (1860) he published a fat volume entitled Archaia; or, Studies of the Cosmogony and Natural History of the Hebrew Scriptures, in which he mounted what he insisted was a scientifically documented defence of the Old Testament account of creation. Dawson was never to be swayed from his conviction that "it can easily be shown that there are important points of agreement between the simple story of Eden, as we have it in Genesis, and scientific probabilities as to the origin of man."[14]

Though the Canadian scientific community gradually and quietly came to terms with the Darwinian hypothesis,[15] Principal Dawson, who after the death of Louis Agassiz in 1873 became the leading scientific anti-Darwinian, grew increasingly hostile and shrill. As Darwin's influence spread, Dawson's pen poured forth millions of words designed to stem the tide of the new biological thinking. While his objections continued to be illustrated by geological evidence and interpretation, the essential assumption of his position was that science "is the exponent of the plans and works of the great Creative Will....

Men must know God as the Creator, even before they seek him as a benefactor and redeemer." By the 1870s he had become convinced that by expelling God from science, Darwin had opened the doors to the deluge which, unless diked, would swamp not only true science but also religion, society, and man himself. A profound conservatism animated his condemnation of the "evolutionists": "They seek to revolutionize the religious beliefs of the world," he wrote in *The Story of Earth and Man,* "and if accepted would destroy most of the existing theology and philosophy. They indicate tendencies among scientific thinkers which, though probably temporary, must before they disappear, descend to lower strata, and reproduce themselves in grosser forms, and with most serious effects on the whole structure of society. With one class of minds they constitute a sort of religion, which so far satisfied the craving for truths, higher than those that relate to immediate wants and pleasures. With another, and perhaps larger class, they are accepted as affording a welcome deliverance from all scruples of conscience and fears of a hereafter. In the domain of science evolution has like tendencies. It reduces the position of man, who becomes a descendant of inferior animals, and a mere term in a series whose end is unknown. It removes from the study of nature the ideas of final cause and purpose."[16]

To deny knowledge of the chief end of man and reject the idea of final cause and purpose in nature was, in Dawson's view, subversive. The struggle against Darwin was more than a scientific combat. That was important, for Dawson loved science only slightly less than he loved God, his family, and perhaps McGill University. But Darwinism was more than bad science, for bad science also threatened religious and social certainties. "The mind of our time," he wrote in 1890, "is unsettled and restless. It has the vague impression that science has given it power to solve all mysteries. It is intoxicated with its physical success, and has no proper measure of

its own powers." Here was the making of an undisciplined and therefore dangerous intelligence, one that threatened to break the bounds of that moral authority founded on religion. The social consequences were ominous. "At a lower level," the McGill principal warned, "it is evident that the ideas of struggle for existence, and survival of the fittest, introduced by the new philosophy, and its resolution of man himself into a mere spontaneous improvement of brute ancestors, have stimulated to an intense degree that popular unrest so natural to an age discontented with its lot, because it has learned what it might do and have, without being able to realize its expectations, and which threatens to overthrow the whole fabric of society as at present constituted."[17] These dark forebodings were hardly surprising in a man of Dawson's religious persuasion. A God banished from Nature could hardly expect to remain a bulwark of the social order. Since Dawson believed in the "fundamental unity and harmony of all truth, whether natural or spiritual, whether discovered by man or revealed by God," the denial of God's place in the natural order undermined his role in the social order and promised social chaos. Social conservatism went hand in hand with scientific conservatism, and both were founded on religious conservatism.[18]

Though many late Victorian Canadians joined Dawson in the struggle against godless Darwinism,[19] few were as total in their rejection as the McGill geologist. Outside the scientific world the chief concern was not so much with Darwin's *On the Origin of Species* as with Darwin's *The Descent of Man,* published in 1871. The contention that man was an animal, perhaps just a little above the ape, rather than God's special creation was an "unspeakably momentous" idea which many found too unsettling or too ludicrous to accept.[20] The Toronto magazine *Grip,* whose satire always had a serious Christian purpose, thought the whole idea could be reduced to ridicule. In an 1880 issue

J.W. Bengough, the editor of *Grip*, published a poem entitled "Evolution Made Plain."

Once upon a time
There was a little bit of slime
  In the deep, deep bottom of the sea;
And it commenced to breathe,
Without anybody's leave,
  And that was the beginning of you and me.

It sucked the green sea water, —
It was neither son nor daughter,
  But a little bit of both done up in one,
And from it soon evolved,
While the old world still revolv'd,
  A being which we'll nominate its son.

The son the father hated,
And so 'differentiated';
  Its son in course of time just followed suit, —
So it grew by many stages,
Through fifty million ages,
  Till in the course of time it reached the newt.

The newt was awful gritty,
And *knew't* would be a pity,
  To leave the world no better than his *pater*
So he turned him inside out,
Knowing what he was about,
  And, lo! became an animal much greater.

He, too, went on evolving,
The riddle ever solving
  Of his destiny, and bound to solve it soon;
So he taller grew and fatter,
And one day commenced to chatter,
  And found himself a bouncing big baboon.

While his tail was long and growing,
He wore it quite off rowing
  A la HANLAN on a patent sliding seat;
Then he went and killed his brothers,
Made soup of some, and others
  Served up with roast potatoes and some beet.

The 'survival of the fittest,'
See! reader, as thou sittest,
  Is the proper and most scientific plan —
This ape surprised the others,
Both his sisters and his brothers,
  And in course of time became a gentleman.[21]

Even some prominent scientists found Darwin's conclusions unacceptable when applied to man. Alfred Russel Wallace, the co-discoverer of evolution by natural selection, rejected the materialistic implications of *The Descent of Man* and turned to spiritualism as a method of demonstrating man's spiritual distinctiveness.[22] One of Dawson's fellow Canadian academics, Daniel Wilson, found an equally ingenious method of escape. Wilson, who had scientific training, taught history and literature at the University of Toronto. As befitted a nineteenth-century scholar, his interests ranged widely and included ethnology and anthropology. In 1873 he offered his contribution to the growing list of speculations about man's origins.[23] He turned to Shakespeare's *The Tempest*, arguing that Caliban was the missing link, neither man nor animal, separating man, with his mind, intelligence, morality, and spirituality, from even the higher animals. "In so far as it is a strictly physiological and anatomical question, let physical science have untrammelled scope in deciding it," Wilson argued, "but when it becomes a psychical question, it is not a mere matter of sentiment that the mind revolts at a theory of evolution which professes to recognize its own emanation as no more than the accumulation of impressions and sensations of the nervous organization gathered in the slow lapse of ages, until at last it has culminated in a moral sense. Our belief in a First Cause is inextricably bound up with our belief in the human soul." Wilson was willing to accept almost the whole of evolutionary theory, but he insisted on keeping man distinct. And nothing more convincingly demonstrated that distinctiveness than man's capacity for religious belief, "especially the immortality of the soul and Christian morality."[24]

Wilson's rejection of scientific naturalism, his determination to save religion and morality from the grasp of materialism, was an understandable and not illegitimate strategy.[25] In adopting it he was joined by John Watson, who argued that "the attempt being made to explain moral and social phenomena by the doctrine of Evolution is an instance of the effort to apply a hypothesis to a totally new class of cats." Neither Darwinian nor Spencerian evolutionary theory appealed to the Queen's philosopher when applied outside science's legitimate realm. He was here pointing to the way that modern biological theory and Christian teachings might both be preserved, even made to work advantageously together, in a system of philosophical idealism.[26]

A similar approach was adopted by the conservative editor of *The Christian Guardian,* the Reverend E.H. Dewart. For him some formulations of evolutionary thought were acceptable, provided they were restricted to natural phenomena and made no pretence to reveal the "mystery of mysteries." Dewart adopted much of Dawson's outlook, relying especially on the Presbyterian scientist's geological evidence and his insistence that no provable links existed between inorganic and organic life.[27] But gradually he focused his attention on ways of combining evolution and Christianity. He summarized his conclusions in an editorial marking Darwin's death in 1882. "The utmost that evolution can be said to do," he argued, "is to carry the design a little further back and make it a little more comprehensive. The teleological value of each particular adaptation in nature is not destroyed but magnified when it is referred to a universal law, working out a universal harmony and adaptation. It is a shortsighted philosophy, indeed, which in the presence of the far-reaching law, forgets the lawgiver."[28] In this fashion the essence of the Paleyite argument could apparently be preserved from Darwin's purposeless evolutionary scheme. Dr. Dewart also took comfort from Alfred Russel Wallace, whom he heard speak at the University of Toronto in 1887. "In these statements Dr. Wallace maintains that there is nothing in evolution inconsistent with man's spiritual nature and immortal destiny. Many on the contrary think that Darwin's theory of evolution lands in sheer materialism. Our own idea has always been that there is nothing inconsistent with Christianity in admitting natural development as one of God's methods of working out his plans."[29] For Dewart, unlike Dawson, Darwinism and Christianity were quite compatible. But then Dawson actually understood Darwinism, while Dewart defined it to meet his needs.

E.H. Dewart, like many other Canadians—Goldwin Smith, Salem Bland, Mackenzie King, and W.C. Good, for example—had found great assistance in his effort to adapt evolution to Christianity in the works of the Scottish theologian and naturalist Dr. Henry Drummond. His *Natural Law in the Spiritual World* (1888) and other works harmonized Christianity and evolution in a general doctrine of progress.[30] Yet Dewart was not unaware that such a mixture had its dangers. When the American liberal preacher, Henry Ward Beecher, author of *Evolution and Religion,* appeared in Toronto, *The Christian Guardian* contended that his message had its greatest appeal among "the unbelieving and anti-Christian part of the audience." The American had reconciled evolution and Christianity only by making the latter "thin and vapory." "The Christianity he portrayed," the paper remarked, "was largely a sentimental humanitarianism without doctrinal background or definite scriptural form."[31]

Implicit in this defence of traditional Christianity was Dewart's belief that if too much ground was conceded to the new science, the door would be opened to materialism and secularism; each denied God and insisted that only the affairs of this life mattered. "Secularism is practical agnosticism," *The Guardian* maintained in a warning against the dangers of secular influences among the working classes, "as its professors hold that whatever religious and moral principles men have should be restricted to this present world without regard to future judgment and the life to come." But what sanction would be left to morality if the existence of a transcendent and judging God was denied? In Dewart's view there could be no other effective sanction. "Men live best in this world who live most for the world to come,"[32] he wrote in a summation that would have delighted, or infuriated, Karl Marx.

In his criticism of Henry Ward Beecher and in his insistence that morality was dependent upon religious belief Dewart was defending Christianity against the inroads of a modernism that insisted upon the immanence of God in the world and the primary ethical and social meaning of Christianity.[33] This was certainly the route that John Watson hoped his combination of idealism and evolution would follow. For that was the road "of progress towards higher forms of individual, social and political life."[34] A young Presbyterian graduate student, Mackenzie King, drew a similarly optimistic conclusion. "The doctrine of evolution," he recorded in his diary after reading one of Herbert Spencer's works, "makes man one with the universe, he glories in all because he is greater than all, he finds himself the supreme product of creation...all evolution points to immortality, creation alone finds completion only in immortal life and perfection."[35]

This "new theology," as Dr. William McLaren of Knox College pointed out to the readers of *Canadian Presbyterian* in 1886, taught "the immanence of God in the Universe and united it with the doctrine of evolution."[36] But he and others anxious to defend traditional Christian teaching realized that the "new theol-

ogy"—which they suspected of being old Unitarianism—drew its inspiration from other sources, too.

II

Professor McLaren, in his temperate and scholarly analysis of the sources of the "new theology," naturally had quite a lot to say about biblical criticism. Principal Dawson had also, less temperately, fixed upon this enemy. "It is plainly shown by recent controversies," he wrote in his *Modern Ideas of Evolution*, "...that the agnostic evolution and the acceptance of the results of German criticism in disintegrating the earlier books of the Bible, are at the moment combining their forces in the attack on Evangelical Christianity."[37] Certainly by 1890, when Dawson published that warning, the debate over the higher criticism had reached a crescendo in Canadian Protestant circles. Higher, or historical, criticism, which had originated in Germany early in the century, raised questions about the authorship and even the authenticity of certain books of the Bible and particularly about the relationship of the synoptic Gospels to the Gospel of John. By insisting that biblical texts had to be understood in their historical context, that archeological and linguistic analysis had to be taken into account when interpreting biblical writing, these scholars were "conducting a revolution in thought comparable to the Reformation itself," for "the dogma of the inerrancy of scripture" was being destroyed. To some, the higher critics were laying secular hands on a sacred book, "reducing the Bible to the level of a mere product of natural law."[38] That the higher criticism was often connected with the names of such writers as D.F. Strauss and Ernest Renan, who were openly sceptical about Christian teachings, led some to condemn it as nothing but "the new Negation School." J.W. Bengough used the term in a poem satirizing the higher critics as purveyors of "modern doubts and theories" who told believing Christians:

> In short, my simple brother, you *must* not feel
> so sure;
> The Book you think inspired is only Jewish
> literature.
> Its authorships, chronologies and dates are
> quite astray;
> You must wait and hear what future excavations
> have to say.[39]

Like evolution, the higher criticism, or a somewhat popularized version of it, was a topic of fairly widespread discussion in Canada at least by the 1870s. It probably first made itself felt by the arrival from overseas of men like George Paxton Young, who already in the 1850s was introducing the new scholarship into his sermons.[40] His subsequent career, first as a professor of theology at Knox College in Toronto and, following his resignation from the Presbyterian ministry, as a professor of philosophy at the University of Toronto, may have confirmed the suspicions of conservatives about the inevitable drift of "scientific" biblical scholarship.[41] The case of the Reverend D.J. Macdonnell, a Canadian educated at Queen's University and later in Scotland and Germany, added further to this suspicion. In 1875 his expressed doubts about the meaning of predestination led to heresy charges, several years of controversy and investigation, and finally to acquittal. That angry debate made a wider public aware of the theological controversies that were disturbing the church; the acquittal only made conservatives more anxious.[42]

In fact, historical criticism appears to have been absorbed by Canadian Presbyterians, or at least a section of them who took their educational direction from Queen's University, with relative ease. The Reverend G.M. Grant, who became principal in 1877 and held the post

until the end of the century, was already a "modernist" when he arrived from the Maritimes. Indeed, one of his close Nova Scotia friends, himself under the influence of liberalism, felt constrained to rebuke Grant mildly for the sentiments expressed in his inaugural address. "I infer that your theology is somewhat halting and uncertain," he observed. "I think that if you concede so much to the critics as to reduce to unauthenticated myths any portion of the Bible it will be of little use to cry out 'Believe! Believe the spiritual truth the myth contains!' But this spiritual truth must be authenticated by something. If you allow the outward authority to go by the board, there is nothing but an inward something to appeal to; and this may vary from man to man...I am not inclined to concede as much to German and other criticism as you."[43]

Grant, deeply influenced by romantic idealists like Coleridge and Carlyle,[44] warmly welcomed most modern intellectual developments. He was convinced that the discoveries of modern science and the scientific method worked to the benefit of mankind and presented no unanswerable threat to religious belief.[45] Certainly the higher criticism caused him no unease. "Just because Christianity is emphatically a historical as well as an ideal religion," he wrote in answer to an opponent of the new biblical scholarship, "it welcomes the new science of history which has given us new methods. In applying these methods to the early history of all nations, we discover that the legends or myths, once accepted literally, cover events, thoughts, and periods grander than the story; but in giving them a new interpretation we do not destroy but fulfill."[46] If that comment was complacent, it was more often a spirit of optimism that infused Grant's writing. Certainly his study *The Religions of the World* (1895) not only revealed a remarkably tolerant attitude to non-Christian beliefs, but also underlined the extent to which Grant identified Christianity with contemporary liberal civilization. His message was that the Christian church should "rise above that sectarianism which exhausts its strength, and go forward as one body to make the kingdoms of the world the Kingdom of God and His Christ."[47] He knew that his liberalism might raise some eyebrows, but, he told a friend, "everything depends on the spirit in which a book is written that deals with other religions. It must aim at getting a view of them from within and not from the outside; and such a point of view we are now somewhat prepared for, though to the theologians of the eighteenth century it would seem unChristian."[48]

Grant was a popularizer, not a profound or even a systematic thinker. He spoke persuasively, wrote with clarity and directness, and, perhaps most important, never gave the slightest hint that he doubted anything he said. In 1879 a New Brunswick minister wrote him a long, anxious letter about the intellectual doubts which the higher criticism and liberal theology were causing him. "Is it not obvious that the Churches are walking in the dark of night, and disputing about ways they cannot see but only guess?" he asked plaintively.[49] Grant's reply, unfortunately, is lost, but its contents can be imagined. Optimist and activist that he was, he almost certainly told his correspondent to quell his doubts and offer a straightforward, practical message. As he told a similar correspondent a few years later, "The people will take anything from a Minister they trust, and who deserves to be trusted."[50] Character rather than doctrine was what counted.

Certainly there were Presbyterians who had to struggle harder than the principal of Queen's before accepting the new theology. But on the whole the transition was made without any profound public crisis. In 1894 Professor John Campbell of Presbyterian College, Montreal, was accused of heresy as a "higher critic," but the charges were never heard. There could hardly have been much evidence against a man who had already dismissed German biblical scholarship with a quip: "Get a man behind a Meerschaum pipe and a flagon of Piltzener," he wrote, "and he can think himself right, and all the prophets and apostles wrong." In 1898 Knox College appointed to a professorship John McFadyen, whose German education and commitment to historical methodology were well known. His careful scholarship, undoubted piety, and attractive personality helped to ensure that modern biblical scholarship was accepted quietly. By the turn of the century John Scrimger, professor of exegesis at Presbyterian College, reflected the new outlook when he argued for a revision of the creed endorsing the fundamentals of liberalism. "The new creed," he predicted, "will recognize that Christianity is more a life than a creed, and will acknowledge the real presence of the Spirit of God in the hearts of many who are not disposed to trouble themselves much with creeds of any kind, but who are following in the footsteps of Christ, trying to do good as they have opportunity."[51]

The Methodists found the transition more difficult, noisier, and of longer duration. Doubtless that partly reflected a difference in personality. If there was a Methodist with the power and influence of G.M. Grant, he was the Reverend Dr. Albert Carman, the Methodist general superintendent. But in contrast to the Kingston liberal, Carman was a conservative in matters of biblical interpretation, though not on social questions. Carman, ably seconded by the Reverend E.H. Dewart, editor of *The Christian Guardian,* was determined to scotch the serpent of liberalism at every opportunity— and there were several. But there was more to it than mere personality. For Canadian Methodists the doctrines of biblical inspiration and inerrancy were crucial, for their church had never developed a theology as systematic as that of Calvinism. Some Methodists appeared to fear that if the Bible was questioned there would be little to fall back on.[52]

The first round in the battle over the higher criticism in the Methodist church ended when the German-trained Professor George C. Workman was relieved of his post in the theology faculty of Victoria College in 1892. Workman's views, the result of five years of Old Testament study at Leipzig, appeared first in the form of a lecture on "Messianic prophecy," which was subsequently published in *The Canadian Methodist Quarterly*. The reaction was immediate and hostile. As Workman admitted ruefully, "Neither the country nor the church seems to have been so well prepared for scientific investigation of Prophetic scriptures as I had naturally supposed."[53]

The essence of Workman's contention in 1890 (presented in fuller detail in two subsequent books) was simply that the Old Testament should be read in its historical context. Once that approach was accepted, it could no longer be argued that the Old Testament was full of predictions that would later be fulfilled in the New Testament. The Bible, in brief, should not be read literally. "While...the Scripture writers acted under a Divine impulse in apprehending and communicating their religious ideas," he explained, "we must not assume that every part of the Bible contains a divinely inspired statement or expresses a divinely inspired sentiment...It is only the moral truths and spiritual principles of the Bible that are divinely inspired; and it is only these truths and principles taken together that constitute a trustworthy guide to life, and form a sufficient rule of practice." Naturally, Workman was convinced that he was defending Christianity, for he was satisfied that any attempt to retain the literal account of the Bible's contents brought Christianity into an unequal conflict with modern scientific and historical knowledge.[54]

Carman and Dewart, however, believed that Workman's defence of Christianity amounted almost to unconditional surrender. In the columns of *The Christian Guardian* and *The Canadian Methodist Quarterly*, in books and pamphlets and in the church courts, the traditionalists counter-attacked and finally, though only temporarily, won. In Dewart's view the higher criticism could be valuable, but it too often led to extreme and unacceptable conclusions. For him, Old Testament prophecy was exactly what Workman denied: a foretelling of the Messiah's advent. To accept any other conclusion was to contribute further to an already threatening climate of intellectual doubt which, Dewart believed, had been sapping the vigour of Christian belief for several decades. "We live in times of great mental unrest," he wrote, introducing his detailed attack on Workman in 1891. "The spirit of enquiry which has distinguished modern research in physical science, has made itself felt in all departments of thought. This is notably the case in regard to Biblical and theological subjects.... A spirit of doubt and questioning seems to pervade the intellectual atmosphere." Dewart and his allies were unwilling to exchange certainty for what they saw as their opponents' offer of a better method of searching for the truth.[55]

To conservatives like Dewart and Carman, a full-scale defence of the dikes was called for. The seepage of modernism, whether carried by science or the new biblical criticism, could only dilute the full meaning of what they called "evangelical Christianity." There could be no retreat from the traditional teaching: God's transcendence, Christ's divinity, man's sinfulness, faith as the sole means of salvation, the life of holiness. These doctrines, Carman insisted, "derived from a Bible whose divine inspiration must be unquestioned."[56] To doubt these verities meant the deluge. "The natural effect of these teachings [the higher criticism and liberal theology] with the ordinary man in the long run," a Methodist writer contended, "would be stealthily to unsettle his faith, produce disrelish and consequent disregard for the Word of God, engender want of confidence in the authority of

Christ and his apostles, arouse doubt, if not denial of the inspiration of sacred writers, cause neglect of public worship, cut the nerve of evangelistic effort and, in short, promote the general lowering of the religious life of the people."[57]

These apprehensions, though exaggerated, were not without foundation. Certainly the conservatives were correct in fearing that their version of orthodoxy was losing its appeal. By 1910, when the tumult over the higher criticism erupted again because of the teachings of the Reverend George Jackson, Dewart was gone, his *Christian Guardian* fallen into liberal hands. Carman, still filled with righteous wrath, stood defiant but nevertheless defeated. Nathanael Burwash, natural scientist turned theologian and chancellor of Victoria College, shared the hope that the old man "would refrain from attacking the millionaires [sic]" at the General Conference in Vienna, where the Jackson case was finally settled in the liberal professor's favour. Burwash and other leading Toronto Methodists apparently agreed, as Chester Massey put it, that up-to-date businessmen "are not going to give liberally to a church whose institutions are not up-to-date, and who do not turn out up-to-date men...." But Carman was not silenced, convinced as he was that in conceding the field to the theological modernists Methodism surrendered its soul to the monied middle classes—the Rowells, Masseys, Flavelles, Fudgers, and Eatons—who he believed found comfort in the attenuated doctrines of modern theology. "Here is possibly our greatest danger," he told an uncomfortable General Conference. "We are becoming wealthy and may easily lose the vigour and tension of spiritual life and voice and tone of aggressive evangelism.... At such times and under such conditions novelties are preached for the well-proven doctrines of converting grace and sanctifying power.... Even good men are dazzled by the glitter of theories, and befooled with empty speculations."[58] The aging

general superintendent would soon be replaced by the energetic Dr. Dwight Chown, for whom sociology took precedence over theology. Carman's worst fears were being realized.

III

The experience of the Reverend W.S. Rainsford perhaps epitomizes the transformation of Canadian protestantism in the late Victorian age. Rainsford, who served Toronto's fashionable St. James's Cathedral in the late 1870s and early 1880s, was born in Great Britain. He had been caught up in the so-called evangelical revival of the mid-century. In 1876 he travelled to North America to conduct a mission first in New York and Boston and later in Toronto and London, Ontario. His mission, according to his own account, was a huge success and resulted in a call to St. James's. It was during his Toronto pastorate that he absorbed "the cataclysmic change...the evolutionary hypothesis has effected in religious belief." His newly adopted liberalism at first brought him into sharp conflict with the congregation that had earlier responded so warmly to his evangelical message, but he gradually won most of them over. Even Goldwin Smith, Rainsford remembered with pride, joined his congregation. William Hume Blake, a leading evangelical, moved out. By the mid-1880s, having built up a "great free and open liberal church for the people," Rainsford accepted a call to St. George's in New York, where he ministered to J.P. Morgan and others of economic power and social prominence. His 1913 book, *The Reasonableness of the Religion of Jesus,* displayed all of the fatal flaws that an Albert Carman (had he been willing to read a book by an Anglican), or a William Hume Blake would have expected from a theological liberal. "By so much as Jesus is pronounced as supernatural by His birth, or death or rising from the dead," he wrote soothingly, "by so much are we robbed of our elder Brother, robbed of a real son of man who is a real practical guide and example; one we can follow and imitate down here on earth."[59]

What Rainsford was saying—and in this he spoke for many of his and a later generation—was that the practical application of Christ's teachings was more important than theological controversy. Indeed, the new science and the new scholarship had left doctrine in the midst of shifting sands that might best be avoided. That was certainly the conclusion of the regular religious columnist of *The Toronto Mail* when in 1885 he asked the central question: "Now what we demand is the authority by which these iron bound creeds and confessions are imposed?" He responded immediately: "It certainly was not the Saviour, whose teaching was utterly free from even the suspicion of theology."[60] Professor John Watson, whose Christian Hegelianism reduced the church to an organization for social betterment (he wrote a troubled Presbyterian minister in 1914: "No creed or any Church can be accepted, and I don't think a church can be based on any belief except that it is an organization for making men better"[61]), explained the meaning of modernism to the readers of the *Knox College Monthly* in 1891: "Christianity does not conceive of the future world as different from this, but as the present world in its ideal aspect; what a man is then, he is now, and what he is now is determined by the degree in which his life breathes the spirit of love. Christianity is above all things a religion of this world.... It is nothing if it is not social."[62]

The young W.C. Good, the future intellectual leader of a succession of agricultural reform movements in Ontario, spent a good many of his spare hours as a science student at the University of Toronto in the 1890s listening to sermons and struggling with religious questions. He concluded that the conservative stand of the Dawsons and Carmans was indefensible and a waste of time. Instead he arrived, without the aid of Hegel, at a conclusion close to that of Professor Watson: "the sooner people learn," he wrote his sister in the self-confident tone that would characterize his whole career, "that religion has a foundation quite apart from the Bible—though the Bible is a *means of grace*—the sooner will they quit worrying about comparatively trivial matters. The new historical criticism of the O.T. writings has made them once more a living book, when they were becoming dead to many people on account of foolish and unreal distinctions between secular and sacred etc. It is a transition period just now, and some friction is inevitable."[63]

Good proved an astute observer. By the end of the Victorian age the foundations of religious orthodoxy had been shaken. And if the "sacred" and the "secular" were no longer distinct, then perhaps religion, rather than being the opiate of the masses, would become a recipe for social regeneration. The criticism of religion led, sometimes by sinuous routes, to the criticism of society.

Notes

1   Karl Marx, "Towards the Critique of Hegel's Philosophy of Law: Introduction (1844)," in *The Essential Karl Marx: The Non-economic Writings*, edited by Saul K. Padover (New York, 1978), 286–7.

2   Owen Chadwick, *The Secularization of the European Mind in the Nineteenth Century* (Cambridge, 1975), 48–87.

3   Stanley Ryerson, "Mark Szalatnay," in *Dictionary of Canadian Biography* vol. 10 (Toronto, 1972), 670–1.

4   *The Victorian Crisis of Faith*, edited by Anthony Symondson (London 1970); Paul Carter, *The Spiritual Crisis of the Gilded Age* (DeKalb, 1971).

5   John Watson, "Science and Religion," *Canadian Monthly and National Review* (September 1876): 384–5.

6 William Leitch, *Introductory Address at the Opening of Queen's College,* 8 November 1860, cited in A.B. McKillop, *A Disciplined Intelligence: Critical Inquiry and Canadian Thought in the Victorian Era* (Montreal, 1979), 8.

7 John Watson, "Science and Religion: A Reply to Professor Tyndall on 'Materialism and Its Opponents,'" *Canadian Monthly and National Review* (May 1876): 384.

8 Robert J. Taylor, "The Darwinian Revolution: The Responses of Four Canadian Scholars," PhD thesis (McMaster University, 1976); P. Roome, "The Darwinian Debate in Canada, 1860–1880," in *Science, Technology, and Culture in Historical Perspective,* edited by L.A. Knaffla, M.S. Staum, and T.H.E. Travers (Calgary, 1976), 183–206; Carl Berger, *Science, God and Nature in Victorian Canada* (Toronto, 1983).

9 Sir William Dawson, *Fifty Years of Work in Canada: Scientific and Educational* (London and Edinburgh, 1901); Stanley B. Frost, *McGill University, 1801–1895* (Montreal, 1980), chaps. 8, 10, and 11; Charles F. O'Brien, *Sir William Dawson: A Life in Science and Religion* (Philadelphia, 1971). To place Dawson in context it is necessary to consult James R. Moore, *Post-Darwinian Controversies* (London, 1979).

10 C.C. Gillispie, *Genesis and Geology* (New York, 1959), 96.

11 J.W. Dawson, "The Present Aspect of Inquiries as to the Introduction of Genera and Species in Geological Time," *Canadian Monthly and National Review* (August 1872): 154.

12 David L. Hull, *Darwin and His Critics: The Reception of Darwin's Theory of Evolution by the Scientific Community* (Cambridge, Mass., 1973), 451.

13 E.J.C., "Review of 'On the Origin of Species by Natural Selection,'" *The Canadian Journal* new series 38 (July 1860): 367–87.

14 J.W. Dawson, *Archaia; or, Studies of the Cosmogony and Natural History of the Hebrew Scriptures* (Montreal, 1860); J.W. Dawson, "Points of Contact between Science and Revelation," *Canadian Methodist Monthly* (March 1883): 232.

15 Berger, *Science, God, and Nature,* 72.

16 J.W. Dawson, *The Story of Earth and Man* (Toronto, 1873), 318.

17 Sir William Dawson, *Modern Ideas of Evolution* (1890; reprint New York 1977), 54, 11.

18 J.W. Dawson, "Points of Contact between Science and Revelation," part 2, *Canadian Methodist Monthly* 16 (April 1883): 380. On the relation of science and society see Robert Young, "Malthus and the Evolutionists: The Common Context of Biological and Social Theory," *Past and Present* 43 (May 1969): 109–41, and "The Historiographical Ideological Contexts of the Nineteenth-Century Debate on Man's Place in Nature," in *Changing Perspectives on the History of Science,* edited by M. Kulas Teich and Robert Young (London, 1973), 344–8; Keith Thomas, *Man and the Natural World* (New York, 1983), 70–1; Raymond Williams, *Problems of Materialism and Culture* (London, 1980), 70–1.

19 Taylor, "The Darwinian Revolution," passim.

20 Goldwin Smith, "The Ascent of Man," in *Lectures and Addresses* (Toronto, 1881), 89; Loren Eiseley, *Darwin's Century* (New York, 1961), 257.

21 *Grip,* 13 March 1880.

22 Malcolm Jay Kottler, "Alfred Russel Wallace: The Origin of Man and Spiritualism," *Isis* 65 (June 1974): 145–92; Stephen Jay Gould, "Natural Selection and the Human Brain: Darwin vs Wallace," in *The Panda's Thumb* (New York, 1980), 47–58.

23 A. Ellegard, *Darwin and the General Reader 1859–72* (Göteborg, 1958), 296 et seq. On Wilson see Bruce Trigger, "Sir Daniel Wilson: Canada's First Anthropologist," *Anthropologica* 7 (1966): 3–37 and Bennett McCardle, "The Life and Anthropological Works of Daniel Wilson (1816–1892)" (MA thesis, University of Toronto, 1980).

24 Daniel Wilson, *Caliban: The Missing Link* (London, 1873), 93–4, 133, 104.

25 Morse Peckham, "Darwinism and Darwinisticism," in *The Triumph of Romanticism* (Columbia, SC, 1970), 184–8.

26 John Watson, "Darwinism and Morality," *Canadian Monthly and National Review* 11 (October 1876): 319; J.A. Watson, "The Evolution of Morality," ibid. (May 1877): 491–501; John Watson, "The Ethical Aspect of Darwinism," ibid. (June 1877): 638–9; Perry Miller, *American Thought: Civil War to World War I* (New York, 1963), xiv; Maurice Mandelbaum, *History, Man, and Reason: A Study in Nineteenth-Century Thought* (Baltimore, 1971), chap. 1.

27 *The Christian Guardian,* 28 May 1878, 261.

28 Ibid., 10 May 1882, 148, and 22 October 1879, 340.

29 Ibid., 16 March 1887, 168, and 20 January 1892, 401.

30 Henry Drummond, *Natural Law in the Spiritual World* (New York, 1888); James McArthur, "Professor Henry Drummond, FRSE, FGS, LID," *Methodist Magazine* 38 (October 1893): 352–5; John Dillenberger, *Protestant Thought and Natural Science: A Historical Interpretation* (New York, 1960), 243–8; Richard Hofstadter, *Social Darwinism in American Thought* (Boston, 1955), 96–7; John Laing, "Drummond's 'Ascent of Man' and Christianity," *Knox College Monthly and Presbyterian Magazine* 17 (April 1895): 537–51. For a revealing attempt to combine Darwinism and theism, see Gerald Killan, *David Boyle: From Artisan to Archeologist* (Toronto, 1983), 58–61.

31 *The Christian Guardian,* 4 June 1884, 184.

32 Ibid., 22 February 1888, 121, and 3 October 1877, 316.

33 William R. Hutchison, *The Modernist Impulse in American Protestantism* (Oxford, 1982), 2.

34 John Watson, "Christianity and Modern Life," *Knox College Monthly and Presbyterian Magazine* 14 (July 1891): 164.

35 Public Archives of Canada (PAC), W.L.M. King Papers, *Diary* 1, 1 July 1894, and 111, 12 November 1898. On evolution and the idea of progress see Robert Young, "The Impact of Darwin on Conventional Thought," in Symondson, *Victorian Crisis of Faith,* 27–31. That Darwinism did not necessarily lead to liberal Christianity is shown in Moore, *Post-Darwinian Controversies, 349.*

36 William McLaren, DD, "The New Theology and Its Sources," *The Canadian Presbyterian,* 15 (13 October 1886): 662; McLaren was criticizing the Andover theologians who only two years earlier had founded the *Andover Review,* the vanguard of liberal theology in the United States. See Daniel Day William, *The Andover Liberals* (1941; reprint New York, 1970).

37 Sir William Dawson, *Modern Ideas,* 21.

38 John Dillenberger and Claude Welch, *Protestant Christianity* (New York, 1954), 195; McLaren, "New Theology," 663.

39 J.W. Bengough, "The Higher Criticism," in *Motley: Verses Grave and Gay* (Toronto, 1895), 163–5; H.G. Wood, *Belief and Unbelief Since 1850* (Cambridge, 1955), 63–81.

40 D.C. Masters, *Protestant Church Colleges in Canada* (Toronto, 1966), 46.

41 Leslie Armour and Elizabeth Trott, *The Faces of Reason: An Essay on Philosophy and Culture in English Canada, 1850–1950* (Waterloo, 1981), 85–105.

42 J.F. McCurdy, *The Life and Works of D.J. Macdonnell* (Toronto, 1879); Joseph C. McClelland, "The Macdonnell Heresy Trial," *Canadian Journal of Theology* (October 1958): 273–84; Rev. D.J. Macdonnell, *Death Abolished: A Sermon Preached at St. Andrew's Church, Toronto, in connection with the Death of Professor George Paxton Young* (Toronto, 1890) and Robert S. Weir, *Review of Rev. D.J. Macdonnell's Sermon Entitled Death Abolished* (n.p.p., n.d.).

43 G.M. Grant, *Sermon Preached before the Synod of Nova Scotia and Prince Edward Island, 26 June 1866* (Halifax, 1866); PAC, G.M. Grant Papers, S. Macdonald to Grant, 7 May 1879.

44 G.M. Grant, *Reformers of the 19th Century: A Lecture Delivered before the Young Men's Christian Association of Halifax, January 29, 1867* (Halifax, 1867). Though he praised Coleridge and Wordsworth, the highest encomium was saved for Carlyle: "no prophet has spoken with so an authoritative voice since Luther's time, if then" (at 28).

45 W.L. Grant and Frederick Hamilton, *George Monro Grant* (Toronto, 1905), 212–15.

46 Grant Papers, undated review of George H. Towers, *Studies in Comparative Theology.*

47 G.M. Grant, *The Religions of the World* (London and Edinburgh, 1895), 51. On the role of comparative religion in the development of theological liberalism, see Carter, *The Spiritual Crisis of the Gilded Age,* 199–222.

48 Grant Papers, Grant to J.A. McClymont, 5 January 1893.

49 Ibid., Rev. P. Melville to Grant, 2 December 1879.

50 Ibid., Grant to Mrs. McClymont, 25 December 1901; see also Hilda Neatby, *Queen's University, 1841–1917* (Montreal, 1978).

51 John Moir, *Enduring Witness* (n.p.p., n.d.), 174–5; *Presbyterian College Journal* 11 (February 1892): 318; ibid., 21 (January 1902): 207.

52 Goldwin French, "The People Called Methodists in Canada," in *The Churches and the Canadian Experience,* edited by John Webster Grant (Toronto, 1963), 78; Tom Sinclair-Faulkner, "Theory Divided from Practice: The Introduction of Higher Criticism into Canadian Protestant Seminaries," in *Canadian Society of Church History Papers* (1980), 33–75.

53 George C. Workman, "Messianic Prophecy," *The Canadian Methodist Quarterly* 2 (October 1890): 407–78, and "Messianic Prophecy—A Sequel," ibid., 3 (October 1891): 407–55.

54 George C. Workman, *The Old Testament Vindicated as Christianity's Foundation Stone* (Toronto, 1897), 39, 85.

55 *The Christian Guardian,* 31 December 1891, 824; E.H. Dewart, "A Brief Examination of Professor Workman's Teaching and Methods," *Canadian Methodist Quarterly* 3 (January 1891): 74–86; E.H. Dewart, *Living Epistles* (Toronto, 1878), 97; E.H. Dewart, *Jesus the Messiah in Prophecy and Fulfillment* (Toronto, 1891), vi; William, *Andover Liberals,* 105–6.

56 A.R. Carman, "What Are the Church's Working Doctrines?" *Canadian Methodist Magazine* 28 (July–December 1888): 540–88.

57 Rev. J.S. Ross, *A Review of George Jackson's Lectures on the Early Narratives of Genesis* (Toronto, 1909), 20.

58 United Church Archives, Burwash Papers, Margaret to Nathanael, 14 August 1910; PAC, Rowell Papers, Chester Massey to Rowell, 2 August 1910; "The General Superintendent's Address to the General Conference, 1910," *Christian Guardian,* 22 August 1910. On the controversy see George A. Boyle, "Higher Criticism and the Struggle for Academic Freedom in Canadian Methodism" (BTh thesis, Victoria University, 1965), which sets the tone for the standard liberal interpretation found in Margaret Prang, *N.W. Rowell* (Toronto, 1975),

70–87 and Michael Bliss, *A Canadian Millionaire* (Toronto, 1978), 200–2. Studies that demonstrate a better understanding of the theological issues include Lawrence Burkholder, "Canadian Methodism and Higher Criticism," United Church Archives (1976); Tom Sinclair-Faulkner, "Theory Divided from Practice,"; Paul Neilson, "The Struggle in the Methodist Church over Higher Criticism and Modern Thought 1889–1910" (research paper, York University, 1974); and Michael Gauvreau, "The Taming of History: Reflections on the Canadian Methodist Encounter with Biblical Criticism," *Canadian Historical Review* 65 (September 1984): 315–46.

59 W.S. Rainsford, *The Story of a Varied Life: An Autobiography* (New York, 1922), 179, 187–95, 376.

60 *The Toronto Mail,* 18 March 1881.

61 McKillop, *A Disciplined Intelligence,* cited at 216.

62 John Watson, "Christianity and Modern Life," *Knox College Monthly and Presbyterian Magazine* 14 (July 1891): 163.

63 PAC, W.C. Good Papers, Good to Ethel, 18 March 1901. One of the principal influences on Good's religious thinking was Professor J.F. McCurdy, a leading exponent of the "higher criticism" at the University of Toronto and a member of the Canadian Society for Psychical Research. See ibid., Good to mother, 31 March 1901. On McCurdy and the development of the "higher criticism" generally, see J.S. Moir, *A History of Biblical Studies in Canada: A Sense of Proportion* (Chico, Calif., 1982).

Three Ideas of Nature in Canada, 1893–1914

GEORGE ALTMEYER

The interaction between man and his natural environment is an integral part of the Canadian experience. Economically, Canada has been developed through the exploitation of a series of natural resources: cod, beaver, timber, and, most recently, mineral deposits. Certain geophysical characteristics of the country have served as the basis for both national and continental political models; an east-west waterway functioning as the underlying premise of the former, four north-south "barriers of nature, wide and irreclaimable wildernesses or manifold chains of mountains"[1] utilized as the rationale of the latter. In its rude beginning, Canadian writing—explorers' diaries, natural histories, guide books, immigration tracts and essays on hunting and fishing—centred upon the practical aspects of man's relationship with wilderness. In subsequent years a persistent theme of Canadian literature has been to discern what effect life in that wilderness has had on the collective national consciousness.[2] Likewise, Canadian painting, from Paul Kane to the Group of Seven and Emily Carr, has found its most enduring expression in the portrayal of Canada's natural heritage. When viewed in this perspective, it is with some consistency that Canada is identified by two wilderness symbols: the beaver and the maple leaf.

Yet, no matter how thoroughly one documents the significant role played by the natural milieu in Canada's economic, political, literary and artistic development, an important question remains: how have Canadians themselves perceived their relationship with Nature? According to the given interpretation, Canadians view Nature in a negative, even frightening manner. Based primarily on literary sources, this viewpoint depicts Nature as a hostile, terrifying monster, which threatens the very existence of those who dare intrude upon its domain. In a review which appeared in 1943, Northrop Frye first set forth the central thesis of this interpretation. After reading the selections in A.J.M. Smith's *Book of Canadian Poetry*, Frye somberly concluded that "Nature is consistently sinister and menacing in Canadian poetry";[3] that, in fact, "the outstanding achievement of Canadian poetry is in the evocation of stark terror"[4] in regard to Nature. Frye identifies the immediate source of this terror as the frightening loneliness of a huge and thinly settled country. But, as he explained in more detail elsewhere, at a more profound level, the "tone of deep terror in regard to Nature...is not a terror of the dangers or discomforts or even the mysteries of Nature, but a terror of the soul at something that these things manifest."[5] The reason for this deeper fear of Nature, Frye claims, is historical. Canada began as a group of small, outpost communities set amidst a menacing continent which could be penetrated, but, unlike the American example, could not be pushed back. The all-pervasive

---

George Altmeyer, "Three Ideas of Nature in Canada, 1893–1914," *Journal of Canadian Studies* 11, 3 (August 1976): 21–36. Reprinted courtesy of George Altmeyer.

insecurity inherent in such isolation compelled Canadians to retain a psychological, as well as a political and economic connection with England. Forced always to cling to the mother country for security, Nature became, for Canadians, the evil antithesis of all they most cherished in English society: order, security and, above all, civilization. In short, Frye's thesis claims that, because Canadians did not make the psychological break with Europe through revolution, they could not face the harsh realities of North American Nature with the same positive attitude as the Americans.

Frye's conception of Nature as a reservoir of a "vast unconsciousness" of sinister intent has coloured all subsequent attempts to investigate the theme of Nature in Canadian literature.[6] In her book, *Beyond the Land Itself,* Marcia B. Kline uses the idea of Nature as a malevolent force to explain the differences between Canadian and American attitudes toward Nature. Contrasting the romance novels of John Richardson and James Fenimore Cooper, the works of Susanna Moodie and the American, Caroline Kirkland, and various other nineteenth century poets and novelists, she finds that, unlike American literateurs who exhibit a positive attitude towards Nature, Canadian writers see Nature as "part of a world that is terrifying, hostile to human values and human endeavour, and inferior to civilization."[7] In a similar manner, Margaret Atwood, in advancing her thesis that Canadians have seen themselves primarily as victims, asserts in a chapter aptly entitled "Nature the Monster" that in Canadian literature Nature is "often dead and unanswering or actively hostile to man."[8] Following the accepted thesis, D.G. Jones, examining the theme of evil in Canadian literature, posits that the Canadian image of Nature is pregnant with the "threat of disorder, irrational passion and violence, the crude, the mortal, and the absurd."[9]

While this interpretation may be useful in examining literary works, it nonetheless obscures the immense complexity characteristic of the Canadian attitude towards Nature. Certainly, at the turn of the century, many Canadians, even in their literature, did not view Nature in the way these literary critics suggest. Indeed, as a reaction against certain distressing tendencies in their society, many Canadians wanted to get "back to nature," to better manage her resources and to use her as an instrument of religious expression. It is the intention of this essay to show that, from the mid-eighteen-nineties to the First World War, one facet of the Canadian attitude towards Nature was positive and typically North American. This positive perception involved the ideas of Nature as a Benevolent Mother capable of soothing city-worn nerves and restoring health, of rejuvenating a physically deteriorating race and of teaching lessons no book learning could give; as a Limited Storehouse whose treasures must in the future be treated with greater respect; and as a Temple where one could again find and communicate with Deity.

I

It is commonplace to depict the Laurier years as a time of optimism, a period in Canadian history when the national future looked so bright as to merit the dictum that the twentieth century would belong to Canada. While this scenario is no doubt accurate for many aspects of Canadian life, it tends to conceal a certain uneasiness about what this new era of industrialization, urbanization and materialism meant for people on a personal level. This apprehension manifested itself in a number of ways: "The papers are filled," wrote the Women's editor of the *Canadian Magazine* in 1908, "with advertisements of tonics and nerve pills, the magazines learnedly discuss 'Worry: the Disease of the Age,' and the doctors who are canny enough to establish rest cures are millionaires in no time, while the lady who exploits a 'don't worry' religion is a benefactor to the race."[10] Others, more exotic in temperament, dabbled in various forms of Occultism and Spiritualism. In such an atmosphere it was not unusual for the major English-Canadian journal of the day to publish a series of five articles on "Worry: the Disease of the Age."[11] The author of these articles, Dr. C. W. Saleeby, submitted that "worry is preeminently the disease of this age and of this civilization, and perhaps of the English-speaking race in particular."[12] Worry was the price for the advancement of civilization; each successive step intensified the type and tempo of the struggle for existence, culminating in the present society whose chief malady was stress. One of the most important causes for the anxious state of the Anglo-Saxon race, the doctor explained, was city life.

While Saleeby's social analysis no doubt appealed to many readers, his comment on city life came closest to identifying the source of this anxiety. By the early 1900's Canada was in the midst of a demographic revolution of enormous proportions. Comparison between the 1891 and 1911 censuses shows that Montreal and Toronto more than doubled in size, Vancouver and Winnipeg increased fivefold, while Calgary, Edmonton and Regina arose from nowhere.[13] During the decade 1901–1911, Canada's urban population increased by 62 per cent and the rural population by only 17 per cent. In the Maritime Provinces and in Ontario, the rural population actually decreased. In 1901, urban dwellers formed 38 per cent of the total population; in 1911, this proportion had been increased to 45 per cent.[14]

Canadian response to rapid urbanization was generally unfavourable.[15] A recurring motif in contemporary journals portrayed city life as artificial: the city was seen as a place of "stone and mortar," "of rattlin', roarin' streets," and of clanging telephones.[16] The artificiality of modern urban life created what one journalist called, "jaded minds," wanting only to satisfy, what

another one called, "jaded tastes."[17] In a poem titled "A Voice From the City" a Vancouver poet succinctly expressed the frustration and tension felt by many urban dwellers:

> I am tired of the shifting City,
> And the ceaseless cry of the streets
>
> Sing me a song of the free life
> When a man is a man again
> When the joy of life calls madly
> And the pain is a lesser pain.[18]

To find personal contentment, the Ottawa poet, Archibald Lampman, maintained that one had to escape from the horror of the city,

> Out of the heat of the usurer's hold,
> From the horrible crash of the strong man's feet;
> Out of the shadow where pity is dying;
> Out of the clamour where beauty is lying,
> Dead in the depth of the struggle for gold;
> Out of the din and the glare of the street.[19]

Paradoxically, "high-tuned" city life evoked in many people a sense of monotony, isolation and, above all, the feeling that the "artificial method of life we call civilization"[20] produced a basically unhealthy mode of living. In this age of anxiety who among the tense yet bored inhabitants of larger Canadian cities could resist the beckoning question put forth by a writer in *Rod and Gun,* "Do you want to rest a season from the Life Artificial and live the Life Natural?"[21] Who among them could doubt the wisdom of Adam Shortt's advice that Canadian social life could best be ameliorated through an "improvement in the whole physical setting of our social life, involving the relations of man and nature"?[22]

The thousands of urban Canadians who took to the out-of-doors at the turn of the century in a movement "back to nature" provided a positive response to this query.[23] As early as 1894, a Canadian journalist observed it to be "one of the characteristics of modern times" that, as the competition in all aspects of life becomes keener, people "seek recreation and restoration in a closer approach to nature than can be found in the busy street or crowded mart."[24] For much the same reasons, J. W. Dafoe, in 1899, took solace that: "In these days the country has been discovered anew. No fact of contemporary life is more significant or more hopeful than this return to nature, for breathing space, for those whose daily walk is the tumultuous city streets."[25] At its mildest, "back to nature" meant leisurely rides into the countryside astride a bicycle on Sunday afternoons, tramping through a marsh or hillside thicket to get the perfect "kodak" snapshot of some animal or bird,[26] or taking up the popular sport of birdwatching. Somewhat more strenuously, it meant hiking, camping, canoeing and alpine climbing.[27] Reflecting the general interest in Nature, at least ten journals—*Canadian Athletic* (Toronto, 1892), *Pastoral* (Toronto, 1901), *Rod and Gun* (Montreal, 1899), *Athletic Life* (Toronto, 1895), *Canadian Outdoor Life* (Toronto, 1907), *Outdoor Canada* (Toronto, 1905), *Western Canadian Sportsman* (Winnipeg, 1904), *Sports* (Halifax, 1908), *Canadian Sport* (Montreal, 1911) and *Canadian Alpine Journal* (Banff, 1907)—devoted exclusively or in part to out-of-door activities, began publication.[28] Moreover, the animal stories of Ernest Thompson Seton, Charles G. D. Roberts and W. A. Fraser, whose first books in this genre appeared in 1898, 1900 and 1902 respectively, ranked among the best read Canadian books.

In this awakening to the benefits of out-door life, the countryside, which a half century before had been thought of as "an absolutely uninteresting wilderness, only fit for men and women of no mind,"[29] took on new and added significance. It became the haunt of that "Old Dame Nature, that great, placid, untroubled Mother of us all," who, as one canoeist wrote, was capable of taking

...us quietly to her bosom,
and, as a mother sooths and 'gentles'
a tired and fretful child, had
quietly and completely cleared away
the mists and cobwebs from the
mind, soothed the tired spirits,
and induced in both mind and body
a comprehensive and deep reaching
peace and an unconcern for the
things of the too busy world.[30]

For Lampman, Nature was the

Mother of all things beautiful, blameless,
Mother of hopes that her strength makes
   tameless,
Where the voices of grief and of battle
   are dumb,
And the whole world laughs with the light
   of Her mirth.[31]

Yet, no matter if her voice be expressed as "the call of the wild," "the lure of the woods," "the lure of the wild," "the lure of the open," or any of a dozen other idioms, what Nature promised was always the same:

Leave the city; it is soiling
Leave your worry and your toiling,
Seek the camp beside the river,
Haunt of bear and home of beaver,
It will cool the world's mad fever,
Won't you come, won't you come?[32]

The conception of Nature as a healing mother rested on her purported ability to provide city dwellers with what they most lacked: health and relief from boredom. Her supporters did not question for a moment her ability to provide these conditions. "Health and strength go hand and hand beneath the trees," guaranteed a camping veteran in *Rod and Gun*.[33] "Almost anyone will tell you today," said another, "that the open air is the great remedial agent for badly strung nerves."[34] According to one writer, at a time when sanitariums are much in vogue, "a trip to the woods is the very best kind of sanitarium," one better than any doctor or institution.[35] Similarly, Nature was the home tonic prescribed for boredom. Instead of turning to alcohol, tobacco or silly fads for relief from urban monotony, L.O. Armstrong noted that "the right thinking turn to Mother Nature, and she cures them of boredom."[36] One of the chief benefits of alpine climbing, maintained the secretary of the newly-formed Canadian Alpine Club, was that "a new and unknown world is unfolded to dwellers in cities and places where life is either an eternal grind or an eternal show."[37] The list of testimonials such as these literally fill the articles and speeches on outdoor activity at the turn and early part of the century. Again, it was Lampman who expressed most directly the therapeutic benefits derived from close contact with Nature:

> Are you broken with the din
> Of the streets?
> Are you sickened of your thin
> Hands and feet?
>
> Are you bowed and bended double
> With a weight of care and trouble,
> Are you spectral with a skin
> Like a sheet?
>
> Take your body and your soul
> To the woods,
> To the tonic and control
> Of its moods,
> Where the forest gleams and quivers,
> Where the only roads are rivers,
> And the trunk-line bears the whole of
>   your goods.[38]

When seen in this light, it is not as strange as it might seem today that Banff, Canada's first national park, was originally established to pro-tect the hot spring geysers, or that the words "health resort" should appear prominently in the list of reasons for the establishment of provincial parks such as Algonquin (1894) and Quetico (1909).

The curative benefits ascribed to Nature were, of course, not limited to adults. J. E. Atkinson, publisher of the *Toronto Star*, after touring some of the poorer sections of Toronto during the terrible heat wave of '91, established The Star Fresh Air Fund.[39] The avowed purpose was to provide slum children with a dose of clean air at least for a few weeks in the summer. "Fresh Air!" declared the *Star* article that kicked off the drive, "what can those words mean to a child whose experience of pure atmosphere is limited to the breezes which creep about the dusty lanes or rise from the sun-heated pavements of the city."[40] The *Montreal Star* soon followed Atkinson's lead and set up a similar fund.[41] For children of wealthier families, boys' camps became the vogue. Camp Temagami, or as it was affectionately known, "Cochrane's Camp," was probably the first summer camp in Canada devoted to boys. Set up by an Upper Canada College teacher who wanted to find a productive way to occupy his young charges during summer vacation, Cochrane's Camp offered camping, canoeing, swimming, all manner of sport and plain wholesome food.[42] At about the same time, Ernest Thompson Seton, the Toronto-based artist, naturalist and animal story writer, founded the Woodcraft Indian club for boys, an organization dedicated to tracking, camping, canoeing and woodcraft.[43] First proposed in a series of articles in *Ladies Home Journal*, hundreds of Woodcraft Indian groups soon sprang up all over the United States and Canada.[44]

The idea of Nature as a refuge from the ills of city living also underlay the development at this time of the cottage syndrome. While, at least in Ontario and Quebec, summer cottages date back to the mid-nineteenth century, it was not until the 1890's that the practice of spending a part of the summer in the woods came into wider practice.[45] In 1900, the *Canadian Magazine* pointed out: "The growth of the Canadian urban population has increased the number of people who are desirous of getting 'back to nature' for at least one month of the year. Hence, in the neighbourhood of each city there are one or more special districts where the summer cottage is in increasing evidence...."[46] The Lake of the Woods region of Manitoba, the Georgian Bay and Muskoka Lakes region of Ontario, the Lower Lakes region of Montreal and certain beach areas around St. John and Halifax were listed as examples of cottage districts. Whether one lived in a tent, a modest cottage or a luxurious summer home,[47] the custom of getting "back to Nature" for short and frequent holidays was becoming, in the words of J. W. Dafoe, "firmly established as a factor of city life."[48]

Some social critics, however, looked to Nature for more than mere relief from the anxiety, boredom and general unhealthfulness associated with urban living. Taking stock in the overall physical condition of Canadian manhood, they saw in Nature a way of rejuvenating a rapidly degenerating race. Again the cause of this malady was urban, industrial life. "One of the most serious problems that confront the British Empire," wrote R. Tait McKenzie in 1907, "is the physical deterioration of the people in towns and cities." McKenzie attributed this deterioration to the increase in the number of factories and other industries incidental to the demands of trade. "These conditions," he warned, "are beginning to show even in Canada."[49]

While McKenzie, and others such as F. E. Dorchester, John Kelso and J. A. Cooper,[50] looked to athletics, physical culture and frugal dietary habits to stem the trend towards physical degeneracy, others looked to Nature. "Are we Anglo-Saxons degenerating?" asked *Rod and Gun* in 1904. "Is the Englishman, the American, and the Canadian less hardy than his forefathers?" To dispel any doubt on this important question, the editorial suggested that canoeing and camping be made the "national pastimes." It urged every Canadian male to get into the woods and lakes at least once a year in order to prevent them from becoming "helplessly soft and luxurious."[51] Similarly, fear of the deleterious effects of urban living on the nation's youth led to the formation of Boy Scout packs in Canada. According to the movement's founder, Lieutenant-General Robert Baden-Powell, "scouting," which for Canadian boys meant the emulation of "the work and attributes of backwoodsmen, explorers and frontiersmen," was the best way to counter the trend towards physical deterioration.[52] Through outdoor activities such as "pioneering," "camping," "tracking" and "woodcraft, or knowledge of animals and Nature," Baden-Powell contended Canadian boys might prepare themselves physically and mentally to defend their empire in time of peril.[53]

The idea of Nature as a teacher of youth was not confined to scouting movements or summer camps. By 1910, chiefly through the efforts of Natural History and Field-Naturalist Societies, farm organization and the staff of the Central Experimental Farm,[54] nature study classes were introduced into the public schools of British Columbia (1900), Alberta (1908), Winnipeg (1903), Ontario (1904), and Nova Scotia (1901).[55] As part of the Froebelian doctrine of progressive education,[56] the central theme of these courses was "primarily and essentially the study of the out-of-doors."[57] Why was it important to study Nature? A member of the Ottawa Field-Naturalists' Club explained it this way:

> The foundation of all education is the training of the senses, but in this artificial and introspective age we are losing sight of this objective influence of nature, ignoring the plan by which the human race has been nourished and developed for untold generations.[58]

That modern society had atrophied or stunted the senses was an often expressed idea associated with nature study. As one Toronto teacher said, "Nature study is a method rather than a subject."[59] It was a way of sharpening blunted senses; it provided students, according to the editor of the St. John *Educational Review,* with "eyes to see."[60] Perhaps C. J. Atkinson of Toronto best articulated the meaning of the Nature Study movement when he said:

> ...the unnatural surrounding and conventionalities of city life dwarf the boy physically and mentally, and [so] that to have the boy at his best [we] must counteract the influence of man-made environment by getting him back to Nature.[61]

For all these reasons, then, the idea of Nature as a Benevolent Mother, acting as a refuge from the boring and unhealthy aspects of urban life, as a means of stiffening the backbone of a slacking race and as a teacher of natural values, appealed to many Canadians at the turn of the century. It would be a mistake, however, to see this positive attitude towards Nature as uniquely Canadian. As many studies have shown, interest in camping, hiking, birdwatching, nature study, wildlife photography, scouting and summer cottages was keen in the United States during these years.[62] Indeed, to put it into its proper perspective, the Canadian "back to nature" movement must be viewed in its North American context. This is not to say, however, there were not important motivational differences between the two movements. Many writers have identified as one of the main sources of the American desire for a closer relationship with Nature, the "perceived" closing of the American frontier and all its attendant psychological consequences. This surely is not the case in Canada, where exactly at this time, the lands of New Ontario and the "last, best West" of the prairies were opening up. Instead, it

seems likely that the impetus for the Canadian "back to nature" movement came from three sources: first, from a reaction against urban, industrial life; secondly, from the influence of the movement in the United States; and thirdly (and this is highly speculative), from a desire on the part of some eastern urban Canadians to share in some limited way with the national excitement accompanying the opening up of the Canadian West. Yet, whatever were the motivational differences between the United States and Canada in this regard, the general movement for closer contact with Nature was similar in substance in both countries. This point was not lost to the railroad company directors, resort operators and other interest groups, who promoted the notion that Canada was rapidly becoming "the natural playground of the world."

The potential of Canada as a tourist haven was not a new idea in the 1890's. It had been discussed at least as far back as the Confederation period. But with the shift in vacationing preference at the turn of the century from seaside resorts to woodland retreats, the idea took on new importance. "It is certain," predicted J. A. Cooper in a special issue of the *Canadian Magazine* in 1900, "that Canada shall become more and more the resort of the summer traveller, especially from the United States. Her thousands of lakes and rivers afford plenty of sport after pleasant excitement, her vast forest preserves are still well stocked with the finest game in the world, and the natural beauty of the many regions, which the prosaic hand of civilization has not touched, affords rest to the tired man or woman of the world."[63] In a series of articles which followed Cooper's introductory remarks, every region of Canada from Vancouver to Prince Edward Island was portrayed as a wonderful tourist area, each stressing their particular advantage as a natural retreat from the work-a-day, urbanized world.

Other interests also picked up the theme. Arthur O. Wheeler, president of the Canadian

Alpine Club, described Canada's mountain ranges as "a great national playground" where those who were tied to desks and shut behind closed city walls might escape their "prison environment."[64] Other Alpine enthusiasts christened the Canadian Rockies as the "great international playground,"[65] as the "playground of the world,"[66] and, in a label used extensively in C.P.R. advertisements, as "50 Switzerlands in One." The founder of the Ontario Fish and Game Protective Association even maintained that, if Ontario could get proper hunting regulations, it would become the "Scotland of North America."[67]

The practical motif of Nature as a playground rested upon the willingness of Canadians to use their natural heritage as a means of economic development. In the latter part of the nineteenth century the entire concept of the use of natural resources was in transformation, the idea of Nature as a bottomless Horn of Plenty, which one could indiscriminately exploit, giving way to the more positive idea of Nature as a Limited Storehouse.

II

The Canadian Conservation Movement defies any simplistic analysis. On one level the movement to conserve Canada's natural resources was pragmatic, financially motivated and a continuation of previous policy; on another it was idealistic, devoid of monetary considerations and a break from traditional approaches. Two different philosophies, the "doctrine of utilization" and the "doctrine of unselfishness" underlay its two main impulses. Yet in defining the movement in this manner, a fundamental point must be made. These two aspects of the Canadian Conservation Movement were not mutually exclusive. They were not opposites separated by some unbridgeable divide. They did not represent in the Conservation Movement the "purist" and the "realist" positions. Rather, they were

expressions of the same impulse on two distinct levels. On the first level this impulse took the form of wanting to use Nature's bounty in such a manner as to ensure that it could be exploited again in the future. Yet the feeling underlying even this most practical consideration was a sharp departure from previous assumptions.

The purpose of the economic policy of the Macdonald government was to create a national economy based on the exploitation of Canada's natural resources. This National Policy was predicated on the idea that Canada possessed these resources in unlimited quantity.[68] The philosophy of "usefulness" on which this economic strategy rested was clearly elucidated by Macdonald in a speech given on his return from a trip through Western Canada. Describing the Canadian Rockies, Macdonald observed:

> The mountains are rich in gold, and silver and all description of minerals, and clothed with some of the finest timber, an inexhaustible means of supplying the treeless expanse of prairies in the Northwest.[69]

As the historian, R.C. Brown, queries: "Could anyone in Macdonald's audience, anyone who knew John A., believe for a minute that the tapping was not about to begin?"[70] A storehouse of unlimited natural wealth was there for the taking; the only real question was who should direct the operation. This problem quickly solved, a pillage of Canadian forests commenced. So great was the rate of cutting that, according to one critic, the only question remaining was whether "the idea of boundless wealth of woodland—of forest with exhaustless supplies of timber—would survive the forests themselves."[71]

Gradually in the 1890's, the idea of unlimited abundance came under reappraisal. The shift of attitude surfaced first in occasional articles appearing in popular journals on the danger of unregulated cutting to forests.[72] In these articles, and in many others like them in the following decade, the solution proposed was not of ending or even limited lumbering activity but of employing "scientific techniques," based on German models, to eliminate the wanton and largely unnecessary wasteful characteristics of contemporary forestry methods. This new outlook of forest resource management found a focal point in the Canadian Forestry Association.

Founded in 1900, the Canadian Forestry Association sought "to advocate and encourage judicious methods in dealing with our forests and woods" and "to awaken public interest to the sad results attending the wholesale destruction of the forest."[73] Through the pages of its official organ, *Rod and Gun*,[74] the C.F.A. expounded its position that in a commercial age it was good business to farm scientifically the nation's lumber wealth, rather than simply to work it as a mine until exhausted. Emphasizing that Canadian forests were in no immediate danger of depletion, the Association warned Canadians that they could not afford to repeat the mistakes made by American foresters. This hard-nosed, business attitude toward resource development dominated the C.F.A. first national convention in 1906. Presided over by Sir Wilfrid Laurier and addressed by such notable American conservationists as Gifford Pinchot, the C.F.A. convention of 1906 gave the Canadian Conservation Movement a legitimacy it had previously lacked and propelled the issue into public prominence. The convention led to regular annual meetings which provided the only national forum where resource professionals, the Government and conservationists could exchange views and ideas, the founding of schools of forestry at the University of Toronto in 1907 and at the University of New Brunswick in 1908, and the establishment of forest services by various provincial governments.[75]

The same philosophy of scientific utilization rather than sheer exploitation pervaded the work of the Canadian Commission of Conservation. Like the Washington Conference (1909) from which it emanated, the Canadian Commission preached the ideals of efficient resource management in the areas of forestry, lands, water, minerals and fuels and public health. In his opening address to the Commission, Clifford Sifton, its Chairman and chief spokesman, set the business-oriented tone maintained throughout its twelve year history:

I have heard the view expressed that what Canada needs is development and exploitation, not conservation. This view, however, is founded on erroneous conceptions which it must be our work to remove. If we attempt to stand in the way of development our efforts will assuredly be of no avail, either to stop development or to promote conservation. It will not, however, be hard to show that the best and most highly economic development and exploitation in the interests of the people can only take place by having regard to the principles of conservation.[76]

For Sifton, as for this part of the Conservation movement in general, no contradiction existed between development and conservation, the latter only being an aspect of the former. Conservation meant simply the sound business principle of planning ahead for tomorrow's needs. "Canadians," wrote one conservationist in 1910, "have lived for many years in a fool's paradise as to their natural resources."[77] Canadian businessmen, fully realizing the unprofitability of living in a fool's paradise, were quite willing to change their exploitative technique from one of unlimited "use" to the more gentle approach of scientific "utilization."

The practical considerations that led lumbermen to take a fresh look at their relationship with the forests prompted sportsmen to take renewed action to protect fish and game. In this new effort the idea of harvesting rather than wantonly killing wildlife became the sportsman's ideal.[78] Concern for the well-being of fish and game supplies was not new in Canada. For example, Upper Canada passed laws on salmon fishing in 1807 and deer hunting in 1827.[79] But season and limit regulations such as these, enacted in many parts of Canada over the next half century, were seldom enforced. In the early 1890's both the Royal Commission on Game and Fish and the Royal Commission of Forests and National Parks lamented the fantastic desecration of wildlife occurring in Canada.[80] The focal point of agitation for better and rigorously enforced hunting and fishing regulations was *Rod and Gun*. Used by sporting organizations in much the same way as C.F.A.,[81] *Rod and Gun* urged its readers to adopt a new and more responsible attitude towards wildlife. It advocated stricter enforcement of game and fish laws, carried news of Fish and Game Protection societies in all the provinces and even launched the League of Canadian Sportsmen in 1899.[82] The efforts of *Rod and Gun* and provincial sporting fraternities were not without result: specific Game Acts were secured in Prince Edward Island (1906), Nova Scotia (1912), New Brunswick (1909), British Columbia (1919), Manitoba, Saskatchewan and Alberta, while in Ontario and Quebec more stringent bounty and season laws were put on the books.

For the hunting and fishing sportsmen, as for the lumbermen, Nature did not in itself possess any intrinsic value. It was merely a storehouse of animate and inanimate wealth to be exploited for their own needs. For very pragmatic reasons their attitude towards Nature's storehouse had changed. Yet it would be a mistake to equate the Conservation Movement in Canada only with this practical aspect. For the Conservation Movement, involving as it did a complexity of elements, had a humanitarian side whose philosophy was not "utilization" but "unselfishness."

Two events, more than any others, symbolized for many North Americans the need for wildlife preservation. In a Cincinnati zoo, in 1911, the last passenger pigeon died—the sole survivor of a species which had once numbered in the billions.[83] Meanwhile, on the prairies, the last remnants of the once vast herds of buffaloes were rounded up and placed into protected areas. The main reason for this unbelievable pillage of Nature's creatures, held the Naturalist, C.W. Nash, echoing a current sentiment, was the greed of the so-called civilized whiteman. Warning that animal life in Canada was being depleted so rapidly that the next generation would know them only through a few skins in museum cases, Nash pleaded with his fellow Canadians to enact laws for the survival of the remaining wildlife.[84] Nash's call for wildlife conservation, like that of thousands of naturalists and nature lovers across the country, was not premised upon economic motives. Rather, it rested on the idea that Nature itself should be protected. This custodial attitude towards Nature embodied itself in what one naturalist called the "gospel of unselfishness."

"Conservation," contended the Dominion Entomologist C. Gordon Hewitt in 1911, "is nothing more than the gospel of unselfishness," a gospel whose most fundamental tenet is the "protection of Nature."[85] Fully recognizing that it was a pragmatic age in which he lived, Hewitt nonetheless posited that conservation contained an "aesthetic and ethical side" as well as a practical one.[86] He insisted that national well-being could not be equated with material progress alone:

> Nature is not ours to squander, to amass wealth at her expense, and enjoy a transient prosperity; it is ours to protect, and the protection of Nature is more or less the ensuring of a national happiness.[87]

The national happiness demanded the "use without waste, or with as little waste as possible" of Canada's natural resources.[88] Hewitt's doctrine of conservation was not in conflict with the doctrine of utilization expounded by Sifton. It merely added another dimension—the moral and aesthetic one.

The campaign to substitute animal photography for hunting is a good example of the naturalists' desire to inject moral considerations into the conservation debate. In a speech reprinted in *Rod and Gun,* Ernest Thompson Seton, who, like his fellow animal story writer, Charles G. D. Roberts, had forsaken hunting on humanitarian grounds,[89] urged hunters to take up the morally and aesthetically superior sport of animal photography where the "weapon is the camera, not the rifle."[90] Seton's plea for a more humane method of hunting found advocates in many contemporary journals.[91] But probably the most vocal proponent of camera-hunting was Bonnycastle Dale, who popularized the message in journals across Canada that the "noiseless, houndless, barrelless, merciful camera" was a more manly way of hunting.[92] For all its advocates, then, photography was seen as a way of conserving Nature by sublimating a destructive, wasteful impulse towards Nature with a more humane method of possessing her.

Of more immediate concern for naturalist conservationists was the establishment of bird and wildlife sanctuaries. The first governmental birdlife sanctuary in North America was set up by the Canadian Government in 1887 in Saskatchewan.[93] Although this particular sanctuary failed, it provided the impetus for greater efforts in bird protection. In 1904, Jack Miner established his first bird sanctuary in Kingsville, Ontario, beginning for him a life devoted to fowl preservation.[94] Encouraged by the Kingsville sanctuary, local Naturalists' Clubs in Ottawa and Vancouver secured legislation setting aside public parks in those cities as bird preserves.[95] The example of pioneering efforts such as these eventually led to greater action for wildlife protection by Federal and Provincial Governments.[96]

While naturalist conservationists often stressed the practical aspects of wildlife protection in soliciting aid for these projects, their primary concern was to protect Nature from the exploitative instincts of man. Lieut.-Colonel William Wood, an avid naturalist conservationist, expressed the essence of this concern when he defined a wildlife sanctuary as "a place where man is passive and the rest of Nature active."[97] His plan to set aside a section of Labrador as a massive fish and game preserve simply does not fit into the argument that the Canadian Conservation Movement was simply an extension of the National Policy. For Wood, Hewitt, Miner and countless other naturalist conservationists, Nature was more than a resource to be exploited. For them, it was important as well to protect Nature for moral and aesthetic reasons. The moral duty to preserve Nature for future generations, the aesthetic beauty inherent in Nature, even Colonel Wood's desire to conserve a part of Labrador as a unique "stage on which the prologue and living pageant of Evolution can be seen together from a single and panoramic point of view"[98]—all demanded the conservation of Nature for more than monetary reasons. In their desire to protect Nature for "higher reasons" the naturalist conservationists were akin in feeling to those, at the turn of the century, who looked to Nature for religious meaning.

III

The closing years of the nineteenth century were a portentous time in the religious development of Canada. The general religious atmosphere of the day might best be described as spiritual uncertainty. The reason for this uneasiness lay in the assault mounted by the Higher Criticism, the Darwinian hypothesis and the seemingly endless advances of science against the tenets of traditional beliefs. While for some this apprehension was swiftly quieted by disclaimers such as Sir John Dawson's assertion that "as applied to man, the theory of the struggle for existence and survival of the fittest...is nothing less than the basest and most horrible superstition,"[99] others sought spiritual reassurance in Nature.

On its simplest level the search for religious meaning through Nature took the form of seeing in the natural environment the hand of God. Although nature lovers of all descriptions found spiritual inspiration in contact with the out-of-doors, it was alpine climbers who expressed most clearly the idea that Nature was God's Temple. "Do you not hear the Gospel of Nature preached anew from these perfect hills?" asked one Western mountain climber. "Do you not...feel that God's pulpit is up there on the massive crags?"[100] It was in the spirit of the Gospel of Nature that the secretary of the Canadian Alpine Club urged Canadians to become mountain climbers so that they might stand "face to face with Infinitude" and learn spiritual truths which would be otherwise denied them.[101] She further declared that the "large spiritual vision" afforded in alpining was a more potent force in offsetting the materialism of the age than all the long-winded sermons put together.[102] Yet, however strong Miss Parker's faith might be in the spiritual value of mountain climbing, it was the Club's President who put most bluntly the religious significance of alpining. "The one spot above all others where there is no place for an atheist," claimed Wheeler, "is on the summit of a mountain peak."[103]

On a more profound level, Canadian poets of the 1890's such as Charles G. D. Roberts, Bliss Carman and Archibald Lampman, attempted to define more precisely the nature of the new relationship among man, Nature and God necessitated by Darwinian theory. The importance of Darwinian theory for understanding the way these poets looked at Nature can hardly be overemphasized, for evolutionary science at once struck down the long-standing barriers erected between man and the natural world by the teachings of the medieval Christian church. In the older Hebrew and Greek traditions, the natural world had been seen as a positive component of the order of things: for the Jews of the Old Testament, it

manifested the power of the Deity and revealed His purpose; for the Greeks, it stimulated the mind and fed a love of beauty. According to the medieval church, however, man was primarily a spiritual being, inherently distinct from and superior to the non-spiritual world of Nature.[104] After the publication of Darwin's *On the Origin of Species* in 1859, things were much different. Man was seen now not as a product of special creation, which, by definition, separated him from the rest of physical existence, but as a part of an evolutionary process common to all. In the post-Darwinian world, man was not a foe of Nature but her off-spring.

Moreover, for Canadian poets, who in an earlier period may have indeed used sentimental romantic concepts such as the "picturesque," the "sublime," and "grandeur" to mask the stark reality of life in the wilderness, evolution provided the tool by which they could penetrate the overwhelming presence of Canadian Nature. According to Stevenson, evolution allowed them "a glimpse of unity pervading nature and the control directing her mysterious ways." It provided a standpoint from which they "might obtain a vision of life in which man's puny figure and Nature's brooding power assumed a conceivable proposition, both subordinate to a supernal plan."[105]

The terms most often used to describe the new relationship between man and Nature were "kinship" and "companionship." For Lampman, companionship with Nature demanded:

> Let us be much with Nature; not as they
> That labour without seeing, that employ
> Her unloved forces, blindly without joy;
> Nor those whose hands and crude delights obey
> The old brute passion to hunt down and slay;
> But rather as children of one common birth,
> Discerning in each natural fruit of earth
> Kinship and bond with this diviner clay.[106]

For Roberts, in a poem entitled "Kinship," the new bond with Nature commanded them:

Back to the bewildering vision
And the borderland of birth;
Back into the looming wonder,
The companionship of earth.[107]

Carman entitled one of his most important works, *The Kinship of Nature*.[108]

The sense of kinship with the natural world extended to the "lower orders" of nature, that is, animal and plant life. In many of his poems Bliss Carman identified himself totally with the natural object he describes, resulting in poems portraying how a tree or flower might think or feel:

Between the roadside and the wood,
Between the dawning and the dew,
A tiny flower before the sun,
Ephemeral in time, I grew.[109]

The same technique of integration is employed in Charles G. D. Roberts' "realistic" animal stories which are told from the animal's point of view. In them we are asked to think and feel as a bear, fox and any other animal might, in a given situation. Similarly, Lampman, whom the president of the Ottawa Field-Naturalist Club called "in the truest sense of the word a naturalist,"[110] felt so strongly the sense of kinship between man and the "lower orders" of Nature that he could not condone even the picking of wild flowers.[111]

If evolution provided man with a new and closer tie to the natural world, it also threatened to separate him from the traditional spiritual one. Lampman and Roberts, both sons of clergymen, sensitive to this tension, found it difficult to live within the religious boundaries of their youth.[112] Roberts, whose "slightly heterodox religious convictions" prevented him from teaching a Sunday School class at his father's church,[113] directly challenged the traditional view of Deity in "O Solitary of the Austere Sky":

How small am I in thine August regard!
Invisible,—and yet I know my worth!
When comes the hour to break this
    prisoning shard,
And reunite with Him that breathed me forth,
Then shall this atom of the Eternal Soul
Encompass thee in its benign control![114]

Likewise, Lampman, who had serious doubts about the validity of established faiths, described the feeling he received from city churches:

O Life! O Life! I kept saying,
And the very word seemed sad.[115]

Yet, even in rejecting traditional religion, neither Lampman nor Roberts, nor any other Canadian poet, embraced scientific materialism. Instead, they alleviated their spiritual anxiety by employing Nature as a medium for communing with Deity. Vague transcendentalism, based loosely on the teachings of Emerson and Thoreau, may be the best way to depict the religious position of Roberts, Lampman and Carman. That they came to hold these beliefs is understandable on three counts. First of all, as has been often noted, New England, the birthplace of the North American variant of transcendentalism, served during this period as a path for currents of thought into Canada.[116] Secondly, both Roberts and Carman proudly claimed family lineage (through the Bliss family) with Emerson.[117] And thirdly, as Georges Ross Roy points out,

Emerson et l'école des transcendantalistes étaient originaires de la partie des Etats-Unis qui ressemble le plus aux régions d'où venaient les poètes du Groupe de Soixante, c'est-à-dire des Provinces Maritimes, de Québec et de l'Ontario.... Ce fait est important, car les descriptions de la nature que les poètes canadiens trouvaient chez leurs ainés de l'autre côté de la frontière traitaient plus ou moins des mêmes phénomènes qu'eux mêmes voyaient et voulaient chanter; aussi, quand Emerson ou un autre de son école traite de l'hiver, c'est une réalité pour les Canadiens; quand Keats ou Wordsworth le font, il n'en est pas de même.[118]

The influence of Emerson's central principles that "behind nature, throughout nature, spirit is present," and that "spirit, that is, the Supreme Being, does not build up nature around us but puts it forth through us"[119] is readily observable in the works of Roberts and Lampman. For Roberts, the spirit present in Nature is named the "enigmatic Will,"[120] the "Control"[121] or simply the "force" underlying the cyclic movement of all life; while the idea that man is an element of a world soul is explicitly put forward in "Autochthon" and "O Solitary of the Austere Sky." For Lampman, the omnipresent spirit in Nature is alternately christened "energy," "force," and "spirit"; while in regard to man's connection with that spirit, Lampman boldly contends: "We know with the fullest intensity of sympathy that we are of one birth with everything about us, brethren to the trees, and kin to the very grass that now...flings the dew about our feet."[122] Finally, the later writing of Carman, according to his biographer, possesses:

> The transcendental belief in the essential identity of man's soul with the Soul of the universe, the belief in man's consequent kinship with Nature, and...the reliance upon intuition as the means whereby man becomes aware in ecstatic moments of his mystical union with the Oversoul.[123]

It was, then, on this more sophisticated level that Canadian transcendental poets used the idea of Nature as a Temple.

IV

The mid-1890s through the First World War were years of economic, political and social transformation in Canada. Beneath the buoyant optimism which accompanied this transition was a feeling of loss emanating from the realization that there was a price to be paid for the benefits accruing from a modern urban and industrial society. In this cognition many Canadians became aware that the serenity, robustness and simplicity of country living was the price exacted for the comforts and accruements of city life. They gradually understood that the practice of gross exploitation which, in the past, had characterized their use of natural resources was no longer tenable; and they saw that, in an age of materialism and evolutionary science, traditional religions were inadequate for fulfilling their spiritual needs. In seeking solutions for each of these problems many Canadians, in a way unaccounted for by the literary explanation, turned to Nature, seeing her in a new, more positive light.

This paper has attempted to examine this positive attitude toward Nature. Through the inspection of three specific motifs, this positive attitude was found to be a protective reaction against the unsettling tendencies in modern society. The idea of Nature as a Benevolent Mother was a reaction against the effects of urban life. The idea of Nature as a Limited Storehouse was a result of the death of the myth of abundance. The idea of Nature as a Temple was an attempt to alleviate religious uncertainty. For each of these themes, Nature served as a medium through which one might deal with the complexities of a nation in transformation.

Notes

1 Goldwin Smith, *Canada and the Canadian Question,* University of Toronto Press edition (Toronto, 1971), 4.

2 The titles of the two most recent thematic studies of Canadian literature are suggestive of this preoccupation: "Survival" and "Patterns of Isolation."

3 Northrop Frye, "Canada and Its Poetry," *Canadian Forum,* XXIII (Dec., 1943), 210.

4 Ibid., 209.

5 Northrop Frye, "Conclusion," in Carl F. Klinck, ed., *Literary History of Canada* (Toronto, 1965), 821–49.

6 A notable exception to the Fryean conception of Canadian Nature is found in John Moss' recently published work, *Patterns of Isolation in English Canadian Fiction* (Toronto, 1974). Moss rejects completely all anthropocentric conceptions of Canadian Nature. "Nowhere in our literature," he contends on page 111, "is adequate support to be found for these obstrusive assumptions. With few exceptions, Canadian writers have perceived nature to be amoral, impassive, indifferent. The landscape and its seasons have no ethics, no consciousness. Nature is neither willful nor benign, malevolent nor beneficent. Some of our writers respond to it with hostility, some with reverence, or hope, or fear, but the emotion is in their response—neither emotion nor conscious design is apparent in nature itself."

7 Marcia B. Kline, *Beyond the Land Itself: Views of Nature in Canada and the United States* (Cambridge, 1970), 25.

8 Margaret Atwood, *Survival: A Thematic Guide to Canadian Literature* (Toronto, 1972), 49.

9 D.G. Jones, *Butterfly on Rock: A Study of Themes and Images in Canadian Literature* (Toronto, 1970), 90.

10 Jean Graham, "Camping Out," *Canadian Magazine,* XXXI (July, 1908), 272.

11 C.W. Saleeby, "Worry—the Disease of the Age," *Canadian Magazine,* XXXIII (Dec., 1906), 118–20; (Jan., 1907), 225–30; (Feb., 1907), 347–53; (March, 1907), 452–7; (April, 1907), 537–43.

12 Ibid. (Jan., 1907), 225.

13 From figures cited in Robert Craig Brown and Ramsay Cook, *Canada, 1896–1921: A Nation Transformed* (Toronto, 1974), 98–9.

14 "The Back-to-the-Land Movement," *Conservation of Life,* I (Oct., 1914), 30.

15 Paul Rutherford, "'Tomorrow's Metropolis: The Urban Reform Movement in Canada, 1880–1912," *Canadian Historical Association Papers, 1971,* 203.

16 C. A. B., "Camping Out," *Rod and Gun,* III (Aug., 1901), 19; F. W. Wallace, "The Lure of the Open," *Rod and Gun,* V (Oct., 1911), 518; F. W. Wallace, "The Lure of the Wild," *Rod and Gun,* XII (July, 1910), 178.

17 Julian Durham, "Summer on the Pacific Coast," *Canadian Magazine,* XV (May, 1900), 6; "The Rest Cure in a Canoe," *Rod and Gun,* XII (Oct., 1910), 619.

18 D.C. Ireland, "A Voice from the City," *Westward Ho! Magazine,* II (March, 1908), 52.

19 "Freedom," in D.C. Scott, ed., *The Poems of Archibald Lampman* (Toronto, 1905), 17.

20 C.W. Nash, "The Bass of Ontario," *Canadian Magazine,* XVII (Aug., 1901), 333.

21 "The Rest Cure in a Canoe," *op. cit.,* 619.

22 Adam Shortt, "Some Aspects of the Social Life of Canada," *Canadian Magazine,* XI (May, 1898), 8. For Shortt's personal attempt to break down the "artificialities between himself and nature" see: Adam Shortt, "Down the St. Lawrence on a Timber Raft," *Queen's Quarterly,* X (July, 1902), 16–34.

23 The "back-to-nature" movement differed from the "back-to-the-land" movement. The former was the sentiment of urban Canadians to return to nature for short periods of time; the latter was part of the movement to have people live permanently in rural areas. Bliss Carman: Going back to nature does not mean "going back to savagery nor to barbarism nor to any pestilential past; it only means opening the doors and the windows." (*The Making of Personality* [Boston, 1908], 315.) For "back-to-the-land" movement, see: John A. Cormie, "Back to the Land," *University Magazine,* XVII (1918), 197–203; Canada, "The Back-to-the-Land Movement," *Conservation of Life,* I (Oct., 1914), 30–1.

24 Thomas W. Gibson, "Algonquin National Park," *Canadian Magazine,* III (Sept., 1894), 543.

25 J.W. Dafoe, "A Day in the Laurentians," *Rod and Gun,* I (Aug., 1899), 51.

26 The trouble to which amateur photographers went to get "natural" pictures of wildlife at close range prompted a journalist in *Canadian Magazine* to satire. With tongue-in-cheek, three methods of concealment were listed: a bogus tree-trunk made of

27 The Canadian Alpine Club was organized in Winnipeg in 1906.

28 *McKein's Directory of Canadian Publications* (1892, 1899, 1901, 1905, 1907, 1909, 1911, 1913). Of these journals, *Rod and Gun* was by far the most popular, its circulation reaching over 18,000 in 1913.

29 L.O. Armstrong, "Boredom and One of Its Antidotes," *Rod and Gun,* VI (Oct., 1904), 241.

30 "The Rest Cure in a Canoe," *op. cit.,* 623.

31 "Freedom," *op. cit.,* 17.

32 Donald Black, "The Call of the Wild," *Rod and Gun,* XII (Nov., 1910), 769. Women also responded to the call of the out-of-doors: "It is almost as necessary for a woman to be an enthusiast for outdoor games as it is for her to be beautiful and well-dressed." ("As She Sees It," *Westward Ho! Magazine,* II [April, 1908], 57.)

33 "Camping Out," *op. cit.,* 19.

34 "Our Medicine Bay," *Rod and Gun,* VI (Oct., 1904), 249.

35 H.G. Wilson, "The Pleasures and Benefits of Camping," *Rod and Gun,* VII (Dec., 1905), 721–2.

36 L. O. Armstrong, *op. cit.,* 241.

37 Elizabeth Parker, "Mountaineering in Canada," *University Magazine,* XI, 135.

38 "An Invitation to the Woods," in Arthur S. Bourinot, ed., *Archibald Lampman's Letters to Edward William Thompson* (Ottawa, 1956), 59–60.

39 Ross Harkness, *J.E. Atkinson of the Star* (Toronto, 1963), 70–1.

40 June 28, 1901, 3.

41 Paul Rutherford, *op. cit.,* 204.

42 "A Boys' Camp in Temagami," *Rod and Gun,* X (June, 1908), 49–51; Roy I. Wolfe, "The Summer Resorts of Ontario in the Nineteenth Century," *Ontario History,* LIV (Sept., 1962), 159. Also see: C. B. Powter, "A Boys' Camp in the Laurentians," *Rod and Gun,* IX (July, 1907), 168–72; Harold G. Salton, "A School Boy's Search for an Ideal Vacation," *Rod and Gun,* X (July, 1908), 154–8.

43 Ernest Thompson Seton, *Trail of an Artist-Naturalist* (New York, 1940), 374–85.

44 Fred Bodsworth, "The Backwoods Genius with the Magic Pen," *Maclean's Magazine,* LXXII (June 6, 1959), 40.

45 R. I. Wolfe, *op. cit.,* 149–50, 157.

46 J. A. Cooper, "Canada and the Tourist," *Canadian Magazine,* XV (May, 1900), 4. Also see: "The Outdoor Life of Canada," *Canadian Pictorial,* IV (June, 1909), 1.

47 In Muskoka the term "camping" was expanded to include "picturesque wooden homes, large or small, ornamental or plain" as well as the traditional "bed or branches and a canvas roof." (Catherine Blindfield, "Muskoka Days and Doing," *Canadian Magazine,* V [Sept., 1898], 486–7.)

48 J. W. Dafoe, *op. cit.,* 51.

49 R. Tait McKenzie, "The University and Physical Efficiency," *University Magazine,* VI (April, 1907), 168.

50 Both Kelso and Dorchester were advocates of using physical culture for putting Canadians back into shape. See: Frank C. Dorchester, "Physical Culture: A Nation's Need," *Rod and Gun,* XI (Sept., 1907), 347–9. J. A. Cooper: "If Canadians are to be physically strong there are some reforms to be effected. They must eat less pastry, they must breathe more fresh air, they must encourage still more athletic sports and physical culture...." (*Canadian Magazine,* CMXXII [April, 1904], 588.)

51 "A Word of Caution," *Rod and Gun,* VI (July, 1904), 60–1. Also see: L. O. Armstrong, "Out of Doors," *Rod and Gun,* VI (June, 1904), 15.

52 Sir Robert Baden-Powell, *The Canadian Boy Scout* (Toronto, 1911), ix.

53 Ibid., *passim.* Baden-Powell's manual was a thinly disguised rewrite of Seton's Woodcraft Indians guide, *The Birch Bark Roll,* only with Seton's emulation of the Indian thrown out and Baden-Powell's militarianism inserted.

54 W. Lockhead, "Agencies for the Promotion of Nature-Study in Canada," *The Ottawa Naturalist,* XX (Dec., 1906), 193–6.

55 Charles C. Phillips, *The Development of Education in Canada* (Toronto, 1957), 435; J.B. Wallis, "Nature Study in the Winnipeg Schools," *The Ottawa Naturalist,* XVIII (May, 1904), 61–4; J. F. Power, "The Importance of Nature Study, with Some Suggestions as to Methods," *The Ottawa Naturalist,* XXII (Nov., 1908), 145–53; A. H. MacKay, "Nature Study in the Schools of Nova Scotia," *The Ottawa Naturalist,* XVIII (Feb., 1905), 209–12.

56 C. C. Phillips, *op. cit.,* 421–35.

57 Frank T. Shutt, "Nature Study and the Camera," *The Ottawa Naturalist,* XVIII (Nov., 1904), 161–4. The Nature Study Movement was also heavily influenced by the desire to keep rural children on the farms. See: W.T. Macoun, "The Practical Aspect of Nature Study," *The Ottawa Naturalist,* XVII (Jan., 1904), 181–4; J. W. Hotson, "Nature Study and Rural Education," *The Ottawa Naturalist,* XVII (March, 1904), 221–4.

58 D. A. Campbell, "The Need of Nature Study," *The Ottawa Naturalist,* XVII (June, 1903), 61.

59 W. Scott, "What Is Nature Study?" *The Ottawa Naturalist,* XVII (Nov., 1903), 148.

60 G. U. Hay, "It Is the Spirit Which Gives It Effect," *The Ottawa Naturalist,* XVII (Nov., 1903), 148.

61 C. J. Atkinson, "Mother Nature and Her Boys," *The Ottawa Naturalist,* XIX (Feb., 1906), 215.

62 Russel B. Nye, "The American View of Nature," in *This Almost Chosen People* (East Lansing, 1966); John Higham, "The Reorientation of American Culture in 1890's," in H. J. Weiss, *The Origins of Modern Consciousness* (Detroit, 1965); R. Nash, "The American Cult of the Primitive," *American Quarterly,* 18 (Fall, 1966), 517–37; R. Nash, "The American Wilderness in Historical Perspective," *Forest History,* VI (Winter, 1963), 3–13; Peter J. Schmitt, *Back to Nature: The Arcadian Myth in Urban America* (New York, 1969); Hans Huth, *Nature and the American: Three Centuries of Changing Attitudes* (Berkeley, 1957).

63 J. A. Cooper, "Canada and the Tourist," *op. cit.,* 4.

64 Arthur O. Wheeler, "Canada's Mountain Heritage." Address delivered before the Toronto Canadian Club (Dec. 20, 1909), 63.

65 J. W. A. Hickson, "Climbs in the Canadian Rockies," *The University Magazine,* IX (Oct., 1910), 438.

66 T. A. Langstaff, "The Canadian Mountain Regions as a National Asset." Address delivered before the Toronto Canadian Club (Oct. 13, 1910), 43.

67 A. Kelly Evan, "Fish and Game Protection in Ontario," *Rod and Gun* (Aug., 1905), 310.

68 The historical development of the Conservation Movement is discussed in: Thomas L. Burton, *Natural Resource Policy in Canada* (Toronto, 1972), 23–46; F. J. Thorpe, "Historical Perspectives on the 'Resources for Tomorrow' Conference," *Resources for Tomorrow Conference, Background Papers,* I (1961), 1–13; R. C. Brown, "The Doctrine of Usefulness: Natural Resource and National Park Policy in Canada, 1887–1914," in J. G. Nelson, ed., *Canadian Parks in Perspective* (Montreal, 1970), 46–62; C. Roy Smith and David R. Witty, "Conservation, Resources and Environment," *Plan,* XI (1970), 35–70, XI (1972), 199–216.

69 Cited in Brown, *op. cit.,* 48.

70 Ibid.

71 E. J. Toker, "Our Forests in Danger," *Canadian Magazine,* I (July, 1893), 336.

72 *Ibid.,* 336–40; Phillips Thompson, "Forestry—A Neglected Industry," *Canadian Magazine,* VIII (Nov., 1896), 24–9.

73 "Constitution of the Canadian Forestry Association," *Rod and Gun,* I (April, 1900), 204. In these aims, the C.F.A. followed closely its sister organization in the United States, the American Forestry Association, which had been established in 1875.

74 At the first meeting of the C.F.A., *Rod and Gun* was designated as the official organ of the Association. Thereafter, the magazine devoted a special section to forestry. See: *Rod and Gun,* II (March, 1900), 1.

75 F.J. Thorpe, *op. cit.,* 3.

76 Commission on Conservation, Canada, *First Annual Report, 1910* (Ottawa, 1910), 6.

77 *Ibid.,* 16.

78 William T. Hornaday, "The Ideals of Sportsmanship," *Rod and Gun,* X (March, 1909), 10. Adopted by North American Fish and Game Protective Association.

79 J. K. Reynolds, "One Hundred Years of Fish and Wildlife Management in Ontario," *Rod and Gun,* LXVIII (Jan.–Feb., 1967), 14.

80 C. Roy Smith and David R. Witty, *op. cit.* (1970), 58.

81 For example, *Rod and Gun* carried the news of almost all Forest and Fish and Game Associations across Canada. See: "Our Ninth Birthday," *Rod and Gun,* X (June, 1908), 3.

82 "League of Canadian Sportsmen," *Rod and Gun,* I (July, 1899), 1.

83 "The Last Wild Pigeon," *Rod and Gun,* XII (Sept., 1911), 429. Also see: C.W. Nash, "Passing of the Pigeons," *Canadian Magazine* (Feb., 1903), 315–7.

84 C.W. Nash, *op. cit.,* 317.

85 C. Gordon Hewitt, "Conservation, or the Protection of Nature," *The Ottawa Naturalist,* XXIV (March, 1911), 221.

86 Ibid., 210.

87 Ibid., 209.

88 Ibid., 221.

89 See: James Polk, *Wilderness Writers* (Toronto, 1972), 45–6, 64–7.

90 Ernest Thompson Seton, "Hunting with the Camera," *Rod and Gun,* II (June, 1900), 259.

91 For example, F.B. Doud, "Still Hunting with a Camera," *Rod and Gun,* XI (Aug., 1909), 213–5; John Innes, "Buffalo Hunting: Modern and Ancient," *Canadian Magazine,* XIX (May, 1902), 9–17; H.M. Johnston, "Another Use for the Hand Camera," *Rod and Gun,* IV (Feb., 1903), 324–5.

92 Bonnycastle Dale, "The Opening of the Season," *Westward Ho! Magazine,* I (Oct., 1907), 33. Dale published extensively on this theme in *Westward Ho!, Canadian Magazine* and *Rod and Gun.*

93 H. F. Lewis, "Wildlife Conservation Through the Century," *Rod and Gun* (Jan.–Feb., 1967), 12.

94 Harry McDougall, "Jack Miner's Bird Sanctuary," *Canadian Geographical Journal,* LXXXIII (Sept., 1971), 108.

95 Stanley Park in Vancouver and Rockcliffe Park in Ottawa. The establishment of a bird sanctuary in Rockcliffe Park was a result of an impassioned speech delivered by Hewitt to the Ottawa Field-Naturalist Club. See: "The Protection of Birds in and Around Ottawa," *The Ottawa Naturalist,* XXVII (March, 1914), 161–71.

96 C. Gordon Hewitt, *The Conservation of the Wild Life of Canada* (New York, 1921), 258–77, 300–9.

97 Lt.-Colonel William Wood, "Animal Sanctuaries in Labrador," *An Address Presented Before the Second Annual Meeting of the Commission of Conservation* (Quebec, 1911), 5. In the preface to the written publication of the address, Wood appealed to: "All to whom wild Nature is one of the greatest glories of the Earth, all who know its higher significance for civilized man today, and all who consequently prize it as an heirloom for posterity,...to help in keeping the animal life of Labrador from being wantonly done to death."

98 Ibid., 36.

99 Cited in W.E. Colin, *The White Savannahs* (Toronto, 1936), 8.

100 Julia Henshaw, "A Summer Holiday in the Rockies," *Canadian Magazine,* XX (Nov., 1902), 3–4.

101 E. Parker, "The Alpine Club of Canada," *The Canadian Alpine Journal,* I (1907), 8.

102 E. Parker, "The Mountain Ideal," *Rod and Gun,* Viii (July, 1906), 146.

103 Arthur O. Wheeler, "Canada's Mountain Heritage." Address delivered before the Toronto Canadian Club (Dec. 20, 1909), 63.

104 Alec Lucas, "Nature Writers and the Animal Story," in Carl F. Klinck, ed., *Literary History of Canada* (Toronto, 1965), 364; Charles G.D. Roberts, *Kindred of the Wild* (Toronto, 1902), 13–4.

105 L. Stevenson, *Appraisals of Canadian Literature* (Toronto, 1924), 78–9.

106 "On the Companionship with Nature," D.C. Scott, ed., *The Poems of Archibald Lampman* (Toronto, 1905), 258–9.

107 "Kinship," in Charles G.D. Roberts, *Poems* (Boston, 1907), 17–8.

108 *Kinship of Nature* (Boston, 1903).

109 "Wind-flower," cited in Odell Shepard, *Bliss Carman* (Toronto, 1923), 80. Shepard: "Carman identifies himself, so to speak, with the object, merging himself into it, seeming to pierce to the heart and inner nature of flower and tree and to become, as it were, a thinking tree, a feeling flower."

110 John Macoun, cited in A.S. Bourinot, *op. cit.,* 70.

111 Carl G. Connor, *Archibald Lampman: Canadian Poet of Nature* (New York, 1929), 149.

112 On Lampman, see: Barrie Davies, "Lampman and Religion," *Canadian Literature* (Spring, 1973), 40–60.

113 E.M. Pomeroy, *Sir Charles G.D. Roberts: A Biography* (Toronto, 1943), 42.

114 Roberts, *op. cit.,* 69.

115 "Life and Nature," in Scott, *op. cit.,* 138.

116 Pomeroy, *op. cit.,* xx.

117 Shepard, *op. cit.,* 114; Pomeroy, *op. cit.,* 98.

118 G. R. Roy, *Le Sentiment De La Nature Dans La Poésie Canadienne Anglaise, 1867–1918* (Paris, 1961), 99–100.

119 Cited in Hans Huth, *op. cit.,* 88.

120 "Imminence," Roberts, *op. cit.,* 41.

121 "Origins," Roberts, *op. cit.,* 18.

122 Cited In Connor, *op. cit.,* 162.

123 Shepard, *op. cit.,* 115.

The Just War

JONATHAN VANCE

Daybreak on 11 November 1918 found the units of the Canadian Corps clustered around the Belgian city of Mons. Previously the scene of the war's first important skirmish between troops of Germany and the British Empire, Mons had been captured hours earlier by elements of the Royal Canadian Regiment and the 42nd Battalion of Montreal. At about 6:30 AM, Canadian Corps headquarters received a message that an armistice had been signed and that hostilities should cease at 11:00 AM. Over the next few hours, the news was transmitted down through the units of the Corps, and by 9:00 AM most of the soldiers had been informed. The war was over.

The troops reacted to the news with anything from stoic resignation to mild jubilation. Vincent Goodman, a New Brunswicker in the 2nd Canadian Motor Machine Gun Brigade, recalled that the men in his unit "took the news calmly, almost passively." Artillery officer H.C. Pullen wrote to his sister from his battery's billets at Marly that "the troops let a yell out of themselves and then turned in to clean harness as usual."[1] Private Pat Wyld of the Canadian Forestry Corps celebrated with his mates by bouncing flares down the cobbled streets of Valenciennes. Will Bird related a different but perhaps more characteristic response to news of the Armistice. An officer had been dispatched to an isolated outpost to convey the cheering news that the war was over, but the sergeant who commanded the post was unmoved. "Beg pardon, sir," he said after a slight pause, "but 'oo's won?"[2]

Bird's sergeant may have had his doubts, but there was no such scepticism in Canada's collective memory of the war. That vision affirmed November 1918 as a clear and unequivocal victory for the Allied cause. The Hun had been vanquished, and civilization had been saved from the threat of barbarism. Still, there was no guarantee that the salvation was permanent, and the memory of the war accepted that such a struggle might well have to be waged again. In this way, it acted as a powerful antidote to pacifism, for it assumed that the truest lovers of peace were those people who were willing to fight for it. Because the country had gone to war to preserve peace, Canada could look back with pride at its first world war. The nation had fought a good fight; it had been a just war.

I

While the men of the Canadian Corps reacted to news of the Armistice with restraint, their friends and families at home erupted into spontaneous celebrations. "Never again to most of us will come the exaltation of the morning of November 11," predicted a Fredericton newspaper. Students at Acadia University started a huge bonfire on campus and then paraded through Wolfville, Nova Scotia, to rouse any residents who lingered in their beds. In Brandon, Manitoba, jubilant townspeople in various states of undress jammed the streets, singing, dancing, and waving flaming torches. The quiet

---

Jonathan Vance, "The Just War," Chapter 1 of *Death So Noble: Memory, Meaning and the First World War* (Vancouver: UBC Press, 1997), 12–34. Reprinted with the permission of the publisher. All rights reserved by the Publisher.

of St. George, New Brunswick, was shattered by the ringing of church and school bells and the blowing of whistles, a cacophony that continued for the rest of the day. In the small town of Burford, Ontario, four-year-old Mel Robertson and his sister were awakened before dawn by the sound of church bells, a factory whistle, and a babble of voices in the street: "When we called out our hired girl came in with a lamp and told us the War had ended. She then brought us tin dish pans and we beat on them with curling tongs until our parents got up. Then we were dressed and went outside where we found people everywhere—some with coats over their night-clothes. On the main corner a woman with an accordion was playing 'Praise God from whom all blessings flow.'"[3]

Once relative calm had been restored, Canadians gathered in a more orderly fashion to give thanks for the nation's deliverance. A service held at Toronto's St. James Cathedral was entirely typical of celebrations convened across the country. "O God Our Help in Ages Past" and "A Hymn of Victory (Now Praise the Lord of Glory)" rang through the nave as worshippers expressed their gratitude in song. For the lesson, the minister chose a reading from the First Book of Chronicles, in which the people of David offer thanks to God for their deliverance. In a combination of misconception and wishful thinking, the order of service proclaimed "the signing of the Armistice by Germany Signifying her Unconditional Surrender."[4]

Of course, there had been no unconditional surrender, and even the Treaty of Versailles, which officially ended the war in Europe, would not be signed for another eight months. That event gave Canadians an excuse to repeat the revelries in celebration of Peace Day on 19 July 1919. In Guelph, Ontario, a civic procession ended at a huge bonfire and fireworks display, while in Revelstoke, British Columbia, as many as 25,000 people gathered to watch an evening peace pageant staged by local women. One

source estimated that three-quarters of Vancouver's population turned out for the peace celebration in that city. In Saskatoon, a two-mile-long parade of veterans, schoolchildren, local service clubs, and police and firemen wound its way through the streets; at the parade's conclusion, thirty white doves were released as emblems of peace.[5]

The most striking characteristic of Peace Day, however, was its similarity to Armistice Day. Indeed, many Canadians evidently looked upon Peace Day as another opportunity to celebrate victory. In one British Columbia newspaper, most of the advertisements marking Peace Day were titled "Victory and Peace." An advertisement for Woodward Department Stores depicts a woman holding a shield that lists Canadian victories on the battlefield, while the Hudson's Bay Company used St. George standing triumphant over a dragon wrapped in a banner marked "Militarism." In more than one city, municipal officials borrowed captured German field guns from the Department of Militia and Defence to tow through the streets as part of Peace Day parades.[6] It was perhaps the last time that Canadians copied the ancient practice of parading with the trophies of war, a practice that had more to do with proclaiming triumph over the enemy than celebrating the return to peace. Residents of Saskatoon had their own reminder that German military might had been vanquished. After watching the doves of peace flutter into the afternoon sky, they could adjourn to the Thélus Theatre (formerly the Strand, it had been renamed in honour of a village near Vimy Ridge that had been captured by Prairie battalions in 1917) for a seven-reel war film entitled *Crashing through to Berlin,* a chronicle of Germany's defeat at the hands of "the 'Treat 'Em Rough' Boys."

The desire to mark the defeat of imperial Germany, then, was central to the celebrations of both Armistice Day and Peace Day. The spontaneous outbursts of 11 November 1918 reflected the joy of a society's recognition that the years of sacrifice had paid off in victory. The events of 19 July 1919 were more carefully contrived and orchestrated yet were underpinned by the same assumption. Despite attempts by planners to focus on the symbols of peace, notions of military victory were so prevalent that they overshadowed everything else. The sincere thanks tendered to God for the triumph in battle, the advertisements that placed victory ahead of peace, the constant reminders of the defeat of imperial Germany—all indicated a broad acceptance of the idea that Canadians were really celebrating not the return to peace, but a victory of arms over the enemy.

Indeed, it was victory that dominated the discourse about the end of the war. Rather than graciously accepting victory and celebrating instead the return to peace, Canadians were determined to enjoy their day in the sun by trumpeting their triumph at every occasion. After four years of tragedy, it was difficult to resist the temptation to gloat. "Victory is ours," crowed the principal of Queen's University in 1918, "victory far more complete than we had dared to hope for." Even the historian, poet, and ex-soldier Edgar McInnis, generally one of the more moderate commentators on the war, came close to gloating in his 1920 collection *The Road to Arras:*

> They have not passed! Their scornful, sneering lies,
> Their senseless hate and blind brutality,
> Their ranting boasts and unctuous blasphemies
> Have naught availed — to us the victory![7]

In the postwar years, every conceivable aspect of the war was interpreted as a symbol of victory. The fallen became "the morning stars that herald the day of Victory—of the victory of good over evil, kindness over cruelty, justice over tyranny." They were not simply casualties of war; they were signs of triumph over "the boasting war-lord's might."[8] William Rothenstein's *The Watch on the Rhine,* a Canadian War Memorials

Fund painting of a huge artillery piece louring silently over the river, did not symbolize the ascendancy of technology or the fact that the guns had been stilled. For observers such as Hector Charlesworth, the critic and associate editor of *Saturday Night,* it was "singularly suggestive of conquest." By the same token, Alfred Bastien's *Canadians Passing in Front of the Arc de Triomphe* was in no way allegorical; its only message was "the thrill of victory."[9]

It would be a mistake to ascribe the emphasis on victory simply to the enthusiasm of the immediate postwar years. Throughout the 1920s and 1930s, the language of commemoration was dominated by the figures of Winged Victory and the rejoicing soldier, symbols of earthly triumph that constituted the single most important theme in war memorials erected by Canadians. While there may have been some spiritual side to these elements as symbolizing a victory over death, the temporal significance should not be understated. Both the artistic context and the contemporary views of these memorials confirm that they marked, more than anything else, an earthly triumph.

The figure of Winged Victory had been thrust firmly into twentieth-century iconography in 1863, when a statue of the goddess Nike was discovered by French archaeologists at Samothrace, in the Aegean Sea. Scholars concluded that it had been erected to mark a Rhodian naval triumph over the Syrians in the second century BC. With its beauty, grace, and dynamism, the Nike of Samothrace quickly captured the public imagination, and the winged female figure as a symbol of earthly victory immediately re-entered the artistic vocabulary. North Americans of the early twentieth century would most likely have been familiar with the image from Augustus St. Gaudens's statue of Winged Victory leading General William T. Sherman, unveiled in New York City in 1903.[10]

Because the figure was such a fresh motif in 1914, it is hardly surprising that Canadians took it into their language of commemoration. In doing so, they commissioned many memorials that strongly echoed the Sherman statue. A bronze relief in the Montreal suburb of Notre-Dame-de-Grâce shows the figure of Victory exhorting a rank of soldiers, while G.W. Hill's Westmount memorial features a winged figure pointing the way to a marching infantryman. In Beamsville, Ontario, the Angel of Victory urges on a soldier, while in Sherbrooke, a winged female stands above three soldiers, spurring them to victory with the laurel wreath she holds. In each case, the artistic context clarifies the meaning: the winged figure is not an angel shepherding the fallen into heaven but a personification of victory showing warriors the way to triumph on the battlefield.

Another image of victory that proliferates in memorial sculpture is the soldier holding his hat or rifle aloft in jubilation. There has been a tendency to interpret this too as symbolizing a spiritual victory, but a different meaning emerges when the context is taken into account. One of the most well-known images to come out of Canada's participation in the Boer War was Richard Caton Woodville's *The Dawn of Majuba Day*, which depicts members of the Royal Canadian Regiment celebrating their victory at Paardeberg in February 1900. In the middle ground are visible the surrendering Boer soldiers, but attention is drawn most forcefully to the Canadian soldiers, the most prominent of whom holds his helmet aloft and raises a cry of triumph at the defeat of the enemy. The image was adapted for Ottawa's Boer War memorial and, in 1915, was echoed by Bernard Partridge's famous illustration in *Punch* to commemorate the Canadian defence of Ypres. One of the most reproduced illustrations of the war, the Partridge etching shows a soldier clutching the Red Ensign and holding his hat aloft on the muzzle of his rifle; his head is bandaged and a cry of exultation is on his lips. Like Caton Woodville's painting, Partridge's etching was a very human expression of joy for a victory over the enemy.

When it came time to commemorate the dead of the Great War, many Canadian communities turned to this popular image of temporal victory, and the celebrating soldier became as prominent as the Winged Victory in the language of commemoration. He graced the welcome-home medal presented to soldiers from Shawinigan Falls, Québec, and was immortalized in stained glass in Kingston's Memorial Hall. G.W. Hill adapted the figure for the war memorial in Lachute, Québec, described by the Commission des Monuments Historiques as "un soldat d'infanterie tenant sa carabine dans sa main gauche et acclamant la victoire des Alliés."[11] Memorials in Longueuil, Québec, and Kingston, Shelburne, and Chatham, Ontario, feature variations on the theme: the soldier, arm raised triumphantly, gazes upwards to raise a cry of victory or utter thanks for the enemy's defeat.

Just as striking as the degree to which metaphors for victory dominated the language of commemoration was the lack of any meaningful challenge to this practice. In 1925, H.W. Hart of Victoria, disturbed by memorials that glorified victory instead of pointing to the evils of war or the blessings of peace, suggested raising a different sort of monument, one that would have had more in common with the later Vietnam Memorial in Washington. It would consist of a panel listing the number of dead, wounded, widows, and orphans from all nations, accompanied by the simple inscription, "Wherein is the glory of war?" Despite assiduous efforts, Hart had to admit that his scheme failed to generate any interest whatsoever; Canadians evidently had no taste for such gloomy commemorations.[12] The glow of victory was no time to raise awkward questions about whether the triumph had been a pyrrhic one. Dwelling on the cost of the war merely diverted attention from what had been won or, just as importantly, from what might have been lost.

II

Victory remained such a precious possession simply because of the consequences of defeat. As Canadians remembered it, the war had been a struggle between civilization and barbarism in which the Allied armies held the ramparts against the spread of brutality and ruthlessness. It was for good reason that "Hun" remained the most popular epithet for the enemy: a German victory would have meant nothing less than the descent into a new Dark Age. For this reason, the losses that concerned Hart were irrelevant, for they were a small price to pay for the survival of the free world. In Canada's memory, the war had not destroyed "the happy equation between civilization and victory," as A.J.P. Taylor suggested.[13] On the contrary, civilization had been preserved by the victory over imperial Germany.

Of course, a few Canadians insisted on muddying the waters by looking for villains in all the wrong places. Some pinned blame on "the avaricious financier, and none too honest politician." Equally loathsome were Stephen Leacock's Mr. Spugg, who selflessly sent to war his chauffeur, his gardener, and finally his valet, and Mr. Grunch, who complained that the government's war income tax was unfair because it let off the man without an income.[14] "Were we on God's side then? was God on our side?" wondered the prolific Maritime writer Theodore Goodridge Roberts. "My dear duffers, we were working for fat tradesmen who had shells and bacon and hot air to sell." Leslie Roberts, an ex-soldier like his New Brunswick namesake, was just as cynical in marvelling "that countless lives might be snuffed in the name of the Prince of Peace, so that the politician, profiteer, man of wealth and sometime even the rector himself, may sip tea or whiskey in patriotic ease."[15]

As insightful as they seem to modern minds, these conclusions found little room in Canada's memory of the war. In 1925, the Reverend Charles W. Gordon, better known to the world as the novelist Ralph Connor, affirmed that a war between civilized people was wicked but inferred that this rule of thumb did not apply to the late conflict, because only the Allied side could call itself civilized.[16] Germany, on the other hand, represented all that was opposed to civilization: Prussianism, Junkerdom, militarism, or any other pejorative term that came to mind. There was no point in searching the nineteenth-century alliance structure, imperial expansion, or the rise of industrial competition for the causes of the war. It "had its foundation in German autocracy," proclaimed an Ottawa cleric matter of factly; any other theory about the war's causes merely diverted attention from this self-evident truth.[17]

The myth of the war, then, placed the enemy in precisely the same place it had been in 1914. Furthermore, despite the popular notion that there was no desire to be "beastly to the Boche," only a few Canadians openly expressed a willingness to be conciliatory towards Germany for its wartime conduct. The poet Norah Holland asked her readers to "Cheer if you will the brave deed done, with laurels the victor crown, / But keep one leaf of your wreath of bay for the men who are lost and down."[18] Holland called for forbearance and forgiveness; few Canadians were as generous.

Indeed, there was little abatement of interest in the atrocity tales that had so chilled the blood of readers during the war. Terms like Hunnishness and *schrecklichkeit* (frightfulness) lost little of their potency in the postwar years and were repeated to confirm the real nature of the enemy that the Allies had faced. Though tales of a crucified Canadian soldier were discredited, writers were not shy about reminding their readers of other war crimes committed by the Central Powers.[19] German abuse of prisoners of war remained a sore point with Canadians, and the memoirs of former captives sold well in the years immediately following the war. Far from scolding such works for perpetuating wartime hatreds, Canadians reviewers often praised them for doing just that. The tale of one private who escaped from captivity, for example, was lauded for leaving the reader "in no doubt of the basic brutality of German militarism."[20] Some of the more notorious misdeeds remained popular fodder for writers, and the execution of British nurse Edith Cavell and the torpedoing of the British passenger liner *Lusitania* were staples of poetry collections through the 1920s and 1930s. In Saint John, hundreds of people braved the cold of February 1920 to line up for a film about wartime atrocities called *Auction of Souls,* while Frank Carrel, the editor of the Québec *Daily Telegraph,* devoted an entire chapter of his book *Impressions of War* to "Hun Heinousness." Other chapters were liberally sprinkled with horrors like a crucified kitten wired into a booby trap and the rape of Belgian nuns.[21]

Even the physical damage of the war was taken as proof of German evil. Photographs of ruined Belgian and French cities were common in postwar illustrated volumes, including some published by the government; the 1918 report of the Overseas Military Forces of Canada, for example, includes photographs captioned "An Abiding Record of the Enemy's Wanton Destruction" and "The Hand of the Hun in Cambrai." Poetry, too, often dwelt on these tangible signs of German evil. "Rheims," written by the poet and Bishop's University language professor Frank Oliver Call, was addressed to the shattered cathedral in that city: "Do thy mute bells to all the world proclaim / Thy martyred glory and thy foeman's shame?" The destruction of the city of Ypres, though a legitimate target for German artillery, was also taken as a sign of German wantonness. Commenting on the rebuilding of the city, the editor of the *Globe* expressed hope that the new Ypres would have a better fate than the old one, which fell victim to "frightfulness."[22] James Kerr-Lawson's canvas of the ruined Cloth Hall in Ypres was

occasionally exhibited under the title *The Footprint of the Hun.* The word "cloven" was implicit.

Most of these accounts date from the years immediately after the war, but such enmity was not confined to the period of postwar hysteria. Indeed, Canadians demonstrated a long memory when it came to the war's excesses. Despite later Allied experiments with poison gas, Canadians never forgot that the Germans had used it first. In 1928, Vancouver poet Kate Colquhoun decried the "foul methods" that Germany resorted to at Ypres in 1915 when they could not win by fighting fairly. The following year, Kim Beattie, a regimental historian and writer of popular trench doggerel, published "The First Gas," an even more bitter commentary on the battle:

> The cowardly bastard! He done this job;
> They're strangled an' choked wi' gas;
> An' they had no chance to croak
> Like a fightin' sojer bloke
> — God'll never let this pass![23]

Nor were Canadians willing to forget the murders of women and children in occupied France and Belgium. The 1926 history of the Canadian Grenadier Guards cited "definite and authentic information" that the Germans had slaughtered Belgian civilians, and in a 1936 piece by a Nova Scotia playwright, the dramatic action turns on the murder of Belgian women and children.[24] German attacks on hospitals and hospital ships, the destruction of French cities in the summer of 1918, the adoption of unrestricted submarine warfare—all continued to enrage Canadians well into the 1930s. Even Canada's "official" war film was generously dosed with references to northern France being "ruthlessly violated" and "defenceless vessels sinking on the desolate wastes of the ocean." On the eve of the next war, journalist Pierre van Paassen, who had been shamed into enlisting while a divinity student in Toronto in 1914, lamented the continuing credulity of Canadians when it came to wartime atrocity tales: "hundreds of thousands of easy-going citizens of the Dominion are firmly persuaded that... Belgian babies were currently carried on the point of German bayonets, that Bavarian yodelers took a particular delight in cutting off the breasts of Flemish nuns, that the Huns boiled enemy corpses in order to extract grease for the soap in the Kaiser's bath."[25]

Most Canadians knew full well where to lay blame for these excesses—not upon war as a social act or on the darkness in the human heart, but squarely on the shoulders of Germany, and often on the head of Kaiser Wilhelm himself. As a consequence, representations of the kaiser came to be characterized by extreme bitterness. An amateur poet in rural Ontario envisioned the Devil giving up his dominion over hell to his rival from imperial Germany: "It breaks my heart to leave a job that I love so well, / But the kaiser knows better how to run a real hell."[26] A disgruntled Nova Scotian had a different fate in mind for Wilhelm Hohenzollern:

> For a man of any nation
> Guilty of this conflagration
> How much lenience would you deem the
>   proper scope?
> Viewed aright from any angle,
> In your vision he will dangle
> From a tough and solid piece of hempen rope.

Even on Peace Day 1919, when Canadians might have taken the opportunity to exercise a spirit of forgiveness, many people were in no mood to be charitable. The venerable journalist and caricaturist J.W. Bengough, in his "Lines for the Peace Day Celebration," gloated that "the Teuton despot, panting with dismay, / Lies helpless in the dust his vileness stains."[27] At the festivities in Hamilton, Mayor Charles Booker, still grieving the death of his only son at the front in October 1918, demanded that the kaiser and his warlords face justice for their crimes. "I have come to believe," he confided to the cheering crowd, "that the only good German is a dead German." The people of Guelph, Ontario, would have applauded the mayor's comments. The Peace Day parade in that city included a mannequin of the kaiser, complete with a rope around his neck; the crowd roared as the effigy was consigned to the bonfire.[28]

Not everyone felt this degree of antipathy towards Wilhelm on a personal level. It was more common to indict Germany in a more general sense, often by objectifying the enemy in ways that perpetuated propagandized wartime stereotypes. Every conceivable term of opprobrium was repeated in the interwar years, from "the horrible Hun and the unspeakable Turk" to "Germany, like an unchained beast, plung[ing] across defenceless Belgium to devour France."[29] The German armies continued to be referred to as "Hun hordes" or fiends "mad with the lust of conquest and dead to every sense of honour," and the Reverend Wellington Bridgeman was certainly not alone in declaring that "the Austro-Hun has forfeited the right to dwell among decent people."[30]

Even those Canadians who were dubious about atrocity tales and reluctant to fasten blame upon the Germans, individually or collectively, still had little doubt that the war had been justified. Shortly after the Armistice, a Methodist minister in Ontario predicted that veterans would need "time to analyze and relate their experiences...[before they] are able to present the inner truth and meaning of it [the war]."[31] Many Canadians had no need of such reflection; for them, the truth and meaning of the war had always been manifest, and remained so after the victory had been won. In the view of the *Globe*'s editor, a decade of peace gave no reason to look any deeper into the meaning of November 1918 and the war it ended: "Twelve years have elapsed since the world conflict armistice was announced, and during this period of retrospection there has been no alteration of view in regard to the justness of the war. Rather, the conviction has grown that, while the years of battle presented the tragedy of the ages, it was all necessary to the prevention of a still greater and more lasting tragedy."[32] On the eve of the war, British Foreign Secretary Sir Edward Grey stood in his Foreign Office window and watched the lights being extinguished as a precaution against air raids. "The lamps are going out all over Europe," he is reputed to have said in a remark that has become part of the iconography of 1914. As far as Canadians were concerned, there remained little doubt that the war had been necessary to prevent the tragedy of eternal darkness.

Some Canadians continued to insist through the 1920s and 1930s that the country had gone to war to avoid German domination. If Britain fell, wrote Colonel George Nasmith, "Canada would be next...[The soldiers] were fighting for their own homes." A Toronto veteran agreed, maintaining that the volunteers of 1914 had enlisted because they visualized German troops reaching Calais, from where they would embark for Canada. As an ex-soldier in Guelph, Ontario, put it, "there would now be a German flag flying over our "Old Canadian Home" instead of the Union Jack," if not for the sacrifice of 60,000 Canadian lives.[33] For this reason, many war memorials suggested that the country had narrowly escaped German occupation. The deaths of Canadian soldiers "helped under God to save their country," proclaimed the memorial in Bedford, Nova Scotia. "The men were very good unto us and we were not hurt," stated a number of other memorials. "They were a wall against us born by night and day."

The image of German *uhlans* trotting up Dorchester Street or Yonge Street was less common than the contention that certain fundamental principles had to be defended. There were, in the words of an Ontario cleric, "princi-ples that we / Have on the field of conflict seen well tried, / For which our loved ones spent themselves and died."[34] In some cases, these principles were given no more specific identity than Right or Good. "I will go forth to battle for the right," declared a character representing the youth of Acadia University going to war, and few Canadians would have disagreed with him.[35] An Armistice Day supplement to Canadian newspapers in 1928 asked Canadians to feel "thankfulness that our cause was a righteous one," and even ten years later, a Prairie divinity student was able to interpret the war in simple terms of right and wrong: "They gave their all in the belief that thus / Must human rights be saved, and states yet rife / With wrong be raised to nobler planes of life." This was the simple reason, according to the chancellor of Toronto's Victoria University, why the lives of Canadians had not been wasted: the Allies were right, and Germany was wrong.[36]

Other Canadians preferred to interpret the war not just as a defence of good or right, but as a defence of humanity and civilization. "They left their homes to safeguard humanity and to add a bright band to the chaplet of history," declared Chancellor A.L. McCrimmon of McMaster University. "Young and full of promise! What an offering at the Altar of Liberty!" This notion, that the fallen had given their lives "in defence of those principles which all good citizens regard as worth preserving in the best interests of humanity," was one of the most common refrains in Canada's memory of the war.[37] Listeners tuning in to the General Motors of Canada radio program in 1931 heard it, and ex-soldiers in the Brotherhood of Railroad Trainmen found it on the welcome-home medals presented to them by their union.[38] The sacrifice of Canada's sons and daughters had helped to save humanity from barbarism.

This theme also dominated the language of commemoration, often through the use of a figure representing Humanity or Civilization. This affirmed what had been at stake during the war and, in transforming humanity into a ward of the Allied governments, also confirmed that Germany was inhuman and uncivilized. This is especially evident in the work of sculptor Walter Allward. *Saturday Night* described his war memorial in Peterborough, Ontario, as representing the collapse of barbarism in the face of civilization: "civilization stands in a commanding position, with outstretched hand, the idle shield worn on the back of the figure and an idle sword expressing the idea that there can be no further conflict...the figure of strife or barbarism, beaten and retreating before the strength of civilization, the sword has fallen to the ground and the flambou [*sic*] has been extinguished." His sketch for the Bank of Commerce memorial was similar, depicting a male figure who "plants his strong foot upon the neck of a recumbent and still struggling brute beast of wilful war waged by a misguided nation."[39] The victory of civilization over Hunnishness was thus validated in bronze.

It was also validated by the inscriptions that hundreds of Canadian communities chose for their monuments. They frequently affirm that the war had been fought for civilization, humanity, or ideals like Liberty, Truth, Justice, Honour, Mercy, or Freedom. Such inscriptions, which list the specific principles at stake and confirm the value of fighting for those principles, proliferate in every Canadian province. Often listed as a trinity, there is apparently little logic in the values that any given community chose to list. A plaque in St. Paul's Church in Charlottetown recorded that Lieutenant Frederic John Longworth, killed in action a day before the Armistice, died "For Liberty, for Honour, for Righteousness." The fallen of Mahone Bay, Nova Scotia, gave their lives for truth, justice, and liberty; in Orangeville, Ontario, it was freedom, truth, and righteousness. Only occasionally is an inscription more revealing of local sensibilities. On the bilingual

memorial in Lac-Mégantic, Québec, the French text notes that the soldiers had died "pour la défense de la liberté et de la civilisation," two concepts nearer to the Gallic heart than the "freedom and righteousness" listed in the English text.

It went without saying that any sacrifice, including the supreme sacrifice, was more than justified in defence of these eternal principles. In this regard, virtually every Canadian war memorial can be considered a patriotic memorial (to use Antoine Prost's phrase), one whose inscription renders a value judgment on the sacrifice.[40] Such monuments affirm the nobility and rectitude of the struggle waged by Canadian soldiers and honour those people who were willing to lay down their lives to check the spread of militarism and barbarism. By their service, they had helped to banish the darkness into which the world had been plunged in 1914.

III

In the face of this inspiring vision of the Great War, a few faint voices tried to shape an alternate vision. Neutralists, non-interventionists, and isolationists, many of them intellectuals like Frank Underhill, Arthur Lower, and Escott Reid, railed against involvement in wars that, in their view, little concerned Canada directly. Because they conducted their campaign in the rarefied atmosphere of *Canadian Forum,* university campuses, and the Canadian Institute of International Affairs, however, these elites posed little real threat to the just war theory. More dangerous was the very vocal pacifist lobby, which carried a critique of war into the streets, churches, and public schools. The poet Wilson Macdonald, whose patriotic verse, such as "The Girl behind the Man behind the Gun," had given way to impassioned and slightly overdone pacifist poetry, painted the war not as a righteous defender of civilization but as a hideous beast:

His feet are rotting
From a slow gangrene;
His tusks are yellow
And his eyes are green.
But the church of god
Calls him sweet and clean.[41]

In Saskatoon, Violet McNaughton eschewed Macdonald's poetic excesses and developed instead a more rational critique of the war, using the women's page of the *Western Producer* to disseminate a mixture of traditional pacifism and western cooperative ideals. The Women's International League for Peace and Freedom (WIL), headquartered in Vancouver and led by Laura Jamieson, Lucy Woodsworth, and Agnes Macphail, organized lectures, festivals, and a range of other activities intended to "make peace as interesting as war." WIL peace conferences, often held to coincide with Armistice Day, featured addresses by prominent pacifists such as J.S. Woodsworth and Rabbi Maurice Eisendrath, as well as the obligatory poetry reading by Macdonald. The lectures were often complemented by church services, discussion groups, and ceremonies to decorate the graves of nurses, firefighters, and other "heroes of peace."[42]

Despite such efforts, adherents to the pacifist movement remained a small minority in Canadian society. The leading organizations never had a large membership, and their communitarian ventures were pitifully small. Even the movement's peak, when it brought together a rough coalition of pacifists, social gospellers, and liberal internationalists, lasted only a few years, from the late 1920s to the mid-1930s. With the rise of fascism in Europe, allied groups melted away, many under the pressure of having to choose between preserving democracy and social justice and holding to the ideals of non-violence.

But if fascism stood in the way of a strong Canadian pacifist movement, so too did the memory of the Great War. According to that memory, August 1914 had given the civilized world (in other words, the Allies) a choice: either fight to preserve the values that were deemed to underlie society, or sacrifice those values in the interests of preserving peace. By opting to fight in 1914, Canada had made the only possible choice. The slaughter of the next four years did little to shake the nation's faith that the choice had been right. It would temper their public displays of enthusiasm when the choice had to be made again in 1939, but it would serve as no brake on enlistment, unity, or less obvious shows of patriotism.

That the war had been a necessary evil was accepted by most veterans. E.L.M. Burns, who would command Canadian troops in the field during the Second World War, quoted approvingly a line from Ernst Jünger, the ex-soldier and reluctant darling of the German political right: "There are ideals in comparison with which the life of an individual or even of a people has no weight."[43] In 1934, a former nursing sister agreed: "Our only choice in the last resort is to be prepared to defend ourselves, or accept slavery and extinction.... Is it to be our creed that *nothing* is worth dying for?" Vancouver veteran F.W. Bagnall, a former YMCA worker and a very devout man, abhorred war but admitted its necessity if greater evils were to be avoided; he did not understand how others failed to grasp this fundamental reality.[44]

It was not simply that old soldiers wanted to justify a war in which they suffered and that took the lives of so many of their comrades. On the contrary, the belief that Canada had been right to fight to defend a set of principles was widespread in society. When the Woman's Christian Temperance Union suggested in 1925 that the Anglican Church reconsider its support for cadet training in public schools and Anglican universities, a synod committee disagreed. Military training was imperative, concluded the committee, because it was the duty of every Christian to be ready to defend sacred principles like freedom, justice, and truth. It was not enough to avoid an aggressor and hope the threat would pass. "War is a bad thing," wrote a Toronto cleric, "but when a mad dog runs amuck [sic] it must be met with proper methods."[45] At a Montreal Armistice Day service in 1933, Sir Andrew Macphail concurred, declaring that "peace and war is not the antithesis. The antithesis of a slothful peace is not war but massacre. That has always been the fate of every docile, passive and submissive people." War was an evil, but it was not the supreme evil; it was infinitely preferable to a peace purchased by the abandonment of a society's most treasured values and principles. In response to Neville Chamberlain's "Peace in our Time" speech on the signing of the Munich agreement, Sir Charles G.D. Roberts read his poem "Peace with Dishonour" to the University of Guelph's 1938 Armistice Day service. In it, Roberts held that he did not shrink from the "red flame of war, the anguish of women, / The dropped bomb, the gas-choked breath," because all of these eventually passed. His soul, however, cringed from the "long dishonour, brief cowed peace. / For freedom stripped and cast to the loud pack. / *This* stain endures."[46] For Sir Charles "God Damn," pacifism was flawed simply because it asked Canadians to jettison every philosophy they valued most highly rather than take up arms against another nation.

Roberts was not the only Canadian to believe this. On Armistice Day, the Canadian Youth Congress (CYC) made a practice of soliciting messages in support of world peace from prominent Canadians. The responses received in 1937 are revealing. Certainly many politicians, clerics, and educators expressed wholehearted support for the efforts of the CYC, but a number of individuals pointed out the inherent weakness of pacifism, its refusal to recognize the existence of a just war. Derwyn T. Owen, the archbishop of Toronto, stressed that "in all our efforts to promote peace we should remember the claims of justice," while Adele Plumptre,

the Toronto politician, educator, and philanthropist, noted that "there can be no peace without a foundation of justice in international relations." General Alex Ross, president of the Canadian Legion, responded at greater length: "I am convinced of the fact that we who took up arms under similar circumstances [in 1914] played our part in a manner which history will proclaim as adequate.... [W]e fought no war of conquest but we fought sincerely and honestly to secure the peace of the world. But we failed in that purpose and therefore it is with this sense of failure and in a spirit of humility I speak and say that it is futile and hopeless to simply proclaim our desire for peace." Pacifism was not enough, maintained Ross. People had to be willing to fight to defend what they valued.[47]

The widespread acceptance of the just war thesis through the 1920s and 1930s was, as much as Nazism, the rock upon which the ship of pacifism came to grief. For Armistice Day 1935, *Saturday Night* printed a thoughtful reflection on the relationship between memory, pacifism, and the Great War. The editor decided that there was little honour to those who served or died "by the constant reiteration of the thought that their sacrifice was vain and mistaken, and that no such sacrifice should ever have to be repeated." The contention that all war was futile was irritating at the best of times, but especially so on the anniversary of the Armistice "which marked the saving of Europe from the possibility—at any rate for a generation or so— of complete domination by one of the least humane, least tolerant, and least freedom-loving of its races." Furthermore, pacifists achieved nothing with their protests against war: "If those who hate war—and its hatefulness we have no wish to deny—would content themselves with making every effort that lies in their power to ensure that the behaviour of their nation shall be so wise, so just and so humane that no other nation can possibly make war on it without gross injustice and inhumanity, we should have no word to say against them. Unfortunately, we see little sign of any such effort on their part."[48] In short, even Canada had not yet reached that level of spirituality that freed people from the need to go to war. For this reason, the pacifist position was entirely too simplistic. No one could deny that universal cooperation and love were the ultimate goals of the human race. However, it was folly to suggest that this state of grace could be achieved without sacrifice.

That the Great War represented one of the sacrifices along the road to universal amity is evident in Canada's memory of the war. Allward's sketch for the Bank of Commerce memorial, the male figure with its foot upon the neck of the beast of war, was intended to be constructive, not destructive. It stressed "the ameliorating forces of re-creation, which by the power of benevolent ideas in evolution will tend to make the savagery of war impossible."[49] In this interpretation, the war waged by the Allies had been a force for good, because its only goal was the prevention of future conflict. The sculptor's memorial on Vimy Ridge carried the same message, according to *Saturday Night*: "There is in the symbolism of this monument no suggestion of that characteristic element of the shallower popular philosophy of our post-war day, the emotional rebellion against all forms of human strife, the strident clamour for the immediate establishment of the millennium on the basis of the present division of the world's surface among the existing sovereign states." Allward's figures demonstrated that the pacifist position was untenable, for in the 1930s the most it could realistically hope for was an artificial peace that was legalistic and treaty-based. Instead, the true goal should be a peace that was spiritual in nature. That peace "will be brought nearer only as we each and every one learn...to be actuated by a much livelier sense of the universal brotherhood of man and the relative unimportance of racial and national divisions."[50]

The mythicized version of the war, then, proved that pacifism was a bankrupt philosophy, because only those people who were willing to fight for peace and freedom would be able to secure it. With this, the soldier became the foremost advocate of peace; as someone who was willing to fight and die to secure peace, he was the ultimate pacifist. Criticism of Armistice Day or war memorials on the grounds that they perpetuated wartime hatreds missed the point, for such commemorations marked not a war, but a quest for peace. As the Canadian Legion put it, "all the living sacrifices made upon the fields of battle, and commemorated on all our War Memorials were made in the truer interest of Peace, and not in those of war."[51] The decorated hero had no "passion for war"; the men who enlisted in 1914 were not warmongers who joined up "because they enjoyed the prospect of slaughtering foreign men who had nothing to do with war being declared." On the contrary, "it was through his love of peace that he shouldered the burden of kit and accoutrements and went forth to do battle—a struggle that should have been made lighter and shorter by the assistance of those professed so-called pacifists who are decrying him today."[52]

What was true of the soldier was even more true of the veteran; he was not "pugnacious and anxious for war" but rather was "the greatest and sincerest pacifist extant." Only the veteran, who had experienced first-hand the horror of war, could fully appreciate the need for a true pacifism. "We know war and its aftermath," said former Canadian Corps commander Sir Arthur Currie at the unveiling of the Peterborough memorial in 1929. "We speak of peace with the authority of service." Veterans were men who "deplored war, its military discipline, its hardships, its trail of suffering, but who to-morrow, if their country needed their services, would immediately respond to the call, would make any sacrifice to ensure a more lasting peace."[53] The pacifist-soldier, then, was not a contradiction in terms. The veteran of the Great War was a truer pacifist than Wilson Macdonald or any WIL member, for only the veteran had been willing to risk death on the battlefield in defence of peace.

When H.G. Wells coined the phrase "the war that will end war," he intended "war" as a euphemism for Prussianism or militarism.[54] In this sense, he was entirely correct, and Canadians never lost sight of the fact that November 1918 marked a victory over the forces of barbarism. Yet Wells's phrase was also interpreted in a literal sense: the Great War would put an end to the human activity of war. The fact that this assertion proved optimistic in no way compromised its basic validity within the context of the myth. It was unfortunate that the Great War had not marked the dawn of eternal peace, yet there was no reason to believe that this dawn would not eventually come. The war only verified what many people already knew, that the road to peace might well lead humanity through conflict. If aggressors were met on that road, they had to be faced and defeated. Only by fighting for the principles that Canadians valued could they one day enjoy a state of peace founded on universal love and cooperation.

That did not mean, of course, that the nation should leap at every chance to go to war. Were the majority of Canadians willing to fight for the League of Nations over Manchuria and Ethiopia? Probably not. Did they support Neville Chamberlain, the self-proclaimed "go-getter for peace," in his efforts to appease Nazi Germany? Almost certainly. Yet when appeasement had been tried and had failed, they accepted war as a last resort, an unfortunate but necessary evil. They did so for a number of reasons, not the least of which was the fact that the notion of a just war against an intransigent and dangerous aggressor had been nurtured in the public consciousness in the two decades after 1918.

Clearly, the journey to everlasting peace would take humanity through a number of just wars. The true pacifist, then, was not the publicist who railed from a soapbox against every form of war, but the soldier who was prepared to stand in the vanguard. One could never achieve peace simply by talking about it; one had to be willing to sacrifice more than a few well chosen words and the odd poem for something so precious. The only way to demonstrate a real commitment to peace was to be willing to fight and die for it. In Canada's vision of the war, the soldier was the twentieth-century version of the Prince of Peace.

Notes

1   David Beatty, *Memories of the Forgotten War: The World War I Diary of Pte. V.E. Goodwin* (Port Elgin, NB: Baie Verte Editions 1988), 199; NAC, H.C. Pullen Papers, Pullen to Ernestine Gilman, 14 Nov. 1918.

2   Gordon Reid, *Poor Bloody Murder: Personal Memoirs of the First World War* (Oakville, ON: Mosaic Press 1980), 239; Will Bird, *Thirteen Years After: The Story of the Old Front Revisited* (Toronto: Maclean 1932), 180.

3   *Daily Gleaner* (Fredericton), 10 Nov. 1932, 6; St. Stephen Public Library, Saint Croix Courier, *Journey Through Time,* 14 Nov. 1918; letter from M.N.W. Robertson, Burford, 10 Feb. 1994.

4   TFL, "United Service of Thanksgiving and Prayer on the Occasion of the Signing of the Armistice by Germany Signifying her Unconditional Surrender held in St. James' Cathedral, Toronto, Tuesday, November 12th, 1918."

5   *Guelph Evening Mercury,* 21 July 1919, 1; *Vancouver Daily Sun,* 21 July 1919, 3, and 20 July 1919, 1; *Phoenix* (Saskatoon), 21 July 1919, 3.

6   *Vancouver Daily Sun,* 19 July 1919, 7, 14; *Globe* (Toronto), 19 July 1919, 2.

7   Lorne Pierce Special Collections, Queen's University, "Memorial Service held at Queen's University, Kingston, Canada, for Queen's Men who have given their Lives in the War, December

1st, 1918"; Edgar McInnis, "Triumph" in *The Road to Arras* (Charlottetown: Irwin 1920), 27.

8 TFL, "The Message from Mars, being a Christmas greeting from the Officers, NCOs and Men of the 4th Canadian Division to friends the wide world over. In the field—December 1918," 55–6; Bernard McEvoy, "When the Cenotaph Was Unveiled" in *Elvira and Fernando, and Other Selections* (Montreal: private 1927), 85.

9 *Saturday Night*, 18 Sept. 1920, 2.

10 Marina Warner, *Monuments and Maidens: The Allegory of the Female Form* (New York: Atheneum 1985); 140–2.

11 Pierre-Georges Roy, *Monuments commémoratifs de la province de Québec* (Quebec City: Commission des Monuments Historiques 1923), 2:121.

12 NAC, Arthur Currie Papers, vol. 10, f. 29, Hart to Currie, 13 Oct. 1925.

13 Quoted in John Ferguson, *The Arts in Britain in World War I* (London: Stainer and Bell 1980), 40.

14 Capt. W.H. Talbot in *Salute* 4, no. 6 (Oct. 1936):3; Stephen Leacock, "The War Sacrifices of Mr. Spugg" and "Some Just Complaints about the War," in *The Hohenzollerns in America, with the Bolsheviks in Berlin and Other Impossibilities* (Toronto: S.B. Gundy 1919).

15 Theodore Goodridge Roberts, "What Price Military Glory?" *Canadian Bookman* 15, no. 3 (March 1933):36; Leslie Roberts, *When the Gods Laughed* (Toronto: Musson n.d.), 202.

16 UMA, Charles W. Gordon Papers, box 30, f. 2, review of Owen McGillicuddy's *Sir Arthur Currie*, 16 Oct. 1925.

17 Erskine Church Archives, Ottawa, "Erskine Church War Memorial," n.d., 3.

18 Norah M. Holland, "The Defeated" in *Spun Yarn and Spindrift* (London: J.M. Dent 1918), 94.

19 On the crucified soldier, see Maria Tippett, *Art at the Service of War: Canada, Art, and the Great War* (Toronto: University of Toronto Press 1984), 81–7.

20 Review of Nellie McClung's *Three Times and Out* in *Saturday Night*, 29 March 1919, 9.

21 Mark Blagrave, "Garbo Talks...Thespis Listens: The Impact of Cinema on Live Theatre in Saint John, N.B. between the Wars" in *Myth and Milieu: Atlantic Literature and Culture, 1918–1939*, ed. Gwendolyn Davies (Fredericton: Acadiensis Press 1993), 37–8; Frank Carrel, *Impressions of War* (Québec: Telegraph 1919).

22 Frank Oliver Call, "Rheims" in *Acanthus and Wild Grape* (Toronto: McClelland and Stewart 1920), 27; *Globe,* 26 July 1927, 4.

23 Kate Colquhoun, "The Battle of St. Julien" in *The Battle of St. Julien and Other Poems* (Toronto: Ryerson Press 1928); Kim Beattie, "The First Gas" in *"And You!"* (Toronto: Macmillan 1929), 8.

24 *A Brief Outline of the Story of the Canadian Grenadier Guards and the First Months of the Royal Montreal Regiment in the Great War* (Montreal: Gazette 1926), 21; W.C. Hancock, "Fate," *Acadia Athaneum* 61, no. 7 (May 1936): 26–9.

25 NAC, Department of National Defence Records, vol. 1819, f. GAQ 4–11, script for "Lest We Forget"; Pierre van Paassen, *Days of Our Years* (Garden City, NJ: Garden City Publishing 1939), 62.

26 David Burns, "The Devil Resigns to the Kaiser" in *Random Writings* (Brooklin, ON: private 1920), 2: 100.

27 PANS, MG 100, vol. 85 #66, J.E. Slocomb, "Wanted—The Kaiser's Explanation," 14 Dec. 1918; *Globe,* 19 July 1919, 4.

28 *Hamilton Spectator,* 21 July 1919, 5; *Guelph Evening Mercury,* 21 July 1919, 1.

29 "A Memorial Hall for OAC Guelph," *OAC Review* 31, no. 10 (June 1919):459; foreword to *Canada in the Great War: An Illustrated Record of the Canadian Army in France and Flanders during the Years 1915 to 1918* (Ottawa: Heliotype 1919).

30 Rev. A. O'Malley, "The Hun" in *Sonnets of a Recluse* (Barrie: Gazette n.d.), 2:36; Lieut.-Col. D. Donald, "The War Memorial: An Appreciation," *Caduceus* (Canadian Imperial Bank of Commerce) 1, no. 12 (March 1921):23; Rev. Wellington Bridgeman, *Breaking Prairie Sod: The Story of a Pioneer Preacher in the Eighties* (Toronto: Musson 1920), 158, 188.

31 Rev. Basil W. Thompson, in *Trinity War Book: A Recital of Service and Sacrifice in the Great War,* ed. Oliver Hezzelwood (Toronto: Ontario Press 1921), xiii.

32 *Globe,* 11 Nov. 1930, 4.

33 George G. Nasmith, *Canada's Sons and Great Britain in the World War* (Toronto: John C. Winston 1919), 82; Charles Stebbing, *Globe,* 6 June 1930, 4; NAC, Robert Manion Papers, vol. 67, f. s-300, G.E. Speight, Guelph to Manion, 20 Nov. 1938.

34 Leonard S. Klinck, introduction to *Record of Service 1914–1918: University of British Columbia, McGill*

British Columbia, Vancouver College (Vancouver: Faculty Association Editorial Committee 1924); T.D.J. Farmer, "Accomplishment Not Years" in *A History of the Parish of St. John's, Ancaster* (Guelph: Gummer Press 1924), 254.

35 Mary Kinley Ingraham, *Acadia* (Wolfville: Davidson Brothers 1920), act 4.

36 PANS, MG 100, vol. 79 #25, Armistice Day supplement, 11 Nov. 1928; N. Willison, Lutheran College, Saskatoon, "Remembrance Day," *Kitchener Daily Record,* 11 Nov. 1938, 6; *Acta Victoriana* (Victoria University, Toronto), War Supplement (1919):6.

37 Address at the unveiling of the memorial tablet in Castle Memorial Hall, 9 Dec. 1921, in *McMaster University Monthly,* 31, no. 4 (Jan. 1922):142; Lieut.-Col. H.V. Rorke, in D.J. Corrigall, *The History of the 20th Canadian Battalion* (Toronto: 20th Battalion Association 1935), ix.

38 DFC, #203. 1 G.B. Castle, "Canada on Parade / Le Canada en Parade" (Waterloo, ON: Waterloo Music 1931).

39 *Saturday Night,* 13 Nov. 1920, 5; "Sculpture and the War," *The Lamps* (Arts and Letters Club of Toronto), Dec. 1919, 84.

40 Antoine Prost, "Les Monuments aux morts: Culte républicain? Culte civique? Culte patriotique?" in *Les Lieux de mémoire,* vol. 1, *La République,* ed. Pierre Nora (Paris: Gallimard 1984), 202.

41 Wilson Macdonald, "War" in *A Flagon of Beauty* (Toronto: Pine Tree Publishing 1931), 131.

42 Thomas P. Socknat, *Witness against War: Pacifism in Canada, 1900–1945* (Toronto: University of Toronto Press 1987), 111, 128.

43 Review of Ernst Jünger's *Storm of Steel* in *Canadian Defence Quarterly* 7, no. 3 (April 1930):428.

44 Mabel Clint, *Our Bit: Memories of War Service by a Canadian Nursing Sister* (Montreal: Barwick 1934), 175–6; F.W. Bagnall, *Not Mentioned in Despatches* (Vancouver: North Shore Press 1933).

45 Richard E. Ruggle, "Some Canadian Anglican Attitudes to War and Peace, 1890–1920," *Journal of the Canadian Church Historical Society* 35, no. 2 (Oct. 1993):139; Canon W.J. Loucks, rector of Holy Trinity Church, *Globe,* 10 Nov. 1930, 1.

46 NAC, Sir Andrew Macphail Papers, vol. 6, f. 2, "Armistice Address to Westmount Women's Club," 10 Nov. 1933; University of Guelph Archives, Sir Charles G.D. Roberts Papers, XMI MS A003, letter and poem, Nov. 1938.

47 MU, Canadian Youth Congress Papers, box 12, f. 1, Owen to CYC, 22 Oct. 1937; Plumptre to CYC, 14 Oct. 1937; Ross to CYC, n.d. [Oct. 1937].

48 "Armistice Oratory," *Saturday Night,* 16 Nov. 1935, 3.

49 "Sculpture and the War," 85.

50 *Saturday Night,* 1 Aug. 1936, 1.

51 NAC, Royal Canadian Legion Papers, vol. 7, f. 8, circular #31/10, message from Conference of Presidents of Veterans Organizations, 3 Nov. 1931.

52 NAC, J.L. Ralston Papers, vol. 165, f. 1, speech at Pictou war memorial, 11 July 1935; Charles Stebbing, *Globe,* 6 June 1930, 4.

53 Quoted in *Toronto Daily Star,* 2 July 1929, 32; *Toronto Daily Star,* 10 Nov. 1928, 22.

54 Adrian Gregory argues this point very persuasively in *The Silence of Memory: Armistice Day, 1919–1946* (Oxford: Berg 1994), 122.

Transitional Years: Canada, 1919–1945

The period from 1919 to 1945 was one of turbulent change for most Canadians. It began with a post-war recession that lasted until early 1924, giving way to an uneven prosperity for about six years, followed by the most severe and enduring economic depression that the country has experienced to date (1930–1939), and finally the Second World War (1939–1945). The pace of industrialization and urbanization that had marked the pre-war period and wartime quickened, and social values moulded in earlier periods gradually gave way to "modern" values, characteristic of societies in transition from rural to industrial life.

Our first reading explores, in miniature, why the new industrialism, characterized by corporate control with little government regulation, delivered inconsistent results for Canada's regions and social classes. David Frank traces closely the development of the coal and steel industries in Cape Breton, demonstrating why these potential catalysts for industrial development in the Maritimes proved instead to be examples of vicious external exploitation of the people and resources of the region. Frank's painstaking recreation of the financial machinations of the monopolistic companies that controlled Cape Breton explains why these industries failed either to become stable and competitive, or to pay their workers decent wages.

While the Maritimes endured economic depression throughout the 1920s, much of the rest of the country enjoyed considerable economic growth from 1924 to 1929. During the Dirty Thirties, however, that growth gave way to unprecedented economic decline in the face of a worldwide economic depression that robbed Canada of external markets for its resources. Single men without work were particularly viewed as a potential threat to law and order. In 1932, Prime Minister R. B. Bennett decided to remove these individuals from the cities and place them in relief camps under the control of the Department of National Defence. Laurel MacDowell's article examines the austere lives that

the authorities imposed on the inmates of the camps in one province, Ontario, as well as the efforts of the young men to make their camp lives happier and more independent of the camp authorities.

The pursuit of happiness and autonomy by young people in the inter-war period is the subject of Cynthia Comacchio's article. To the chagrin of their elders and particularly clerics, many young people seemed to be creating a peer culture in which the sober values of earlier generations gave way to what appeared to be hedonism. Sparked by new forms of communication, particularly the radio and movies, young people created their own spare-time activities, resisting parental and church efforts to organize their lives.

The economic turmoil of the inter-war period, along with the challenge by youth to established social values, created a longing among older folk for the ways of the past. The war was increasingly viewed as a time when people were more noble and unselfish than they were in the time of peace that followed, and the people who lived in the pre-industrial age were idealized as being closer to nature and less greedy and competitive. This approach even extended to a degree to Canada's Native people, who had always been regarded ambivalently by their conquerors as both "savages" requiring assimilation to Europe's supposedly more civilized culture for their moral good, and "noble savages" whose way of life was close to nature and fundamentally admirable though doomed to fall before European "progress." Emily Carr, as examined by Douglas Cole, led a number of painters who, from one point of view, honoured the country's First Nations by depicting their oneness with their natural surroundings, in the process bemoaning the separation from nature of her contemporary Euro-Canadians. Such depictions of Native lives, however, tended to ignore the history of European colonialism, which had shaped First Nations for several centuries, and gave little sense of Native realities, which in Carr's lifetime were marked by an effort to achieve a semi-autonomous existence within the larger society rather than an attempt to return to an irretrievable past.

Efforts to rediscover an earlier, supposedly better life in Canada's past, so evident in English Canada in the inter-war period, were equally marked among the intelligentsia in French Canada. Quebec's francophone elites, led by the Roman Catholic Church, joined their Protestant English counterparts in reviling the new secular culture heralded by radio and films. They regarded such innovations as a threat to the traditional influence of the church over popular attitudes and behaviour among francophones, and ultimately to the Roman Catholic religion. The desire to limit the spread of the new forms of culture and the subversive ideas that they propagated led to both an intensification of French-Canadian and Quebec nationalism. While the church and the elites railed against all forms of modernism, ordinary francophones, especially the young, quietly embraced much of the new secular culture, thereby reinforcing a sense of crisis among the elites. The latter's resistance to the transition to a more secular society led them to embrace reactionary political programs that appeared to have the potential to limit the ravages of modernism.

In the context of this social climate, many of Quebec's Francophone intellectual leaders, old and young alike, flirted with the fascism of Mussolini's Italy and the Nazism of Hitler's Germany. Even the young Pierre Elliott Trudeau, who would later actively fight against anti-democratic tendencies in Quebec political life, was attracted to the rhetoric of the fascist regime of General Pétain in France, which collaborated with the Nazi regime in Germany from 1940 to 1945. Authoritarian, race-based, anti-democratic ideologies seemed to many to be the only way to resist the abyss of secularization. Interestingly, as Esther Delisle argues, once the full horrors of Nazism were revealed after the Second World War, Quebec's elites, while embracing different ideologies, tacitly agreed to cover up their common pro-fascist past.

In English Canada, as well, political and intellectual elites had subscribed to anti-democratic ideologies before the Second World War. While few opinion makers openly opposed the right of Canadians to choose their leaders and determine their own national destiny, many conservatives believed that Canadian nationalism was best served by a close identification with the onward march of British imperialism. Britain was supposedly the fount of civilization and culture, and Canadians could do no better than extolling that nation and joining its military adventures as it imposed British values and trade upon the benighted nations of Asia and Africa. The alternative, conservatives argued, was not, in any case, an autonomous Canadian economy and culture but absorption by the American monolith to the south. As J. L. Granatstein's article suggests, the Second World War considerably weakened the conservatives' case because it weakened the economic and political power of Great Britain. In turn, the Americans became the undisputed imperial power of the western world, and Canadians, their economy and culture already perched somewhere between the old and new imperial powers, inevitably came under the complete sway of the rising American star.

While much of inter-war thinking on Canadian nationalism pitted British imperialists against French-Canadian nationalists, Harold Innis proposed that Canadians think of their nation in terms of territory rather than blood. He believed that this nation could expand the territory under its effective control by looking north and making the Canadian North a "crucible of development." Although Innis hoped to transcend French–English bickering, his vision was not without racial or gender limitations. The image that he conjured up, according to Matthew Evenden, was one of white male conquerors establishing dominion over a hostile geographic region. Both women and Natives were shut out of this vision.

The Cape Breton Coal Industry and the Rise and Fall of the British Empire Steel Corporation *

DAVID FRANK

Our understanding of regional underdevelopment in Atlantic Canada has been slow to develop. For more than 50 years we have had extensive documentation of the existence of serious regional inequality in Canada. Attempts to explain the reasons for this have been less common. In the 1920s politicians active in the Maritime Rights movement catalogued the "unfilled promises" and "betrayals" of Confederation and demanded increased federal subsidies as compensation.[1] A less subjective interpretation was proposed by S. A. Saunders, C. R. Fay and Harold Innis, who attributed the region's troubles to the new era of industrialism. For the Maritimes it was "prosperity so long as their face was towards the sea, and... struggle against adversity when the pull of the land increased." Like an "economic seismograph," the Maritimes registered the shockwaves of a "rising tide of continental forces that were destined to dominate the economy of the Maritime Provinces."[2] Recent studies have questioned this approach: an economic historian has challenged the myth of the "Golden Age"; an historical geographer has traced the domination of the region by outside forces during the colonial era; an economist has pointed

out that during a decisive period in the 1830s and 1840s local entrepreneurs neglected the region's industrial potential.[3]

The most important revisionist studies were those published in the early 1970s by Bruce Archibald and T. W. Acheson. In 1971 Bruce Archibald applied a sweeping metropolis/satellite interpretation to the economic history of the region. He argued that the region has "always existed in a dependent relationship with a larger controlling metropolis" and the region must be seen as "the back yard of a dominant economic centre rather than an autonomous but struggling unit." His survey stressed the role of outside exploitation in the underdevelopment of the region: the extraction of resources and capital in response to the needs of outside forces divided the loyalties of local entrepreneurs and produced growing regional underdevelopment.[4] In 1972 T. W. Acheson challenged the view that the Maritimes did not experience economic growth after Confederation; his study found that the Maritimes sustained a significant amount of industrial expansion in the late nineteenth century, as a group of "community-oriented" entrepreneurs transferred capital from traditional pursuits to new industrial invest-

David Frank, "The Cape Breton Coal Industry and the Rise and Fall of the British Empire Steel Corporation," *Acadiensis* 7, 1 (Autumn 1977): 3–34.

* For their constant support and critical comments, I would like to thank Michael Cross, Judith Fingard, Craig Heron, Gregory Kealey, Don Macgillivray, Ian McKay, Del Muise, Nolan Reilly and David Sutherland.

ments. By the 1920s, however, this industrial structure had collapsed, mainly because no "viable regional metropolis" had emerged to take leadership and central Canadian business and finance had asserted control over the region's economic life.[5]

In the light of these studies, it seems clear that a new framework is necessary for understanding regional underdevelopment. A tentative approach may be drawn from the Marxist analysis of regional inequalities under industrial capitalism, which explains uneven development between regions as a natural feature of capitalistic economic growth. The continuing search for new economic surpluses, better rates of profit, new raw materials, markets and sources of labour supply, all caused an expansion in the scale of capital accumulation. As part of this process, the operation of the free market system generally led to the concentration and centralization of capital; economic wealth and power tended to become concentrated in fewer hands and centralized in fewer places. Once the structure of an inter-regional market in goods, labour and capital was established, relationships of domination and dependency emerged between regions. As the process continued, regional disparities deepened and the subordinate communities entered a cycle of capital deficiencies, population losses and economic powerlessness.[6]

By the 1880s industrial capitalism had become well-established in central Canada and began to extend its hegemony over regions and sectors where the growth of industrial capitalism was less advanced. The emergence of this trend towards the concentration and centralization of capital had devastating consequences for economic development in the weaker regions and communities of the country.[7] The concentration and centralization of the Canadian economy affected these regions, especially the Maritimes, in several ways. First, national economic policies under Confederation promoted regional underdevelopment. The political hegemony of central Canada helped shape state policy to aid central Canadian goals and to injure or neglect regional interests, especially in tariff, railway, trade, marine and fisheries matters. The completion of the railway network added a key instrument of national economic integration; the railways brought western goods in and took eastern people out. The creation of a national market in goods undermined local industry as outside competitors conquered the regional market, and the creation of an inter-regional labour market tended to make the region a reserve pool of labour for neighbouring regions. A fourth aspect was the growing division of labour between regions, which often took the form of the export of raw materials and specialized products to the metropolitan market, but also resulted in the location of resource-based and labour-intensive industries to take advantage of raw materials and low wages in the underdeveloped region. A corollary was the emergence of economic sectors, which, because they were not important to the national economy, suffered capital deficiencies (the fisheries) or were absorbed into other economic empires (the forest industries). A fifth aspect of the "Canadianization" of the region was the steady import of central Canadian social and cultural norms; by the time they reached Ottawa, political figures like W. S. Fielding and R. L. Borden readily accepted the assumptions of central Canadian hegemony. Finally, the most effective form of regional subordination was the extension of direct metropolitan financial control over the region. Through competition and credit manipulation, and mergers and takeovers in all important industries and financial institutions, the domination of central Canada over the Maritimes was consolidated by the 1920s. Much of the social and political turmoil of that decade expressed the community's response to the crisis of the regional economy.

Nowhere can the results of these developments be seen more clearly than in industrial Cape Breton, where the process of national economic integration was of decisive importance in the exploitation of one of the region's richest natural resources, the coal-fields. At the beginning of the twentieth century, industrial Cape Breton seemed a dynamic and prosperous industrial community. The population of the industrial area, which numbered 18,005 people in 1891, had increased to 57,263 people by 1911.[8] The largest and most valuable in eastern Canada, the Sydney coal-field stretches about 30 miles along the northeastern shore of Cape Breton Island and in the 1920s the field's proven reserves were known to exceed one billion tons. The accessibility and quality of the coal supply gave the Sydney field considerable economic importance. Cape Breton's bituminous coal compared favourably with other industrial coals, although it was no rival for anthracite as a domestic fuel.[9] The inexpensive water route to Quebec enabled Cape Breton coal to penetrate the central Canadian market, and the extensive iron ore reserves at Bell Island, Newfoundland, generated the establishment of an iron and steel industry in Cape Breton; these two markets consumed the bulk of the coal industry's output. By the time of the First World War industrial Cape Breton occupied an important place in the national economy. The coal mines supplied more than 44 per cent of Canada's annual coal production, and the iron and steel industry produced more than one-third of the country's pig iron.[10]

Although the condition of the local economy at the peak of its fortunes inspired widespread optimism, at least one thoughtful observer was troubled by the emerging pattern of industrial development. A Yorkshire mining engineer who had immigrated to Cape Breton, Francis W. Gray, lamented in 1917 the underdevelopment of the coal resources:

Nova Scotia, as a province, has not reached the stage of industrial and manufacturing activity that should have accompanied a coal mining industry 100 years old.... It must be confessed that the potentialities of Nova Scotia have been but meagrely realized. Take away the steel industry from Nova Scotia, and what other manufacturing activity has the Province to show as a reflex of the production of 7,000,000 tons of coal annually?... The coal mined in Nova Scotia has, for generations, gone to provide the driving power for the industries of New England, Quebec and Ontario, and has, in large part, been followed by the youth and energy of the Province. For almost a century, Nova Scotia has been exporting the raw material that lies at the base of all modern industry....

"Briefly," Gray concluded, "Nova Scotia has achieved the status of a mining camp, whereas its full stature should be that of a metropolis of industry."[11] Gray's worries proved well-founded. After the First World War, the local economy experienced a crisis from which it has never recovered. In 1921 the British Empire Steel Corporation assumed control of the coal and steel industries in Nova Scotia. The outcome of a well-established pattern of regional underdevelopment in Atlantic Canada, the rise and fall of the British Empire Steel Corporation marked a decisive turning point in the economic history of industrial Cape Breton.

Before the 1860s the growth of the coal industry in Nova Scotia was restricted by imperial policy. In 1826, under a royal charter, the General Mining Association (GMA) of London took exclusive control of the mineral resources of Nova Scotia, but advocates of colonial economic development, including Abraham Gesner and Joseph Howe, helped lead a popular campaign against the monopoly. In 1858 the Association's rights were restricted and control of mineral rights was vested in the colony. This successful revolt against colonial underdevelopment opened the way for expansion of the coal industry. Numerous mining companies were formed and a brief boom followed. Under the unusual conditions of the 1854 Reciprocity Treaty and the high demand for coal during the American Civil War, Cape Breton coal entered the long-coveted United States market on a large scale. The boom ended in 1867, however, when Congress restored prohibitive import duties.[12]

The collapse of the export trade led to growing protectionist sentiment in the coal industry. The example of British industrial growth, where the coal resources fueled the industrialization of the Black Country, provoked hopes for a large local market based on "home manufactures."[13] But the dominant protectionist impulse was support for a federal tariff to enable Nova Scotia coal to enter the central Canadian market. The idea was influential among pro-Confederates in the 1860s.[14] A short-lived duty in 1870 demonstrated the effectiveness of a coal tariff, and during the 1870s the Cape Breton coal operators campaigned for "the same just and reasonable protection as has been afforded to other Dominion industries."[15] This agitation was successful in 1879 when the National Policy established a 50¢ per ton duty on coal imports, which was raised to 60¢ the next year. Nova Scotia's coal sales in Quebec rose sharply, and the local market also became important, as the Maritimes experienced industrial expansion under the National Policy. Based on this twin foundation, the coal industry's long expansionist cycle continued until the First World War.

During this expansionist period the growth of the coal industry demonstrated several aspects of the uneven development between regions which characterized the emergence and consolidation of industrial capitalism in Canada. The growing concentration and centralization of capital in the Canadian economy created a national economic structure based on inter-regional linkages and dependencies. National economic policies encouraged the expansion of the coal industry, but did not promote stability or prosperity for the hinterland resource area. The creation of national markets led to a division of labour between regions, which established the Cape Breton coal industry as a source of industrial energy filling the needs of the central Canadian market. With the growth of strong Canadian financial centres, a corporate consolidation movement unified the coal industry into a few large companies and delivered control of the industry into the hands of powerful financial interests in central Canada.

The division of labour between regions established the coal industry in Nova Scotia as an important—but vulnerable—source of industrial energy in Canada. After the 1870s, imports of British coal into Canada declined sharply. Under the tariff, shipments of Nova Scotia coal to the Quebec market grew from 83,710 tons in 1878 to 795,060 tons in 1896 and 2,381,582 tons in 1914. Simultaneously, imports of American coal into Canada increased heavily, from 331,323 tons in 1878 to 1,451,508 tons in 1896 and 18,145,769 tons in 1913. By the eve of the First World War, Nova Scotia supplied 54 per cent of Canada's coal production—but 57 per cent of the coal consumed in Canada was imported from the United States.[16] Although the tariff promoted expansion of the domestic coal industry, it provided only partial protection. The Ontario market remained beyond the economic reach of the industry, and in Quebec, Nova Scotia coal continually faced keen competition. Despite protests from Nova Scotia, the tariff on bituminous coal was reduced to 53¢ per ton in 1897 and remained at this figure until 1925. As coal prices approximately doubled during this period, the effect of the fixed duty, which had amounted to more than 20 per cent in the

1880s, was seriously diminished.[17] Under a national policy that was never truly national, the coal trade occupied a vulnerable position in the Canadian market.

The coal market in the Maritimes also grew during this period, reaching a peak of more than three million tons in 1913,[18] but the key factor in the coal market was a single customer. In 1913 the steel plant at Sydney consumed 1,362,000 tons of coal, more than half the total coal sales in Nova Scotia.[19] A vital customer for the coal industry, the Nova Scotia steel industry suffered from chronic instability throughout its history; dependence on this market was a source of further vulnerability for the coal industry.[20] In general, the industrial structure of the Maritimes was limited in scope and suffered seriously from its own pattern of underdevelopment and deindustrialization.[21]

The second main trend in the coal industry was the growth of a consolidation movement in the coal-fields. Completion of the railway to central Canada in the 1870s was followed by mergers dominated by Montreal interests in the mainland coal-fields in 1884 (Cumberland Railway and Coal Co.) and 1886 (Acadia Coal Co.). Plagued by the insecurities of seasonal operations, distant markets and inadequate capital, the Cape Breton coal operators also turned to mergers. The formation of the Provincial Workmen's Association prompted a short-lived defensive alliance among the coal operators in the early 1880s, the Cape Breton Colliery Association.[22] The battle for "survival of the fittest" continued, however, and of the 20 mines opened in Cape Breton after 1858, only eight remained in operation in 1892. The coal operators welcomed the formation of the Dominion Coal Company.[23]

The Dominion Coal Company played an important part in integrating the Cape Breton coal industry into the national structure of industrial capitalism in Canada, although ironically, this was not the original aim of the compa-

ny's promoters. The formation of Dominion Coal in 1893 was sponsored by an alliance between Boston financier Henry M. Whitney, who promised to invest capital and revive the lost coal trade to New England, and a group of Nova Scotia coal operators and politicians anxious to expand the coal industry and restore dwindling provincial revenues. An experienced promoter, in 1886 Whitney had created Boston's West End Street Railway Company, the first extensive electrified rail system in the country, and energy for the railway was supplied by his coal-burning New England Gas and Coke Company. Whitney's interest in Cape Breton was designed to secure an inexpensive coal supply and improve the financial position of his other companies. The financial arrangements indicate that the formation of Dominion Coal was a typical episode in an age of corporate carpetbagging.[24] Dominion Coal also received considerable encouragement from the provincial government. The legislature approved a 99-year lease on all the unassigned coal resources of Cape Breton and the company was permitted to purchase any others; in return Dominion Coal guaranteed a minimum annual royalty at a fixed rate of $12\frac{1}{2}$¢ per ton for the duration of the lease. Premier W. S. Fielding predicted the coal industry would grow tenfold as Whitney accomplished "what nature intended...the shipment of large quantities of coal to the United States."[25]

The creation of Dominion Coal marked the integration of the coal industry in Cape Breton into a metropolitan network of financial control. The composition of Dominion's first board of directors revealed an alliance of New England, Nova Scotia and Montreal capitalists under Whitney's presidency.[26] The establishment of the merger also marked the triumph of the strategy of exporting the province's coal resources in large volume. Dominion Coal soon acquired control of all the existing operations in the Sydney coal-field, except the GMA's holdings at Sydney Mines. The unification of the south Cape Breton field under one management rationalized exploitation of the coal resource and the new coal company applied a much-needed infusion of capital and technology. Hopes of capturing the New England market were disappointed,[27] but the trade into the St. Lawrence ports continued to grow rapidly and Dominion Coal established an extensive network of railways, shipping piers, coal carriers and coal yards to serve this market.

Control of the coal industry again changed as the integration of the regional economy into the national economic structure accelerated after the 1890s. In 1901 Whitney sold control of Dominion Coal to James Ross, the prominent Montreal capitalist. Dominion Iron and Steel, another Whitney company launched with great fanfare in 1899, was abandoned to central Canadian interests at the same time. Ross and his backers briefly controlled both the coal and steel companies, but in 1903 separate control was established, with J. H. Plummer of Toronto as president of the steel company.[28] Ross and Plummer were both important figures in Canadian business circles: in 1906 Ross held 15 directorships in addition to Dominion Coal, including seats on the Bank of Montreal and Montreal Rolling Mills boards, and Plummer, formerly assistant general manager of the Bank of Commerce, held seven directorships in addition to Dominion Iron and Steel.[29] The two companies quarrelled continually; Ross attempted to take over the steel company in 1907, but in 1910 Plummer triumphed and merged the two companies into the new Dominion Steel Corporation. The merger also took over the Cumberland Railway and Coal Company, but failed to win control of the Nova Scotia Steel and Coal Company, the New Glasgow industrial complex.[30] With Plummer as president and Sir William C. Van Horne as vice-president, Dominion Steel represented a powerful alliance of Toronto and Montreal interests. Closely linked to the Bank of Montreal and the Bank of Commerce, the Dominion Steel directors as a group held more than 179 company directorships.[31] Thus, by the eve of the First World War the Cape Breton coal industry had become not only an important source of industrial energy for the Canadian economy, but also an attractive field of investment for Canadian businessmen. These two aspects of the Canadianization of the region's economic life would contribute heavily to the crisis of markets and corporate welfare which gripped the coal industry in the 1920s.

The emergence of the British Empire Steel Corporation (Besco), which was incorporated in the spring of 1920, was the result of extended manoeuvres for further consolidation of the coal and steel industries in Nova Scotia. By 1917 American financial interests had gained control of the Nova Scotia Steel and Coal Company (Scotia) and were actively pursuing a merger with the much larger Dominion Steel Corporation. The same idea attracted interest in Britain at the end of the war, and in 1919 a syndicate of British industrialists began to buy control of Dominion Steel. At the same time, a third group also appeared on the scene; based in Canada Steamship Lines and led by two Montreal entrepreneurs, J. W. Norcross and Roy M. Wolvin.

The Nova Scotia Steel and Coal Company boasted a strong reputation for cautious management, technical excellence and financial success. From humble beginnings in the 1870s in New Glasgow, the Scotia companies had pioneered the growth of the Canadian steel industry, smelting the first steel ingots in Canada in 1883. In 1899 Whitney had attempted to include Scotia in his new Dominion Iron and Steel Company. In 1900 Scotia entered Cape Breton by taking over the GMA's holdings at Sydney Mines and building a steel plant there. Despite growing links with Toronto interests, especially through customers like Massey-Harris and financial backers like the Bank of Nova

Scotia, the company remained dominated by Nova Scotia financiers and industrialists.[32]

In 1915 a number of steps signaled the closer integration of Scotia into the metropolitan financial structure. President since 1905, Robert Harris, the prominent Halifax financier, resigned to take a seat on the province's Supreme Court. He was replaced as president by Thomas Cantley, Scotia's longtime general manager. W. D. Ross, a native Cape Bretoner active in Toronto financial circles (and ultimately Lieutenant-Governor of Ontario), became financial vice-president, and N. B. McKelvie of New York joined the Scotia board as a representative of the New York investment house of Hayden, Stone and Company. In 1917 McKelvie's group supplied a large investment of working capital for Scotia and secured control of the company. Cantley was replaced as president by Frank H. Crockard, formerly vice-president of a Tennessee coal and steel company, "one of the bright stars of the United States Steel Corporation's galaxy of subsidiary corporations."[33] The New York investment banker, Galen L. Stone, became chairman of Scotia's finance committee. Speculation in the press suggested the giant U.S. Steel Corporation was behind the influx of American investment, but Scotia denied this rumour.[34] President Crockard explored plans for amalgamation with Dominion Steel, which he regarded as "absolutely essential" to develop local resources "along broad lines as followed in the States in the Iron and Steel industry."[35] Efforts to purchase shares in Dominion Steel met resistance and direct negotiations for a merger also failed in the spring of 1918. Dominion Steel President Mark Workman commented favourably on the idea, but insisted that control must remain in Canadian hands.[36] Soon Scotia recruited the general manager of Dominion Steel to its side. A native Cape Bretoner, D. H. McDougall had worked for the Dominion companies for almost 20 years, rising from mechanic's apprentice to

general manager, but in 1919 he accepted an appointment as president of Scotia.[37] A mining engineer, McDougall strongly favoured a merger of the coal operations in the Sydney coalfield, as the haphazard distribution of submarine coal leases threatened to cause mine closures and costly duplication of effort by the two rival companies.[38]

The next steps towards merger took place within Dominion Steel. In 1916 a Montreal clothing manufacturer, Mark Workman, had succeeded Plummer as president, but otherwise the controlling group remained stable. In October 1919 new merger rumours circulated; the "inside story," denied by Workman, was that Lord Beaverbrook had accomplished a merger of the Scotia and Dominion companies.[39] Soon it was revealed that a British syndicate had purchased a large quantity of Dominion Steel shares and that a London Advisory Committee had been formed to represent the British interests.[40] The London syndicate included a blue-ribbon committee of industrialists from the British steel and shipbuilding industries: Viscount Marmaduke Furness, chairman of the Furness iron, steel and shipbuilding companies; Benjamin Talbot, managing director of the Furness group; Sir Trevor Dawson, managing director of Vickers Ltd.; Henry Steel, chairman of the United Steel Companies of Great Britain; and Sir William Beardmore (soon Lord Invernairn), chairman of the large Glasgow shipbuilding company.[41] The most active members of the London group were Sir Newton Moore and Lt. Col. W. Grant Morden. Prominent in the Australian mining and steel industries, Moore had been active in Australian politics before removing to London during the war. There he sat in the House of Commons and pursued his business interests, especially in General Electric and various empire mining and steel companies. Chairman of the London group was Lt. Col. Morden, a Toronto-born entrepreneur who first came to prominence as promoter of the Canada Steamship Lines (CSL) merger in 1912, which had been backed by Vickers and Furness. Morden himself had moved to London, engaged in industrial espionage in Germany and Switzerland during the war, chaired a British chemical firm and sat in the House of Commons. And according to a sketch in the *Sydney Record*, Morden was also "above all an accountant to the nth degree, lightning-like in his grasp of detail."[42]

During 1919 a third group also displayed interest in Dominion Steel. Led by J. W. Norcross and Roy Wolvin of Montreal, this group appeared to be working independently of the London syndicate. Norcross had started steam-boating on Lake Ontario as a youth and eventually became managing director of Canada Steamship Lines. In a bitter battle early in 1919, Norcross insisted on a distribution of common shares dividends and supplanted CSL president James Carruthers. Vice-President of the Collingwood Shipbuilding Company, Norcross was also a director of the Canadian branch of Vickers. Like Norcross, Wolvin was an aggressive young entrepreneur who came to prominence on the Great Lakes. Born in Michigan in 1880, Wolvin became a leading transportation expert in the shipping trade. As early as 1902, when he was working out of Duluth, Wolvin was known in Halifax as "one of the shrewdest shipping men on the lakes" and praised for his efforts to improve the capacity of the St. Lawrence canal system. Later Wolvin established the Montreal Transportation Company and joined Norcross in CSL and Collingwood Shipbuilding.[43] In the wake of the Halifax Explosion, Wolvin was invited by the Minister of Marine to consider the potential for establishing steel shipbuilding at Halifax, long a fond local hope. The result was the formation of Halifax Shipyards Ltd. in 1918 under the control of Wolvin, Norcross and their associates. Events then proceeded rapidly. Wolvin was impressed by the immense advantages of the Nova Scotia coal and steel industries

and hoped to link them to his shipbuilding and shipping concerns. Following a chance shipboard conversation with Mark Workman, Wolvin began to purchase shares in Dominion Steel and entered the board as a director in July 1919. At some point during the year, Wolvin later recalled, he established "a friendly understanding, you might say," with the London interests. In January 1920 Norcross also entered the board and in March 1920 the London group proved their control of Dominion Steel by installing Wolvin as the new president. A "silent revolution" had taken place in the affairs of Dominion Steel.[44]

Plans for creation of the British Empire Steel Corporation were unveiled in a speech by Morden at a meeting of the Empire Parliamentary Association in Ottawa on 14 April 1920. "If we can combine the capital and experience of the Old Mother Land with the resources of our Overseas Dominions," he explained, "we are going to put ourselves in an economic position that will forever maintain us as the greatest Empire in the world. I have long felt that the so-called 'silken thread of sentiment' should be reinforced by 'golden chains of commerce,' but the difficulty was how to do it."[45] In its earliest form, the proposal was to create a $500 million merger which would join Canadian coal, iron and steel resources to the British steel and shipbuilding industries; the frankly predatory design was to use Canadian resources to revitalize British industry in the face of American competition. The proposal involved nine companies. In addition to the Dominion and Scotia companies, the merger would include three companies controlled by Wolvin's group (CSL, Halifax Shipyards and Collingwood Shipbuilding) and four smaller companies (Canada Foundries and Forgings, Port Arthur Shipbuilding, Davie Shipbuilding and Repairing, and the Maritime Nail Company). The book value of the corporation's assets was set at $486 million, including an estimated valuation of the coal and ore reserves at $200 million. The plan was to issue four types of shares, to a total value of $207 million: 8 per cent cumulative first preference ($25 million), 7 per cent cumulative second preference ($37 million), 7 per cent non-cumulative preference ($68 million) and common shares ($77 million). The first class of shares was reserved to raise new capital on the British financial market and the remainder were to be issued at advantageous rates of exchange for the securities of the merging companies.[46]

The proposal generated immediate controversy, including a three-hour debate in the House of Commons on the subject of "cosmopolitan grafters." "Members are afraid that it is some great stock jobbing scheme," reported the *Monetary Times*. "They will have to be convinced that there is no huge watered stock promotion job." Rather than face a threatened investigation, Besco quickly reincorporated in Nova Scotia, where the province was pleased to receive a $75,000 fee and granted a charter specifying wide powers.[47] The proposed basis of share exchanges aroused criticism from directors of the Dominion and Scotia companies, who questioned the inclusion of the lesser companies, on which they lacked adequate financial information and on which the promoters of the merger stood to gain substantially through the merger. In response, the organizers made several revisions, dropping Halifax Shipyards and allowing better terms for the Scotia shareholders. But by the time of Dominion Steel's annual meeting in June 1920, a small group of veteran directors were in open revolt against the merger. In addition to Workman and Plummer, the dissident group included E. R. Wood and Sir William Mackenzie of Toronto and George Caverhill, William McMaster and Senator Raoul Dandurand of Montreal. A stormy session followed, as Wood, a Bank of Commerce director, pinpointed irregularities in the Besco balance sheet and protested the dilution of the

steel company shares by the inclusion of the weaker companies.[48] Relying on the backing of the British group and his own holdings, Wolvin was able to control the outcome of the meeting.[49] The old board was defeated and only five members were retained on the new board: Wolvin, Norcross, Senator Frederic Nicholls and Sir Henry Pellatt (both vigorous defenders of the merger), and the aging Sir William Mackenzie. New members of the Dominion Steel board included Stanley Elkin, manager of the Saint John Maritime Nail Company, Senators Sir Clifford Sifton and C. P. Beaubien, and three of Wolvin's associates from the CSL, Halifax Shipyards, Collingwood and Davie Shipbuilding group. Three representatives of the London group also entered the board at this time: Moore, Talbot and Furness. In July D. H. McDougall of Scotia and Senator W. L. McDougald of Montreal, both directors of companies involved in the merger, were also added to the board.[50]

Ratified by the three principal companies, the merger was never completed.[51] First, an uproar took place over the arrangements with CSL. Cantley suddenly learned that instead of bringing the shipping firm in as one of the merging companies, Wolvin now planned to sign a 25-year lease guaranteeing a fixed return of 7 per cent to CSL shareholders. In effect, this would make dividends to Steamship shareholders a fixed charge on the earnings of Besco, to be paid ahead of returns to other Besco shareholders. Enraged, Cantley protested that Scotia was being "jockeyed out of its property and its resources and earnings" and denounced the lease as a violation of the merger terms; Galen Stone in New York agreed the news was "a tremendous shock" and suggested the merger might be voided as a result.[52] Furthermore, the new corporation encountered great difficulty in raising capital; completion of the merger remained conditional on the issue of the $25 million first preference shares, shown on the balance sheet as available working capital. The London financial market was not receptive. Besco had earned a poor reputation on the London "street." Initially enthusiastic, the *Financial Times* grew exasperated at the repeated revisions in the plans and in July 1920 denounced Besco's "Merger Mysteries." The lack of adequate information on the merging companies revealed that "so far as British investors are concerned, they have been very cavalierly treated" and the editors warned investors to be cautious:

> The efforts of the promoters of the deal seemed to have been concentrated to rush the matter through as quickly and with as little discussion as possible.... We do not like this way of doing business, and those interested in Canadian enterprise and anxious to secure the good opinion of the public on this side cannot learn the fact too quickly.[53]

Moreover, the collapse of the postwar speculative boom during the spring and summer of 1920 caused a contraction of British capital markets and, under an adverse exchange situation, Canadian borrowing in London became more difficult. Wolvin later estimated that the Besco merger "missed the boat" by about two weeks.[54] [...]

Firmly convinced his corporation possessed "the greatest known deposits of coal and iron ore, splendidly situated," Wolvin hoped to implement a programme of capital expansion and enlarge the scope and capacity of the steel industry at Sydney.[55] Under Besco in 1922, the Sydney steel plant for the first time in its history made a brief entry into foreign markets for finished steel.[56] Symbolic of the steel industry's aspirations for diversified production was the opening of Canada's first ship plate mill in February 1920; producing steel plate for shipbuilding, the mill represented a key addition to the industrial structure of the Maritimes. The federal government encouraged establishment of the mill during the war by contracting advance orders and in 1920 the new mill had some success in selling plate to British yards. But in 1920 the federal government cancelled its orders and a long dispute ultimately yielded Besco a $4 million settlement. The plate mill closed and was forgotten for 20 years.[57] Another desultory symbol of Besco's expansionist hopes was an unfulfilled agreement to construct a steel plant in Newfoundland by 1926.[58] Demand for the output of the Nova Scotia steel industry fell sharply after 1919. During the 1920s the steel industry at Sydney eked out a hand-to-mouth existence as it lobbied for orders to keep the plant open for months at a time. The smaller Scotia plant at Sydney Mines, though equipped with a new blast furnace at the end of the war, was closed in November 1920 and never reopened. Pig iron production at Sydney dropped from a near-capacity output of 421,560 tons in 1917 to 296,869 tons in 1920 and 120,769 tons in 1922; production then rose slowly but did not exceed 250,000 tons again until 1928. In 1922 the export to the Ruhr of more than 720,000 tons of iron ore, about three-quarters the annual production of the Bell Island mines, signified clearly the failure of Besco's hopes for expansion of the local steel industry.[59]

The coal industry also suffered seriously at the end of the war. The sharp drop in steel production curtailed the coal industry's largest single market; by the end of 1920 the Sydney steel plant's consumption of coal had fallen from more than 100,000 tons per month to 40,000 tons.[60] The war itself had also disrupted the traditional pattern of markets for coal. The loss of the coal fleet to war service closed the St. Lawrence market, though this loss was compensated during the war by the vigorous local demand and the wartime shipping trade. When the war ended, readjustment was necessary. The return of coal vessels was slow and the Quebec market could not be entered aggressively until the 1921 season. Always costly, the alternative of rail shipments was uneconomic and the capacity of this route was limited by the Canso Strait. Also, high prices in the postwar bunker trade and potential export markets in France, Belgium and Britain tempted the coal operators more than the resumption of sharp competition in Quebec.[61] Recapturing Nova Scotia's share of the Quebec market took place slowly and with difficulty. The most formidable obstacle was the entrenched position of American coal suppliers, who shipped more than 3.5 million tons of coal to Quebec in 1920. Overexpansion of the U.S. coal industry during the war had led to the entry of large quantities of cheap coal into the Canadian market and the Nova Scotia coal industry did not regain its former share of this market until 1927.[62] In the Sydney coal-field, where production had reached a peak of 6.3 million tons in 1913, output fell to 4.5 million tons in 1920. The number of man-days worked in the coal industry plunged by one-third, from a peak of 4.5 million man-days in 1917 to 3.0 million in 1921; for the next two decades the level of activity never exceeded 3.3 million man-days per year and the industry was marked by irregular employment and a declining work force.[63]

Wage reductions in the coal industry promised substantial savings for Besco. The coal industry remained surprisingly labour-intensive and the potential for generating surpluses from the coal operations without new capital investment or a large amount of working capital, was attractive. Furthermore, since Whitney's time the coal operations had supplied hidden subsidies to allied companies, through below-cost contracts for coal (which the New England Gas and Coke Company and the Sydney steel plant enjoyed) or through the transfer of credits and surpluses within mergers (which took place within Dominion Steel after 1910).[64] Wolvin made no secret of the fact that he regarded all assets within the merger as common ones and the transfer of earnings or materials from one to the other was the equivalent of changing money from one pocket to the other.[65] The Duncan Commission criticized this policy in 1926 and revealed that Dominion Coal had remained a profitable operation during most years in the early 1920s, in spite of Besco's claims that losses had required wage reductions.[66] David Schwartzman has reconstructed a series of estimates to show the financial position of Dominion Coal during the period when Besco did not issue separate reports for its constituents. When set beside the corporation's financial record, these figures reveal that in the merger's first years the coal operations contributed profits to the merger; by 1923, however, Besco could no longer lean on the coal operations to sustain the corporation.[67]

The coal miners' resistance to Besco's campaign of wage reductions made it impossible for Besco to implement this strategy of survival. In 1920 Wolvin reluctantly signed an agreement for substantial increases for the coal miners. When this contract ended, Besco began its campaign to reduce wages. In 1922 the corporation sought a reduction of about one-third, but after a dramatic struggle was able to win only half this amount. In 1924 and 1925 Besco sought 20 per cent reductions; in 1924 the coal miners won a small increase and in 1925, after a long and bitter strike, a royal commission allowed the corporation a ten per cent reduction. The outstanding feature of industrial relations in the coal-fields in the 1920s was the tenacity of the coal miners' resistance to wage reductions. Besco's notorious labour policies did little to endear the corporation to public opinion and the coal miners' determined resistance placed an insuperable obstacle in the path of Besco's survival.[68]

To improve the competitive position of the coal and steel industries in the national market had long been a goal of the coal industry in Cape Breton. The coal duty never provided effective protection for a national market in coal. Wartime shortages alerted central Canadian consumers to the vulnerability of their fuel supply, as did postwar disruptions in the coal trade. Sentiment for an all-Canadian coal market rose high during the early 1920s, but had little impact on public policy.[69] After a thorough review of proposals for more protection for coal, the *Monetary Times* concluded that higher duties would "restrict the operation of Ontario and Quebec industries and increase general living and production costs throughout these provinces."[70] In Nova Scotia improved protection for coal was a major theme of the Maritime Rights movement, a coalition which harnessed various regional grievances to the political ambitions of the Nova Scotia Conservative Party. The main demand was for an increase of the 14¢ per ton duty on slack coal to the general level of 53¢ and for a programme of subsidies to help Nova Scotia coal penetrate deeper into the central Canadian market.[71]

The relationship of Besco to this agitation was a complex one. In 1924 and 1925 the corporation did not participate in the large Maritime Rights delegations, which visited Ottawa. In February 1925, however, Besco commenced publication of the *Besco Bulletin*, which campaigned for a "Bluenose tariff" to protect local industry. Besco's campaign grew most active in 1926, when the federal government appointed a tariff board to consider changes in protection for iron and steel. Wolvin in 1926 appealed for a 75¢ duty on coal and blamed the deteriorating protection for primary iron and steel over the previous two decades as the chief difficulty facing his corporation.[72] Yet Besco's enlistment in the ranks of Maritime Rights did not present a credible appearance. "At once the giant and the ogre of the Maritimes," Besco earned frequent attacks from local politicians and small businessmen who regarded the corporation as an embodiment of the outside exploitation which had destroyed the region's economy.[73] When Arthur Meighen came out "flat-footed for protection"

for the coal industry in February 1925, he provoked dismay among party leaders in Nova Scotia. Gordon Harrington, the Glace Bay lawyer and future premier, warned Meighen that it would be unwise to become associated with protection for Besco, "until some very severe restrictions are placed upon it in the handling of the monopoly it has obtained of the industries based on the natural resources of our country. The absurdity of this corporation asking for tariff concessions on the one hand, and the reduction in already too meagre wage scales on the other hand, must be apparent. Further, the corporation appears to be financially hopelessly unsound and its direction is beyond comment."[74]

The campaign for state intervention in the coal industry did meet some success by the end of the 1920s. In 1924–25 a limited system of rail subventions was tested, but abandoned. The intense lobbying in the winter of that year, the bleakest and most desperate months in the coalfields in the 1920s, caused the Liberal government that spring to standardize the duty on all bituminous coal at 50¢ per ton. While the Duncan Report failed to endorse tariff changes or subsidies, it called for wider use of Canadian coke in central Canada. The report concluded with an eloquent personal appeal by commissioner Hume Cronyn, a native Maritimer and Ontario businessman, who called on residents of Ontario and Quebec to make sacrifices to help this important Maritime industry. In the comfort of a steamship en route to Nassau that winter, Cronyn also penned a second addendum to the report in a private letter to Sir Robert L. Borden:

> There are two main difficulties in Nova Scotia which could not be set forth openly in a public document. In the first place the industry is economically unsound and must remain so until the cheaper Virginian and Kentucky coals cease being dumped on our market. Next

(quite confidentially) the company (Besco) is in the wrong hands. If it could be re-organized under a new President and staff and could obtain some relief by way of duties or bounties there would be hope for the future. Otherwise I can see nothing ahead but liquidation with all its attendant distress and loss.[75]

As a result of the tariff board hearings, protection for iron and steel was raised substantially in 1930 and 1931, and the coal duty was increased to 75¢ in 1931. Railway subventions were renewed in 1928 and soon became a large factor in the transportation of coal to central Canada.[76] But these important changes came too late to help Besco, and too late to rescue industrial Cape Breton from a condition of economic dependency and decline.

At stake in Besco's strategy of corporate survival was the corporation's inability to raise new capital or to return a satisfactory profit. As Besco's fortunes deteriorated, internal tensions grew. To one observer, Besco in the 1920s was "a vicious circle of ancient rivalries and new antagonisms."[77] The battle on the board of Dominion Steel in the summer of 1920 was followed by new manoeuvres two years later, at Besco's first annual meeting. The most powerful financial figure in Canada, Royal Bank President Sir Herbert Holt, was reportedly ready to assume the presidency of Besco and provide the financial backing the corporation needed. Besco stock values rose with this speculation, but the London group continued to support Wolvin and retained control of the corporation for him.[78] In November 1922 Wolvin raised new capital by issuing Dominion Iron and Steel mortgage bonds worth $4.6 million, which were financed by director Galen Stone's investment house.[79] At the next annual meeting, in an effort to make the corporation more attractive to investors, Wolvin reduced the corporation's authorized capital by half to $250,000.[80] The intense labour conflict of the summer of 1923

created more anxieties for the corporation. The popular vice-president and general manager, D. H. McDougall, resigned and was replaced by E. H. McLurg, general manager of Halifax Shipyards.[81] The most influential of the directors, Moore and Stone, remained active behind the scenes attempting to raise capital. In September 1923 Moore pleaded with Prime Minister Mackenzie King not to obstruct their efforts by appointing a royal commission to investigate the summer's labour strife. Moore sounded a plaintive note:

A good many of us have put the savings of years into this Canadian enterprise and have been bitterly disappointed that the Company has not been able to return some interest on the capital invested...the present market value of our shares represents only 1/4 of the amounts of the purchase money.[82]

The turning point in the rise and fall of Besco was evident in the record of financial success. Operating profits fell sharply from $4.4 million in 1923 to $.9 million in 1924, when the corporation lost $2.3 million. In March 1924 the directors suspended dividend payments on all stock. Though additional capital was secured through the issue of Dominion Coal bonds, the year ended with a net loss of $1.3 million.[83] Besco's dividend policy awakened shareholder dissatisfaction. Wolvin received a "great many" letters criticizing the non-payment of dividends on the second preference stock and with the suspension of all payments, complaints multiplied.[84] The condition of Besco grew worse in the winter of 1924–1925, and the hardship and suffering of the local community starkly dramatized the plight of the coal industry. After the annual meeting in March 1925, a dejected Besco shareholder and director, *Montreal Herald* publisher Senator J. P. B. Casgrain, poured his heart out to Mackenzie King:

I am a director of the British Empire Steel Corporation, and an unfortunate shareholder for a very large amount. I have never had one cent of dividend on that merger-stock. However, that is my own affair.... I do not plead for myself—although since the merger I have very foolishly invested, in money, in that enterprise $123,000. My wife, 25 years ago, after a visit to Sydney with Sir Laurier, Lady Laurier and myself, invested of her money $40,000. I know all this has nothing to do with the question of bounties and duties and it is not for that that I write. Forget about us but think of the 22,500 men who will be out of work when we close up. With their families, there will be over 100,000 who will probably have to leave Nova Scotia.[85]

Wolvin's intransigence in the 1925 strike, when he and McLurg refused to meet union leaders and closed company stores, further damaged the corporation's reputation. In July 1925 the Liberal government was overwhelmingly defeated in a provincial election, partly as a result of their association with the corporation.[86] Tory premier E. N. Rhodes, who had promised to settle the five-month strike, now found it impossible to deal with Wolvin; "Wolvin is, I think, the most stubborn man with whom I have ever come in contact," he complained to Borden, "and his stubborness [sic] is increased by the fact that his Companies are almost bankrupt."[87] E. R. Forbes has found that Wolvin finally came to terms as a result of financial pressure from Bank of Commerce chairman Sir Joseph Flavelle, whose bank threatened to deny short-term money to Dominion Coal.[88] The strike ended with a temporary agreement and the appointment of a provincial royal commission, which, under the chairmanship of British coal expert Sir Andrew Rae Duncan, vice-president of the British Shipbuilding Employers' Federation, criticized Besco's unrealistic capital structure and financial policies.[89]

In the spring of 1926 the Bank of Commerce and Bank of Montreal refused Besco additional short-term financing, and Wolvin resolved to allow Dominion Iron and Steel, the weakest part of the merger, to go into receivership. In July 1926 Dominion Iron and Steel defaulted on bond payments and National Trust, closely linked to the Bank of Commerce, was appointed receiver for the company. No surprise, the collapse nevertheless caused a sharp fall in Canadian bond prices that summer and marked the beginning of Besco's disintegration.[90] Bondholders' committees were appointed to guard the interests of various investors, and early in 1927 National Trust began court proceedings for the winding up of Besco and Dominion Steel.[91] The Supreme Court of Nova Scotia refused to wind up Besco, but agreed to the liquidation of Dominion Steel, appointing Royal Trust, which was allied to the Bank of Montreal and the Royal Bank, as the receiver. In July 1927 Wolvin submitted a reorganization scheme to his shareholders, but could not win their support.[92] Soon Wolvin agreed to sell his holdings to Herbert Holt and a group of his Royal Bank associates. At the annual meeting in January 1928 Wolvin resigned as president of Besco.[93]

Wolvin's successor as Besco president was C. B. McNaught, a Toronto director of the Royal Bank. With the entry of seven new directors onto the Besco board in 1928, the coal and steel industries passed into the hands of a financial grouping dominated by the Royal Bank. The group began plans to reorganize the corporation. McNaught and J. H. Gundy visited London to reach agreement with the British investors. In March 1928 the group incorporated a new holding and operating company, the Dominion Steel and Coal Corporation, which was capitalized at $65 million and took over the Besco properties.[94] With the completion of this transfer in May 1930, the British Empire Steel Corporation ceased to exist. The new company represented an alliance of old and new interests. The Royal Bank group held half the seats on the Dosco board, but Sir Newton Moore and Lord Invernairn remained as directors to represent the continued British interest; Moore served as vice-president and from 1932 to 1936 was president of the corporation. The new company ended a decade of financial turmoil and disappointment and placed the corporation in a strong position to weather the troubles of the 1930s.

As an episode in Canadian economic history, the development of industrial Cape Breton between the 1880s and the 1920s revealed a pattern of rapid growth culminating in severe crisis. Far from a backwater of economic inactivity, industrial Cape Breton performed important and useful functions for the national economy. Through the coal industry, the region supplied a basic industrial raw material, supported the local iron and steel industry and provided a lucrative arena for the financial wizardry of various investors. But industrial capitalism could not provide balanced and harmonious economic growth between regions; on the contrary, the national economic structure which emerged in Canada during this period promoted uneven development and regional dependency. This pattern of uneven development led to the crisis of markets and corporate welfare in the coal industry during the 1920s. Vulnerable in its distant markets and unable to rely on a stable local market, the importance of the Cape Breton coal industry declined. At the same time, the metropolitan search for economic surpluses continued, and in the case of Besco, reached unrealistic proportions. After the 1920s, the main functions of industrial Cape Breton in the national economy changed; the community was now called upon to provide a large pool of labour for the national labour market, and, in time of need, to supply reserve capacity for the national energy and steel markets. The rise and fall of the British Empire Steel Corporation provided the occasion, though not the root cause,

for a structural turning point in the economic history of industrial Cape Breton.

The growth of the coal industry in Cape Breton expressed above all the financial opportunism of its successive owners, rather than any commitment to principles of regional economic welfare. Spokesmen for the coal industry from Richard Brown to Roy Wolvin endorsed local industrial development as a strategy for utilization of the local coal and iron resources, but in practice they sought trading links with distant markets and pursued policies of rapid resource depletion. The local business class offered no effective resistance to the integration of the coal industry into the national economy; native Cape Bretoners like D. H. McDougall and W. D. Ross were capitalists foremost and proved no more loyal to the region's welfare than Whitney, Ross, Plummer or Wolvin. The experience of industrial Cape Breton also suggests that in the period between 1890 and 1930 Canadian capitalism featured a powerful and aggressive business class, associated in common purposes although often divided by rivalries. The resources of industrial Cape Breton attracted the interest of American and British investors, but except for the frustrated intentions of Whitney in the 1890s and the London syndicate in 1920, they preferred to leave direct control in Canadian hands. The passage of control over the coal industry from Bank of Montreal circles to a Bank of Montreal-Bank of Commerce alliance before the war, and ultimately to the Royal Bank in the 1920s, paralleled the successive domination of Canadian capitalism by these financial groupings. The route from Van Horne and James Ross to Sir Herbert Holt was interrupted in the 1920s by the intervention of Roy Wolvin and his allies on the Great Lakes and St. Lawrence and in London. But the extreme brevity and catastrophic failure of their regime during the 1920s indicated the distance that separated this group from the real seats of power in Canadian capitalism.

The most important conclusions to this episode in Canadian economic history were those reached by the local community in industrial Cape Breton. At a time when the labour movement was on the defensive across the country, the resistance of the coal miners to the British Empire Steel Corporation caused the eventual collapse of that enfeebled enterprise. The emergence of a militant labour movement in Canada helped begin a new stage in the history of Canadian capitalism. After the 1920s and 1930s, an ever closer collaboration between state and capital was needed to maintain the essential structure of the national economy. In industrial Cape Breton the deteriorating local economy would be propped up by government subsidies, enabling private capital to continue profitably to exploit the region's economic assets, while the deepening underdevelopment of the region would drive Cape Bretoners to leave their homes and enter the national labour market. The local working class continued to resist the progressive destruction of their community by campaigning for improved social standards and equitable national policies, and for public ownership of the coal and steel industries, which was achieved in 1968. In 1928 hopeful members of the Cape Breton Board of Trade celebrated the arrival of the new Besco president, C. B. McNaught, with a ceremonial banquet. But the rise and fall of the British Empire Steel Corporation left most Cape Bretoners with a permanent distrust of outside capitalists.

Notes

1   Nova Scotia, *A Submission of Its Claims with Respect to Maritime Disabilities within Confederation* (Halifax, 1926); Nova Scotia, *A Submission on Dominion-Provincial Relations and the Fiscal Disabilities of Nova Scotia within the Canadian Federation* (Halifax, 1934).

2   C.R. Fay and H.A. Innis, "The Economic Development of Canada, 1867–1921: The Maritime Provinces," *Cambridge History of the British Empire* (Cambridge, 1930), vol. VI, 657–71; S. A. Saunders, "Trends in the Economic History of the Maritime Provinces," *Studies in the Economy of the Maritime Provinces* (Toronto, 1939), 245–65.

3   P.D. McClelland, "The New Brunswick Economy in the 19th Century," *Journal of Economic History*, XXV (1965), 686–90; A. H. Clark, "Contributions of Its Southern Neighbours to the Underdevelopment of the Maritime Provinces Area, 1710–1867," in R. A. Preston, ed., *The Influence of the United States on Canadian Development* (Durham, N.C., 1972), 164–84; R. F. Neill, "National Policy and Regional Underdevelopment," *Journal of Canadian Studies*, IX (May, 1974), 12–20.

4   Bruce Archibald, "Atlantic Regional Underdevelopment and Socialism," in Laurier LaPierre *et al.*, eds., *Essays on the Left* (Toronto, 1971), 103–20; Archibald, "The Development of Underdevelopment in the Atlantic Provinces" (M.A. thesis, Dalhousie University, 1971); Archibald's work was based on an application of Andre Gunder Frank, "The Development of Underdevelopment," *Monthly Review*, XVIII (September, 1966), 17–31.

5   "The National Policy and the Industrialization of the Maritimes, 1880–1910," *Acadiensis*, I (Spring, 1972), 3–28. Similar in approach was J. M. S. Careless, "Aspects of Metropolitanism in Atlantic Canada," in Mason Wade, ed., *Regionalism in the Canadian Community 1867–1967* (Toronto, 1969), 117–29.

6   Karl Marx, *Capital* (New York, 1967), vol. I, especially ch. XXV; Paul Baran, *The Political Economy of Growth* (New York, 1968); Ernest Mandel, *Capitalism and Regional Disparities* (Toronto, 1970); Henry Veltmeyer, "The Methodology of Dependency Analysis; An Outline for a Strategy of Research on Regional Underdevelopment" (unpublished paper, Saint Mary's University, 1977).

7   Recent work on regional underdevelopment includes E. R. Forbes, "The Maritime Rights Movement, 1919–1927: A Study in Canadian Regionalism" (Ph.D. thesis, Queen's University, 1975); David Alexander, "Newfoundland's Traditional Economy and Development to 1934," *Acadiensis*, V (Spring, 1976), 56–78; see also the

contributions by C. D. Howell, Carman Miller, E. R. Forbes and T. W. Acheson to D. J. Bercuson, ed., *Canada and the Burden of Unity* (Toronto, 1977).

8   D.A. Muise, "The Making of an Industrial Community: Cape Breton Coal Towns, 1867–1900" (paper presented to the Atlantic Canada Studies Conference, Fredericton, 1976), Appendix I.

9   M.J. Patton, "The Coal Resources of Canada," *Economic Geography,* I (1925), 84–5; A. L. Hay, "Coal-mining Operations in the Sydney Coal Field," American Institute of Mining and Metallurgical Engineers, *Technical Publication No. 198* (New York, 1929), 3–6.

10 F. W. Gray, "The Coal Fields and Coal Industry of Eastern Canada," Canada, Mines Branch, *Bulletin No. 14* (Ottawa, 1917), 14; W. J. Donald, *The Canadian Iron and Steel Industry* (Boston, 1915), Appendix B. In 1913 Nova Scotia produced 8,135,104 short tons of coal; of this total the Sydney field supplied 6,313,275 tons. For production data see Canada, *Report of the Royal Commission on Coal, 1946* (Ottawa, 1947), 64–5.

11 Gray, "The Coal Fields of Eastern Canada," 13–14. The same question puzzled historians V. C. Fowke, S. A. Saunders and Harold Innis, who briefly examined the coal industry in the 1920s and 1930s. They observed that Canada's coal industry was located at the ends of the country, while most industry was clustered at the centre. They stressed the difficulties in shipping a cheap, bulky commodity like coal long distances to market and lamented the inadequacy of local markets within the region. By failing to attract other production factors to generate industrial growth in its own geographic locale, the coal industry seemed to follow an anomalous growth strategy. To explain this, Innis and his associates began to point out the dominant role of central Canada in the construction of the national economy. This approach was supplemented by economist David Schwartzman and labour historian C. B. Wade, who drew attention to the manipulative and exploitative financial policies of the coal companies. They found that the ideas of O. D. Skelton's "financial buccaneers" had blossomed handsomely in the coal-fields and concluded that the industry's chronic instability and mismanagement stemmed largely from this source. See V. C. Fowke, "Economic Realities of the Canadian Coal Situation—1929" (M.A. thesis, University of Saskatchewan, 1929); S. A. Saunders, *The Economic Welfare of the Maritime Provinces* (Wolfville, 1932), 30–46; H. A. Innis, "Editor's Foreword," in E. S.

Moore, *American Influence in Canadian Mining* (Toronto, 1941), v–xvii; C. B. Wade, *Robbing the Mines* (Glace Bay, 194-?); Wade, "History of District 26, United Mine Workers of America, 1919–1941" (unpublished manuscript, Beaton Institute of Cape Breton Studies, Sydney, 1950); David Schwartzman, "Mergers in the Nova Scotia Coal Fields: A History of the Dominion Coal Company, 1893–1940" (Ph.D. thesis, University of California, Berkeley, 1953).

12 Abraham Gesner, *The Industrial Resources of Nova Scotia* (Halifax, 1849); Richard Brown, *The Coal-Fields and Coal Trade of the Island of Cape Breton* (London, 1871); C. B. Fergusson, ed., *Uniacke's Sketches of Cape Breton* (Halifax, 1958), 117–29; J. S. Martell, "Early Coal Mining in Nova Scotia," *Dalhousie Review,* XXV (1945–1946), 156–72; Saunders, "The Maritime Provinces and the Reciprocity Treaty," *Dalhousie Review,* XIV (1934), 355–71; Phyllis Blakeley, "Samuel Cunard," and David Frank, "Richard Smith," *Dictionary of Canadian Biography,* IX (Toronto, 1976), 172–84, 730–2.

13 C. O. Macdonald, *The Coal and Iron Industries of Nova Scotia* (Halifax, 1909), 42; G. A. White, *Halifax and Its Business* (Halifax, 1876), 108–9.

14 B.D. Tennyson, "Economic Nationalism and Confederation: A Case Study in Cape Breton," *Acadiensis,* II (Spring, 1973), 39–53; D. A. Muise, "The Federal Election of 1867 in Nova Scotia: An Economic Interpretation," Nova Scotia Historical Society *Collections,* XXXVI (1967), 327–51.

15 J.R. Lithgow, *A Letter to the House of Commons of Canada on Behalf of the Coal Interests of Canada* (Halifax, 1877), 9.

16 *Importance of the Canadian Coal Industry* (n.p., n.d., probably 1897), 50–5; Canada, Dominion Bureau of Statistics, *Coal Statistics for Canada, 1927* (Ottawa, 1928), 27.

17 *Importance of the Canadian Coal Industry,* 21. Tariff changes on coal are summarized in *Royal Commission on Coal, 1946,* 575–7.

18 *Report of the Royal Commission on Coal Mining Industry in Nova Scotia [Duncan Report],* Supplement to the *Labour Gazette* (January, 1926), 13.

19 E. H. Armstrong, untitled manuscript on the coal industry in Nova Scotia, 1921, E. H. Armstrong Papers, Box 41, Public Archives of Nova Scotia [PANS].

20 Basic accounts of the steel industry include Donald, *The Canadian Iron and Steel Industry;* E. J.

McCracken, "The Steel Industry of Nova Scotia" (M.A. thesis, McGill University, 1932); W. D. R. Eldon, "American Influence on the Canadian Iron and Steel Industry" (Ph.D. thesis, Harvard University, 1952).

21 Important studies of this process are Acheson, "Industrialization of the Maritimes," and Nolan Reilly, "The Origins of the Amherst General Strike, 1890–1919" (paper presented to the Canadian Historical Association Annual Meeting, Fredericton, 1977).

22 *Canadian Mining Review* (August, 1894), 131.

23 Robert Drummond, "Appendix," in Richard Brown, *The Coal Fields and Coal Trade of the Island of Cape Breton* (reprint, Stellarton, 1899), 123–5.

24 Robert Drummond, *Minerals and Mining, Nova Scotia* (Stellarton, 1918), 192–205; *The National Cyclopedia of American Biography*, X (1900; Ann Arbor, 1967), 155; *Who Was Who in America*, I (Chicago, 1943), 1340; Schwartzman, "Dominion Coal," 109–21.

25 Nova Scotia, *Debates and Proceedings of the House of Assembly*, 1893, 15. Conservative Party critics attacked the generous lease provisions and warned that the future of the coal industry would now depend "upon a thousand and one financial considerations...and not upon any consideration for the coal mines or for the people of Nova Scotia." One protectionist critic opposed the export of a single ton of coal: "This commodity is essential to our success as a manufacturing centre. If we jealously guard this commodity, the day may yet dawn when Nova Scotia will become to the Dominion of Canada what Manchester is today to England, Ireland and Scotland." *Debates*, 1893, 41–2, 71–3.

26 *Canadian Mining Review* (August, 1894), 131–3. In addition to Whitney, the board included his brother-in-law H. F. Dimock, a Mr. Winsor representing Kidder, Peabody and Company, the Boston investment house, and F. S. Pearson, a Boston engineer employed by Whitney. The Canadians included two local coal operators, J. S. McLennan, who became treasurer, and David McKeen, resident manager, two Halifax lawyers, W. B. Ross and B. F. Pearson, and three Montreal capitalists, Hugh McLennan, Donald Smith and Sir W. C. Van Horne.

27 Reduced in 1894, the U.S. coal duty was restored near full strength in 1897; except for long-term contracts with Whitney's coke company, shipments to the U.S. remained small. Donald, *The Canadian Iron and Steel Industry*, 200.

28 *Canadian Mining Review* (March, 1902), 45–6; *ibid.* (December, 1903), 241–2. The rapid transfer from American to Canadian control is often overlooked, as in R. T. Naylor, *The History of Canadian Business* (Toronto, 1975), II, 176–7, 210.

29 W. R. Houston, ed., *Directory of Directors in Canada* (Toronto, 1906).

30 Acheson, "Industrialization of the Maritimes," 25–7, discusses the struggle for Scotia.

31 W.R. Houston, ed., *Directory of Directors in Canada, 1912* (Toronto, 1912). In 1912 the Dominion Steel directors included from Toronto, J. H. Plummer, George Cox, Frederic Nicholls, William Mackenzie, James Mason, Henry Pellatt, and from Montreal, W. C. Van Horne, J. R. Wilson, William McMaster, H. Montagu Allan, George Caverhill, Robert MacKay, W. G. Ross, Raoul Dandurand. David McKeen of Halifax was the lone Maritimer. The board of Dominion Coal was very similar; Toronto: Plummer, Cox, Mason, Pellatt, Mackenzie. W. D. Matthews, E. R. Wood; Montreal: Wilson, Van Horne, Dandurand, MacKay, McMaster, Lord Strathcona (formerly Donald Smith), F.L. Wanklyn, W. R. Houston, comp., *The Annual Financial Review, Canadian* [*Houston's Review*], XII (1912). An important study of the Canadian financial community in 1910 graphically situates Dominion Steel between financial groupings surrounding the Montreal and Commerce banks. The board of Dominion Coal had four or more directors in common with the following: Bank of Montreal, National Trust, Canadian Pacific Railway, Toronto Railway Company, Electrical Development Company, Canada Life Assurance Company, Gilles Piédalue, "Les groupes financiers au Canada, (1900–1930)." *Revue d'Histoire de l'Amérique Française*, XXX (1976), 28–9.

32 J. M. Cameron, *Industrial History of the New Glasgow District* (New Glasgow, 1960), ch. III; Donald, *The Canadian Iron and Steel Industry*, 194–9, 254–6. The Scotia board included J. W. Allison, Robert Harris, Thomas Cantley, G. S. Campbell, Frank Stanfield, G. F. McKay, J. D. McGregor, J. C. McGregor, all of Nova Scotia; W. D. Ross and Robert Jaffray, Toronto; Lorne Webster and K. W. Blackwell, Montreal; Frank Ross, Quebec City; J. S. Pitts and R. E. Chambers, St. John's, Newfoundland. *Houston's Review*, XII (1912). The Scotia board was closely linked to the Bank of Nova Scotia and the Eastern Trust Company, itself also close to the Royal Bank; Piédalue, "Les groupes financiers," 28. From

1902–1909 Lyman Melvin-Jones, president of Massey-Harris, was a director of Scotia; according to Cantley, half of Scotia's sales were to agricultural implement manufacturers; Eldon, "The Canadian Iron and Steel Industry," 489.

33 *Financial Post* (Toronto), 30 June 1917; *Monetary Times* (Toronto), 22 February 1918, 22 June 1917. The new directors included D. C. Jackling, New York, and W. Hinckle Smith, Philadelphia, capitalists interested in mining investments and associated with Boston banker Charles Hayden, prominent in Kennecott Copper, Utah Copper and the International Nickel Company. *Who Was Who in America*, I, 538; II (Chicago, 1950), 498; III (Chicago, 1963), 195, 440–1.

34 *Montreal Herald*, 10 July 1917.

35 F.H. Crockard to N. B. McKelvie, 6 February 1918, Thomas Cantley Papers, Box 175, PANS.

36 *Montreal Gazette*, 5 February 1918; *Canadian Annual Review 1918; Monetary Times*, 22 February 1918.

37 *Canadian Mining Journal* (30 April 1919); *ibid.*, (14 September 1923); *Who's Who and Why, 1921* (Toronto, 1921), 885.

38 Dominion Steel resisted accommodation with Scotia and both the provincial government and the Dominion Fuel Controller were forced to intervene in the dispute. Armstrong Papers, vol. II, Folders 3, 4, 5, PANS.

39 *Sydney Post*, 3 October 1919. Evidence for Max Aitken's involvement is circumstantial. In February 1919 Aitken was meeting with both Cantley and Workman in London, and in June 1919 he was accompanied on his trip to Canada by W. D. Ross. "Daily Memorandum Covering European Visit, 1919," Cantley Papers, Box 167, PANS; *Montreal Star*, 25 June 1919. Grant Morden, the main Besco promoter, admitted in a New York interview that he was an associate of Aitken; *Sydney Post*, 13 February 1920. The rhetoric of the Besco promoters reflected Beaverbrook's vision of imperial economic cooperation.

40 *Monetary Times*, 28 November 1919; *Sydney Post*, 15 December 1919, 10 January 1920.

41 *Houston's Review*, XX (1920), 166; *Who Was Who, 1929–40; Who Was Who, 1941–1950; Who's Who, 1920* (London, 1920).

42 *Who Was Who, 1929–1940*, 963, 965; clipping, 1920, in Stuart McCawley Scrapbook, 6, Miners' Memorial Museum, Glace Bay; *Sydney Record*, 1 May 1920; *Canadian Mining Journal* (March,

1934). Two ships in the CSL fleet reflected the links with Vickers: the *W. G. Morden* and the *Sir Trevor Dawson*, clipping, Cantley Papers, Box 175, PANS.

43 *Monetary Times*, 14 February 1919; *Sydney Post*, 16 October 1919, 31 March 1920; *Monetary Times*, 26 March 1920; H. J. Crowe to G. B. Hunter, April 1902, H. Crowe Letterbook, PANS.

44 Nova Scotia, Royal Commission on Coal Mines, 1925, "Minutes of Evidence," 2061; *Sydney Post*, 22 March 1920; *Monetary Times*, 26 March 1920.

45 *Saturday Night*, 8 May 1920; *Salient Facts of the Steel Merger* (n.p., 1 June 1920); *Press Opinions of 'Empire Steel'* (n.p., 1 July 1920). The crisis of the British economy in the post-war period led to efforts by prominent industrialists to revitalize the national economy, but they could not always rely on the support of the London financial community. For short summaries, see Sidney Pollard, *The Development of the British Economy, 1914–1950* (London, 1962), and John Foster "British Imperialism and the Labour Aristocracy," in Jeffrey Skelley, ed., *The General Strike, 1926* (London, 1976), 3–16. According to Wolvin, the two financiers in the original Besco promotion, Morden and an Austrian banker named Szarvassy, also tried to recruit American support; Duncan Commission, "Minutes of Evidence," 2063.

46 *Monetary Times*, 7 May 1920.

47 Canada, House of Commons, *Debates*, 1920, 1945–67; *Monetary Times*, 7, 28 May 1920. Letters patent authorizing a capitalization of $100,000 were obtained from the federal government on 15 March 1920; the increase to $500 million was obtained in Nova Scotia on 22 May 1920; *Besco Bulletin*, 11 April 1925.

48 *Monetary Times*, 18 June 1920; *Sydney Post*, 15, 16, 18 June 1920.

49 By this time the London group held about 180,000 shares in Dominion Steel; Wolvin held 50,000 himself and as President controlled another 50,000. The dissident directors polled only 3,000 shares against the merger, which received 298,000 votes. Newton Moore to W. L. Mackenzie King, 1 September 1923, W. L. Mackenzie King Papers, Public Archives of Canada [PAC]; *Sydney Post*, 23 June, 16 July 1920.

50 *Monetary Times*, 25 June, 2 July 1920; *Sydney Post*, 23 June, 19 July 1920.

51 W.D. Ross and D. H. McDougall encountered little resistance in gaining approval for the merger from Scotia shareholders. In New Glasgow their argument

was that "the merger is going through with or without us," that the smaller company could not withstand the competition and that Scotia needed the capital which would be available through the merger; "Special Meeting, Scotia Shareholders, YMCA Building, New Glasgow, 25 June 1920," Cantley Papers, Box 175, PANS. The controlling interest in Scotia was held by the American investors, but the character of U.S. interest in Scotia had changed by 1920; during the inter-war period the American steel industry favoured a policy of retrenchment and did not engage in expansionist policies abroad; Mira Wilkins, *The Maturing of Multinational Enterprise: American Business Abroad from 1914 to 1970* (Cambridge, 1974), 151, 153.

52 Cantley to Stone, 21, 26 July 1920: Stone to Cantley, 26 July 1920; Cantley Papers, Box 175, PANS. Also, before entering the merger, CSL shareholders purchased Wolvin's Montreal Transportation Company; *Monetary Times*, 2, 30 July 1920.

53 *Sydney Post*, 28 July 1920; *Financial Times* (London), 23, 24, 29 July 1920, 4 May 1920.

54 *Monetary Times*, 9 January, 2 July, 1 October 1920, 7 January 1921; Duncan Commission, "Minutes of Evidence," 2070.

55 *Monetary Times*, 2 July 1920.

56 Ibid., 14 July 1922.

57 McCracken, "Steel Industry," 154–66; *Monetary Times*, 17 September, 26 November 1920.

58 *Monetary Times*, 9 June 1922.

59 *Monetary Times*, 13, 27 May 1921; McCracken, "Steel Industry," Appendix; *Houston's Review*, 180. Overexpansion, competitive disadvantages and deteriorating tariff protection caused a general problem of excess capacity in the Canadian steel industry during the 1920s; the hinterland steel plants at Sydney and Sault Ste. Marie, specializing in basic steel and rails and located at a distance from the industrial heartland, suffered the greatest contraction; Eldon, "The Canadian Iron and Steel Industry," 132.

60 Armstrong, untitled manuscript, 1921, PANS.

61 *Sydney Post*, 28 November 1919, 26 February, 27 March 1920.

62 The Quebec market normally obtained two-thirds of its coal supply from Nova Scotia, but in 1920 Canadian coal accounted for only 250,880 tons; by 1923 Canadian coal accounted for 1,540,284 tons and U.S. coal 2,922,991; by 1927 the more normal proportions were re-established: Canada 2,307,185, U.S. 1,572,692 tons. As late as the 1940s, central Canada continued to derive half its energy needs from coal. See Canada, DBS, *Coal Statistics for Canada*, 1922, 23–4; *ibid.*, 1927, 22–7; J. H. Dales, "Fuel, Power and Industrial Development in Central Canada," *American Economic Review*, XLIII (1953), 182–3.

63 Nova Scotia, *Journals of the House of Assembly*, 1940, App. 9, 148.

64 Donald, *The Canadian Iron and Steel Industry*, 257; Schwartzman, "Dominion Coal," 113, 125–37.

65 Canada, Special Committee of the House of Commons on the Future Fuel Supply of Canada, *Official Report of Evidence* (Ottawa, 1921), 137.

66 *Duncan Report*, 15. The financial data convinced the commissioners that no reduction of miners' wages was justified in 1922, that a reduction in 1923 would have been suitable, that the 1924 increase was not unjustified and that a ten per cent reduction was appropriate in 1925.

67 Schwartzman, "Dominion Coal," 182, estimates that for the year ending March 1921 Dominion Coal's profits were $4.2 million gross ($2.9 net), for December 1921 $3.4 million gross ($2.4 net), for December 1922 $2.6 million gross ($1.3 net), for December 1923 $1.4 million gross ($.1 net), for December 1924 $.7 million gross ($-.6 net).

68 Don Macgillivray, "Industrial Unrest in Cape Breton, 1919–1925" (M.A. thesis, University of New Brunswick, 1971); David Frank, "Coal Masters and Coal Miners: The 1922 Strike and the Roots of Class Conflict in the Cape Breton Coal Industry" (M.A. thesis, Dalhousie University, 1974); David Frank, "Class Conflict in the Coal Industry: Cape Breton 1922" in G. S. Kealey and P. Warrian, eds., *Essays in Canadian Working Class History* (Toronto, 1976), 161–84, 226–31.

69 *Monetary Times*, 3 January 1919, 15 September 1922. "Canada can only be politically independent so far as she controls and supplies her own bituminous coal," warned F. W. Gray; by his estimate Nova Scotia was producing two million tons less than capacity during the 1920s and with adequate capital investment could supply 10 million tons of coal per year. F. W. Gray, "Canada's Coal Supply," Canadian Institute of Mining and Metallurgy and the Mining Society of Nova Scotia, *Transactions*, XXIII (1920), 300–1, 304; Gray, "Canada's Coal Problem," *ibid.*, XXV (1922), 293–300.

70 *Monetary Times*, 6 March 1925. To economic historian J. H. Dales, the coal tariff "appears to be nothing but a mischievous hidden tax on Canadian manufacturing" whose effect was to "retard the industrial development" of central Canada; Dales,

"Fuel, Power and Industrial Development in Central Canada," 183.

71 Forbes, "The Maritime Rights Movement," 147–9, 222–7, 280–2; Associated Boards of Trade of the Island of Cape Breton, *Memorandum with Regard to the Conditions Presently Existing in the Coal and Steel Industries of the Province of Nova Scotia* (n.p., 1925). Slack coal provided 1/5 of imported coal in 1920, but almost 2/5 in 1923. The lobby also sought abolition of the 99 per cent rebate on the coal duty allowed since 1907 to consumers using coal for steelmaking. Cantley favoured a duty of $1.50 per ton; *Monetary Times,* 10 February 1928.

72 *Besco Bulletin,* 6 June 1925; *Houston's Review,* 1926, 165–6; Canada, House of Commons Special Committee Investigating the Coal Resources of Canada, *Minutes of Proceedings and Evidence* (Ottawa, 1926), 105–23.

73 *Monetary Times,* 25 March 1927; *Halifax Herald,* 14 March 1924.

74 G.S. Harrington to Arthur Meighen, 16 March 1925, Arthur Meighen Papers, PAC.

75 Duncan Report, 30–1; Hume Cronyn to R. L. Borden, 14 February 1926, Robert L. Borden Papers, PAC.

76 Eldon, "The Canadian Iron and Steel Industry," 366; F. W. Gray, "The History of Transportation Subventions on Nova Scotia Coal" (unpublished manuscript, Miners' Memorial Museum, Glace Bay, 1944); O.J. McDiarmid, *Commercial Policy in the Canadian Economy* (Cambridge, 1946), 276.

77 *Canadian Mining Journal* (26 August 1927).

78 *New York Times,* 21, 27 June 1922; *Financial Post,* 30 June 1922; *Financial Post Survey,* 1927, 233, 235.

79 *Monetary Times,* 8 December 1922.

80 *Monetary Times,* 30 March 1923.

81 *Houston's Review,* 1924, 175.

82 Newton Moore to W. L. Mackenzie King, 1 September 1923, King Papers, PAC.

83 *Monetary Times,* 4 April, 29 August 1924.

84 Roy Wolvin to E. H. Armstrong, 4 March 1924, M. C. Smith to Br Emp S Co [sic], 1 March 1924, Armstrong Papers, PANS.

85 J.P.B. Casgrain to W. L. M. King, 19 March 1925, King Papers, PAC.

86 Paul MacEwan, *Miners and Steelworkers* (Toronto, 1976), 145.

87 E.N. Rhodes to R. L. Borden, 3 August 1925, Borden Papers, PAC.

88 Forbes, "The Maritime Rights Movement," 263–8.

89 *Who Was Who, 1951–1960,* 326; Duncan Report, 26–8.

90 Forbes, "The Maritime Rights Movement," 392–7; *Monetary Times,* 11 June 1926; *Houston's Review,* 1926, 165–6; *Financial Post Survey,* 1927, 233.

91 *Monetary Times,* 10 September 1926, 25 March 1927.

92 *Houston's Review,* 1928, 216–7; ibid., 1927, 182–3; *Monetary Times,* 28 October 1927.

93 *Monetary Times,* 3 February 1928. Wolvin re-established himself in the Canadian shipping and shipbuilding industry and on his death was chairman of the executive board of Canadian Vickers Ltd.; *New York Times,* 8 April 1945.

94 *Monetary Times,* 30 March, 18 May 1928.

Relief Camp Workers in Ontario during the Great Depression of the 1930s

Laurel Sefton MacDowell

The 1930s were harsh years for Canadian workers who faced wage cuts, layoffs, and unemployment, because "in 1929 the onset of the Great Depression brought development to an end for almost a decade." By 1933 the nearly complete economic collapse resulting from a rapid decline in exports of wheat, raw materials like lumber, and major manufactured goods like cars and newsprint was followed by a halting recovery until the outbreak of war in 1939 stimulated economic growth.[1] In Ontario, between 1929 and 1932, overall employment fell by 32 per cent, as companies closed down and left thousands dependent on relief services.[2] Early in 1932 federal inspector Frank LaFortune reported that the unemployment situation in Ontario communities was severe. In Orillia township, for example, he found fifteen families on direct relief. Meaford, with its population of 2700, had used up its public works budget by November 1931, as the Beaver Bran and Hardwood Floor companies had closed in June, throwing forty-seven families on direct relief. As a result, "there is no work of any kind going on at present at Meaford," he wrote. Conditions in the larger town of Midland (population 8000) were "fairly good," but 535 married men, 310 single men, and 50 single men with dependants were registered as unemployed. Conditions in

Cornwall were "fairly good," largely because its three cotton mills were running at full capacity and there was a public relief works project for some of the 450 registered unemployed men. "The town is trying to take care of the most needy by using them for street cleaning and quarry work, but as the finances cannot stand this very long, the Council are considering whether they would apply for some additional grant to carry on stone crushing work." In Peterborough, where 559 married men and 77 single men were registered as unemployed, there was a public works relief program.[3]

The Ontario government's approach to unemployment initially was to introduce public works in urban and isolated areas. In 1931, for example, public works relief camps were established in northern Ontario under the jurisdiction of the Northern Development Branch of the federal Department of Lands and Forests; they were inspected by the federal Department of Labour and were staffed by Ontario government employees to maintain workers as they built sections of the Trans-Canada Highway. For some small northern communities like Kenora and Dryden, the work provided was a blessing, but single men from southern centres like Hamilton, Oshawa (which sent large numbers), and Brantford (which sent 140) arrived as well.

Laurel Sefton MacDowell, "Relief Camp Workers in Ontario during the Great Depression of the 1930s," *Canadian Historical Review* 76, 2 (June 1995): 205–228. Reprinted by permission of the University of Toronto Press.

These camp jobs in the province were stopgap measures intended as temporary. From Fort William, an inspector reported that many of the men sent to the road camps left vacancies in the town's work project which could be filled immediately.[4] Work relief projects became too expensive for municipalities and, in 1932–3, the proportion of direct relief increased to more than $25 million. Despite large expenditures on relief, the unemployed got shunted about, relief recipients had to contend with the prevailing public notion that "the dole" was shameful and an indication of moral shiftlessness, and relatively little help reached single unemployed men.[5]

The Depression put immense stress on everyone, but young single men were particularly vulnerable. Society expected them to take care of themselves, as it was assumed that such men would not burden their families if they contributed no wages to the household and would feel obliged to leave. As one man expressed the prevailing attitude, "I couldn't expect my mother to feed me so I went to the farm. I walked five or six miles just to work for my board."[6]

Overburdened municipalities, which were responsible for all unemployed men in their communities, gave priority to married men with dependants. In Guelph, for example, where 717 married men and 513 single men were unemployed in 1931 but "had work of some kind from time to time," those with dependants were given two days work a week, whereas single men with no dependants were given two days work every second week. As work and money became scarcer, single men worked two days every three weeks and were paid half in cash and half in relief vouchers.[7] As there was never enough money, municipal officials were often hostile towards single men who sought relief, urging them to pack up and go, sometimes in blunt terms. In February 1932 Mayor Max Armstrong of Hanover told such a group that appeared before council asking for work, "You need not sit down and expect the town to feed and clothe you. The town is at the end of its tether so far as money is concerned...[we] will have to combine to provide food, clothing and fuel-not to single, or even married men, but to the latter's families." In September 1932 Mayor Hayman of London stated, "We will look after our own men but we cannot do anything more and we should not spend a nickel to try to do anything more."[8] In many Ontario communities, there was little work for single men, as both the local governments and private industry doled it out to married men first. Joy Parr found that in Hanover, for example, the single men were the first to be laid off at the Knechtel Furniture Company, and this pattern was apparent in other communities. Consequently, when the federal relief camps were established, they eased the pressure on municipalities somewhat by providing single men with an alternative to roaming and scrounging to survive.

Before the Department of National Defence camps were set up, families were disrupted as youths drifted across the country and rode from place to place atop freight cars, sometimes a hundred or more on the same train looking for non-existent work. They became transients and were increasingly recognizable, if Victor Howard's portrait is accurate. He described them with "knapsacks strung across their backs, floppy fedoras and soft billed caps tugged low, usually with a pair of goggles attached, pants and shirts and coats frayed, boots and shoes scratched and broken. Quite a few carried a kitten or puppy stuffed in a pocket for company over the long haul."[9] Some young men went north to work in the mines that continued to operate profitably, but there was such an oversupply of available labour that the companies picked "the cream of the crop" for their workforces.[10] Others moved on and continued their vain search for employment. Some found temporary resting places in missions, immigrant hotels, and hostels run by the "Sally Anns," where a man could get a meal and a bunk for the night.[11] In Toronto, for example, a Parliament Street Mission dispensed sandwiches and weak cocoa, and men slept on the floor. The Salvation Army on Jarvis Street provided facilities for washing clothes, and the Toronto Reference Library provided sanctuary from the cold. Single men of all ages learned that if they walked to residential districts in many communities, an occasional kind housewife would provide food at the door. Others stopped in the "jungles" on the outskirts of rail yards, which consisted of crude huts made from tin sheets, packing crates, boxes, and other debris hauled from garbage dumps. Some took to the bush for fear of being arrested for vagrancy, as many were. This fear was particularly urgent among immigrants, who could be threatened with deportation.[12] The enforced mobility of these unemployed worsened their plight, for if they moved about they could not qualify for assistance under the relief system since most municipalities demanded at least six months residency.

Society came both to sympathize with and to fear the growing restless throng of roaming men. Policy-makers worried about this unused youth and virility, particularly as the communists by 1932 were aggressively organizing the unemployed to demand their rights and an unemployment insurance scheme. The federal government had been concerned enough about this visible activism to outlaw the Communist Party in 1931. Out of this dilemma about what to do, and fear of what might happen if nothing were done, the idea of work camps for single unemployed males emerged.[13]

In 1932, when Major-General Andrew McNaughton, the chief of the General Staff, toured and inspected the military districts, there were an estimated 70,000 mostly young, single, unemployed, homeless men in Canada. McNaughton saw many of them—wasted, malnourished individuals suffering from low morale and little self-esteem. He sympathized with them

and was motivated to act because, as he said, "We were destroying physically and mentally the very best of our people, the people that we would need the moment we got over this temporary depression...to get the economy on the rails again." As a soldier, he sought to conserve the nation's manhood, because he was appalled that these young men "in their ragged platoons were the prospective members of Canada's armed forces should the country become involved in war."[14] As the person responsible for maintaining law and order in the country, he wanted to remove causes of unrest and the possibility of having to use force to resist insurrection and "prevent the unemployed going to rack and ruin and being driven into the arms of the Communists." Also as an experienced administrator, "frustrated by the parsimony of government towards defence...[he] seized the opportunity offered by unemployment relief to add to Canada's defence equipment."[15] McNaughton's idea was to establish work camps for young unemployed men to provide food, clothing, a bed, and medical treatment to "build up morale through work." This solution was meant to be a temporary measure to salvage youth and reduce the danger of disorder. To save money, the camps would use the existing facilities, personnel, and administrative experience of the Canadian Armed Forces as much as possible.

McNaughton first put his plan to W.A. Gordon, the minister of labour, and H. Hereford, the commissioner of unemployment relief. He was invited to present his idea to Cabinet and, in October 1932, the Bennett government agreed to inaugurate the scheme by order-in-council PC 2248. This order was the first of twenty-three concerning the relief camps, and it established a worker's allowance of 20 cents a day, authorized up to $3000 for relief projects to 31 March 1933, and gave the minister of national defence the authority to administer the projects in consultation with the minister of labour. The government viewed the camp idea as a constructive solution to provide for homeless single men on the move among communities. They would be sheltered, provided with work to fill their days, and would be quarantined in most cases from political "agitators" in urban communities. From the beginning of the federal camps, McNaughton dominated both the conception and the execution of the relief projects, which operated until 1936.[16]

Much has been written about the camps in western Canada and especially in British Columbia. Their wards participated in the dramatic On-to-Ottawa Trek, which culminated in the Regina Riot of 1935.[17] Relatively little is known of the Ontario camps, but, next to British Columbia, which had 53 projects, Ontario had the second largest number, with 37 of a total of 144 (123 actual work projects and 21 administrative), and handled 52,432 men of a Canadian total of 170,248.[18] On 4 August 1933 the minister of national defence, in consultation with the minister of labour, approved the works projects, some of which were already underway. The thirty-seven Ontario projects consisted of building five aerodromes, twenty-four intermediate landing fields, three air stations, three barracks, one training camp, and one land-clearing project. Of the total, five projects were completed (a hangar in Emsdale, three radio-beacon stations in Ottawa, Emsdale, and Dane, and a caretaker's quarters in Reay); thirty-two were closed as relief projects before the work was accomplished, but several were near completion and continued on a wage basis until they were finished. These included hangars in Kapuskasing and Wagaming, a radio-beacon station in Kapuskasing, and operators' living quarters in Dane, Kapuskasing, Wagaming, and Emsdale.[19]

In November 1932 the camps had opened across Canada, with 2000 men working. Men could enter a camp through any office of the National Employment Service (NES). In Ontario they were inundated with applicants,

and by June 1933, 8000 men were employed and their number kept growing. The federal government supported such growth, as it had no alternative policies for single men and the municipalities were glad to have a place to send them.[20] There were selection criteria for the projects undertaken, which had to be useful and to Canada's advantage. Labour had to be available and of little expense, but not every man could enter a camp; workers were supposed to qualify as young, single, in relatively good health, and motivated. Over the next four years, however, the camps also sheltered older men.

Many applicants were turned away for medical reasons, and even then project administrators complained that the men were often not given proper medical examinations in municipalities before they were dispatched. From Project 91 in Round Lake a foreman wrote: "It seems to be regarded as the correct thing to foist men into the relief camps merely to get rid of them and this creates a very distressing condition when it becomes necessary to reject them here."[21] Older men from Toronto had been sent back from Project 94 in Tudhope because they could not stand up to the rigours of the northern autumn weather. Even among those who remained in the camps, who were considered healthy, there were problems. Administrators found it difficult to keep within the low medical budget of 3 cents per man per day because, in 1933, in some camps, nearly 50 per cent of the men required some medical care.[22] The Depression had exacted its toll, but most newcomers adapted. Dr. L.W. Rice, who provided care at Petawawa, noted, "there is invariably a number of men who are not physically fit on arrival but who rapidly round into shape and are able to, and do, carry on satisfactorily at work after one or two weeks of acclimatization."[23] It was soon apparent that the camp workers' health improved steadily and the men gained weight. McNaughton wrote privately, but with considerable confidence, to W.D. Herridge,

Canadian ambassador to Washington: "The more experience I have with this form of relief the more I am convinced that we are on the right lines. We are able to take the men off the streets who want to work; to feed them adequately and to clothe them properly, and we should be able to keep up morale and return them eventually to the economic life of the country unimpaired bodily and mentally. In addition, we are adding works of substantial value to the capital equipment of the country and ones on which there will be no heavy annual maintenance charges."[24]

The Ontario camps provided for large numbers of men who came from the cities and towns of Ontario; one project at Petawawa was established to relieve the unemployment situation in Montreal; and Project 51 at Lac Seul was set up specifically to ease the relief situation in Winnipeg.[25] Most of Ontario's camps were isolated in the north in such places as Kowkash, Vermilion Bay, Pagawa, and there were groups of camps at Lac Seul, Petawawa, North Bay, and Nakina. But there was also a project at the Royal Military College in Kingston, work done on an air station at Trenton, a camp at Barriefield, and a work project in Ottawa to improve facilities at Rockcliffe airport.

There are a number of contentious points about the relief camps-the military discipline, their voluntary nature, the productivity of the workers, the "20 cent allowance" but lack of wage payment, and the value of the work performed by relief workers. However flawed the camp idea may have been in the long run, it was well implemented; in general, the camps were administered efficiently by officers who gained experience in handling large numbers of men. Swettenham, McNaughton's biographer, claimed that "much of the administrative excellence of the Canadian army in the Second World War sprang from the hungry thirties."[26] The camp administrators were motivated by McNaughton's idealism and by the fact that they had jobs which they wanted to keep by performing well. Both military personnel and relief workers wore civilian clothes in camp, as the army recognized that the unemployed were not soldiers, but the claim that there was a complete absence of military discipline is exaggerated, as the administration of the camps reflected the training of its personnel.[27] There was order and routine on the work projects; the structure of the camps was hierarchical and not consultative; individuals could take a grievance to an officer, but there could be no committees. Discipline by persuasion was preferred, but there were dismissals "for cause," and any men who were in a disturbance were dealt with summarily. As the Department of National Defence's *Final Report* to the government on the camps put it, individuals were "discharged" if they were insubordinate, refused to work, or were malingering.[28] Sometimes camp administrators invoked the aid of the civil police "in enforcing the removal of disturbing elements from some of the camps."[29]

The claim that the camps were voluntary is an overstatement. Swettenham writes, "No man was held in the camps against his will. Anyone wishing to go was given clothing if he needed it and transportation to his prospective place of work; if he failed to find it, as many did, he was taken back."[30] In fact, transportation of the men was free from the place of acceptance to the project. It was free when a man left the camp for roughly the same distance from where he entered if the project was completed, he was "discharged" for medical reasons, or he had accepted a bona fide offer of employment. For men who got fired or homesick or fed up, as many did, they had to wait for transportation or walk or hitch a train ride, and they were supposed to turn in their work clothes, which sometimes were forcibly seized if they did not. The average length of time a man spent in a camp was 107 days, or about three-and-a-half months, but some men, if necessary using assumed names, re-entered the camp system.[31]

In the circumstances, the camps were relatively productive and very inexpensive. The *Final Report* claimed that average labour productivity in output per person-hour was half that of a labour force working for wages under ordinary conditions. It attributed the difference to the "class of men and their physical condition on entering the camps," but undoubtedly a very important reason was that relief workers were not paid and they sometimes were ill equipped. Organized labour criticized the camps because of concern that work done by relief workers might deprive union members of employment. The labour movement favoured only unskilled manual labour being performed in the camps. In the early stages of these projects, the bulk of the relief work was done by hand labour "in order to employ the maximum number of men usefully."[32] McNaughton refused to waste the men on primitive tasks, but, as a concession to labour, he directed that a minimum amount of equipment be used on the projects in order to employ as many men as possible. As useful work progressed in grading landing fields and building permanent buildings, the army provided machinery and trucks to assist in getting such jobs done, and also for the sake of the men's morale. As McNaughton reported, "The relief personnel quickly recognized that the work was proceeding inefficiently and became apathetic and listless." Where suitable machinery was provided, the men were more productive and the work advanced quickly.[33] In the purchase of machinery, the army was frugal; it economized by using second-hand machinery, which constantly needed repairs, and even horses, and spent at a rate of 7.5 cents per workday of relief compared with 13 cents on an American scheme, the Civilian Conservation Corps. Under a dominion-provincial agreement, the province supplied machinery, which was used on work of provincial advantage. These conditions affected productivity on the projects. With proper equipment, the relief workers did

accomplish good work. By 30 September 1934, for example, relief workers had excavated 53,000 cubic yards of material at the intermediate landing field in Diver, Ontario, so that the field could be used for summer and winter aircraft landings, but where there was no machinery, even on smaller projects, the fields were not ready even for easier winter landings. Colonel J.L.H. Bogart reported from Project 40 in Petawawa at that time that twenty-three buildings were standing where previously there had been seven. Repairs had been made to the main camp, brush had been cleared and stumps removed, and there was ongoing bridge and road construction. The men had also planted a garden to grow potatoes.[34]

The camps were run cheaply. Taxpayers were promised the cost per man would not exceed $1.00 a day, and this amount was exceeded only slightly.[35] For an estimated 18,156,213 days of relief work on what the authorities determined were desirable projects, the federal government paid $24,517,012, or an estimated $1.30 per man per day, which is inexpensive by any standard. The camp administrators considered the men's conduct as generally satisfactory with a reasonable amount of work completed, except when the pace slowed when "agitation" unsettled them. As the level of unrest in Ontario camps was relatively low, compared with British Columbia, and the amount of work completed was relatively high, the army had reason to continue the camps despite growing public criticism. In response to attacks on the camps, McNaughton was passive, and he followed the lead of politicians who did not close the camps until there was a change of government.

The men's main complaint was the low allowance (the military never intended it as a wage) of 20 cents a day, which prevented them from setting aside any money for the future.[36] When they left a camp, they were left destitute without even their work clothes. The lack of wages lowered productivity, morale, and was the basis for the charge by the Relief Camp Workers' Union that they were "slave camps." The labour was physically demanding, was undertaken even in very cold weather, and, when the amount of work done is considered along with the government's satisfaction with it, this charge by "radicals" was not as extreme as it appeared to contemporary politicians. The *Final Report* indicated that the administrators were fair to the men, and it may be that the physical condition of the men in the camps was better than it had been when they were transients; this was the original rationale for the camps. Clearly, the government deliberately ran the camps as cheaply as possible, which made the gruelling work in a difficult situation worse for the relief workers.

The value of the work performed by relief workers has been seriously underestimated by historians, who have either dismissed their labour as "make-work" or have been preoccupied primarily with the disturbances in the camps.[37] Most single, unemployed men in the Ontario camps did not do make-work. Prime Minister Bennett spoke publicly of the non-military tasks accomplished by the men-miles of road construction, trees planted, railway crossings improved-but McNaughton gave priority to the construction of airfields and barracks.

One of the most important achievements of the work camps was the Trans-Canada Airway. By 1930 the western section from Winnipeg to the Rockies had already been built. Now, the need for its completion, if Canada were to keep pace with world developments in both military and civil aviation, was urgent. The rest of its construction—the intermediate landing fields and the aids to navigation—was undertaken in 1933 as projects by the relief camp workers. By early 1934, a report to McNaughton indicated that there had been remarkable progress made in northern Ontario in the initial work of clearing, grading, and finally surfacing the aerodromes. When they were finished, the plan was to initiate air-mail services across the country.[38] In 1936 C.D. Howe, the new minister of transport in Mackenzie King's government, was taken on a trip over the airway and he expressed amazement at the work that had been accomplished. Howe told McNaughton that "Canada would certainly not have had an airway for many years if we had not gone ahead and made it under the relief projects."[39] In 1937 Trans-Canada Air Lines, a crown corporation, began operations. McNaughton appreciated Howe's comments, as the relief camps had become controversial after their inception.

The living and working conditions of all the camps were organized on a similar basis, but life within them varied because the personnel and tasks differed. The men were housed in barracks on the work sites. There was fuel for stoves, and cold and often hot running water. Each man was issued work clothes, shaving gear, and a towel, was assigned a bunk, and given three meals and a 20-cent a day allowance for tobacco and personal needs. When the payment became controversial, the men satirized themselves as "the Royal 20 Centers." They had medical, dental, and eye care, which was provided by the Royal Canadian Army Medical Corps, and spiritual services offered by various churches on a voluntary basis.

Unlike the other provinces, which established correspondence courses and sent teachers to the relief camps, Ontario refused to organize and administer an educational program. Such services theoretically could be arranged by local camp officers with local boards of education, but they were not. The gap was filled to some extent by Frontier College.[40] McNaughton viewed their labourer-teachers as "estimable young men" who were providing valuable services in many camps and were serving their generation "in a most excellent manner." They were paid $15 a month in the smaller camps and $20 in the larger camps.[41] Frontier College provided classes in basic elementary-school subjects like reading, writing, and math, taught immigrant workers English, and gave some advanced subjects to small groups. Besides boosting morale, the classes apparently encouraged a few relief workers to improve their education. While some men benefited from such classes, especially in small isolated camps that were conducive to study, the program was not extensive and the high turnover in the camps did not facilitate the educational process.[42]

When a camp opened, the first men to arrive laid out a campsite, built the bunkhouses, mess halls, storage rooms, privies, roads, and parking areas, and cut trails out of the bush. When work began on a project, the men were under a supervisor (often a civil engineer), a foreman, and a number of gang bosses. The other personnel in a camp were the store or supply clerk and, of course, a cook. The men were not only isolated but vulnerable in their poverty and dependency, and they sometimes ran into problems. Some gang bosses were harsh and a few foremen were incompetent; some store clerks were "crooks"; not every cook could cook. Such difficulties were corrected eventually, but they could cause disturbances.[43]

The administration was very precise about food, and the food budget for relief workers was considerably less than for soldiers in training camps after 1939. As Howard details, a daily ration per man consisted of 1 pound each of bread, meat, and potatoes, 6 ounces of fresh vegetables, 3 ounces of bacon and sugar, 2 ounces of beans, jam and butter, 1 ounce of tea, and 1/3 ounce of pepper.[44] This was not a great deal of food for a full-grown man doing manual labour all day in cold weather. As an administrator on Project 40 in Petawawa reported, "for the men employed on heavy work—such as logging operations during the winter months—the existing ration scale was not sufficient." It was not increased.[45] There were many complaints about the food, which was a big issue in the monotonous days of the men. If a cook had

skill, he could make something out of the meagre supplies; if not, the situation could cause rebellion, as it often did. In Project 28 (Trenton), it was reported that the quality of the food was good, but that "the cooking is so *poor* that much of the food is left untasted on the men's plates." The situation was frustrating, as some of the camp workers were cooks and bakers, but "they were not in a position to offer either assistance or advice. The chief cook in kitchen #1 is an ex-railroad foreman, which would seem to explain much of the trouble."[46] In the last analysis, there was not much with which to work. According to Swettenham, in the final accounting the cost of feeding a man was 26 cents a day, and judging by the consistent complaints, the food budget was inadequate to feed the men properly.[47]

There were few recreational supplies in the camps and there was no money allocated for such purposes. Donations from charities went to the Unemployment Relief Comforts Fund to purchase sports equipment, books, magazines, and radios. "Even so, the men had to improvise their own checkers and checkerboards and borrow horseshoe sets from farmers." Voluntary gifts sent on this haphazard basis were not always suitable. Project 109 in Kenora received a shipment of mostly ladies' and religious magazines "for which there is no demand." The superintendent requested fiction and comics, and suggested that if such items were not available the army might as well save on the freight and express charges. In some camps located near a town, the men themselves organized public boxing bouts and wrestling matches which they greatly enjoyed, and which were supported by local citizens and raised funds for other forms of recreation.[48]

There was unrest in the camps for a variety of reasons, which differed from camp to camp. In the four years the camps were running, there were a total of 359 recorded strikes, riots, demonstrations, and disturbances in all projects across Canada. In Ontario, there appear to have been about thirty outbreaks that were sufficiently problematic to be reported; so there was a relatively low level of conflict in the Ontario camps compared with those in British Columbia. Of the total disruptions in Ontario, thirteen occurred in the Lac Seul project, which was the largest in the province and housed 2000 men in fifteen camps. The men's task, which was different from the usual construction projects, was to clear the wooded foreshore along 1400 miles of shoreline so that when the water level was raised as the result of the installation of a new dam, the timber would not be ruined. The conditions were trying, as the men worked in isolation, the food was poor (although the fishing was good), the black flies were a menace, and the only way out was by scow in the warm season and by tractor across the ice in winter. The higher level of conflict in the Lac Seul camps was attributable to some unusual aspects of the project, including the unrealistic nature of the task resulting from political conflicts among the federal, Ontario, and Manitoba governments, the extremely cold weather, arbitrary discipline by the camp administration, and the transiency of the men.[49] Of the thirteen eruptions, eight involved food. In 1933 strikes for better meals in Camps 3, 4, 6, and 10 resulted in "discharges"; in Camp 11, a strike of seventeen men resulted in a cook being fired and one man discharged. On 26 March 1934 in Camp 14, a strike of Chinese workers occurred because there was insufficient food, and two men were arrested.[50] Other incidents involved a strike of seventeen men in Camp 5 in November 1933, when the men refused to work during a snowstorm, and in Camp 3 in April 1934, when twenty-five men were allowed to leave after they quit work because their tobacco rations were short. These small sparks, which set off outbursts, resulted from the discomfort of the camps and the sometimes heavy-handed treatment meted out to the men. There were a few

more organized disturbances in 1934 and 1935 when, for example, forty-one men in Camp 5 refused to work until their grievances were heard and their demands met. At Lac Seul, however, where there was the most conflict, the presence of professional organizers was limited compared with the high-conflict situation in British Columbia.

In Ontario camps where conflict was lower, there were minor outbreaks in 1933 at Pagawa, Kowkash, and Ogahalla over similar issues of basic comfort, food, and clothing, and in 1934 brief strikes occurred in Emsdale, Nakina, and Porquis Junction. In June at Ramore camp, two men refused to give up their government clothing when they were leaving the camp, and the civilian police were brought in to secure it from them.

Some strikes indicated the presence of organizers, judging by the numbers of men or the issues involved, though they were not always mentioned. For example, when men stationed at the Royal Military College in Kingston refused to work in wet weather, twenty-one were discharged. There were "major" disturbances at Long Branch in 1933, when nearly 700 relief workers were discharged because they refused to work and the supervisors could not maintain control, and at Rockcliffe, where in July 1935 150 were discharged after workers expressed general dissatisfaction and demanded $1 a day in wages. The military attributed these disruptions to the agitation and active propaganda by "subversive" elements, which was plausible as these camps were located in urban centres, not isolated in the bush. As the Relief Camp Workers' Union (RCWU), which was established by the Workers' Unity League (WUL) and associated with the Communist Party, became more organized, it used its experience of organizing the unemployed in the cities and applied it in the camps. "Agitators went from camp to camp breeding discontent and creating discord among the men"[51] and distributing radical literature. Some but not all of these organizers were identified by camp officials and expelled. Others evaded camp personnel, survived expulsion, changed their identity, and kept moving.[52] In June 1935 a strike at Vermilion Bay was out of sympathy for two men discharged for disciplinary reasons, and it resulted in twenty-four more being discharged. In July 1935, at Barriefield, there was dissatisfaction in the mess room over the quality of the fish being served. The four "agitators" were dismissed as the military reported that the complaint was unfounded.

At Tudhope on Project 94, the plight of restless relief workers influenced T.B. Higginson, a young teacher-labourer working there. Project foreman Joseph Found reported to Frontier College's Principal Bradwin that Higginson was polite and had performed satisfactorily, but that "during his sojourn here, there were two strikes—the men agitating and refusing to work for very trivial reasons." Though he had not taken part in these strikes, the foreman admonished Higginson for not discussing the situation with him and for "following the agitators." Apparently Higginson left the project without warning, did not return to his home in Hawkesbury, but travelled to Frater, north of the Sault, where he resigned from Frontier College. Found concluded that "the influence of these agitators on the young is great." Bradwin regretted this incident and expressed his view that when there was trouble, Frontier College representatives in the camps were to support the camp administration and not the relief camp workers; they were to avoid all discussions of debatable questions, especially those relating to "social readjustments." He wrote, "Frontier College realizes something of the problems that confront all superintendents and officials handling men in unemployment camps at this time and we are desirous always that the representative of Frontier College will hold himself aloof from the internal problems of the camp, taking no sides. And, if a decision is unavoidable, they should be found lined up with the officials who carry the responsibility at the camp."[53] Had young Higginson not resigned, he would have been fired.

In November 1935 a disturbance at Trenton air station occurred when "agitators" led 300 men to demand their October allowances (as yet unpaid) so they would have cash to spend over the weekend. The officer in charge spoke to the men about the policy concerning the payment of allowances, apparently the crowd dispersed, and several leaders were discharged. At Kapuskasing, five men were discharged and five men left voluntarily over the issue of an "agitator distributing Communistic literature."[54] Compared to British Columbia, strikes in the Ontario camps did not reach as serious proportions partly because there were fewer organizers influencing smaller numbers of men. At the Lac Seul camps, for example, there is evidence that the extreme isolation of the project and the severe weather helped prevent the effective infiltration of the camps by organizers and the politicization of relief workers. As a result, the Department of National Defence's strategies to cope with disturbances were more effective. Disciplinary action was prompt; leaders and strikers who refused to work were dismissed and not re-engaged on projects. These control mechanisms worked with a fragmented, transient, and impoverished workforce at a time when any work was considered a privilege and demand to enter the camps remained steady.

Between December 1934 and March 1935, the RCWU tried to organize all the camps to strike simultaneously for a living wage. It failed in Ontario, but in British Columbia the result was the On-to-Ottawa Trek across the West, which was forcibly stopped by the RCMP in Regina. During the trek, "other bodies of marchers in Eastern Canada began to organize"; strikers left Nakina, North Bay, Petawawa, and

Rockcliffe camps out of sympathy for the "trekkers." Of those men marching from Vancouver to Regina, seventy-one were sent home to Ontario with the assistance of the Saskatchewan government. The military's *Final Report* to the government condemned "agitators," but understood the camp workers' frustration. "The long continuance of depressed labour conditions discouraged a large proportion of the men, particularly the younger element, many of whom had never obtained remunerative employment."[55] Men existing so long in this position lost patience and rebelled.

The work camps, which opened in November 1932, expanded in 1934, and then began to contract in 1935 and 1936. As a result of the "Regina Riot," they were investigated by a committee in the autumn of 1935 which consisted of R.A. Rigg[56] from the federal Department of Labour, E.W. Bradwin, the principal of Frontier College, and Humphrey Mitchell, who in 1942 became the minister of labour. The committee toured fifty Canadian camps and many camps in the United States,[57] and on 31 January 1936 it reported to Minister of Labour Norman Rogers.

The original idea behind the camps had been to provide work relief for an undetermined but presumably short time to young, single, unemployed males. In the camps the committee identified four distinct groups of workers, all of various nationalities. They found some young men eager to work. They also found that many of the relief workers were "mature men" who "yearn for the opportunity to independently maintain themselves" through regular private or public employment. They identified a third group of intelligent young men (eighteen to twenty-five years of age), who had held only casual jobs and had not developed the habit of working, who were very frustrated, and who lacked "hopes for the future." They judged these men to be the "easy prey" of communist organizers and a menace for the administrators:

They are viciously rebellious against and defiant to authority; they shirk work and are determined to continue to do so; they assert that society owes them a living and are oblivious of the obligations they owe to society; they are acquiring undesirable habits, especially by moving from camp to camp, often under assumed names, staying in each camp long enough to secure a complete issue of clothing and then leaving camp, selling the issued clothing and shoes and donning ordinary, cheap mufti clothing; they disturb and irritate more reasonable and stable-minded men and are a constant source of trouble to camp authorities.

The committee also identified a substantial group of older men, who, in a normal economy, would have been marginal unskilled labourers, but in the depression, after years of relief, had nowhere else to go and were unemployable.[58] Many of the men in the relief camps were "unsuited by background, training and adaptability for regular camp life," which in the main consisted of work in lumbering and construction. The camps had become a stop-gap measure for men at different stages of life with different needs and aspirations.

The committee was preoccupied with the low morale of the men in the camps, and suggested that a work-and-wages policy would be an improvement because it would encourage individual initiative and self-respect. The men could buy their own clothes (some resented being dressed alike), pay their own expenses, and be expected to give an honest day's work. The investigators also recommended that men should be in the camps no longer than six months.[59]

The committee's report was based on its own observations of the camps, but also on information about the men and camp conditions gleaned from a questionnaire to Frontier College teachers. Their responses revealed that there were some married men in the camps, although they all represented themselves as single. Some had deserted their wives or been left. The questionnaire was biased towards some concerns of the Frontier College employees, many of whom were United Church reformers raised on social gospel Protestant beliefs. There was, for example, a question on liquor and gambling, but little evidence of either "vice" in the camps except occasionally among the staff. As Clarence Parker with Project 141 in Grant reported, "the labourers at Grant and Sunstrum were not necessarily any more virtuous than the members of the staff; they simply had not the money or the opportunity to indulge themselves." The questionnaire wanted to know if the men were frugal and saved, even though the camp workers were impoverished. Some immigrants saved a little even in these meagre circumstances, but as one teacher responded, "I have seen little evidence of any saving on 20 cents a day."[60]

In all the camps, there were cases of "jumping," when men quit camp without permission for a variety of reasons. Some resented the 20 cent allowance, others protested the food or sanitary conditions, but most moved on out of restlessness; they wanted a change or wished to return home. They "had nothing to lose," or were looking for something better. Apparently Canadian-born workers were somewhat more on the move than immigrants. As one teacher/labourer, P.C. Perry, working at Emsdale concluded, "The inner driving forces of a normal life do not permit contentment in relief camps without wages, away from society. The men go out to look for work, usually get none, drift into another camp, driven there by hunger and exposure. Then, merely to change camps breaks the monotony for a while."[61] Winton Budgeon, working at Barriefield, was less charitable. He wrote, "Bumming has become a habit. These men came to the camp for a few days rest and never intended to stay."[62] George Andrews, in Hudson, believed the camps were detrimental to the men because they held out no hope for the future. "Possibly the vast majority can look for-

ward to only a purposeless life."[63] A.T. Newby, writing twenty miles north of Hudson, noted a slow degeneration of thought and action among men who remained in the camps for long. Some teachers were concerned that very young men were exposed to older, hardened, sometimes illiterate men with bad habits, and thought that youth really belonged at home and in school and should only stay in the camps a short time.[64]

For some of the skilled men in the camps, frustration was a problem. At Trenton, some outside workers were hired to construct new buildings, and this provoked some camp workers. "The project men's complaints is [sic] that, while many of them are skilled at various trades, they have to see poor workmen being paid prevailing rates of wages for work they could do and also seeing these same skilled men 'bumming' on the job...or else doing work that falls down or has to be pulled down and rebuilt. The project men, rightly or wrongly, refuse to work at their trades for 20 cents a day." The resident Frontier College teacher, William F. Hunt, also alleged that "the camp has been made a political football by both parties apparently." After the change of government in 1935, there was "out and out graft" and political patronage in this camp, as the Liberal MP at Belleville "seems to have more to say as to the personnel of the camp than anyone else; even men fired for legitimate reasons by the new liberal foremen have had to be reinstated," and there was "absolute incompetence on the part of some of those in charge." He reported to Bradwin that work which he presumed was "being done as a relief measure to help the unemployed single men is being spoiled by political patronage and the desire for a few who want to 'get rich quick' at the government's expense. The 20 cent a day man who is responsible for the work having been started seems to have been left out of the picture in the scramble after soft jobs and easy money."[65] This situation suggests that, in 1935, the uncertainty about the future of the camps was a destabilizing factor.

W.J. Wishart, the foreman of Project 57 with experience in both the federal and provincial camps, provided the Rigg committee with a thoughtful analysis of what the camps were supposed to do and what had gone wrong. He wrote: "the primary idea of the establishment of relief camps was to take care of single unemployed men until such time as they were able to be absorbed back into the normal industry of the country; apparently this time was expected to be short. If the time had been as short as expected, the camps as organized would have fulfilled their objective admirably. Unfortunately, the time has now been four years with prospects of continuing indefinitely." The men seldom got hired out of the camps, they received little money, and had no hope. As a result, Wishart believed that "a long-range attitude should be taken with respect to these camps."[66] He proposed several changes in their administration, such as a sliding scale of hourly wages, and greater self-reliance for relief workers, who should pay for and care for their own clothes. He opposed the free issue of tobacco, and thought that some camps could grow some of their own provisions. He favoured training men in trades and higher pay. This idea had appealed to McNaughton, but it was opposed by both business and labour, who insisted that no work or training in the camps could be done which might compete with private-sector jobs or wages.[67] Wishart's brief was constructive, though unrealistic, on this latter point, and in any case it came too late.

On 11 January 1936 the Rigg Committee recommended that the camps be run temporarily on a work-and-wages basis and then be closed. The Department of Labour assumed their administration and there were no new admissions. In February 1936 the railways agreed to employ 10,000 men on deferred maintenance work (subsidized by the federal government), and some camp workers went to farms. The allowances of 20 cents a day were replaced with wages of $15 a month, which amounted to 50 cents a day in cash, but increasing numbers continued to be "placed" elsewhere, so that, in this period of transition, the camps did not increase the expenses of the government.

After Mackenzie King assumed office late in 1935, the camps closed on 1 July 1936.[68] The news that the camps had been abolished was welcomed by many, but, as J.W. Buckley, secretary of the Toronto District Labour Council remarked, "We're naturally glad they are not going to reopen the camps, but what is the alternative?"[69] It was a good question, for, after the camps closed, single men persisted in searching for non-existent jobs and continued to be kept under surveillance until 1939, when the war effort absorbed them.[70]

The federal camps had been established to relieve unemployment, avert revolution, and provide public works of permanent benefit to Canada. They were intended as a short-term solution for single, unemployed men, but, as the Depression dragged on for years, they became intolerable for the men. Their longevity was a factor in their demise because the camps became a political liability. When the communists organized relief workers in opposition to the 20 cent allowance, this created problems of maintaining order. As the public came to sympathize with relief workers, especially after the trek, increasingly Canadians disapproved of the government's administration of the camps. Despite the accomplishments of relief workers, particularly in building airfields, the tasks were limited by business and labour's insistence that no work or training in the camps could compete with private-sector jobs or wages. As the camps came to symbolize the wastage of youth in the depression years, the government eliminated this reminder of the persistence of economic ills and of its inability to bring about recovery.

Notes

1 Ian Drummond, *Progress without Planning: The Economic History of Ontario* (Toronto 1987), 148; R.B. Bryce, "The Canadian Economy in the 1930s: Unemployment Relief under Bennett and Mackenzie King," in Duncan Cameron, ed., *Exploration in Canadian Economic History: Essays in Honour of Irene M. Spry* (Ottawa 1985), 7.

2 Bryan Palmer, *Working Class Experience: The Rise and Reconstitution of Canadian Labour, 1800–1980* (Toronto 1983), 207; *Canadian Annual Review* 1932.

3 National Archives of Canada (NA), RG 27, vol. 2070, file Ontario Inspectors' Reports, Part I, 1931–2, LaFortune to Carter, assistant dominion director, Dominion Unemployment Relief, Department of Labour, 13 and 14 Jan. 1932; LaFortune to Carter, 19, 14, and 7 Dec. 1931; RG 27, vol. 2264, file Relief Works, Ontario 1931–4, T.M. Birkett's report, 10 Feb. 1931.

4 Ibid., vol. 2071, file Ontario Inspectors' Reports, Part 5, 1932–3, inspector to Harry Hereford, 9 Jan. 1932.

5 There were fewer single unemployed women and they were regarded entirely differently by society, which saw women's role in the labour force as marginal, temporary, and not entirely essential—particularly in recessionary times. The prevailing ideology of the "family wage" assumed that a male was the head of every household and that married women would be supported by husbands or fathers, and hence need not be unemployed. It was also assumed that women in need could always work as domestics. Both assumptions were wrong. When it became necessary for municipalities to assist single women, they did so only gradually, often informally, and they involved private social organizations. Thus, in structural terms, women were not really part of the organized employment relief system. See Veronica Strong-Boag, *The New Day Recalled: Lives of Girls and Women in English Canada 1919–1939* (Toronto 1988), chap. 2.

6 Joy Parr, *The Gender of Breadwinners: Women, Men, and Change in Two Industrial Towns, 1880–1950* (Toronto 1990), 201–2.

7 NA, RG 27, vol. 2253, file Department of Labour Employment Services, Annual Report, Supt. H.C. Hudson, Brantford, 17 Nov. 1931.

8 Parr, *The Gender of Breadwinners*, 202; H.M. Cassidy, *Unemployment and Relief in Ontario 1929–1932* (Toronto 1932), 208.

9 Victor Howard, *"We Were the Salt of the Earth": The On-to-Ottawa Trek and the Regina Riot* (Regina 1985), 2.

10 L.S. MacDowell, *"Remember Kirkland Lake": The Gold Miners' Strike, 1941–1942* (Toronto 1983), 51

11 Howard, *"We Were the Salt of the Earth,"* 2.

12 Barbara Roberts, *Whence They Came: Deportation from Canada, 1930–1935* (Ottawa 1988).

13 For details about increased communist activity among the unemployed in the early 1930s see Ivan Avakumovic, *The Communist Party in Canada: A History* (Toronto 1975), chap. 3; Howard, *"We Were the Salt of the Earth,"* chap. 1; Ronald Liversedge, *Recollections of the On to Ottawa Trek* (Ottawa 1973), chap. 3.

14 John Swettenham, *McNaughton*, vol. 1 (Toronto 1968), 270.

15 Ibid., 271, 274, 284. The military projects included emergency landing fields on the Trans-Canada Airway routes, six aerodromes, and forty-two intermediate landing fields, three RCAF air stations (one in Ontario), four barracks, including one at the Royal Military College, and four training camps, including one at Petawawa.

16 NA, Photograph Collection, Peter Robertson, "The Department of National Defence Relief Projects Collection," 1.

17 Existing literature on the camps includes Howard, *"We Were the Salt of the Earth"*; Liversedge, *Recollections of the On to Ottawa Trek*; and Lorne A. Brown, "Unemployment Relief Camps in Saskatchewan 1933–1936," in Michiel Horn, ed., *The Depression in Canada* (Toronto 1988).

18 NA, McNaughton Papers, series II, vol. 98, *Final Report on Unemployment Relief Scheme for the Care of Homeless Men*, vol. 1, 4, 97.

19 Ibid., 61, 98. "On a national scale the men at the relief camps carried on the following public works: a) restoration work at several historic sites; b) the development of 6 aerodromes and 42 intermediate landing fields on the trans-Canada airway; c) the development of one provincial and 3 municipal airports; d) the general development of 5 RCAF air stations; e) highway construction in conjunction with the provincial governments of British Columbia and Alberta; f) forestry operations in conjunction with the Department of the Interior; g) the clearing of the foreshores of Lac Seul in preparation for raising the water level of the lake; h) the

construction or expansion of 4 rifle ranges; i) the development of 4 army training areas; j) barrack construction at various army bases across Canada." Robertson, "The Department of National Defence Relief Projects Collection," 2.

20 NA, RG 24, vol. 2974, Administrative Report, Project 91, file 46.

21 Ibid.

22 Ibid., vol. 3091, Memo, 18 July 1933, file HQ 1376-11-5-2 (vol. 2).

23 Ibid., vol. 3090, Memo of L.W. Rice MD, file HQ 1376-11-5-2 (vol. 1).

24 Swettenham, *McNaughton,* 273, 284.

25 McNaughton Papers, vol. 98, *Final Report,* vol. 1, 98.

26 Swettenham, *McNaughton,* 298.

27 In the case of a few large projects with numerous camps, like Lac Seul, there were civilian staff employed who were selected from among qualified unemployed persons, as well as the military officers.

28 NA, RG 24, vol. 3091, H.B. Gordon to Military District No. 10, 21 July 1935, file HQ 1376-11-5-2 (vol. 2). The federal government considered establishing Camps of Discipline for the incarceration of agitators and people who did not cooperate with relief officials. Brown, "Unemployment Relief Camps in Saskatchewan," 88.

29 NA, RG 24, vol. 2972, Memorandum, 25 Jan. 1934, file 43.

30 Swettenham, *McNaughton,* vol. 1, 27.

31 McNaughton Papers, vol. 98, *Final Report,* vol. 1, 23.

32 NA, RG 24, vol. 4872, Draft Report, file 43.

33 Ibid., vol. 2969, Report of A. McNaughton, 7 Jan. 1935, file Unemployment Relief-Machinery Requirements.

34 Ibid., vol. 3090, Report of J.L.H. Bogart, nd, and Bogart to secretary, DND, 19 May 1934, file HQ 1376-11-5-2 (vol. 1).

35 Desmond Morton, *Working People: An Illustrated History of the Canadian Labour Movement* (Ottawa 1986), 146.

36 McNaughton Papers, vol. 98, *Final Report,* vol. 1, 7, 24.

37 For the view of the camps as "makework," see Barry Broadfoot, *Ten Lost Years, 1929–1939: Memoirs of Canadians Who Survived the Depression* (Markham 1985), 93. For the focus on disturbances, see Brown, "Unemployment Relief Camps in Saskatchewan."

38 NA, RG 24, vol. 4872, Draft Report, file 43.

39 Swettenham, *McNaughton,* 298.

40 NA, RG 24, vol. 2972, Administrative Report, 1 Aug. 1935, file 43 (vol. 2A).

41 NA, Frontier College Papers, vol. 198, McNaughton to Bradwin, 14 June 1935, file Unemployment Relief Camps 1935; Bradwin to secretary, DND, 26 June 1935.

42 Ibid., McNaughton to Bradwin, 29 May 1935.

43 There are many examples of the problems the men faced. Forty men in Camp 5 of the Lac Seul project presented a list of grievances to the superintendent for his consideration; they included complaints about the issuance of tobacco and papers and the lack of pipe tobacco, the lack of enough lamps in bunkhouses, the laundry facilities, the absence of toilet paper, mistakes in the price of canteen goods "always to the detriment of purchasers" and working in wet snowy weather. NA, RG 24, vol. 3128, file WR-31-11.

44 Howard, *"We Were the Salt of the Earth,"* 12–13.

45 NA, RG 24, vol. 2972, Administrative Report, Project 40, file 46.

46 NA, Frontier College Papers, vol. 198, Report of William F. Hunt, 12 Jan. 1936, file Relief Camps-Questionnaire 1935.

47 Swettenham, *McNaughton,* 283.

48 Howard, *"We Were the Salt of the Earth,"* 10; NA, RG 24, vol. 2972, Administrative Report, Project 109, file 46; Draft Report, file 43.

49 McNaughton Papers, vol. 98, *Final Report,* appendix 22.

50 Laurel Sefton MacDowell, "Canada's Gulag: Project #51—Lac Seul (A Tale from the Great Depression)," *Journal of Canadian Studies,* 28, 2 (summer 1993). The Chinese workers were segregated from the whites and, from this incident, it became clear that there was racial discrimination from the highest levels to the local level in the administration of the camps.

51 McNaughton Papers, vol. 98, *Final Report,* vol. 1, 25.

52 Morton, *Working People,* 147. NA, Frontier College Papers, vol. 198, Rigg Committee Report, 5, file Relief Camps—Questionnaire re 1935. This committee concluded that "Communist agitators, that is the agents of the WUL and its subsidiaries, are expert in the art of inoculating the minds of relief camp workers, particularly the younger element, with the virus of discontent. The policy is not nec-

essarily to teach the doctrines of communism openly, but rather to suggest them covertly and as being of secondary importance. The principal and direct object sought is to fan to flame the sense of injustice which is felt by these men and especially to incite the young fellows to disobedience."

53 NA, Frontier College Papers, vol. 198, Joseph Found, Foreman Project 94, to Bradwin, 7 July 1935; Bradwin to Foreman MacGregor (Petawawa), 3 Feb. 1934, file Relief Camps Questionnaire re 1935.

54 McNaughton Papers, vol. 98, *Final Report,* appendix 22.

55 Ibid., vol. 1, 26.

56 R.A. Rigg was secretary of the Winnipeg Trades Council in 1913, an army corporal in the Great War, and became a leading member of the Great War Veterans' Association in Winnipeg. At the time of the Winnipeg General Strike in 1919, he was among the veterans who actively supported the workers. D.J. Bercuson, *Confrontation at Winnipeg* (Montreal 1974).

57 There is no overall history of American work relief, but information on various New Deal schemes for the unemployed is included in Anthony J. Badger, *The New Deal: The Depression Years 1933–40* (New York 1989), chap. 5; William D. Reeves, "PWA and a Competitive Administration in the New Deal," *Journal of American History* 60 (1973); Donald S. Howard, *The WPA and Federal Relief Policy* (New York 1943); Forrest Walker, *The Civil Works Administration: An Experiment in Federal Work Relief 1933–34* (New York 1979); Bonnie Fox Schwartz, *The Civil Works Administration 1933–34: The Business of Emergency Employment in the New Deal* (Princeton 1984); Mark Naison, *Communists in Harlem during the Depression* (Urbana 1983); William W. Bremner, "Along the American Way: The New Deal's Work Relief Program for the Unemployed," *Journal of American History* 42 (1975); Richard D. McKinzie, *The New Deal for Artists* (Princeton 1973); John A. Salmond, *The Civilian Conservation Corps* (Durham, NC 1967). The motives behind the American projects were similar to the Canadian—a concern to provide work relief to the unemployed, to relieve mass distress, and to contain the threat of radical social disorder. Compared with the Canadian camps, the American projects were more eclectic, self-critical, and creative, more generously funded (especially at

the national level), more oriented to civilian life, and they applied to a broader range of people (including both males and females).

58 This finding confirms James Struthers's view in *No Fault of Their Own: Unemployment and the Canadian Welfare State, 1914–1941* (Toronto 1983).

59 NA, Frontier College Papers, vol. 198, Rigg Committee Report, 8.

60 Ibid., Parker to Bradwin, 8 Jan. 1936; Report of Charles Welch, Algonquin Park, nd; Report of William Hunt, Trenton, 12 Jan. 1936, file Relief Camps—Questionnaire 1935.

61 Ibid., Report of R.C. Perry, Emsdale, 11 Jan. 1935.

62 Ibid., Report of Winton Budgeon, 4 Jan. 1936.

63 Ibid., Report of George Andrews, 18 March 1935; Report of A.T. Newby, 10 March 1935; Report of C. Anderson, 16 March 1935; Report of A.J.H. MacDonald, Canoe Lake, 14 March 1935; and George Lantz, Kinmount, 9 March 1935.

64 This worry may have reflected a concern about homosexuality, but the subject was not mentioned.

65 NA, Frontier College Papers, vol. 198, Report of William F. Hunt, 12 Jan. 1936.

66 Ibid., W.J. Wishart, "Suggestions for Changes in the Relief Camps," file Commission, January–February 1935, 1936.

67 For the opposition of the Trades and Labour Congress, see H.A. Logan, *Trade Unions in Canada* (Toronto 1948), 477.

68 McNaughton Papers, vol. 98, *Final Report,* vol. 1, 6.

69 *Ottawa Citizen,* 18 July 1936.

70 NA, RG 27, vol. 2256, J. Batza Report, 7 May 1939, Confidential File, Police Report, 1938–9. In May 1939 Constable J. Batza reported on the Ottawa Single Unemployed Men's Association that "yesterday A.M. this Association held a parade from the Ukrainian Hall to the employment office, where they registered in a mass." On the way, he fell in at the rear of the parade, but was recognized by a man whom he had met at the Manitoba relief camp at Lac du Bonnet several years before. He was instructed by his inspector "to keep an eye on the men and report their movements" until further notice, but he was frustrated at being "exposed at a time when I just got to know the leaders and their various angles of the game."

Dancing to Perdition: Adolescence and Leisure in Interwar English Canada*

Cynthia Comacchio

In October 1921 a "large gathering" reportedly collected in Guelph, Ontario, to hear a local preacher discuss the social and spiritual repercussions of the "youth dance craze." Determined to awaken "the civic conscience" to the "debauchery and degrading circumstances" festering in the town's dance halls, the Reverend detailed—presumably from hearsay rather than personal witness—the "reeking atmosphere" and "absolutely inevitable stirring of sexual passion entailed in the so-called jitney and other similar dances." These young dance hall patrons were invariably "failures in classroom and physical culture." Could "responsible citizens" do any less than immediately "lend their influence in remedying these conditions"?[1]

This small-town preacher's dismay about the antics of modern youth was replicated across a multiplicity of discourses, religious and secular, "expert" and non-expert during the interwar years. Their common language of moral outrage and foreboding only thinly veiled the real issue: the youthful autonomy symbolized by these modern "palaces for pleasure." Moreover, these anxieties materialized in a regulatory network of social policies addressing such prominent components of the "youth problem" as recreation, labour, schooling, "social hygiene" and juvenile criminality.
[...]

This essay is about the shaping of a modern adolescence during the interwar years through the regulation of youthful pastimes. Its focus is the public discourses of the period's English-Canadian professional journals, mass-circulation magazines and newspapers and government studies. I have attempted to match these against less "public" historical sources—records of clubs and associations, private memoirs, social surveys and high school yearbooks. We see taking form a notion of modern citizenship that, for all its makers' insistence on its "modernity," was premised on a familiar white, middle-class, Christian domestic ideal. Their specific experiences of class, gender and race informed ideas about how best to regulate a young, industrial-urban and increasingly—frighteningly—heterogeneous nation. Demonstrating the curious mix of nostalgia and progressivism that characterized this response to modernity, concerned adults attempted to cultivate an "acceptable" modern adolescence for Canadian youth.

Cynthia Comacchio, "Dancing to Perdition: Adolescence and Leisure in Interwar English Canada," *Journal of Canadian Studies* 32, 3 (Fall 1997): 5–35. Reproduced by permission of Dr. Cynthia Comacchio.

*Appreciation is expressed to the Social Science and Humanities Research Council, and to the Office of Research, Wilfrid Laurier University, especially Dean Barry McPherson, for ongoing research support. This essay is part of a larger project on adolescence in English Canada, 1880–1950.

The "youth problem" thus gained currency because of a double-edged public uneasiness about the declining viability of the traditional sources of sociocultural reproduction represented by family, church, school, community and workplace, but also about their modern replacements. By the early-twentieth century, Canadian adolescents were spending much of their leisure time apart from their families. They were enjoying greater social freedom in the streets, in clubs, through organized entertainments and new commercial amusements, shaping a youth culture expressed through leisure activity.[2] With children at school, and adults occupied by housekeeping and paid labour, truly "free" time was the dominion of the in-between age. Modern leisure and modern adolescence were thus deliberately connected in a multifarious critique that entwined these "problems" with larger issues of citizenship, national welfare and the nature of modernity.[3]

[...]

What to Do About Flaming Youth: Sources and Solutions

Topping the list of factors contributing to the youth problem was the "modern home," source of all good and all evil, and especially the moral vacuum to which could be attributed so much of the "extravagance" of contemporary youth. Toronto's chief of police declared "the prevalent lawlessness" a direct result of the breakdown of familial authority. The modern home was a mere "parking place between shows and dances." Irresponsible and negligent, modern parents did not know how their children spent their leisure hours, who their companions were, or where they went after school.[4] When were young people most likely to get into trouble if not on their own time and in their own unsupervised company?

In families of non-British origin, whether the children were themselves immigrants or first-generation Canadians, the relationship between adolescents and parents was seen to be characterized by a "clash of ideals." Generational tensions were magnified by parents' commitment to old-world ways and family relations, while children had few personal memories of those ways and a strong desire to "fit in" with their peers—which meant being as "modern" and "Canadian" as they were. A major source of familial discord was the issue of contributions to the family economy, specifically, control over the adolescent's pay. Many parents did not recognize the Canadian custom of paying "board," preferring to take command of all wages and return some spending money to the earner. Young wage-earners, not surprisingly, were reluctant to part with their hard-earned money. Local family welfare agencies were sometimes called to intervene in such domestic disputes.[5]

Flappers and their male counterparts caused much consternation in the homes of immigrants devoted to the concept of filial obedience. A Montreal-born son of Italian immigrants told a social worker that "My parents keep after me every time I go out; they want to know why I can't stay at home but I've just got to be going somewhere...they shout and shout but I go just the same."[6] From the other side, parents naturally worried about their children's safety, physical and moral. "He probably knows more at 16 than I do at 50," charged one Italian immigrant of his young son: "I ask him where he has been or where he is going and he won't say." The demeanour and behaviour of daughters, whose personal morality represented familial honour and reputation, were a special concern. An Italian-born Montreal girl, already working from 7:00 a.m. to 5:00 p.m. in a macaroni factory at the age of 13, complained that all she seemed to do was "eat, work and sleep... it was a fight every time I wanted to go out." She and her sisters were occasionally permitted to attend a movie—always chaperoned by other family members—but never a dance.[7] A Macedonian girl growing up in Toronto remembered that "We could never do anything... always had to be with our parents." But she held no grudge against them because they just "didn't seem to know that in Canada you don't have to act that way with your kids."[8] While most young people probably complied with their parents' wishes, if grudgingly, contemporary sociologists theorized that this generational clash forced the breakdown of parental authority in the immigrant home, and brought about the "undoing" of the child. The result, they contended, was often juvenile delinquency, especially where boys were concerned.[9]

The legal classification of "juvenile delinquent" for those 16 and under was established in 1908. By the interwar years, new attention was being paid to the peer group as a contributory factor, especially in its manifestation as the street gang. It was understandable why the gang should appeal to the adolescent boy, with "its social spirit, its power of suggestion, its mob psychology, its scope for leadership and hero worship, its spirit of adventure and method of spreading responsibility upon many shoulders." Boys from economically deprived and socially marginalized homes could feel like "big fellows" in their gangs, which were recognized as dangerous training grounds for working-class masculinity. The most respected, most feared, most manly of gang members were those who committed the most daring crimes, such as stealing cars. The issue was "a lack of adequate social and recreational guidance," which permitted the gang's association of manly bravado and petty criminality. Conversion of these "instincts" and associations into healthy sports and club activities would remedy the gang's criminal potential, "for most of its wrong-doings are traceable to the play instinct."[10] The family court instigated in several provinces during the 1920s met the perceived need for an institutional apparatus to address the problems of wayward youth. It was intended as a specialized remedial environment that combined legal regulation and social casework to the best effect. Codification of crime labelled "juvenile," and the creation of a judicial machinery to deal with it, led to a corresponding rise in arrests. The statistics were interpreted as direct evidence of rising juvenile criminality, further inciting public alarm. Whatever the relationship between number of prosecutions and actual levels of crime, law and order were served by clearing the streets of problem youth and delivering a strong message to their peers about the preferability of alternative forms of leisure.[11]

Family and peer group were significant influences, but the true demon was mass culture, misshapen offspring of modern technology and the modern social outlook. The movies stood unchallenged as the most potent of the new cultural forces affecting youth. A recreational survey of Montreal in 1912 found 50 cinemas, and proclaimed the moving picture show "by far the dominant type of amusement in the city...an integral part of neighbourhood life."[12] Professional journals, popular magazines and the daily press resounded with moral indignation about the vivid screen images that planted "wrongful notions" in young minds, the new "talkies" using dialogue to magnify their nefarious effect. While boys were driven to crime, the movies' effects on young girls were "constantly and seriously demoralizing" in the literal sense. Anxieties about crime and sexual license were entwined none-too-subtly with suspicions about the youthful misuse of "free time" associated with movie attendance.[13]

Despite admonitions and attempts at regulation, going to the movies was dear to the hearts of modern youth. The cinema was relatively affordable, accessible and tame. It also permitted a convenient (and dark) setting for the rituals of adolescent meeting and courtship, as these, too, were removed from the home and transformed into "dating," an activity both more public and more private (unchaperoned) than in their parents' time. Thus, while regular church attendance drew "scarcely half our people," over 90 per cent were evidently regular movie-goers, and fully 60 per cent of these were under the age of 18. Even during the Great Depression, most movie-goers attended once a month; in larger centres, the average attendance was 20–35 times per year.[14]

Evidently few Canadians of any age were deterred by negative prophecy about a "filmized" popular culture. In the aftermath of a 1919 fire at Montreal's Laurier Palace cinema that killed 78 children, provincial governments tightened their regulations for licensing, inspection, ages and hours of admission.[15] Ontario's were the most stringent, as befitting the province with the highest rate of cinema attendance. No child under 15 unaccompanied by an adult was allowed admission "except on Saturday of each week, between the hours of 9 a.m. and 6 p.m.," during which hours a "matron" was to be present. But such legislation left considerable space for adolescent attendance, and consequently for unrelieved adult anxieties about how movies influenced budding sexual and criminal proclivities.[16] A "young Italian lady" told a Montreal social worker that she and her friends loved the movies because they liked to copy the actresses' "way of make-up, dress and style, as well as beaucoup de snobiness."[17]

There was seemingly little faith in the censor boards that were in place in most provinces by 1914. By the 1920s, public pressure had obliged amendments both more specific and more encompassing. Most provinces echoed Manitoba's law, which not only prohibited the standard "immoral or obscene" scenes, but also any picture deemed "injurious to public morals, suggestive of evil to the minds of children and young people or against the public welfare."[18] The nation's largest social service tribunal, the Canadian Council on Child and Family Welfare, in collaboration with the Canadian Motion Picture Distributors Association, began circulating lists of approved films for those under adult age in 1927. Copies were distributed to every motion picture theatre in Canada and published in family-oriented mass-circulation magazines such as *Chatelaine*. Despite such earnest efforts, there was little hope of slaying the Hollywood dragon—especially since filmmakers and cinema managers were keenly aware of the importance of catering to the tastes of their dedicated young clientele.[19]

As the opening narrative suggests, the so-called "dance craze" was a close second on the list of modern leisure evils. Dancing as a social activity was hardly new, but it now appeared to have "a grip on our young people such as it never had before."[20] It was the style of dancing ("whirling") that so bothered observers. Involving close bodily contact in darkened rooms, such "fevered" dances as the tango, the fox trot, the jitney, the Lindy Hop, the Bunny Hug and the Charleston were performed to the "uncivilized" strains of jazz and other "Negro" music, all American cultural imports of questionable value/virtue. Commentary, both bemused and alarmed, singled out such fads as the "codfish cuddle": "named doubtless because no one but a fish would make bold to attempt it.... It is an opportunity, hitherto undreamed of, for the transfer of rouge that would make any pale young man glow...the til-death-do-us-part grasp is used, also mincing steps that take the dancer nowhere in particular." It was reasoned that these dance-hall devotees "in the flower of their youth" saw "eccentricity" as their greatest triumph, and "so they go on dancing themselves to perdition."[21]

Probably the dance hall's detractors never dared set foot in one, so much were they part of a youth scene that scorned and scared those even a little past adolescence, as well as those who, not socially favoured, were simply "ginks." The dance hall was a favoured stage for young people playing out their cultural style and trying on sexual personae—cultivating a personal "aura," as the marketers of "sex appeal" called it, with due attention to appearance and technique. For contemporary youth-watchers, it was the chief symbol of troubling new attitudes towards leisure, sexuality and personal fulfilment.[22] Modern "dance hall girls" were surrendering to the odious flapper influence: "the very clothing worn is an indication of the character and the ideals which are actuating our growing girls." The gauzy, strappy, short "flapper" costume that bared chest, shoulders and back, designed to twirl scandalously in motion, revealing legs all but naked in the new flesh-toned rayon stockings, testified to "a degradation in the minds of young women suggestive of a return to animal instinct and opposed to the dictates of what we are pleased to call civilization." The "risks" taken by immodestly dressed girls were quite simply "enough to make a mother's heart stop."[23] The boyish look of the day, deliberately downplaying traditional conventions of feminine beauty and freeing both "preparation" time and physical movement, was a special generational marker. For the first time in history, youth set the fashion pace. Along with other elements of style such as smoking, drinking, and "loose" attitudes towards fun and sex (if not necessarily loose behaviour), dress and coiffure signified the thoroughly modern girl. Much flouting of gender-defined "bourgeois" convention remained at this level of the symbolic. Very real restrictions on women's lives continued, especially for girls still largely dependent on their families. But "the look" at least signalled their commitment to differentiating themselves from previous generations by being modern women, and for some, "Canadian" as well. Confronting her immigrant mother's adamant disapproval of evening clothes, shorts, bathing suits and "going without stockings," one young woman declared that "we are Canadian-born and are not different from others."[24]

The anti-dance set proposed "adequate philanthropic or civic provision for the normal demand for rhythm and music in recreation." Until this noble objective was realized, control could be approached through licensing that established hours of operation and ages of admittance. But the "thing that would really alter them" was supervision of each by a chaperone "who was doing it because of her motives and not for the money entailed." The chaperone would have "control of the dances" and "of correct methods of dancing," clearly intended in the moral and not the aesthetic sense of correctness. Despite persistent resolutions endorsed by the Council on Child and Family Welfare and a variety of other groups, regulating public dance halls as "a menace to the physical and moral life of youth" was piecemeal and ineffective. Requiring public halls to be registered, licensed and inspected by provincial agencies at least kept them under watch, a surveillance that could be extended by permitting municipal by-laws that were often more stringent.[25] In Ottawa, the two dance halls that existed in 1929 were licensed by both city and province, with the municipality prohibiting the admittance of "any unescorted woman." They were also chaperoned and had to close at midnight. Kitchener and Galt each hired a policewoman expressly to keep an eye on "moral conditions," especially those in and around the towns' dance halls. But Guelph citizens lamented that no provision was made in its three dance halls "to prevent, say, a drunken man from annoying girls...there is no paid chaperone, there is not even a 'chucker-out.'"[26]

The dominant class could not oblige Canadians to enjoy themselves in the manner it declared appropriate. In prompting and legislating certain standards for work and leisure, individual and group behaviour; its members did have sufficient authority for some influence on the way that Canadians passed their time.[27] By regulating commercial amusements through legislation and intrusive adult supervision, and by summoning up wholesome alternatives to these through school, church and club, worried adults tried to limit the transgressive potential of adolescent leisure: an inappropriate crossing into the jealously guarded realm of adult privilege without the socially prescribed attainments that signified maturity and "citizenship," and without adult sanction and supervision. However much, and however dangerously, their independence appeared to be growing, adolescents remained largely under the governance of parents, teachers, employers, lawmakers and other authoritative adults. Beneath "the age of majority," they had neither voice nor visibility in decision-making circles. While their critics feared the growing autonomy and market power of the young, it was, ironically, the latter's lack of power that made them focus their lives on fun and on the politics of play.[28]

It was clearly the moral implications of this emergent youth culture, with its blatantly sexual overtones and its association with working-class, immigrant, uncultured and possibly "unrespectable" adolescents, that offended middle-class observers. "Modern leisure" was a social problem that challenged established class distinctions, the work ethic, order and morality, traditional authority and gender and familial roles and relations. It seemed that young moderns were all too keen to participate in constructing these troubling new models of behaviour, conveniently forgetting that "the indices we need to consult most carefully are moral indices."[29] Images of adolescence as a "dangerous time" were rife in discussions of the "youth problem," but they were generally countered by hopeful theories about adolescence as a malleable period receptive to educative influence. Modern youth was conceptualized and institutionalized as both a negative outcome of modernity, and as an instrument for attaining the best that the modern represented. The "adventurous instinct" intrinsic to adolescence was proclaimed the same spirit "that grips the heart and soul in passionate devotion to the national ideal." Its proper channelling required wholesome recreation organized under "capable and inspiring leaders" and, above all, "constructive education in citizenship and the ideals of national and individual life."[30] A key objective of the period's expansive campaign for social order, consequently, was to get young people off the streets, out of the gangs, cinemas and dance halls, and into adult-supervised "educational" venues: high schools, vocational programmes, organized sports, clubs and associations offering up "character training" and equivalent lessons in citizenship. [...]

Group Work: Apprenticeship for Citizenship

Outside the walls of home and school, an ever-expanding system of structured and supervised recreation for youth was being elaborated. The result was a "pedagogy of vigilance," a formalized apprenticeship for citizenship under the guise of good, clean, Christian fun.[31] Utility and productivity were the heart of the proposed index of purposeful leisure, with three additional motifs discernible. The idea—ideal, in effect—of community was central. The community needed to formulate "constructive principles for social education" in the interests of "reaching out toward the social vision of the normal." The concept of community that stood for service, obedience and respect for authority operated at every level to maintain and confirm the status quo.[32] Christianity was another common thread weaving together the various plans for productive youthful pastimes. The churches' developing interest in youth issues derived from the activist Christianity of the Social Gospel, but it was also a direct response to the threat of secularization posed by mass culture. Organized religion would have to intercede "to recover lost ground and safeguard the future by properly organized and supervised recreation."[33] To retain any degree of social influence, the churches would have to compete for young people's attention for "whenever doctrines or religious customs cannot be interpreted to hold the interest of youth, the end of those doctrines and customs is in sight."[34] Finally, there was much insistence on expert planning and supervision of play, in keeping with the modern faith in professional expertise. A new vocation of "leisure time leadership," ideally taught through university courses, would arm leisure experts with a clear understanding of adolescent needs. The experts would steer young people into creative, fulfilling, productive, Christian pastimes, to provide "wholesome satisfaction" and prevent "mental and moral indigestion."[35]

The simplest way for the community to meet its recreational responsibilities was through the encouragement of carefully directed youth clubs in close association with the churches and schools. "Group work" was declared a vital reinforcement of family and society, contributing much to "the team play necessary to democracy and unselfish cooperative living." It took advantage of the gang instinct, offered worthwhile activity "under the guidance of wise counsellors," and most important, provided "an experience for life in a democracy." A member's involvement in the club, in its council, and then in the wider council of clubs, paralleled the young citizen's relationship with community and nation, imparting "the responsibilities of social living which no adult can teach him."[36]

Proper guidance of adolescent boys outside school hours was "so vital a need, so tremendous a task, and a problem of such compelling interest" that there were some calls for "boyology" as a legitimate subfield of psychology. Boys in "the most plastic period of their lives" were in particular need of the example of "men of calibre" to help them achieve "sterling man-

hood."[37] The growth of the Big Brothers Association during this period reflects social expectations about the importance of healthy male role models to prevent juvenile delinquency among fatherless boys, diagnosed as its prime candidates. Boys were believed to need substitute fathers more than did girls, because the father-son relationship was supposed to be chiefly about transmitting the ideas and behaviour that constituted manliness.[38] In Winnipeg, the Rotary Club financed the salary of a "boy worker" and the operation of a community-wide programme for boys. Carried on in four schools, it provided lectures, movies on evenings and Saturdays, instruction in such useful hobbies as aircraft building and Morse Code, chess and checkers, special drawing classes and "character building talks," all geared to "the maintenance of wholesome interests and citizenship."[39] Healthy recreation, healthy masculinity and good citizenship were a package that boys' clubs could effectively deliver.

In 1914 the first National Committee on Boys' Work was formed, comprised of representatives from all Protestant denominations and the YMCA. The committee sponsored "Leaders' Training Camps" and three "Boys Conferences" the following year. The outcome, in 1917, was the Tuxis and Trail Rangers' programmes across Canada.[40] By 1933, 24,850 boys in 613 communities were organized. "Older Boys' Parliaments," conducted by 16- to 18-year-old members in provincial legislative buildings, were held annually in capital cities. In these mock parliaments, the Tuxis boys decided their own programmes for the year. They also passed earnest resolutions condemning the use of tobacco, alcohol and drugs, and urging Sunday observance and club activity, "because youth generally fails to use his leisure time in activities that really re-create."[41] Many of the groups, in the interests of "world brotherhood," resolved "to establish friendly relationships with boys of foreign parentage," in order to demonstrate "the exercise of sympathy and friendliness even if we cannot grant social equality."[42] The Tuxis and Trail Rangers were particularly enthusiastic about "Father and Son" activities, in that "a noble character is a father's best gift to his son."[43]

During the interwar years, the Young Men's and Young Women's Christian Associations in Canada also made concerted efforts to lure adolescents, especially those of the working class. The national leadership of the YMCA felt that "social education" should be their principal aim: they wanted to make young people "aware of changing forces in order that we may be better prepared to work toward a more Christian Social Order."[44] Both YMCA and YWCA conducted recruiting drives, sending staff members into local factories to present "health talks" and lectures on various social topics, and to encourage membership.[45] The associations also created special ties with high school students through their "Hi-Y" programmes. Their purpose was "to create, maintain and extend throughout the school and community high standards of Christian character," in addition to fostering a "better school spirit" for boys and girls over 16 and "of good character." The Girls' Hi-Y also had the particular objective of "uniting in an effort to assist those less fortunate," usually by acting as counsellors at summer camps for underprivileged children.[46]

Club activities under religious or community leadership were believed to be especially important for working-class girls, whose home lives might be deficient for suitable character formation, especially regarding sexual self-control. Instead of dressing "in the extreme" or "being noisy on the street" to attract notice, purposeful discussion groups would satisfy their need for attention.[47] Hoping to promote a common standard of "healthy girlhood" the Canadian Girls in Training, a group for 12- to 17-year olds connected to both the YWCA and the Protestant churches, held its first conference in Kingston in 1917. By 1924, the CGIT,

premised on the same "Canadian Standard Efficiency Training" as the Tuxis, counted over 30,000 members. Its avowed purpose was "to take a united stand on personal and group standards which will make it possible for the Canadian Girls in Training as a body to influence the standards of dress, behaviour in public and in school of the girls in the community." The "training" aspects emphasized Christianity and citizenship within a non-competitive setting, recognizing that girls' needs were different than those of adolescent boys.[48] A 1932 survey indicated that its membership, as a percentage of eligible girls in each province, ranged from a high of 12.05 in Manitoba to a low of .73 in Quebec; the second-lowest enrolment was in the Maritimes, with 6.63 per cent.[49]

These church-affiliated, gender-segregated community groups taught their young members middle-class, Protestant, Euro-Canadian standards of social relations in all their manifestations—domestic, productive, public, recreational, religious, sexual. They also provided opportunities for adolescents to get together in "mixed company," usually on Sunday evenings, for refreshments, talks, games and at times "wholesome" films, under "proper supervision" and within "a favourable and safe environment." It was argued that the activity, excitement and association with the opposite sex "craved" by all adolescents were better met under community auspices than under commercial ones. These events also introduced "a very natural opportunity to discuss some of the important questions of family life and home building," since adolescents were "sure to be thinking much about these things." The "wise leadership" that recognized this interest and gave "something of the radiance and inspiration of religion" to discussions on sexuality was "doing much to guide and enrich the lives of these young people."[50] The Tuxis boys, resolving that "cheap ideas of friendship with girls is all too common," that sex education was of "vital importance in boy life," and that much harm was being wrought "in the whole community" by ignorance, implored their group mentors to include sex education in their programmes.[51]

At bottom, the question that obsessed youth-watchers during the interwar years was whether young Canadians had changed dramatically in the span of a few generations. For all their suspicions about "flaming youth," it was generally believed that "they only reflect the times they live in." This was simply an extravagant age "that shakes off the trammels of bygone conventions, that takes short cuts and lives at a pace never before possible in the history of the world." Recognizing the role of modernization in stirring up the youth problem, critics generally pleaded for a measure of compassion towards young people in this rapidly changing world: "How would you feel today if you were a boy or girl in a world which seems to be reeling and rocking ceaselessly, without any apparent intention of ever again returning to rest and peace?" Modern youth was evidently suffering from the necessarily painful adaptation process, as were its critics.[52]

"The Wall of Blank Negation": Youth in the Great Depression

During the unemployment crisis of the 1930s, concerns about "idle time" made the "youth problem" all the more visible and pressing. As they reached the life stage that would ordinarily have found them preparing for adult independence, pursuing education or training opportunities, and commencing work, young people were instead forced into a waiting zone with little promise of a quick exit. The Depression's persistence saw social agencies reiterating, with ever more conviction, that unemployed youth were the greatest challenge facing Canada. Young

people were turning to street gangs to while away the time, diverting their youthful energy into vice and crime. A 1931 survey of unemployed boys reported that "even as late as 11 o'clock, not only older boys, but young children literally appear to swarm in the streets, indicating that they are not able to find sufficient satisfactions in their home life."[53]

Solutions espoused to this point had leaned heavily towards the didactic and the utilitarian. They now took on a "therapeutic" rationale that belied a repressive objective. The mad dark world of anarchy, sexual depravity, racial degeneration and criminality that had been conjured with reference to some incalculable future moment now appeared imminent. Previously subtextual, fear of the future was palpably conveyed in Depression-era discourses on youth and idleness, widening even more the generational divide. There were dire warnings about the "rumble of an approaching storm" that would "surely destroy the order which is," as the young generation looked to its parents to justify its current plight. Refusing to be forever oppressed "by the weight of a dead hand in politics, religion, business, education, amusement, conduct of private and public affairs," young people would demand "the right to make a world to their own satisfaction."[54] In a new "Youth Tells All" column in *Maclean's* magazine in 1934, one young woman declared that "our sense of values is slipping." She envisioned a "complete revolt against old traditions—traditions which seem to have failed not only the older people but youth as well."[55]

Commentators veered between compassion and castigation, at times self-blaming, at times blaming young people themselves for the national predicament. Some believed that the young were enjoying their newly tragic status, as they lay about, "inert, immature and inclined to indolent theorizing." They were "lazy and indifferent at a time when our national life needs everything we have to give."[56] More common, however, was the sense that "it is an appalling price we are paying for folly and youth has borne and is bearing the heaviest brunt of it all."[57] The stark forces of economic deprivation did bear down especially hard on the young. Among youth between the ages of 14 and 20, even the unreliable statistics of the period indicate an unemployment rate of more than 50 per cent, surpassing that of any other age category. Single unemployed men were regarded with particular dread as a subversive underclass; witness, for example, the "work camps" established to isolate and contain them. The ill-fated "On to Ottawa" trek to protest the federal government's indifference was filled with boys who moved to pity even those prepared to condemn their exercise. These young men, "our sons and nephews," had not "known the love of a family or the warmth of a home for many years," in addition to not knowing the right to work for their own support: "the effects of this cannot be the regeneration of the ideals of youth, but their degeneration."[58] Single, unemployed young women fared even worse, while attracting less sympathy. There was no public recognition of their "right" to work in view of the Depression's hardening of lines about the primacy of the idealized male breadwinner.[59]

Those who could manage to hold on stayed in school, feeling shame as their deteriorating family circumstances compelled them to attend in ever-shabbier attire at a moment in their lives when appearance counted for so much.[60] High school students themselves noted the overall "seriousness" of tone, the dampening of "school spirit" wrought by the Depression: "in fact, depression seems rampant in the school, as much in esprit de corps as in anything else." Participation in extracurricular activities dropped decidedly. At Guelph Collegiate, a 1933 drama club production of "Julius Caesar" was "sadly handicapped" when students failed to show up for rehearsals, or withdrew before the play's opening. There was evidently difficulty in

getting members of the school sports teams, especially the senior teams, out to practise.[61] The school yearbook, an honoured and much-anticipated yearly tradition, was suspended that year due to a shortfall in contributions by local businesses, previously its primary source of funding. Some young people, less fortunate or perhaps less patient than those who stayed in school, took to the streets and to the rails, collectively embodying the archetypal "lost generation." Having attained the threshold of adulthood in this time of international crisis, they were forced to confront "the wall of blank negation that can neither be climbed nor cast down."[62]

In the midst of raging, and largely futile, debates over state provision for the unemployed, the only other palliatives that could be offered were to postpone the date of unemployment through extended schooling, and "when unemployment comes, to ensure to the young people participation in some definite activity." Canadian delegates to the League of Nations committee on youth unemployment argued the equal importance of vocational training and recreational opportunities, especially sports and games. The 1935 League report stressed that one of the worst "moral results" of youth unemployment was social isolation, from which invariably grew disaffection and alienation. Any recreational activity based on "a broad social view" would represent a step towards reintegration of alienated youth into the social mainstream: "To offer such people words only when their whole being is demanding something to do is another example of giving stones for bread."[63]

The problem of "idle youth" thus subsumed that of "flaming youth" during the Depression decade. Yet the public discourses regarding youth and associated "problems" still underscored the issue of youthful pastimes. Commentaries on the subject continued to suggest that "immorality"—usually defined along the lines of "a loosening of moral fibre in respect to sex relationships"—was a more serious outcome of youth unemployment than were poverty and thwarted ambitions.[64] Despite fretting about the absence of worthwhile occupations for unemployed youth, whether work or leisure, some regarded the Depression as a necessary antidote—perhaps a necessary atonement—for the excesses and extravagances of the flaming youth of modern times. Like the mythical Icarus, they had flown too close to the burning sun of commercialism, consumerism, materialism, even hedonism. Deprivation delivered a lesson in sober responsibility, bringing them back to earth, away from "the easier way of paying to be amused." This was the very moment for young people to prove their value to the nation by absorbing and recreating its acknowledged ideals, so undermined by modern cultural forces.[65]

By some reports, those who would direct modern youth on the straight path to citizenship were achieving a measure of success. In 1933, a Winnipeg social worker could boast that the club movement had made "integrated social groups" out of "anti-social gangs" through 25 local boys' clubs and 12 girls' clubs. The boys' clubs drew 16,203 boys to meetings over the course of that year: "to many boys these clubs might be the big event of the week, and in many cases it was noticed that there was a gradual sprucing up in their clothing and the care exercised in their general appearance."[66] By 1936, the Boy Scouts, Camp Fire Girls, CGIT, YMCA and YWCA, and Tuxis had enrolled over two million boys and girls across the nation. In that year, the formation of the Canadian Youth Congress, intended as a national tribunal for youth organizations, also provided hope that the spirit of organized and disciplined youth could be put to constructive nation-building purposes.[67]

Despite such optimistic assessments, it was clear even to social workers on the front lines of the "youth problem" that the adolescents who were reached looked much like their own children: white, middle-class, Protestant high school students who were rarely "problems" to begin with. While community and church agencies performed "an outstanding service in the modelling and shaping of our youth," and while they "touched many strata of society," contemporary surveys indicated that they were not "in anything like full measure" reaching the underprivileged boys and girls whose recreational needs should be "first and foremost." Nothing of lasting benefit could be attained unless such clubs could "gather those who roam the streets, those who congregate in gangs, around stores, poolrooms, and other hangouts" and bring these "stray boys and girls into organized closely bound neighbourhood clubs." The real youth problem was being inadequately handled. There was "little or no machinery in the city" to bring needy boys and girls into contact with the very recreational agencies designed to serve them best. Of the eligible population of adolescent girls across the nation, the CGIT, for example, attracted only 6.17 per cent to its fold.[68] Furthermore, legislative and voluntary attempts at regulation of cinemas, dance halls and other public places of amusement may have been helpful in keeping these social spaces "on the level," but they were not dissuading adolescents from frequenting them—even during the Depression. Young people were formulating their own rites of passage into adulthood in newly important, if not altogether new, informal leisure institutions. School, club and church activities largely failed to provide appealing alternatives.

By impressing its views and standards on the rest of society through its exercise of both formal and informal power, the dominant class can use leisure activities to affirm cultural patterns. At the same time, leisure can serve as an arena for the articulation of different, even opposing, values and behaviours.[69] With money in their pockets, time on their hands, and the desire to participate in new and interesting social activities, young people demanded that certain kinds of pastimes be provided for their amusement. They used new modes of leisure to create an identifying subculture that both borrowed, and consciously strove to differentiate itself, from the wider mainstream (adult) culture.

Good Christian Fun: The Balance Sheet

The socioeconomic transformations of the early-twentieth century opened up new worlds to youth, reconfiguring adolescence in ways that made it significantly different from the experience of previous generations, including the parents of those "coming of age" in 1900 and thereafter. Adolescents came to identify, and to be identified, more with leisure than with work. The dramatic development of youth culture consolidated peer group influence over the socialization of adolescents. By the 1920s, the combined popular image of health, sport and youth had crystallized into the ultimate symbol of status and modernity.[70] The "cult of youth" was reflected in cinema and advertising, influencing not only pastimes but also incidentals such as fashion, hairstyles, popular music and choice of popular icons. A degree of role reversal occurred as young people increasingly set the sociocultural pace previously the prerogative of their elders. By the Second World War, "teenagers"—a category that did not exist before this time—had become true cultural trendsetters.[71]

Even intensified age-identification did not obliterate hierarchies within generations, as suggested by the culture of the modern high school, with its status cliques and "exclusionary" divides, defined even more precisely by the new focus on "style." Youth from families that were not acceptably middle class and Anglo-Celtic, must have felt the particular pressures of not "fitting in." Young women of all classes and backgrounds, however "modern" their appearance and tastes, still faced many of the gender-defined limitations that had tied their mothers and grandmothers so closely to the fortunes of men. Urban and rural distinctions in youth culture were mitigated by the automobile and the mass media, but they may also have appeared starker to the young people of the countryside who envied their city counterparts for their easy access to fascinating diversions.

It is intriguing to think that the generational divide is especially gaping during periods of rapid and intensive structural change, such as was occurring at the beginning of this century with mass industrialization, during the 1960s with the "sexual revolution," and at the close of the twentieth century with the so-called "information revolution."[72] At such times, the similarities between the older generation's own adolescence and that of their children are diminished. The changes in material reality, and consequently the ways in which that reality is taken in, made sense of, and adapted to, really do signify vastly different adolescences. Struggling to cope with these changes on their own level, parents are at a loss to guide their children—to perform their role as adults and parents—because these experiences are as new to them as to their children. The level of adult anxiety and social consternation regarding "the youth problem" increases dramatically as the generation gap widens. A true inability to understand across that gap, an inadvertent absence of empathy, manifests itself on both sides of the relationship. Adolescents take advantage of their "difference" from their parents by making that difference all the more felt, all the more recognized, in the one part of their world that they can reasonably call their own: the world of play. But it is a world that remains their own only until some of its pieces are broken off and reintegrated into mainstream popular culture.

Early-twentieth-century Canadians, with one eye to a worrisome future and the other to a sentimentalized past, attempted to define "modern youth" with reference to their own experiences and aspirations. At base was a common view of the increasing disorder that characterized modern life, and a common will to impose structure, to confine and regulate, even what was supposed to be "free time." The real problem with free time, they would find, was that it tended to defy regulation, because the amount of policing required was beyond the capacity of a non-police state. In the end, even adults possessed of political voice and economic clout were powerless to deter the spread of mass culture. Modern amusements were seductive and virtually irresistible to modern youth, who were actively contributing to the ongoing process of cultural innovation. As in so many other of the period's reformist schemes, there was a marked ambivalence about modern life, a tension between old and new that could not be successfully accommodated despite all apocalyptic predictions. Social critics acknowledged the difficulties of cultural adaptation, but they could not accept that disorder could neither be avoided nor prevented. As an historical process, it simply has to be endured—much as does adolescence.

Notes

1 "Guelph Pastor Scores Dancing," *Guelph Daily Mercury* (3 October 1921). The Reverend eventually backed down, saying that he had heard the story from the mayor, and that it was perhaps a "malicious misrepresentation," 10 October 1921. The story ends with a formal letter to the editor by the Rev. T.J. Hind retracting his statement, 11 October 1921.

2 W. Scott Haine, "The Development of Leisure and the Transformation of Working-Class Adolescence in France," *Journal of Family History* 17.4 (1992): 451; K. Peiss, *Cheap Amusements* (Philadelphia: Temple University Press, 1986) and for Canada, Strange, *Toronto's Girl Problem,* discuss the relationship between urban amusements and young women early in this century.

3 T.R. Robinson, "Youth and the Virtues," *Social Welfare* (October 1928): 9; H. Dobson, "Youth: Scapegrace or Scapegoat," *Social Welfare* (July 1929): 228; K. Alaimo, "Shaping Adolescence in the Popular Milieu: Social Policy, Reformers, and French Youth, 1870–1920," *Journal of Family History* 17.4 (1992): 420; Haine, "The Development of Leisure and the Transformation of Working-Class Adolescence," 451. Although used occasionally in the media during the interwar years, the term "teenager" did not come into popular usage until the 1950s. I am defining "adolescence" as encompassing the years 13 to 18, with particular emphasis on the 16–18 category, because it was defined in this manner by the period's social reformers and policy makers.

4 "Forum: Are Parents What They Used to Be?" *Maclean's* (15 August 1927): 12, quoting S.J. Dickson, Toronto Chief of Police; also "Parental Delinquency," *Canadian Child Welfare News* (August–December 1924): 38; A. Plumptre, "What Shall We Do With Our Flapper?" *Maclean's* (1 June 1922): 66; P.J. Bend, "Juvenile Delinquency: Its Causes," *Social Welfare* (March 1919): 126; Judge E. MacLachlan, "The Delinquent Girl," *Social Welfare* (December 1921): 56.

5 C.M. Bayley, "The Social Structure of the Italian and Ukrainian Immigrant Communities in Montreal." (MA thesis: McGill University, 1939): 85–7, 242. Bayley spent 15 months living among Italians and seven months among Ukrainians in Montreal between 1935 and 1937 as a Research Fellow in Sociology at McGill, under the supervision of Carl Dawson. He contends that social workers knew of "many cases" where children simply refused to turn over their wages.

6 Interview cited in Bayley, "The Social Structure of the Italian and Ukrainian Immigrant Communities in Montreal," 282.

7 Ibid., 71; ibid., Case Study 7, Miss E., 278. On generational conflict in immigrant families, see F. Swyripa, *Wedded to the Cause* (Toronto: University of Toronto, 1993), 90–5.

8 National Archives of Canada, MG 28, I 10, Canadian Youth Congress, 3, file 599, 1942–44, Interview, "Vi," Toronto, August 1944. These "intensive interviews" were conducted by the CYC as part of a national survey on citizenship and youth services.

9 H. Atkinson, "Boys in Trouble," *Child and Family Welfare* 7.6 (March 1932): 2.

10 K.H. Rogers, *Street Gangs in Toronto* (Toronto: Macmillan, 1945), 111–16; J.M. Wyatt, "Causes of Juvenile Delinquency," *Social Welfare* (July 1920): 10; A.E. Dodds, "What Can Our Cities Do in Their Leisure Hours?" *Social Welfare* (July 1920): 180. Few of the street-gang members in the working-class Point St. Charles district of Montreal had gone beyond fourth grade, all were out of work, and "spare time occupation" was seen to be their biggest problem; "Study of the Need of Recreational Facilities in Point St. Charles," 18.

11 D. Chunn, *From Punishment to Doing Good* (Toronto: University of Toronto Press, 1992) details the reformist discourses on delinquency, and the resulting framework of family courts that was constructed to address those anxieties about youth criminality; see also Judge H. Gregory MacGill, *The Work of the Juvenile Court* (Vancouver: 1943); "Judicial and Penitentiary Statistics: Juvenile Delinquency," *Canada Yearbook* (1939): 1067–8. The statistics for 1922–37 showed a definite upward trend overall, for all offences and all ages; however, the 16 to under 21 group showed a much higher crime rate than the juvenile group (7–16) or the total young persons group (7–21).

12 "Recreational Survey of the City of Montreal," 24

13 G. Dickie, "The Menace of Delinquency," *Social Welfare* (April 1921): 185; "Children at the Movies," *Child Welfare News* (February 1930): 266. On film in Canada, see T. Magder, *Hollywood's Canada* (Toronto: University of Toronto Press, 1993).

14 W.M. Bellsmith, "What of the Movie Censor," *Social Welfare* (April 1931): 143. In 1930 there were 910 theatres in Canada, with receipts posting an unprecedented $38,479,500; in 1934, for Canada as a whole, attendance reached a total of 107,718,000, with Ontario accounting for almost half that [45,747,000] and Quebec, one-quarter [24,466,000]; see *Census of Merchandising and Service Establishments: Motion Picture Statistics* (Ottawa: Dominion Bureau of Statistics, 1934). On the emergence of "dating" in the 1920s, see Modell, *Into One's Own,* 85–97; also Bailey, *From Front Porch to Back Seat.*

15 NAC, CWC files, 8, file 41, *Montreal Gazette* clipping, "New Theatre Law Draft Commenced," (17 March 1919); for example, *Statutes of Nova Scotia,* 10–11 George V, c. 44, 1920, "An Act to Amend Chapter 9, Act of 1915, Respecting Theatres and Cinematographs"; *Statutes of Manitoba,* 11 Geo. V, c.

46, 1921, "An Act to Amend the Public Amusements Act [1916]"; *Statutes of Saskatchewan,* 11 Geo. V, c. 81, 1920, "An Act to Amend Theatre and Cinematographs Act"; *Statutes of British Columbia,* 14 Geo. V, c. 45, 1924, "Act to Amend Moving Pictures Act [1914]." For Ontario, see *Statutes of Ontario,* 9 Geo. V, c. 66, 1919, "An Act to Amend the Theatre and Cinematographs Act [1917].

16 The age was raised to 16 in 1930, and attendance was also permitted between 9 a.m. and 6 p.m. on legal and public holidays; "Amendments to the Theatre and Cinematographs Act," *Child and Family Welfare* (November 1930): 30.

17 Interview cited in Bayley, "The Social Structure," 87.

18 There were about 40 members, altogether, on the eight provincial boards; see N. North, "What Can the Movies Teach?" *Social Welfare* (15 January 1922): 15; also "Deceiving the Censor," *Maclean's* (15 December 1919); 56–9, R.L. Briscoe, "What the Censor Saves Us From," *Maclean's* (1 November 1929): 28–9. *Statutes of Manitoba,* 11 Geo. V, c. 46, 1921, "An Act to Amend the Public Amusements Act"; for similar wording, see Saskatchewan, 21 Geo. V, c. 70, 1931, "An Act Respecting Theatres and Cinematographs." On censorship in Manitoba, see J. Skinner, "Clean and Decent Movies: Selected Cases and Responses of the Manitoba Film Censor Board, 1930–50," *Manitoba History* 14 (Autumn 1987).

19 Editorial, "Experiment in Approved Motion Pictures," *Social Welfare* (April 1927): 395; also NAC, CWC, Proceedings and Reports of Annual Meetings, Report of the Executive Director, [Charlotte Whitton] (1 November 1929–31 March 1931): 9; Briscoe, "What the Censor Saves Us From," 28; Nasaw, "Children and Commercial Culture," 19–25.

20 J. Strothard, "The Most Urgent Reform Needed," *Social Welfare* (May 1920): 283.

21 "Dancing Craze Is on Increase," *Guelph Daily Mercury* (1 February 1922).

22 Peiss, *Cheap Amusements,* 88–90.

23 Strothard, "The Most Urgent Reform," 285; Editorial, "Home Authority Is Lax," *Guelph Daily Mercury* (21 March 1921).

24 Interview cited in Bayley, "The Social Structure," 90.

25 Strothard, "The Most Urgent Reform" 285; "National Conference on Child Welfare," *Social Welfare* (November 1922): 31. See, for example, *Statutes of Nova Scotia,* 17–18 Geo. V, c. 42, 1927, "An Act to Amend Theatres, Cinematographs and Amusements Act"; Ontario, 9 Geo. V, c. 66, 1919,

"An Act to Amend Theatre and Cinematographs Act," expanded in 12–13 Geo. V, c. 72, 1922, Municipal Institutions Act; expanded again in 21 Geo. V, c. 50, 1931, Municipal Institutions Act.

26 NAC, CWC, 28, file 143, "City of Ottawa Survey: Recreation," Memorandum to Captain Bowie, Recreation Division Advisory Committee (1929): 4; "Mary Marston's Own Column," *Guelph Daily Mercury* (28 January 1921).

27 R. Williams, *Culture and Society* (London: Chatto and Windus, 1982) 298–300.

28 M. Brake, *Comparative Youth Culture* (London: Routledge, 1985), 148.

29 Editorial, "A World of Change," *National Home Monthly* (December 1934): 3.

30 Ibid., 4.

31 Alaimo, "Shaping Adolescence," 421–3.

32 C. Whitton, "Ontario's Immediate Problem in Child Welfare," *Social Welfare* (June 1924): 1; "Present Day Problems in Social Life," *Social Welfare* (June–July 1926): 192; NAC, CWC papers, MG 28 110, Canadian Council on Child and Family Welfare, Report of the Executive Director (1 November 1922–31 March 1923): 10; also Special Issue on Recreation, *Child and Family Welfare* (July 1931): 329. On "community" concepts, see Williams, *Culture and Society,* 328.

33 Rev. G.A. Woodside, "The Ideal for the Child," *Social Welfare* (May 1919): 191–2. See also M.L. Marr, "Church Teen Clubs, Feminized Organizations?" *Historical Studies in Education* 3.2 (1991).

34 "Flappers Interpret Religion?" *Maclean's* (15 July 1923): 131.

35 "Leisure Hours," *Social Welfare* (July 1923): 206.

36 Ibid., 203; V.K. Brown, "Street Play," *Social Welfare* (July 1931): 201; "The Boys' Club," *Social Welfare* (July 1931): 204.

37 "The New Profession: Boy Leadership," *Social Welfare* (November 1923): 37; Editorial, "Building Boyhood," *Social Welfare* (July 1923): 195; J.H. Hodgins, "Fitting Our Sons for Tomorrow," *Maclean's* (15 July 1924): 82–3. The University of Toronto instigated one such course for social workers; University of Toronto Archives, Department of Social Service, B84-1089, Special Course in Work with Boys, n.d. See also Sir William Hearst, Premier, Ontario, "The Strength of the Nation Is the Character of Its Men," *Proceedings of the 1st Ontario Tuxis Boys Parliament,* Toronto (1917): 1.

38 "Big Brothers Movement," *Canadian Public Health Journal* 47 (1922): 104; University of British Columbia Archives, *Journals of the Tuxis, 9th Annual Boys Parliament,* Calgary, Alberta (1928): 5; also *10th Annual Boys Parliament*, Victoria, British Columbia (1929): 24; also pamphlet promoting "Father and Son Week, 3–10 February 1929." On sex-role modelling, see J. Pleck, "The Theory of Men's Sex Role Identity," *In the Shadow of the Past: Psychology Views the Sexes,* ed. M. Lewis (New York: Columbia University Press, 1983) 206–7.

39 NAC, CWC papers, Winnipeg Survey, Autumn–Winter 1933–34, 9–11.

40 University of British Columbia Archives, Boys Parliament Collection, Typescript, "21 Years of Teenage Work."

41 Ibid., *9th Annual Older Boys Parliament of Alberta,* Calgary (1928), Resolution no. 12: 10; *ibid.* (1929) no. 10: 10; *6th Annual Saskatchewan Boys Parliament,* Regina (1928), Resolution no. 10: 12; *7th Annual Manitoba Boys Parliament,* Winnipeg (1928), "The Christian's Attitude to the Use of Alcohol: Summary of General Discussion," 7–9; *ibid.* "The Christian's Attitude to His Leisure Time: Summary of General Discussion," 11.

42 "Resolution Regarding the Race Problem," *Journals of the Maritime Tuxis Parliament,* Sackville, New Brunswick (1928), 10; also *6th Parliament, BC,* Victoria (1928), 8.

43 *Journals of the Tuxis Parliament of Alberta,* Calgary (1928), 5; *6th Annual Saskatchewan Boys Parliament,* Regina (1928), 12.

44 Guelph Public Library Archives, Guelph, Ontario, YMCA papers, General Secretary's Report, July–August 1937.

45 Ibid., Minutes of Third Regular Meeting, Board of Directors, 11 November 1913, 2; General Secretary's Report, February 1937, 1; YWCA papers, General Secretary's Report, Summer 1925. See also Mrs. N.W. Rowell, President, Dominion Council, YWCA, "The Young Women's Christian Association," *Social Welfare* (October 1922): 20–2.

46 Guelph Collegiate and Vocational Institute, *Acta Nostra* 2 (1927): 50; *ibid.* (1930): 45; *ibid.* (1931): 87. Also McGill University Archives, Montreal High School files, B.I. Rexford, I. Gammell and A.R. McBain, *History of the High School of Montreal* (1950): 159, indicates that the Boys' Hi-Y was operating in 1914.

47 E. Pearce, "The Girl and the Group," *Social Welfare* (July 1929): 230; K. MacPherson, "The Delinquent

Girl and the Rescue Homes," *Social Welfare* (April 1921): 152; I. Dingman, "Your Teenage Daughter," *Chatelaine* (October 1934): 19. See Strange, *Toronto's Girl Problem,* for full treatment of the discourses/policies in one Canadian city between 1880 and 1930.

48 Rowell, "Young Women's Christian Association," 20–1; "Resume of Cooperative Girls Work in Canada," *Canadian Child Welfare News* (January–March 1925): 52. On the CGIT, see M. Prang, "The Girl God Would Have Me Be: The Canadian Girls in Training, 1915–39," *Canadian Historical Review* 66.2 (June 1985).

49 I. LePage, "Group Organization and the Development of the Adolescent Girl," (MA thesis: McGill University, 1932): 49.

50 NAC, CWC papers, York Township Survey, Autumn–Winter 1933–34, 10; Bowie, "The Value of Supervised Recreation," 442; L.F. Ward, "The Opportunity of the Pastor in Family Guidance," *Social Welfare* (December 1933): 12.

51 UBC Archives, Boys Parliaments Collection, *British Columbia Tuxis 2nd Older Boys Parliament,* Victoria, (1924), 9–10.

52 M. Middleton, "Give Modern Youth a Hearing," *Maclean's* (15 November 1925): 169; Editorial, "Go... Teach," *Social Welfare* (July 1930): 9; W.J. Healy, "Worry About the Rising Generation," *National Home Monthly* (November 1938); L.M. Willison, "Hectic Modern Youth," *Maclean's* (1 May 1938): 24.

53 McGill University Archives, Montreal Boys Work Council, "Survey of Unemployed Boys" (1931): 23.

54 Editorial, "The Revolt of Youth," *National Home Monthly* (June 1934): 3.

55 "A Woman's Opinion," Youth Tells All column, *Maclean's* (1 January 1934): 23.

56 G. Arnold, "Flaming Youth," *Maclean's* (1 July 1934): 13.

57 D.L. Ritchie, "The Plight of Youth," *Social Welfare* (June 1934): 50.

58 Advertisement, "To the Citizens of Vancouver and District, Statement of the Conference Committee on Relief Camp Workers," *Vancouver Sun,* 27 May 1935. On the camps, see J. Struthers, *No Fault of Their Own* (Toronto: University of Toronto Press, 1983), 100, 132–35.

59 R. Pierson, "Gender and the Unemployment Insurance Debates in Canada," *Labour/Le Travail* 25 (Spring 1990): 82–4.

60 See the letters to R.B. Bennett in M. Bliss, L. Grayson, *The Wretched of Canada* (Toronto: University of Toronto Press, 1971); also W. Johnson, "Keeping Children in School: The Response of the Montreal Catholic School Commission to the Depression of the 1930s," Canadian Historical Association, *Historical Papers* (1985): 197.

61 GCVI, Editorial, Acta Nostra, 1933, 11.

62 "The Revolt of Youth," 3.

63 M. McLeachy, "The Effect Upon Young People of the Economic Depression and Unemployment," *Child and Family Welfare* (November 1935): 15; E. Muncaster, "Strengthening Family Ties Through Recreation," *Child and Family Welfare* (November 1933): 47; see also Canadian Council on Child and Family Welfare, Division on Leisure Time and Educative Activities, "Relief Is Not Enough: The Idle Time of Compulsorily Idle Canadians," *Bulletin No. 1* (25 September 1933): 1–4.

64 F.T. Sharpe, "Stopping Before Starting," Child Welfare News (January 1934): 43–4; Editorial, "Moral Standards," *Social Welfare* (September 1936): 94; "Youth Tells," *Maclean's* (15 December 1933): 8.

65 W. Bowie, "The Character of a Nation," *Social Welfare* (July 1931): 199; "Leisure Time Problems in the Isolated Home," *Child and Family Welfare* (January 1934): 46; W.R. Cook, "Getting Down to Brass Tacks in Community Planning for Leisure Time," *Social Welfare* (March 1938): 10–11; S. Brent, "Reinforcing Family Strengths by the Provision of Leisure-Time Activities," *Child and Family Welfare* (September 1931): 53.

66 NAC, CWC papers, Child Welfare in Manitoba, typescript, "Community Clubs for Boys and Community Clubs for Girls," Winnipeg, 12 April 1933, 4–7.

67 In the late 1930s, the CYC had a total constituent membership of over 400,000, mostly in the 18–24 years age range; see P. Axelrod, "The Student Movement of the 1930s," *Youth, University and Canadian Society,* eds. P. Axelrod and J.G. Reid (Kingston/Montreal: McGill-Queen's University Press, 1989), 219–20.

68 NAC, CWC papers, Survey of Social Agencies: Ottawa, 1929. Montreal Boys Council, "Survey of Unemployed Boys," 19, noted that only 39 per cent of the 1,009 boys participating had any club affiliation; the majority spent their time on the streets. On the CGIT, see LePage, "Group Organization and the Development of the Adolescent Gift," 51.

69 Wetherell Kmet, *Useful Pleasures* xxi; Williams, *Culture and Society,* 320; Peiss, *Cheap Amusements,* 4–8.

70 See S.A. Riess, *City Games: The Evolution of American Urban Society and the Rise of Sports* (Urbana, Illinois: University of Illinois, 1991) especially chs. 4 and 5, 127–71; also K.B. Raitz, "Introduction," *The Theatre of Sport* (Baltimore: University of Maryland Press, 1995), ix; on Canada, B. Kidd, *The Struggle for Canadian Sport* (Toronto: University of Toronto Press, 1996).

71 On Canada, see D. Owram, *Born at the Right Time: A History of the Baby Boom Generation,* especially ch. 6; see also G. Palladino, *Teenagers: An American History* (New York: Basic Books, 1996).

72 Note, for example, the resentment expressed in the commentary by Christina Holder, "Generation X Faces a Barren Harvest," *Globe and Mail* (15 February 1996). Holder argues, among other things, that "senior citizens are a group that has never hesitated to take out of the coffers more than it has ever put in," seemingly forgetting that these were the generations that came of age during the Depression and the Second World War.

The Invented Indian/
The Imagined Emily[*]

DOUGLAS COLE

Emily Carr was a dedicated artist and writer. She was not a very politically or socially conscious person. Raised in cultivated gentility and respectability, as an adult she lived on inherited capital as a *rentier* and small-scale entrepreneur involved in private teaching, dog breeding, and souvenir making. She even speculated a little in real estate. Aside from contractual teaching in private schools for a few years in Vancouver (and working as a decorator in California), she never had a "job." Indeed, the thought of entering the labour force—as public school teacher, for example, or stenographer, retail clerk, teller, or telephone operator—was one she never seems to have entertained. Her unmarried sisters were similarly independent, Alice running her own elementary school classes and Lizzy being a physiotherapist.

Carr was, all her idiosyncrasies and eccentricities aside, a woman of conservative temperament. She did do some politically charged cartoons for the *Western Women's Weekly*, a women's rights magazine, but otherwise her comments on the economic order, on class relations, and on political questions are very rare. We have no idea how, after women received the franchise, she cast her vote in any election (or, indeed, whether she voted at all).

Few public events—national, provincial, or municipal—seem to have troubled her. World wars enter her concerns, of course, as did recessions, for they affected the rents she received. We know that she had harsh words for the single unemployed men who occupied the Vancouver Art Gallery in 1938, but, had it not been the gallery they occupied, we might never have heard even those.[1] By character she seems apolitical, and her views (with the exception of those on religion) seem conventional and conservative.

It is hardly surprising, then, to find Carr virtually silent about the relations between the Canadian government and its Aboriginal peoples. Part of this may be due to the unevenness of our sources. Few of Carr's letters written before 1927 have survived, and it is only after that date that we have her journals. So it is impossible to judge whether she had anything to say, or what it might have been, about such matters as the moving of the Kitsilano from their south shore reserve, agitation over the land question and the McKenna-McBride Commission, or the attempt to suppress the Kwakwa̱ka̱'wakw potlatch during and immediately after the Great War. Nor is it at all surprising that Carr's view on the history and future of Aboriginal peoples in many ways conformed to the prevailing ideas

Douglas Cole, "The Invented Indian/The Imagined Emily," *BC Studies* 125/126 (Spring/Summer 2000): 147–162.

[*] This paper was a draft in progress at the time of Douglas Cole's death. Some minor editing was required to prepare it for publication. Special thanks go to Brian Dippie, Heather Gleboff, Alex Long, Gerta Moray, Jay Stewart, and Wendy Wickwire for their assistance.

of the times. Like others, she believed in the prevailing myth of the "vanishing Indian." She has recently been criticized for this by scholars who have judged her by contemporary standards. They, in turn, have imagined another Emily, for Carr's own writings, especially *Klee Wyck,* suggest a more complicated portrait of both Emily Carr and Aboriginal peoples.[2]

In 1907, after a holiday in Sitka, Emily Carr decided to make a record of Aboriginal villages and poles. Her decision resonated with what has become known as "the salvage paradigm," a broad phenomenon that moved anthropologists and museums frantically to collect the remnants of endangered Aboriginal societies and cultures. Behind the salvage paradigm was a realization that time was essential, that civilization was everywhere pushing Aboriginal peoples to the wall, destroying their material culture and even extinguishing the Aboriginal stock itself. "What can be done must be done now," wrote Germany's Adolph Bastian. "In a few years it will be impossible," the American John Wesley Powell commented, "to study our North American Indians in their primitive history." Anthropologist Franz Boas saw that the cultures of the Pacific Northwest were rapidly disappearing "and the whole work is becoming more difficult from year to year."[3]

The assumption behind salvage anthropology was that the traditional, pre-contact languages, customs, and societies of Aboriginal North America were rapidly disappearing. So too, it seemed, were the Aboriginal peoples themselves. Thus, the salvage paradigm shared in the larger intellectual tradition of the "vanishing Indian."

The "disappearing Indian" was an entrenched belief, one that has been dealt with superbly by University of Victoria historian Brian W. Dippie. He shows that a fully rounded version of the "vanishing American Indian" had won public acceptance in the United States by 1814. By its logic, Indians were doomed to "utter extinction." Poets, novelists, orators, and artists found the theme of a dying Aboriginal race congenial, while serious students of "the Indian problem" provided corroboration for this particular construct. Opinion was virtually unanimous: extinction was inevitable.[4]

The "vanishing Indian" was, of course, a construction, a "cultural myth," but that does not mean that it was a falsehood. In writing of the "vanishing Indian" as a constant in American thinking, Dippie's concern was not with "historical reality—the actual number of Indians, the actual causes and extent of population decline"—but with White perceptions of the Indian. While gathering a life of its own and prophesying the future, the concept of the "vanishing Indian" was "based on what was thought to be irrefutable evidence."[5] Indeed, the evidence did seem overwhelming. The disappearance of the familiar Native American was empirically verifiable. There had been a drastic decline in the Aboriginal population, a large-scale replacement of their material existence by European goods, and widespread conversion to Christianity. This was undeniable.

British Columbia's Aboriginal population had declined precipitously, the result of epidemics of introduced diseases such as smallpox and measles, and of less dramatic but no less deadly ones such as tuberculosis and venereal diseases. Warfare, impoverishment, and other consequences of social, economic, political, and cultural disruption had taken their toll. The Northwest Coast population may have declined by 80 percent in the first century of contact. British Columbia's Aboriginal numbers reached a low point of 22,605 in 1929. Some regions saw a modest reversal of the decline, though the Northwest Coast did not. The decline was halted there only later—as late as 1939 for the Nuu-chah-nulth. The Haida reached their low in 1915 when there were less than 600 people concentrated in two towns, with dozens of deserted villages having been left behind.[6] In 1912 most

Aboriginal languages were still alive, but some had disappeared: Salishan Pentlatch as well as Athapascan Tsetsaut and Nicola. The people, when still living, had been absorbed into neighbouring populations. Language decline continued long after the population had begun to rebound. Art production seemed to have drastically fallen off, replaced by trade goods, European-style homes, and Christian concepts and ceremonialism. By 1910 the majority of British Columbia's Aboriginal peoples were adherents, however nominally, of one Christian church or another. To the outside world, the "Indian" did seem to be "vanishing."

As a phenomenon of both the past and the present, the myth of the "vanishing Indian" seemed a reasonable extrapolation in Carr's age. Even if populations were stabilizing and in some places rebounding, the demographics of non-Aboriginal immigration and natural increase so tilted the ratio that Aboriginal peoples seemed inevitably swamped. In 1901, when Carr was already thirty, Aboriginal peoples still made up over 16 percent of the provincial population. The boom years of the next decade changed that; by 1911 they made up only slightly over 5 percent of the provincial population.

Carr's sense of the "vanishing Indian" was not imagined. It seemed an inexorable truth verified by all known experience. She saw the deserted villages—they were no myth—and she was witness to the tilted and rotting poles. She regretted their demise, whether to the forces of nature or to museum collectors.

Traditional Aboriginal life in British Columbia was in decline. It grieved her, but she accepted it, with resignation, as inevitable. "I began to realize that these things were passing," she recalled, "and I started in earnest to make a collection of paintings of the villages and totem poles."[7] She thus participated in the salvage paradigm, "reflecting a desire to rescue 'authenticity' out of destructive historical change."[8] Her travels in 1928, during which she revisited some of the sites she had seen over a decade before, confirmed her view that "the old places and people are passing away rapidly" in the north. Few poles were left, few old-type houses, and very few old people.[9]

In drawing these conclusions, Carr was not an uninformed or superficial observer. She had grown up in nineteenth-century Victoria, where Aboriginal people were a ubiquitous presence. As a child, she saw the family's laundress weekly and accompanied her mother to "Wash Mary's" funeral. Aboriginal people were frequent visitors to her father's store. She visited a West Coast village as a young woman, something that remained an indelible memory. She was close enough to the people to gain an appellation—"Klee Wyck"—which she treasured, perhaps romantically, all her life. "We seemed to understand each other," she wrote; they called her Laughing One "because they said they could not understand my talk, but they understood my laugh."[10]

Over the course of her life, she visited reserves throughout Vancouver Island and the Lower Mainland, in particular those of the Songhees, Squamish, and the Nuu-chah-nulth. She also visited the old and new Haida villages on the Queen Charlotte Islands as well as a number of villages among the Kwakwaka'wakw, the Nisga'a, the Coast Tsimshian, and the Gitksan. She met numerous Interior peoples during trips to the Cariboo (in 1904) and Lillooet (in 1933). In her Vancouver years, she made friends with Sophie Frank, a Squamish basket maker.

Ideas of salvage and of the "vanishing Indian" brought with them a tendency to think that Aboriginal cultures existed only in the past, that Aboriginal peoples ceased to be "authentic" as soon as they altered their way of life or adopted, or adapted to, non-Aboriginal ways. "In spite of centuries of contact and the changed conditions of Native American lives, Whites picture the 'real' Indian as the one before contact or during the early period of the contact." Indianness was conceived of as ahistorical and static, with adoption of White ways making the Indian "ipso facto less Indian."[11] Such adaptations were, moreover, often seen as contaminating, or degrading, the "real Indian." Aboriginal peoples sometimes appeared to accept White vices as much as their virtues and so became "those imperfect creatures, the degraded or reservation Indian," neither noble nor savage but possessed of the vices of both societies.[12]

Carr's painting, from 1907 to 1912 (and perhaps to a lesser extent from 1928 to 1933 or so), was within the salvage paradigm. It was premised on the "vanishing Indian." While this is indubitable, it would be misleading to think that she accepted the associated idea that "Indianness" was ahistorical, static, or that the Aboriginal peoples in British Columbia were necessarily any less "Indian" because of the altered conditions of their lives. Indeed, Carr's recorded perceptions defy that stereotype.

Carr's *Klee Wyck* (1941) records her experience with British Columbia's Aboriginal peoples from her childhood through to her 1928 northern journey to the Queen Charlottes and the Skeena Valley.[13] It is her only sustained literary treatment of Aboriginal life, which makes it all the more remarkable that several recent commentators on Carr and Aboriginal peoples have almost ignored it.

Carr's portraits are of a people living in a transient present, caught in conflicts between old and new, between traditional and colonized modern, who are making their way as best they can. The span of the impressionistic stories is some fifty or so years, and its locales move from Victoria, the Cariboo, and Vancouver, to the Charlottes and the North Coast. The narration is personal, the voice variously mischievous, ironic, and wistful. Carr wrote the twenty-one "short sketches or glimpses" over a long period, sifting her memories, filling in "gaps" with "research" and invented dialogue, using all the literary devices available to her. She wanted, she said, to be "true to the places as well as to the

people"—though it was difficult "to avoid slopping over to fill up [the gaps]."[14]

What emerges is an apparently unselfconscious portrait that records, with the artful eye of a sensitive observer, the Aboriginal people she meets. They live in Carr's present, not in an ahistorical past. The Haida she describes are not "imagined," seldom traditional, and certainly not stereotyped into a false authenticity. An occasional note of wistful regret over the disappearing past intrudes, but the people she describes live in partitioned houses, engage in the commercial fishery, even prepare herring roe for the Japanese market. They live in a world of missionaries, cannery bosses, schools, policemen, and Indian agents.

Her friends, Jimmie and Louisa (William and Clara Russ), who talk "Indian" together, seem thoroughly modern yet still "Indian." "Louisa's house was the best in the village."[15] It had a garden and veranda, a large kitchen with a cook-stove and sink, a living room and double parlours. The outer parlour had become a music room with player piano, organ, a cabinet for the player rolls, and a bench, sofa, and rocking chairs for seating, leaving "scarcely any space for people." Carr's bedroom contained a brass bed (fitted with heavily embroidered pillowslips) and a fine drawer, on top of which was a candle in a beer bottle and a tin pie plate for hairpins.[16] The asides are mischievous but not malicious; the incongruities are light touches, not lapses into "half-civilized" discourse.

Juxtaposed to the modern Louisa and Jimmie was Louisa's mother, the more traditional Mrs. Green (in real life, Mrs. Brown). "A remarkable woman," she lived in a cabin in Skidegate and "clung vigorously to the old Indian ways." Carr saw the older woman outside her home preparing herring roe and helped her put the roe-filled trunk on a boy's wagon and trundle it to the wharf, there to be transported to Prince Rupert for sale to Japan. Carr assisted Mrs. Green with her store order: groceries, a plaid shawl, some pink print, a silk handkerchief, and a tobacco pipe with a little tin lid.[17] Mrs. Green's "old Indian ways," Carr tells us, "sometimes embarrassed Louisa." Louisa was uncomfortable when her mother spit in the woodpile behind the cook-stove in Carr's presence, and she was "a little ashamed too, of her mother smoking a pipe; but Louisa was most respectful of her mother—she never scolded her."[18] Now much of this may be invented—most certainly much of the dialogue is. Carr was writing years later, from memory, constructing a marketable storyline for a non-Aboriginal public. But her portrayal of generations, of differential acculturation, of ambivalence and embarrassment is a sensitive acknowledgment of human predicaments. It is a literary construction, rekindled from memory, that captures the intimate, the transitory, the ambiguities and conflicts of colonization and change.

Other mixtures of old and new can be found. Carr travels to Yan in a tippy little canoe that carried a ragged flour sack as a sail. She remembers the "Indian" attributes of the young girl who paddles her, but she also, passingly, remembers her print dress.[19] At Skedans non-Aboriginal halibut fishers had constructed rude driftwood tables in an old bighouse, but the Haida "use[d] the floor for their tables and seats."[20]

Carr's most moving story is about her friend Sophie Frank. There is something untouchable about this relationship. Sophie is an urban woman living in a three-room home on the Squamish reserve on the north shore of Burrard Inlet. She crosses the water by ferry to sell baskets in Vancouver. Her kitchen has a cook-stove, a coal-oil lamp, and, at least in winter, the family bed—though Sophie herself sleeps on a mattress beside the stove. The kitchen floor, Carr emphasizes, was scrubbed clean.[21]

Cleanliness is obviously a primary virtue to Carr. Sophie's friend, Mrs. Johnson, the widowed Squamish wife of a non-Aboriginal man, keeps her house clean "beyond words," "the cook-stove was a mirror, the floor white as a sheet from scrubbing." Each of Mrs. Johnson's kitchen chairs had its own antimacassar and cushion, and her bed had a tautly pulled crocheted spread and embroidered pillowslips—all the work of Mrs. Johnson's hands.[22] Neither Sophie nor her friend are stereotyped as "authentic," romanticized, invented "Indians," nor are they "degraded, half-civilized savages." They are, in Carr's emphasis on cleanliness, perhaps subversive counter-stereotypes, but they are certainly not essentialized Aboriginal women.

Carr also writes of Sophie's hospitalization and of her friend being put into a "little Indian ward." (Carr does not omit this segregation, but she makes no comment on it.) She visits Sophie there, poking fun at herself for thinking that Sophie would find it more comfortable than her kitchen floor. Sophie quickly puts her right. "Me ole'-fashion, Em'ly. Me like kitchen floor fo' sick."[23] The irony is light, even unintended. Old-fashioned here means sleeping on a kitchen floor mattress, not on a longhouse mat.

While we learn something of Sophie's milieu in the Squamish community across the shore, what we remember most about Sophie is her children, some twenty-one (according to Carr), who were carefully nurtured but, nonetheless, died. (One is reminded that infant mortality was high among Aboriginal peoples.) They were buried in coffins, their graves marked with tombstones. When Sophie, a Roman Catholic, took Emily to see the tombstones, she wore her "best plaid skirt" and a "yellow silk handkerchief" round her head. "She wore her shoes when she walked with me," Carr wrote, "if she remembered."[24] The point is not that Sophie is "half-civilized"—only that she is Sophie.

Carr's memory sometimes leads us in other directions. She has Sophie, apparently jealous, telling her friend that:

"I don' want you know Mrs. Chief Joe [Capilano]."

"Why?"

"You fliend for me, not fliend for her."[25]

Local rivalry resonates here. This is no "imagined Indian"; this is the discourse of everyday life.

Some of Carr's villages are " 'going modern,' [with] new buildings replacing the old community houses"; women bake bannock, fathers are out with whalers; boys play football in a village street. Some Aboriginal people have schooling, many do not. Carr has Sophie say that her husband had learned "school English. Me, no. Frank laugh my English words."[26] And Carr does not miss the residential school experience.

Louisa and Jimmie's Methodist pastor wanted Carr "to influence them into sending their boys to the Industrial boarding school for Indians." Carr refused. "In Louisa's house now there is an adopted child, a lazy, detestable boy, the product of an Indian Industrial School, ashamed of his Indian heritage." The two remaining boys were not well, and there was a school in the village. Carr told the pastor that Louisa "can send them there and own and mother them during their short lives. Why should she give up her boys?" The pastor raised the advantages; Carr countered with "And the disadvantages!" A poignant scene follows over young Joe's too pink cheeks and too shiny eyes, symptoms of tuberculosis. Louisa asks, "If he were your boy Emily, would you send him away to school?" The vignette ends with Carr's resounding "NO."[27]

The past is there too—not just tilted poles but the haunting presence of the great smallpox epidemics. And Carr slips in a comment concerning how the missionaries came and "took the Indians away from their old villages and the totem poles and put them into new places where life was easier, where they bought things from a store instead of taking them from nature."[28] *Klee Wyck* is a testament to an outsider's perception of the transitions in Northwest Coast Aboriginal life during Carr's lifetime.

All the more remarkable, then, that some recent observers have condemned Carr for accepting the whole "vanishing Indian" paradigm, including the associated ideas of an idealized past now lost in contamination and degradation. Carr was an artist, writes Daniel Francis, "who took for granted that Indians were vanishing and sought to preserve an idealized image of them, and not the reality of Native people."[29] Scott Watson judges that Carr's "life's work involved the presentation of the ruins rather than the living fabric of First Nations people."[30] The rapport she sought with the ruins and the allegory of nature overwhelming the old totem poles "eclipsed the possibility of any understanding of the social, political and cultural struggles that are involved in the territories she depicted."[31] Art historian Robert Linsley finds that her work "has perhaps contributed to the false perception that native culture had effectively died out by the twenties and thirties."[32] Carr "mourns, in paint, the loss of a culture that she and others of European descent believed was dead or dying," reads the wall poster for Vancouver Art Gallery curator Andrew Hunter's dialogic encounter between Carr's work and that of contemporary Salish painter Lawrence Paul Yuxweluptun. (The exhibition was originally planned to consider "the problems of perpetuating Carr's view as an authentic view of "Indianness.") Carr, Hunter writes, had a religion that was "balanced" by anthropology's perpetrated belief that "when cultures adopt and incorporate aspects of another, they die—the only authentic culture being a fictional 'pure' culture."[33]

Among the most widely cited critiques of Carr has been Marcia Crosby's criticism of her as an artist whose

> paintings of the last poles intimate that the
> authentic Indians who made them existed
> only in the past, and that all the changes
> that occurred afterwards provide evidence of

racial contamination, and cultural and moral deterioration. These works also imply that native culture is a quantifiable thing, which may be measured in degrees of "Indianness" against defined forms of authenticity, only located in the past.[34]

There is, of course, some truth in this criticism, but it is more half than whole. Carr did mourn the passing of the old ways and did feel that Aboriginal peoples had lost something. The poles were passing—"only a few more years and they will be gone forever, into silent nothingness."[35] And, when she went north again in 1928, for the first time in sixteen years, she saw everywhere "miserable change creeping, creeping over villages." The Indians, having lost faith in their totems, were selling the best poles to museums and doing meaningless work for tourists.[36] The young were fast absorbing White ways, not valuing the poles "as the old ones did."[37] She could also fall into the discourse of moral decline. In 1913 she spoke of Aboriginal peoples being unable to differentiate between the good and the bad among Whites: "there is so much bad, and they copied it."[38] And she did believe that Aboriginal peoples were losing touch with their traditional cultures.

What she did not do, however, was assume that Aboriginal peoples would necessarily disappear or that change necessarily challenged their authenticity. *Klee Wyck* makes that abundantly clear. Louisa, Jimmie, Sophie, and Mrs. Johnson are "modern," Westernized people who are nonetheless "Indian." Whatever one wishes to read into Carr's paintings, her writing does not imply "that Native culture is a quantifiable thing, measured in degrees of 'Indianness' against defined forms of authenticity only located in the past."[39] This is incongruent with *Klee Wyck*. Her writing contests the judgments of her commentators.

The critique seems to have hit a chord in postmodern and post-colonial thought. "Words

like those of Emily Carr," writes Judith Mastai, "have been used by Canadian society to point out the diffusion of Native culture into Canadian culture in order to deny Native peoples' claims for Aboriginal title."[40] But this description, even if it can be read into Carr's paintings, is contested by her writings. Carr, in her carefully crafted stories and vignettes, in her journals, and even in her autobiography, writes of the "real Indians" as she knew them. In these I find little evidence of the kinds of things that Crosby, Francis, and others allege. They have "invented Emily."

In doing so, they are ironically guilty of the same offense of which they charge her. They have taken the commonplace ideas of our time and invested them upon her. They have read of "the White man's Indian," of "the vanishing American," of the salvage paradigm, of "the imagined Indian," and of various other constructions and inventions, and they have superimposed these upon Carr. They have essentialized her as the White colonizer. It all makes for a superficial fit. She did paint "for history"; she did mourn the loss of the old poles and the old ways; she did talk of "relics"; she did have a sense of the traditional past; and she did regret its passing. But *Klee Wyck,* her most intimate portrait of Northwest Coast Aboriginal peoples, contradicts the new bottle into which some wish to pour her. This book is not about a passing, dying race. It is not even about "the past."

Even in urban Victoria, Carr was able to observe and to note the cultural continuity of Aboriginal British Columbians. In February 1931 she wrote:

> Went to a dance and potlatch at the Esquimalt reserve, stayed from 8 to 11:30 p.m. It was *grand*—the great community house and smoke holes both pouring sparks into the sky, and the rhythmic victory of tom-toms, the inky darkness outside, then the sea of faces—Indians seated on benches in tiers to the roof, many of

them with painted faces, two enormous fires which were fed fast and furiously by the young men with huge pieces of cord wood. The different reserves were all allotted places.[41]

What does one make of this? Here she celebrates the living tradition of the Coast Salish in a zone of urban contact and assimilation. Carr's journal entry directly contests Linsley's comment that "the glamour of the noble savage that surrounds the Haida and other northern tribes in her work could not belong to the natives of the Songhees reserve in Victoria."[42] Carr's potlatchers *were* Songhees.

Even in her formal lectures and writing, where she assumes a different authorial voice than the one she uses in her journals or *Klee Wyck* stories, there is a sensitivity to continuities amidst change. She writes of totem poles and beliefs as situated in the past, then goes on to describe Aboriginal people as she knows them in the present. Indians, she writes in 1929, move from place to place, fish, make oolichan oil, smoke salmon, potlatch, follow the canneries.

Though she accepts the hegemonic attitudes of her time—"The old places and the old people are passing away rapidly."[43]—she cannot quite embrace them. She had painted her pictures "for history," but "[she] hoped that some day they would be put in a place where their children's children could see them and admire the work of their ancestors."[44] Although the young seemed to be fast absorbing White ways and were half ashamed of these things now, she resisted extrapolating from such tendencies. "By and bye when the white race has absorbed them, something deep down within them must surely respond to the great art of their past."[45] As she says to Mrs. Douse of Kitwancool: "I want to make pictures of them, so that your young people as well as the white people will see how fine your totem poles used to be."[46] Here Aboriginal people remain distinct, unabsorbed, a category separate from "white people."

Six months before she attended the Esquimalt potlatch, Carr made a journal entry about a visit to Quatsino Sound. Her reflections on this visit reveal a mood almost post-modern in its ambiguous sense of the transitory nature of culture: "The Indian watches his race disappear yet not disappear, appearing in a new civilization new manners new customs new looks yet with a thing in them of himself, the new Race gathering sifting sorting."[47]

Underlying some of the criticism of Carr is the fact that she did not take a more political stance against colonial oppression. "Carr's failure, and that of her contemporaries, was the failure to recognize or value non-traditional political activities of the various First Nations communities they depicted in decline."[48] Carr, according to Watson, "seemed to have little knowledge of the real legislative oppressions of her First Nations friends and encouraged the view that they were part of natural, rather than human, history."[49] First Nations peoples and cultures were being done in "by government policy and unbridled entrepreneurial greed," and he faults Carr "for, in the end, not knowing where she lived."[50] According to Francis, Carr was "no social worker; nowhere does she ask her audience to confront social reality."[51]

Again, while none of this is wrong, to a degree it condemns her for not sharing the contemporary political views of her critics. To expect Carr to have been a crusading social and political reformer is to ask her to have assumed a role to which she was intellectually and temperamentally unsuited and uninterested. They are imagining an Emily that could never have existed.

On the other hand, they miss whatever is critical in her art, especially in her writing. In juxtapositions between White and Aboriginal, Carr's partisanship was clearly with the colonized. Missionaries are almost invariably condemned, as are residential schools. The subtlety of her subversion of authority in her "Kitwancool" story could pardonably be missed by those unfamiliar with the long history of that village's resistance.

> At a moment when government and settler interests lay in minimizing Native claims and grievances, the acquisition of such a vivid and positive testimony to Native culture could hardly be seen as expedient. In addition, Carr clearly sought to change her audience's preconceptions about Native peoples. Both her lectures and her images did, in many respects, contradict the ideas about Native culture propagated by other agencies of White society—agencies that sought to regulate Native affairs.[52]

Carr's concern with poles was an act of respect. She worried that their fate was either to "rot and topple to the earth" or, perhaps worse, to be taken by Whites to museums where "they would be labelled as exhibits, dumb before the crowds who gaped and laughed and said, 'This is the distorted foolishness of an uncivilized people.'"[53] Again, there is a subversion, a contestation, even a partisanship in Carr's writing that goes against the grain of White colonization.

Certainly Carr appropriated Northwest Coast Aboriginal peoples in that she incorporated them into her conceptions of Canada and the West. Carr's celebration of the "primitive greatness" of the province's Aboriginal inhabitants gave them "a meaning that has to do with her national identity, not the national identity of the people who own the poles." "The induction of First Nations peoples' history and heritage into institutions as a lost Canadian heritage," continues Marcia Crosby, "should be considered within the context of the colonization of aboriginal land." Daniel Francis makes something of the same point. "By appropriating elements of Native culture, non-Natives have tried to establish a relationship with the country that pre-dates their arrival and validates their occupation of the land."[54] While the implications that Crosby and Francis draw are contestable, the fact that Carr incorporates Aboriginal peoples into her own conception of who she is is not contestable, nor, for that matter, is the fact that Canadians incorporate Carr's images and writings into their conception of what Canada is—or ought to be. Drawing upon distinctive regional or national attributes during the act of identity-formation is a widespread phenomenon, one that continues in such trivial ways as wearing engraved silver bracelets or buying calendars or silk-screen prints made by Aboriginal artists. This process, as it occurs in Carr, deserves to be highlighted and examined.

One last act reflecting Carr's relationship to Aboriginal peoples needs to be mentioned. Carr willed her paints, brushes, and unused canvasses to George Clutesi, a young Nuu-chah-nulth artist whose ability to tell stories would rival hers. What exactly Carr had in mind we do not know. But she must have recognized in Clutesi an artist, an Aboriginal artist, a living one, younger than she. This posthumous contesting of post-colonial tropes by the Imagined Emily has been largely unnoted.

Notes

1   "I suppose they are *cleaning the gallery* how thankful they must [be] to get those brutes out. we have them here. now. They are like the grass hopper scourge." Carr to Nan Cheney, 23 June 1938, in *Dear Nan: Letters of Emily Carr, Nan Cheney, and Humphrey Toms*, ed. Doreen Walker (Vancouver: UBC Press, 1990), 91.

2   Editor's Note: The original manuscripts of Emily Carr's *Klee Wyck* are currently located in the E. Carr Papers, British Columbia Archives (BCA), MS-2181, box 6, fols. 11–32. These typed manuscripts are Carr's final drafts prior to publication and include minor handwritten revisions. According to Kathryn Bridge (Manager of Access Services at

BCARS) and Maria Tippett (a recognized Carr scholar), many of Carr's journals and manuscripts were significantly revised by her editor, Ira Dilworth, and therefore differ from the published versions. But for *Klee Wyck,* unlike these other writings, handwriting analysis shows that Carr made most—if not all—of the revisions on the manuscript. There are two published versions of *Klee Wyck:* the 1941 edition and the 1951 edition, both of which Dilworth edited. For the 1941 edition, Dilworth made minor changes in punctuation but did not alter the voice, tone, or substance of the stories. For the 1951 edition, which still circulates today, he included a foreword and took greater editorial liberties, not only shortening Chapters 1 and 16 but also removing a chapter entitled "Martha's Joey." In this essay, Douglas Cole relied on the limited 1941 edition—the edition closest to Carr's original manuscript—for his interpretations.

3 Douglas Cole, *Captured Heritage: The Scramble for Northwest Coast Artifacts* (Vancouver/Seattle: Douglas and McIntyre/University of Washington Press, 1985), 288; Franz Boas to M.K. Jesup, 19 January 1897, F.W. Putnam Papers, box 16, Harvard University Archives. The use of the term "salvage" for such activities occurred much later and was probably derived from "salvage archaeology," where it has only very recently been replaced by "urgent archaeology."

4 Brian W. Dippie, *The Vanishing American: White Attitudes and U.S. Indian Policy* (Middletown, CT.: Wesleyan University Press, 1982), 10–11.

5 Ibid., xi–xii.

6 Robert T. Boyd, "Demographic History, 1774–1874," in *Northwest Coast: Handbook of North American Indians,* vol. 7, ed. Wayne Suttles (Washington: Smithsonian Institution Press, 1990), 135; Wilson Duff, *The Indian History of British Columbia.* Vol. 1, *The Impact of the White Man* (Victoria: Provincial Museum of Natural History and Anthropology, 1964), 39–45.

7 Emily Carr, "Modern and Indian Art of the West Coast," Supplement to *McGill News,* June 1929, 21.

8 James Clifford, "Of Other Peoples: Beyond the 'Salvage' Paradigm," in *Discussions in Contemporary Culture,* ed. Hal Foster (Seattle: Bay Press, 1987), 121.

9 Carr, "Modern and Indian Art of the West Coast," 22.

10 Ibid., 21.

11 Robert F. Berkhofer, Jr., *The White Man's Indian: Images of the American Indian from Columbus to the Present* (New York: Vintage, 1979), 28–9.

12 Ibid., 29–30.

13 Emily Carr, *Klee Wyck* (London: Oxford University Press, 1941).

14 Maria Tippett, "Emily Carr's Klee Wyck," *Canadian Literature* 72 (Spring 1977): 55, 52–3.

15 Carr, "Friends," in *Klee Wyck* (London: Oxford University Press, 1941), 101.

16 Ibid., 100–1.

17 Ibid., 102–4.

18 Ibid., 102.

19 Carr, "Sailing to Yan," in *Klee Wyck.*

20 Carr, "Skedans," in *Klee Wyck.*

21 Carr, "Sophie," in *Klee Wyck.*

22 Ibid., 43.

23 Ibid., 44–5.

24 Ibid., 36.

25 Ibid., 41.

26 Carr, *Klee Wyck,* 50, 62, 99, 35.

27 Carr, "Friends," in *Klee Wyck,* 106–7. This conclusion to "Friends" is omitted from the 1951 and 1965 Clarke-Irwin paperback editions.

28 Carr, *Klee Wyck,* 91, 31, 73.

29 Daniel Francis, *The Imaginary Indian: The Image of the Indian in Canadian Culture* (Vancouver: Arsenal Pulp, 1992), 38.

30 Scott Watson, "Disfigured Nature: The Origins of the Modern Canadian Landscape," in *Eye of Nature,* ed. Daina Augaitis and Helga Pakasaar (Banff: Walter Phillips Gallery, 1991), 109.

31 Ibid.

32 Robert Linsley, "Painting and the Social History of British Columbia," in *Vancouver Anthology: The Institutional Politics of Art,* ed. Stan Douglas (Vancouver: Talonbooks, 1991), 232.

33 Andrew Hunter, Yuxweluptun-Carr Exhibition, Vancouver Art Gallery, 1997.

34 Marcia Crosby, "Construction of the Imaginary Indian," in *Vancouver Anthology: The Institutional Politics of Art,* ed. Stan Douglas (Vancouver: Talonbooks, 1991), 276.

35 Emily Carr, "Lecture on Totems," 1913, Carr Papers, BCARS, MS-2181, box 7, fols. 33–4.

36 Emily Carr, *Growing Pains: The Autobiography of Emily Carr* (Toronto: Clarke, Irwin, 1966 [1946]), 237.

37 Carr, "Kitwancool," in *Klee Wyck,* 142.

38 Carr, "Lecture on Totems."

39 Crosby, "Construction of the Imaginary Indian," 276.

40 Judith Mastai, "Hysterical Histories: Emily Carr and the Canadian West," in *Inside the Visible: An Elliptical Traverse of 20th Century Art in, of, and from the Feminine,* ed. M. Catherine de Zegher (Cambridge, MA: MIT Press, 1996), 314.

41 Emily Carr, Unpublished Journal, February, 1931, quoted in Gerta Moray, "Northwest Coast Native Culture and the Early Indian Paintings of Emily Carr, 1899–1913" (PhD diss., University of Toronto, 1993), 393. Dr. Moray's dissertation offers a superb analysis of Carr's work, milieu, and shifting reputation.

42 Linsley, "Painting and the Social History of British Columbia," 232. There is a half-truth to Linsley's comment. The Songhees, like the Squamish, did not have poles, such as those of the central and northern coastal peoples and, following its removal from Victoria Harbour in 1911, the new Songhees village probably did not retain the distinctive Salish house posts. On the other hand, Carr took note of the change incurred by the dismantling of their permanent village. In a "Lecture on Totems," delivered in Vancouver in April, 1913, she drew attention to a small painting of the former Songhees reserve she had made prior to 1911, noting that with the construction of a new village in a new locale, "a phase of Indian life...has now passed into history." (Maria Tippett. *Emily Carr: A Biography.* [Toronto: Oxford University Press, 1979]), 114.

43 Ibid., 22.

44 Ibid.

45 Ibid.

46 Carr, "Kitwancool," in *Klee Wyck,* 142.

47 Emily Carr, Unpublished Journal, 19 August to 11 September 1930, quoted in Gerta Moray, "Northwest Coast Native Culture and the Early Indian Paintings of Emily Carr, 1899–1913," 396.

48 Hunter, Yuxweluptun-Carr Exhibition, Vancouver Art Gallery.

49 Watson, "Disfigured Nature," 109.

50 Scott Watson, Letter to the Editor, *Canadian Art,* March 1994.

51 Francis, *Imaginary Indian,* 37–8.

52 Moray, "Northwest Coast Native Culture," 128–9, see also 340, 354–5.

53 Carr, "Greenville," in *Klee Wyck,* 73–4.

54 Crosby, "Construction of the Imaginary Indian," 276–7; Francis, *Imaginary Indian,* 190.

The Northern Vision of Harold Innis*

MATTHEW EVENDEN

In the spring of 1924, the Mackenzie River loomed largely in Harold Innis's thinking. At the end of the academic term, Innis, a junior assistant professor of political economy at the University of Toronto, would travel the river and begin to reorient his career and scholarship in a northern trajectory. The river would become a point of entry into a new northern vision.

Although Harold Innis remains one of Canada's most celebrated and studied social scientists, relatively little is known of his early career or northern scholarship.[1] The limited attention granted to Innis's interest in northern Canada invariably centres on his field expeditions conducted in the 1920s to investigate the fur trade, mining, transportation and communications. Innis travelled, with companion John Long, along the Peace, Slave and Mackenzie rivers in 1924; down the Yukon River in 1926 with his former student, W.K. Gibb; to various towns of northern Ontario, Quebec and the Maritimes in 1927; and to Hudson Bay in 1929.[2] These four busy summers have been enshrined as mythic instances in the history of Canadian historiography. Donald Creighton's biography of Innis devotes four pages in a slim volume to the Mackenzie voyage alone. He suggests that the trip marked a turning point in Innis's personal development: the limping junior scholar, still showing the marks of war in 1924, returned from the North an invigorated, healthy man, no longer in need of a cane.[3] The North served as a context for the redefinition of self: from ill health to vigorous manhood; from uninitiated scholar to renowned field researcher and economist.

Parsing this image of Innis and the North—by inquiring into the constructed nature of the idea of the North and Innis's role in developing it; by asking what Innis sought to learn and earn from his northern experiences; and by considering how Innis's northern research altered his development as a scholar in the 1920s—this paper seeks to redraw this mythic instance, to focus the problem of the social creation of nordicity in the context of intellectual biography. Innis imagined the North before arriving there, grafted ambitions onto the region, inscribed ideas in field notes and represented the North to popular audiences in southern Canada on his return. In the process of creating a northern vision that stressed the importance of the North as a frontier for industrialism and a binding agent for national unity, Innis adopted and refashioned popular ideas of Canada's northern regions and remade himself as a public intellectual and nationalist thinker.

Matthew Evenden, "The Northern Vision of Harold Innis," *Journal of Canadian Studies* 34, 3 (Fall 1999): 162–184. Reprinted by permission of Matthew Evenden.

*I would like to thank Daniel Drache for allowing me to use certain research materials collected as his assistant. Anne Innis Dagg, Daniel Drache, Kirsty Johnston, H.V. Nelles, Alan MacEachern, Marlene Shore, Robert Sweeney, Bill Waiser and the *JCS* reviewers provided helpful comments on drafts. I would like to acknowledge the support of the Social Sciences and Humanities Research Council.

Imagining North

In the winter of 1924, Harold Innis began to plan his northern career. Letters fanned north seeking advice about canoe routes along the Mackenzie and the North Saskatchewan. Contacts were made with officials in the Department of the Interior and the Hudson's Bay Company, with missionaries and geographers.[4] In a research prospectus written for R.M. MacIver, his department head, Innis outlined his interest in the settlement of the Peace River region, the fur trade and mining development. His research was not solely focussed on the fur trade at this early stage, as is often assumed.[5] The ultimate goal, he explained to MacIver, would be a book-length study of the Mackenzie River basin; a knowledge of the fur trade would also help his teaching.[6] His interest in the fur trade at this time was intimately bound up with the idea of the importance of rivers in Canadian history. Only months before he had corresponded with H.G. Moulton of the Institute of Economics in Chicago about writing a history of the St. Lawrence.[7] Since the publication of his thesis on the Canadian Pacific Railway the previous year, he had the uneasy feeling that he had begun the economic history of Canada in *medias res*.[8] While he had analyzed the unification of Canada through the steel rail, he had come to believe that the river networks utilized by the fur trade had established Canada's original political space.

Innis's subject of research was still evolving when he left for the Mackenzie in June 1924. However, two important strands of thought bounded his general approach: one drew on an amorphous sense of nationalism, tinged with northern imagery; another, more narrowly intellectual, was based on Thorstein Veblen's theories of industrialism. Innis's attitudes towards nationalism shifted over his career, but in the 1920s they were largely enthusiastic, a product of recent experience and an envisioned

future. During the war, Innis was appalled by the disregard shown to Canada and Canadian soldiers by the British, and lost whatever sentimental affection he may have once felt for Britain and Empire.[9] Similarly, while completing graduate school in Chicago, he expressed frustration at the lack of recognition paid to the Allies by the Americans and voiced concern about a growing American arrogance in world affairs.[10] By the early 1920s, his disillusionment with Britain and the United States produced a complementary counterpart: an enthusiasm for the growth of Canada as a nation, with the ability to create itself as a dominion through internal territorial conquest.

The territorial aspect of Innis's nationalism intersected with a long tradition of treating the North as a site of national imagining. Dating at least to the late nineteenth century and the nationalist tracts of Canada Firsters, an imagined North played an important role in Canadian nationalism, as a defining element of Canada and as a site of national self-realization.[11] Contemporaneously expressed in the paintings of the Group of Seven, in popular literature on the possibilities of northern development and in the mythic presence of northern adventurers, such as Vilhjalmur Stefansson, the nordicity element of Canadian nationalism complemented Innis's desire to help Canada realize itself as a nation. Innis's nationalism thus evolved as a northern nationalism, one that would offset the degrading influence of Britain and the United States by finding Canada's meaning in its own mythic North.

Yet to study Canada as a distinctive place, Innis would have to draw on metropolitan scholarship in order to define his own way of seeing. His analysis of Canadian development drew on discursive theoretical approaches. He built on the example of J.M. Clark on the theory of overhead costs; C.S. Duncan on the effects of the physical properties of commodities on marketing; the teachings of Frank Knight on the theory of value;

and, debates over the frontier thesis, the model of metropolitan dominance and W.A. Mackintosh's staples approach.[12] Each of these theories yielded important insights for Innis, but by far the most important influence was the scholarship of Thorstein Veblen, particularly his writings on industrialism. Innis had studied the works of Veblen as a student at the University of Chicago and would publish an appreciative review of Veblen's life's-work in 1929. Veblen's theory built on an institutional analysis of economic growth. He distinguished between industry and business, as productive and ritualistic sides of capital, and highlighted the growth and decay effects of industrialism, particularly in settings of recent capitalist development. His approach suggested a broad conceptual framework for studying the frontier margins of Canada where the marks of integration within the world economy stood beside signs of apparent decline.

An integral aspect of Innis's imagining of the North related to career opportunities. Becoming a student of the North meant building a career as well as a new national vision. Although, by 1924, Innis's thesis had been published and he had three years of teaching experience, he had yet to attain a permanent position, and his annual salary sat modestly at $2,000.[13] As he wrote to H.G. Moulton when requesting research funds for the St. Lawrence study, "These expenses are slight but so too is a salary at the University of Toronto."[14] And yet, opportunities were opening up. In the Fall of 1922 he wrote enthusiastically to his wife in Chicago about "a very great shock."

> The President is anxious to appoint a man in Geography, preferably from the University. This would mean a considerable chance to travel at the University's expense, a chance for rapid promotion and the possibility of establishing a chair. He asked me what I thought about it. It looks very nice especially as it fits in with the general approach which

you know only too well. It would be a wonderful chance to open up something that has never been done in Toronto and which needs doing very badly. What do you think about it?[15]

Mary Quayle Innis had plenty of time to think about the matter that summer as she and her husband travelled around Europe at the University's expense, investigating geography programmes and meeting prominent scholars.[16] Innis had some misgivings about the idea. The next year he admitted while preparing some geography lectures that "I know nothing about economic geography."[17] His self-deprecation had its point; despite reading widely in geographical literature, he had no formal training in the field.[18] When he left for the Mackenzie it was in the hope that the trip would not only build his research programme, but also educate him about the geography of Canada and advance his career. Shortly after his departure, he received a letter announcing his promotion to the position of assistant professor.[19]

The Mackenzie voyage and subsequent northern excursions seemed like great adventures to Innis, his family and friends. Newspapers across the country carried short announcements of his first adventure.[20] Friends asked whether he had decided to survey railroads now, as well as write their histories.[21] Weeks before he left he watched *Call of the Wild* at the local cinema, an adaptation of one of his favourite novels at the time.[22] It would have been only a short step to imagine his own journey through Jack London's optic. Only Innis's mother lamented the fact that he liked to "take such wild trips."[23] But despite her different opinion, the idea of the North at the root of her concern was the same as the one Innis and his friends shared: the North was a wild place where mystery lurked.

And yet, the trip was not as wild as all that. Innis's route was well known, and the trip was planned cautiously. Innis had been told by the Hudson's Bay Company (HBC) Manager of the

Mackenzie District that the first section of his trip would be what they liked to call the "'Tourist Trip' when an opportunity is afforded to view the midnight sun and that along the huge river natives can be seen."[24] F.C.C. Lynch of the Department of the Interior gave the opinion that Innis's full route could be made "quite easily."[25] The majority of his trip to Aklavik, in fact, would be made sitting on the deck of the *Liard River*, an HBC supply ship.[26] Unlike an ethnologist's field-work where time was set aside to take circumstances as they came, a long stream of correspondence arranged details in advance.[27] A canoe was commissioned in Edmonton, routes worked out and alternatives sketched. In his pack he included letters of introduction provided by officials at the Department of the Interior.[28]

What made this trip special, and caused his mother worry, was not the physical exertion involved, but the "wild" location in the North. In subsequent years, Innis would receive numerous requests to give public talks on this and other excursions to the North, to which he heartily complied. During the 1920s the North held a privileged position in discussions about the future of Canada: new Ontario beckoned with resource potential, and the Arctic cast a spell of mysterious possibility over media commentators. When Innis packed his gear on the night of 29 May, with his head "in very much of a whirl," as he put it, he was preparing to become a northern expert for southern Canada. His role would be that of a metropolitan "seeing man," in Mary L. Pratt's evocative phrase: an individual who represents the periphery to the centre, who defines and situates the Other through the genre of travel literature.[29]

Inscribing North

Harold Innis kept two records of field notes of his northern excursions: one of his Mackenzie River trip in 1924, the other of his 1929 trip to Hudson Bay.[30] The typed copies of these notes are 89 and 100 pages long, respectively. The entries in the notes are uneven. Innis wrote more about particular portions of his voyages and engaged in different styles of note-taking between trips. The first reads like point form and contains reports of conversations and facts and figures about the fur trade. The second adopts a more seamless approach; observations and interviews are embedded within a descriptive narrative of transportation developments on Hudson Bay. Field notes, as anthropologists have shown, are many-sided documents: they are personal creations, made for future reference; they are inscriptions of cultural interpretation; they contain transcriptions of the views of others.[31] A point of entry into Harold Innis's emergent northern vision is through the making of his observations.

The view from Harold Innis's canoe was not neutral. As each fact from his two sets of field notes is sifted and its source unveiled, a series of unstated conventions of interpretation may be constructed.[32] His selection of informants set boundaries of exclusion and inclusion: the views of women are recorded but once; and only three short notes report the observations of Native peoples.[33] One of these notes is followed by the terse dismissal: "but this is difficult to credit."[34] Métis fare more favourably. At least seven male Métis, or "half-breeds," as he called them, had their views recorded, including a man named Alexander Mackenzie, who claimed descent from the explorer.[35] Other individuals, who defied classification, such as the Hawaiian trapper "Fiji Jim," grace his notes once or twice.[36] Yet, the overwhelming majority of Innis's informants (by my account over 80 per cent) were white men, generally in positions of authority.[37] Those whose views were recorded at greatest length included district agents of the HBC, railway company officials, missionaries and government employees. Innis's observations were made using a primarily white male optic.

The representation of persons in Innis's notes parallels his approach to informant selection. Women are rarely mentioned specifically. In the instances when their actions are described, they are performing domestic functions or are the victims in stories of male sexual predation.[38] If women are nearly completely out of sight, then Native peoples inhabit the margins of Innis's notes. They are rarely differentiated by group affiliation, and their actions are always recorded at a distance: they are viewed on the shore, approaching the supply ship or across a room.[39] There is a definite sense that a barrier stands between Innis and Native peoples, be it language or a cultural divide. Yet, this does not mean that he assumes their unimportance. His later writings on the fur trade place Native peoples in central positions of importance in the working of the trade.[40] His notes also express sympathy for the plight of Native peoples, under the pressures of disease and "civilization."[41] In one passage he avers that "Indians [are] better in some ways than white."[42] However, this sympathy and respect is tempered when one considers that Natives are represented as a necessary aid for northern development: "Eskimo of utmost fundamental importance to opening up North," Innis notes while on Hudson Bay.[43] Native peoples, he writes on a number of occasions, must be "conserved."[44] "Spend less time on cruelty to dumb animals," he argues, criticizing the Indian department, "and more on cruelty to dumb Indians."[45] The juxtaposition of Native peoples with endangered wildlife demonstrates the ambiguous boundary position of Native peoples in his representation: they exist near to "nature," beyond the reach of civilization, but nevertheless experience the "white man's" corrupting effects.

Against these margins, the central characters in Innis's notes stand out. Métis appear with greater frequency than aboriginal peoples and are favourably described. On a number of occasions he writes that they are "good people."[46]

They appear in a middle ground of Innis's racial representation. They do not need conservation, like Native peoples, but are prone to the corruption of whites: "civilization spoils them for hunting."[47] This in-between position is not neutral, however; it is tied up in a historical logic. The "Half-breed," he writes, is the "forerunner of white man."[48] This historical logic leads to Innis's main characters: white men. Curiously, he does not note their appearance, as he occasionally does with others. White men exist in his representation as purveyors of ideas, rather than as physical beings who must be described. Their ideas command the space of Innis's notebooks, with little censure or criticism, even when the views expressed appear to contradict his own beliefs noted elsewhere. The only cases where he criticizes white men are for instances of institutional neglect (as with the Department of Indian Affairs, or missionary churches) and moral depravity.[49] He blames white men for "corrupting" Native peoples, or turning to "amber colored wine, slow horses and fast women."[50] While in Red Lake, a "tough place," he concludes his comments on the base life of the town with the question, "Why not YMCA?"[51] The North, he points out a number of times, can be "very immoral...plenty of VD."[52] Innis's observations on northern mores suggest his class position and the legacy of his Baptist upbringing.[53] More broadly, his concerns represent a moral discourse on the North in the early twentieth century that described the region as sexually depraved social space.[54]

One can only speculate as to the reasons Innis created such exclusions and inclusions in the making of his observations. Unlike an anthropologist, he was not in the practice of "writing culture"; he was in search of economic facts and on a tight schedule. It is likely that such concerns led him to contact local "big men," as a way of cutting to the quick. This, nevertheless, made for important distortions in his method. Predominantly, Innis relied on informants who held positions of authority. Indeed, the planning of his Mackenzie trip was only made possible by the cooperation of Department of the Interior and HBC officials. The relationships formed with such officials lasted long after his journeys. He maintained correspondence with figures like T.W. Harris, Indian inspector at Fort Simpson, and depended on the Department of the Interior offices in Ottawa to supply him with maps, lantern slides and statistics.[55] He was not a client of these individuals or institutions, but he reciprocated good will shown. He sent books to Harris on request, sent reprints of his publications to interested officials and wrote a confidential memorandum on the conservation of resources in the Mackenzie basin for the Department of the Interior in 1924.[56] As a researcher, Innis remained closely bound to state authority and company power.

While Innis's research practice engaged official views, it excluded the views of Native peoples and women. Neither of these exclusions can be explained simply by noting the kind of information he sought or his hurried schedule. The role of aboriginal peoples and women in the fur trade was too important to allow for their views to be blithely passed over. Innis's approach to Native peoples was bounded by the fact that he lived in a racist culture and saw aboriginal peoples through filters of its making.[57] His notes contain numerous complaints by white informants about natives and their trapping "privileges."[58] His own descriptions suggest ambivalence toward, and distance from natives. At least once, his friendships with white men in the North involved him in racist caricature. On the Yukon in 1926, he became a member of the "Squawmen's Union," a farcical organization that instructed its membership that one "should not covet thy neighbor's klootch."[59] His union membership card was one of the few tokens from the journey that he saved. Innis may have seen past such racism, but his subjectivity was conditioned in relation to it.

Like the thoughts of Native peoples, those of women were rarely recorded, even if their voices were occasionally heard.[60] Three women correspondents wrote the most of any individuals Innis met on his excursions. Rachel Harris, an acquaintance made on the *Liard River,* wrote affectionately, recalling the beauty of starry nights, for two years following his return from the Yukon.[61] Clara Rogers and Gwen Doreen Smith, encountered on the Yukon River in 1926, became frequent correspondents, visited Innis in Toronto and discussed the idea of a joint trip to Labrador.[62] Even though it would appear that Innis respected certain women he met, their views were not noteworthy. In contrast to Innis's interaction with white women, little evidence suggests that he mingled on a social level with Native women. Indeed, the women he did meet defined themselves in contradistinction to Native society. Rachel Harris complained to Innis of the lack of whites in her neighbourhood in northern Alberta, and Clara Rogers, a globe-trotting Brit, romanticized the North as a place of magnetic attraction, a background against which her adventures could be realized. Innis's approach to women intersected with Native-white relations.

If Innis's research practice contained instances of gender and cultural selection, it nevertheless provided the basis for his conclusions about economic life in the North. His ideas about northern society and economy recorded in his field notes are connected in all their diversity by a unifying theme: that the North was a world in motion, marked by rapid growth and decay. Particular attention is devoted to the transportation networks that underlie specific trades: the river transportation of the fur trade and the railway transport and shipping routes of mineral development. These routes are described as the keys to the spatial organization of economic development. Under their sway, cultures grow in the North and others decay; certain trades are made viable, and others no longer profitable. Still others, in his estimation, await the peculiar combination of technique and capital investment to make innovation out of geographical endowment. His 1924 and 1929 notes provide a telling contrast in the evolution of his northern vision by their focus on different aspects of northern development.

Innis's Mackenzie field notes demonstrate his attention to the close relationship between water routes and the economic geography of the fur trade. "Whole arctic civilization a capitalization of advantages of a swift river," he noted somewhere near Fitzgerald in 1924. The town, he observed, was a product of the fur trade; it reflected the spatial organization of river transport and the geography of its situation. "Tremendous advantage," he remarked, "of swift current load provisions heavy material going in and light coming out—adaptation of trade (furs) to river."[63] The theme of the adaptation of the trade to the means of transport had earlier been noted at Peace River, where he described the river as a "highway."[64] He postulated that there was a tendency for settlement to "spread northward up river and toward Peace River." The reason was the "effect of swift current on direction of growth of town."[65] The notes of Innis's Mackenzie trip contain many other detailed observations about prices, rivalries between trappers, and graft in the HBC, to note three recurring interests. Yet, it is the sweeping statements concerning rivers and transport that suggest the geographical basis of his interpretation. In a subsequent, published account of his trip, he quoted almost verbatim some of the passages selected above.[66] The observations arguably represent the meeting of expectation and experience: his thesis concerning the importance of river transport in the early history of Canada was affirmed, in his mind, by the economic geography of the Mackenzie basin. On one day he mused to his field book that the "River is very important determining factor in the direction of econom-ic development of early period."[67] His northern laboratory was turning out to confirm his historical hypotheses. "The rivers," he wrote later, "hold sway."[68]

Innis's field notes from his trip to Hudson Bay reflect five years of further thought about northern conditions. Since his Mackenzie River trip, he had travelled down the Yukon River and paid close attention to mining developments, and he had examined resource development facilities in northern Ontario, Quebec and the Maritimes. Although his *Fur Trade in Canada* was still a year away from publication, his research programme had changed direction. His focus was on what he would later describe as the foreground of Canadian unity: mineral development. The field notes suggest that Innis had come closer to developing a coherent analytical approach to the study of staple commodities since his 1924 Mackenzie trip. Dispersed reflections on costs, social conditions and technology are hemmed in by conclusions about the meaning of such data and by specific references to economic theory. On one level, he had come to a more focussed statement of forward and backward linkages. "A mine is an economic explosive," he postulated near the end of his tour, "developing in its train lumbering, agriculture, hunting, industry, transport facilities in a remarkably short period of time."[69] This new staple commodity was made possible by a new transportation technique. "Overwhelming importance," he insisted, "of gasoline and hydroelectric and water transport contrasted with steam, rail, and coal. New revolution in the gasoline tank."[70] In certain respects, this observation was predictive and looked beyond the railway link to Churchill that served ostensibly as his subject of study during the trip. The prediction, however, helps to reveal his sense of the meaning of development. Development occurred when new commodities could be exploited through more advanced forms of transportation and technique. His conception of development drew directly from his reading of Veblen.[71] In one cryptic passage, Innis points to Veblen's "distinction [between] business and industry..." which was spelled out in detail in Veblen's *Theory of Business Enterprise,* and which can be related to Innis's analysis of mineral development as an example of industrialism and its effects.[72] Veblen's distinction, wrote Innis in his 1924 review essay, asserted "that machine industry was overwhelmingly, and increasingly productive, and that the problems of machine industry were incidental to the disposal of the product."[73] Innis's notes mirror this assumption of a basic cleavage between marketing and industrial development in their attention to the details of technical change. His photographs taken during the trip focus on physical structures, transportation devices and gasoline tanks.[74] Innis's later analyses of mineral development would stress the central place of the engineer in development and the all-encompassing effects of the machine process in dissolving institutions and forging new ones in their wake. More tangibly than in 1924, Innis's notations on Hudson Bay show the marks of a more theoretically engaged empirical approach. It was an approach that he advocated in his review of Veblen: "Any substantial progress in economic theory must come from a synthesis between economic history and economic theory."[75]

Innis's field notes suggest how he asked questions, who he found important and how he came to view the North. But it was not until he returned from "the field" that he composed his refined reflections of what he had seen and attempted to synthesize this material with archival research and secondary reading. In the 1920s he engaged in three kinds of public engagement with his refined reflections about the North: he wrote for popular audiences and gave public lectures; composed private memos to persons in authority; and wrote scholarly books and articles advancing the theories and

arguments at the basis of his popular claims. In these different forms, Innis clarified and crystallized his northern vision: he combined the concepts of development and nation into a necessary and progressive relationship. By examining his views and representations of the North, an understanding of his role as a public intellectual may be developed. The point is not to offer a close textual analysis of Innis's most famous works (a well-trodden path), but to point out some of his lesser-known ideas, buried in popular publications, and find the parallels and distinctions they created with his better known interpretations.

Representing North

Harold Innis sought out the role of public intellectual in the 1920s. The message he delivered to public gatherings was optimistic; his North was the future. A typical engagement occurred on a cold night in Hespeler in February, 1924. The talk had been arranged by the University of Toronto Extension Department, after a request by a group in Hespeler for a public speaker.[76] The group wished to develop an organization like the Canadian Club; its correspondent hoped for something "above average."[77] Innis showed some lantern slides on loan from the Department of the Interior, and then began to outline his views of the North.[78] The reporter covering the event for the *Mail and Empire* noted approvingly that Innis

> had an abiding faith in the future of Canada and the opening of the north country, further exploration and means of conservation of the large supply of minerals, furs, timber and pulpwood. As to why he had this belief he stated that the advent of modern machinery and mechanical methods dated back only about 150 years and that minerals were the background for this vast industry.[79]

Pointing to maps, Innis suggested the possibility of agriculture; this land, he insisted, was not a "frozen waste." After offering these opinions, he stated his credentials for judgement. He described his trip down the Peace and Slave rivers, across Slave Lake and down the Mackenzie. By way of conclusion he gave a ringing endorsement of the building of the Hudson Bay Railway. The railway, he argued, would not depend on the exports of the grain trade via Hudson Bay, as was popularly assumed, but would act as a point of access to developing the North. Through the refraction of his northern vision, an outlet for prairie agriculture became a means of penetrating the North. Before stepping down, he enthused that Canada is "THE country of the twentieth century on account of her vast mineral resources...he felt perfectly safe in saying 'Go sell your boots and buy Government Bonds.'"[80] The performance earned Innis a little over $9.00.[81]

There were other nights like the one in Hespeler. Between 1924 and 1931, Innis delivered at least 16 public lectures on the theme of the North in Canada.[82] Throughout the decade he spoke to groups such as the YMCA, the Canadian Institute and the Brotherhood of the United Church of Davenport Road in order to advance his public standing and to proselytize about the North. In the late 1920s and early 1930s there was increasing interest in the Canadian North, Canadian history and the plight of the nation's explorers in opening up the land. Innis's biography of Peter Pond, whom he anachronistically described as a "Father of Confederation," was one such expression of this interest.[83] In his lectures on the North he responded to this mood by telling the future of Canada in a manner that paralleled its romantic and heroic past and charted its progressive future.

On one level, his representations of the North portrayed the region as an anti-modern enclave, safe from the din of the industrial revolution. In a lecture to an association of furriers

meeting in Toronto in 1930, he stated that the fur trade in the North remained "romantic" despite changes in transportation technology.

"In the work of the trapper," he says, "the emphasis is still on the individual as in the days of the French Regime. The men of the north have substantially the psychology of the men of the wilderness of former times. And I think as long as the fur trade lasts it will still put a premium on the individual and produce a race of men who are unlike the factory organized wage-earning industrialists of the south."[84]

The northern fur trade was not a relic of history, Innis suggested; it was Canada's heroic past incarnate. Other popular descriptions highlighted the institutions that the fur trade had bequeathed to the making of the nation. Central government and Canadian institutions were rooted, he claimed, in the fur-trade past.[85] "An understanding of our economic background," he told an audience at the Canadian Institute in 1930, "is a certain antidote to those who worry about American penetration.... Historically, Canada is an economic unit, not a series of provinces."[86] The fur trade thus existed in his popular descriptions as an escape from modernity on one level, and as the solid base of the past on which the present and future of the nation could be constructed.[87]

His lectures also drew a subtle parallel between himself, as the modern searcher of knowledge, and the explorers of the past. Opinions of the North's possibilities were interspersed with his own travel narratives. In his published account of his trip down the Mackenzie, he made no mention of the fact that he had travelled mainly on a supply ship.[88] The picture of Innis in a canoe that accompanies the article, and his frequent references to canoeing in the composition, tell another story. While Innis may have been subtle in juxtaposing his experience with that of earlier explorers, it was drawn in high relief by reporters in search of good copy. "Professor Innes [sic]," wrote reporter Henry Lynn-Folke in 1929, "has the eye of the true explorer." "Directness of manner and a breadth of shoulder betoken an ability to handle situations and men, and he has the calm gaze which indicates deep penetration."[89] Lynne-Folk had a way with unselfconscious Freudian turns of phrase. When he described Innis's research method, he wrote that Innis went "armed with a voluminous notebook, a camera, and his extremely retentive memory."[90] Penetrating, armed and retentive, all at once: here indeed was a true explorer. The representation of Innis as explorer demonstrates the force of popular narratives of nordicity in shaping his public image.

In his role as public intellectual, Innis focussed attention both in popular and academic writings on the notion that the North was a crucible of development, a land where growth and decay marked progress. In his popular engagements he promoted development; in his academic publications he analyzed it. The concept was protean in his hands: it melted boundaries between past, present and future, as well as nature and culture. In one popular article, for example, he read rivers as historical objects, subject to the power of development. The spirit of capitalism under his pen metaphorically drove the Mackenzie. "Violent seasonal changes and the swiftness of the current," he wrote, "are tremendous forces making for pronounced and rapid geological action."[91] Like the violent price swings that commanded the course of resource exploitation in the North, seasons could usher in rapid transformations.

> Constant carrying away of the soil, especially in the bends of the river where the water flows with greatest speed, provokes land slides, and leaves typical fresh surfaces known as "cut banks".... Channels are constantly changing, islands are being built up and torn down, deltas are in process of formation, and the bays about the entrances to the lakes, as at Chipewyan and

> Resolution, are being filled in.... Large trees constantly undermined slap into the river. These are carried down and piled into great heaps on the heads of islands or scattered around the deltas.[92]

Nature revealed itself, in this passage, as the contradictory process of development, where growth and decay are inseparable oppositions.

Although some have argued that Innis was a geographical determinist, his few writings on landscape suggest, to the contrary, a metaphorical social determinism. Nature affected human affairs, in his analysis, but it functioned according to cycles that paralleled human institutions and economies conceptually as well as metaphorically. Beaver lodges, in *The Fur Trade in Canada,* could be described as "fixed capital," while the rapid decline of beavers could be suggested on the basis of the "Depreciation through obsolescence of the beaver's defense equipment...."[93] What is forgotten in the debate about Innis's geographical determinism is that he did not hold fast to a boundary separating nature and culture.[94] It is only criticism of Innis since the 1970s that has forced scholars to take positions on Innis as a boundary keeper between the assumed dichotomy. In Innis's approach, nature and culture commingled, affected each other dialectically and could be analyzed with a common language.

The language of growth and decay extended from landscape to the historical and spatial analysis of economies. The productive and destructive aspects of the river, for example, parallel his description of staples.[95] Staples, he argued, arose out of a combination of geographical endowment and technique driven by the export markets of industrialized countries. They developed economies through linkages, but also destroyed much in their path. The fur trade created a continental transportation network, institutions of central government and the political space of Canada. In the process, however, it diminished Native culture and showed every sign of destroying its resource base. The succession of staples, in turn, reproduced the logic of growth and decay at a different level. Lumbering succeeded the fur trade in the East, and mining promised to overtake it in the North. Thus, Innis's appeal to the history of the Canadian fur trade as a continuity in the development of the nation was paradoxical. The fur trade's progressive aspects, he suggested, were largely spent; its significance arose out of the basis it laid for the rise of further staple industries. The background of Canadian unity, Innis wrote, was found in the fur trade; its foreground, on the other hand, lay in the development of minerals. Both developments were marked by growth and decay. Time and space collapsed into continuity.

In his present-minded discussion of northern development, railroad building and mineral exploitation rose out of a decaying fur economy. Water routes faded in significance; railroads, airplanes and gasoline took their place. Throughout the late 1920s and early 1930s Innis promoted to various audiences the causes of mineral development and the Hudson Bay Railway.[96] The railway served to focus his ideas about the future of the North. It had been built as a competitive route for the export of prairie wheat, but Innis saw its possibilities in the development of local traffic and minerals. Such an economy would only be developed by struggle, he suggested; but its rewards would be a new national political economy. "In the whole of Canada as well as in northern Canada," he wrote in one popular publication, "we shall probably have closer integration and more sane and balanced growth."[97] The significance of the railway, he insisted, "lies much deeper than in the immediate development of traffic and in the evolution of transportation technique. It is the keystone of the arch in the development of northern Canada. It will bring together the hitherto isolated and independent areas of the Northwest."[98] The railway promised to unleash the North's economic potential, he argued, as well as spur national unity.

Innis's advocacy of railway and mineral development complemented his career strategy. After his research expedition to Hudson Bay in 1929, Innis pressed President Falconer of the University of Toronto to appoint a geographer with an expertise in northern Canada. His motivation in the matter had overtones of career ambitions, as well as a nationalist zeal for the Canadian North. Innis had found his home department of political economy confining in the late 1920s.[99] In 1926 he pursued the possibility of a joint position as an advisor with a financial institution; three years later he resigned from the University when a colleague was promoted over his head.[100] Throughout the decade he was drawn to the idea of establishing an independent geography department. His interest in geography gained him the President's ear as an ad hoc advisor at a time when most communication would have been directed through department heads.[101] After his Hudson Bay trip in 1929, he spelled out his northern vision as a strong reason for supporting geography. "I am very much impressed," he wrote in a confidential memorandum to the President,

> after this summer's experience of the growing importance of the Hudson Bay area. We must follow up along these lines 1, Scientific work on the Arctic and Archipelago, 2, Closer relations between the maritimes and the West by Hudson Bay, 3, Closer relations with Newfoundland. My fear is that the Americans will precede us and that we shall lose our one chance at broadening out in our own country. This may appear beside the point but to me it makes more urgent the problem of geography.[102]

The study of geography, northern development and national self-realization were all of a piece in his mind.

As an advisor on geography and the North, Innis strengthened his position within the university. Although he dropped his earlier interest in becoming a geographer, he did not abandon his advocacy of the subject: in 1928 he attended the International Geographical Congress and delivered a lecture on northern Canada; and he continually pressed Falconer for the appointment of Griffith Taylor, an Australian geographer at the University of Chicago.[103] Under the encouragement of the president in 1930, Innis set aside earlier reservations and almost took up the position.[104] He was already listed as an economic geographer in official documentation, and the move may have appeared as the logical institutional recognition of his intellectual progression. But the appointment never occurred, perhaps for financial reasons. In later years, he continued his "geography crusade," as John Watson dubs it, and finally succeeded when in 1935 President H.J. Cody, Falconer's successor, followed Innis's advice and hired Taylor.[105] Innis's role in the advocacy of geography and the North placed him in a strong position for career advancement and allowed him to travel internationally at the university's expense. His connection to the president helped him to win departmental battles. When he resigned in frustration in 1929 the president reappointed him and promoted him against the wishes of his department. The North and geography had their uses.

Innis's advocacy of the North within the university was buttressed by a defense of the university in public discussions of the North. In 1927 Innis became involved in a dispute between University of Toronto academics and the *Financial Post* and *The Globe* over the role of academics in representing the Canadian North.[106] The dispute arose when the *Financial Post* and then *The Globe* carried editorials criticizing an "article" published in the *Canadian Historical Review* (CHR) that besmirched the developmental possibilities of the Canadian shield.[107] The offensive passage stated that

While to the north and northwest of Lake Superior there lies only a continuation of that endless dreary waste which forms the dead heart of the eastern half of Canada, to the south of Lake Michigan there is a land of far greater possibilities.

The Globe concluded the quotation with a fierce rebuke: "The 'dead heart' is very much alive."[108] Both editorials mentioned that the *CHR* had a close relationship with the University of Toronto. The implication seemed to be that the university was not pulling its patriotic weight.

No one could doubt the editorial stance of the newspapers, but for historians of a fact-grubbing persuasion the situation was appalling. George Brown took issue with the implied slander of the *CHR* and the University of Toronto. The "article," he clarified, was in fact a book review. And the reviewer, W.A. Mackintosh, had simply quoted the book's author, the Scottish geographer Marion Newbigin, in her analysis of the economic value of the regions in question in the seventeenth and eighteenth centuries.[109] Innis chimed in next, pointing out his annoyance "that the University of Toronto is attacked in this fashion."[110] He listed the work done in the practical sciences at the university and his own research as proof of a commitment to northern development. In response, the *Financial Post* published a partial retraction, which noted the complaints and then reiterated the newspaper's commitment to the development of the Canadian shield.[111]

The episode is testimony to the uncritical boosterism of the Canadian North that infected the Toronto press in the 1920s but also suggests the complicity of Canadian intellectuals.[112] While the stance of the newspapers points to the power of the mining interest in the politics of the province, the position of the University of Toronto academics was not as different as one might have expected. Innis and Brown defended their positions as fellow northern boosters. As Brown put it, "the *Canadian Historical Review* is in sympathy with *The Globe*'s desire to dispel false notions regarding the value of Northern Canada's resources."[113] The character of Innis and Brown's defense suggests the length to which Canadian academics, and Innis, in particular, were convinced disciples in the task of northern development.

Innis's northern vision thus developed in close relation with his career ambitions and institutional affiliation. Yet, the tone of its enunciation with respect to mineral development owed little to this context. Innis's advocacy of northern mineral exploitation and railway development owed more to the northern boosterism that filled the newspaper pages he felt bound to criticize than to any institutional politics. While he had described the fur trade as a reminder of the past and as an example of growth and decay in the hinterland, his present-minded focus on the Hudson Bay region adopted a rhetoric of war. In a lecture on the railway to the Canadian Engineering Institute, he observed that

> We have only begun the advance to the north. To the engineer belongs the task of forging the weapons by which the vast northern territory made accessible by the railway may be conquered. The railroad itself is an auspicious omen of success and already the aeroplane and the tractor have shown important possibilities.[114]

The military metaphors had their point: nations were forged in battle. "It remains to be seen," he stated in 1930,

> whether the front line which has been pushed forward in the first attack on the last vast stretch of the Canadian shield will be occupied and consolidated; but it seems reasonable to suppose that Canada will continue to take advantage of the industrial revolution based on

gasoline and to broaden out toward the north. The political framework of the Dominion worked out under the fur trade will be gradually filled in economically.[115]

Innis's northern boosterism bred a rhetorical militarism.

At the basis of this rhetoric lay a particular interpretation of the course of national development. Spelled out in its most advanced form in the conclusion to *The Fur Trade in Canada*, the interpretation held that Canada was not invented "in spite of geography, but because of it."[116] Canada's national boundaries, Innis instructed, followed fur trade routes across the continent. However, this established political space served only as a sufficient cause in his formulation; it was space yet to be consolidated. In his argument, mineral development and railway construction acted as the means of consolidation, as the necessary causes of national integration.[117] In the intellectual context of the 1920s, when Innis first made these claims, his argument was idiosyncratic and original. The argument stood Oliver Goldwin Smith's claim that Canada was bound to disintegrate under the ineluctable forces of continental geography on its head.[118] Nationalist arguments about the historical integrity of Canada could now be based on a myth of territoriality as well as weaker ones of blood. Like nationalist histories of the late nineteenth century produced by historians Frederick Jackson Turner and Sergei Mikhailovich Solov'ev, Innis's interpretation of national development integrated a strong territorial element.[119] It treated national history as a narrative of geographical transcendence.

Harold Innis was integrally part of his own northern vision. At the centre of his northern vision was a belief that national self-realization followed economic development. He imagined nation, not as a community, but as a geo-body that would be given life when its territory was filled in economically. This fundamental belief was buttressed by a series of secondary positions: that the North's development depended upon a progression from one mode of transportation to another; that the background of the fur trade provided the basis for the foreground of mineral development. Mineral development, in his estimation, would be one of the most important staple industries of the twentieth century. In its wake, the Canadian economy would reorient itself along a northern axis; railway links to Hudson Bay would rebalance the transportation economy of the nation. As Innis studied the North and crafted these positions, he became more and more tied to his own vision. His research practice and the popularization of his ideas to various audiences made him into a northern prophet, with links to the forces of development. When he studied northern peoples and places, he took the view of the conquerors. Native peoples and women did not tint his optic. Innis gave meaning to his observations from his field research within a narrative of unceasing and benevolent development. When he presented his ideas to different publics, he could only advocate development and more of it. Within the university, he called for the establishment of a geography department and studies of the North; he parlayed his northern expertise into rapid career advancement. In public forums he defended the position of the University as one of the agents of northern development in its knowledge-producing capacity. Canada's epitome of the ivory tower scholar was, in fact, a northern booster. In creating a North, Innis recreated himself.

Notes

1   In a related article, I have examined Innis's involvement with a social scientific survey of the Arctic during the 1940s: "Harold Innis, the Arctic Survey and the Politics of Social Science during the Second World War," *Canadian Historical Review* 79.1 (March 1998): 36–67.

2   Another field excursion was made to Newfoundland in 1930.

3   Donald Creighton, *Harold Adams Innis: Portrait of a Scholar* (Toronto: University of Toronto Press, 1978 [1957]), 61–64. See also Carl Berger, *The Writing of Canadian History: Aspects of English-Canadian Historical Writing since 1900* (Toronto: University of Toronto Press, 1986), 89–90.

4   University of Toronto Archives (UTA), Department of Political Economy Papers, A76-0025, Box 2, File 7, Chalifaut (sp?), Chief Geographer, Department of the Interior, to Innis, 13 March 1923; A. Brabant, Hudson Bay Fur Trade Commissioner, to Innis, 22 March 1923; File 8 Innis to Hon. Charles Dunning, n.d.; Reverend C.E. Whittaker, to Innis, 29 March 1924; Bishop I.O. Stringer to Innis, 29 April 1924; F.H. Kitton, Natural Resources Intelligence Service, to Innis, 14 May 1924; F.C.C. Lynch, Department of the Interior, to Innis, 21 March 1924; Alberta Motor Boat Co., to Innis, 28 April 1924; Innis Papers, B72-0003, Box 4, File 11,

L. Romand, Acting District Manager, Mackenzie River District, HBC, to Innis, 26 March 1924.

5   Creighton, *Harold Adams Innis: Portrait of a Scholar*, 60–61.

6   UTA, Department of Political Economy Papers, A76-0025, Box 2, File 9, MacIver to Falconer, 18 March 1924 (copy). Innis's proposal was quoted in MacIver's letter seeking funds for the Mackenzie trip. The request was turned down: UTA, Presidential Papers (Falconer), A67-0007, Box 84, File 2, Falconer to MacIver, 19 March 1924. It is unclear whether Innis received any other funding for the trip.

7   UTA, Department of Political Economy Papers, A67-0025, Box 2, File 8, Innis to H.G. Moulton, 11 January 1924; Innis Papers, B72-0003, Box 4, File 11, Innis to Moulton, n.d.

8   UTA, Innis Family Papers, B79-0056, Box 2, Harold Innis, "Autobiography," 126–27.

9   Ibid., 126.

10 UTA, Innis Papers, B72-0003, Box 4, File 4, Innis to Mother and All, 6 July 1918.

11 On the history of nordicity in Canada, see for example: Carl Berger, "The True North Strong and Free," *Interpreting Canada's Past, Vol. 2*, ed. J.M. Bumstead (Toronto: Oxford University Press,

1986); Douglas A. West, "Researching the North in Canada: An Introduction to the Canadian Northern Discourse," *Journal of Canadian Studies* 26.2 (1991): 108–119 and the special issue, "Representing North," *Essays in Canadian Writing* 59 (Fall 1996). On the popularity of Stefansson at the end of the First World War, see: Morris Zaslow, *The Northward Expansion of Canada, 1914–1967* (Toronto: McClelland & Stewart, 1988), 1–2.

12 UTA, Innis Family Papers, B79-0056, Box 2, Harold Innis, "Autobiography," 97–98; 125.

13 UTA, Presidential Papers (Falconer), A67-0007, Box 58(B), Hunter-Johnston File, Falconer to Innis, 11 May 1920. The president's offer of appointment stated that the job was not permanent and set the salary as $2,000 per annum with no mention of raises.

14 UTA, Innis Papers, B72-0003, Box 4, File 11, Innis to Moulton, n.d.

15 UTA, Innis Papers, B72-0003, Box 4, File 9, Innis to Mary Quayle Innis, 7 October 1922. The "he" in this quotation is R.M. MacIver.

16 Berger, *Canadian History*, 90–91.

17 UTA, Innis Papers, B72-0003, Box 4, File 10, Innis to Mary Quayle Innis, n.d. [1923].

18 Gary S. Dunbar, "Harold Innis and Canadian Geography," *Canadian Geographer* 29.2 (Summer 1985): 160; UTA, Innis Papers, B72-0003, Box 4, File 9, Innis to Mary Quayle Innis, 29 September 1922.

19 UTA, Department of Political Economy Papers, A76-0025, Box 2, File 8, F.A. Mouré to Innis, 27 June 1924. He had received informal notice of the appointment as early as April: UTA, Innis Family Papers, B91-0029, Box 57, File 2, Mary Quayle Innis Diary, 12 April 1924 entry.

20 Announcements appeared, for example, in the St. John *Globe*, 20 August 1924, and the *Christian Science Monitor*, n.d. Another unidentified paper in Innis's papers announces their voyage with the statement, "Easterners to Attempt Canoe Trip to Arctic," UTA, Innis Papers, B72-0003, Box 6, File 5.

21 UTA, Department of Political Economy Papers, A76-0025, Box 2, File 8, Norman Clark to Innis, 2 March 1924.

22 UTA, Innis Family Papers, B91-0029, Box 57, File 2, Mary Quayle Innis Diary, 12 April 1924 entry.

23 UTA, Department of Political Economy Papers, A76-0025, Box 2, File 6, Mother to Innis, 10 June (n.d.).

24 UTA, Innis Papers, B72-0003, Box 4, File 11, L. Romand, Acting District Manager, Mackenzie River District, HBC to Innis, 26 March 1924.

25 UTA, Department of Political Economy Papers, A76-0025, Box 4, File 8, F.C.C. Lynch to Innis, 21 March 1924.

26 In a later trip down the Yukon River, Innis travelled a substantial leg of the journey by car, from Circle, Alaska, to Fairbanks. UTA, Innis Papers, B72-0003, Box 4, File 13, Innis to Mary Quayle Innis and Donald, 22 July 1926; Innis to Mary Quayle Innis and Donald, 2 August 1926.

27 UTA, Department of Political Economy Papers, A76-0025, Alberta Motor Boat Company to Innis, 28 April 1924; HBC receipt to Innis, Box 2, File 9, 14 June 1924.

28 UTA, Department of Political Economy Papers, A76-0025, Box 2, File 8, F.H. Kitto to Innis, 14 May 1924. Kitto gave Innis eight separate letters to specific individuals, all employed in official capacities.

29 UTA, Innis Papers, B72-0003, Box 4, File 11, Innis to Mary Quayle Innis, 29 May 1924; Mary Louise Pratt, *Imperial Eyes: Travel Writing and Transculturation* (London and New York: Routledge, 1992).

30 The following analysis refers to the typed copies of his originals. They appear to have been typed after his return, either by F. Hahn or his wife, and contain incidental corrections, sometimes in Innis's handwriting. The typed versions were cited because the originals are barely legible in parts, and the typed copies generally contain page numbers, which allow for precise citations. All originals and typed notes may be found in UTA, Innis Papers, B72-0003, Box 6. Other field notes were kept of trips to Newfoundland and British Columbia. An account of his trip down the Yukon River was written by his companion and former student, W.K. Gibb. "Eight Hundred Miles on the Yukon," *Canadian Geographical Journal* VIII.3 (March 1934): 123–34.

31 The literature of self-reflexive anthropology is enormous; the following lists works I have found particularly stimulating: James Clifford and George E. Marcus, *Writing Culture: The Poetics and Politics of Ethnography* (Berkeley: University of California Press, 1986); Clifford Geertz, "Thick Description: Toward an Interpretive Theory of Culture," *The Interpretation of Cultures* (New York: Basic Books, 1973); Roger Sanjek, ed. *Fieldnotes: The Makings of Anthropology* (Ithaca: Cornell University Press, 1990); George Stocking Jr., ed. *The Observers Observed: Essays on Ethnographic Field Work* (Madison: University of Wisconsin Press, 1983); James Clifford, "Notes on (Field)notes," in Roger Sanjek, ed. *Fieldnotes*, 47–70;

David Plath, "Fieldnotes, Filed notes and the Conferring of Note," in Sanjek, 371–84.

32 A number of problems attend the analysis of Harold Innis's field notes that should be considered: first, it is difficult in parts to distinguish Innis's remarks from the transcriptions of the views of others. On the whole, Innis attempted to distinguish these views, but occasionally, attribution is not clear. I have tried to avoid passages that could not be precisely attributed. Second, the heritage of Innis's informants was not consistently stated; in over half of the cases he stated their ethnicity or provided a clue of their general background. I have therefore tried to make my comments on the heritage of informants sufficiently general, but do make specific statements of numbers where possible.

33 The female interviewed was Mrs. J.M. Bolinger, whom he met on a train going North in 1929, on the subject of the wheat trade in North Dakota. The Native peoples interviewed, all on his Hudson Bay trip, were unidentified. UTA Innis Papers, B72-0003, Box 6, File 7, 5, 7, 59. While in Skagway, Alaska in 1926, Innis wrote to his wife about talking with local Native peoples. Box 4, File 13, Innis to Mary and Donald, 22 June 1926.

34 Ibid., 5.

35 UTA, Innis Papers, B72-0003, Box 6, File 3, 8.

36 Ibid., File 7, 73.

37 See note 32.

38 UTA, Innis Papers, B72-0003, Box 6, File 3, 6; File 4, 11–12, 27, 29, 32, 49; File 7, 18, 54, 57, 98.

39 Ibid., File 3, 9, 11, 21, 31; File 4, 22, 29; File 7, 5, 11, 54.

40 Berger, *Canadian History*, 100; Bruce Trigger, *Natives and Newcomers: Canada's "Heroic Age" Reconsidered* (Montreal and Kingston: McGill-Queen's University Press, 1985), 38. Trigger points out that Innis treats Native peoples narrowly as *homo economicus.*

41 UTA, Innis Papers, B72-0003, Box 6, File 4, 3.

42 Ibid., File 3, 16.

43 Ibid., File 7, 66.

44 Ibid., File 7, 3, 14, 66.

45 Ibid., File 7, 14.

46 Ibid., File 3, 14; File 4, 11–12.

47 Ibid., File 3, 16.

48 Ibid.

49 Ibid., File 4, 49; File 7, 3, 14, 52, 65, 68.

50 Ibid., File 7, 4.

51 Ibid., The original quotation did not include a question mark.

52 UTA, Innis Papers, B72-0003, Box 6, File 3, 8.

53 Michael Gavreau, "Baptist Religion and the Social Science of Harold Innis," *Canadian Historical Review* LXXVI.2 (June 1995): 187.

54 Karen Dubinsky, *Improper Advances: Rape and Heterosexual Conflict in Ontario, 1880–1929* (Chicago: University of Chicago Press, 1993): 154–58.

55 UTA, Department of Political Economy Papers, A76-0025, Box 2, File 6, Innis to F.C.C. Lynch, 13 January 1926; Innis to Lynch, 21 January 1926; Innis to Lynch, 16 February 1926; File 12, T.W. Harris to Innis, 6 September 1925.

56 UTA, Department of Political Economy Papers, Box 2, File 9, Hoyes Lloyd to Innis, 24 October 1924. In this letter Lloyd thanked Innis for his "confidential memorandum on the question of wildlife conservation in the Mackenzie District. This will be of great value, and I hope will assist in carrying out improvements in that area." A follow-up letter by Innis on the subject of the memorandum was received by Lloyd. File 11, Hoyes Lloyd to Innis, 8 January 1925.

57 On Native-White relations in the Yukon in this period, see Ken Coates, *Best Left as Indians: Native-White Relations in the Yukon Territory* (Montreal and Kingston: McGill-Queen's University Press, 1991), 86–107. During the 1920s, Innis made a number of references to the concept of race that implied a belief in innate characteristics. In a memorandum to R.M. MacIver on possible thesis topics, he suggested "The negro population in Canada." He hoped that such a thesis would "show something as to the adaptability of the negro to northern latitudes." UTA, Department of Political Economy Papers, Box 2, File 9, Innis to MacIver, 17 March 1924. In his review of the work of Thorstein Veblen, he pointed out Veblen's racial background, and discussed certain theories of racial mixing, that had made the idea of racial groups redundant. Harold Innis, "The Work of Thorstein Veblen," *Essays in Canadian Economic History*, ed. Mary Quayle Innis (Toronto: University of Toronto Press, 1956), 17–18. Innis was not peculiar in thinking that races existed, but, on the whole, displayed a more progressive attitude to the relevance of presumed racial characteristics than was general at the time.

58 UTA, Innis Papers, B72-0003, Box 6, File 4, 6, 23.

59 Ibid., File 1, Membership Card, Squawmen's Union No. 1, 26 June 1926.

60 Besides the three women mentioned below, Innis received a letter from Anne Tamminen, whom it appears he met on his 1926 trip. UTA, Department of Political Economy Papers, A76-0025, Box 2, File 14, Anne Tamminen to Innis, 28 October 1926.

61 UTA, Department of Political Economy Papers, Box 2, File 9, Rachel Harris to Innis, 30 August 1924; Harris to Innis, 30 September 1924; Harris to Innis, 10 November 1924; File 12, Harris to Innis, October (n.d.) 1925.

62 There are a total of 16 pieces of correspondence from Clara C. Rogers to Innis in UTA, A76-0025 and B72-0003. On the Labrador idea, see: UTA, Department of Political Economy Papers, A76-0025, Box 4, File 1, Clara C. Rogers to Innis, 26 January 1928; Rogers to Innis, 11 July 1928; Gwen Doreen Smith to Innis, 12 July (n.d.); Rogers to Innis, 30 July 1928; Rogers to Innis, 14 August 1928.

63 UTA, Innis Papers, B72-0003, Box 6, File 4, 4.

64 UTA, Innis Papers, B72-0003, Box 6, File 3, 20.

65 Ibid.

66 Harold Innis, "A Trip Through the Mackenzie River Basin," *University of Toronto Monthly* XXV.4 (January 1925): 151–53.

67 UTA, Innis Papers, B72-0003, Box 6, File 3, 9.

68 Ibid., 152.

69 UTA, Innis Papers, B72-0003, Box 6, File 7, n.p.

70 Ibid., 15.

71 Robin Neill, *A New Theory of Value: The Canadian Economics of Harold Innis* (Toronto: University of Toronto Press, 1972), 22–27; Michael Cowen and Robert Shenton, *Doctrines of Development* (London and New York: Routledge, 1996), 216–19.

72 UTA, Innis Papers, B72-0003, Box 6, File 7, n.p.; Thorstein Veblen, *The Theory of Business Enterprise* (New York: New American Library, 1963 [1904]).

73 Harold Innis, "The Work of Thorstein Veblen," 23.

74 Many of Innis's photographs and lantern slides are contained in: UTA, Innis Family Papers, B91-0029.

75 Harold Innis, "The Work of Thorstein Veblen," 26.

76 UTA, Department of Political Economy Papers, Box 2, File 6, Harriet M. Latter, University of Toronto Extension Department to Innis, 28 January 1926; File 13, Latter to Innis, 19 February 1926.

77 UTA, Department of Political Economy Papers, A76-0025, Box 2, File 13, H.L. Trapp quoted in Harriet M. Latter to Innis, 17 February 1926.

78 Ibid., F.C.C. Lynch to Innis, 17 February 1926. Lynch was Innis's main contact at the Department of the Interior.

79 UTA, Innis Papers, B72-0003, Box 3, File 1, "Hespeler Men Hear About the North," *Mail and Empire,* 18 February 1927.

80 Ibid.

81 UTA, Department of Political Economy Papers, A76-0025, Box 2, File 13, Harriet M. Latter to Innis, 1 March 1926.

82 I determined this number by cross-referencing newspaper articles, speech announcements, letters from the University of Toronto Extension Department, and entries in Mary Quayle Innis's diary. Following is a list of the sites at, or the groups to which, Innis spoke on northern subjects. The dates accompanying this list are approximate, as they generally list the newspaper coverage date rather than the actual speaking date. Speaking engagements: Rose Avenue School, 31 October 1924; Marmora, 27 November 1924; Eaton Club, 20 November 1924; Hespeler, 18 February 1926; Memorial Hall, Elora, Girl Guides Association, 25 January 1927; Women's Art Association, 18 February 1927; Canadian Institute, 27 January 1930; Central YMCA, 20 February 1930; Furriers' Convention, 29 March 1930; Engineering Institute of Canada, 31 October 1930; Hart House, 3 March 1931; Canadian Institute, 25 April 1931; Toronto YMCA, 27 September 1932; Davisville Home and School Club, 1923; Brodie Club, Royal Ontario Museum, n.d.; United Brotherhood of Davenport Road, n.d. Innis may also have spoken to the Appleby Community League and the Women's Club at T. Eaton and Co. in 1924, but the only evidence is letters of request. UTA, Innis Papers, B72-0003, Box 3, File 1; Innis Family Papers, B91-0029, Box 57, Files 2, 3 and 5; Department of Political Economy Papers, A76-0025, Box 2, Files 6, 9 and 13.

83 Harold Innis, *Peter Pond: Fur Trader and Adventurer* (Toronto: Irwin and Gordon, Ltd., 1930), ix.

84 UTA, Innis Papers, B72-0003, Box 3, File 1, R.C. Reade, "Fur Trade in Canada Centres in Toronto," *Star Weekly,* 29 March 1930.

85 UTA, Innis Papers, B72-0003, Box 3, File 1, "Fur Trade Is Origin of Many Institutions Peculiar to Canada," *The Globe,* 27 January 1930; "Importance of Fur in Canada Outlined," *Montreal Gazette,* 27 January 1930.

86 UTA, Innis Papers, B72-0003, Box 3, File 1, "Says Fur Trade Made For Canadian Unity," *Toronto Star*, 25 January 1930.

87 This perspective contrasts markedly to the one taken in a short primer on the modern trade published on the basis of a series of research papers written by his students as *The Fur Trade of Canada* (Toronto: University of Toronto Library, 1927).

88 Harold Innis, "A Trip Through the Mackenzie River Basin." The article contains a picture of the *Liard River* and refers to it once, but does not give the impression that Innis took passage on it.

89 UTA, Innis Papers, B72-0003, Box 3, File 1. This article was printed twice, it would appear, once under the title "From the Classroom He Ranges Far North," presumably in 1929, although no date or paper title is listed; and again five years later as Henry Lynne-Folk, "Professor-Explorer Ranges Far Afield in Chosen Work," *Ottawa Citizen*, 3 March 1934.

90 Ibid.

91 Harold Innis, "A Trip Through the Mackenzie River Basin," 151.

92 Ibid.

93 Harold Innis, *The Fur Trade in Canada: An Introduction to Canadian Economic History* (New Haven: Yale University Press, 1930), 4.

94 Berger, *Canadian History*, 93; Daniel Drache, "Celebrating Innis: The Man, The Legacy and Our Future," in Harold A. Innis, *Staples, Markets and Cultural Change: Selected Essays* ed. Daniel Drache (Montreal and Kingston: McGill-Queen's Press, 1995), xxix.

95 See, for example, *The Fur Trade in Canada* and *Settlement and the Mining Frontier* (Toronto: Macmillan, 1936).

96 Harold Innis, "The Hudson Bay Railway," *Geographical Review* XX.1 (January 1930): 1–30; "The Canadian North," *University of Toronto Monthly* XXX (January 1930): 163–168. "Economics of the Hudson Bay Railway," *The Canadian Engineer* (25 November 1930): 659–60; "The Engineer and the Hudson Bay Railway," *Canadian Railway and Marine World* 34 (April 1931): 224; "The Canadian North," in *Problems of Staple Production in Canada* (Toronto: Ryerson Press, 1933). A number of the speaking engagements noted above concerned the Hudson Bay Railway.

97 Harold Innis, "The Canadian North" (1930), 168.

98 Ibid. 167.

99 Creighton, *Harold Adams Innis: Portrait of a Scholar*, 69–70.

100 UTA, Department of Political Economy Papers, Box 2, File 14, Innis to J.P. Crysdale, Cochran Hay & Co. Ltd., 13 December 1926; *Ibid*.

101 John Watson, "Marginal Man: Harold Innis' Communication Work in Context," PhD thesis (Toronto: University of Toronto, 1981), 219.

102 UTA, Presidential Papers (Falconer), A67-0007, Box 120, Innis to Falconer, 15 November 1929.

103 UTA, Presidential Papers (Falconer), A67-0007, Box 120, Falconer to Innis, 14 November 1929; Falconer to Innis, 19 November 1929; Falconer to Innis, 18 January 1930; Innis to Falconer, 6 February 1930; Innis to Falconer, 3 April 1930; Falconer to Innis 7 April 1930; Innis to Falconer, 29 April 1930; Innis to Falconer, 2 May 1930; Falconer to Innis, 3 June 1930; Innis to Falconer, 19 June 1930. The paper presented to the International Geographical Congress was later published as "The Canadian North" in *Problems of Staples Production in Canada*. For an account of Taylor's life, see Marie Sanderson, *Griffith Taylor, Arctic Scientist and Pioneer Geographer* (Ottawa: Carleton University Press, 1988).

104 UTA, Presidential Papers (Falconer), A67-0007, Box 120, Falconer to Innis, 7 April 1930; UTA, Innis Family Papers, B91-0029, Box 2, File 3, Innis to Mother and All, 2 February 1930.

105 Watson, "Marginal Man," 218–25.

106 The dispute is partially documented, though with occasionally incorrect dates, in Innis's scrapbook: UTA, Innis Papers, B72-0003, Box 3, File 1.

107 *Financial Post*, 12 August, 1927; *The Globe*, 16 August 1927.

108 Ibid.

109 George Brown, Letter to the Editor, *The Globe*, 19 August 1927. The book under review was Marion Newbigin's *Canada, the Great River, the Lands and the Men* (London: Christophers, 1927). The review was published in the *Canadian Historical Review* VIII.2 (June 1927): 142–44.

110 Harold Innis, Letter to the Editor, *The Globe*, 26 August 1927 (dated 18 August).

111 UTA, Innis Papers, B72-0003, File 1, clipping undated.

112 On the promotion of New Ontario from the late nineteenth century, see: H.V. Nelles, *The Politics of Development: Forests, Mines and Hydro-Electric Power in Ontario, 1849–1941* (Toronto: Macmillan, 1974), 48–62.

113 George Brown, Letter to the Editor, *The Globe*, 19 August 1927. On aspects of the *CHR*'s editorial policy in the 1920s and 1930s, see: Marlene Shore, " 'Remember the Future': The *Canadian Historical Review* and the Discipline of History, 1920–95," *Canadian Historical Review* 76.3 (September 1995): 417–23.

114 Harold Innis, "Economics of the Hudson Bay Railway," *Canadian Engineer* (25 November 1930), 660. The speech was also published in slightly different form as, "The Engineer and the Hudson Bay Railway," *Canadian Railway and Marine World*, April 1931.

115 Harold Innis, "The Hudson Bay Railway," *Geographical Review* XX.1 (January 1930), 30.

116 Innis, *The Fur Trade in Canada*, 397.

117 Innis, "The Hudson Bay Railway," *Geographical Review*; *Settlement and the Mining Frontier*.

118 W.L. Morton quoted in: Ramsay Cook, *The Maple Leaf Forever: Essays on Nationalism and Politics in Canada* (Toronto: Macmillan, 1976), 143.

119 Mark Bassin, "Turner, Solov'ev and the 'Frontier Hypothesis': The Nationalist Signification of Open Spaces," *Journal of Modern History* 65 (September 1993): 473–511.

Introduction to *Myths, Memory, and Lies*

Quebec's Intelligentsia and the Fascist Temptation, 1939–1960

Esther Delisle

The recent history of Quebec resembles a tragicomedy: the manifestations of repressed memory are often comical while the past that is strenuously denied is tragic. A three-and-a-half metre high statue of the late premier Maurice Duplessis, who for sixteen years ran the Province of Quebec, can disappear without a trace, and not even a commission of inquiry can discover its whereabouts. And a world war (the Second) can cover the planet with blood and flames, but no one in Quebec seems to recall it.

At the beginning of the 1960s, the young guard of the Quebec sovereignty movement and the older, federalist guard, together created the myth of the Quiet Revolution and its necessary corollary, the Great Darkness. The former were anxious to dissimulate the extreme right-wing ideological origins of their political views; the latter wanted to forget that in their youth they had shared them. It was an exercise in occultation of the recent past which gave both groups want they wanted. The young sovereigntists could pose as revolutionaries having broken with the clerical obscurantism, while the federalists could pretend that they led the way by their opposition to the Duplessis regime. These two groups are the architects of the official memory of Quebec. Their success is astonishing

when one thinks of the size of the mystification, and can be explained in part by the fact that both the sovereigntists and the federalists had the wind in their sails during the sixties and were settling in to command positions of political and intellectual power. The myths they created and which served them so well would, however, quickly turn into an orthodoxy as "quiet" as it was tenacious.

Viewed from the outside, the generation of René Lévesque and Pierre Elliott Trudeau seems to be a generation that had no youth. But it was not banal to be twenty years old when World War II broke out. What did they think of this conflict without precedent in human history, what were their feelings, which belligerents did they support? Reading the memoirs of Pierre Elliott Trudeau, Gérard Pelletier and Gérard Filion, among other French Canadians promised to prestigious careers, one could conclude that they saw nothing, heard nothing, and said nothing at the time, and that they were only interested in (and marginally, at that) the struggle against conscription. René Lévesque became a war correspondent in Europe, but would lie about some of his activities of that time. It is remarkable to find that both Pierre Elliott Trudeau and René Lévesque express in very similar terms their regret at not having participated in what they perceived as the great adventure of the men of their generation. Nevertheless, there is more to the silence and lies than a simple narcissistic scratch. There is the need to hide positions which the Allied victory made unspeakable. These men would have to forget, and make others forget, their attraction to the siren songs of fascism and dictatorship in the worst cases, and in the best, their lack of opposition to them.

Omission and lies became the principal tools used to conceal the facts of their youth. They were well served in this demeanor by the lessons of their intellectual guide, Lionel Groulx, and of their mentor, André Laurendeau. In his memoirs, Groulx covers the war in but a few pages, an astonishing feat when one thinks of his exalted pre-war pro-Mussolini, pro-fascist tirades, and he clearly shows the way by speaking only of the referendum on conscription and the Bloc Populaire Canadien.

In the same perspective as that adopted by Lionel Groulx, André Laurendeau would write the quintessential tragicomical book, *La crise de la conscription 1942*.[1] In it, trying to justify his lack of criticism of the Vichy regime, he resorts to lying absurdly, pretending to have been ignorant of the conditions of life in occupied France. Laurendeau then appropriates the drama of which he is apparently ignorant and writes, quite seriously, that Québec also sank beneath the fascist yoke during these terrible years. In the words of this able magician, Canadian Prime Minister William Lyon Mackenzie King takes on the role of "führer" or "il duce," and Adélard Godbout (premier of Quebec) has the attributes of a "collaborator." Of which abominable crime were these two guilty? According to Laurendeau, it was nothing less grave than legalizing a system of universal unemployment insurance. While the poor Europeans were shaking at the thought the Gestapo might come knocking at midnight in their occupied lands,

Quebeckers were apparently trembling at the mere thought that an unemployment insurance cheque might show up in their mail boxes! Different countries, different fears, one must believe! Laurendeau became less and less rational as the years went by, saying to the national convention of the Bloc Populaire Canadien on February 4, 1944: "This meeting is taking place in tragic circumstances, in the middle of a war that has sown disorder, misery and death."[2]

There is something indecent in the appropriation of the misfortunes of others, all the more so when one also supports the agent of their ills. In the same year of 1944, the same André Laurendeau harangued the masses, pushing for a National and Social regime for the Province of Quebec which would free it from the nightmare of the parliamentary system and give due punishment to its politicians. The use of the expression "National and Social" regime (as in National Socialism), pronounced in 1944 only a few short months before the Normandy invasion, is hardly innocent, especially when it comes from the lips of a political leader who was the head of a nationalist magazine, a man who had lived for some years in France during the crucial 1930s. The journal of the Bloc Populaire Canadien, of which he was secretary, overflowed with admiration for the Portuguese dictator Salazar, and described the war as the work of the Anglos and the "kikes." Can we believe that Laurendeau never read the publications of his own political party? More credible is another explanation, that the people who joined the ranks of the Bloc Populaire Canadien, motivated by their hatred of the old parties and by their nationalism much more than by simple opposition to conscription, were not mistaken in choosing a party that had a similar agenda. In fact, the Bloc Populaire Canadien was founded after the referendum on conscription, which clearly shows it had other fish to fry. The truth of the matter is that Laurendeau would use the war to renew the fascist convictions of his youth, if in fact he had ever abandoned them in the first place.

By characterising the conscription issue as the principal, if not the only one surrounding World War II that concerned French Canadians, Laurendeau penned the fable around which would crystallise Quebec's historical memory. But he himself was not taken in by his own mystification. "In the full and formal sense, there was no conscription: was this long debate only in fact a sinister joke?"[3] he asks at the conclusion of *La crise de la conscription 1942*. Moreover, the book itself came out in 1962, at the very moment when the myths of the Quiet Revolution and the Great Darkness were being written. The mystification would be endorsed by older federalists about to become ministers in Ottawa and by the nationalist young Turks who believed they were moving in for good in the citadels of the provincial state and of the universities of Quebec. In their hasty attempts to recast a pure past for themselves and for the nation, their view of the conscription crisis quickly acquired the status of dogma. André Laurendeau, showing great prowess at conjuring information became, unsurprisingly, a political icon whose popularity was high in both camps.

But what were the noteworthy from the *Ligue pour la Défense du Canada* and the *Bloc Populaire Canadien* up to during the war, whenever they had a few minutes to spare from their noble combat against conscription? The archives of the State Department in Washington and the Royal Canadian Mounted Police in Ottawa offer a partial response to the question. We learn from the reports to the State Department of Rollin R. Winslow, American consul in Quebec City, that two young men, hardly twenty years old, were arrested in March 1942 for distributing Nazi propaganda. Raymond Chouinard and Lauréat Tardif belonged to a subversive clandestine organization with a sinister, evocative name: The Iron Guard. Documents seized at Tardif's home by the RCMP revealed that he and his accomplice were but the small fry in a movement run by some of the most eminent nationalist figures of the time: Lionel Groulx, Philippe Hamel, René Chaloult, Oscar Drouin and Paul Gouin, among others.

Raymond Chouinard explained to an RCMP agent that financing The Iron Guard posed no problem until the USA entered the war. From that time on, young Chouinard confessed, things became more difficult, but the organization was still able to obtain the funds it required. This information suggests that The Iron Guard was financed by a foreign power, and in fact the address book belonging to Lauréat Tardif contained the names and addresses of many foreign individuals and organizations. Among them was Eugène Deloncle, a former member of *l'Action française* and a highly-placed partisan of the Nazi order in occupied France who founded the *Mouvement Social Révolutionnaire* during the war in order to put his convictions into violent practice.

These activities took place on a background of Radio-Vichy and Radio-Paris short-wave radio broadcasts, easily captured in Quebec, which announced the progress in the struggle to eliminate the Jews of Europe, bragged of the formation of a chaste and virtuous youth under the guidance of Marshal Pétain and his National Revolution and constantly denounced an England rotted to the core by the bankers and consumed by its imperialist ambitions in Europe. Messages also travelled back the other way. Radio-Algiers reported the words of the rector of the Université de Montréal, Mgr. Olivier Maurault, who announced the news of the creation of the *Ligue pour la Défense du Canada* and who reminded listeners in the same breath that in 1942, France and Quebec shared the same ideals, more so than ever. It is certainly not by chance that during this period the American consul Winslow observed a rekindling of fervour for Laurentia (an idealized kind of independent Province of Quebec governed by a dictatorial regime) and for its unofficial flag, the Carillon.

Winslow and other observers feared the creation of an independent French-Canadian state modelled on European extreme right-wing or fascist regimes. It is more reasonable to believe that Groulx and his acolytes would only have been able to take power as Pétain had: in the suitcase of an invader. Winslow also believed that the Province of Quebec constituted a danger for the security of the North American continent, probably an unfounded conclusion. The consul's anxious exaggerations, however, do not mean that the currents he described did not exist in fact, nor that the acts and the activities of the people he observed did not take place. His interpretation of events, while interesting, was not necessarily exact and just.

In any event, it is very interesting to observe the consul at work. He had at his disposal a variety of means he could use to unmask spies and to obtain information on people suspected of being hostile to the Allied cause. Even J. Edgar Hoover, director of the Federal Bureau of Investigation, got involved: a reading of his agents' reports throws some light on the agency's procedures.

The fact that the partisans of Laurentia and Vichy were in many cases the same persons who welcomed and defended the French Nazi collaborators who sought refuge in the Province of Quebec after the war tends to confirm Winslow's interpretation of wartime Quebec nationalism.

During the war, these Frenchmen joined the ranks of the Militia run by Joseph Darnand, and swore to fight against "democracy, Jewish leprosy and dissident Gaullism." They were judged in absentia by the French courts established after liberation, and given various sentences, from death to loss of citizenship. In every case, their property was also confiscated. They hid in monasteries, obtained false papers and French Government Orders of Mission

and/or received Canadian visas at the Canadian Embassy in Paris. Not just anybody had the connections to obtain these "Orders of Mission," nor for that matter the means to defray the cost of crossing the Atlantic. Where, one wonders, did they find the money needed to come to [Canada]? Some possessed French passports with consecutive serial numbers, all illegally issued by a single prefecture of police. Others, unable to find their way to such "collaborative" prefectures, somehow received passports from the Order of Malta, made out in the name of fictitious persons.

It is difficult not to conclude that some well-placed persons in the upper echelons of the French state apparatus facilitated the post-war evasion of these fleeing militiamen. Worse: when their situation became tenuous in Canada, the government of France never officially requested the extradition of the condemned collaborators, and the French Minister of Justice proved unwilling to forward to the Government of Canada the information it had requested concerning these war criminals who had entered the country illegally. If the French government or its officers did not actively assist their clandestine departure from France, it was now clear that there was obviously no wish to bring these collaborators back to face justice in their own country.

In almost every case, their narrow exit channel would flow through the Canadian Embassy in Paris, which issued them entry visas. General Georges Vanier was then ambassador of Canada in France; his biographer and his wife recount the events as they took place in almost identical terms, with one important exception: Pauline Vanier gives herself the role that Robert Speaight maintains was played by her husband. According to their story, a number of people came to the embassy in Paris on an emergency basis, proclaimed their innocence to Georges or Pauline Vanier and asked for their assistance in escaping France. The names of the fleeing collaborators were submitted to French Justice

Minister Pierre-Henri Teitgen, who made enquiries and gave recommendations to one Vanier or the other. Canadian visas were then promptly issued to the innocent, while those guilty of minor offenses were advised to turn themselves in to the French authorities. Parties guilty of grave crimes were told that it would be better for them to hide for the time being. Pauline Vanier admits that the handling of the case of Jacques de Bernonville was a serious blunder. It is difficult to swallow the affirmation that an inquiry led by the French Justice Minister did not come up with the fact that Bernonville was (among other claims to infamy) military governor of Lyon, a superior of Paul Touvier and a member of the Waffen SS. Many hypotheses are possible in this affair: Teitgen was misinformed and in turn, misinformed ambassador Vanier; Teitgen knew the truth about Jacques de Bernonville and lied to the Vaniers; or, Teitgen knew the truth and so informed the Canadian ambassador, who under political or personal pressure, admitted Bernonville to Canada despite his crimes.

Another interesting case concerned a Doctor Michel-Lucien Seigneur, 42 years old, an important militiaman in the Vienne region of France. If the French Justice Minister was ever in fact consulted about this man, the inquiries made were of necessity quite lax. Using the assumed name of Vincent Desgarets, Seigneur obtained a student visa to pursue his studies at Montreal's Collège Stanislas, a private and well-known high school! It is frankly incredible that such an absurdity would not have been noticed by Vanier. In addition, Michel-Lucien Seigneur, like a number of other refugee claimants who knocked at the embassy's door, had been hidden at the Château d'Ars, and like the others, assumed the name of the lords of the manor which gave them refuge. This entire operation just could not have been conducted without the approval, be it tacit, of Georges Vanier. Finally, both the wife of

Michel-Lucien Seigneur, Geneviève Seigneur, and Julien Labedan, former militia member condemned to death after the Liberation affirmed in a summer 1984 interview that Georges Vanier simply pretended not to know that their papers were fake.

The reasons that caused General Vanier to facilitate these French militiamen's road to Canada remain obscure. Vanier was a constant supporter of the allied armies throughout the war and showed no sympathy for the Vichy regime, the National Revolution, or Marshal Pétain. Was he continuously duped or misinformed by Pierre-Henri Teitgen, French Minister of Justice, who was his friend? Or, as devout Catholics, were he and his wife showing an obligatory Christian charity by assisting fellow Catholics in trouble, who they believed had been unjustly accused victims of the kangaroo court justice that sprung up in France right after Liberation? Were they pressured by the religious orders who were hiding and protecting these militia members? It is quite remarkable to discover that the Vaniers advised those guilty of grave crimes to hide, rather than give themselves up to the police. In any case, no thought seems to have been given to turning them in to the French police authorities.

From 1946 to 1948, a rag-tag band of Nazi collaborators, French for the most part, arrived in Montreal. Among them were a world-famous writer, a doctor (formerly Vice-Mayor of Annecy and a friend of some very wealthy Americans), a former military governor of Lyon, close to Klaus Barbie and a superior of Paul Touvier, a Radio-Paris journalist, a French Nazi propagandist from *Solidarité française* (one of the principals of the antisemitic movement in the Alsace region before the war) and militiamen protected by a family of manor lords who during the nineteenth century were the protectors of the parish priest of Ars.

In the Montreal area, the doors of the best houses in Outremont and Westmount were flung open to the Nazi collaborators. They were suddenly acclaimed as the real heroes of the war. In Quebec City, some of them were received in the panelled salons of the residences of René Chaloult, Philippe Hamel and Noël and Frédéric Dorion, the very same people who had only recently gaily toasted the Vichy regime with the city's French consul. Out on the town, these collaborators could always find a good table at the celebrated Kerhulu Restaurant, owned by one Joseph Kerhulu, an unconditional supporter of Pétain. Father Simon Arsenault, former director of the newspaper *La Droite* which saw its publication suspended in 1941 by the RCMP, would often join these feasts. American war-time consul Rollin Winslow's suspicions finally found a postwar confirmation in these activities.

These elegant soirées of the "right" crowd would soon be unfortunately disrupted when five former French militiamen, instead of their anticipated Canadian residence visas, were served with deportation orders. A street-fighter's trench war ensued, between the federal government and the defenders of the collaborators; in the end, four of the five fugitives were allowed to remain in Canada. It is worth noting however, that the group of fugitives who had arrived from the Ars Château were never bothered by Canadian immigration authorities, and none of them would ever receive deportation advices.

Through their defence of the French collaborators, René Chaloult, the Dorion brothers, Philippe Hamel, André Laurendeau and Robert Rumilly exposed their pro-Pétain, even fascist convictions, convictions apparently not curtailed by the Allied victory. A curious re-writing of history began to come to light: according to André Laurendeau and Philippe Hamel, it was Poland, destroyed by the Nazi blitzkrieg which found itself in the box of the accused, for having been too intransigent towards Hitler, who really had no other option but to attack, thus provoking the worldwide conflagration. Mindlessly repeat-

ing the ideological clichés of the Révolution Nationale so dear to Pétain, the fumbling Quebec defenders of the exiled collaborators lashed out at the Jews, the Communists and the fanatical Anglophiles who had it in for their protegés here and in France. André Laurendeau was aware of the contents of the police file concerning Bernonville; one would hardly suspect it from the way he supported this war criminal in the pages of *Le Devoir*. Philippe Hamel, for his part, wasted no time in rushing to the defence of Maurice Bardèche, the brother-in-law of Robert Brasillach, a man who had been the secretary of the publication *Je suis partout* and an unrepentant fascist, who was having problems, not surprisingly, with French justice.

Prime Minister Louis St. Laurent appeared reticent to become publicly involved in the business of the refugee war criminals in exile in the Province of Québec. He bent in the face of the combined pressure of French and Canadian prelates, of Quebec public opinion and of immediate political imperatives. After all, on the eve of the June 1949 federal elections, what good could possibly come from alienating all those devout and opinionated voters, especially since *Le Devoir* and Robert Rumilly did not conceal their intentions of using that particular card in the defence of the collaborators. Still, the question of who exactly protected these illegal immigrants who were never bothered by Canadian authorities remains open. As time went by, for example, the members of the Château d'Ars-sur-Formans group all abandoned the Desgarets pseudonym and began to use their real names in order to legalize their status in Canada. Their true identities were then out in the open, so why was there no attempt made to deport them? Another question with no answer, as yet: why were the contents of the criminal file on Jacques de Bernonville never fully revealed in public? On June 5 and 6, 1951, Immigration Minister W.E. Harris swore under oath that the contents of the file were a state secret and refused to divulge its contents in a Montreal Superior Court. To this day, we still do not know the precise and complete nature of the information in that dossier.

Then there is the case of Paul Erwin Eberhard Reifenrath, alias Paul-Éverard Richemont, alias Paul Dumont, alias Paul Leyzen, alias Paul Chambord, alias Tonton, who never tried to acquire permanent residency in Canada. It didn't stop him from becoming the personal and confidential ambassador to the Vatican of the premier of Quebec, Maurice Duplessis. A Nazi propagandist in war-time France, Paul Reifenrath arrived in Quebec after the war using the name Paul Leyzen. He then assumed the name Paul-Éverard Richemont and quickly became associated with the *Association professionnelle des industriels (API)* and Maurice Duplessis in their struggle against the Communists, the Jews, the Freemasons, the Christian democrats and all the other "subversive elements at work in the world and in the province." The role Richemont played as a paid Duplessis propagandist during the famous asbestos strike shows him in a different light than the one generally presented by historiography. Duplessis responded to this labour conflict by launching an ideological war that took no prisoners and gave no quarter, aiming to eliminate once and for all the subversive threat as he saw it in the above description. As the many-tentacled beast reached even into the very heart of the Vatican, according to Duplessis, he decided to send Richemont to Rome in order to throttle it. As Duplessis saw it, if a cat's paw segment of the Church in Quebec supported the asbestos miners' strike and lobbied the Vatican to denounce the collusion of the provincial government with the mining companies, the true puppet masters were surely those subversives hiding as much over there as right here in Quebec. Richemont's stay in Rome would be a lengthy one, and he tirelessly sought support for Duplessis from whichever cardinal who would

listen to him. In the *Bulletin de Custos* that Richemont edited in Rome, he portrayed Duplessis as the Franco du Nord and the head of the "only Catholic government in North America," a phrase coined by Duplessis himself.

The astonishing thing about the propaganda penned by Richemont and his acolytes, be it in the Custos Report, the *Bulletin de Custos* or the diatribes of On. Lezaura, is its crude nature. Crude, first and foremost, was their methodology, for who would take seriously their articles signed with obvious pseudonyms, quoting anonymous sources? The arguments they used were equally simple-minded: the Comintern was controlling the asbestos strikers, and the Jews, in cahoots with Christian democrats were dragging the world down to ruin, and so forth and so on. That the premier of the province and eminent members of the clergy were content with such vulgar propaganda is stupefying. Our astonishment though, is tempered by the knowledge of the crude, virulent and vulgar antisemitism of *Le Devoir* during the thirties, which was also published using patently unbelievable pseudonyms. That the same tired methods were used over and over from one decade to the next still provides researchers with some surprises, not the least of which is to see how a third-rate Nazi propagandist and illegal alien could gain direct access to the cabinet of the premier of Québec.

Duplessis belonged to an icon of accepted dogma, the Great Darkness, and as such, was classified and any contradictory information consigned to dusty archives. His statue remained hidden for 16 years until, in 1977, the Parti Québécois erected it in a grand ceremony in front of the National Assembly in Quebec. The dignitaries invited to the event represented the mainstream of provincial politics: the Parti Québécois, Liberals, and Union Nationale all attended. On a cold and grey November morning, the children of the Quiet Revolution all recognized the Duplessis in themselves and in close ranks, formed a true "national union." They celebrated his defence of provincial autonomy and excused his dictatorial regime. One notable difference did separate the father from the children, though. In a break with the past the Union Nationale party name no longer referred to a political ideology but to the Nation, without, however, overtly naming it. The Parti Québécois, going a step further on the path opened by the Union Nationale, chose an ethnic denomination. Thus, while the Great Darkness put the idea of a nation on the political agenda, the Quiet Revolution, named it without defining it but rendered it exclusivist all the same.

Of course, this does not in any way mean that the Parti Québécois presented a clear political option. Many competing formulas were proposed, such as sovereignty, sovereignty-association, independence, autonomy, last-chance federalism, to name only a few, some even at one and the same time. Not wanting to be left in their dust, the political adversaries of the Parti Québécois came up with their own abstruse proposals: cultural sovereignty, special status, renewed federalism, asymmetric federalism, etc. During the sixties, the constitutional status of Quebec became a hive of business for a great number of francophone intellectuals and politicians, and for a surprising number of anglophones. Media access was virtually guaranteed to anyone with a word or two to say on the question, as long as they showed the serious demeanor the subject called for.

But the blush on the rose of the sixties has long since faded. The young sovereigntist rebels of that time now see the spectre of retirement approaching at a brisk clip; for some, the rubicon has already been crossed. But they want one last kick at the can before they go. The trouble is, they never stop kicking, and worse, they have taken on the pontificating tone of the priests who educated them and against whom they had the illusion of having rebelled. Their federalist elders, somewhat more on in years, see their

ranks dwindling ineluctably, but never miss a chance to valiantly sing the old refrain whenever an opportunity presents itself.

On the eve on the new millennium, it is clear that the fables and the myths of the Quiet Revolution have long since become an orthodoxy riddled with dogma and hackneyed tales that even those who spout them no longer believe. But what thinking person would voluntarily relinquish such a lucrative trademark? The fables of the Quiet Revolution and the constitutional three-ring circus ensured the successful careers of a whole class of bureaucrats, intellectuals and politicians, who had no interest in considering other interpretations of history nor other political agendas. Their dust-covered orthodoxy now shivers with mean-spiritedness, and sees in any new idea a threat to its monopoly of the truth and to the fortunes of those whose interest it defends. Cringing, it fears for the future, and lashes out at those who challenge its tenets, like all orthodoxies that have run out of breath.

This behaviour resembles that of the Roman Catholic Church in the two decades before Vatican II. The Holy See had so often thundered against any heterodox idea that the simple mention of its name sufficed to gag any potential audacious spirit. In Quebec, the clergy rivalled the Holy See in its zeal, abusing its power so flagrantly that it looks comical in today's light. While the excommunications spewed in all directions and the speeches flew fast and furious, opposing currents of thought grew in influence until the day when Vatican II sounded the death knell of a power that its tenants had thought eternal. The triumphant trumpet call usually signals nothing more than the beginning of defeat.

According to an unwritten but implacable law of historical research, the historian often finds something quite different from what he or she was looking for. But this "something else" is more interesting than what the researcher was hoping to find. For example, I went looking for traces of collaborators exiled in Canada in the American National Archives, but came up empty-handed. However, I did discover the existence of a nestful of spies and fascist sympathizers in Quebec City that was reported by the American consul, Rollin R. Winslow, and this discovery formed the basis for *Sleepless in Quebec City*. The other chapters in the book *Sounds of Silence, A Tale of Two Statues* and *Loony Tunes,* were written to order for academic journals. University publication being what it is, *Sounds* was not accepted because it was deemed too tract-like, with an "anti-scientific, polemical" tone where "gratuitous and unfounded affirmations ran rampant," the second was accepted but the special issue of the review in which it was to appear was pulled from publication sine die. As for *Loony Tunes,* it appeared in the distant and solicitous down under, in Australia, where a few hardy souls yet study the affairs of our nation.

Notes

1   André Laurendeau, *La crise de la conscription 1942,* Éditions du Jour, Montréal, 1962.

2   *Le Devoir,* 4 February 1944.

3   André Laurendeau, *op. cit.,* p. 155.

Staring into the Abyss

J. L. GRANATSTEIN

"History repeats itself." That is a popular view of the past, but it is not, I suspect, a view shared by most historians. The differences in personalities, in context, in subtleties and shadings usually combine to persuade historians that the crisis of one decade or century is different in class and kind from that of another. But, sometimes, history really does seem to repeat itself.

In the First World War, as we have seen, the United Kingdom's weakened financial condition led Whitehall to pressure Canada to turn to the United States to raise money. At the same time, Britain proved unable or unwilling to take all the food and munitions produced by Canada unless Ottawa picked up a greater share of the costs, and the Canadian government had little choice other than to agree. In an effort, both politically and economically inspired, to keep munitions factories working at full blast in Canada, the Imperial Munitions Board, a Canadian-operated imperial procurement and production agency, actively sought contracts from the U.S. War Department. At the same time, other arms of the Canadian government lobbied in Washington to get their share of scarce raw materials. The net effect of the First World War on Canadian-American relations was to strengthen the links across the border and to increase the number and complexity of the ties of economics, politics, and sentiment that bound the two North American nations together. The defeat of reciprocity in the 1911 election, therefore, seemed only a temporary check, one virtually nullified by the greater necessity of wartime integration and cooperation.

It should have been no surprise, then, that Canada entered the 1920s with Conservative Prime Minister Arthur Meighen urging Britain to seek an accommodation with the United States and not to renew the Anglo-Japanese Alliance.[1] Nor was it a surprise that Canada welcomed more investment from the United States while, despite repeated efforts by the Liberal governments of Mackenzie King to enhance trade with the United Kingdom, its commerce with its neighbour continued to increase.[2] The Great Depression and the massive increases in the American tariff put in place by a protectionist Congress and then matched by Canadian governments, however, temporarily cut into Canadian-American trade.

While these restrictions led many Canadians to look overseas with renewed imperial fervour, some Britons nonetheless feared for Canada's survival as a British nation in the face of the power of the United States. One example of the first tendency was Harry Stevens, soon to be minister of trade and commerce in R.B. Bennett's government, who told the voters in 1930 that "My ambition for Canada is that she may become a unit of the Empire and concerned not with a few petty tariff items, but with all the great problems confronting the Home Government." No worse fate could have befallen Canadians! In contrast, Leo Amery, the dominions secretary in 1928, returned from a trip to Canada worried that "the din and glare of

J.L. Granatstein, "Staring into the Abyss," in *How Britain's Weakness Forced Canada into the Arms of the United States* (Toronto: University of Toronto Press, 1989), 21–40. Reprinted by permission of the author.

the great American orchestra" might drown out Canada. His hopes were bolstered, however, by the conviction that there was "no deeper fundamental instinct of the Canadian national character than dislike of the United States as belonging to an inferior political civilisation."[3] For their part, officials of the United States government, as Peter Kasurak has noted, began "from a single point of view in the area of Canadian affairs—fear that Britain was forging its Empire into an international colossus which would dominate world trade."[4] To Washington, that fear seemed to be realized after the Ottawa Conference of 1932.[5]

But not even the Imperial Economic Conference and the imperial preferences agreed on at Ottawa could truly reverse the historic trend towards North American continentalism that had accelerated during the Great War. The two "hermit kingdoms," to use Charles Stacey's phrase uttered from this platform a dozen years ago,[6] had a great deal in common in an era when British trade as a percentage of world trade continued its decline and Britain's overall military power ebbed. Mackenzie King had begun the transformation of the empire into the Commonwealth during the Chanak affair of 1922 and at the Imperial Conference of 1923, where "the decisive nature of the English defeat at Mackenzie King's hands" was nothing less than a "surrender, which changed the course of the history of the empire."[7] Those apocalyptic phrases were the considered judgment of Correlli Barnett, "the Jeremiah of British historians," or so Noel Annan has recently called him.[8] They sound very similar in tone to the words of Donald Creighton, the Jeremiah of Canadian historians, who wrote that King, "a stocky barrel-like figure, with an audible wheeze when in full voice," was no "bulky St. George confronting a slavering imperial dragon." He was "a citizen of North America...determined to destroy" the Commonwealth.[9]

When Mackenzie King came back to power in the middle of the Great Depression in 1935,

the Ottawa agreements had demonstrably not restored Canada's economic health. Prime Minister Bennett had seemingly recognized the failure of the imperial initiative by launching his own somewhat desultory efforts to strike a trade agreement with Washington, but his attempt at an accommodation with the United States could not come to fruition before the voters eagerly dispensed with the Tory government's services.[10] It fell to the new prime minister, choosing what he described to the United States minister in Canada as "the American road," to negotiate that trade agreement with the Roosevelt administration.[11] Mackenzie King reinforced it with another trade pact with the United States three years later.[12] Simultaneously, King and his advisers in the Department of External Affairs looked with dismay at the wide-ranging rivalry between London and Washington, most pronounced in the Pacific where the two English-speaking powers jostled for economic and political dominance with each other and an aggressive Japan. Conflict between Canada's mother country and its nearest neighbour held out only the prospect of terrible divisiveness in Canada.[13] Nonetheless, the prime minister gladly accepted and immediately reciprocated President Franklin Roosevelt's assurances, delivered at Queen's University in Kingston on 18 August 1938, "that the people of the United States will not stand idly by" if Canada were ever threatened.[14] That guarantee had to be called upon just two years later.

By 1939, as the Nazis prepared to plunge Europe into the war that was to ensure America's half century of world economic hegemony, U.S. companies and investors and the American market had already established their pre-eminence in Canada. The United States provided 60 per cent of the foreign capital invested in Canada while British sources put up only 36 per cent. In 1914 the figures had been 23 and 72 per cent, respectively. In terms of Canadian exports, shipments to the United States in 1939 exceeded those to

Britain by 20 per cent; in 1914 exports to Britain had been 10 per cent higher than those to the United States. Similarly, in 1914 Canada had imported three times as much from the United States as from the United Kingdom; in 1939 Canada imported four times as much.[15] The years of the Great War had provided the impetus for Canada's shift from the British to the American economic sphere.

During the Second World War, the events of the Great War were repeated with a stunning similarity. To be sure, different men from different political parties were in charge in Canada. Mackenzie King, that most unadmired of Canadian leaders, was at the helm in Ottawa, and his attitudes and prejudices were certainly far different from those of Sir Robert Borden.

Ramsay Cook predicted almost two decades ago that King was certain to become the subject of a book of readings for students under the title "Mackenzie King: Hero or Fink?" Cook knew that the fink side of the debate would be easy to document. He suggested that King had become the central figure in the Canadian mythology, the most convenient one of all, because he was the "cause of all our failings," including the decline and fall of the British Empire in Canada.[16] Cook was certainly correct in assessing the little man's place, and few have yet come forward to argue that Mackenzie King was a great Canadian hero. Charles Stacey, in the last words of his Joanne Goodman lectures in 1976, however, did say—and I expect he was only half-jesting—that he would "not be altogether surprised if he turned up, one of these days, as the patron saint of the new nationalism."[17]

Still, King is difficult to elevate to sainthood. Even (or especially) those who observed or worked intimately with him had scant admiration for him. Tom Blacklock, a Press Gallery member in the 1920s, complained that King was "such a pompous ass that an orang-outang that would flatter him could choose its own reward."[18] Leonard Brockington wrote speeches

for King for a time during the early years of the Second World War, and when he quit in exasperation he told a friend that he was "sick and tired of being mid-wife to an intellectual virgin."[19] Senator Norman Lambert ran elections for the Liberal leader, and Mackenzie King gratefully elevated him to the Upper Chamber. Nonetheless, Lambert told Grant Dexter of the *Winnipeg Free Press* that "he simply can't stand the worm at close quarters—bad breath, a fetid, unhealthy, sinister atmosphere like living close to some filthy object... But," the senator added, "get off a piece and he looks better and better."[20]

That last comment on Mackenzie King I have always thought the nearly definitive one. Up close, there was little that was admirable about the Liberal leader, much that was slippery and sleazy. But acquire some distance, get off a piece, as Lambert said, and the dumpy little laird of Kingsmere—and Canada—began to look not unlike a giant. To bring us back to Earth, I might point out that the fine Canadian novelist Hugh Hood has his main character in *The Swing in the Garden* note, "I think always of W.C. Fields when I think of Mackenzie King."[21] That may be *the* definitive description.

I have no intention of trying to paint Mackenzie King as a super-hero here, though, despite years of reading Donald Creighton and W.L. Morton, I cannot yet bring myself to see him as a filthy object or even as a fink. For me, the crucial factor in assessing the common charge that Mackenzie King sold us out to the Americans is that the prime minister during the Second World War faced similar, but greater, problems to those Sir Robert Borden had had to confront a quarter century before. But though he had more resources at his disposal than his predecessor in the Prime Minister's Office, King had no greater freedom of action when British military and economic weakness forced his country into grave difficulties. When it came to directing the weak corner of the North Atlantic Triangle in its efforts to stay safe and secure in a world suddenly unstable, King, much like Borden before him, had to turn to the United States for assistance.

One major factor was different in the Second World War. In the Great War, Britain and France lost battles but they did not suffer catastrophic defeats that placed their survival as nation-states at stake. In May and June 1940, of course, Hitler's astonishingly effective armies defeated Britain and France in the Low Countries and in France, the French capitulated, and the British Army, without equipment, found its way home thanks only to a miracle at Dunkirk.

For Canada in that terrible summer of defeat and despair, the changes in the military balance of power were catastrophic. The country had gone to war with the idea that it could fight as a junior partner with "limited liability." The government had hoped that its war effort could be small, balanced, and relatively cheap, and Quebec and the country had been promised that there would be no conscription for overseas service. Now, the planning of late 1939 had to be scrapped. Canada, with its population of eleven million and suddenly Britain's ranking ally, was in the war to the utmost—except for conscription, which was still politically unacceptable. Moreover, a huge proportion of this country's under-equipped and partially trained air, army, and naval forces was already in the United Kingdom, and if—or when—Britain fell they were certain to be completely lost. The Royal Navy had its hands full in trying to protect home waters and block the expected Nazi invasion. The aircraft necessary to operate the centrepiece of the Canadian war effort, the British Commonwealth Air Training Plan, had been scheduled to come from Great Britain, but now would not arrive. If Britain fell and, especially, if the Royal Navy passed into German hands, Canada was likely to be subject to Nazi attack.[22] Britain's military weakness in July and August 1940 was exposed for all to see; so too was Canada's.[23]

The military weakness of the United States was also apparent, but there can be no doubt that President Franklin Roosevelt's country was the only hope of the Allies—and of Canada. Many in Canada recognized this truth in the days after Dunkirk, and they realized the new obligations this would force on the dominion. Donald Creighton, writing years later, noted that for many Canadians—and he had his despised colleague Frank Underhill in mind—the war's course "hastened the growth" of Canada's "new North American nationality by proving that...Great Britain...could no longer act as Canada's main defence against danger from abroad."[24]

At the time, the bureaucratic response to the new state of affairs came from Hugh Keenleyside of the Department of External Affairs, who set out the fullest statement of the likely Canadian situation as France surrendered to Hitler. It was improbable, he wrote, that the United States would protect Canada without "demanding a measure of active cooperation in return. It is a reasonable expectation that the United States will expect, and if necessary demand, Canadian assistance in the defence of this continent and this Hemisphere." Canada, he noted, would feel some obligation to participate; "thus the negotiation of a specific offensive-defensive alliance is likely to become inevitable."[25]

President Roosevelt himself was thinking along these lines. In August, Loring Christie, the Canadian minister in Washington, reported to Mackenzie King that the president "had been thinking of proposing to you to send to Ottawa 3 staff officers...to discuss defence problems... He had in mind their surveying [the] situation from [the] Bay of Fundy around to the Gulf of St. Lawrence. They might explore [the] question of base facilities for United States use."[26] But on 16 August Roosevelt asked King to meet him at Ogdensburg, NY, the next day to discuss "the matter of [the] mutual defence of our coasts on the Atlantic."[27]

What the president wanted was the creation of a Permanent Joint Board on Defence with equal representation from each country and a mandate limited to the study of common defence problems and the making of recommendations to both governments on how to resolve them. Delighted at the prospect of forging a military alliance with the United States, King queried only Roosevelt's desire that the board be "permanent." "I said I was not questioning the wisdom of it," King noted, "but was anxious to get what he had in mind." According to King's diary, Roosevelt replied that he wanted "to help secure the continent for the future."[28] The Canadian leader sometimes suffered from "the idea," in the superb Australian novelist Thomas Keneally's phrase, "that the only empire you need to suspect is the British."[29] Mackenzie King probably ought to have asked whose empire and whose future, but in August 1940 that question was virtually impossible even to raise—when the fear was that it might be Adolf Hitler's empire and Germany's future if no action were taken.

The decision to create the PJBD was an important one. The board sprang into existence within two weeks and began surveying defences on both the Atlantic and the Pacific coasts. A Joint Canadian-United States Basic Defence Plan, produced by the board's military members, aimed to meet the situation that would arise if Britain were overrun. In that event, strategic control of Canadian forces was to pass to the United States. A second plan, produced in the spring of 1941 and called ABC-22, looked at Canadian-American cooperation in a war in which the United States was actively engaged on the side of the Allies. The Americans again sought strategic control of Canadian forces and to integrate the Canadian east and west coast regions directly into their military commands. It was one thing to agree to American military direction in a war that saw North America standing virtually alone; it was another thing entirely

in a war where Britain remained unoccupied and the United States was a partner. "The American officers," to use Keneally again, "listened...with that omnivorous American politeness...we poor hayseeds would come to know so well and mistrust, perhaps, not enough."[30] Nonetheless, Canada refused to accept Washington's aims for ABC-22 and won its point, thereby demonstrating that Mackenzie King's government could and would fight for its freedom of action.[31] Whether such independence could have survived a German or Japanese invasion happily never had to be tested.

The significance of the PJBD in its context of August 1940 was that a still-neutral United States had struck an alliance with Canada, a belligerent power. That had to be seen as a gain for Britain—and for Canada, too. Important as that was for the war, the true meaning of the Ogdensburg meeting was that it marked Canada's definitive move from the British military sphere to the American. The British had lost whatever capacity they might have had to defend Canada, and, in August 1940, their ability even to defend the British Isles successfully was very much in doubt.[32] In the circumstances, Canada had no choice at all. Canada had to seek help where help was to be found, and that meant Washington.

Few people truly realized the significance of the Permanent Joint Board on Defence and the Ogdensburg Agreement that had created it in the summer of 1940. Some Conservatives grumbled at Mackenzie King's actions, former Prime Minister Arthur Meighen being the most caustic. He had noted that "I lost my breakfast when I read the account this morning and gazed on the disgusting picture of these potentates"—that is, King and Roosevelt—"posing like monkeys in the very middle of the blackest crisis of this Empire."[33] Most Tories and almost all the Canadian press showed more sense.[34]

The one critic who shook Mackenzie King, however, was Winston Churchill. The new

British prime minister, in office only since 10 May 1940, had replied to King's telegram on the Ogdensburg meeting by stating "there may be two opinions on some of the points mentioned. Supposing Mr. Hitler cannot invade us...all these transactions will be judged in a mood different to that prevailing while the issue still hangs in the balance."[35] Churchill, disgustedly seeing Canada scurrying for shelter under the eagle's wing, evidently realized that a major shift had occurred. What he would have had Canada do, what he would have done differently had he been Canadian prime minister, was never stated. Certainly he failed to recognize that with its security now guaranteed by the United States, Canada could send every man and weapon possible to defend Britain, something it dutifully and willingly did.

As for me, no matter how often I try to appraise the situation, I cannot see any other option for Mackenzie King. The issue potentially was the survival of the Canadian nation in face of an apparently defeated Great Britain and a victorious Nazi Germany. King did what he had to do to secure Canada's security. The reason Mackenzie King had to strike his arrangement with Roosevelt was the military weakness of Great Britain in the summer of 1940.[36]

The immediate result of the Ogdensburg Agreement was wholly beneficial to Canada and Canadian interests. But we can see now that the long-term implications included the construction of major American installations and the presence in substantial numbers of American troops in the Canadian Northwest from 1942,[37] the 1947 military agreement with the United States that continued joint defence cooperation, the North American Air Defence Agreement of 1957–8, and eventually even Cruise missile testing and the possibility of Star Wars installations in the Canadian North.

Many Canadians may be less than happy with the way matters turned out. In his *Lament for a Nation,* George Grant wrote:

In 1940, it was necessary for Canada to throw in her lot with continental defence. The whole of Eurasia might have fallen into the hands of Germany and Japan. The British Empire was collapsing once and for all as an international force. Canada and the United States of America had to be unequivocally united for the defence of this hemisphere. But it is surprising how little the politicians and officials seem to have realized that this new situation would have to be manipulated with great wisdom if any Canadian independence was to survive. Perhaps nothing could have been done; perhaps the collapse of nineteenth-century Europe automatically entailed the collapse of Canada. Nonetheless, it is extraordinary that King and his associates in External Affairs did not seem to recognize the perilous situation that the new circumstances entailed. In all eras, wise politicians have to play a balancing game. How little the American alliance was balanced by any defence of national independence![38]

Much of Grant's assessment is correct. Certainly, Canada had no choice in August 1940 in the situation in which it found itself. But to me, Mackenzie King's actions in August 1940 were an attempt to protect Canadian independence—and ensure Canada's survival—in a world that had been turned upside down in a few months by the defeat of Britain and France. Grant, writing a quarter century after the event, does not say what King might have done after Ogdensburg to achieve a balance to the American alliance. Nor did Churchill in 1940. In the remainder of this essay, I will try to show how King successfully struggled to preserve at least a measure of financial independence for Canada.

Those who believe, like George Grant and Donald Creighton, that the Ogdensburg Agreement and its aftermath were a virtual sellout to the United States have an obligation to offer an alternative vision. If there was "a forked road" in August 1940 and if Canada went in the wrong direction, where might the other road have led? What should Mackenzie King and his government have done that they did not do? I await the response.

The Ogdensburg Agreement had secured Canada's physical defences, but it had done nothing to resolve the country's economic difficulties. As in the Great War, the problem came about because Canada was caught between a strong United States and its desire to help an economically weak Great Britain. Indeed, Britain was weak. The ambassador in Washington, Lord Lothian, summed it up when he told a group of reporters: "Boys, Britain's broke. It's your money we want."[39] It was soon to be Canada's money that London wanted too.

Britain had begun the war in 1939 convinced that purchases had to be switched away from North America to conserve scarce dollar exchange. That laudable goal threatened Canadian tobacco, fruit, and wheat exports and provoked extraordinary outrage in Ottawa and threats that such a policy might hurt what Mackenzie King delicately called "our ability to render assistance." Similarly, British munitions orders in the Phoney War months were less than expected; that too angered the King government. But the same German victories that forced Canada to seek assistance to the south also obliged London to look to Canada for more—more money, more food, more munitions, more of everything.[40]

By February 1941, therefore, the Department of Finance in Ottawa estimated that the British deficit with Canada was $795 million, an amount that had been covered by transfers of gold, debt repatriation, and a large sterling accumulation in London.[41] Ottawa also predicted that war expenditures for the year would amount to $1.4 billion and that $433 million was needed for civil expenditure. A further $400 million would be required to repatriate additional Canadian securities held in Britain, in

effect a way of giving Britain additional Canadian dollars with which to pay for the goods it bought in Canada. At the same time, the mandarins in Finance estimated that the provincial and municipal governments would spend $575 million for a total governmental expenditure of almost half Canada's Gross National Income.[42] Could the country function, they asked, if half of all production were devoted to government operations?

Historically, Canada's economic position had depended on the maintenance of a "bilateral unbalance within a balanced 'North Atlantic Triangle.'"[43] That meant, in effect, that our chronic trade deficit with the United States was covered by a surplus with Britain. Pounds earned in London were readily converted to American dollars, and thus the bills could be paid. But now sterling was inconvertible, and as Canada built up large balances in London, these could no longer be used to cover the trade deficit with the United States.

Compounding the problem was that as Canada strained to produce greater quantities of war material and food for Britain, more components and raw materials had to be imported from the United States. Every time, for example, that a truck, built in Canada by General Motors or Ford, went to Britain, it contained an imported engine, specialty steels, and a variety of parts brought in from south of the border. Almost a third of the value of a tank, ship, or artillery piece had to be imported. The result was a classic squeeze. Canadian goods went to Great Britain where the British could pay for them only in sterling, which was of little use to Canada outside the British Isles (though we could buy New Zealand lamb or Malayan tin, for example, with it). In effect, Canada was financing the British trade deficit. But at the same time and as a result of war production for Britain, Canadian imports from the United States were expanding rapidly, far more so than exports to the United States. The result was a huge trade deficit with the United States, one that grew worse the more Canada tried to help Britain. In April 1941 Ottawa's estimates of the deficit for that fiscal year were $478 million; by June, officials argued that imports from the United States had risen by $400 million a year while exports to the south had increased by only half that sum.[44]

Canada had been trying to grapple with this problem for some time. Efforts had been made since September 1939 to control foreign exchange, to promote Canada as a tourist mecca for Americans ("Ski in a country at war," the advertisements could have said), and by devaluing the dollar to 90 cents U.S. to restrict imports from and encourage export sales to the United States. Each measure had some positive results, but together they amounted to very little against the flood of components pouring over the border for an expanding war industry. Soon, Ottawa slapped stringent controls on the U.S. dollars Canadian travellers could acquire, and a wide range of import prohibitions were put in place in December 1940 on unnecessary imports. Those measures, strong enough to anger the American government and American exporters, also failed completely to reverse the steady growth in the deficit with the United States.[45]

What else remained? A loan from the United States government? O.D. Skelton, the undersecretary of state for external affairs until his death in January 1941, told Pierrepont Moffat, the very able American minister in Canada, that "it would be disastrous to face a future of making heavy interest payments to the United States year after year in perpetuity, or alternatively having a war debt controversy."[46] Canada was physically too close to the United States to owe debt directly to Washington, or so Skelton and his colleagues in the Ottawa mandarinate believed. What then? Could Canadian investments in the United States, estimated at $275 million to $1 billion in worth, be sold off to raise American dollars? They could, but those

investments cushioned Canada from the strain of her foreign indebtedness, and there were obvious political problems in forcing private investors to sell their holdings at wartime fire-sale prices.[47] That was not a feasible route for the Mackenzie King government.

At this point, the situation altered dramatically. The United States Congress accepted President Roosevelt's proposal for Lend-Lease, a scheme to permit the United States to give the Allies war materiel effectively free of monetary cost, though there were political costs of which the British were all too aware.[48] The initial appropriation accompanying the bill was $7 billion. This was, as Churchill called it, "the most unsordid act," an extraordinarily generous step by the still-neutral United States. But Lend-Lease posed terrible problems for Ottawa. First, the Canadian government did not want to take charity from the United States—"the psychological risk," two historians noted, "of becoming a pensioner of the United States was too great."[49] Second, if Britain could get war materiel from the United States free of charge, what was to happen to the orders it had placed in Canada and for which it had to pay, even if only with inconvertible sterling? C.D. Howe, presiding over Canada's war production as the minister of munitions and supply, told the Cabinet War Committee that he was "gravely concerned" that those orders might be shifted to the United States.[50] If that happened, what would the impact be on Canada's war employment and wartime prosperity? It was the spring of 1917 all over again, and history repeated itself.

The British characteristically and quickly saw the advantages offered by the situation and began to press Canada. Although junior ministers in Churchill's cabinet bemoaned what they saw as Canada's accelerating drift out of the Empire,[51] the hardheaded officials at the Treasury knew what they wanted. Cut purchases of non-essential goods in the United States, Ottawa was told. Accept Lend-Lease. Sell off

Canadian securities held in the United States. Such a regimen meant higher taxes and inflation for the Canadians, the British knew, but as the Treasury officials said, "It is as much in their interests as in ours to act along these lines, seeing that our only alternative, if we are unable to pay for our orders in Canada, is to place them instead in the United States in cases in which we should be able to obtain the goods under the 'Lease and Lend' Act."[52]

Thus Canada's problem. Some way had to be found to keep the British orders, so essential for wartime prosperity, without selling the country lock, stock, and barrel to the United States. Though the Liberal government faced no immediate election, as had Borden in 1917 in similar circumstances, the retention of prosperity was every bit as much a political necessity. At the same time, and again the parallel with Sir Thomas White's refusal to borrow from the U.S. government is clear, the King government was adamant in its refusal to take Lend-Lease. That was little better than a loan and, while relations with Franklin Roosevelt's Washington were very good, no one wanted to be quite so indebted to the great nation with which Canada shared the continent. The Americans, as Clifford Clark, deputy minister of finance, noted fearfully, might later drive a very hard bargain on tariffs.[53] Nonetheless, Canada's trade with the United States somehow had to be brought into balance.

The ideal solution, as Canadian officials came to realize in the spring of 1941, was an arrangement that would see the United States increase its purchases in Canada and, in addition, supply the components and raw materials Canada needed to produce munitions for the United Kingdom. Those components could be charged to Britain's Lend-Lease account, a clever device that could let Canada keep its war economy going at full blast without bankrupting itself in the process. In the meantime, desperate to ensure the continuation of orders in Canada, Ottawa agreed to finance the British deficit with Canada.[54] That was again a repetition of the events of 1917. Though there is no sign in the files that anyone realized this parallel, so too was the Canadian proposal to the United States.

The Hyde Park Declaration, signed by Mackenzie King and Franklin Roosevelt on "a grand Sunday" in April, put the seal on the Canadian proposal. The United States agreed to spend $200–300 million more in Canada, largely for raw materials and aluminum. "Why not buy from Canada as much as Canada is buying from the United States," Mackenzie King said he had told the president, "—just balance the accounts. Roosevelt thought this was a swell idea."[55] In addition, the president agreed that Britain's Lend-Lease account could be charged with the materials and components Canada needed to produce munitions for export.[56] That too dealt the trade deficit a mighty blow.

The declaration signed at Hyde Park was a splendid achievement for Canada. Howe told Mackenzie King that he was "the greatest negotiator the country had or something about being the world's best negotiator," the prime minister recorded.[57] Howe soon created War Supplies Limited, a crown corporation with E.P. Taylor as its head, to sell Canadian-manufactured war equipment and raw materials in the United States.[58]

The Hyde Park Declaration allowed Canada to do its utmost for Britain without fear of financial collapse. Most important, King had won Roosevelt's agreement without having to give up anything tangible—in the short-run. Unlike Great Britain, Canada was not obliged to sell off its investments prior to receiving U.S. aid; nor was Canada to be required to take Lend-Lease, both measures that the government sought to avoid.[59] Knowing that the desperate plight of the British had forced him to seek assistance for Canada from the United States, Mackenzie King had secured that help on the very best terms. For his part, Roosevelt could agree to King's proposals (incidentally, entirely on his own without any consultation with Congress or the State Department) because they cost the United States almost nothing, because he was friendly to Canada, and because he considered that his country's long-term interests would be best served by having an amicable and prosperous Canada on his northern border, a nation tightly linked to the United States. Undoubtedly, Roosevelt was correct. He served his country's interests well.

In retrospect, however, we can see that the inextricable linkages created or strengthened by the Second World War were the key long-term results of the 1941 agreement. The Hyde Park Declaration effectively wiped out the border for war purposes, allowing raw materials to pour south while munitions components came north. To help the war effort, to produce the goods for a desperate Great Britain, Mackenzie King's Canada tied itself to the United States for the war's duration. There is no point in complaining about this almost a half century later. The Hyde Park Declaration was one of many actions that were necessary to win the war against Hitler, and everything done to further that end was proper and right. But neither is there any point in blinking at the facts. Canada tied itself to the United States in 1941, just as it had done in 1917 because Britain was economically weak. That weakness forced Canada to look to Washington for assistance, and the Americans provided it, freely and willingly. It served Washington's interests; it served Canada's immediate interests; above all, it served the cause of victory.

The short-term results of the Hyde Park Declaration were much as the Canadian government had hoped. American purchases in Canada rose rapidly, and Canada's dollar shortage came to an end in 1942; indeed, the next year controls had to be put in place to prevent Canada's holdings of U.S. dollars from growing too large. The wartime prosperity that Hyde Park solidified was such that in 1942 Canada could offer Great Britain a gift of $1 billion, and the next year Canada created a Mutual Aid program that eventually gave Britain an additional $2 billion in munitions and foodstuffs. The total of Canadian aid to Great Britain during the war was $3.468 billion[60]—and a billion then was really worth a billion. That was help to a valued ally and friend, of course, just as much as it was an investment in continued high employment at home. As an official in the Dominions Office in London noted, "Per head of population the Canadian gifts will cost Canada about five times what lend lease costs the United States. Canada's income tax is already as high as ours; it may have to go higher.... Canada is devoting as large a proportion of her national income to defence expenditure as any other country; in no other country is the proportion of defence expenditure which is given away in the form of free supplies anywhere near so high as in Canada."[61] The war had cost Canada about $18 billion, and almost one-fifth of that staggering total was given to Britain in the form of gifts. That Canada could offer such assistance freely was the best proof possible that Mackenzie King's policy in 1941 had been correct and successful.

Still, there can be no doubt that the Hyde Park Declaration reinforced the trends that had begun to take form during the Great War. Some of those were psychological. Two bureaucrats who dealt with the United States regularly during the war had gushed fellowship in an article they published in the *Canadian Journal of Economics and Political Science* at the end of the war. "There has been the open exchange of confidence between the Americans and Canadians, the warm welcome, the freedom from formality, the plain speaking and the all-pervading friendship," Sydney Pierce and A.F.W. Plumptre wrote. This was the result of "our common background of language and culture, and to the close trade and industrial relationship: in part it is due to the fact that our approach to problems is similar."[62] That was all true, too.

Other trends were financial and commercial. By 1945 American investment had risen to 70 per cent of the total foreign capital invested in Canada. Exports to the United States were more than three times what they had been in 1939 and were 25 per cent greater than war-swollen Canadian exports to Britain. Imports from the United States were now ten times those from Britain.[63] The war undoubtedly had distorted Canada's trade figures, but the direction was clear and it would be confirmed by the events of the reconstruction period.

By 1945 Canada was part and parcel of the continental economy. It was a two-way North American street now, and the North Atlantic Triangle, if it still existed at all, was a casualty of the world wars. Despite this, the Canadian government tried desperately, if unsuccessfully, to restore the traditional balance in the postwar years.

Notes

1 See Philip Wigley, *Canada and the Transition to Commonwealth: British-Canadian Relations 1917–1926* (Cambridge 1977), 129ff. D.C. Watt erroneously saw "geographical or racialist factors" responsible for "the pro-American orientation" of Canadian foreign policy, and he argued that British actions here were taken "for the sake of keeping Canada in the Empire." *Succeeding John Bull: America in Britain's Place 1900–1975* (Cambridge 1984), 50, 52.

2 King expressed strong support for the effort to widen imperial preferences at the Imperial Economic Conference of 1923. See R.M. Dawson, *William Lyon Mackenzie King*, vol. I: *A Political Biography 1874–1923* (Toronto 1958), 469ff. The 1930 Liberal budget lowered the duties on 270 British goods exported to Canada and threatened countervailing duties against the United States. See H. B. Neatby, *William Lyon Mackenzie King*, vol. II: *The Lonely Heights* (Toronto 1963), 323–4. On reaction to U.S. investment in this period and after see Peter Kresl, "Before the Deluge: Canadians on Foreign Ownership, 1920–1955," *American Review of Canadian Studies* 6 (spring 1976), 86ff.

3 Quoted in Norman Hillmer, "Personalities and Problems in Anglo-Canadian Economic Relations between the Two World Wars," *Bulletin of Canadian Studies* 3 (June 1979), 5, 8.

4 Peter Kasurak, "American Foreign Policy Officials and Canada, 1927–1941: A Look Through Bureaucratic Glasses," *International Journal* 32 (summer 1977), 548.

5 The best study of the Ottawa Conference, including its origins and aftermath, is in Ian Drummond, *Imperial Economic Policy 1917–1939* (London 1974), chap. 5ff.

6 C.P. Stacey, *Mackenzie King and the North Atlantic Triangle* (Toronto 1976), chap. 2.

7 Correlli Barnett, *The Collapse of British Power* (London 1972), 195. Barnett's index reference under Mackenzie King refers to this episode as "destroys imperial alliance." Stacey's judgment is more sensible and accurate: King "challenged this idea of a common foreign policy and, essentially, destroyed it." Stacey, *Mackenzie King*, 33.

8 "Gentlemen vs Players," *New York Review of Books* (29 Sept. 1988), 63.

9 Donald Creighton, "The Decline and Fall of the Empire of the St. Lawrence," *Historical Papers 1969*, 21.

10 Within a year of giving up the Conservative party leadership, Bennett left Canada to live in England. "It's grand to be going home," the New Brunswick-born Bennett said as he left for the mother country. That may have been the most revealing comment ever made about Canadian Conservatism prior to the Second World War. Bennett soon violated Canadian law by accepting a peerage.

11 F.D. Roosevelt Library, Roosevelt Papers, PSF, box 33, Armour to Phillips, 22 Oct. 1935.

12 On the decline in British trade see Paul Kennedy, *The Rise and Fall of the Great Powers* (Toronto 1987), 316. On the Canadian-American trade agreements see J.L. Granatstein, *A Man of Influence* (Ottawa 1981), chap. 3, and R.N. Kottman, *Reciprocity and the North Atlantic Triangle, 1932–1938* (Ithaca 1968).

13 This is the subject of Gregory Johnson's York University doctoral dissertation in progress on the relations of Canada, the United States, and the United Kingdom in the Pacific from 1935 to 1950.

14 R.F. Swanson, *Canadian-American Summit Diplomacy, 1923–1973* (Toronto 1975), 52ff. According to D.C. Watt, Mackenzie King was "yet another channel by which disguised isolationist ideas could be fed to the president." *Succeeding John Bull,* 78.

15 M.C. Urquhart and K.A.H. Buckley, eds., *Historical Statistics of Canada* (Toronto 1965), F345–56; F.H. Leacy, ed., *Historical Statistics of Canada* (Ottawa 1983), G188–202. I have used 1939 data, though Canada's trade with the United States was higher then than throughout the rest of the decade since that was the first year that showed the impact of the 1938 trade agreement. In other words, had the Second World War not distorted trade patterns, the 1939 trends would likely have continued.

16 *Globe Magazine,* 15 Aug. 1970, quoted in Norman Hillmer, "'The Outstanding Imperialist': Mackenzie King and the British," Part I of *Britain and Canada in the Age of Mackenzie King,* Canada House Lecture Series No 4 [1979], 3–4.

17 Stacey, *Mackenzie King,* 68.

18 National Archives of Canada (NA), Robert Borden Papers, Note by Loring Christie, nd, f 148398.

19 L.L.L. Golden interview, 3 Oct. 1965.

20 NA, John W. Dafoe Papers, Grant Dexter to Dafoe, 18 April 1941.

21 Hugh Hood, *The Swing in the Garden* (Toronto 1975), 165.

22 The fate of the Royal Navy naturally concerned the United States and involved Mackenzie King in an excruciating role between Churchill and Roosevelt. See David Reynolds, *The Creation of the Anglo-American Alliance 1937–1941* (Chapel Hill, NC 1982), 115ff, for an American historian's view.

23 Barnett nonetheless argues that the presence of a Canadian corps in England did not make up for the dispatch of British troops to the Middle and Far East. "The nations of the empire were true 'daughters' of the Mother Country in that at no time during the war did their contributions defray the cost of their own strategic keep." Barnett, *Collapse,* 586. In his later book, *The Audit of War* (London 1986), 3, he adds that the empire produced only 10 per cent of the munitions of war supplied to British and imperial forces. So much for Canada's unstinted contribution to the war.

24 D.G. Creighton, "The Ogdensburg Agreement and F.H. Underhill," in C. Berger and R. Cook, eds., *The West and the Nation* (Toronto 1976), 303.

25 NA, Department of External Affairs Records (EAR), vol. 781, file 394, "An Outline Synopsis," 17 June 1940.

26 NA, W.L.M. King Papers, Black Binders, vol. 19, Christie to King, 15 Aug. 1940. Reynolds, *Creation,* 118, describes FDR's request for the Ogdensburg meeting as being necessary to formulate "contingency plans in case Britain lost control of the North Atlantic." See also Reynolds, *Creation,* 132, 183.

27 J.W. Pickersgill, ed., *The Mackenzie King Record,* vol. I: *1939–44* (Toronto 1960), 130–1.

28 Ibid., 134.

29 Thomas Keneally, *The Cut-Rate Kingdom* (London 1984), 125. This novel of Australia's experience with, among other things, the United States in the Second World War has some useful and suggestive parallels for the Canadian case.

30 Ibid., 14.

31 J.L. Granatstein, *Canada's War: The Politics of the Mackenzie King Government, 1939–45* (Toronto 1975), 131–2.

32 Gerard S. Vano has suggested that there had been a reversal of military obligation within the empire by this period. No longer was Canada under the British military shield, but "Britain was, to a degree, falling under a Canadian shield." *Canada: The Strategic and Military Pawn* (New York 1988), 87. Reynolds, *Creation,* 136, notes that Australia and New Zealand, as well as Canada, were forced closer to the United States by the events of the summer of 1940.

33 NA, R.B. Hanson Papers, file S-175-M-1, Meighen to Hanson, 19 Aug. 1940.

34 Professor Underhill, who spoke the truth about the changed Canadian relationships produced by the war, almost lost his job at the University of Toronto as a result. See Creighton, "Ogdensburg Agreement," 300ff, and Douglas Francis, *F.H. Underhill: Intellectual Provocateur* (Toronto 1986), chap. 10.

35 NA, Privy Council Office Records, Cabinet War Committee Records, Documents, Churchill to King, 22 Aug. 1940.

36 Even the usually shrewd observer of Canadian-American relations, Gordon Stewart, has missed this key point. He noted that in the 1940s, Canada "participated willingly in military and defense integration...it is inaccurate to regard American policy as being imposed on an unwilling and unknowing country. If the United States is judged guilty of imperialism, then Canada must accept a ruling of contributory negligence." "'A Special Contiguous Country Economic Regime': An Overview of America's Canada Policy," *Diplomatic History* 6 (fall 1982), 354–5. True enough, but Britain aided and abetted the process. John Warnock in *Free Trade and*

the New Right Agenda (Vancouver 1988), 255, notes similarly that "The Mackenzie King government chose to conduct the war effort on a continental basis" and thus "greatly undermined Canadian sovereignty." Some choice in August 1940!

37 The King government was slow to recognize the dangers posed to Canadian sovereignty by the U.S. presence. But once it was alerted to the problem (by the British high commissioner to Canada!), it moved quickly to appoint a special commissioner in the northwest and, at war's end, Canada paid the United States in full for all facilities built in Canada—quite consciously in an effort to ensure that its rights were fully protected. See Department of External Affairs, Records [DEA], documents on files 52-B(S), 5221-40C, the records of the special commissioner (NA, RG 36–7), and Granatstein, *A Man of Influence,* 120ff.

38 George Grant, *Lament for a Nation* (Toronto 1965), 50.

39 Cited in David Dilks, "Appeasement Revisited," *University of Leeds Review* 15 (May 1972), 51.

40 Based on Hector Mackenzie, "Sinews of War: Aspects of Canadian Decisions to Finance British Requirements in Canada during the Second World War," Canadian Historical Association paper 1983, 3.

41 King Papers, W.C. Clark to King, 9 April 1941, ff 288021ff.

42 H.D. Hall, *North American Supply* (London 1955), 230. Later, more accurate assessments put war spending in 1941–42 at $1.45 billion, aid to the United Kingdom at $1.15 billion, and civil expenditures at $1 billion. With a national income of $5.95 billion, public expenditure amounted to 60.5 per cent. King Papers, "Canada's War Effort," 4 April 1941, ff 288088ff.

43 The phrase is R.S. Sayers's in *Financial Policy, 1939–45* (London 1956), 322–3. The balance, however, was less than real for the British. They had large peacetime trade deficits with the United States and could pay Canada in U.S. dollars only because they received them from other parties in a pattern of multilateral settlement that ended with the outbreak of war. I am indebted to Professor Ian Drummond for this information.

44 King Papers, Clark to King, 9 April 1941, ff 288014ff. The actual figures were even worse than these estimates. See Urquhart and Buckley, eds., *Historical Statistics,* F334–47. But whether the situation was as bleak as government officials believed at the time is less certain. Although munitions exports to Britain did stimulate the growth of imports from the United States, still more came

from the war effort itself, which stimulated imports directly (in the form of components) and indirectly (by increasing consumer demand and domestic investment in plant and equipment). I am again indebted to Professor Drummond.

45 Granatstein, *Canada's War,* 135–6; Granatstein, *A Man of Influence,* 94ff.

46 EAR, vol. 35, "United States Exchange Discussions," 20 Nov. 1940.

47 Urquhart and Buckley, eds., *Historical Statistics,* F164–92; King Papers, Clark to King, 9 April 1941, ff 288018ff; Queen's University Archives, Grant Dexter Papers, Memorandum, 11 March 1941.

48 On the costs to the United Kingdom see Barnett, *Collapse,* 591ff. Churchill was asked if Britain would be able to repay the United States for its aid: "I shall say, yes by all means let us have an account if we can get it reasonably accurate, but I shall have my account to put in too, and my account is for holding the baby alone for eighteen months, and it was a very rough brutal baby." Quoted in David Dilks's introduction to Dilks, ed., *Retreat from Power,* vol. II: *After 1939* (London 1981), 14.

49 Robert Bothwell and John English, "Canadian Trade Policy in the Age of American Dominance and British Decline, 1943–1947," *Canadian Review of American Studies* 8 (spring 1977), 54ff. A.F.W. Plumptre commented that "Ottawa apparently believed that it is well to keep Canada as independent as possible and to avoid borrowing or begging as long as may be." *Mobilizing Canada's Resources for War* (Toronto 1941), 80. Cf R.W. James, *Wartime Economic Cooperation* (Toronto 1949), 32.

50 Cabinet War Committee Records, Minutes, 18, 26 Feb. 1941.

51 Public Record Office (PRO), London, Prime Minister's Office Records, PREM4/43B/2, Cranborne to Churchill, 5 March 1941; ibid., Treasury Records, T160/1340, Amery to Kingsley Wood, 10 May 1941.

52 Ibid., T160/1054, "Canadian Financial Assistance to this Country," nd [14 March 1941].

53 Granatstein, *Canada's War,* 139.

54 Cabinet War Committee Records, Minutes, 12, 13 March 1941; Sayers, *Financial Policy,* 338ff.

55 Dexter Papers, Memo, 21 April 1941.

56 The text of the Hyde Park Agreement is printed as an appendix to R.D. Cuff and J.L. Granatstein, *Canadian-American Relations in Wartime* (Toronto 1975), 165–6.

57 Pickersgill, ed., *Mackenzie King Record*, I, 202.

58 C.P. Stacey, *Arms, Men and Governments* (Ottawa 1970), 490; Richard Rohmer, *E.P. Taylor* (Toronto 1978), 106.

59 This was seen as a virtual miracle. See *Financial Post*, 26 April 1941.

60 See J.L. Granatstein, "Settling the Accounts: Anglo-Canadian War Finance, 1943–1945," *Queen's Quarterly*, 83 (summer 1976), 246.

61 PRO, Dominions Office Records, DO35/1218, Minute by A.W. Snelling, 26 Jan. 1943; Sayers, *Financial Policy*, 350ff.

62 S.D. Pierce and A.F.W. Plumptre, "Canada's Relations with War-Time Agencies in Washington," *Canadian Journal of Economics and Political Science* 11 (1945), 410–11.

63 Urquhart and Buckley, eds., *Historical Statistics*, F345–56; Leacy, ed., *Historical Statistics*, G188–202.

PART IV

Reinventing
Canada, 1945–1975

Canada emerged from the Second World War as a prosperous nation. Wartime mobilization of the economy had ended the 10-year economic depression and massive unemployment of the 1930s. Canadians were determined not to allow a repetition of the Depression and pressured governments to ensure that market forces were sufficiently regulated by state policies to maintain high levels of employment and to ensure a degree of state support for those whom the private economy could not provide a minimum income.

Gradually, a set of social policies emerged that, in the eyes of some Canadians, made Canada a "welfare state," a country where governments guaranteed a minimal income to all citizens regardless of whether they participated in the formal economy or not. Old-age pensions, medical insurance, unemployment insurance, and federal sharing of costs for provincial programs to assist the destitute all formed part of this incipient "welfare state."

But the post-war period also ushered in the "warfare state," as the Americans and Soviets, allies during the Second World War, quickly became enemies. A "cold war" split much of the world into two camps, pro-Communist and pro-America, each claiming to provide a political and economic model for all nations to follow. With each side possessing an arsenal of nuclear weapons capable of blowing up the world, the war between the two opposing camps was largely conducted in skirmishes in countries such as the two Koreas and the two Vietnams rather than on the territories of Europe or the Americas, where they might have led to nuclear conflict.

Canada had become part of the American camp during the war and in its immediate aftermath. While Canadian governments sometimes regarded American actions and rhetoric as extreme, they limited themselves to attempts to convince the American authorities to moderate their behaviour rather than giving serious consideration to neutrality between the two camps of the Cold War. While the "welfare state" largely promoted a more tolerant and humanistic Canada, the "warfare state" sowed the seeds of paranoia as Cold War dissenters were treated much as dissenters were treated in wartime—that is, as traitors.

In the early post-war period, psychologists earned themselves a great deal of official and popular respect as the arbiters of "normal" and "abnormal" behaviour. Unlike the disapproving clerics of the inter-war period, psychologists claimed that science, rather than religious morality, guided their analyses. But, as Mona Gleason suggests, the judgments of psychologists, while presented in scientific guise, were largely a defence of the same institutions, social roles, and morals that the churches had long defended as normal. Though the wartime period had witnessed a major temporary boom in wartime employment for married women, including their assumption of skilled industrial jobs once reserved for men, the psychologists joined the state and business in pressuring women to leave the paid workforce after marriage. For the "experts" in human behaviour, it was important that children should be raised to view differentiated sex roles as natural rather than social creations. Similarly, heterosexuality was to be viewed as normal and homosexuality as deviant.

While sexual orientation and political beliefs may seem rather discrete categories, the desire of elites in the post-war period to fight "deviance" of all kinds often caused them to make a curious link between homosexuality and communism, respectively a proscribed form of sex and a political philosophy espoused by "the enemy." The government spied upon large numbers of people in an effort to ensure that neither gays nor Communists held government jobs. The logic that barred homosexuals from government employment was interesting: until the Criminal Code was amended in 1968, homosexual sex constituted an illegal activity in Canada, no matter the circumstances. Therefore, reasoned government officials, Communist agents might seek to blackmail these "deviants" into betraying the Canadian state so as to avoid being betrayed by the Communists to the Canadian state. So keen was the government to root out Communists from its ranks that at one point, as Gary Kinsman explains, it experimented with a device that was meant to measure sexual arousal to pinpoint gays and then fire them. Only the defective functioning of the "fruit machine" in test runs prevented "scientific" sexual-orientation examinations from becoming a standard part of the routine for obtaining many government jobs.

While Cold Warriors in the federal government fretted about Communists and homosexuals, and sometimes proclaimed that "Communist agitation," rather than real social inequalities, precipitated militancy in Canada, other divisions based on region, class, and gender intensified. Canada's First Nations meanwhile remained at the bottom of the social ladder. Joan Sangster demonstrates that rather than attempting to let indigenous peoples share in postwar prosperity, the Canadian state left them wallowing in poverty, and then incarcerated them when they broke the colonists' laws.

In Quebec, the alliance of church and state was challenged by both trade unions and middle-class groups throughout the long rule of the conservative Union Nationale, headed by Maurice Duplessis. During the so-called Quiet Revolution of the 1960s, a Liberal government redefined Quebec nationalism in secular terms, focusing on economic growth and an educated Francophone labour force as the means of creating a nation in fact if not in law within Quebec. At first, the supporters of this new, secular nationalism seemed content to have Quebec remain within Confederation and to benefit from federal social and economic programs meant to aid underdeveloped provinces. Fearing the growth of separatism, the federal government initially seemed willing to allow Quebec to establish its own programs in many areas with federal grants and without federal intervention. But, under Pierre Trudeau's prime ministership (1968–1984, with one brief interruption of nine months in 1979–1980), Quebec's right to "opt out"

of new federal programs was curtailed. The movement for Quebec sovereignty burgeoned as the nationalist middle class became convinced that Ottawa's policies stymied Quebec's economic development. Alain Gagnon and Mary Beth Montcalm examine sympathetically the complaints that various groups of Québécois made regarding their province's relationship with the Canadian economy as a whole.

Atlantic Canadians, judging by their lower average incomes than Québécois throughout this period, had similar cause for complaint, with Newfoundlanders, who had become Canadians in 1949, experiencing the lowest living standards. James Overton examines critically the mythology that Newfoundlanders' "culture," as opposed to larger economic forces mostly outside the control of Newfoundlanders, had created the economic disparities of which Newfoundlanders were victims. Similarly, James Walker, by examining the lives and aspirations of the African-Canadian residents of the poor community of Africville, demonstrates that the bigoted individuals who controlled city council in Halifax, rather than the residents of this vibrant community, were responsible for many of its problems. Nonetheless, the city leaders claimed that the destruction of Africville and the dispersal of its population would benefit its former residents.

The drums of economic progress, which the mayor and councillors of Halifax beat as they destroyed Africville, are assessed critically by George Grant. He argues that Canadians' efforts to establish a separate national identity from the Americans in the post-war period were doomed because of their wholesale embrace of the commercial values of the Americans, and their abandonment of older values of community and sharing. Neil Earle, however, provides a glimmer of hope for Canadians retaining a degree of difference from Americans in his analysis of the ways in which Canadians' sustained devotion to hockey reflects and reinforces a unique Canadian identity.

Psychology and the Construction of the "Normal" Family in Postwar Canada, 1945–60

MONA GLEASON

We need a psychology of personality which is derived from the study of normal people.... A research centre for the study of normal people is less easy to organize than is a psychological clinic in a mental hospital; yet until we have such centres we shall not be able to make our contribution as scientists to the cause of mental health.[1]

In the years following the Second World War the mental health of Canadians, along with other aspects of life, attracted the attention of a variety of commentators. After years of fighting, separation, and death, citizens were told to prepare for a considerable amount of strain in their postwar relationships with family and friends. From family life, to the relationship between men and women, to the difficult process of growing up, a potent mixture of social scientists, journalists, and other commentators maintained that the experience of war had significantly challenged, even altered, the conventional meaning and character of family life in Canada.[2] The assumption framing these discussions was that the long years of economic depression and war had left Canadian families shaken and in need of strengthening. While they assumed that Canadians longed for security and happiness, commentators also warned that satisfaction in these pursuits could be easily thwarted. The

postwar world was cast as changing all too rapidly. Canadian society, the experts warned, was paying a high price for a modern way of life in the form of rising divorce rates, juvenile delinquency, increases in the number of married women in the workforce, and general anxiety about the threat of communism and nuclear annihilation as the Cold War loomed.[3]

Rather than offering strictly a history of the postwar family or a history of postwar psychology, this study analyses how popular psychological discourse shaped attitudes towards family life during this period. In particular, I am concerned with the ways in which psychology constructed the "normal" Canadian family, what it had to say about living in a normal family, what a normal family was supposed to be like, and how normalcy in family life was supposed to be conceived and ultimately achieved. I argue that psychologists' discussions of normal families and normal family members were shaped not by objective, unchanging scientific "truths," but by the hegemonic values and priorities of the middle class in postwar Canada. This focus helps explain, at least in part, the considerable amount of agreement among psychologists writing for a popular audience about what constituted normal family relations. Popularized psychological discourse reinforced traditional

Mona Gleason, "Psychology and the Construction of the 'Normal' Family in Postwar Canada, 1945–60," *Canadian Historical Review* 78, 3 (September 1997): 442–477. Reprinted by permission of the University of Toronto Press.

civic qualities necessary to sustain the social order, such as industriousness, obedience, and happiness, by reinterpreting them in "psychologized" terms. To the traditional dichotomies used to characterize families, such as bad or good, weak or strong, was added another binary opposition: normal or abnormal. The considerable amount of agreement among psychologists regarding normalcy, however, did not reflect nor accommodate the fact that a variety of Canadian families existed with a variety of needs and priorities. This was especially true after the Second World War, when large numbers of eastern and southern European refugees from Poland, Estonia, Hungary, Italy, and other wartorn countries were grudgingly allowed entry into Canada.[4] Cultural traditions regarding family life and parenting deemed "un-Canadian" were discouraged in popular psychological discourse on the grounds that they jeopardized children's ability to adjust successfully to society.

Popular psychology's definition of normalcy and normalizing worked to level important differences between and across individuals, ethnic groups, and classes. The normal child, teenager, and family was equated with the idealized, and more socially acceptable, Anglo-Saxon, middle-class child, teenager, and family. This normalized ideal consolidated the diversity of family life into the confines of an *a priori* model and had significant consequences in a number of areas, including the entrenchment of traditional gender roles for women and men. The normal family that this discourse constructed had mothers who stayed at home and raised well-adjusted, bright, industrious children, and white-collar fathers who skilfully divided time between the office and home. In this way, an idealized "every family" became the standard against which the unique needs and circumstances of those outside the ideal, such as immigrant, working-class, non-nuclear, or female-headed families, were measured and judged.

Nevertheless, psychologists writing in the popular arena—predominately male, Anglo-Saxon, middle-class professionals such as William Blatz, Samuel Laycock, and Karl Bernhardt—assumed that their audience either shared their social standing or aspired to it. Blatz, founder of the Institute of Child Study in Toronto, introduced Canadian parents to the psychological tenets of childrearing in the late 1920s. He became one of the general public's "main interpreters" of child psychology for the next forty years.[5] Laycock, an educational psychologist at the University of Saskatchewan, was also a well-known promoter of mental health in the field of parenting, education, penal corrections, and medicine. According to Gordon A. McMurray, one of his successors at the University of Saskatchewan, Laycock was popularly known as "Mr. Psychology" in the province and beyond.[6] Laycock dispensed a great deal of advice to Canadian parents before his death at the age of eighty-nine in 1971. A year earlier, he received the Medal of Service Order of Canada for his contributions in the area of education and gifted children and in clinical practice.[7] Despite the extent of his involvement in advising parents, Laycock never married or raised children of his own. He acted as godfather to seventeen children "scattered across Canada and overseas," and was reportedly known as "Uncle Sam" to many others.[8]

Although a less public persona, Bernhardt also contributed substantially to the dissemination of psychological advice about the family and parenting in postwar Canada. In 1938, he became head of the Parent Education Division at the Institute of Child Study and published many popular articles in the journal initiated under his direction, *Bulletin of the Institute of Child Study*. When Blatz retired, Bernhardt temporarily took over directorship of the Institute until poor health forced him to step aside.[9] Bernhardt captured something of psychology's appeal for Canadian parents when he wrote in

1947: "Why study child development? Why construct more and more tests? There can be only one answer in terms of purpose; and that is so that more people can be more happy."[10] In the opinion of Bernhardt and others who shared his views, psychological knowledge represented the means by which the future would be secure. The horrors of the Second World War encouraged human relations experts like psychologists to teach citizens the world over to manage and negotiate problems more successfully in the "modern age." Canadians, experts such as Blatz, Laycock, and Bernhardt reasoned, needed new coping strategies to ensure a peaceful, contented, and normal future.

Renaming problems perceived to be plaguing the family in psychological terms, Canadian psychologists represented part of a process by which "a certain idea or model of man [sic] became normative, self-evident, and supposedly universal."[11] In other words, by describing, defining, and diagnosing family problems in terms of "normal personality" and "behaviour adjustment," psychologists "psychologized" family and family life. In so doing, they solidified their niche as professionals in postwar society. With their specialized knowledge determining normalcy, psychologists not only singled out and diagnosed deviance but also "proactively predicted and pre-empted its development."[12] Michel Foucault suggests five overlapping components or strategies that constitute normalizing power. According to him, normalizing power compares, differentiates, hierarchizes, homogenizes, and excludes—each of these strategies adding to its rhetorical and social power.[13] Popular postwar psychology's normalizing, as I demonstrate throughout this study, relied on these strategies of comparing, differentiating, hierarchizing, homogenizing, and excluding to ensure its power and relevancy. Numerous examples of this power at work abound within psychological discourse: personality inventories compared and differentiated the proper adjustment of children; definitions of normalcy estab-lished static boundaries and homogenized differences among families; and the legitimization of traditional gender roles hierarchized the spousal relationship in postwar marriages.

[...]

The role that psychology played in shaping attitudes towards the postwar family is particularly important because its practitioners claimed expertise in normal human adjustment and interaction. This expertise set it apart from related disciplines such as psychiatry, which concerned itself with pathological human adjustment and interaction. As psychologist J.S.A. Bois succinctly stated in 1948, "the psychologist is interested in normal growth, not in pathological deviations...he is an educator, a trainer; he is not a non-medical psychiatrist."[14] Despite Bois's insistence, the social function of psychology remains the subject of scholarly debate. Pioneering studies on the impact of the helping professions on family life in the American context, carried out by scholars such as Christopher Lasch, introduced the suggestion that psychology's ideological and professionalizing goals—like other "helping professions"— were hidden behind objective science and expertise.[15] Lasch's thesis continues to be influential, but it has been criticized for suggesting too "simple and straightforward a shift from familial autonomy to state surveillance" and for underrepresenting the degree to which constraints based on class, gender, and ethnicity complicated the notion of home as a "haven."[16] Studies that focus more minutely on the nature of psychology's knowledge claims argue that its focus on the constitution, transmission, and reproduction of normal behaviour made it a powerful social tool for the purpose of entrenching the status quo.[17] Conceptualizing psychology as a "chapter in the utopianism of social science," other scholars have concentrated on the place that family and childrearing professionals have had in modern intellectual history.[18] Although my analysis owes a considerable debt to each of these approaches, I have tried to offer a more focused critique of the normalizing power of psychological discourse and how it was used to shape ideas about postwar family life in the Canadian context. Understanding the discourse's "technologies of normalcy" illuminates how arbitrators of convention, such as psychologists, influenced social interaction and the cultivation of particular social values, along with the consequences this influence had for ordinary Canadians in postwar society.[19]

The post-Second World War debate on the emotional health of the family signified a reaction not against familial breakdown per se but against the rapid changes and transformations which it represented and which social leaders found uncomfortable, improper, or threatening.[20] The family, like other social institutions, reflected the anxieties and desires of those with something to gain or lose by its swaying fortunes. Dorothy Chunn has pointed out that "crises of the family" seem to crop up whenever a gap between middle-class and non-middle-class conceptions of proper family life became too wide. When this chasm occurs, middle-class efforts aimed at "upgrading standards to family life" follow.[21] In fact, the recurring or cyclical incidence of family crises has been a feature of Canadian society since the nineteenth century, fostering the emergence of the welfare state and shoring up the "ideology of familialism" that characterized the interwar period.[22] While the contexts are unique, each instance demonstrates the powerful potential of family crisis rhetoric to influence definitions of acceptable family life. [...]

Historians in Canada have begun to tackle and dispel many myths surrounding family life after the war.[23] The notion that the 1950s marked a high point of social optimism, prosperity, naivety, and innocence obscures many of the era's complexities and says more about the tendency to look back at this period with nostalgic eyes than about the period itself.[24]

Women, as workers, wives, and mothers, for example, received highly contradictory directives that betrayed a considerable degree of anxiety about their changing roles after the war. Popular stereotypes tended to paint all women, regardless of their unique circumstances, as quintessential "angels of the house," at the same time that growing numbers of them sought and found new opportunities for paid employment outside the home.[25] Recent studies have also dispelled myths surrounding women's idyllic experiences in postwar suburbs, focusing instead on the strategies they forged to help cope with isolation and loneliness.[26] The nostalgic image of the 1950s as a time of willing conformity among all Canadians, often associated with suburban living, flies in the face of the findings of scholars such as Franca Iacovetta. In her important work on Italian immigrants in postwar Toronto, Iacovetta demonstrates that attempts to "Canadianize" newcomers, though often only partially successful, were grounded in a desire to assimilate cultural outsiders into a mainstream Anglo-Saxon and middle-class world view that dominated postwar Canada.[27] Exploring and exposing the experiences of those outside the dominant discourse, these studies complicate and revise our understanding the postwar years.

In the postwar atmosphere of change and dislocation, psychological discourse suggested that the normal and happy adjustment of Canadians was in jeopardy. It was important for psychologists writing for a popular audience, therefore, to focus attention on the degree to which postwar conditions fostered or prevented the normal family from functioning. From the point of view of postwar psychology, the health of the Canadian family was determined by the emotional and behavioural maturity of its members. Psychological discourse, however, was appropriated by journalists, social commentators, doctors, and governmental officials to explain how the family had been dislocated during the war.[28] A whole spectrum of familial pathologies was discussed using psychological jargon, from unwed motherhood, unfulfilled housewives, absent fathers, child abuse, and family desertion to the threat of the sexual deviant, often assumed to be homosexual, stalking young children.[29] The causes of problems were described in various ways: poor parenting, the absence of the father as the traditional familial authority figure, the death of a relative or family friend in the war; the increased bombardment in movies, radio, newspaper, and, later television, of the horrors of battle; the absence of working mothers from the home; the increased freedom, and concurrent disobedience and rebelliousness, of teenagers; and increasing urbanization.[30] Speaking to his listening audience over the CBC in 1954, psychologist David Ketchum suggested that "no Canadian institution, not even education, is viewed with more alarm today than the Canadian family."[31]

By popularizing it and making it much more accessible, psychology became more relevant in Canadians' everyday lives. Through it, for example, Canadians were informed about the importance of healthy personality development: "mental health," as one writer pointed out, "like physical health, is not necessarily a permanent condition—it must be safeguarded."[32] Personality, for example, was defined in such broad terms that it impinged on practically any aspect of life: "it is the *sum total of the individual's characteristic habits, attitudes and persistent tendencies*...almost everything a child does or is able to do is a function of his [*sic*] personality."[33] Psychologists took great pains to identify the connections between emotional stability, personal fulfilment, happiness, and civic order to their audience. These connections helped to present psychological health as a basic consideration, not a frivolous self-indulgence. Achieving some control over sound personality development was promoted as a means of ensuring a happy family and a happy future for the country. As Laycock declared over the radio:

"We don't need to sit down in the face of crippled personalities and fold our hands in resignation and blame the Deity for our troubles. As we do a better job in the home and school we don't have so many crippled personalities—the kind who create problems in family, community, national and international life."[34] Laycock presented psychological sensitivity and know-how, suggested in the euphemistic phrase "doing a better job," as the key to a peaceful future. Making clear the connections between psychological health and peaceful co-existence, he further encouraged Canadians to put this know-how into immediate use.

The divorce rate, cited as a symptom of the declining strength of the family, seemed to support the need for psychological expertise. In the province of Saskatchewan, for example, statistics gathered by the Department of Public Health and the Registrar General indicated that the number of divorces and annulments granted in the province rose steadily from a total of 127 in 1940 to 285 in 1945. In 1946 this number rose dramatically to 518, peaking in 1947 with 520. By 1948, however, the total number of divorces or annulments granted dropped to 339.[35] Saskatchewan was not a unique case. This general pattern of rising divorce rates following the end of the war was repeated throughout the country. At the end of the war, divorce rates nationally had tripled: in 1941, 2471 divorces were granted in Canada, and by 1946 the number had risen to 7683.[36] By 1948, however, the number dropped to 6881, and, in 1949, fell further to 5934.[37] Between 1948 and 1958, despite population growth, the number of divorces in Canada did not rise above 6300.[38]

Few commentators acknowledged the steady decline in divorce rates after the early postwar years. Nor did they acknowledge the same increases in divorce, and the same lamentations about the state of the family, which accompanied the end of the First World War.[39] The same assumption that prolonged separation of spouses resulted in marital estrangement and increased extra-marital activity underscored discussions of rising divorce and separation rates in both eras.[40] Lorne Stewart, a Toronto judge, interpreted the post-Second World War increase in divorce as symptomatic of the larger problem of general social breakdown, rather than as simply an increasingly popular solution to unhappy marriages. Signalling society's "problem of disorganization," Stewart, in a typical manner, lumped Toronto's rising divorce rate with other problems perceived to be on the rise—such as the number of neglected and delinquent children.[41]

Psychologists interpreted postwar marriage breakdown as symptomatic of improper emotional and behavioural adjustment. Divorce, as Laycock understood it, was the result of emotional immaturity on the part of one or both marriage partners.[42] It might seem absurd that the bachelor Laycock should offer advice on these subjects to Canadians, but it was perfectly in keeping with the psychologists' belief that experience in these areas was not only unnecessary as a prerequisite, but could be a hindrance. Superior spousal and familial interaction was learned, not gained through experience. In a course on marriage given to the Two-by-Two Club of the Metropolitan United Church of Saskatoon, for example, Laycock based his discussion on "several research studies" on the "psychological factors in marriage happiness."[43] Among the factors that helped make a marriage successful (or, if absent, unsuccessful), Laycock included "a happy childhood, lack of conflict with the mother, home discipline that was firm but not harsh, strong attachment to the mother without being dependent on her, strong attachment to the father without being childishly dependent, parental frankness about sex, and a premarital attitude to sex which is free from disgust."[44] Two recurring themes in postwar psychological discourse generally are contained in Laycock's discussion of childrearing: first, the Freudian view that the first five years of a child's life established his or her personality and determined adult behaviour and, second, the notion that parents hindered or guaranteed their children's chances for happiness, depending on how they performed their duties.[45] These two interconnected themes, the importance of a child's early experiences in shaping personality and the determining role of parents in this process, established a powerful rhetorical position for psychological discourse. It created the impression that the success of important future events, like marriage, was determined very early in a child's life. The earlier parents paid attention to the psychological health of their children, the stronger the guarantee of future happiness for both. By positioning psychological advice in this way, practitioners like Laycock made this expertise attractive and indispensable to conscientious Canadian parents.

Whether they were responding to this promotion or not, Canadians were marrying in greater numbers during the mid-1940s. Douglas Owram has suggested that a "cult of marriage" characterized the era.[46] During the early years of the Depression, the marriage rate had fallen below 65,000 per year or 5.9 marriages for every thousand people. In 1944, 104,000 couples were married, or 8.5 marriages per thousand people. By 1945, this number rose to 8.9 marriages per thousand people, and by 1946, 10.9 marriages per thousand people took place.[47] The marriage rate was, by the end of the war, unprecedented.[48] Between 1951 and 1952, however, marriage rates gradually declined from 9.2 to 8.9 per thousand population.[49] In 1958, statisticians pointed out that 7.7 marriages per thousand population took place, the lowest marriage rate in twenty years. This trend continued in 1960, with 7.0 marriages per thousand.[50] Although more Canadians were marrying than in the darkest days of the Depression, "marriage-mania" was cooling near the end of the 1950s. Those who did marry, however, did so at an increasingly younger age. Between 1941 and 1961, the average age of marriage for women dropped from 25.4 years to 22.0 years, while for men, the average age dropped from 26.4 years to 24.8 years.[51]

Marriage, postwar Canadians were told, was more complex and tenuous than in the past; it needed to be self-consciously studied and prepared for. Given the anxiety over divorce, juvenile delinquency, and the meaning of family in these years, preparation for marriage seemed all the more urgent. Not surprisingly, the introduction of a marriage course, one of the first at the college level in Canada, occurred at the University of British Columbia in 1945.[52] Offered through the Extension Department, the Marriage and Family Life Course was aimed at "ironing out the wrinkles in the lives of newly-weds, and smoothing the path ahead for the husbands, wives and children who will have to face the rocky days of the postwar era."[53] Professional marriage instructors, initially popular in the United States, also became well known in Canada during this period.[54] Paul Popenoe, "one of the most-demanded marriage lecturers in the 1940s," wrote on the subject of good marriages for Canadian magazines such as *Maclean's*.[55]

Psychologists, along with other social commentators, argued that just as the family had been "democratized" by the lessons of the war, so too had marriage become a more democratic institution.[56] However, while terms such as "modernized" and "changed" pervaded the psychological discourse on postwar marriage, it ultimately legitimized traditional and unequal gender roles for wives and husbands. Ideally, nonetheless, modern marriage was no longer based on the sole authority of the husband: "For in making the authoritarian type of marriage structure obsolete," promised Toronto psychologist David Ketchum, "it will give us a chance to rear a generation free from many of our shortcomings."[57] Although Ketchum did not specify from which shortcomings he and his generation suffered, he played on postwar anxiety surrounding perceptions of increasing

divorce and juvenile delinquency. Moreover, Ketchum's rhetoric conjured up provocative postwar images of dictatorship and freedom. Postwar marriage, like postwar society, he insinuated, should respect the lessons of the Second World War. "Democracy" and all things associated with the term characterized everything from the proper marriage arrangement and proper parenting attitudes to the proper classroom atmosphere in these years.[58] The horrors and triumphs of the war, psychologist Karl Bernhardt argued, opened the doors for a new articulation, a new ideal, in healthy marital relations.[59] In turn, the reasoning went, healthy marital relations ensured healthy family life.

In the popularized writings of psychologists, democratic marriages did not necessarily mean equality between the sexes. As part of a series of *Chatelaine* articles on the state of marriage in postwar Canada, Blatz told his readers that "in every human relationship there is a dominant and a submissive party."[60] In past marriage practices, he argued, the husband was always dominant and the wife always submissive. Blatz pointed out that with the lessons of the war and heightened awareness of psychology, husbands and wives learned to shift between dominant and submissive roles, depending on the situation at hand. Detailing the specific workings of such an agreement, Blatz suggested, "...they could agree that the husband will dominate in certain fields such as the handling of the family's finances while the wife will dominate in the handling of the children. In other words they must assign spheres of influence to each other if this modern concept of partnership in marriage is going to work."[61] Blatz promoted the notion of the modern democratic marriage based on his idea of spousal cooperation, not equality. As the above quotation suggests, this negotiation between dominance and submission did not necessarily subvert traditional gender roles for men and women. In Blatz's conception, men still interacted with the public world of finance and breadwinning, while women looked after the children. Similarly, Laycock presented the idea of democratic marriages in the rhetoric of separate spheres. He chastised women who "refused to accept the responsibility of managing a household and of building a happy home."[62] Equally unsubtly, this rhetoric made its way into government-issued parenting pamphlets boosting the legitimacy of this approach to so-called democratic marriage: "Because the man usually earns the income for the whole family, he may feel like the boss and dole out money to others. However, most thinking men today accept the woman's role as that of an *equal* partner even if she isn't a salaried one. Women have a lot of training in buying and most families manage better and more amiably if decisions are made jointly."[63] The so-called democratic marriage model, as this comment implies, was often used to keep women in an unequal position vis-à-vis their husbands. The rhetoric of "partnership" used in this example did not substantially alter or threaten the traditional roles of the sexes. Psychologist and sex-hygienist Mildred Horn encouraged women to focus on the physical attributes they contributed to marriage, exemplifying once again contradictory notions of "democratic" marriages: "Marriage is a partnership and to make it a success both partners must put into it the best that is in them both spiritually and physically. First of all, the wife should keep herself clean. Every portion of the body should be kept immaculate from head to foot.... Don't allow yourself to become fat. Nothing so destroys a woman's appearance as unsightly rolls of flesh."[64] While the obligations of husbands were not discussed by Horn, wives were to keep their end of the marriage partnership by maintaining an attractive appearance for their husbands.

In his marriage series for *Chatelaine,* Blatz focused on negative qualities like nagging, quarrelling, and jealousy as prime dangers to a suc-cessful marriage.[65] He psychologized marriage, presenting it to women in particular as a matter dependent on their psychological maturity and emotional deference to their husbands: "When you lose your temper with your husband you run the risk of losing the marriage itself. Married people usually lose their tempers when they both want different things at the same time and they can't reconcile their conflict. Frustrated because they can't get what they want, they give way to anger."[66] Like Laycock, Blatz presented marital problems in terms of emotional weaknesses and inability to avoid conflict.[67] That he placed the main responsibility for the emotional climate in marriage on women, however, garnered mixed reactions from his readers. Madeline Mann from Toronto praised Blatz for a "very fine and understanding" article. Likewise, K. Waites from Woodbridge thanked Blatz for "helping us to solve the current problems of modern living." Some readers, sensitive to the plight of many unfulfilled women in the strictly gendered postwar society, were not impressed with Blatz's advice. Responding to his article on wives who "bore" their husbands, E. Ross wrote: "So everybody is bored with the housewife, that poor unfortunate whose only excuse for existence is survival of the race. No wonder! Has it ever occurred to anyone that we, who may be handicapped by the possession of a few brains, are bored with ourselves and our boring jobs, from which there is no escape?"[68] Mrs. E.B. from Ottawa maintained that quarrelling with her spouse actually improved her marriage. She confided that while she and her husband had had many quarrels over the years, "we can honestly say that there has grown a deep and sympathetic bond between us which would not necessarily have been had we not known the true feelings of each other."[69] These varied responses to Blatz's articles show that not all Canadian women accepted his version of women's submissive role in marriage. The comments by E. Ross, in particular, suggest that she recognized and disagreed with the political consequences of Blatz's legitimization of women's inferiority. She clearly resented the fact that husbands were encouraged to be economically dominant, while wives were told to be dependent on a male breadwinner.

The contradiction inherent in a "democratic" marriage built on the traditional hierarchies of power was not acknowledged by psychologists. They presented the democratic marriage as a means of enforcing the separate roles for men and women based on the constraints of gender. While marriage was characterized in psychological discourse as an important relational state sustained by the satisfaction of the "basic psychological needs" of both partners, its discussion reflected hegemonic social values rather than scientific certainty. Laycock's pronouncements, while based on "the results of research studies and the best findings of clinicians," centred on the proper nature of marital qualities such as affection, belonging, independence, achievement, approval, and sense of worth.[70] He warned of the psychological problems associated with interracial marriages, thereby cloaking the socially unacceptable in the guise of psychological pathology. Cultural differences between spouses in any or all areas of life, Laycock warned, were "apt to cause trouble." "Mixed marriages" were discouraged simply on the grounds that they too often ended in divorce.[71]

The problems of marriage and divorce were not the only topics featured in postwar debates over familial and social stability. Children and teenagers were also identified as suffering from "crippled personalities," and this problem helped justify a great deal of discussion regarding their proper place in postwar society.[72] Concern about the actions of teenagers signalled anxiety, based at least in part on generational differences, about the deterioration of the social status quo.[73] During the war, for example, although employment oppor-

tunities for teenagers provided financial rewards, freedom, and personal expression, they also created new tensions: "Many of these young people, with too much money to spend, were supposedly making a mockery of the taboos and standards that had hitherto governed their conduct. The war, in effect, was producing an unsavoury, and unstructured climate on the homefront that threatened the health, education and morals of impressionable teenagers."[74] Social leaders, as these comments suggest, were concerned because young people were not acting as they were supposed to act. Although they were perceived to be more independent, brash, and undisciplined, teenagers were also made to seem more vulnerable than they had been before the war.[75]

Although the perception of a youth problem received substantial attention in the popular press at the time, historians have argued that the incidence of criminal activity on the part of the country's juveniles during the postwar years was not, in strict statistical terms, on the increase.[76] In the writings of psychologists, however, delinquency represented a threat to traditional qualities of compliance and obedience and was far from simply equated with crime statistics. For them, the term conjured up a much broader set of problems—combining truancy, anti-social behaviour, and habitual challenges to authority—that subverted the acceptable paradigm of adult authority.[77]

Rather than criminalizing suspect behaviour, psychologists were much more eager to reinterpret it using their terms—to focus on the emotional and behavioural pathology of juvenile delinquency. As was the case with the problems of marriage and divorce, psychologists portrayed juvenile delinquency as symptomatic of impaired psychological development. Moreover, they often traced this impaired psychological development back to the family: "Delinquency occurs when adults in home, school and community fail to provide children with the environment they need in order to grow up straight and strong. Delinquency, then, is really an adult problem. In other words, it isn't a case of delinquent children; rather it is a case of delinquent adults."[78] The failure on the part of parents to create a satisfactory environment, according to postwar psychologists, was more to blame for juvenile delinquency than bad children, hard economic times, or inadequate social support. This line of reasoning, that parents and communities were to blame for the inadequacies of children, significantly widened the audience for psychologists' discourse. Not only did it provide a focused source of children's problems but it made possible a powerful preventive orientation. A "failed environment," for example, referred to a home in which children's psychological needs were unfulfilled, ignored, and/or frustrated by parents.[79] Thus, psychological discourse did not focus simply on studying, describing, and administering to delinquent behaviour; rather, its prime objective was to disseminate a new ideal regarding family life, thereby including parents under its professional gaze.[80] Families could be judged acceptable or not acceptable according to psychological criteria, and this helped open the door to the normalizing activities of any intervening helping professionals, such as public health nurses, social workers, or case workers from juvenile courts.

Divorce, unhappy marriages, and juvenile delinquency symbolized family breakdown, and by extension social breakdown, for many commentators in postwar Canada. Psychologists maintained that disruptions in family life, regardless of the particular form they took, had to do with the changing function of the postwar family.[81] A reading assigned as part of a Parent Education Course at the Institute of Child Study delineated this so-called new development stating that "many functions have been taken out of the home, for example, protection and education...the function which is emotional or affective is still left and can be given due

prominence now that it has not so many other duties."[82] Ketchum suggested that postwar problems were simply part of a complex change in the psychological goals of family living:

> The forces which for so many centuries made the family a cohesive and permanent unit are gone or are going, and no substitute has clearly emerged. Divorces naturally increase. But at the same time we've also become acutely aware of the child's urgent need for a stable, close-knit, affectionate group around him. So we have what is really a new problem for mankind: how to form durable family groups on a *voluntary basis;* how to get men and women to live together harmoniously for twenty or thirty years when they are no longer compelled to do so (by law or convention).[83]

Ketchum suggests here that a break with the past had occurred in terms of the family life. While the modern family was at a crossroads, traditional forces, such as the law, the church, and economic exigencies no longer kept it bonded together. Despite this claim, the family's relationship with these significant outside forces had hardly disappeared.[84] Not only did Ketchum claim that these regulating constraints had disappeared, but that they had done so at the worst possible time—a time when psychologists increasingly recognized the emotional vulnerability of children. The crux of the matter was clear and was passed on to parents: children needed stable, affectionate homes in order to develop normally. In the absence of traditional forces of cohesion, families required new reasons to stay together. If the central bond of the family was no longer legal, religious, or economic, Ketchum pronounced, it was psychological and emotional.[85]

That the modern family was based on emotional ties was not, however, a new claim in the postwar era.[86] This myth was, nonetheless, perpetuated through psychological discourse.

Using the war as a powerful rhetorical backdrop, Samuel Laycock used this strategy when he wrote: "Modern family life makes highly important and very heavy demands on the family. There has been merely a shifting of functions. Instead of *making things,* the modern family has as its chief function *the building of personality.* While the building of personality in its members has always been a function of the family, its task at the present is insistent and urgent."[87] The essential function of the modern family, Laycock argued, had shifted from "making things" to "building personality," even though the latter had always been important. He suggests, however, that far more than simply representing a renaming of the family's function, "building personalities" had become "insistent and urgent"—the implication being that it was more difficult to achieve in the postwar years, yet more crucial than ever before. Through this rhetorical strategy, Laycock reinterpreted the family as the main passageway through which Canadians travelled towards normalcy. This conception of the family's main function situated psychological expertise as a preventative strategy, thereby increasing its opportunity to exercise its normalizing powers.

Shaping attitudes towards normal families and normal children preoccupied psychologists' efforts throughout the postwar years. How did psychological discourse construct the normal child? Normalcy and normal personality development in children signified a set of attributes first constituted and ultimately determined by the psychologists themselves. Particular psychological theories, popular throughout the period, provided explanatory models for normal personality development in children. Normal childhood constituted not only a separate stage of life but was characterized by successful negotiation through separately defined stages. These childhood stages had specific behavioural characteristics and usually corresponded to the age of the child. This orientation was most clearly articulated, with differing emphases, in the work of psychologists Arnold Gesell and Jean Piaget. Gesell compiled detailed and precise descriptions of the behaviour that normal children exhibited at numerous points in their early lives. Piaget went beyond descriptions of children's development, offering the theory that as experience with the world unfolded, the mind was changed and transformed as it took on more complex and difficult tasks. This stage approach could also be found, with greater emphasis on psychosexual characteristics, in the work of Sigmund Freud. Freud emphasized infantile sexuality as a measuring stick of a child's development—the movement from the oral to the phallic to the latent to the genital stage of development.[88]

Popularized Canadian psychological writing borrowed heavily from the stage orientation articulated in the work of Gesell, Piaget, and Freud.[89] A textbook written by two educational psychologists at the University of Alberta, for example, told readers: "At one, you were sociable and enjoyed a pat-a-cake; at two you said 'no' more frequently than 'yes'...at three, in your parents' opinion, you were beginning to be more human...at four your mother paused occasionally, no doubt, to wonder how she could have given birth to such a little monster."[90] Understanding and appreciating children, this particular example suggests, depended to a large extent on an *a priori* set of normative standards and expectations. Informed parents anticipated well ahead of time what to expect in their growing child—they had a blueprint for normalcy.

This presentation of a growing child's development, however, necessarily oversimplified the process. In turn, this oversimplification necessarily homogenized children—all normal children at a particular age displayed the same tell-tale characteristics. The paradox inherent in this aspect of psychological discourse is exemplified in a parenting pamphlet issued by the Department of National Health and Welfare:

When your baby arrives you will soon realize that he is not just a little pink bundle to be fed and changed and cuddled, but a tiny individual.... He has psychological needs— mental, emotional and spiritual needs, just as much as physical needs.... If, as a parent, you have some idea of what is considered normal behaviour at various age levels, you will find bringing up your children much easier. There is much to be learned.[91]

The normal child, in psychologically informed advice such as this, personified an oxymoron: he or she was an individual who conformed to external standards. Psychologists seemed unaware of this inherent contradiction as they admonished parents to treat children as individuals by ensuring that they conformed to a well-scripted repertoire of normal behaviour. It is also suggested here that parents who utilized psychological knowledge in "decoding" their children had an advantage over parents who did not. The endorsement of psychological principles by a governmental agency, moreover, added both legitimacy and clout to this view of childhood.

Psychologists in the postwar period also tended to define normality and normal personality development in children by highlighting its opposite attributes. They informed Canadians what normalcy was, in other words, by focusing on what it was not. And the characteristics of a pathological personality were considerably broad. A study of children aged six to twelve years referred by teachers and parents to mental health clinics in Vancouver between 1945 and 1949, for example, demonstrates this point and suggests that the message was getting through to adults. The reasons for referrals reflected a mixture of overt difficulties and simple transgressions against the sensibilities of those in authority.[92] The first referral category, "socially unacceptable behaviour," included "temper tantrums, teasing, bullying, rebellion against authority, cruelty to persons or animals, destruc-

tiveness, bragging, seeking bad company, precocious sex activities, lying, stealing and truancy." No further definition of what exactly constituted some of these unacceptable attributes, like "seeking bad company" or "precocious sex activities," was offered by the author. Yet 38.91 per cent or 100 out of the 257 children examined, were referred to the clinics for these reasons. The next category, "personality reaction," afflicted some 31 per cent, or 80 of the 257 children. It was defined, albeit only superficially, as "seclusiveness, timidity, sensitiveness, fears, cowardliness, excessive imagination and fanciful lying, nervousness, excessive unhappiness and crying... overactivity and unpopularity with other children."[93] Children referred to the clinics for problems of "habit formation," the third category, totalled 15 per cent, or 30 of the 257 children examined in the Vancouver area clinics. "Habit formation" included those with "sleeping and eating difficulties, speech disturbances, thumb sucking, nail biting, masturbation, prolonged bed wetting and soiling." The final category of "special school disabilities" was left undefined, but nonetheless was said to afflict the remaining 15 per cent of the children studied.

The Vancouver clinic examples demonstrate that characteristics considered to be worthy of psychological treatment, such as temper tantrums, timidity, nailbiting, and masturbation, walked a fine line between the socially unacceptable and the clinically abnormal. In psychological discourse these two phrases often meant the same thing. While some of the characteristics described above were undoubtedly displayed by all children at some point in their lives, anti-social behaviour was pathologized in psychological discourse and thus judged harshly. The Vancouver clinic referrals suggest that normal children were controlled by adults and displayed compliance, obedience, happiness, and sexual innocence. Abnormal children, conversely, were difficult to control, anxious, and aware of their sexuality. By linking the normal with the ideal child, psychologists bolstered their own power, their own vision of normality, and their own conception of society's proper order.

While personality pathologies were certainly not limited to small children in psychological discourse, teenagers were taught to evaluate and even improve their own psychological maturity. A high school textbook used in Canadian classrooms, for example, instructed young readers to steer clear of immature personality traits, such as "irresponsibility, self-centredness, and blowing up easily." The mature alternatives to these undesirable traits included "responsibility, concern for others, controlling your emotions."[94] This example suggests that the psychological conception of normality served to entrench the traditional balance of power between teenagers and adults. It endowed the traditional notion that the former defer to the wishes of the latter with psychological legitimacy. Thus an obedient teenager or child was much more than simply good—he or she was normalized through this discourse. It described how the ideal child, the ideal teenager, or the ideal family would or should cope rather than how the majority of children, teenagers, or families coped with life. Any kind of familial conflict, this kind of reasoning suggested, was a sign of abnormality and was best avoided.

In postwar psychological discourse, it was parents, ultimately, who determined whether children enjoyed normal personality development or had personality pathologies. Psychology's recognition of this important influence in children's lives, however, did not mean that parents were to be left to their own devices. On the contrary, the need for psychologists' guidance and advice was promoted more vigorously than ever before. Just as children and teenagers were susceptible to personality pathologies, adults too could fall away from the boundaries of normalcy. For adults, especially parents, the stakes were even higher. In a lecture entitled "Good Parents," psychologist Robert

Jones told his audience: "The moral is plain—the best way to take advantage of a child's suggestibility and imitativeness is to put your own life in order so that you can set an example worthy of impressing the child. If you argue, pout, quarrel, cry, or curse your child will pick up on these traits."[95] Jones's comments suggested that the psychological mishandling of children eventually came back to haunt ill-prepared parents. Children of these inadequate parents eventually acted, in a manner rather like psychological blackmail, as humiliating billboards of familial failure. The kind of behaviour that caused abnormalities in children, as described briefly by Jones, is reminiscent of that displayed by the abnormal teenagers discussed previously—behaviour that threatened the reproduction of contented families. Parents, therefore, were to monitor their own behaviour closely and be on constant guard against unfavourably influencing the personality development of their children. It is significant to note, however, that Jones represented reactions such as arguing, pouting, and crying as character "traits" and not as common reactions to disappointment or injury. The possibility of doing emotional damage to children, given that unpleasant yet common human emotions like anger, disappointment, and frustration were not to be openly displayed by adults, seemed inevitable. Jones's caveats suggested that an essential, prototypical "good" parent, like an essential, prototypical "good" child, existed somewhere "out there." He suggested further that Canadians either were or were not good parents, depending on their knowledge of psychology and their willingness to put it into practice. Behaviour characterized by variety, individuality, and spontaneity, in light of Jones's position, could be considered suspect.

Undoubtedly, mothers were acknowledged as centrally important in the emotional lives of their children, but the issues surrounding this were complex and often contradictory. Some psychologists turned to the physical fact of pregnancy as a logical explanation for their identification of mothers as the primary caregiver.[96] Women, rather than men, the argument went, had a closer, more meaningful bond with their infants because mothers and babies shared the physiological process of pregnancy and birth. "Residues of the original unity," one student wrote in 1955, "always remain in the mother-child relationship."[97] This perception was even more pronounced in Quebec where, combined with the Catholic belief that propagating children was a religious duty, "'maternal instinct' was invoked so frequently that the qualities associated with it seemed innate."[98] The next logical assumption, that mothers naturally made gifted parents, was nevertheless denied in psychological discourse. Even before the war, psychologists were carving out a niche for their knowledge claims by asserting that the proper approach to mothering was learned from psychologists; it did not exist innately.[99] Blatz proclaimed in 1928 that while it was "formerly believed that mother instinct or mother love was a safe basis for the problems of training," scientific mothering had to be learned.[100] Similarly, Laycock, reacting in 1944 to an unfavourable Edmonton newspaper editorial regarding the necessity of parent education, stated that "one would think that this writer, if he goes about with his eyes open, must see that "natural instinct" does not tell mothers how to look after their children either physically or psychologically."[101] These reactions against women's "instincts" for proper mothering did not mean that psychologists had an enlightened view of women's diverse roles or their power to choose their life course. By differentiating between psychological insight and "natural" ability, psychologists made their expertise in the area of parenting all the more palatable and possible. A central tension in the psychological discourse concerning mothers, therefore, was reconciled: because mothers were the most important person in the child's life, they needed the most guidance to do their job well.

Psychologists considered mothers to be "the most important person" because it was during the early years that young children developed their "basic personality pattern."[102] Based on this interdependency between mothers and children, mothers were usually to blame if something went wrong. Case histories of school children referred to child guidance clinics around the country consistently blamed the inadequacies of mothers for causing emotional problems in children. Mothers were found to be "outgoing, talkative, and rather domineering in manner," someone who "made too much of the patient's misdemeanours."[103] Roberta Bruce concluded in her 1953 study of delinquent girls counselled at Montreal's Mental Hygiene Institute that "the primary factors which lead to anti-social behaviour are to be found in the relationship of the mother, and later on, of the father, to the child."[104] Besides knowing when to refrain from nagging and bossing their children, women were also supposed to know when to stop indulging their children with play and fun. Dr. Benjamin Spock, the author of the bestselling childcare manual, *Baby and Child Care*, warned mothers not to raise children who were overly dependent on them for their creative outlets. He instructed that "if a new mother is so delighted with her child that she is holding him or making games for a him a good part of his wakeful period, he may become quite dependent on these attentions and demand more and more of them."[105]

Instead of focusing on wider social problems as possible explanations for family troubles, psychologists suggested other remedies to an unhappy situation. The importance of the father figure was of particular interest to the psychologists in this regard. In keeping with the often contradictory meanings attached to democratic marriages in psychological discourse, fathers were encouraged to use their positions of authority to ensure and protect children's sense of confidence and security.[106] The psychologists' solution to the problem of "overmothering," for example, was simple: evoke the calming presence of the father.[107] A father who played with his children, read them stories, and took an interest in their lives, psychologists counselled, helped counteract the dangers posed by an overly zealous mother: "The closeness with a father as well as a mother during early childhood is of great importance. It doubly enriches a child's life to know and love two people instead of one. Children whose fathers as well as their mothers take an active part in their lives need not feel that home is a woman-dominated place where a man is either too stupid or too aloof to find his way around."[108]

These comments suggested that the "woman-dominated" home had inherent dangers for the normal upbringing of postwar children. They also exemplified the gendered thinking so prevalent in psychological discourse. The problem of overmothering, women's tendency to be prone to frustration and selfishness, and the loss of male dominance in the postwar home were recurrent themes in discussions of the importance of mothers and fathers. Children brought up by mothers alone, psychologists warned, ran the risk of developing abnormal attitudes towards the proper roles of the sexes. Psychologist Anna Wolf, frequently cited as a source of childrearing advice for Canadian parents, noted that children raised in "fatherless" homes grew up believing that "women are born to be the world's real bosses; such a belief tends to breed passive men and aggressive women."[109] Psychologists were often blunt in their condemnation of postwar women who refused the idealized, and therefore submissive, middle-class feminine role: "The man wants a partner in marriage, not a competitor. The woman, in her fight for her rights, has put herself too much into a competing position. She has tried to turn man instead of remaining woman. A man does not want to marry another man."[110]

Fathers were told that they, not mothers, represented "figures of strength, of security, of wisdom."[111] They were encouraged to explore their natural leadership role more actively in the family and to provide a counterpoint to the domineering tendencies that mothers were believed to possess.[112] Fathers were portrayed in psychological discourse as having something unique to offer to children, apart from mothers. Whereas mothers were a necessary evil satisfying the physical needs of young children, fathers were crucial for the development of maturity in older children: "Father has an important place in the family...that of a participating member of a partnership, an understanding friend and guide to his children, an entertaining member of a group, and an example of adult adjustment."[113]

A Montreal doctor writing on the subject of mental hygiene and childhood characterized this relationship between parents and children in hierarchical terms. According to him, properly developed toddlers first learn from their mothers "how to love and be loved." When the child reached a certain level of maturity, however, it was the father's lessons about "how to respect and feel respected" that allowed the child to move on to the realization of "logical thinking" and "rational judgement."[114] Whereas the expression of maternal emotion was seen as fraught with all sorts of potential excesses, paternal instruction was noble, mature, and often valorized in psychological discourse on parenting.[115] This notion of a hierarchy of normal parenting based on the constraints of gender was echoed in a textbook used by educational psychology students at the University of Saskatchewan: "As long as a boy stands alongside his mother and looks with wondering eyes at his father's activities, he seems to his father to be still a child. But when he steps over the line and stands alongside his father, he begins to behave like a man in his relationships with both his parents, and wins the respect of his father particularly."[116] As the passage suggests, a boy grew up and reached maturity only when the immature succour of his mother was bravely rejected for the mature confraternity of his father. In the case of the daughter-father relationship, the father also represented the key to her growing up. His attention could, as one author argued, "show in many ways that he approves of her not only as a person, but as a person who will some day be a woman."[117] As was the case with boys, girls were to look to the most powerful figure in the family hierarchy, the father, for final approval and acceptance.

In broader terms, this tendency to construct a hierarchy of parenting functions within psychological discourse worked to reproduce traditional attitudes towards gender and legitimized the belief that, although prone to "overparenting," women were best suited to look after very young children.[118] Furthermore, it reinforced the idea that while a mother's attention was useful, it was a father's crowning guidance that made the real difference in a child's normal development. Constructing "father" as a correcting foil to the corrupting indulgence of "mother," psychological discourse reinforced and legitimized the traditional position of fathers as rightful "heads" of families. [...]

Notes

1   Robert Macleod, "Can Psychological Research Be Planned on a National Scale?" *Canadian Journal of Psychology* 1, 4 (Dec. 1947): 190.

2   Canadian Broadcasting Corporation, *School for Parents: A Series of Talks Given on the National Network of the Canadian Broadcasting Corporation* (Toronto: National Committee for Mental Hygiene 1945); Canadian Broadcasting Corporation, *The Soldier's Return* (Toronto: Publications Branch 1945); Canadian Youth Commission, *Youth, Marriage and the Family* (Ottawa 1945); S.R. Laycock, *Education for a Post-War World* (Toronto: Home and School Association 1945); Karl Bernhardt, "Tomorrow's Citizens," *Parent Education Bulletin* 40 (1947): 2–5; Brock Chisholm, "Tell Them the Truth," *Maclean's*, 15 Jan. 1946, 42–4; Benjamin Spock, "What We Know about the Development of Healthy Personalities in Children," *Canadian Welfare* 27, 15 April 1951, 3–12; C. Wesley Topping, "How to Stay Married," *Chatelaine*, Feb. 1946, 10–11, 47; A.P. Luscombe Whyte, "Psychologists Go to War," *National Home Monthly*, 44 Nov. 1943, 12–13, 22.

3   Often negatively associated with communist tendencies, homosexuality and homosexuals were especially demonized in the paranoid political climate of the Cold War era in Canada. See especially Gary Kinsman, *The Regulation of Desire: Sexuality in Canada* (Montreal: Black Rose Books 1987); Daniel J. Robinson and David Kimmel, "The Queer Career of Homosexual Security Vetting in Cold War Canada," *Canadian Historical Review* 74 (1994): 319–45; and Gerard Philip, "From Subversion to Liberation: Homosexuals and the Immigration Act,

1952–1977," *Canadian Journal of Law and Society* 2 (1987): 1–27. The political threat of women's sexuality is explored in Donna Penn, "The Sexualized Woman: The Lesbian, the Prostitute, and the Containment of Women's Sexuality in Postwar America," in Joanne Meyerowitz, ed., *Not June Cleaver: Women and Gender in Postwar America, 1946–1960* (Philadelphia: Temple University Press 1994), 358–81; Mary Louise Adams details postwar discourses about concern for youth and "normal" sexuality in "Youth, Corruptibility, and English-Canadian Campaigns against Indecency, 1948–1955," *Journal of the History of Sexuality* 6, 1 (1995): 89–119; see also Mary Louise Adams, "The Trouble with Normal: Postwar Youth and the Construction of Heterosexuality" (PhD dissertation, University of Toronto 1994).

4   Franca Iacovetta, "Remaking Their Lives: Women Immigrants, Survivors, and Refugees," in Joy Parr, ed., *A Diversity of Women: Ontario, 1945–1980* (Toronto: University of Toronto Press 1995), 135–67; Valerie Knowles, *Strangers at Our Gates: Canadian Immigration and Canadian Immigration Policy, 1540–1990* (Toronto: Dundurn Press 1992), 118–36.

5   Jocelyn Motyer Raymond, *The Nursery World of Dr. Blatz* (Toronto: University of Toronto Press 1991), 3–24.

6   Gordon A. McMurray, "Psychology at Saskatchewan," in Mary J. Wright and C.R. Myers, eds., *History of Academic Psychology in Canada* (Toronto: C.J. Hofrefe 1982), 181–2; Theresa R. Richardson, *The Century of the Child: The Mental Hygiene Movement and Social Policy in the United States and Canada*

(New York: State University of New York Press 1989), 156.

7 Mary L. Northway, "Child Study in Canada: A Casual History," in Lois M. Brockman, John H. Whiteley, and John R. Zubek, eds., *Child Development: Selected Readings* (Toronto: McClelland & Stewart 1973), 22–3.

8 Ibid., 22.

9 Raymond, *The Nursery World of Dr. Blatz,* 144, 200.

10 Karl Bernhardt, "Canadian Psychology: Past, Present and Future," *Canadian Journal of Psychology* 1, 2 (1947): 57.

11 Rux Martin, "Truth, Power, Self: An Interview with Michel Foucault," in Martin H. Luther, Huck Gutman, and P. Hutton, eds., *Technologies of the Self: A Seminar with Michel Foucault* (Amherst: University of Massachusetts Press 1988), 15; John Newson and Elizabeth Newson, "Cultural Aspects of Childrearing in the English-Speaking World," in M.P.M. Richards, *The Integration of the Child into a Social World* (London: Cambridge University Press 1973), 52–65; Andrew Abbott, *The Systems of Professions: An Essay on the Division of Expert Labor* (Chicago: University of Chicago Press 1988).

12 As Mariana Valverde observes, "social regulation is best understood not as the control of already distinct areas of social activity but rather as a process which first constitutes the object to be administered." "Representing Childhood: The Multiple Fathers of the Dionne Quintuplets," in Carol Smart, ed., *Regulating Womanhood: Historical Essays on Marriage, Motherhood and Sexuality* (London: Routledge Press 1992), 19, 143.

13 Michel Foucault, *Discipline and Punish: The Birth of the Prison* (New York: Pantheon 1977), 177–84.

14 J.S.A. Bois, "The Psychologist as Counsellor," *Canadian Journal of Psychology* 2, 3 (Sept. 1948): 121. Generally, both psychologists and their clients were referred to as "he" unless addressing a specific case involving a female. Although it was a male-dominated profession, women did act as psychologists, especially during the Second World War. See Mary Wright, "Women Ground-breakers in Canadian Psychology: World War II and Its Aftermath," *Canadian Psychology/psychologie canadienne* 33, 4 (Oct. 1992): 674–82.

15 Christopher Lasch, *Haven in a Heartless World* (New York: Basic Books 1977).

16 Chunn, *From Punishment to Doing Good,* 192–3.

17 David Ingleby, "The Psychology of Child Psychology," in Richards, *The Integration of the*

Child into a Social World, 296; see also Ruby Takanishi, "Childhood as a Social Issue: Historical Roots of Contemporary Child Advocacy Movements," *Journal of Social Issues* 34, 2 (1978): 8–27; Kathleen Janet McConnachie, "Science and Ideology: The Mental Hygiene and Eugenics Movement in the Inter-war Years, 1919–1939" (PhD dissertation, University of Toronto 1987); Fred Matthews, "The Utopia of Human Relations: The Conflict Free Family of American Social Thought, 1930–1960," *Journal of the History of the Behavioural Sciences* 24 (Oct. 1988): 343–62; Cathy Urwin and Valerie Walkerdine, eds., *Language, Gender, and Childhood* (London: Routledge & Kegan Paul 1985), 164–202.

18 Matthews, "The Utopia of Human Relations," 343.

19 I refer here to Foucault's phrase "technologies of the self." Foucault explains the evolution of discipline as a movement from physical punishment of the body to incarceration and surveillance. Over the course of this evolution, discipline becomes internalized and self-perpetuating. We cooperate, are coerced, and willingly conform, all technologies of the self, to forces exercising various degrees of control over our free will. See Martin, "Truth, Power, Self," 15; Martin Hewitt, "Bio-Politics and Social Policy: Foucault's Account of Welfare," in M. Featherstone, Mike Hepworth, and Bryan S. Turner, eds., *The Body: Social Process and Cultural Theory* (London: Sage Publications 1991), 225–56.

20 In "Family Matters: The Canadian Family and the State in Postwar Canada," *left history* 1, 2 (1993): 9–50, Annalee Gölz suggests that "socio-economic and gender dislocations" after the Depression and the war spawned a "concerted effort" to "restabilize" the family. See also Adams, "Youth, Corruptibility, and English-Canadian Postwar Campaigns against Indecency, 1948–1955," 93–6.

21 Chunn, *From Punishment to Doing Good,* 40–1.

22 Jane Ursel, *Private Lives, Public Policy: 100 Years of State Intervention in the Family* (Toronto: Women's Press, 1992), 205–6; Cynthia Comacchio, *"Nations Are Built of Babies": Saving Ontario's Mothers and Children, 1900–1940* (Montreal and Kingston: McGill-Queen's University Press 1993); James G. Snell, *In the Shadow of the Law: Divorce in Canada, 1900–1939* (Toronto: University of Toronto Press 1991), 28.

23 Parr, ed., *A Diversity of Women;* Adams, "Youth, Corruptibility, and English-Canadian Campaigns against Indecency"; Franca Iacovetta, "Making 'New Canadians': Social Workers, Women and the Reshaping of Immigrant Families," in Franca

Iacovetta and Mariana Valverde, eds., *Gender Conflicts: New Essays in Women's History* (Toronto: University of Toronto Press 1992), 273; Charles M. Johnson, "The Children's War: The Mobilization of Ontario Youth during the Second World War," in Roger Hall, William Westfall, and Laurel Sefton MacDowell, eds., *Patterns of the Past: Interpreting Ontario's History* (Toronto: Dundurn Press 1988), 365–6; Gölz, "Family Matters," 24–6; Owram, "Home and Family at Mid-Century"; Veronica Strong-Boag, "Home Dreams: Women and the Suburban Experiment in Canada, 1945–1960," *Canadian Historical Review* 72, 4 (1991): 471–504.

24 Referring to women's experiences, for example, Joanne Meyerowitz points out that the tendency to view the postwar years in this way "flattens the history of women, reducing the multidimensional complexity of the past to a snapshot of middle-class women in suburban homes." "Introduction: Women and Gender in Postwar America, 1945–1960," in Meyerowitz, ed., *Not June Cleaver*, 2. Similar caveats are offered in Mariana Valverde, "Building Anti-Delinquent Communities: Morality, Gender, and Generation in the City," in Parr, ed., *Diversity of Women*, 19–45; Adams, "Youth, Corruptibility, and English-Canadian Postwar Campaigns against Indecency," 89–117.

25 Veronica Strong-Boag, "Canada's Wage Earning Wives and the Construction of the Middle-Class, 1945–1960," *Journal of Canadian Studies* 29, 3 (1974): 5–25; Joan Sangster, "Doing Two Jobs: The Wage-Earning Mother, 1945–1970," in Parr, ed., *A Diversity of Women*, 98–134; Susan M. Hartmann, "Women's Employment and the Domestic Ideal in the Early Cold War Years," in Meyerowitz, ed., *Not June Cleaver*, 84–101.

26 Strong-Boag, "Home Dreams," 471–504, and "'Their Side of the Story': Women's Voices from Ontario's Suburbs, 1945–1960," in Joy Parr, ed., *A Diversity of Women*, 46–74.

27 Franca Iacovetta, *Such Hardworking People: Italian Immigrants in Postwar Toronto* (Montreal & Kingston: McGill-Queen's University Press 1992) and "Remaking Their Lives," 135–67.

28 See, for example, Gölz, "Family Matters," 24–6; Owram, "Home and Family at Mid-Century," 2–6; Strong-Boag, "Home Dreams," 471–504; George Kisker, "Why You Fight with Your Wife/Husband," *Maclean's*, 60 1 Aug. 1947, 1, 36–7; Paul Popenoe, "First Aid for the Family," *Maclean's*, 60 1 May 1947, 19; Topping, "How to Stay Married," 10, 11, 47.

29 Mildred Horn, *Mothers and Daughters: A Digest for Women and Girls, which Completely Covers the Field of Sex Hygiene* (Toronto: Hygienic Productions 1946), 91. Despite the absence of documented sources, Horn contends that "one high school in a small town with an enrollment of 68 girls reported 53 pregnancies in one year...another school with 281 girls reported 112 pregnant between the opening of school in September and Christmas holidays"; Kisker, "Why You Fight with Your Wife/Husband," 37; Sidney Katz, "Are We Growing More Cruel to Our Children?" *Maclean's*, 61 15 July 1948, 42; Lotta Dempsey, "We the People vs. The Sex Criminal," *Chatelaine*, Jan. 1948, 6. See also the discussion of sexual delinquency in the 1950s in Christabelle Laura Sethna, "The Facts of Life: The Sex Instruction of Ontario Public School Children" (PhD dissertation, University of Toronto 1993), 262–9.

30 Becki L. Ross, *The House That Jill Built: A Lesbian Nation in Formation* (Toronto: University of Toronto Press 1995), 12–15; W.D. Ross, "Mental Hygiene and Reconstruction," *Public Affairs* 6, 4 (1943): 200; Dyson Carter, "Treating Our Minds Tomorrow," *National Home Monthly*, Dec. 1944, 11; Samuel Laycock, "What Can We Do About Juvenile Delinquency?" in *Education for a Post-War World*, 84, and "What Are Families For?" *National Parent-Teacher* 41, 3 (Nov. 1946): 10; C.M. Hincks, "Postwar Women," in CBC, *The Soldier's Return*, 17.

31 The text of the radio program reappeared in J.D. Ketchum, "The Family: Changing Patterns in an Industrial Society," in *Canadian Family Study, 1957–1960* (Toronto: Canadian Home and School and Parent-Teacher Federation 1961), 16.

32 Anonymous, "Simple Rules for Mental Health," *Canadian Congress Journal* 21 (Aug. 1942): 109.

33 J.D.M. Griffin, S.R. Laycock, and W. Line, *Mental Hygiene: A Manual for Teachers* (New York: American Book Company 1940), 9. Emphasis in original. In most of the psychologists' advice surveyed in this study, the generic term "child" or "children" is equated with the masculine "he."

34 University of Saskatchewan Archives (USA), Samuel Laycock Papers, Publications—Articles and Addresses, No. 271, "Radio Address—Mental Hygiene in the School and Home," (nd), 4.

35 James M. Pitsula, *Let the Family Flourish: A History of the Family Service Bureau of Regina, 1913–1982* (Regina: Family Service Bureau of Regina 1982), 72.

36 Canada, Dominion Bureau of Statistics, *Canada Year Book, 1945* (Ottawa: King's Printer 1945),

150–1; *Canada Year Book, 1950* (Ottawa: King's Printer 1950), 232.

37 *Canada Year Book, 1955* (Ottawa: King's Printer 1955), 224.

38 *Canada Year Book, 1960* (Ottawa: King's Printer 1960), 254.

39 Snell, *In the Shadow of the Law,* 9–10.

40 Gölz, "Family Matters," 13.

41 V. Lorne Stewart, "Family Breakdown," in *Canadian Family Study, 1957–1960,* 10–11; Journalist Max Braithwaite, in an interesting twist to this postwar discussion, argued that the Canadian family was strong, despite "doleful pronouncements of hundreds of speakers and writers who keep hinting, insinuating and even declaring outright that the good old institution of the family is on the skids." Braithwaite, "The Family Is Here to Stay," *Chatelaine,* Oct. 1951, 110.

42 S.R. Laycock, "New Approaches to Sex Education," *The School,* Dec. 1945, 312, and "Psychological Factors in Marriage," *The Prairie Messenger* 28 (Jan. 1950): 1; Harry C. McKown, *A Boy Grows Up* (New York: McGraw-Hill 1949), 300. Although an American publication, McKown's book was recommended for guidance training in Laycock's Educational Psychology courses at the University of Saskatchewan.

43 Laycock, "Psychological Factors in Marriage," 12.

44 Ibid., 12–13.

45 Northway, "Child Study in Canada," 14; S.R. Laycock, "How Parents Hinder Their Adolescents' Adjustment to the Opposite Sex," *Understanding the Child* 14, 2 (1945): 35–9.

46 Owram, "Home and Family at Mid-Century," 9.

47 *Canada Year Book, 1950,* 227–9.

48 Owram, "Home and Family at Mid-Century," 16–17.

49 *Canada Yearbook, 1955,* 220–1.

50 *Canada Yearbook, 1960,* 261.

51 Alison Prentice et al., *Canadian Women: A History* (Toronto: Harcourt Brace Jovanovich 1988), 311; Owram, "Home and Family at Mid-Century," 17.

52 Kay Montgomery, "Family Relations in B.C.," *National Home Monthly,* July 1945, 27.

53 Ibid.

54 Owram, "Home and Family at Mid-Century," 21.

55 Paul Popenoe, "First Aid for the Family," *Maclean's,* 1 May 1947, 19, 45, 47. Popenoe, Angus McLaren reminds us, was an early proponent of the eugenics movement in the United States. McLaren, *Our Own Master Race: Eugenics in Canada, 1885–1945* (Toronto: McClelland & Stewart 1990).

56 Gölz, "Family Matters," 15–16; Owram, "Home and Family at Mid-Century," 23–5; Laycock, "Psychological Factors in Marriage," 10; Karl Bernhardt, "The Father in the Family," *Bulletin of the Institute of Child Study* 19, 2 (1957): 2; Guy Roche, "Le Père," *Food for Thought* 14, 6 (March 1954): 9; McKown, *A Boy Grows Up,* 203.

57 Ketchum, "The Family," 19.

58 S.R. Laycock, "What Are Families For?" *Canadian Home and School* 6, 2 (1946): 10, and "Psychological Factors in Marriage," 10; Harold W. Bernard, *Mental Hygiene for Classroom Teachers* (New York: McGraw-Hill 1952), 4. Bernard's book was recommended reading for Canadian teachers-in-training. William Blatz, *Understanding the Young Child* (Toronto: Clarke, Irwin 1944), 127, 240; Karl Bernhardt, *What It Means to Be a Good Parent* (Toronto: Institute of Child Study 1950), 2; Baruch Silverman and Herbert R. Matthews, "On Bringing Up Children," *Canadian Home and School* 10, 1 (1950): 5.

59 Bernhardt, "Canadian Psychology," 58.

60 William Blatz, "Why Husbands and Wives Nag Each Other," *Chatelaine,* Nov. 1955, 17.

61 Ibid., 82.

62 Laycock, "Psychological Factors in Marriage," 10.

63 Canada *Up the Years from One to Six* (Ottawa: Department of National Health and Welfare 1961), 80. Emphasis in original.

64 Horn, *Mothers and Daughters,* 33.

65 W.E. Blatz, "The Greatest Menace to Marriage Today," *Chatelaine,* Oct. 1955, 13, 119, 120–1, 123; "Why Husbands and Wives Nag Each Other," 16–17, 82–4; "Why You Bore Your Husband," *Chatelaine,* March 1956, 21, 53–6; "Why You Should Never Quarrel with Your Husband," *Chatelaine,* Nov. 1956, 11, 54–5; "What Makes a Woman Jealous?" *Chatelaine,* May 1956, 24, 30–2.

66 Blatz, "Why You Should Never Quarrel with Your Husband," 11.

67 Blatz's own forty-year marriage to Margery Rowland ended in 1960. Jocelyn Motyer Raymond suggests that the decision to do so had been made early in their married lives and was to take place after their daughter, Margery, nicknamed Gery, had grown. They were reportedly "devoted parents and each other's good friends, willingly taking the con-

sequences of an earlier, younger decision in order to give their daughter a stable childhood" *The Nursery World of Dr. Blatz,* 197.

68 "Letters to Chatelaine," *Chatelaine,* May 1956, 3.

69 E.B., Ottawa, "Quarrels Beat the 'Road Blocks': Letters to Chatelaine," *Chatelaine,* Jan. 1957, 2.

70 USA, Samuel Laycock Papers, Publications: Articles and Addresses, "Psychological Factors in Marriage," 1951, 4.

71 Ibid.

72 Linda Ambrose has suggested that fear and paranoia over communism and fascism, along with postwar opportunities for work, made young people a presumably volatile and unpredictable population in the eyes of some governmental and social leaders in these years. Mary Louise Adams has focused our attention on the opportunity for moral and sexual regulation that discourses about the "corruptibility" of youth presented. See Linda McGuire Ambrose, "The Canadian Youth Commission: Planning for Youth and Social Welfare in the Postwar Era" (PhD dissertation, University of Waterloo 1992), especially chapter 1, "Approaches to Youth: The Context of the CYC," 30–66; Adams, "Youth, Corruptibility, and English-Canadian Postwar Campaigns against Indecency."

73 Valverde, "Building Anti-Delinquent Communities," 19–20.

74 Johnson, "The Children's War," 366.

75 Johnson notes that in Toronto, 15 per cent of the school population under fourteen were "working into the late night hours at restaurants, theatres, bingo halls, and that object of middle-class puritanical loathing, the pool hall" (365).

76 Augustine Brannigan, "Mystification of the Innocents: Crime Comics and Delinquency in Canada, 1931–1949," *Criminal Justice History* 7 (1986): 110–44, and "Delinquency, Comic and Legislative Reform in Postwar Canada and Victoria," *Australian-Canadian Studies* 3 (1985): 53–69; Janice Dickin McGinnis, "Bogeymen and the Law: The Crime Comic and Pornography," *Ottawa Law Review* 20, 1 (1988): 3–25; Mona Gleason, "Disciplining Children, Disciplining Parents: The Nature and Meaning of Psychological Advice to Canadian Parents, 1948–1955," *histoire sociale/Social History* 29, 57 (1996): forthcoming.

77 The standard definition of juvenile delinquency in the postwar years was taken from the 1949 *Encyclopedia of Criminology.* It defined the term as "habitual truancy from home or school; conduct that injures or endangers the morality or health of others; infractions of laws; and habitual disobedience or waywardness that is uncontrolled by parent, guardian or custodian." See, for example, Roberta M. Bruce, "Parent-Child Relationships of 23 Delinquent, Adolescent Girls: A study of the emotional factors in parent-child relationships of 23 adolescent girls referred to the Mental Hygiene Institute and of the role of the social worker in the treatment plan" (MSW, McGill University 1951), 4.

78 Laycock, *Education for a Post-War World,* 94; J. Alex Edmison, "Gang Delinquency," *Canadian Forum* 29 (April 1949): 7.84.

79 See, for example, Bernhardt, *What It Means to Be a Good Parent,* 7–8; Samuel Laycock, "Development of a Normal Personality," *British Columbia Parent-Teacher News* 11, 4 (1949): 4. The basic psychological needs repeated by psychologists over the course of the postwar period included the need for affection, belonging, independence, social approval, self-esteem, and creative achievement.

80 Samuel Laycock, for example, wrote that a "great deal of delinquency is due to the fact that the child does not feel emotionally secure in his own home," in "Discipline and Supervision: How Much Freedom?" *Home and School Quarterly* 14, 1 (1945): 6.

81 Ketchum, "The Family," 16; Gölz, "Family Matters," 26–7; Rocher, "Le Père," 6–10; W.B. Baker, "A Home on the Prairie," 22–6; Laycock, "What Are Families For?" 8–10; *Canadian Family Study, 1957–1960,* 28–33.

82 University of Toronto, Thomas Fisher Rare Book Room, William Blatz Collection, MS 134, box 25, Parent Education Courses, 1928–1951, "The Modern Home," 13 Jan. 1941.

83 Ketchum, "The Family," 18. Emphasis in original.

84 The Canadian Youth Commission, for example, debated rigorously on the nature of these and other factors in shaping family life after the war. Ambrose, "The Canadian Youth Commission," 212–48.

85 See also Gölz, "Family Matters," 15–17; S.R. Laycock, "Parents Are Such Problems," *Maclean's,* 15 Oct. 1946, 13; Baker, "A Home on the Prairie," 22–6; Rocher, "Le Père," 6–10.

86 For discussions of the importance of sentiment in family life in Canada in the nineteenth and early twentieth century, see Peter Ward, *Courtship, Love, and Marriage in Nineteenth-Century English Canada* (Montreal-Kingston: McGill-Queen's University Press 1990); Comacchio, *"Nations Are Built of Babies."* Classic studies which trace the importance

of attachment and rejection in family life include Philippe Ariès, *Centuries of Childhood: A Social History of the Family* (New York: Knopf 1962); Edward Shorter, *The Making of the Modern Family* (New York: Basic Books 1975); Lawrence Stone, *The Family, Sex and Marriage in England, 1500–1800* (London: Weiderfled and Nicolson 1977); Michael Anderson, *Approaches to the History of the Western Family, 1500–1914* (London: Macmillan 1980).

87 Laycock, "What Are Families For?" 9. Emphasis in original.

88 Morton Hunt, *The Story of Psychology* (New York: Anchor Books 1993); Arnold Gesell, *Child Development: An Introduction to the Study of Human Growth* (New York: Harper & Row 1949); *The First Five Years of Life: A Guide to the Study of Preschool Children* (London: Methuen 1959); Jean Piaget, *The Moral Judgement of the Child,* translated by Marjorie Gabain (Glencoe: Free Press 1948), and *Judgement and Reasoning in the Child,* with E. Certalis (New Jersey: Littlefeld, Adams 1959); Sigmund Freud, *Three Essays on Sexuality* (New York: Avon 1965).

89 See, for example, S.R. Laycock, "Every Child Brings His Home to School," *Alberta School Trustee* 13, 12 (June 1943): 23, "Educating the Six-to-Twelve-Year-Old for Family Living," *Canadian Home and School* 10 (March 1951): 22, and "What Can We Do about Juvenile Delinquency?" 82; Marguerite W. Brown, *It Takes Time to Grow* (Toronto: Board of Christian Education, Women's Missionary Society of the United Church of Canada 1953); S.C.T. Clarke and J.G. Woodsworth, *Youth and Tomorrow: A Guide to Personal Development in the Early and Middle Teens* (Toronto: McClelland & Stewart 1956); Blatz, *Understanding the Young Child.*

90 Clarke and Woodsworth, *Youth and Tomorrow,* 6.

91 Department of National Health and Welfare, *You and Your Family* (Ottawa: Information Services Division Department, National Health and Welfare 1949), 35.

92 Evelyn Marie Roberts, "Mental Health Clinical Services: A Study of Children between 6 and 12 years of age examined by the Mental Health Clinics in Vancouver from 1945 to 1947 inclusive" (MSW, University of British Columbia 1949), 31.

93 Ibid., 31–2.

94 Clarke and Woodsworth, *Youth and Tomorrow,* 28–9.

95 Robert O. Jones, "Good Parents," in *School for Parents: A Series of Talks Given on the National Network of the CBC* (Toronto: National Committee for Mental Hygiene (1944), 2.

96 See Donald G. Finlay, "The Mother-Child Relationship after Treatment in a Child Guidance Clinic" (M.A. thesis, University of Toronto 1955); M. Prados, "On Promoting Mental Health," *Canadian Psychiatric Association Journal* 2, 1 (1957): 44.

97 Finlay, "The Mother-Child Relationship," 6. The concept of maternal instinct, the notion that women have a "natural" desire to have and nurture children that is inextricably meshed with the dictates of their bodies, has had a long articulation in Canada, especially among doctors. The adherence to this belief—that a woman's bond with children is "naturally" stronger than a man's because of biology—has been used to justify both the exclusion of women from the public realm and women's politicization of the private. See Wendy Mitchinson, *The Nature of Their Bodies: Women and Their Doctors in Victorian Canada* (Toronto: University of Toronto Press 1991), especially chapters 1, 2; Carol Bacchi, *Liberation Deferred? The Ideas of the English-Canadian Suffragists, 1877–1918* (Toronto: University of Toronto Press 1983).

98 Andrée Lévesque, *Making and Breaking the Rules: Women in Quebec, 1919–1939,* translated by Yvonne M. Klein (Toronto: McClelland & Stewart 1994), 24; Evelyn M. Brown, *Educating Eve* (Montreal: Palm Publishers 1957), 7.

99 For more on the experts' construction of motherhood, see especially Katherine Arnup, *Education for Motherhood: Advice for Mothers in Twentieth-Century Canada* (Toronto: University of Toronto Press, 1994).

100 William Blatz and Helen Bott, *Parents and the Pre-School Child* (Toronto: Dent 1928), viii.

101 Samuel Laycock, "Parent Education Is Adult Education," *Food for Thought* 5, 3 (Dec. 1944): 4–5. A similar view is expressed in Ella Kendall Cork, *A Home of Her Own* (Canada: National Girls' Work Board of the Religious Council of Canada 1944), 54.

102 Baruch Silverman and Herbert R. Matthews, "On Bringing Up Children," *Canadian Home and School* 10, 1 (1950): 4–8.

103 Anonymous, "Some Data on Mental Health Problems in Canadian Schools," *Canadian Education* 3, 2 (1948): 24–7.

104 Bruce, "Parent-Child Relationships of 23 Delinquent Adolescent Girls," 2.

105 Benjamin Spock, *Baby and Child Care* (New York: Pocket Books 1946), 166. Since its appearance, the book has sold thirty million copies. Katherine Arnup has found that while exact sales figures for Canada are difficult to determine, a test marketing of the pocket edition, blamed by Montreal doctor Alton Goldbloom for undermining the sales of his hard-copy manual, sold 3000 copies within six weeks. The New York publisher recommended an initial run of 100,000 copies for the Canadian market. Arnup, "Education for Motherhood: Women and Family in Twentieth-Century Canada" (PhD thesis, University of Toronto 1991), 128.

106 Mary Frank and Lawrence K. Frank, *How to Help Your Child in School* (New York: Signet Books 1950), 121–2. Although an American publication, the Frank manual was recommended to Canadian parents by Samuel Laycock and in governmental publications on childrearing.

107 Janice Drakich, "In Search of the Better Parent: The Social Construction of Ideologies of Fatherhood," *Canadian Journal of Women and the Law* 3, 1 (1989): 73; *Report of the Research Symposium on Mental Health and Child Development,* given to the Section on the Mental Health of Childhood and Youth of the Fifth International Congress on Mental Health, University of Toronto, August 1954, 5–6.

108 Irma Simonton Black, *Off to a Good Start: A Handbook for Parents* (New York: Harcourt, Brace and Company 1953), 101–2, recommended reading in "A Selective List of Books, Pamphlets and Films on Parent Education," *Food for Thought* 12 (Nov. 1951): 66–8. *Food for Thought* was the official organ of the Adult Education Association of Canada.

109 Anna W.M. Wolf, *The Parent's Manual: A Guide to the Emotional Development of Young Children* (New York: Simon and Schuster 1946), 216–17, recommended reading, for example, in "A Selective List of Books," 66–8.

110 Lee Edward Travis and Dorothy Walter Baruch, *Problems of Everyday Life: Practical Aspects of Mental Hygiene* (New York D. Appleton-Century 1944), 233, recommended in "A Selective List," 66–8.

111 Frank and Frank, *How to Help Your Child in School,* 122.

112 Stephanie Shields and Beth Koster, "Emotional Stereotyping of Parents in Child Rearing Manuals, 1915–1980," *Social Psychology Quarterly* 52, 1 (1989): 50.

113 Karl S. Bernhardt, "The Father in the Family," *Bulletin of the Institute of Child Study* 19, 2 (1957): 4.

114 Prados, "On Promoting Mental Health," 45.

115 Shields and Koster, "Emotional Stereotyping of Parents," 51.

116 McKown, *A Boy Grows Up,* 61.

117 Brown, *It Takes Time to Grow,* 65; see also Shirley Braverman, "The Father's Role in a Child Guidance Clinic" (MSW, McGill University 1951), 1.

118 This idea was also used to justify female teachers' relegation to overseeing lower grades and young children throughout the nineteenth and into the twentieth century. So powerful was this discourse regarding women's nurturing tendencies that women teachers themselves often accepted their often undervalued positions as "natural." Alison Prentice and Marjorie R. Theobald, "The Historiography of Women Teachers: A Retrospect," in Alison Prentice and Marjorie R. Theobald, *Women Who Taught: Perspectives on the History of Women and Teaching* (Toronto: University of Toronto Press 1994), 6.

"Character Weaknesses" and "Fruit Machines"

Towards an Analysis of the Anti-Homosexual Security Campaign in the Canadian Civil Service

GARY KINSMAN

Introduction

"Sexual abnormalities appear to be the favourite target of hostile intelligence agencies, and of these homosexuality is most often used," stated a 1959 Canadian Security Panel memorandum. The memo went on:

> The nature of homosexuality appears to adapt itself to this kind of exploitation. By exercising fairly simple precautions, homosexuals are usually able to keep their habits hidden from those who are not specifically seeking them out. Further, homosexuals often appear to believe that the accepted ethical code which governs normal human relationships does not apply to them. Their propensity is often accompanied by other specific weaknesses such as excessive drinking with its resultant instabilities, a defiant attitude towards the rest of society, and a concurrent urge to seek out the company of persons with similar characteristics, often in disreputable bars, night clubs or restaurants.[1]

The memo continues pointing out that

From the small amount of information we have been able to obtain about homosexual behaviour generally, certain characteristics appear to stand out—instability, willing self-deceit, defiance towards society, a tendency to surround oneself with persons of similar propensities, regardless of other considerations—none of which inspire the confidence one would hope to have in persons required to fill positions of trust and responsibility.[2]

These quotes are from one of the previously secret government documents on the anti-gay/anti-lesbian security campaigns in the Canadian civil service that Canadian Press secured in 1992 through the Access to Information Act.[3] In the ways these texts were mobilized within state security regime relations they could have been devastating for the lives of those identified as gay or lesbian. They were part of constructing gay men and lesbians as a particular type of social problem and were an integral part of the construction of heterosexual hegemony[4] within Canadian state formation.[5]

During the late 1950s and early 1960s these texts were used to organize problems for

Gary Kinsman, "'Character Weakness' and 'Fruit Machines': Towards an Analysis of the Anti-Homosexual Security Campaign in the Canadian Civil Service," *Labour/Le Travail* 35 (Spring 1995): 133–161. Copyright © Canadian Committee on Labour History. Reprinted from *Labour/Le Travail* with the permission of CCLH.

hundreds of lesbians and gay men who lost their jobs or were demoted to less 'sensitive' positions in the federal civil service. The Royal Canadian Mounted Police (RCMP) collected the names of thousands of possible homosexuals, and the government funded and sponsored research into means to detect homosexuals. Homosexuals were designated a 'national security threat' because of their 'character weakness' which supposedly left gay men and lesbians open to blackmail by Soviet agents. While I analyze the security regime more generally the focus in this paper is on the impact of these campaigns on gay men and lesbians and on the conception of "character weakness" which was used against lesbians and gay men as an integral part of this campaign.

A critical reading of these state security documents as pieces of textually-mediated social organization[6] gives us insights into the social organization of this major anti-gay/anti-lesbian campaign in the history of Canadian state formation.[7] In doing this I am drawing on the social organization of knowledge approach of marxist feminist Dorothy E. Smith and power/knowledge and genealogical approaches derived from the work of Michel Foucault.[8] In this paper these texts of the Security Panel and reports of the RCMP are interrogated from the standpoints of lesbians and gay men who were investigated, transferred and purged. We have to be very critical of this ruling social construction of knowledge—these texts are not neutral or 'objective,'—they were part of the textual practices mandating and organizing problems for gay men and lesbians during these years. Texts do not have power on their own. They are produced through human activities and gain social power through their activation and use by people in specific social relations—in this situation within the security regime. It is through these textual practices that this security campaign was organized.[9]

[...]

Homosexuals as a national security danger

The 1950s and the early 1960s were years of the social construction of homosexuality as a national, social and sexual danger in Canada. This occurred in the context of the reconstruction and transformation of patriarchal and heterosexist hegemonic relations after the 'disruptions' of the war mobilizations. There were at least three aspects of the construction of homosexuals as a danger in Canada during these years: the purge campaigns in the civil service, military and the RCMP; the related immigration legislation changes of 1952 which prevented homosexuals from immigrating to Canada and were tied into 'security' concerns; and the construction of homosexuals as a 'sexual danger' (especially to young people) through the extension of criminal sexual legislation and through mass media coverage.[10] In this paper I focus on this first aspect.

In the context of the Cold War, McCarthyism and 'national security' scares, homosexuals were designated a "threat to national security." The anti-homosexual campaigns were linked to anti-communist and anti-Soviet campaigns in the US and Canada. One of the dominant political themes in much of the western world from the late 1940s through the 1960s and beyond was that of the Cold War and the construction of 'communism' and the 'Soviet empire' as a major threat.[11]

In Canada, the anti-communist campaigns were less public and extensive than in the US,[12] although they made the work of socialists and progressives in unions, the peace movement and community groups extremely difficult and dangerous at times. Immigrants and artists were also targeted. In right-wing, conservative, and often liberal discourse, homosexuals were either associated directly with communism and spying for the USSR or were seen as an easy target for blackmail and therefore a risk to 'national security.' Whose security? we might ask. Homosexuals were often constructed not only as violators of sexual and gender boundaries, but also as violators of class and political boundaries.[13] And there were leftists who were lesbian and gay and early gay organizations such as the Mattachine Society formed in 1951 in the US did have a number of ex-Communist Party members as founders.[14] Through a series of trials and spy scandals in England, homosexuality came to be associated with spying and treason affecting how homosexuality was portrayed in official circles in Canada.[15]

This anti-homosexual campaign was informed not only by 'national security' concerns narrowly defined but by other regulatory practices regarding same-gender sexuality as well. These other courses of action regulating homosexuality were the continuing (and during this period extending) criminalization of male homosexual activity (lesbian practices were not as directly affected by criminalization, although they were first criminalized in 1953) and exclusionary practices against gay men and lesbians in state institutions.

The strategy of extending criminalization included the existing offenses of 'gross indecency' and 'buggery' and the new sentencing procedure of Criminal Sexual Psychopath, especially following 1953 when 'buggery' and 'gross indecency' were added as 'triggering' offenses. This procedure which was continued in Dangerous Sexual Offender legislation enacted in 1961, made consensual homosexual activity discovered by the police (or able to be 'proven' by the police in court) into grounds for indefinite detention. This constructed homosexuality, more specifically, as a criminal sexual danger.[16] These criminalization practices, oriented the work of the RCMP and other police forces. Police work, including the work of the RCMP, is textually-mediated through the criminal code. It was crucially through the criminal code and the activities it mandated for the police that homosexuals were constructed as a criminal problem.[17]

There were also continuing prohibitions against homosexuals within the military and the RCMP. Homosexuality (especially between men) was officially viewed as a threat to discipline and bureaucratic hierarchy. This was especially the case in the military and in para-military forms of organization like the police where heterosexual masculinity was a major organizing ideology. Fighting men were identified with heterosexual masculinity, not with homosexuals who were visualized as 'gender inverts' and not 'real men.'[18]

In the military, lesbianism was seen as a threat to the 'proper' femininity of female recruits and the policing of 'lesbianism' was a way of regulating the activities of all women in these institutions. In the armed forces there were policies and procedures for excluding and 'disposing' of 'sex deviates.'[19]

The organization of this campaign also included the major impact of US state policies on Canadian state practices—especially given the referenced and often derived character of Canadian developments to US 'national security' practices in the post-World War II years. There was considerable pressure from US security elites to get Canadian officials to take up similar 'security' campaigns to those in the US that were more broad-ranging, more public and were specifically directed against 'sex perverts.' Through NATO, Canadian and American officials shared common concerns over 'internal security.' Canadian and US security officials engaged in a common security language, and they shared similar organizing concepts and discourse as well as information.[20]

As part of this interaction the Security Panel sent D.F. Wall, secretary of the Security Panel, along with Professor Wake who was studying detection strategies for homosexuality for the panel, to the US in 1961 to study 'security' procedures there. This included quite centrally policies regarding homosexuals. Wall's report focused on some of the differences between Canadian and US security screening policies and procedures and became one of the texts leading up to the new Cabinet Memorandum on "Security in the Public Service" in 1963.

The Security Panel

In response to official security concerns a Security Panel was established in Canada in 1946. The investigative powers of this new panel were officially authorized by a cabinet directive in 1948.[21] This panel soon formulated a policy of transferring civil servants about whom there were "doubts" to less sensitive posts. The setting up of this interdepartmental panel was influenced by the recommendation for increased co-ordination on security measures that came out of the 1946 Royal Commission into the Igor Gouzenko affair and largely followed British rather than American precedent and procedures. Initially Canadian security officials—with some opposition from officials in the RCMP and the military establishment—opted for a more British influenced security response as opposed to the much more public security campaign then being initiated south of the border.[22] This related to the character of Canadian state formation that was influenced during these years by both British and US developments. Canadian state practices increasingly became influenced by US developments in the 1950s and 1960s, especially in the realm of 'national security.'

In 1948, the departments of national defence and external affairs were designated by security officials as vulnerable to subversion. Dismissals of homosexuals had started by 1952.[23] In the two decades that followed, every homosexual in the civil service had reason to fear discovery and dismissal as hundreds of people were fired or transferred. Hundreds lost their jobs for 'security' reasons but clearly not all lesbians and gay men in the civil service were affected or detected.

The firings and transfers were carried out at the urging of the Security Panel, a small, secret committee of top civil servants, Mounties, and National Defence officials. The panel was chaired by the Secretary to the Cabinet and reported directly to the Cabinet. The panel was part of the ruling regime with important links with broader state relations. Permanent representatives on the panel included the Privy Council and the departments of National Defence, External Affairs and the RCMP with others more occasionally represented.[24] The RCMP was the investigative agency for the panel and was mandated by cabinet to perform security investigations. The RCMP had the sole authority to make inquiries in all civilian departments (in the armed forces military intelligence was also involved) and the panel had to negotiate with the department involved if an employee was identified as a security risk by the RCMP. Deputy ministers often made the decisions about dismissals or transfers.

The emphasis in the workings of the panel was on secrecy and the proceedings in Canada were much less public and visible than in the US. Given this secrecy there was no appeal from a denial of security clearance. There was no possibility for independent review. In what were seen to be serious cases, civil servants were asked to resign or were dismissed with no opportunity to defend themselves against the allegations that had been made. While initially the Security Panel's focus was on people with political 'disloyalties' the RCMP soon began to uncover civil servants with 'moral' or 'character' failings which, it was argued, made them vulnerable because they had something to hide.

Thousands of lesbians and gay men and suspected homosexuals were affected by this security campaign. A 1961 memo reported that "During the course of these investigations, the R.C.M.

Police have identified some 460 public servants as confirmed, alleged or suspected homosexuals. Of these about one-third have since left the service through resignation or dismissal."[25] In 1961–62 the RCMP reported having identified 850 suspected and proven homosexuals in the civil service.[26] After this, there is no count of the numbers of homosexuals, specifically in the civil service, in these documents.

One of the objectives of the RCMP investigations was to move alleged or suspected homosexuals into the proven category. Alleged homosexuals were seen as "those who have been named as homosexuals by a source or sources whose information is considered to be reliable." Suspected homosexuals were "those who [were] believed to be homosexuals by a source or sources whose information is considered to be reliable." Confirmed homosexuals were defined as those "who have been interviewed and admitted being homosexuals or who have been convicted in court on a charge of sexual deviation with another male."[27]

These investigations were not only conducted in 'high' security areas like External Affairs, or the higher echelons of the military, but also in such 'low' security areas as the Central Mortgage and Housing Corporation, the Department of Public Works and the Unemployment Insurance Commission.[28] This affected not only the middle-class elites in the civil service but also clerical and other workers. Much of the security campaigns were conducted prior to the rise of unions in the civil service. The shape of the security campaigns needs to be explored further regarding its impact on activists in professional associations and early union organizing efforts.[29]

Total RCMP reports of homosexuals—including those outside the civil service—went up from 1,000 in 1960–61, to 7,500 in 1965–66. In the RCMP Directorate of Security and Intelligence (DSI) annual report of 1966–67 it was reported that "Through interviews of known homosexuals and increased co-operation with other police forces, the index of known and suspected homosexuals has been expanded to approximately 8,200 names."[30] By the 1967–1968 report the total reports were close to 9,000, only about one-third of whom were federal civil servants.[31] This was based in the Ottawa area.

The External Affairs Department in Ottawa and its embassies around the world were seen by right-wingers as "a notorious cesspool of homosexuals and perverts" in the 1950s.[32] No department, with the possible exception of the Navy, was perceived to harbour more 'queers.' By 1960 particular scrutiny was being focused on suspected homosexuals in external affairs.

In the Security Panel texts there was a clear sense from all sides that all homosexuals stationed outside Canada were vulnerable to 'blackmail.'[33] These investigations led to the resignation of David Johnson, Canada's ambassador to Moscow, and may have contributed to the death of his predecessor, John Watkins, who died of a heart attack after being interrogated by the RCMP in 1964.[34]

Usually the Security Panel texts and the practices they helped to organize focused on men, given it was predominantly men who were in these 'security' positions in the Canadian civil service during these years and given the more public construction of male homosexuals as a social threat. At the same time more women were being employed in the civil service and the impact of this needs to be investigated more thoroughly. The notion of 'character weakness' did include lesbianism but lesbianism was rarely distinctly written about in these texts. Usually the references to 'homosexuals' referred to gay men. At the same time they seemed to be more specifically concerned with lesbians when it came to developing mechanisms for detecting homosexuals as I suggest later. The RCMP seemed to have little understanding of or contact with lesbians.

[...]

ANALYSIS OF THE SECURITY PANEL TEXTS—THE ACTIVE DEBATE OVER HOW WIDE THE CAMPAIGN SHOULD BE

Possible limitations in previous security procedures[35] were raised in May 1959 in a memo by D.F. Wall, secretary of the Security Panel, to other members of the Panel.[36] This memo was in response to an apparent request from Prime Minister Diefenbaker for clarification. Wall wrote that "It is the Prime Minister's wish that the matter be examined to determine whether it might be possible to treat cases of character weaknesses differently from those involving ideological beliefs, without of course weakening present security safeguards."[37]

This constructed a clearer separation in the security discourse between political disloyalty and character weaknesses. This began to separate out 'communists' from 'homosexuals' who often had earlier been conflated together in right-wing and security discourse. The 1955 cabinet directive had not made such a clear distinction, although it did state in reference to character defects that "such defects of character may also make them unsuitable for employment on grounds other than security."[38]

Wall's memo also began to homosexualize the character weakness category. 'Character weaknesses' almost seem to become homosexuality since it is the main 'character weakness' that is referred to. The title of the memo is "Security Cases Involving Character Weaknesses with special reference to the Problem of Homosexuality." Despite very little cited evidence, Wall established that homosexuality was the most frequently used 'character weakness' and was the major route used by Soviet intelligence.[39] In investigating this, Wall referred to US and United Kingdom procedures and reports. He took up homosexuals as a security risk from US state discourse in the 1950s, and we can see an important US security influence in this text. He mentioned

that the Department of National Defence (DND) believed that homosexuality made a person unsuitable for employment whether there is access to classified information or not.[40] The DND was a major force for pushing further with the anti-homosexual campaign partly because of influence from US military officials.

In this memo we can discern some of the contours of debates and struggles then occurring in and around the Security Panel. There is a separation of 'ideological' and 'character weakness' security threats, a homosexualization of 'character weaknesses' and a debate over how wide-spread the screening and investigation of this 'character weakness' should be.

These were crucial terrains of debate in the Security Panel for the next few years. In 1959 the homosexual screening program had been initiated in the federal civil service. The RCMP struggled to defend and expand this campaign and engaged in an extension of the campaign to investigations outside the civil service where thousands of names were collected. Since all homosexual acts where then against the law, the RCMP approach was also shaped by the criminalization of homosexuality. The RCMP tended to overlay security discourse with the criminalization discourse to create a wider basis for the anti-homosexual campaign.

Others on the panel, including representatives of External Affairs and the Civil Service Commission, articulated a more specific approach which differentiated between a narrower 'security' frame and the broader criminalization frame of regulation. This suggested that the security campaign should be tighter in its scope and impact than the criminalization course of action. These people did not want to extend the security campaign outside the civil service and they only wanted to transfer homosexuals if they were discovered in security positions. This is not to suggest that this more restricted position was supportive of homosexuals or that they took up a 'liberal' position in this historical context. They shared the same general heterosexist assumptions with those who wanted to extend the campaign further, and they never raised the need to partially decriminalize homosexual acts in private, between two consenting adults, along the lines proposed in the liberal 1957 British Wolfenden report.[41] They did, however, believe that the security campaign should be narrower in its impact.

The early 1960s was the beginning of the period when different strategies in Canadian state agencies were taken up in response to the expansion of lesbian and gay networks and community formation. The 1957 British Wolfenden regulatory frame of the partial decriminalization of homosexual acts began to be used to contest the influence of the expanding criminalization strategy by the mid-1960s in Canada. At the same time, in the early 1960s, the hegemonic regulatory strategy was still one that defined homosexuality as a national, social, sexual and criminal danger.

How wide this security campaign should be was the key terrain of debate within the security regime as it addressed homosexuality during these years. This was an active debate and process with struggles over the wording and interpretation of different texts.[42]

In October 1959 there was discussion of Wall's memo at the Security Panel, where the basic debate was again over how narrow or wide the security campaign against homosexuals should be.[43] Robert Bryce, chair of the Panel, argued for a relatively wide-ranging approach but he did not think that homosexuals should be dismissed from the public service but instead should be transferred to less 'sensitive' positions. The RCMP and deputy ministers of Justice and National Defence argued for a wider interpretation with the deputy minister of National Defence questioning "whether persons suspected of homosexuality should be permitted to enter the public service in any capacity."[44] As a result of these disagreements, they could not recommend any change to existing security policy.

A common belief held by all on the Security Panel was that homosexuals were vulnerable to compromise by Soviet agents. This was constructed as taken-for-granted, and as 'common-sense.' This is not to suggest that the fear of blackmail was not an important problem for gay men and lesbians during these years, since we know it was from first hand accounts,[45] but that it was located very differently in their lives. For gay men and lesbians blackmail was often linked with fears of police harassment or official sanction which were being actively constructed precisely through the practices of this security campaign and the policing practices criminalizing same-gender sex. The social space of 'the closet' which makes gay men and lesbians 'vulnerable' to blackmail and 'subversion' was in part constructed through these regulatory practices.[46]

The construction of 'blackmail' as a problem facing homosexuals came from two different directions and was articulated by two different logics. Firstly, it was raised as a concern by early gay activists. They argued that it was only because of laws criminalizing homosexual sex that such blackmail was possible. This was used as part of an argument for law reform to begin to remove the social basis for blackmail threats. But 'blackmail' was also a crucial part of the construction of the 'national security' scares which were often linked with the criminalization of homosexual sex. These practices were part of the construction of the very need for secrecy, and living in 'the closet' that created problems in many lesbians' and gay men's lives.

Through a critical reading of the Security Panel texts we discern an understanding within the security regime of the existence of *and* also their own use of 'the closet.'[47] But how the practices mandated by the security regime actually created some of these secrecy needs is never made visible. They can therefore define the need for secrecy as the 'threat' making homosexuals vulnerable to 'subversion' while not noticing how they are creating and mobilizing this very need for invisibility as part of their security campaign. Rather than removing the social basis for the threat of blackmail through calling for the repeal of anti-homosexual laws and heterosexist social practices, they instead intensify the construction of the need for secrecy as the problem which requires the mobilization of surveillance and detection strategies.

In a Foucaultian power/knowledge sense the security regime was both part of producing the space for 'the closet' and also used this social space for its security investigations, and these practices produced even more reasons for closetry. The security regime fed on the terror produced through the threat of discovery in this very heterosexist social context.

There were different emerging strategies within Canadian state relations, organizing different responses regarding the regulation of same-gender sexualities. Heterosexual masculinity was more integral to the ideological organization of some sites within state relations than others. Generally those most tied into defending 'national security' and policing like the military and the RCMP were the most hostile to 'queers.'

The RCMP—Extending the Campaign

In May 1960 the RCMP submitted its contribution "Homosexuality within the Federal Government Service" to the Security Panel discussion. They requested clearer terms of reference and argued that existing policy restrictions "which prohibit our interviewing homosexuals should be set aside from this type of investigation." They argued that "necessary provision be made for us to interview at our discretion any person who we may consider to be of assistance to our enquiry."[48]

In a slightly earlier text they reported that

During the period under review an extensive investigation was started into the identification of known and suspected homosexuals employed in federal government departments and agencies. The investigation was precipitated by the knowledge that persons with this particular character weakness are highly susceptible to compromise and blackmail.[49]

In the same document they reported that they investigated 393 suspected homosexuals confirming 159 and that "New names continue to come to light and it is felt that only a fraction of the total number of homosexuals in the federal government service has been identified to date. One self-admitted homosexual estimated there are 3,000 homosexuals in the Ottawa area."[50]

RCMP policy was to fire all known homosexuals. The RCMP was an integral part of both the security regime and security investigations. Despite the ebb and flow of Security scares the RCMP along with the military hierarchy were consistent in their stance that homosexuals should not be in government service. The RCMP set up an investigative unit within the force, called A-3, to hunt down and purge homosexuals within its ranks and within the government more generally. Informants would watch bars and parks frequented by gays and they attempted to get homosexual men to inform on others. Reportedly this met with some initial success.[51]

The RCMP also developed interrogation techniques to unearth homosexuals who were then forced to either resign or were transferred. By 1963, the A-3 unit had produced a map of Ottawa using red dots to designate sites where homosexual activity took place. The map was soon covered with so many red dots in so many different parts of the city that it became practically useless.[52] The Security Service investigations extended to the universities and the community at large.

In June 1960 there was a Security Panel discussion on the RCMP memo, "Homosexuality Within the Federal Government Service."[53] There was only a quorum of the Security Panel in attendance as R.B. Bryce reported they tried to keep the discussion "limited to the smallest circle possible."[54] In the discussion the Commissioner of the RCMP reiterated the RCMP request for more explicit guidance especially given how "recent investigations indicated that the problem [of homosexuality] was becoming increasingly widespread, and the accumulation of the names of persons against whom allegations had been made was growing with each new enquiry."[55]

This posed administrative difficulties for the RCMP about how to handle and use this information. There were some initial problems with the 'ideological' construction of homosexuals as a tiny minority with certain identifiable characteristics (like marks of gender inversion) that didn't fully prepare them for the numbers they began to uncover. They were beginning to unearth gay and lesbian networks during a period in which these networks were expanding and becoming more visible.

In response to this extended campaign, the Under-secretary of State for External Affairs pointed to "the danger of this kind of investigation developing into a sociological survey in which the security aspects were lost sight of, and suggested that it did not serve our present purpose to make a determination of the probable proportion of homosexuals in the population."[56] He stressed that the RCMP should only be concerned with investigating homosexuals if it was a security matter.

Although clearly homosexuality was seen to be a problem by all participants, it was recorded that they felt "that the question of prosecutions for homosexual offenses would probably not arise through present investigations...."[57] In the clash between the broader criminalizing and more narrow security frames the majority of the panel members at this meeting sided with the narrower security frame. The minutes stated "that where security was not a factor, there did not appear to be any reason for the RCMP to report allegations of homosexuality to the employing department."[58]

For the RCMP, whose work was also shaped by the criminalization of homosexuality, or for the military with their policies against homosexuals in any position, their practices would also have been shaped by their institutional policies. But at the same time the minutes recorded "that there appeared to be some reduction in the risk to security if the RCMP and the employing department were aware that an employee had homosexual tendencies."[59] This provided an opening for the RCMP extension of the campaign suggesting certain struggles, negotiations and compromises in the panel. This allowed the RCMP to continue its extended investigations without the Security Panel as a whole giving direct approval to what it was doing. The Panel minutes concluded with a call for its secretary to prepare a report setting out these proposals and a further recommendation that direct consultation with the Prime Minister and Minister of Justice begin.

This led to the memo for the Prime Minister and Minister of Justice by R.B. Bryce. In the initial December 1960 version of this memo there was a fairly strong defence of the expanded character of RCMP security investigations, including moving beyond the civil service.[60] This expanded role, however, still did not satisfy the RCMP. In the second version in early 1961 a long section was added which stated:

> The Commissioner of the RCMP has explained that for a number of reasons the scope of these investigations was further expanded to include the investigation of homosexuals who were not employed in the government service entirely. In the early stages it became evident that the homosexual, irrespective of employment, was

the most productive source in identifying and providing factual information on other homosexuals employed in or by the government. Employees not having access to classified information were included in the expanded investigation on the assumption that they obtain access at some future date through promotion or change of employment. Homosexuals outside the government service were interpreted as precluding any extensive interviewing of homosexual government employees on the grounds that as the subject of a security investigation they, as individuals, should not be made aware of the reason for any subsequent action taken against them. Another reason for investigating homosexuals outside the government service was based on the possibility that they could be used by a foreign intelligence service to identify and perhaps otherwise assist in the compromising of homosexuals employed in the government on classified work.[61]

Here the RCMP was attempting to provide a broader reading of 'security' concerns that extended far beyond 'sensitive' positions in the civil service and far beyond the civil service itself. This provided more justification for the RCMP position on extending the campaign and we can see the very active influence of the RCMP in the Security Panel through the addition of this section in the revised version of the memo.

The memo also stated that investigations "should not be widespread, but limited to those persons who were vulnerable to effective exploitation by foreign intelligence services, except in cases where further investigation was necessary to establish the validity of information concerning employees in vulnerable positions" and the government was asked to give the RCMP a clear directive to the effect that, "where security was not a factor, the R.C.M. Police were not required to report allegations of homosexuality to the employing department."[62]

They asked for Ministerial approval for "the following proposed courses of action." The first priority was "that the Security Panel ask those departments with missions abroad to classify according to risk those positions whose nature and location is such that their incumbents might be subjected to pressure for intelligence purposes" and "that these departments, with whatever assistance the RCMP are able to provide, make a careful study of the incumbents of these positions to ensure, in so far as possible, that they are not susceptible to blackmail, either through homosexual activity or other indiscreet behaviour" and "that in cases where the incumbent of a vulnerable position is found to be a homosexual, departments be asked to consult the Secretary of the Security Panel before any action is taken concerning the employee."[63]

The second priority included considering whether positions other than those abroad are vulnerable and that

> consideration be given to setting up a program of research...with a view to devising tests to identify persons with homosexual tendencies. It is hoped that such tests might aid in the identification of homosexuals already employed in the government service, and eventually might assist in the selection of persons who are not homosexuals for service in positions considered vulnerable to blackmail for intelligence purposes. (The Commissioner of the R.C.M. Police feels that these tests should be extended to prevent, where possible, the initial engagement of homosexuals in the government service on the grounds that they are usually practising criminals under Sections 147 and 149 of the Criminal Code of Canada.)[64]

This was the proposal that would lead up to the development of the 'fruit machine' research. The revised memo by Bryce was discussed by the cabinet on 26 January, 1961.

A New Cabinet Directive

These meetings, memos and the cabinet discussion led up to a new Cabinet Directive on "Security in the Public Services of Canada" in December 1963.[65] Public announcements were made by the new Prime Minister and Minister of Justice regarding this. This text referred to good personnel administration and distinguished between those who were politically disloyal and those who were unreliable. At the same time the language used in this text is somewhat different from that used in the Security Panel and RCMP documents. Rather than using homosexual it refers to "illicit sexual behaviour."

In a covering memo to the new Cabinet Directive, the Secretary to the Cabinet stated that "The most important modifications in the new Directive involve an attitude of much greater frankness with employees whose reliability or loyalty is in doubt, and provide related procedures for reviewing such cases both within the responsible department or agency and if necessary by a Board of Review composed of members of the Security Panel."[66] In a number of areas, they attempted to bring Canadian procedures more into line with current US procedures as a partial outcome of Wall's 1962 report.

This directive laid out procedures and a mandated course of action. The course of action went along these lines. A person applied for a position in the civil service where they would have access to what was designated to be 'classified' information or was promoted into such a position. Either the Civil Service Commission or departments and agencies (where the employment is not under the Civil Services Act) would then initiate security investigations. The RCMP would be called in with the possible involvement of a deputy minister or head of the agency concerned.

If the person was discovered to be a homosexual or to have some other sort of 'unreliability' they would then be transferred to a less 'sensitive' position or they would be dismissed. There was now the possibility for review within the department or agency including review by the deputy minister or head of the agency or by a review board of members of the Security Panel.[67] At the time there was also the research on detecting homosexuals that the Security Panel was simultaneously engaged in.

ATTEMPTING TO DEVELOP A 'FRUIT MACHINE'

The Security Panel also mandated research on the detection of homosexuals. In doing this there was an important reliance on psychiatric and psychological knowledge which was premised on the assumption that gay men and lesbians were either psychologically 'abnormal' or suffered from a 'disorder.' As in most other research, the 'normality' of heterosexuality was assumed and homosexuality was defined as the problem.

Following up on the approval for such a study in the Security Panel memo to cabinet in early 1961, Professor F.R. Wake (who died in November 1993) of Carleton University was funded to go to the US by National Health and Welfare to research and study detection tests and technologies regarding homosexuality. Previously Wake had been the first chair of the Psychology Department at Carleton and a researcher for the Royal Commission on the Criminal Law Relating to Criminal Sexual Psychopaths in the 1950s.[68] He produced a report in 1962 which got the actual 'fruit machine' research going. This research was funded by National Health and Welfare. A critical analysis of Wake's special project proposal gives us insight into the social character of this research and its interrelation with the social power relations mobilized through the security campaign.

The 'fruit machine' research arose both from an apparent interest by Wake in doing research on homosexuality (usually articulated as an interest in 'suitability' for employment) and also to establish a more effective and efficient mode of surveillance and investigation than that of costly and labour intensive RCMP field investigations. This research was an attempt to find a more 'scientific' means of detection of homosexuals.

The name 'fruit machine' was given to this project, according to John Sawatsky, by members of the RCMP who did not want to be recruited to be among the 'normals' to be tested on it.[69] The 'fruit machine' project involved psychiatrists, psychologists and the departments of National Defence and Health and Welfare for four years but it never worked and the Defence Research Board eventually cut its funding. The research suffered from major technical problems as well as problems with getting the required numbers of 'research subjects.'

Dr. Wake, in his 1962 "Report on Special Project"[70] focused on the "problem of suitability" in employment, and stressed from his review of the research in the US that there was no single method of tests that could detect homosexuality. Instead, a battery of tests was needed. Wake's report and research were based on a review of the professional literature and his investigations of detection research while he was in the US. He took up a general position that there was something wrong with homosexuals which makes them unsuitable for certain positions, that they can be identified, and their behaviour treated and controlled.

He argued that control of homosexuality is much more likely than cure, and he reported "encouraging trends" working with anti-depressant drugs and reported reversal in direction of desire by means of aversion therapy.[71] He argued that "while a great deal of research needs to be done, much of it might be paid for by early moderate success reducing the current load on investigative staffs."[72]

Under the heading of "The Numbers Involved," he referred to the Kinsey reports. Although he mostly dealt with men, he sometimes brought in women and he focused on how lesbians are different from male homosexuals. In general he suggested that fewer females are 'deviant' perpetuating lesbian invisibility.

As a result of his research, he argued that there is no distinct homosexual personality type. This was part of a shift away from homosexuals as gender inverts and from notions of homosexuals as psychopathic personalities. This paralleled a shift that was then taking place in psychological and sexological circles with the articulation of homosexuality as a 'sexual orientation' based on sexual object-choice.[73]

Since Wake argued there was no single, distinct homosexual personality type there could be no single test. Under "Methods of Detecting Homosexuality" he surveyed the various detection tests and procedures that had been used to try to identify homosexuals. These ranged from psychiatric interviews, to medical examinations, to various tests for changes in emotional conditions. These included the Polygraph (lie-detector) test, which Wake argued had too many problems to be useful; the Plethysmograph which measures blood volume in the finger by electronic or pneumatic means; the Palmer Sweat test, which responds to perspiration; the Projective Tests; Word Association Tests; the Pupillary Response Test; the Span of Attention Test, based on the time spent attending to various images (which Zamansky of Northeastern University had constructed as an apparatus to test for homosexuality in 1956); and Masculinity/Femininity Tests with all their gender and sexuality assumptions.[74]

In his commentary Wake suggested that the Palmer Sweat test would be best used in conjunction with a 'word association' test. Words with definite homosexual meaning according to the appended list include queen, circus, gay, bagpipe, bell, whole, blind, bull, camp, coo, cruise, drag, dike (dyke), fish, flute, fruit, mother, punk, queer, rim, sew, swing, trade, velvet, wolf, blackmail, prowl, bar, house, club, restaurant, tea room, and top men.[75]

Wake found the Pupillary Response test to be quite 'productive' in looking for homosexuals. It measured different interest patterns by means of a machine which simultaneously projected a visual stimulus and photographed the pupil of the eye at half second intervals. This procedure was supposed to produce an involuntary "response that cannot be controlled by the subject." Wake discovered this procedure and technology through his research in the US. E.H. Hess and J.M. Polt, researchers at the University of Chicago, had developed this test and apparatus. Professional and academic knowledge relations were directly tapped into in this security-based research.

Wake's report referred to a study done using the Hess-Polt apparatus by graduate student, Allan Seltzer, who was studying under Hess. In Seltzer's study the "stimuli were slides made of pictures from physical culture magazines (some of which were near pornographic) plus neutral pictures of good paintings and at least one modified picture of Christ on the cross."[76] This use of physique magazines, which often had a large gay male readership,[77] seems to have become common in the US by this point and was used in aversion therapy. This also suggested some awareness of the formation of gay men's cultures during these years. Wake argued that the "Results clearly permitted Seltzer to distinguish the homosexual subject when the results of *all* pictures were compared...." Wake reported that "Not only was the change in size of pupil indicative of the direction of sex interest, but the pattern followed by the eyes (and recorded on film) was very important (e.g. the homosexual who could not take his eyes away from the genital area of the vaguely-seen Christ on the Cross)." Wake went on that "Perhaps the most important incidental finding in this experiment was the confession of a homosexual subject who reported that he had done his best to defeat the machine but knew he had failed." In conclusion Wake stated that "Here, then, is a most promis-

ing instrument for detection, not only of homosexuals but of homosexual potentiality."[78]

In his conclusions Wake argued that more research was needed. He proposed a research experiment that would combine

> the Hess-Polt pupillary test with suitable visual stimuli; a measure of skin perspiration...; the plethysmograph with a modification to measure pulse rate. Subjects: Fifteen normal males; fifteen normal females; fifteen homosexual males; fifteen homosexual females. As the experiment progresses, additional normal and homosexual subjects in unspecified numbers. All subjects to be supplied by the RCMP....[79]

The RCMP, the chief investigative arm of the security campaign, was also to provide the 'research subjects.' Here we have another side of the construction of power/knowledge relations in this research context. Also notice the language through which heterosexuality is constructed as 'normal.' Heterosexuality is not specifically named as such, since this was prior to 'heterosexuality' more fully emerging as a 'popular' term which historically follows the rise of gay liberation and lesbian feminism in the 1970s and 1980s. Also notice the equal emphasis placed on "homosexual females" in the research design.

Then Wake outlined the procedure to be used—

> The experimental stimuli will be pictures designed to elicit the subject's interest in males and females.... The first sixty subjects will be processed to determine the reaction patterns of normals and homosexuals. Then, using these patterns as criteria, the experimenter will attempt to distinguish homosexuals presented by the RCMP, where nothing of the subject is known to the research team. Those methods proving successful will be retained for continuing research.[80]

This research was more psychologically oriented than earlier studies that sometimes focused on biological anomalies (like marks of gender inversion on the body).[81] It was directed at finding a 'scientific' means to test 'involuntary' responses that demonstrated sexual orientation. This was based on a series of assumptions about the relation between stimulus and response, about the power of visual images as simulators, about common responses of homosexuals and heterosexuals as viewers, and an assumption of there being two, and only two, dichotomous and essential sexualities. Men or women who were sexually interested in both men and women would have undermined their assumptions.

Predictably there were many problems in trying to get this experiment to work. In a 1963 memo to the secretary of the Security Panel, J.R.M. Bordeleau, RCMP Assistant Commissioner, and Director of Security and Intelligence, wrote, "We are in the process of contacting known male homosexuals in this area [Ottawa] and soliciting their co-operation in the proposed tests, however, we are not yet in a position to determine how many will volunteer for the project." He went on to point out that "We have no contacts within the female homosexual community in this area and no safe ground upon which an approach might be made to these persons" and that "we would suggest that other government departments... might be requested through your office, to solicit the co-operation of female homosexuals known to them." He also reported that the RCMP had "some doubts also as to the propriety of our soliciting normal females to participate in the tests. We believe that this should be undertaken by some government department or departments which have a large pool of female employees under their control.... Similarly we believe that the required number of normal males should be drawn from the government service at large."[82]

The RCMP seems to have had very little contact with lesbian networks and was quite apprehensive about approaching 'normal' women for this research. This account also suggests that there was resistance to participation in this research from RCMP members themselves. As Sawatsky suggests, RCMP members did not want to be determined to be 'fruits' through participating as 'normals' in this experiment.[83] The RCMP response was to try to get other government departments involved in enroling 'subjects' for the research.

The 1965–66 Directorate of Security and Intelligence (DSI) Annual Report noted that "To date, the tests have been inconclusive, the main obstacle to the Program being a lack of suitable subjects for testing purposes."[84] In the same report of 1966–67 they stated that, "Although the research group has made some progress, the objective has not, as yet been achieved."[85] A major problem in the operationalizing of the experiment was with perfecting the technology itself, which had to be adapted to deal with people of different heights, with different sized pupils and different distances between eyeballs.[86] The 'fruit machine' never worked and it was eventually abandoned in 1967.

Signs of Resistance

From this critical reading of official discourse we begin to get a sense of some of the obstacles the security regime was confronting. To be sure, there are certain signs of resistance within this official discourse. But this resistance, ultimately, had its social basis outside official discourse, in gay and lesbian cultural and community formation.

The RCMP faced problems in its investigations with non-cooperation from homosexual informants. In 1962–1963 they reported that "During the past fiscal year the homosexual screening program" was "hindered by the lack of cooperation on the part of homosexuals approached as sources. Persons of this type, who had hitherto been our most consistent and productive informers, have exhibited an increasing reluctance to identify their homosexual friends and associates."[87]

For 1963–64 they reported a "growing reluctance on the part of homosexuals to identify their associates." In response they put additional emphasis "on establishing close liaison with the morality branches of police forces, particularly in the larger centres...."[88] This reluctance or 'resistance' of homosexuals in the face of this security campaign forced the RCMP to devise a new strategy to secure the cooperation of homosexual informants. The RCMP responded by developing working relationships with the morality branches of various police forces and enlisting local police support to procure homosexual informants. Given the criminalization of homosexual activity this meant that the police could 'lean on' those who had committed 'offenses,' and on street informants, in order to get them to provide information to the RCMP. This extended RCMP powers of surveillance through local police forces and, once again, gives us a sense of the 'power/knowledge' relations actively constructed through this campaign. Later DSI reports suggest that the situation 'improved' in terms of getting homosexual informants to talk after this relation with morality branches was put in place. More research is clearly needed on these forms of resistance and regulatory responses.

We also know that Doug Sanders, on behalf of Vancouver's Association for Social Knowledge (ASK), Canada's first lesbian and gay group, made a submission to the Royal Commission on Security in 1968. In this brief he critiqued two main arguments used to deny homosexuals security clearances—that homosexuals suffer from a character weakness and are not emotionally stable and that they are more subject to blackmail.[89]

Some Conclusions— Heterosexual Hegemony and the Security Regime

This investigation of official texts points us towards an analysis of the social organization of the anti-homosexual security campaign within Canadian state formation. We can begin to see the impact this campaign had on thousands of people's lives and we begin to see aspects of how it was organized through the textually mediated practices of the security regime. There were struggles within the security regime between a broader framework for the anti-homosexual campaign and a narrower security framework. While in general the narrower security frame won out by 1963, there was also an allowance for the wider campaign to take place through the practices of the RCMP. There was also the development of research on the detection of homosexuals as part of the security campaign. We need interviews with, and first hand accounts from those who were directly affected to flesh out and further ground this analysis.

Despite significant changes as a result of social struggles, there remains today a continuing and deeply rooted heterosexism in Canadian state institutions, shaped in part by the active legacies of these conceptions and policies. There continues to be major problems that lesbians and gay men encounter in job-related discrimination. The historical and social roots of these policies need to be exposed more clearly, and much more critical research remains to be done. Finally this historical work also poses important questions of redress and compensation for those whose careers and lives were destroyed by these policies. Doing this research is thereby linked to current struggles to dismantle heterosexual hegemonic relations.

Notes

1   D.F. Wall, Memorandum to the Security Panel, "Security Cases Involving Character Weaknesses, with Special Reference to the Problem of Homosexuality," 12 May 1959, 12. This document was secured through a Canadian Security and Intelligence Service (CSIS), Access to Information Request (AIR).

2   *Ibid.*, 13. In the language used in this excerpt the author is building on earlier notions of homosexuals as psychopathic personalities. See Gary Kinsman, "Official Discourse as Sexual Regulation: The Social Organization of the Sexual Policing of Gay Men," PhD thesis, University of Toronto, 1989, 71–89.

3   See the Canadian Press stories by Dean Beeby which were based on these documents. They were printed in *The Globe and Mail*, 24 April 1992, 1–2 as "Mounties staged massive hunt for gay men in civil service" and "RCMP hoped 'fruit machine' would identify homosexuals." I will refer to the individual documents that the Canadian Press secured the release of through Access to Information requests throughout these notes.

4   On heterosexual hegemony see Kinsman, *The Regulation of Desire* (Montreal 1987) and "Official Discourse as Sexual Regulation."

5   On state formation, see Philip Corrigan and Derek Sayer, *The Great Arch, English State Formation As Cultural Revolution* (Oxford 1985).

6   See Dorothy E. Smith, "Textually-mediated Social Organization" in *Texts, Facts and Femininity* (London 1990), 209–24.

7   There is already some journalistic, historical, sociological and legal investigation of these terrains in Canada. Aside from my own work in my book and PhD thesis see John Sawatsky, *Men in the Shadows* (Toronto 1980), 111–40 and his *For Services Rendered* (Markham 1983); Reginald Whitaker, "Origins of the Canadian Government's Internal Security System, 1946–52," *Canadian Historical Review*, LXV 2, (1984), 154–187 and his, *Double Standard, The Secret History of Canadian Immigration* (Toronto 1987); Len Scher, *The Un-Canadians: True Stories of the Blacklist Era* (Toronto 1992); and Philip Girard, "From Subversion to Liberation: Homosexuals and the Immigration Act, 1952–1977," *Canadian Journal of Law and Society*, 2 (1987), 1–27 and his "Gays, Lesbians and the Legal Process Since 1945," 1985, unpublished paper; and David Kimmel and Daniel Robinson,

"The Queer Career of Homosexual Security Vetting in Cold-War Canada," in *Canadian Historical Review*, 75, No. 3, (1994), 319–45.

8   On Dorothy E. Smith and her social organization of knowledge approach see *The Everyday World as Problematic* (Toronto 1987); *The Conceptual Practices of Power* (Toronto 1990) and *Texts, Facts and Femininity*. On 'power/knowledge' relations and genealogical approaches see the work of Michel Foucault including M. Foucault (ed. by Colin Gordon), *Power/Knowledge* (New York 1980). Also see Adam Ashforth, "Reckoning Schemes of Legitimation: On Commissions of Inquiry as Power/Knowledge Forms," *Journal of Historical Sociology*, 3 (March 1990), 1–22. Unfortunately valuable insights in Foucault's work such as 'power/knowledge' are limited by his lack of attention to social standpoint and the deletion of active subjects from his discourse analysis. Foucaultian derived notions of 'power/knowledge' often tend to be relatively ungrounded from the social practices that produce them. Sometimes 'power/knowledge' almost seems to be self-generating and not produced through social practices. For some useful critical analysis of this see Dorothy E. Smith, "The Social Organization of Textual Reality," in *The Conceptual Practices of Power*, 70, 79–80.

9   In my reading of these security regime texts I am looking for traces of the 'extra-discursive' (or at least what is outside official discourse) within these pieces of ruling discourse. What is outside official discourse shapes the ground upon which ruling discourse is constructed. Aspects of my approach are similar to that developed by Jennifer Terry in her innovative article "Theorizing Deviant Historiography," in *differences*, 3 (Summer 1991), 55–74. She reads the documents she is examining for 'effects' of the violence of dominant discourses (57). At the same time Terry's perspective is limited to a critical reconstructive reading of medical research texts since she is unable to specify the basis for the 'extra-discursive.' She only notes "that the deviants' clash with medicine is not entirely dependent on the medical discourse for its enunciation" in note four on 72. We, however, need more than a critical reading from within dominant accounts. We also need to interrogate critically official discourse from standpoints beyond the confines of ruling discourse. We need to investigate the formation of cultures of resistance among people engaging in same-gender eroticism, along with the social spaces they were able to seize

through the transformation of capitalist and patriarchal social relations. We need to break free from the standpoints of ruling accounts and adopt the standpoints of the 'deviants' themselves.

10 On this general social context see *The Regulation of Desire*, 113–33; "Official Discourse as Sexual Regulation" and Kinsman, " 'Inverts,' 'Psychopaths,' and 'Normal' Men: Historical Sociological Perspectives on Gay and Heterosexual Masculinities," in Tony Haddad, ed., *Men and Masculinities: A Critical Anthology* (Toronto 1993), 3–35. On the immigration law see Philip Girard, "From Subversion to Liberation: Homosexuals and the Immigration Act."

11 On the US experience see U.S. Congress, Senate, Committee on Expenditure in Executive Departments, *Employment of Homosexuals and Other Sex Perverts in Government*, Washington, 15 December 1950, reprinted in Jonathan Katz, ed., *Government Versus Homosexuals* (Arno Reprint, New York 1975); Committee on Cooperation with Governmental (Federal) Agencies of the Group for the Advancement of Psychiatry, "Report on Homosexuality with Particular Emphasis on This Problem in Governmental Agencies," Report No. 30, January 1955; John D'Emilio, *Sexual Politics, Sexual Communities* (Chicago 1983), especially 40–53; John D'Emilio, "The Homosexual Menace: The Politics of Sexuality on Cold War America," in John D'Emilio, *Making Trouble* (New York 1992), 57–73; and Richard Cleaver, "Sexual Dissidents and the National Security State, 1942–1992," in Richard Cleaver and Patricia Myers, eds., *A Certain Terror, Heterosexism, Militarism, Violence and Change* (Chicago 1993), 171–208.

12 Philip Girard has argued that the anti-homosexual witch hunt in Canada was much stronger than the campaign against leftists, socialists, or communists. See Girard, "From Subversion to Liberation," 5. More research is needed to determine whether this claim is justified.

13 See *The Regulation of Desire*, 121.

14 See John D'Emilio, *Sexual Politics, Sexual Communities*, especially 57–91; and John D'Emilio, "Dreams Deferred, The Birth and Betrayal of America's First Gay Liberation Movement," in John D'Emilio, *Making Trouble*, 17–56.

15 *See The Regulation of Desire*, 121. On the English experience also see Simon Shepherd, "Gay Sex Spy Orgy: The State's Need For Queers," in Simon Shepherd and Mick Wallis, *Coming On Strong, Gay Politics and Culture* (London 1989), 213–30 and

L.J. Moran, "The Uses of Homosexuality: Homosexuality for National Security," *International Journal of the Sociology of Law* 19 (1991), 149–70.

16 See "Official Discourse as Sexual Regulation."

17 See George Smith, "Policing the Gay Community: An Inquiry into Textually-mediated Social Relations," *International Journal of the Sociology of Law*, 16 (1988), 163–83.

18 On this see *The Regulation of Desire*; "Official Discourse as Sexual Regulation" and " 'Inverts,' 'Psychopaths,' and 'Normal' Men."

19 On lesbians and women in the military see Cynthia Enloe, *Does Khaki Become You?* (London 1983) and the interview with Cynthia Enloe, "Heterosexist Masculinity in the Military," *Sojourner*, 18 (June 1993), 2–4; Alan Berube and John D'Emilio, "The Military and Lesbians During the McCarthy Years," *Signs*, 9 (1984), 759–75; and Leisa D. Meyer, "Creating G.I. Jane: The Regulation of Sexuality and Sexual Behaviour in the Women's Army Corps During World War II," *Feminist Studies*, 18 (1992), 581–601. More generally see *The Regulation of Desire* and "Official Discourse as Sexual Regulation."

20 See Reginald Whitaker, "Origins of the Canadian Government's Internal Security System," 169–70 and Len Scher, *The Un-Canadians*, especially the interview with Reginald Whitaker, "The FBI and the RCMP," 238–9.

21 This section is generally based on Philip Girard, "From Subversion to Liberation," 6–8 and Reginald Whitaker, "Origins of the Canadian Government's Internal Security System."

22 See Reginald Whitaker, "Origins of the Canadian Government's Internal Security System."

23 Sawatsky, *Men in the Shadows* (Don Mills 1983), 124.

24 Its composition at a meeting in 1959 was— Secretary to the Cabinet (the chair), Deputy Minister of Citizenship and Immigration, Deputy Minister of National Defence, Deputy Minister of Defence Production, Deputy Minister of Justice, Commissioner of RCMP, Under-secretary of State for External Affairs, member of Civil Service Commission, and a member of the Privy Council Office (who was the secretary). Minutes of the 68th meeting of the Security Panel, 6 October 1959 by D.F. Wall, Secretary of the Security Panel.

25 R.B. Bryce, Memorandum for the Prime Minister and the Minister of Justice, "Security Cases Involving Homosexuality," 26 January 1961, 2.

26 Directorate of Security and Intelligence Annual Report, 1961–1962, 22.

27 Bella to RCMP Commissioner, 29 April 1960.

28 Ibid.

29 I will explore this in my SSHRC funded research.

30 Directorate of Security and Intelligence (DSI) Annual Reports from 1960 to 1967. The last quote is from the DSI Annual Report, 1966–67, 27.

31 DSI Annual Report, 1967–1968.

32 For instance see Pat Walsh in *Speak Up* (Toronto), 9 (Aug./Sept. 1981). Walsh was an executive member of the far-right World Anti-Communist League.

33 As can be seen in both the 19 December 1960 and 26 January 1961 versions of the R.B. Bryce, Chair of the Security Panel, "Memorandum to the Prime Minister and the Minister of Justice."

34 See Sawatsky, *For Services Rendered*, 172–83.

35 This was rooted in Cabinet Directive 29, "Security Screening of Government Employees," 1955.

36 D.F. Wall, Memorandum to the Security Panel, "Security Cases Involving Character Weaknesses, with Special Reference to the Problem of Homosexuality," 12 May 1959.

37 Ibid., 1.

38 Ibid. This provided a broader opening for campaigns against homosexuals or others with 'character weaknesses' in the civil service on other than security grounds.

39 Wall memo, 12 May 1959, 12. This was argued even though little evidence was ever put forward to defend this claim. For instance—"In only one of the cases investigated has there been evidence that an attempt has been made to blackmail any of these persons for intelligence purposes." (R.B. Bryce, "Memorandum for the Prime Minister and the Minister of Justice, Security Cases Involving Homosexuality," 19 December 1960 version, 2.) And "there is one case on file where an attempt was made to compromise a Canadian government employee" (Report of the Directorate, 1959–1960, Part II Security Branch "A," Appendix G, Appendix to Annual Report on Homosexuality Among Federal Government Employees, 42).

40 From D.F. Wall, "Security Cases Involving Character Weakness with Special Reference to the Problem of Homosexuality," 12 May 1959, 14.

41 See the Wolfenden Commission *Report of the Committee on Homosexual Offenses and Prostitution* (London 1957). On the Wolfenden Report and its impact in Canada see *The Regulation of Desire*, 139–172.

42 See Dorothy E. Smith, "The Active Text: A Textual Analysis of the Social Relations of Public Textual Discourse," in *Texts, Facts and Femininity,* 120–58.

43 D.F. Wall, Secretary of the Security Panel, Minutes of the 68th Meeting of the Security Panel, 6 October 1959.

44 Ibid., 5.

45 See Axel Otto Olson's testimony to a private session of the Royal Commission on the Criminal Law Relating to Criminal Sexual Psychopaths, "Report of the Private Sessions, Royal Commission on Criminal Sexual Psychopaths, Montreal and Toronto," commencing 6 February 1956, 137–47; also see "Official Discourse as Sexual Regulation," 253–7.

46 This allows us to both recognize and to begin to move beyond Eve Sedgwick's insightful notion of the centrality of 'the closet' in the construction of contemporary western culture. She locates this construction of 'the closet' largely on a literary and 'cultural' terrain. See Eve Kosofsky Sedgwick, *Epistemology of the Closet,* (Berkeley 1990).

47 For instance remember this excerpt from the quote this paper started with—"By exercising fairly simple precautions, homosexuals are usually able to keep their habits hidden from those who are not specifically seeking them out." From D.F. Wall, "Security Cases Involving Character Weakness with Special Reference to the Problem of Homosexuality."

48 Here they are referring to a general prohibition on directly interviewing alleged homosexuals presently in the civil service implied in Security Panel directives. They also wanted the decision over when departments should be provided with information about homosexuals in their ranks left to the RCMP's discretion and "we would also appreciate clarification on whether or not we should provide the department concerned with information on a homosexual who is not employed on duties having access to classified material." These quotes come from Appendix C, "RCMP Request for Terms of Reference—May 1960, Brief for Discussion on Reports of Mr. Don Wall and Dr. F.R. Wake on Personnel Security Matters in the USA," 4 March 1963.

49 "I" Directorate Annual Report, 1959–1960, Report of the Directorate, Appendix G, "Appendix to Annual Report on Homosexuality Among Federal Government Employees," 42.

50 Ibid.

51 Ibid., 42–5 and John Sawatsky, *Men in the Shadows,* 125–7.

52 Referred to in Directorate of Security and Intelligence, Annual Report, 1963–1964, 31, and Sawatsky, *Men in the Shadows,* 127.

53 Security Panel minutes, A special meeting of a quorum of the Security Panel, 24 June 1960, taken by D.F. Wall, issued 26 July, 1960.

54 Ibid., 1.

55 Ibid., 2.

56 Ibid., 2.

57 Ibid., 4.

58 Ibid., 4.

59 Ibid., 4.

60 R.B. Bryce, "Memorandum for the Prime Minister and the Minister of Justice, Security Cases Involving Homosexuality," 19 December 1960 version, 1.

61 R.B. Bryce, "Memorandum for the Prime Minister and the Minister of Justice, Security Cases Involving Homosexuality," 26 January 1961 version, 1–2.

62 Ibid., 3.

63 Ibid., 3–4.

64 Ibid., 4. Notice how the RCMP raises the criminalization of homosexuality course of action in their support for extending the campaign to encompass all government workers.

65 Cabinet Directive No. 35, "Security in the Public Service of Canada," 18 December 1963.

66 R.G. Robertson, Secretary to the Cabinet, "Memorandum for Deputy Ministers and Heads of Agency, Revised Cabinet Directive on Security," 27 December 1963, 1.

67 Cabinet Directive No. 35, "Security in the Public Service of Canada," 18 December 1963.

68 See Bill Walther and David Berndhart, Department of Psychology, "In Memoriam, Robert Wake and Russell Wendt," *This Week at Carleton* (20 January 1994), 3 and *The Report of the Royal Commission on the Criminal Law Relating to Criminal Sexual Psychopaths* (Ottawa, 1958).

69 Sawatsky, *Men in the Shadows*, 133.

70 Dr. F.R. Wake, "Report on Special Project," 19 December 1962.

71 See Dr. F.R. Wake, "Report on Special Project," 16. The aversion therapy he referred to was conducted by B. James in 1962 (16). He also discussed a number of treatments to alter behaviour (14) and stated that "Mental health personnel these days prefer not to speak of a cure (a change from homosexuality to heterosexuality) but rather of a change to controlled sexual behaviour, which would be more comfortable for the subject, for he is now divested of anti-social activities" (15). Wake opted for homosexuality being caused in most cases by "a combination of environmental circumstances during the years of childhood or early youth" (1). He stated that it was "not a matter of heredity or of the individual's perverse choice" (1). He was quite aware of the 'liberal' psychological and sexological work then going on in the US and mentioned the work of Evelyn Hooker who critiqued the notion of male homosexuals as 'unstable' and the Kinsey reports (1–3). He even was aware of the distinction being made between overt and covert homosexuals Hooker used that was developed in the work of Maurice Leznoff on male homosexuals in Montréal. On Leznoff see *The Regulation of Desire,* 117–9 and Maurice Leznoff, "The Homosexual in Urban Society," MA thesis, McGill University, Montreal, 1954. Although Wake knew about and used this more 'liberal' work he articulated it to a more 'investigative' and 'control' oriented perspective. Later he stated that "The general run of opinion...is that homosexuals almost always are maladjusted" (15) even though he referred to Hooker as holding a contrasting opinion.

72 Wake, "Abstract of the Report," for the "Report on Special Project."

73 See *The Regulation of Desire,* 132.

74 On the development of masculinity/femininity tests see Joseph H. Pleck, "The Theory of Male Sex Role Identity: Its Rise and Fall, 1936 to the Present," and Miriam Lewin, "Psychology Measures Femininity and Masculinity" in Miriam Lewin ed., *In the Shadows of the Past: Psychology Portrays the Sexes* (New York 1984).

75 Dr. F.R. Wake, "Report on Special Project," Appendix A, Word Association List, 1–3.

76 Ibid., 12.

77 Physique photos and magazines were ostensibly designed to display the non-erotic physical beauty of the male body but came to be eroticized by and produced by gay men. See Tom Waugh, "A Heritage of Photography," *The Body Politic,* 90 (January 1983), 29–33, his "Photography, Passion and Power," *The Body Politic,* 101 (March 1984), 29–33 and his "Gay Male Visual Culture in North America During the Fifties: Emerging from the Underground," *Parellelograme,* 12 (Fall 1986); Alan Miller, "Beefcake With No Labels Attached," *The Body Politic,* 90 (January 1983), 33; and Michael Bronski, *Culture Clash, The Making of a Gay Sensibility* (Boston 1984), 160–74.

78 Wake, "Report on Special Project," 12–3.

79 Ibid., 17.

80 Ibid. Wake also urged that connections be maintained with the network of sex researchers in the US including Evelyn Hooker, Wardell B. Pomeroy, William H. Masters and John Money. He suggested that the Department of Health and Welfare assume this liaison role. It was clear that this liaison was not to take place on security grounds as Wake wrote that "anyone effecting this liaison probably will have to have a front to cover his interest in 'suitability'" (18). A critical reader can get a sense here that 'suitability' was a term that could be coded with security concerns and also with more 'liberal' research concerns. It seems that the sex researchers Wake had contact with in the US would have had little idea of who was supporting his research or of its direct security connections.

81 This can be contrasted with the research technologies and strategies examined in Jennifer Terry's previously mentioned article, "Theorizing Deviant Historiography," 60.

82 A memo to D.F. Wall, Secretary of the Security Panel, 25 January 1963, from J.R.M. Bordeleau, Assistant Commissioner, Director, Security and Intelligence, RCMP, 1.

83 See Sawatsky, *Men in the Shadows,* 133–6.

84 Directorate of Security and Intelligence Annual Report, 65–6, 33.

85 Directorate of Security and Intelligence Annual Report, 66–7, 27.

86 Sawatsky, *Men in the Shadows,* 135–7.

87 Directorate of Security and Intelligence Annual Report, 1962–1963, 19.

88 Directorate of Security and Intelligence Annual Report, 1963–1964, 30.

89 See *The Regulation of Desire,* 157, and Doug Sanders, Association for Social Knowledge submission to the Royal Commission on Security, 29 February 1968.

Criminalizing the Colonized

Ontario Native Women Confront
the Criminal Justice System, 1920–60[*]

Joan Sangster

Over the past decade, Aboriginal women's conflicts with the law and their plight within the penal and child welfare systems have received increasing media and government attention. Framed by the political demands of Native communities for self-government, and fuelled by disillusionment with a criminal justice system that has resolutely failed Native peoples— both as victims of violence and as defendants in the courts—government studies and royal commissions have documented the shocking overincarceration of Native women.[1] At once marginalized, yet simultaneously the focus of intense government interest, Native women have struggled to make their own voices heard in these inquiries. Their testimony often speaks to their profound alienation from Canadian society and its justice system, an estrangement so intense that it is couched in despair. "How can we be healed by those who symbolize the worst experiences of our past?" asked one inmate before the 1990 Task Force on federally sentenced women.[2] Her query invokes current Native exhortations for a reinvention of Aboriginal traditions of justice and healing; it also speaks directly to the injuries of colonialism experienced by Aboriginal peoples.

Although we lack statistics on Native imprisonment before the 1970s, overincarceration may well be a "tragedy of recent vintage."[3] This article explores the roots of this tragedy, asking when and why overincarceration emerged in twentieth-century Ontario; how legal and penal authorities interpreted Aboriginal women's conflicts with the law; and in what ways Native women and their communities reacted to women's incarceration. Drawing primarily on case files from the Mercer Reformatory for Women, the only such provincial institution at the time,[4] I investigate the process of legal and moral regulation that led to Native women's incarceration from 1920 to 1960. Admittedly, such sources are skewed towards the views of those in authority: inmate case files are incomplete and partisan, strongly shaped by the recorder's reactions to the woman's narrative. Arrest and incarceration statistics are also problematic: they homogenize all Native and Métis nations under the designation "Indian,"[5] and they predominantly reflect the policing of Aboriginal peoples and the changing definitions of crime. However partial, these sources reveal patterns of, and explanations for, increasing incarceration; women's own voices, however fragmented, are also apparent in these records, offering some clues to women's reactions to incarceration.[6]

Native women's criminalization bore important similarities to that of other women, who

Joan Sangster, "Criminalizing the Colonized: Ontario Native Women Confront the Criminal Justice System, 1920–60," *Canadian Historical Review* 80, 1 (March 1999). Reprinted by permission of the University of Toronto Press Incorporated.
[*] I want to thank Peter Kulchyski, Bryan Palmer, and Jean Manore for their comments on an earlier version of this paper.

were also arrested primarily for crimes of public order and morality, who often came from impoverished and insecure backgrounds, and whose sexual morality was a key concern for the courts. The convictions of Aboriginal women are thus part of a broader web of gendered moral regulation articulated through the law—the disciplining of women whose behaviour was considered unfeminine, unacceptable, abnormal, or threatening to society. This "censuring" process of distinguishing the immoral from the moral woman was also sustained by the medical and social work discourses used within the penal system; these attitudes constituted and reproduced relations of power based on gender, race, and economic marginality.[7] Granted, the law was one of many forms of regulation—accomplished also through the church, the school, and the family—but it remained an important one. As the "cutting edge of colonialism,"[8] the law could enact the "final lesson" and perhaps the most alienating one for Aboriginal women: incarceration.

The experiences of Native women were also profoundly different from those of other women: they were shaped by racist state policies of "overregulation" linked to the federal Indian Act, by the racialized constructions of Native women by court and prison personnel, and by the cultural chasm separating Native from non-Native in this time period. In short, the legal regulation of these women was an integral component of the material, social, and cultural dimensions of colonialism.[9]

Native women's increasing conflicts with the law thus reflect overlapping relations of power, based on gender, class, and race. Masculinist and class-biased definitions of crime, already inherent in the criminal justice system, were further complicated by the relations of colonialism and race. As Colin Sumner argues, colonialism often sparks the clash of two cultures and legal regimes, with unequal power relations operating *within* as well as *between* those cultures. The supposedly "modern" Western legal regime often dominates, displacing older modes of regulating behaviour, and converting "attempts to preserve the old ways, resist the new order and accommodate to its hardships...into criminal behaviour."[10]

Arguing for a separate Aboriginal justice system, activists and scholars have recently stressed the fundamental, perhaps unbridgeable, differences between Euro-Canadian and Aboriginal value systems.[11] While I have found evidence of culturally distinct notions of wrongdoing, justice, and sanction, my conclusions also highlight some complications in this picture. Though certainly alienated from the dominant criminal justice system, some Native families, leaders, and communities also used this system to address social problems and effect social controls in desperately difficult times. As a result, they also participated in the incarceration of their own wives, daughters, and mothers.

As the only provincial reformatory for women, the Mercer, located in Toronto, took in women from across the province who received sentences varying from three months to two years.[12] Although extreme caution should be exercised in using the Mercer numbers, they do suggest patterns of emerging overincarceration.[13] The most striking fact of Native women's imprisonment at the Mercer was its increase over time. In the 1920s, few Native women appear in the prison registers; three decades later, Native women were listed on virtually every page. Of overall "intakes" (women admitted, repeaters or not) in the 1920s, only thirty-nine were Native women, or about 2 per cent of the prison population. Every decade thereafter, the number of Native women taken in not only doubled but increased as a proportion of admissions—from 4 per cent in the 1930s to 7 per cent in the 1940s to just over 10 per cent in the 1950s. Yet over these years, the Native population remained constant at about 1 per cent of the general population.[14] The turning point clearly came after the Second World War when the number of Native women admitted increased substantially.[15] A survey of minor charges in Kenora supports this pattern; by the 1950s the number of Native women incarcerated in the local jail was increasing rapidly, with the vast majority of repeaters charged with alcohol offences.[16]

Although the patterns were amplified in certain areas, Aboriginal women's incarceration followed the trends of sentencing for all women at the Mercer. There were increasing numbers of women sentenced over time, more and more liquor offences by the 1950s, and a larger number of recidivists with shorter, definite sentences. Younger women, particularly those in their twenties, dominated at the Mercer in the interwar period; in the 1940s and 1950s, women from twenty to forty were still the majority, though slightly more women over forty were being sentenced. Most offenders were listed as housewives or domestic workers, or gave no occupation, and they were primarily sentenced for crimes of public order and morality. By the 1950s, however, Native women were overrepresented in liquor charges. Overall, alcohol offences represented about 50 per cent of the admissions, but for Native women they were as high as 70 per cent.[17]

For Native women, crimes of public poverty and moral transgression always dominated over crimes against private property or the person. Vagrancy, an elastic offence that included everything from prostitution to drunkenness to wandering the streets, dominated as the most significant charge for Native women in the 1920s (50 per cent) and 1930s (31 per cent). In both these decades, prostitution and bawdy house charges came second, and, by the 1930s, breach of the Liquor Control Act (BLCA), especially the clause prohibiting drunkenness in a public place, was assuming equal importance. In the next two decades, alcohol-related charges came to dominate as the reason for incarceration (32 per cent in the 1940s, and 72 per cent in the 1950s), with vagrancy and prostitution convic-

tions ranking second. Theft, receiving stolen goods, and break and enters comprised only 6 per cent of the convictions in the 1940s and 1950s, while violence against the person represented only 2 per cent of the charges in these years. That issues of sexual morality and public propriety were central to Native incarceration can be seen in the increasing use of the Female Refuges Act (FRA), which sanctioned the incarceration of women aged sixteen to thirty-five, sentenced, or even "liable to be sentenced," under any Criminal Code or bylaw infractions for "idle and dissolute" behaviour. While this draconian law was used most in Ontario in the 1930s and 1940s, for Native women it was increasingly applied in the 1940s and 1950s.[18]

A higher proportion of charges was levelled against women for neglecting, abandoning, or "corrupting" their children (5 per cent and 9 per cent in the latter two decades) than for assaults against adults.[19] Prosecutions under this charge point to a crucial theme found within the case files: even if the official charge was not alcohol related, the crime was often attributed to alcohol consumption. One woman charged with both assault and contributing to juvenile delinquency, for instance, had struck another woman on the street while intoxicated, and in the presence of her own fourteen-year-old daughter.[20] Women often lost custody of their children when both alcohol problems and poverty indicated neglect to the authorities; sometimes the children were deserted, sometimes they were left in the hands of relatives who, poor themselves, could not cope easily. One poverty-stricken woman left her children aged three to nine in a tent, and they were later found looking for food in garbage cans. Incarcerated for intoxication, she immediately lost her children to the Children's Aid Society (CAS).

Theft charges were also linked to poverty and alcohol consumption. Two Native women found themselves severely punished when they "destroyed private property"; after drinking in a bar in a northern mining town, they asked two men for a ride home. Refused, they threw matches into the car and destroyed it. In another case, a woman "helped herself to $19.00 from the wallet of an intoxicated bushworker drinking with her." As she was five-months pregnant, she reasoned that "she needed it more than him." The link between prostitution charges and women's poverty was also clear; despite the fact that a woman might be literally "malnourished and destitute," incarceration was deemed the appropriate response.[21] Even the few violent crimes were often explained in the files by alcohol problems; in one tragic case, a woman who was drunk unknowingly assaulted her sister with a beer bottle and killed her. She served less than two years for manslaughter, the judge noting her lack of murderous intent and her own mental anguish. Other women attacked family members in anger or frustration, or attempted suicide; their violence was often unsuccessful or half-hearted, desperate but not calculated.

One reason that liquor charges dominated at the Mercer by the late 1950s was overcrowding in women's cells at the local Don Jail. The crush was relieved by sending some women to the Mercer.[22] This explanation also may account for the increasing number of recidivists: by the 1950s, at least 50 per cent of all the Native women admitted had already been in the Mercer before. A few women, often homeless and sometimes with alcohol problems, were being admitted twenty or thirty times.[23] One recidivist case was typical: in the late 1930s, Susan, a seventeen year old, was brought up before a small-town magistrate on a charge of "corrupting children." An orphaned foster child now working as a domestic, she was arrested for engaging in sex with a local man at his family home in front of children. The initial report also claimed she had no occupation, "has been mixed up in other immorality and was correspondent in a divorce case."[24] After serving her term, and giving birth to a child in prison,

Susan stayed in Toronto, but she had few skills and little education. Two years later, she was incarcerated under the Venereal Diseases Act, perhaps a sign that she had turned to prostitution to support herself. Struggling with alcohol problems, she went back and forth between her home town and Toronto, trying with little success to collect enough relief to survive. When relief officials tried to force her into the local refuge, she went to live in her brother's abandoned hen house. Eventually she was sent back to Mercer for two years, convicted under the FRA as an "idle and dissolute" woman. She remained in Toronto and, over the next fifteen years, was jailed repeatedly under BLCA charges: by 1959 she had thirty-six admissions. Often convicted on the standard thirty days or a $25 fine penalty, she—like many Native women—could not afford the fine, so spent time in the Mercer.

Many women at the Mercer came from families that had suffered significant losses; a parent or siblings had died of pneumonia, gangrene, an accident, or alcoholism. Tuberculosis claimed many lives on reserves, even after it was declining within the general population.[25] When a middle-aged woman, who lost all her eight siblings to disease and her father to alcoholism, told the Mercer doctor that her own drinking is "unfortunate but unchangeable," one can perhaps understand her tone of resignation. Family dissolution, domestic violence, intense poverty, low levels of education, the likelihood of foster care, or CAS intervention in the family were also evident in many women's backgrounds. Despite family dissolution, women struggled, sometimes against great odds, to sustain family ties even when illness, transience, or removal of children made it difficult. "She never knew her parents but she has five younger siblings [spread over residential schools and CAS care]...whom she writes to try and keep the family together," noted the reformatory psychiatrist in one instance.[26]

Women's geographical origins and the location of their convictions are significant, indicating one of the major causes of overincarceration: the spiralling effects of economic deprivation and social dislocation. In the interwar period, the majority of women were convicted in southern Ontario, especially Toronto and Hamilton, or in Sarnia, Sault Ste. Marie, or Sudbury—cities close to many reserves.[27] Following the Second World War, more Native women originally came from more remote areas further north. By the 1950s, even though the majority of convictions were in southern Ontario, the place of origin, in over a third of these cases, was Manitoulin, North Bay, Thunder Bay, or other northern places.[28] This moving "frontier of incarceration" suggests the importance of urbanization and/or deteriorating economic and social circumstances as the stimulus for women's conflicts with the law.[29]

In the interwar period, Natives living on many reserves were finding themselves in difficult economic straits. No efforts were made to encourage new economic development, a reform desperately needed because many reserves had a fixed resource base and a growing population. The Depression accentuated subsistence problems, reducing some Aboriginal communities to relief far below the already pitiful levels in the cities.[30] Similar dilemmas increasingly plagued more isolated reserves after the war, when corporate resource development, the decline of fur prices, and new transportation routes began to have a dramatic impact on northern communities. As the effect of colonization permeated further north, the consequences were increased social dislocation and conflict, and more intervention by Euro-Canadian police forces, especially when Aboriginal peoples were off their reserves.[31] Indeed, women who fled to cities in search of jobs and social services often found little material aid, but faced the complicating, intensifying pressure of racism.[32] One of the most dramatic examples of the colonial "penetration" of the North was that of Grassy Narrows. When this isolated community was relocated closer to Kenora, the community's sense of spatial organization, family structure, and productive relations were all undermined. Proximity to the city brought increased access to alcohol and the malignancy of racism; "the final nail in the coffin" was mercury poisoning of their water and their fish supply.[33]

The stresses experienced by Native families in this time period were never simply material. For example, official federal policies of acculturation, though increasingly viewed as unsuccessful, persisted in projects such as residential schools, which were experienced by as many as one-third of Native youth in the early decades of the twentieth century. While some historians argue that girls may have acquired a few useful skills in the schools, almost all accounts agree that the isolation of children from their communities, the denigration of their culture and language, and the emotional and physical abuse left many women scarred for life.[34] It is impossible to ascertain exactly how many Mercer inmates came through residential schools, but it is clear that when residential school inmates appeared in court, magistrates and judges claimed bluntly that they should know "the difference between right from wrong."[35] Although the legal authorities assumed the moral superiority of the Euro-Canadian, religious instruction of residential schools, Aboriginal leaders now argue that violence, alcoholism, and alienation were actually the direct results of such schooling.[36]

Because alcohol charges were the primary cause of incarceration, it is worth examining them in greater depth: these cases demonstrate how social dislocation interacted with cultural alienation and racism to prompt overincarceration. Despite evidence that prison was no solution to "alcoholism"[37] and may have worsened the problem, penal punishment continued to be the response of the authorities. One important reason for the high numbers of alcohol arrests, especially for women, was their poverty and thus their inability to pay fines. At the same time, the public character of Native drinking made it particularly distasteful to the dominant classes and culture. It was sometimes linked to sexual "misbehaviour," including miscegenation, and, given the image of Native women as weak and corruptible, authorities believed that alcoholism would spread easily by example. Native drinking had for some time been feared as a precursor to alcoholism, and, although consumption of alcohol was increasingly seen as an addiction rather than as evidence of weakness of character, the latter characterization never entirely vanished from the judgments of the legal and medical authorities.

Not a crime as long as it is hidden from view, alcohol-induced behaviour was easier to ignore for the well-heeled drinker than the impoverished one. Moreover, the means of consuming alcohol and the way in which the effects of alcohol are exhibited are socially and culturally specific. By the late 1960s, critics of existing theories of alcoholism among Native peoples argued that there was no direct evidence that "Indians were more susceptible" to alcoholism and that the precise forms that "out-of-control" behaviour took had more to do with culture than biology.[38] Since that time, the dominant interpretations of alcoholism have stressed the social and economic context of colonialism and oppression giving rise to alcohol consumption, some even seeing it as a muted form of "protest."[39] Perceptions of alcoholism as a disease that Natives are especially vulnerable to have not totally disappeared, however, even within Aboriginal testimonies.[40]

Alcoholism may have existed as a problem for some Native women, but magistrates failed to see it as an outcome of systemic social problems. While many regretted the unfortunate background of women brought before the court, pointing to family breakups or alcoholic parents, their laments were specific rather than

structural. They were insensitive to the assaults on Native culture, traditional economic production, and family and community organization that were occurring in the twentieth century. Court pronouncements also divulged a fatalistic equation of Natives and alcohol: "She is an Indian girl and probably will never stay away from the drink," noted one magistrate in 1945. A decade later the same complaint was advanced: "They spend up to 8 months in jail and are the biggest problem I have...I do not know any remedy for this type of person."[41]

The authorities were especially concerned with the links between visible sexual behaviour and alcohol consumption. Native women suspected of prostitution, or who engaged in sex for no money and with no obvious moral regret, were especially vulnerable to incarceration, as were non-Aboriginal women who engaged in "casual" sex and rejected the ritual of confession and moral guilt.[42] Women accused of having sex in public or with multiple partners were targeted by police, who described them in terms tinged with moral outrage: "She is known as a prostitute and often intoxicated...her conduct is disgraceful to say the least, one night she hung around the naval barracks, took off her clothes and jumped in the creek." Alcohol and sexual misbehaviour became so linked in the mind of the police that the mere fact of Aboriginal men and women drinking together suggested sexual immorality; when two women were found in a cabin, drinking with some men, the arresting officer noted "there was no evidence of sex but the proximity of the sexes with intoxicants can have undesirable results."[43]

These descriptions were fuelled by the racist stereotype of the Indian woman easily debauched by alcohol, and lacking the sexual restraint of white women. By the late nineteenth century, political and media controversies had created an image of Native women in the public mind: supposedly "bought and sold" by their own people as "commodities," they were easily "demoralized" sexually, and a threat to both public "morality and health."[44] While the Native was essentialized in the dominant cultural discourse, Aboriginal women did not assume the (male) role of the "noble savage" or the "lazy ingrate," but rather of the licentious "wild woman" symbolizing sexual excess and the need for conquest or control.[45] In one sense, there was less moral panic about Aboriginal women engaging in interracial sex than there was for white women; the latter might even be incarcerated for sexual liaisons with non-white men.[46] This lack of concern with miscegenation, however, emanated from a racist stereotype that saw Native women as less "pure to begin with."

Incarceration was also justified for paternalistic motives: magistrates claimed that, by incarcerating Native women, they were protecting them from becoming an "easy target for the avaricious" or the "victim of unprincipled Indian and white men."[47] A similar rationale of protecting the weak underlay some of the prohibitions against prostitution in the Indian Act.[48] This paternalism was evident in the trial of a young Aboriginal woman from southern Ontario who was sent to the Mercer for two years on FRA charges of being "idle and dissolute." The arresting RCMP officer insisted she was "transient, with no work and has been convicted on many alcohol charges over the past few years." She had been caught "brawling with white men," he continued, "and has been found wandering, her mind blank after drinking." Moreover, it was believed that she was a "bad influence on a fifteen year old who has also been led astray." The magistrate lectured the woman: "My girl, I hope that by removing you from unscrupulous white men and Indian soldiers and alcohol that you will start a new life. It is too bad that such a good looking Indian like you should throw your life away. Other men buy the liquor for you, then you suffer, and they escape."

This example also points to another precipitating factor in many arrests: the public nature

of the woman's alcohol consumption. In large cities, Native women who were jailed were not always recidivists, but simply those targeted by police because of loud, disruptive behaviour or inability to find their way home. One such woman calmly told the psychiatrist that she was not an alcoholic and "only drinks heavily on occasion." He was forced to admit she was right.[49] It is difficult to escape the conclusion that these women were simply more heavily policed because they were poor and Native.[50]

The complaint that women who drank heavily would easily corrupt others was also common. In some cases, it was Native families who feared this prospect: "She should serve her whole term; she is better in there," wrote one father, fearing his daughter, if released, would be influenced by her mother, who also drank. Often, it was the Indian agent or the police who advocated removing the offender so she would not lead others astray. Sentencing one woman to a term in Mercer, a magistrate noted that the woman must be kept away because she was "a bad influence on the girls on the island"; when she was released, he urged that she be sent "away from the Island." Women whose children had been removed because of their mother's drinking were seen as a special burden on the state, and, therefore, a candidate for incarceration. "She has had four children with the CAS," noted one magistrate, "she has chosen the wrong path, now her children are a public charge." Such women were also portrayed as poor material for rehabilitation. As one magistrate noted of a deaf woman charged under the Indian Act: "There is no doubt that children will continue to the end of her reproductive age, or until a pathological process renders her sterile. She is also likely to drink steadily. The prospect of improvement is remote. Institutionalization, if available, is suitable."[51]

Incarceration was thus used as punishment, as banishment from public view, and as an attempt to protect women from further alcoholism or immorality. Declarations of "protection," however, were clearly inscribed with both gender and race paternalism, for they presumed an image of proper feminine behaviour, stressing sexual purity and passivity within the private nuclear family, and the need for Native women to absorb these "higher" Euro-Canadian standards. Similarly, teachers in the residential schools often claimed that Native girls were easily sexually exploited, prone to returning "to the blanket."[52] Aboriginal women were thus both infantalized as vulnerable and weak, and also feared as more overtly and actually sexual.

Unfortunately, a gulf of considerable magnitude divided Native women from those convicting them and from the penal authorities in the Mercer. Indeed, the interpretation of Native crime offered by the legal and penal "experts" contributed to the process of overincarceration by legitimizing an image of Native women as morally weak and easily corrupted. Even after incarceration, these attitudes were significant because they shaped possibilities of parole, alcohol treatment, and rehabilitation; convinced that Native women would be recidivists, little was done to discern their needs. Not surprisingly, many women became even more alienated within the reformatory.

Like other women, First Nations women were separated from prison personnel by class and cultural differences. Inmates encountered revulsion, antipathy, resignation, and sometimes sympathy from the experts whose "scientific" language of clinical analysis and case work often masked subjective, moral judgments. Native women, however, were also seen through the particular lens of race paternalism. For example, the very word *reserve* had a different meaning from words like *poor* or *bad neighbourhood* used between the 1930s and 1950s to describe the backgrounds of white women: reserves were associated with degeneracy, backwardness, and filth. One "progressive" social worker, writing about Indian juveniles in the 1940s, decried

racial prejudice and the poverty on reserves, but at the same time reiterated many racist images, describing Indians as "savage, childish, primitive and ignorant."[53]

A picture of Aboriginal women as weak and lacking in moral fibre followed them through the court and penal systems. Magistrates would comment, "We can't expect miracles from this home," while the presiding prison psychiatrist would often conclude, "It is doubtful if successful rehabilitation could be achieved."[54] The image of the reserve as a place of hopelessness was especially evident in probation reports. Native families sometimes offered probationers accommodation, even when houses were crowded, yet officials equated such offers with a lack of awareness about the need for basic moral and social standards. They were especially critical of congested conditions, likely seeing proximity of the sexes as encouraging immorality. They were also suspicious of those living a transient life, "in the Indian mode,"[55] who might easily succumb to alcohol use, unemployment, and poverty. "Home conditions primitive...the home is a disreputable filthy shack on the reserve," were typical observations. Aboriginal people who did not fit this stereotype were then portrayed as unusual: "Above average Indian home which is adequately furnished, clean and tidy," noted one probation report, while another officer claimed a father was "one of few Indians in the area who does not drink."[56]

Not all these Native women came directly from reserves, but the stigma of primitiveness was carried with them into the city, resulting in overzealous policing and victimization. One older woman was arrested, along with an intoxicated friend, for "indecent exposure"; her crime was simply swimming nude at a lake where nude boys were also swimming. Her claim that she was in prison "unjustly" seemed to be shared by the psychiatrist, but he did not advocate release. A young woman who had stolen a purse she found in a store change room became distraught at the "humiliation" her possible incarceration would cause her siblings, so tried to return some of the money. Her honesty cost her a prison term. Again, the Mercer psychiatrist's report noted she was a "bright, alert, pleasing" woman with a good employment history. She had been incarcerated, however, on the basis of reports from CAS and school officials in Sault Ste. Marie that portrayed her as a "typical" problem Native: she was an orphan, had one illegitimate child, and a "poor" attitude—in their view, she was destined for trouble.[57]

Probation reports also revealed a Catch-22 that Native women faced in terms of rehabilitation. Social workers debated whether reserve or city life would be more corrupting for released women, but they often recommended removing women from their original home or reserve. However well intentioned the effort to isolate her from past problems, this strategy left women in foreign surroundings, alienated by language and cultural differences, often directly faced with racism. This situation was well captured in a parole report that claimed one woman was now "an outlaw on the Reserve" because of her promiscuity, and her parents there were heavy drinkers who lived in a "small, filthy home." It was unwise to return her there, the officer noted, but added: "We realize the extreme difficulty in placing an Indian girl in some other centre, where society is loath in accepting her." Grandmothers often tried to care for children left behind or born in jail, but families were frank about the lack of economic resources and employment available for the released women, and they agonized over the prospects of help with alcohol problems. One mother pointed out that she also drank and that if her adult daughter returned home, "she would lose her mothers allowance and so they would have no money." "The mother really does not want her home," observed the agent, "but she would not say [the daughter] could not return."[58]

If a woman came from a reserve, her incarceration might be the product of the Indian agent's powers to charge her with crimes such as drinking, prostitution, or immorality. Agents were endowed with the powers of justices of the peace under the Indian Act, thus creating an extra layer of oppressive legal regulation for Native women. The level of surveillance of the economic, social, and moral lives of Native families by the agent was astounding. When called on to assess parole, his report might comment on the family's church attendance, the marital status, education, employment, and social lives of siblings and parents, his judgment of their moral standards, and intimate details of the woman's life. The agent could initiate the proceedings sending a woman to the Mercer, or assist police efforts to incarcerate her. He had the power to make or break a case for parole, and might exile her to another area. Moreover, the evidence presented by the agent could be little more than hearsay. "There are complaints that she is hanging around the hotel, going into rooms with men...we hear that she is in the family way," testified the police chief in one case. The Indian agent supported him, claiming he had spoken with her doctor and discovered she was pregnant.[59]

While the agent's power was never absolute, and might be opposed by band members, the mere awareness of his ability to survey and penalize wrongdoers buttressed his authority. His surveillance was also patriarchal in character, for federal Indian policy to "assimilate and civilize" was developed with the specific image of a downtrodden, sexually loose woman in need of domestic education and moral guidance in mind.[60] Criminal charges provided one means for agents to enforce moral standards, and both alcohol consumption and sexual immorality were policed this way.[61] In 1930, for instance, a woman spent a month in a northern Ontario jail after the agent, the RCMP, and the chief charged her with "act[ing] in a profligate manner." Women were the special focus of control, but men could be targeted as well. In one case a woman charged with sexual immorality was given a suspended sentence because she was ill and had a child, while her male "accomplice" in immorality spent a month in jail.[62]

State policies encouraging regulation were buttressed by both social work and psychiatric discourses that claimed to offer expert knowledge of Native women's psyche and character. Inclined to see Natives as weak, impassive, and possibly immoral, social workers and psychiatrists by the 1940s were beginning to attribute such weaknesses to environmental or social conditioning rather than racial traits.[63] Ironically, women sometimes found more sympathy from the magistrates who sentenced them than from the psychiatrists who became increasingly influential after the Second World War: "She has no one to look after her, is badly in need of care and treatment for alcoholism," pleaded one magistrate in his sentencing report.[64] Psychiatrists who examined women's suitability for "clinic" (alcohol) treatment were seldom so supportive. Repeatedly, a woman's silence, a means of coping with alien surroundings (and, in some cases, related to language differences), was read negatively as evidence of a passive personality. It is also revealing that a psychiatrist's assessment denoting "low intelligence" often came immediately after a statement describing the woman as Native, a psychological slip of some consequence.[65] These doctors "saw" only one Native personality type: "taciturn," "the usual Indian reserve," "finds it difficult to verbalize as do most of our Indians," "incoherent and withdrawn," were opinions frequently stated.[66]

There is no evidence that these experts read any of the contemporary anthropological literature, especially on the Ojibwa women who dominated at the Mercer. Irving Hallowell, for instance, argued in the 1940s that culture shaped personality structure and that the Ojibwa were highly reserved emotionally, avoiding direct confrontation or anger with others; this restraint, he argued, was a product of their hunting and gathering way of life, their spiritual beliefs and social organization.[67] Contemporary participant observation has suggested similar conclusions. In both Ojibwa and Iroquois cultures, it is often considered wrong to "speak of your hurts and angers... to indulge your private emotions." Once past, the past should "be buried and forgotten"; moreover, faced with the unfamiliar, "conservation withdrawal" is the best survival tactic: you must "step back into yourself and conserve your physical and psychic energy."[68]

Medical and social work experts at the Mercer had a different measuring stick. What was crucial in their world view, especially by the 1950s, was an embrace of the "confessional" mode, introspection, a critical understanding of one's family background as the "cause" of addiction, and a professed desire to change one's inner self. Native women in the Mercer almost invariably refused to embrace this therapeutic model. Furthermore, their honesty about their drinking simply confounded the psychiatrist. A woman who had both her children taken away because of her drinking and "had never coped with this" spoke doubtfully about whether she could change. "She might use antabuse," he noted, but then was shocked by her final admission: "but she still laughs and says she will go on a big spree when she gets out of here." "She regards her drinking as a feature of her personality which is unfortunate but unchangeable... not motivated to improve, nothing to do to help her when she is discharged," he concluded, as fatalistic as he claimed the women were.[69]

This cultural gap was conversely apparent in Native women's reactions to their incarcerations. Women's silences—perhaps a form of resistance—make it difficult to judge their responses to incarceration. Displaying a level of realism, honesty, acceptance, and stoicism that the authorities interpreted as passive fatalism, Native women often openly admitted to the charge against them, making no excuses. "She freely admits neglect of [her children] and does not make any further comment," a psychiatrist mused; he was even more baffled by a woman's "extraordinary honesty about her unwillingness to work."[70] Several contemporary legal workers noted that honesty about the "crime" and guilty pleas, rather than any demand for the system to *prove* one guilty, distinguished the Ojibwa value system.

Not all women accepted their fate easily; the removal of children was agonizing for some, and a minority sent to the Mercer objected to their punishment. Most commonly it was younger women who tried to run away, or who argued or fought with the matrons. When one "fractious" young woman, already a fugitive from an industrial school and a training school, ended up at the Mercer, she attempted a third escape to her home near Fort William. The more rebellious Aboriginal women sometimes came to the Mercer because they had caused trouble elsewhere, as with the teen accused of trying to "start a riot" at the Galt Training School for Girls. There were women who "denied everything" and argued with the psychiatrist that they did not belong in a reformatory. More often, they resisted by resorting to silence, by answering no to every question posed by the psychiatrist, or rejecting the "help" they proffered: "on the whole seems to be able to run her own show the way she wants it," the doctor commented on a Mohawk woman in the Mercer for one month for alcohol problems. She did not want his advice or any contact with the other Native women, whom she disdainfully dismissed as "primitive Ojibwas."[71]

Families also had mixed responses to women's sentences, but there were some clear distinctions between what families and the authorities condemned as wrong. In contrast to the authorities, many Native families rejected the idea that behaviour caused by alcohol was a crime, a perception that remains strong in many Aboriginal communities today.[72] "I do not believe that my wife should be punished for drinking," wrote one distressed husband; "some soldiers brought the whisky to our reserve and I thought they were our friends." A father and daughter from southern Ontario appeared one day at the Mercer office, asking for the release of the mother. They appealed to the authorities by saying she could get employment in the tobacco fields, and added that there was no reason to keep someone just because of occasional disturbances while drunk: "She is fine unless under the influence of alcohol," they implored, to no effect. Like some white working-class families, relatives also demanded the woman's release so she could resume her familial duties: "We are old and can't look after [our daughter's] two children as well as her sister's fifteen year old," one elderly couple pleaded.[73]

Most Native families and communities failed to see drinking as a crime, and they also had difficulty understanding why incarceration was the punishment. In more isolated Ojibwa communities, the chief and council, or sometimes elders, had imposed different sanctions for wrongdoing than those imposed by the Euro-Canadian justice system. Social control was effected through elders' lectures about good behaviour, connected to spiritual instruction, or through fear of gossip or of the "bad medicine" of supernatural retribution. If a person broke communal codes, shaming and confession were crucial to rehabilitation; indeed, when the confession was public, the "transgression" was washed away.[74] Only in extreme cases was banishment of the individual considered the answer.[75] Similarly, in Iroquois societies, ostracism, ridicule, or prohibitions on becoming a future leader were all used to control behaviour, admittedly an easier prospect in smaller, tightly knit communities in which the clan system also discouraged conflicts.[76]

Many observers claimed that these traditional mechanisms of social control were breaking down in Aboriginal communities at this time owing to the social stresses on reserve life and the debilitating effects of colonialism. Moreover, there is little historical evidence of the gendered applications of sanction,[77] punishment, and social control, or on the way in which traditional values did, or did not, follow women and men into the city. While recognizing the dangers of essentializing or romanticizing "traditional" Aboriginal social control, the cultural gaps between Aboriginal and Euro-Canadian notions of wrongdoing and sanction still remain clear.

On some occasions, local attempts by the families or communities to alter women's behaviour were combined with the strategies of the Euro-Canadian justice system. Maria's case is a good example. Charged repeatedly with intoxication and with neglect of her children, Maria lost them to various institutions: three children were sent to a residential school, one was in CAS care, and one was in the sanatorium. The Indian agent complained to the crown attorney that she resumed drinking as soon as she was released. The chief on the reserve wanted to help her and tried to work out a plan for her rehabilitation promising the return of her children and a house on the reserve if she could refrain from drinking for two months. Her failure to meet his conditions may speak not only to her addiction but to the desolation she still felt about losing her children.[78]

Seldom did the women, their families, or the communities offer a straightforward political critique of the discriminatory nature of the justice system: that is, Natives' lack of access to legal counsel; their limited cultural understanding of the courts' alien legal concepts and rituals; language and translation difficulties; and racist treatment by police or legal officials. Nonetheless, a pattern of estrangement was visible. In a rare case, one mother articulated her anger against what she justly perceived to be overly harsh treatment of her daughter: "I dearly love my daughter, I want my grandson to come home here. This is OUR country, especially Canada, and there is a lot more I could say. [If a] woman anywhere in this country committed murder they would get

out free, but my daughter gets two years for less crime [a drunk charge]."[79]

[...]

In the mid-twentieth century, particularly after 1945, contemporary patterns of overincarceration of Native women became apparent at the Ontario Reformatory for Women. The majority of First Nations women sent to the Mercer were criminalized on the premise of moral and public order infractions linked to alcohol, or for prostitution, venereal disease, or child neglect charges. Like other women sent to the reformatory, the lives of these Aboriginal women were framed by economic marginality, family dissolution, violence, and sometimes previous institutionalization. The background of Aboriginal women, however, was also marked by high levels of ill health and intense poverty, and their experience of the criminal justice system was profoundly shaped by their own cultural alienation and by the authorities' perceptions of their cultural and racial deficiencies. Three crucial, interconnected factors shaped the emerging process of overincarceration: the material and social dislocation precipitated by colonialism, the gender and race paternalism of court and penal personnel, and the related cultural gap between Native and Euro-Canadian value systems, articulating very different notions of crime and punishment.

Unlike the women housed in local jails who were seen as hopeless repeaters, women sent to the Mercer were supposedly targeted for rehabilitation. Yet, before they even entered the Mercer's towered gate, Aboriginal women were exposed to extra layers of surveillance and suspicion, and their reformation was presumed to be unlikely. Women who came from reserves were subject to the authoritarian powers of the Indian agent and the Indian Act, designed to assimilate Native peoples to the more "progressive" patriarchal, Christian, Euro-Canadian culture. If the Aboriginal woman could not be remade in a new image, she would be chastised, hidden, or punished. The process of censuring Native women demarcated colonial and racial power as well as gender hierarchies; legal and moral regulation through incarceration was in turn an integral component of colonialism.[80]

Before the Second World War, Native women were assessed within legal, medical, and social work discourses that assumed that the environmental, even hereditary legacy of their "primitive" origins ran deep. As psychiatry became more influential in the 1950s, Native women were no less disadvantaged: the silences that doctors faulted them for became part of the ongoing racist construction of Native women as lower in moral stature and insight than white women. In neither era did the sentencing or the "helping" authorities really see the structural crises faced by Native women and communities; alcoholism, for example, was still interpreted as a loss of self-control, rather than as a "symptom of cultural devastation, powerlessness, marginality, [also acting] to precipitate those conditions."[81]

The experiences of these women, incarcerated for moral or public-order crimes involving alcohol, indicates the extent to which the very definition of crime is a contested question of political consequence: even the statistics showing the increasing incarceration of Native women reflected interpretations of what the dominant social groups thought was a crime, not what Aboriginal groups believed was wrong. This cultural gap underscores the extent to which the moral regulation of First Nations women through incarceration was first and foremost a "legitimated practice of moral-political control, linked to conflicts and power relations, based on class, gender and race."[82]

While women's actual voices, feelings, and responses are difficult to locate within this regulatory process, the general pattern of Aboriginal alienation from Euro-Canadian justice—particularly for more isolated communities unused to Canadian policing—is a repeated theme in women's stories. However, customary Aboriginal practices could be refashioned and used by Canadian authorities, so much so that Native communities and families might also use the legal system to discipline their own. Native acceptance of Canadian law was one consequence of ongoing attempts to assimilate Aboriginal people, but it was not a simple reflection of European dominance. It also revealed attempts to cope with the negative effects of social change that were devastating individuals and families: in the process of struggling to adjust to the dislocations of colonialism, communities sometimes abetted the incarceration of Native women.

Native women seldom found solace or aid in the reformatory and, tragically, many returned to prison repeatedly. First Nations women often responded to their estrangement from the law and the reformatory with silence and stoicism—perhaps in itself a subtle form of noncompliance—though a very few, along with their families, voiced unequivocal renunciations of this system, their voices a preview to the current sustained critique of the inadequacy of Euro-Canadian "justice" for Aboriginal peoples.

Notes

1   Native women are disproportionately represented in federal prisons—an area *not* dealt with in this article. There are also considerable regional variations in overincarceration. In Ontario, 1980s statistics showed Native people to be about 2 per cent of the population, while Native women comprised 16 per cent of provincial admission to correctional institu- tions; in the North, local arrest rates were far higher. See Ontario, Ontario Advisory Council on Women's Issues, *Native Women and the Law* (Toronto 1989); Carol Laprairie, "Selected Criminal Justice and Socio-Economic Data on Native Women," *Canadian Journal of Criminology* 26, 4 (1984): 161–9; Canada, Royal Commission

on Aboriginal Peoples, *Aboriginal Peoples and the Justice System: Report of the National Round Table on Aboriginal Justice* (Ottawa 1993); Canada, Law Reform Commission, *Report on Aboriginal Peoples and Criminal Justice* (Ottawa 1991); Manitoba, *Report of the Aboriginal Justice Inquiry of Manitoba* (Winnipeg 1991).

2 Anonymous, quoted in Canada, Correctional Services, *Creating Choices: The Report of the Task Force on Federally Sentenced Women* (April 1990), 9.

3 Bradford Morse, "Aboriginal Peoples, the Law and Justice," in R. Silverman and M. Nielsen, eds., *Aboriginal Peoples and Canadian Criminal Justice* (Toronto: Butterworths 1992), 56. In Manitoba it is surmised that Native inmates began to predominate after the Second World War. Manitoba, *Report of the Aboriginal Justice Inquiry*, 1: 87; and John Milloy, "A Partnership of Races: Indian, White, Cross-Cultural Relations in Criminal Justice in Manitoba, 1670–1949," paper for the Public Inquiry into the Administration of Justice for Native Peoples of Manitoba.

4 The Mercer Reformatory for Women was used because it drew inmates from across the province for a variety of common "female" crimes. Few women at this time were sent to the federal penitentiary. City and county jail registers sometimes noted race, but a statistical study of all Ontario's city and county registers has yet to be undertaken.

5 Under "complexion," the Mercer register noted if an inmate was "Indian" or "negress." The designation Indian included Indian and Métis, treaty and non-treaty women. Statistics taken from the Mercer register are also problematic because women might be charged with one crime, but incarcerated for other reasons as well. Women sometimes gave different names and altered their ages. Because of the various problems with statistics, the registers are used primarily to suggest some overall trends.

6 The problems and possibilities of using such case files are explored in Linda Gordon, *Heroes of Their Own Lives: The Politics and History of Family Violence* (Boston: Viking 1988), 13–17; Steven Noll, "Patient Records as Historical Stories: The Case of the Caswell Training School," *Bulletin of the History of Medicine* 69 (1994): 411–28; Regina Kunzel, *Fallen Women, Problem Girls: Unmarried Mothers and the Professionalization of Social Work, 1890–1945* (New Haven: Yale University Press 1993), 5–6.

7 Colin Sumner, "Re-thinking Deviance: Towards a Sociology of Censure," in Lorraine Gelsthorpe and Allison Morris, eds., *Feminist Perspectives in Criminology* (Philadelphia: Milton Keynes 1990) and "Foucault, Gender and the Censure of Deviance," in Sumner's edited collection, *Censure, Politics and Criminal Justice* (Philadelphia: Milton Keynes 1990).

8 Martin Chanock, *Law, Custom and Social Order: The Colonial Experience in Malawi and Zambia* (Cambridge: Cambridge University Press 1985), 4.

9 Many studies of colonialism have focused on the eighteenth and nineteenth centuries, especially on kin and productive relations; fewer carry the story into the twentieth century. Karen Anderson, *Chain Her by One Foot: The Subjugation of Women in Seventeenth Century New France* (New York: Routledge 1991); Sylvia Van Kirk, *Many Tender Ties: Women in Fur Trade Society* (Winnipeg: Watson and Dwyer 1979); Jennifer Brown, *Strangers in Blood: Fur Trade Company Families in Indian Country* (Vancouver: University of British Columbia Press 1980); Carol Devens, *Countering Colonization: Native American Women and Great Lakes Missions, 1630–1900* (Berkeley: University of California Press 1992); Eleanor Leacock, "Montagnais Women and the Jesuit Program for Colonization," in her edited collection, *Myths of Male Dominance* (New York: Monthly Review Press 1981), 43–62; Carol Cooper, "Native Women of the Northern Pacific Coast: An Historical Perspective, 1830–1900," *Journal of Canadian Studies* 27, 4 (1992–3): 44–75; Joanne Fiske, "Colonization and the Decline of Women's Status: The Tsimshian Case," *Feminist Studies* 17, 3 (1991): 509–36. On Iroquois women, see Judith Brown, "Economic Organization and the Position of Women among the Iroquois," *Ethnohistory* 17 (1970): 151–67; Sally Roesch Wagner, "The Iroquois Confederacy: A Native American Model for Non-sexist Men," in William Spittal, ed., *Iroquois Women: An Anthology* (Ohsweken: Irocrafts 1990), 217–22; Elizabeth Tooker, "Women in Iroquois Society," in Spittal, ed., *Iroquois Women*, 199–216. On Ojibwa women, see Patricia Buffalohead, "Farmers, Warriors, Traders: A Fresh Look at Ojibwa Women," *Minnesota History* 48 (1983): 236–44. For interrogation of the dominant emphasis on the decline of women's status, see Joanne Fiske, "Fishing Is Women's Business: Changing Economic Roles of Carrier Women and Men," in Bruce Cox, ed., *Native Peoples, Native Lands: Canadian Inuit, Indians and Metis* (Ottawa: Carleton University Press 1987), 186–98; Nancy Shoemaker, "The Rise or Fall of Iroquois Women," *Journal of Women's History* 2 (1991): 39–57.

10 Colin Sumner, "Crime, Justice and Under-development: Beyond Modernization Theory," in Colin Sumner, ed. *Crime, Justice and Underdevelopment* (London: Heinemann 1982), quotation at 9.

11 The Aboriginal world view is fundamentally different in terms of "culture, tradition, spirituality." Patricia Monture-Okanee, "Reclaiming Justice: Aboriginal Women and Justice Initiatives in the 1990s," in Law Reform Commission, *Report on Aboriginal Peoples and Criminal Justice,* 112.

12 Some women came in with sentences of less than three months.

13 I examined 598 files for basic information on the charge, conviction, age, and place of birth, but many files were incomplete beyond this point, so I concentrated on a core of 300 files as the basis of my analysis.

14 The numbers for the decades are as follows: 39 in the 1920s, 80 in the 1930s, 169 in the 1940s, and 370 in the 1950s. Population statistics taken from Census of Canada, 1931, vol. 2, table 31, show Ontario Indians as 0.9 per cent of the total population; Census of Canada, 1941, vol. 1, table II, lists Indians as 0.8 per cent of the total; Census of Canada, 1951, vol. 2, table 32, also shows 0.8 per cent.

15 A similar trend took place at the Ontario Training School for Girls: in the 1930s, seven "Indian" admissions; in the 1940s, eight admissions, and in the 1950s, fifty-eight admissions. These statistics are drawn from Ontario, *Annual Report of the Ontario Training Schools,* 1933–59.

16 This statement is based on an analysis of the Kenora jail registers, 1920–59. In the 1920s, Indian and half-breed women were about 13 per cent of all admissions; in the 1930s, 16 per cent; in the 1940s, 50 per cent (with the last three years of the decade the most crucial for increases); and in the 1950s, 76 per cent. While most liquor charges at the Mercer came under the Liquor Control Act, the Kenora arrests showed a greater number of women arrested for breach of the Indian Act.

17 Ontario, *Annual Report of the Inspector of Prisons and Public Charities,* 1920–60.

18 Although FRA convictions for Native women remained a small proportion (about 5 per cent) of overall incarcerations from 1920 to 1960, the act was used more in the later period. On the FRA, see Joan Sangster, "Incarcerating 'Bad' Girls: Sexual Regulation through the Ontario Female Refuges Act," *Journal of the History of Sexuality* 7, 2 (1996): 239–75.

19 By "corrupting," I'm referring to charges of contributing to juvenile delinquency.

20 Ontario Archives, Department of Corrections (RG 20), Mercer Reformatory Records (hereafter, OA, Mercer) case file 9869, 1940s.

21 OA, Mercer case file 10328, 1940s; case file 8966, 1940s; case file 15508, 1950s.

22 In the interwar period, recidivists were sent to local jails, and those considered "reformable" to the Mercer, but by the late 1940s this distinction was breaking down, especially for Native offenders. Wendy Ruemper, "Formal and Informal Social Control of Incarcerated Women in Ontario, 1857–31" (PhD dissertation, University of Toronto 1994), 219–20.

23 Changes to the Indian Act in 1951 allowed provinces to legalize the sale and possession of intoxicants (previously illegal) to Indians off the reserve. Sharon Venne, ed., *Indian Acts and Amendments, 1865–75* (Saskatoon: University of Saskatchewan Native Law Centre 1981), 344–5. However, this change made little difference to Native women in the Mercer, who were usually charged, throughout this whole period, under the provincial liquor laws. Local law enforcement may have used the Indian Act more. See note 17.

24 OA Mercer case file 12128, 1940s (the first charge was in the late 1930s). For the initial charge, the man was convicted of selling liquor and received a jail sentence.

25 Pamela White, "Restructuring the Domestic Sphere—Prairie Indian Women on Reserves: Image, Ideology and State Policy, 1880–1930" (PhD dissertation, McGill University 1987), 220. See also George Wherrett, *The Miracle of Empty Beds: A History of Tuberculosis in Canada* (Toronto: University of Toronto Press 1977), chap. 7.

26 OA, Mercer case file 15510, 1950s; case file 16665, 1950s.

27 I recognize that these women came from different First Nations, but the records do not reveal their specific Aboriginal identity. Authorities claimed that women from Ojibwa groups dominated, though there were clearly some Iroquois and Cree women as well.

28 In other cases, the conviction takes place in a northern city—for example, Kenora or Thunder Bay—but the place of origin is a more isolated reserve or town.

29 Some scholars argue that "economic marginalization" was most noticeable in the twentieth century, especially after 1945. See Vic Satzewich and Terry Wotherspoon, *First Nations: Race, Class and Gender Relations* (Toronto: Nelson 1993), 49–50. On the (contrasting) case of the late nineteenth century, see R.C. Macleod and Heather Rollason, " 'Restrain the

Lawless Savage': Native Defendants in the Criminal Courts of the North West Territories," *Journal of Historical Sociology* 10, 2 (1997), 157–83.

30 Robin Brownlie, "A Fatherly Eye: Two Indian Agents in Georgian Bay, 1918–39" (PhD dissertation, University of Toronto 1996), 52, 418.

31 R.W. Dunning, *Social and Economic Change among the Northern Ojibwa* (Toronto: University of Toronto Press 1959), chap. 7.

32 David Stymeist, *Ethnics and Indians: Social Relations in a Northwestern Ontario Town* (Toronto: Peter Martin 1971).

33 A. Shkilnyk, *A Poison Stronger than Love: The Destruction of an Ojibwa Community* (New Haven: Yale University Press 1985).

34 "It seems unlikely that before 1950 more than one-third of Inuit and status Indian children were in residential school." J.R. Miller, *Shingwauk's Vision: A History of Native Residential Schools* (Toronto: University of Toronto Press 1996), 411. On gender, see *Shingwauk's Vision*, chap. 8, and Joanne Fiske, "Gender and the Paradox of Residential Education in Carrier Society," in Jane Gaskell and Arlene Tigar McLaren, eds., *Women and Education* (Calgary: Deslig 1991), 131–46.

35 OA, Mercer case file 9332, 1930s.

36 Assembly of First Nations, *Breaking the Silence: An Interpretive Study of Residential School Impact and Healing as Illustrated by the Stories of First Nations Individuals* (Ottawa 1994).

37 The term *alcoholism* was used at the time in connection with these women, but we don't really know if they were alcoholics, or simply being policed for alcohol use.

38 Craig MacAndrew and Robert Edgerton, *Drunken Comportment: A Social Explanation* (Chicago: Aldine 1969).

39 Nancy Oestreich Lurie, "The World's Oldest On-going Protest Demonstration: North American Indian Drinking Patterns," *Pacific Historical Review* 40 (1971): 311–33.

40 Some family members testified that the women charged were extremely susceptible to alcohol and became "another person" when intoxicated. OA, Mercer case file 11002. For a more recent book including this view, see Brian Maracle, *Crazywater: Native Voices on Addiction and Recovery* (Toronto: Viking 1993).

41 OA, Mercer case file 9955, 1940s; and case file 13139, 1950s.

42 Sangster, "Incarcerating 'Bad' Girls," 251.

43 OA, Mercer case file 9955, 1940s; case file 12081, 1950s.

44 Sarah Carter, "Categories and Terrains of Exclusion: Constructing the 'Indian Woman' in the Early Settlement Era in Western Canada," in Joy Parr and Mark Rosenfeld, eds., *Gender and History in Canada* (Toronto: Copp Clark 1996), 40–1. See also Daniel Francis, *The Imaginary Indian: The Image of the Indian in Canadian Culture* (Vancouver: Arsenal Press 1992), 122. On an earlier period on the Eastern seaboard, see David Smits, "The 'Squaw Drudge': A Prime Index of Savagism," *Ethnohistory* 29, 4 (1982): 281–306.

45 Sharon Tiffany and Kathleen Adams, *The Wild Woman: An Inquiry into the Anthropology of an Idea* (Cambridge: Schenkman 1985).

46 Sangster, "Incarcerating 'Bad' Girls," 257–8.

47 OA, Mercer case file 10978, 1940s; and case file 7393, 1930s.

48 Clauses on prostitution in the Indian Act of 1880 placed more onus on the men encouraging the "use" of Native women in brothels; after 1884, the clauses were more punitive towards aboriginal women. Constance Backhouse, "Nineteenth Century Prostitution Law: Reflection of a Discriminatory Society," *Histoire Sociale/Social History* 18, 36 (1985): 387–423.

49 OA, Mercer case file 9004, 1940s; case file 15489, 1950s.

50 For contemporary parallels, see John Hagan, "Towards a Structural Theory of Crime, Race and Gender: The Canadian Case," *Crime and Delinquency* 31, 1 (1985): 136.

51 OA, Mercer case file 7644, 1930s; case file 11419, 1950s; case file 8646, 1940s; case file 16461, 1950s.

52 That is, Native unions unsanctified by the church. Miller, *Shingwauk's Vision,* 227.

53 Mary T. Woodward, "Juvenile Delinquency among Indian Girls" (MA thesis, University of British Columbia 1949), 2, 21. Similar images of the reserve which stressed a "culture of poverty" can also be seen in the Hawthorn report as late as the 1960s. See H. Hawthorn, *A Survey of Indians of Canada* (Ottawa 1966), 1: 56–7.

54 OA, Mercer case file 14413, 1950s.

55 For example, those living in a tent in the summer when the family was trapping. OA, Mercer case file 15034, 1950s.

56 OA, Mercer case file 14305, 1950s; case file 14768, 1950s; case file 12984, 1950s.

57 OA, Mercer case file 15455, 1950s; case file 16665, 1950s.

58 OA, Mercer case file 14413, 1950s; case file 14305, 1950s.

59 OA, Mercer case file 9332, 1940s. In this case the magistrate corrected police for offering hearsay evidence, but this criticism was rare.

60 White, "Restructuring the Domestic Sphere," chap. 4.

61 Policies on "immorality" on reserves varied over this period and were not uniformly applied. Agents, however, were supposed to discourage adultery, illegitimacy, and sexual "promiscuity." On the local enforcement of Indian policy in general, see Ken Coates, *Best Left as Indians: Native-White Relations in the Yukon Territory, 1840–1973* (Montreal and Kingston: McGill-Queen's University Press 1990); Sarah Carter, *Lost Harvests: Prairie Indian Reserve Farmers and Government Policy* (Montreal and Kingston: McGill-Queen's University Press 1990). On the reservation system, see Brian Titley, *A Narrow Vision: Duncan Campbell Scott and the Administration of Indian Affairs in Canada* (Vancouver: UBC Press 1986), and J.R. Miller, *Skyscrapers Hide the Heavens: A History of Indian-White Relations in Canada* (Toronto: University of Toronto Press 1989).

62 National Archives of Canada (NA), RG 10, Indian Affairs Department, vol. 8869, reel C 9744, file 487, 18-6, Report of agent to Ottawa, 18 Sept. 1930; 14 Aug. 1933.

63 "They are backward, but it is more background than Native intelligence to blame." Woodward, "Juvenile Delinquency among Indian Girls," 18.

64 OA, Mercer case file 14176, 1950s. One 1967 inquiry (which included Native members) claimed that some judges were "in general lenient and compassionate," at least more so than the police. See Canadian Corrections Association, *Indians and the Law* (Ottawa 1967).

65 The comment, "Bright alert and pleasing. Looking only slightly Indian," is yet another example. OA, Mercer case file 16665, 1950s.

66 OA, Mercer case file 14154, 1950s.

67 Irving Hallowell, *Culture and Experience* (Philadelphia: University of Pennsylvania Press 1955). This collection included earlier articles, published in major psychiatric, sociological, and anthropological journals in the 1940s, such as "Some Psychological Characteristics of the Northeastern Indians" (1946), "Aggression in Saulteaux Society" (1940), and "The Social Function of Anxiety in a Primitive Society" (1941).

68 Rupert Ross, "Leaving Our White Eyes Behind," *Canadian Native Law Reporter* 3 (1989): 3.

69 OA, Mercer case files 15214, 15510, 15505, 1950s.

70 OA, Mercer case file 16664, 1950s.

71 This attitude was partly due to a language difference, but she may also have seen her Iroquois heritage as somewhat superior. OA, Mercer case file 16669, 1950s. For other cases cited in this paragraph, see case file 6369, 1920s; case file 8082, 1930s; case files 9161, 10396, 1940s.

72 Shkilnyk, *A Poison Stronger than Love,* 25.

73 OA, Mercer case file 8681, 1940s; case file 11096, 1940s; case file 10328, 1940s.

74 Hallowell, *Culture and Experience,* 272. Sickness could be interpreted as a form of punishment for sexual or moral transgressions; private confession could be the cure. Irving Hallowell, "Sin, Sex and Sickness in Saulteaux Belief," *British Journal of Medical Psychology* 18 (1939): 191–7. Contemporary accounts also suggest that the public confession, not incarceration, is considered the "disciplinary end" in some Aboriginal cultures. See Patricia Monture-Angus, *Thunder in My Soul: A Mohawk Woman Speaks* (Halifax: Fernwood Books 1995), 238–40; Rupert Ross, *Dancing with a Ghost: Exploring Indian Reality* (Markham: Octopus Books 1992); Kjikeptin Alex Denny, "Beyond the Marshall Inquiry: An Alternative Mi'kmaq Worldview and Justice System," in Joy Mannett, ed., *Elusive Justice: Beyond the Marshall Inquiry* (Halifax: Fernwood 1992), 103–8.

75 Hallowell, *Culture and Experience;* Shkilnyk, *A Poison Stronger than Love;* Edward Rogers, *The Round Lake Ojibwa* (Toronto: University of Toronto Press 1962).

76 Michael Coyle, "Traditional Indian Justice in Ontario: A Role for the Present?" *Osgoode Hall Law Journal* 24, 2 (1986): 605–33.

77 Some writers argue that European patriarchal ideals influenced Native cultures. See Teressa Nahanee, "Dancing with a Gorilla: Aboriginal Women, Justice and the Charter," in *Aboriginal Peoples and the Justice system,* 359–82.

78 OA, Mercer case file 11232, 1950s.

79 OA, Mercer case file 15182, 1950s.

80 For more lengthy discussion of the relationship between sexuality and colonial power, see Ann Stoler, "Making Empire Respectable: The Politics of Race and Sexual Morality in 20th Century Colonial Cultures," *American Ethnologist* 16, 4 (1989): 634–60.

81 Shkilnyk, *A Poison Stronger than Love,* 232.

82 Sumner, "Crime, Justice and Underdevelopment: Beyond Modernisation Theory," 10.

Economic Peripheralization and Quebec Unrest*

ALAIN G. GAGNON AND MARY BETH MONTCALM

The Canadian political scene has witnessed a substantial escalation in conflict between the province of Quebec and the federal government since the Second World War. In many aspects of Canadian intergovernmental relations, Quebec has taken noticeably firmer positions in opposition to Ottawa's initiatives than have other provinces. Disagreements at the postwar Reconstruction Conference and Quebec's subsequent opposition to both tax rentals and federal activities in social welfare were early manifestations of this conflictual pattern. Quebec's opting out of many shared-cost programs and the continuing dissension between Quebec and Ottawa over federal management of the Canadian economy are indicators of this conflict.

The strife between Quebec and Ottawa has received much journalistic and scholarly attention. Explanations, however, have more often than not tended to emphasize the cultural and political character of this friction. It is the contention in this chapter that attention to major economic shifts within the North American economy not only gives a useful corrective to what may well be an overemphasis on secondary factors, but also allows a more analytically satisfying explanation of Quebec's unrest within the Canadian federal system.

Since the Second World War, several macroeconomic trends have been evident. First,

the Canadian economy has become increasingly integrated into the American economy. Second, the core of the continental economy has, particularly since the 1960s, shifted to the south and west of the United States. Finally, there has been increasing emphasis on resource-based industries, which has favoured the development of new types of economic activity in Canada's resource-rich western provinces. In fact, there has been an overall westward drift of economic activity throughout North America.

These changes have had a substantial impact on the relative economic importance of Quebec in the Canadian federation. One direct effect of these westward shifts has been the decline of Montreal as an economic centre relative to Toronto and the shift of economic momentum to provinces such as Alberta. While this development need not be devastating for the Quebec economy, the situation is further complicated by the manner in which economic policies are developed. These policies are devised to maximize overall economic growth; in the postwar environment, this means that federal economic policy disproportionately reflects the interests of Ontario, which is Canada's industrial heartland. Thus, the relative decline of the Quebec economy—or its "peripheralization" within the Canadian and North American economic market—is abetted by federal policies. When factors such as the rapid

Alain G. Gagnon and Mary Beth Montcalm, "Economic and Peripheralization and Quebec Unrest," in Alain Gagnon, ed., *Quebec: State and Society in Crisis* (Toronto: Methuen, 1984), 15–30. Reprinted by permission of Alain G. Gagnon.
* This article first appeared in *Journal of Canadian Studies* 17:2 (1982).

social changes within Quebec and the relative unattractiveness of westward migration to Québécois are added to these major economic changes, the pattern of conflict between Quebec and Ottawa is not surprising.

In this study we intend to illustrate how these major economic alterations have lent substantial credibility to claims made by Quebec governmental elites that the Canadian federation has not been economically beneficial to Québécois. In the first part, we offer a brief examination of major economic changes. In the second part, we illustrate the effects of these changes by examining two specific policy areas—namely, the question of the Auto Pact as well as federal and Quebec regional-development policies.

Conflictual Relations between Quebec and Ottawa

In explaining the intergovernmental conflict between Quebec and Ottawa, it is particularly useful to note that at present the Canadian economy can best be regarded as one element of an economy that is primarily capitalist and largely continental in scope. While Wallerstein, for example, argues that what exists today is one world economy,[1] it nevertheless remains true that in order to identify the major economic linkages of the Canadian economy one must begin by analyzing it within a continental perspective. The argument can be made that the Canadian economy is very little more than a minor element in the North American economy. To situate major trends within the Canadian setting, one has to broaden one's focus to include the entire North American economic dynamic as well as acknowledge that the Canadian economy, to the extent that one can identify such a distinct phenomenon, is essentially peripheral to the American economy.

Many scholars have argued that the Canadian economy is comprehensible only with reference to another major centre; it is generally accepted that the Canadian economy has always been a peripheral one. During approximately the first half-century of Canada's existence, the metropolis of the Canadian economy was the British economy. With the decline of Great Britain as a world economic power and the increasing economic strength of the United States, serious changes occurred in the Canadian economy.[2] These changes have been substantial; for example, by 1977 the United States was the principal importer of Canadian goods (close to 70 per cent), while Great Britain accounted for less than 4.4 per cent of Canadian exports. These facts are even more revealing if one recalls that in 1940 Canada exported more than 43 per cent of its goods to Great Britain. (See Table 1.)

With the shift—particularly evident in the post–Second World War period—from British portfolio investment to American direct investment as the major impetus within the Canadian economy, came a move away from an economy based on an east-west axis and toward one based on a north-south axis. The penetration of the Canadian economy by American capital[3] has simultaneously increased the importance of Toronto as a financial and industrial centre and contributed to the erosion of Montreal's position as a major Canadian metropolis. It has also favoured economic developments in Canada's resource-rich provinces of Alberta and Saskatchewan. It has also contributed to a relative decline in the power of interests that benefit from east-west linkages and has facilitated the present ascendancy of interests that stand to gain the most from Quebec's increased autonomy and a growth in Quebec's state sector. The ramifications of this alteration to Quebec unrest have been substantial. The double peripheralization—Canada vis-à-vis the United States and Quebec within the continental economy—is a phenomenon that both underlies much of Quebec's dis-

TABLE 1 | CANADIAN COMMERCIAL EXCHANGES, PERCENTAGES

	Exports to			Imports from		
	Britain	U.S.	Others	Britain	U.S.	Others
1870	38.1	51.4	10.5	56.1	32.4	11.5
1880	48.3	40.6	11.1	48.3	40.3	11.4
1890	48.7	42.5	8.8	38.8	46.0	15.2
1900	57.1	34.2	8.7	25.7	59.2	15.1
1910	50.0	37.3	12.7	25.8	58.9	15.3
1920	39.5	37.4	23.1	11.9	75.3	12.8
1930	25.1	46.0	28.9	15.2	67.9	16.9
1940	43.1	37.6	19.3	14.9	68.8	16.3
1950	15.1	64.8	20.1	12.7	67.1	20.2
1960	17.4	55.7	26.9	10.7	67.2	22.1
1970	8.9	64.7	26.4	5.3	71.1	23.5
1973	6.6	67.8	25.6	4.2	68.5	27.3
1974	5.9	66.3	27.8	3.5	67.3	29.2
1975	5.4	65.3	26.3	3.5	68.1	28.4
1976	4.9	67.6	27.5	3.1	68.7	28.2
1977	4.4	69.9	25.7	3.0	70.2	26.8

Source: Canada Year Books.

content and has affected relations between Ottawa and Quebec. As Gilpin observes:

> What Canada is to the United States both economically and politically French Quebec is to English Canada. Just as the emergence of English-Canadian nationalism is one response to the economic and political forces integrating the periphery with the American core, so French-Canadian nationalism in Quebec is one response to similar forces within Canada itself which are believed to threaten French-Canadian culture and increasingly have made Quebec part of a Canadian periphery centred upon Toronto, the industrial and financial core of contemporary Canada.[4]

Thus, underlying any discussion of the political economy of Canada is the fundamental reality that the Canadian economy is peripheral to the American economy and, second, within this peripheral economy, Toronto is the industrial and financial centre of greatest importance.[5] Substantial changes in the continental economy have seriously exacerbated the economic position of Quebec.[6]

One illustration of this is the relocation of company headquarters from Montreal to Toronto. One study has revealed that in 1952 Montreal had 124 company headquarters for each 100 in Toronto, whereas in 1972 Montreal had only 62.[7] To the extent that Montreal and the overall Quebec economy participate significantly in north-south economic linkages, their ties are primarily with the northeastern United States. As the C.D. Howe Institute indicates, more than 80 per cent of Quebec's exports to the United States are shipped to the Atlantic Centre, Northeast Centre, and New England states.[8] But, as noted earlier, the core of the American economy has meanwhile shifted markedly in the past 20 years to the south and the west,[9] thus eroding the strength of Montreal in relation to that of Toronto. Although this major economic transfer is also affecting Toronto's position relative to the west,[10] Montreal's economic decline does much to place Quebec unrest in an overall perspective. As Fernand Martin states:

> It should not be forgotten that Montreal is at the eastern end of the Quebec-Windsor corridor. Stagnation in U.S. regions near Montreal has therefore worked against Montreal's growth and to Toronto's advantage in that Toronto stands in an intermediary position in Montreal's relations with the new centres of U.S. economic activity, casting what geographers call an "urban shadow" on Montreal.[11]

In fact, despite the frequent observation that Quebec unrest has been a cause of the movement of capital and business headquarters out of Quebec, it is much more cogent to view this unrest as fuelled, at least in part, by the structural economic changes that have contributed to relative economic stagnation in Quebec and the fostering of new types of economic activity, particularly in Canada's west.[12]

Additionally, the "relative dependency" of the Canadian economy on that of the United States and the hold of capitalism leave Ottawa nearly powerless to alter this peripheralizing process. Canadian attempts at countering this trend by fiscal and monetary regulation have proved feeble. The Canadian economy is simply too minor within the continental economy and too subject to external decision making for the federal government to effectively control fiscal and economic policy.[13] It is therefore crucial not to exaggerate Ottawa's policy-making autonomy over major economic decisions. To the limited extent that Ottawa has been able to regulate the Canadian economy, its actions seem to have resulted in major stabilization policies that have favoured the interests of the Canadian industrial heartland of southern Ontario.[14] In its effort to maximize overall economic growth, the federal government has devised stabilization policies which are primarily responsive to major economic indicators that disproportionately reflect the influence of Ontario. Thus, the tendency of business cycles to be more severe in Quebec and the Maritimes than in Ontario has often been overlooked by the federal government as it imposed restrictive policies while these regional economies were still suffering from relatively high unemployment.[15] As the Quebec government described this situation in 1979:

> It is not surprising that the effect of federal stabilization policies has varied regionally. These policies are developed on the basis of Canadian economic indicators that are especially influenced by the situation in Ontario. When the federal government adopts a restrictive policy to slow overly rapid growth, Ontario has attained full employment, whereas Quebec and the Maritime provinces still have high levels of unemployment. This has been the pattern repeated for the past 30 years.[16]

In the face of the powerful forces within the capitalist economy that favour resource extraction in Canada's west and that accord locational advantage[17] to the manufacture of durable goods in southern Ontario, federal policies have tended to leave Quebec's economy inherently dominated by the production of nondurable goods. As well, the greater competition by third-world countries in nondurables has had an increasingly deleterious effect on the Quebec economy.[18]

TABLE 2 | PERCENTAGE DISTRIBUTION OF PERSONS WORKING, BY SECTORS, CANADA AND QUEBEC, 1961–1974

	1961	1971	1974
Primary sector			
Canada	13.9	8.3	8.3
Quebec	11.4	5.6	5.9
Secondary sector			
Canada	29.6	26.0	28.8
Quebec	34.5	30.6	31.4
Tertiary sector			
Canada	54.0	57.7	62.7
Quebec	51.1	56.2	62.9

Sources: Statistics Canada, The Active Population. P. Allen, "Tendances des professions au Canada de 1891–1961," L'Actualité Economique (1965). Census of Canada (1971).

A serious problem is also posed by federal distributive policies, since they can be criticized for having effected little structural change in the Canadian economy. This is illustrated by the distribution of jobs in the primary, secondary, and tertiary sectors in Canada as a whole compared with the levels existing in Quebec during 1961–1974 (Table 2). In addition, one might look at the index of concentration of manufacturing industries in Canada (Table 3).

Not surprisingly, Quebec finds Ottawa's redistributive policies entirely inadequate. As Maxwell and Pestieau state:

> Some Quebecers would also argue that the interregional compensation system has been unfair, for two reasons: first, Quebec was not a significant net gainer from federal revenue and expenditure activities in the province until the 1970s; second, federal expenditures in Quebec have largely taken the form of transfer payments, such as unemployment insurance, that have tended to reinforce Quebec's economic

dependency rather than build its self-reliance.[19]

Since the Second World War, Quebec has been continually faced with what appears to be a multifaceted and cumulative problem. The increasing peripheralization of the Canadian economy by the American economy both favours Toronto and southern Ontario relative to Montreal and the Quebec economy and emphasizes economic growth in the western provinces. Also evident has been the federal government's relative impotence to counter macro-economic forces that seem to be leading to Quebec's peripheralization. Instead, what is obvious is the multiplication of cases in which federal policies have been devised in response to conditions in the Canadian industrial heartland of Ontario and that have effectively worked against any sort of economic *rattrapage* for Quebec.[20] This peripheralization is not only taking place with regard to Quebec; it is even more obvious in the Maritime provinces.[21] Significantly, however, the pattern of Quebec's

TABLE 3 | INDEX OF CONCENTRATION OF MANUFACTURING INDUSTRIES,* CANADA, 1880–1975

	Atlantic	Quebec	Ontario	Prairies	Pacific	Canada
1880	0.67	1.03	1.16	0.43	1.09	1.00
1910	0.58	1.03	1.45	0.34	1.14	1.00
1915	0.63	1.04	1.53	0.32	0.85	1.00
1926	0.40	1.11	1.52	0.32	1.14	1.00
1939	0.43	1.07	1.57	0.31	0.97	1.00
1949	0.37	1.07	1.56	0.34	0.93	1.00
1959	0.33	1.01	1.51	0.43	0.92	1.00
1969	0.36	1.00	1.50	0.40	0.85	1.00
1975**	—	1.00	1.41	—	—	1.00

*This index is simply a location quotient, the ratio of manufacturing value added per capita in a region to that in the country as a whole.

**Roland Jouandet-Bernadat and Alfred Cossette, "Les structures," Annexe 10, *Prospective socio-économique du Québec, Sous-systèmes économiques (2), Collection: Etudes et Recherches* (Québec: Office de planification et de développement du Québec, 1977), 12.

Source: H.M. Pinchin, The Regional Impact of Canadian Tariff *(Ottawa: Economic Council of Canada, 1979), 5, 110, 134–38.*

peripheralization has coincided with deep social changes[22] and has placed increased political resources at the disposal of Quebec governmental leaders who are critical of Ottawa's apparent inactivity and impotence.[23]

The process of economic peripheralization of Quebec has coincided with substantial growth of Quebec's provincially initiated public sector. (See Table 4.) An excellent example of this type of intervention is provided by the expansion of *sociétés d'état* in Quebec. Through such mechanisms, Quebec has attempted to diminish the effects of economic concentration in Ontario.[24] In fact, if not for the tremendous degree of public-sector investment within Quebec (Table 5), Quebec's economic peripheralization might be far more evident.[25]

In sum, the stimulus for economic growth has increasingly come from the Quebec provincial public sector. Also, as a consequence of the shifting continental economic heartland, Ottawa is less and less able to regulate the economy. The increasing fragility of the Canadian federal government in economic and, consequently, in political terms militates against finding a solution to the Quebec question. More and more, one witnesses situations in which the federal government is simply carried along, although this passivity is almost inevitable in the current context, where the shift of private capital encourages the peripheralization of Quebec. Yet it would be mistaken to consider Ottawa as able to do much else, since such an assumption requires that the federal government actually has the necessary political and economic power to do very much. However, within an overall acceptance of the current capitalist economy, such an assumption is debatable.

TABLE 4 | EXPENDITURES MADE BY QUEBEC PUBLIC SECTOR, IN TERMS OF GROSS PROVINCIAL PRODUCT, 1961–1975

	1961	1970	1974*	1975**
Goods and services	16.7	22.8	24.3	25.1
Transfers	11.6	14.1	18.1	20.3
Total	28.6	36.9	42.1	45.3

Excluding transfers between governments.
*Preliminary data
**Temporary data

Source: J. Vézina, "Les gouvernements," Annexe 11, Prospective socio-économique du Québec, Première étape, Sous-systèmes économiques (2), Collection: Etudes et Recherches *(Québec: Office de planification et de développement du Québec, 1977), 14.*

TABLE 5 | PUBLIC INVESTMENT IN QUEBEC, ONTARIO AND CANADA, 1963–79: PERCENTAGE INCREASES IN NONRESIDENTIAL INVESTMENT

	Quebec	Ontario	Canada
Public*	577	315	445
Private	309	425	462
Public and Private	427	379	455

*Public includes public enterprise, government departments, and institutions.

Source: Statistics Canada, Public and Private Investment in Canada *(Ottawa, various years).*

Case Studies

This second section illustrates the argument presented in the first by investigating two test cases, the Auto Pact and regional-development policies.

Regional Development

The Quebec government has of necessity taken an increasing role in the maintenance and expansion of its economy in recent years. Such actions have often involved jurisdictional disputes. The conflictual pattern between the Quebec and federal governments is particularly evident in the context of the policies of regional development undertaken by these respective government levels. In this regard, a recent study reveals a pattern of federal intrusions in provincial jurisdiction.[26] These federal intrusions have had the effect of creating administrative problems and undercutting the effectiveness of programs undertaken by Quebec.[27] The stimulation of the pulp-and-paper industry in Quebec, of the salt mines of Iles-de-la-Madeleine, of the Mont Tremblant ski centre, of the Palais des congrès of Montreal, and the participation of Ottawa in the financing of Sidbec and Pétromont are just a few examples of serious disagreements between the two levels, which often result in a standstill in the undertaking of projects.

The Office de Planification et de Développement du Québec argues that the intrusion of federal bureaucrats in the planning, formulation, and administration of agreements runs the risk of reducing Quebec to a secondary role in the regional development context; it adds that the Department of Regional Economic Expansion (DREE) has become much more an instrument of intrusion into provincial jurisdiction than an instrument leading to the interprovincial redistribution of economic activity.[28]

While the cumulative expenditures of DREE during the period 1969–70 to 1972–73 indicate that 26.5 per cent of total expenditures were in Quebec, it is noteworthy that the Quebec population represented 27.8 per cent of the total Canadian population.[29] It is useful to situate these expenditures within the context of the degree of existing regional disparities. According to the Office de Planification et de Développement du Québec, a close correlation between DREE expenditures and regional disparities per se would lead to an expenditure of close to 50 per cent of the DREE budget within Quebec. Considering that DREE's budget allocation represents only 1 per cent of the total federal budget, it is difficult to argue that the federal government has a serious interest in reorienting the pattern of regional development in Canada.[30] This is also revealed when one scrutinizes the goals set out for DREE when it came into existence. DREE's main function, according to its enabling act, was "to ensure that economic growth was dispersed widely enough across Canada to bring employment and earnings opportunities in the slow-growth regions as close as possible to those in the other parts of the country"; significantly, it further specified "without interfering with a high overall rate of nation-

al growth."[31] Thus, one is entitled to question the real intentions of the federal government. The Quebec government, needless to say, finds such a situation almost incomprehensible:

DREE programs have had no impact on the "pattern" of regional development in Canada. For example, of the 411,000 jobs created in manufacturing in Canada between 1961 and 1977, Quebec received 58,000 (or 14 per cent) and Ontario 244,000 (or 60 per cent). Since 1969, when DREE was created, Ontario has been the site of 66 per cent of the new manufacturing jobs created in Canada (57,000 of 88,000), while Quebec has lost almost 20,000 such positions. In sum, DREE's existence has not even marginally compensated for the negative effects of other federal policies.[32]

At another level, it is notable that from 1969 to 1975 the federal Ministry of Industry, Trade and Commerce (MITC) gave more grants to industry than did DREE ($437 million compared to $256 million). Quebec received an average of $7 per capita from MITC in this period, whereas Ontario obtained $9 per capita.[33] Moreover, per capita DREE expenditures in Quebec for the 1969–70 to 1976–77 period were less than the national average. Table 6 indicates the annual per capita DREE expenditures in Quebec and Canada as a whole. One notes a slight increase in expenditures in Quebec since 1977–78, curiously enough, following directly on the Parti Québécois's accession to power.

Analyzing the federal government's attempt to reduce regional disparities via DREE, the Economic Council of Canada (ECC) states that "The effects of such policies have been modest in reducing per capita income differences among regions."[34] The ECC goes on to say, "Empirical results demonstrate that the Atlantic Region and Quebec are net beneficiaries from the DREE program to a much lesser extent than is commonly supposed. Quebec receives little or no net

TABLE 6 | DREE EXPENDITURES, IN DOLLARS PER CAPITA

	Quebec	Canada
1969–70 to 1975–76 (annual average)	17.27	16.90
1976–77	16.85	20.43
1977–78	26.12	22.53
1978–79	27.35	22.63

Source: Information taken from DREE annual reports (1975–76, 1976–77, 1977–78, and 1978–79).

benefit. Quebec and the Atlantic region will be better off with increased equalization payments rather than the existing DREE program."[35] In addition, the ECC reports that DREE expenditures are only proportional to the percentage of tax paid in Quebec—that is, 24 per cent of the total expenditures in 1969–75 and 25 per cent of federal taxation.[36] Furthermore, as André Raynaud, former Chairman of the ECC, has noted, regional-development policies have stimulated productivity in traditional sectors within each region without effectively modifying industrial structure.[37] Table 7 is highly indicative of such a tendency. In fact, the federal government, as indicated earlier (Table 3), has done little to relocate manufacturing activity in Canada.

Measures taken by the Quebec government in attempting to diminish existing regional disparities between Quebec and the rest of Canada have continually been counteracted by federal policies. For example, as it is noted in *L'Economie du Québec:*

> In the sphere of industrial assistance, the Quebec Ministry of Industry and Commerce put in place a series of incentives or measures of assistance of which the majority were rendered ineffective with the adoption of federal policies for regional development. The latter, in effect, required that all provincial aid be deducted from that given by Ottawa.[38]

One is therefore led to conclude that in the implementation of its regional-development policy, the federal government has contributed to the increasing peripheralization of Quebec in the Canadian economy. This explains how many of the efforts undertaken by the Société de Développement du Québec, a corporation that aims at modifying Quebec's industrial structure, are being undercut by the federal level.[39]

Another serious problem is caused by the different approaches to regional development implemented by the two levels of government. On the one hand, the Quebec government favours the rapid development of key economic sectors, while on the other hand the federal government has adopted a somewhat indiscriminate and fragmented approach aimed primarily at maximizing employment in the short term.[40] This latter approach has been severely criticized by the Quebec government, since it does little to alter the peripheral character of the province's economy.

The Auto Pact

The Canada-U.S. Auto Pact that was signed in 1965 is one illustration of the pattern of what might be considered increasing peripheralization of Quebec's economy as a result of continental economic integration. While the pact was essen-

TABLE 7 | SUBSIDIES PROVIDED BY DREE TO QUEBEC, 1969–1975

	Subsidies to Quebec (%)
Wood, furniture	20.27
Metallic products	17.67
Paper	10.87
Machinery, transportation material	8.28
Electrical products	7.29
Textiles	7.15
Food, beverages	6.55
Nonmetallic mineral	5.41
Rubber	4.05
Chemical industries	2.95
Clothing	2.61
Hosiery	1.81
Various industries	1.81
Printing	1.70
Leather	1.54
Petroleum, coal	0.04
Total	100.00

Source: Roland Jouandet-Bernadat and Alfred Cossette, "Les structures," Annexe 10, Prospective socio-économique du Québec, Première étape, Sous-systèmes économiques (2), Collection: Etudes et Recherches *(Québec: Office de Planification et de Développement du Québec, 1977), 16.*

tially an effort at rationalizing the auto industry,[41] it was also a significant step in North American continental integration. There is much legitimate controversy over the continuing Canadian deficit as a result of this act. Yet, while the Auto Pact has resulted in serious problems for the Canadian economy as a whole, a general discussion of this problem is somewhat beyond the scope of this study. However, two aspects of the Auto Pact are salient: first, the Auto Pact is a major example of economic integration, of integration of the Canadian economic periphery into the American economic core; second, the Auto Pact has been a major sore point between the federal and the Quebec governments, for

Quebec feels strongly that the Canadian benefits derived from the Auto Pact have not been fairly distributed; rather, the Canadian industrial heartland of southern Ontario has benefited disproportionately from its implementation. As the Quebec government has observed:

> The Canada-U.S. Auto Pact, which might be described as a shift away from Canadian protectionist policies, has been to the almost exclusive benefit of Ontario. The safety clauses provided that the companies in question increase their production and investment in Canada, but the regional distribution was not specified in the agreement. As well, again

because of its overall advantage, Ontario has been the principal—indeed, the sole—beneficiary. The recent location of a Ford motor-manufacturing plant in Ontario, thanks to generous subsidies from the federal government, is an example of this policy.[42]

The federal adoption of the Auto Pact has contributed significantly to an increasing intergovernmental conflict in Canada. In fact, it has been claimed that the adoption of such policies as the Auto Pact by the federal government has tended to counterbalance the effects of the much vaunted federal interregional transfers.[43] Under the Auto Pact, the overwhelming benefits have flown to the Ontario economic core;[44] the Quebec government, for one, knows of this disproportion and points out the discrepancy between benefits to Ontario and the relatively minimal benefits trickling down to Quebec.[45]

It is essential, however, to note that the federal government's actions are now being considered here as somehow deliberately harmful to Quebec (or for that matter to other provinces outside the industrial core). In its negotiations, the federal government has obviously wanted to maximize the net benefits to the Canadian economy as a whole. However, since southern Ontario represents the industrial core of the peripheral Canadian economy, the federal policies disproportionately represent Ontario's economic interests. Again, as the C.D. Howe Institute states, the Auto Pact is one example of the ways in which the federal government makes policies that tend to "strengthen the strong,"[46] while they are attempting to maximize net overall economic benefits. As Carl Beigie mentioned in his research on the Auto Pact, negotiators on both sides admitted that they never assessed the regional consequences of the pact during the negotiation period.[47]

The Auto Pact exemplifies the degree to which a peripheral economy, whose orientation is dictated by a politically exterior economic core, has uneven economic development and continuing internal peripheralization. It can be argued that both of these phenomena underlie at least one major conflictual element of relations between Quebec and Ottawa.

Summary

Overall, then, in our examination of the Auto Pact and regional-development policies, two dimensions of the conflictual relationship existing between the federal government and the government of Quebec have been highlighted. The discussion of regional development policies exemplifies one aspect of the conflicting policy approaches of the federal and provincial governments. On the other hand, conflict over the Auto Pact touches closely on the phenomenon of continentalization and illustrates the almost inevitable political conflicts from the tradeoff entailed in continentalization.

It is important to stress that the peripheralization of the Quebec economy has not been diminished by the federal level. In fact, we have argued that distributive and stabilization policies have favoured the industrial heartland of Ontario and that fiscal and monetary regulation, which depend on external factors and are primarily responsive to economic conditions in Ontario, have often proven deleterious for Quebec. This reality is widely alluded to by governmental elites in Quebec and undoubtedly provides ammunition for those who see the Canadian federation as detrimental to the Quebec economy. In addition, while Quebec government intervention in the provincial economy has in part compensated for economic peripheralization, it has probably also contributed to the strengthening of anti-federalist elements. A major byproduct of the increasing scope of Quebec's public sector is the expansion and increasing ascendancy of a bureaucratic and technocratic middle class whose interests are maximized by every step toward decentralization.

Conclusion

The preceding considerations demonstrate that the relationship of Quebec to the Canadian and continental economies is characterized by increasing peripheralization. As Gourevitch observes, "Change in the geographic distribution of economic activity not only encourages separatism in Quebec, but also increases limits on the federal government's ability to deal with it."[48] Moreover, the federal government's inability to regulate the economy for the economic development of Quebec (as in the cases of the Auto Pact and regional-development policies) provides an excellent political resource for the current governmental elite in Quebec.

The impact of this peripheralization poses a serious challenge for national integration in Canada. Gilpin, for one, sees this problem:

> Economic growth tends toward the creation of core-periphery relationship, and where core and periphery represent different cultural, ethnic, and political groupings, the consequence is the intensification of economic nationalism and the emergence of powerful movements toward economic and political disintegration.[49]

This study has shown that Quebec discontent is contributed to by the shift of the continental economy to the south and west as well as by the incapacity of the federal government to alter this trend. Furthermore, it has been underlined that the scope of federal economic activity is severely restricted by macroeconomic trends beyond its control. The likelihood of the federal government's actively countering a major economic shift is remote; the chance of success if it were to undertake such measures is even more distant. Instead, the federal government is largely restricted to piecemeal efforts aimed at maximizing the possibilities of overall economic growth within the Canadian economy. In the postwar environment, this has effec-tively meant that federal economic policy has disproportionately aided the interests of Ontario's industrial heartland.

This state of affairs provides an excellent opportunity for representatives of the Quebec government to use the federal government as something of a scapegoat. Even so, pointing fingers will not alter the evolution of the North American economy, as economist Philippe Garigue warns:

> Le déclin des activités économiques, les diffi-cultés d'un développement socio-économique équilibré, etc., relèvent de l'ensemble de l'évo-lution de l'Amérique du Nord. Il s'ensuit que l'intention du Parti Québécois...pour trans-former les conditions des francophones, ne saurait résoudre fondamentalement les causes des difficultés actuelles.[50]

Nevertheless, it is important to note that the pattern of economic growth in Canada does not meet Quebec's aspirations and that, on the contrary, it constitutes a threat to its very existence as a distinct collectivity on the North American continent. Additionally, the relative unwilling-ness—not to say impossibility—of the Quebec populace to migrate westward further compli-cates an already difficult situation in the light of the westward drift of the Canadian economy.

It is evident that the altered distribution of economic activity has provided ample ammuni-tion for interests that stand to gain from Quebec's autonomy. And, while the linkage between eco-nomic trends and the mobilization of discontent is somewhat problematic, it would appear that the behaviour of elites or classes whose interests are closely allied with increased provincial scope and autonomy provides precisely such a link. In fact, it appears that broad macroeconomic trends within the continental economy have led to a rel-ative stagnation in the Quebec economy and, as well, have provided Quebec elites interested in selling the idea of independence to Québécois with an invaluable political resource.

Notes

1   I. Wallerstein, "The Rise and Future Demise of the World Capitalist System: Concepts for Comparative Analysis," *Comparative Studies in Society and History* 16 (1974), 387–414.

2   Harold A. Innis, *Essays in Canadian Economic History* (Toronto: University of Toronto Press, 1956); Kari Levitt, *Silent Surrender* (Toronto: Macmillan, 1970); Ian Lumsden (ed.), *Close the 49th Parallel etc.* (Toronto: University of Toronto Press, 1970).

3   Wallace Clement, *Continental Corporate Power* (Toronto: McClelland and Stewart, 1977); "Uneven Development: Some Implications of Continental Capitalism for Canada," in J.A. Fry (ed.), *Economy, Class and Social Reality* (Toronto: Butterworth, 1979), 78–96; see also Garth Stevenson, "Canadian Regionalism in Continental Perspective," *Journal of Canadian Studies* 15: 2 (1980), 23.

4   Robert Gilpin, "Integration and Disintegration on the North American Continent," *International Organization* 28: 4 (1974), 867.

5   P. Fréchette et al., *L'Economie du Québec* (Montréal: Les Editions HRW, 1975), 90–91; Maurice Saint-Germain, *Une économie à libérer* (Montréal: Les presses de l'Université de Montréal, 1973), 59–65; R. Gilpin, op. cit., 867.

6   Office de Planification et de Développement du Québec, *Politiques/fédérales et économie du Québec,* 2nd ed. (Québec, 1979), 31–32, 49, 54–55, 61; André Bernard, "Une analyse prospective de la situation canadienne," in *La vie politique au Canada,* Actes du colloque de Mons (April 24–26, 1978), 144; F. Poulin and Y. Dion, *Les Disparités régionales au Canada et au Québec: les politiques et les programmes, 1960–1973,* CRDE (Montréal: Université de Montréal, 1973), 93; Daniel Latouche (ed.), *Premier Mandat,* vol. 1 (Montréal: Les Editions de l'Aurore, 1977), 52–53; Gouvernement du Québec, *Bâtir le Québec* (1979), 23–27.

7   J.H. Chung, "La nature du déclin économique de la région de Montréal," *L'Actualité économique* (summer 1974), 326–41.

8   Judith Maxwell and Caroline Pestieau, *Economic Realities of Contemporary Confederation* (Montreal: C.D. Howe Research Institute, 1980), 97.

9   Benjamin Higgins, "Regional Interactions, the Frontier and Economic Growth," in A.R. Kuklinskis (ed.), *Growth Poles and Regional Policies* (The Hague: Mouton, 1972).

10 "Croissance nulle au Québec et négative en 80," *Le Devoir* (April 25, 1980), 21.

11 Fernand Martin, *Montreal: An Economic Perspective* (Montreal: C.D. Howe Research Institute, 1979), 14.

12 Peter Gourevitch, "Quebec Separatism in Comparative Perspective," in E. Feldman and N. Nevitte (eds.), *The Future of North America: Canada, the United States, and Quebec Nationalism* (Cambridge, Mass.: Harvard University Press, 1979), 242.

13 J. Maxwell and C. Pestieau, op. cit., 43–44; "L'industrie automobile: La politique fédérale du transport empêche toute expansion au Québec," *Le Devoir* (March 25, 1980), 13.

14 Yves Rabeau and Robert Lacroix, "La stabilisation économique et les régions: le dilemme canadien" (Ottawa: Economic Council of Canada, 1978); *Bâtir le Québec,* op. cit., 24–25; *Politiques fédérales et économie du Québec,* op. cit., 33. Ottawa's pursuit of an industrial policy based on resource projects similarly disadvantages Quebec. See, for instance, G. Bruce Doern (ed.), *How Ottawa Spends Your Tax Dollars: National Policy and Economic Development 1982* (Toronto: Lorimer, 1982), 13.

15 J. Maxwell, C. Pestieau, op. cit., 19.

16 *Bâtir le Québec,* op. cit., 24, our translation.

17 For an extensive discussion of locational theory with reference to comparative advantage in manufacturing, see D.C. North, "Location Theory and Regional Economic Growth," in *Journal of Political Economy* 63 (1955), 243–58; J.N.H. Britton, "Location Perspective on Free Trade for Canada," *Canadian Public Policy* 4: 1 (1978), 4–19; and J.M. Gilmour, "Structural Divergence in Canada's Manufacturing Belt," *Canadian Geographer* 17: 1 (1973), 1–18.

18 *Politiques fédérales et économie du Québec,* op. cit., 34.

19 Maxwell and Pestieau, op. cit., 23.

20 *Bâtir le Québec,* op. cit., 24ff.

21 Bruce Archibald, "Atlantic Regional Underdevelopment and Socialism," in L. Lapierre et al., *Essays on the Left* (Toronto: McClelland and Stewart, 1971), 102–20; Robert J. Brym and R. James Sacouman (eds.), *Underdevelopment and Social Movements in Atlantic Canada* (Toronto: New Hogtown Press, 1979).

22 Hubert Guindon, "The Social Evolution of Quebec Reconsidered," *Canadian Journal of Economics and*

Political Science 26: 4 (1960), 533–51; "Social Unrest, Social Class and Quebec's Bureaucratic Revolution," *Queen's Quarterly* 71 (summer 1964), 150–62; "The Modernization of Quebec and the Legitimacy of the Canadian State," in D. Glenday et al., *Modernization and the Canadian State* (Toronto: Macmillan, 1978), 212–46.

23 *Politiques fédérales et économie du Québec,* op. cit., 32.

24 Pierre Fournier, *Les Sociétés d'État et les objectifs économiques du Québec: une évaluation préliminaire* (Québec: Editeur officiel du Québec, 1978), 13–17; L.O. Gerther, *Regional Planning in Canada* (Montréal: Harvest House, 1972), 57–60.

25 Maxwell and Pestieau, op. cit., 99.

26 Lucien Metras, "Quelques aspects de la mise en oeuvre de programmes conjoints de développement régional," communication présentée à l'Association de Science Régionale de la Langue Française (Québec, September 28, 1976).

27 Bernard Descoteaux, "Le budget du MEER au Québec devrait être administré par l'OPDQ (Léonard)," *Le Devoir* (Nov. 23, 1979), 17; see also Paul Morisset, "Le transfert du MEER à l'OPDQ: j'y penserai, dit McKay à Léonard," *Le Devoir* (Nov. 27, 1979), 17.

28 *Politiques fédérales et économie du Québec,* op. cit., 84; Germain Julien and Marcel Proulx, *Le chevauchement des programmes fédéraux et québécois* (Québec: L'École Nationale d'Administration Publique, 1978), A-80, A-81, and A-82.

29 R.W. Phidd, "Regional Development Policy," in G. Bruce Doern and V.S. Wilson (eds.), *Canadian Public Policy* (Toronto: Macmillan, 1974), 187.

30 *Politiques fédérales et économie du Québec,* op. cit., 43–44.

31 A full outline of the act that created DREE can be found in any Canada Year Book from 1969 onward. This quote came from the 1969 one, 1133.

32 *Politiques fédérales et économie du Québec,* op. cit., x, 40, our translation.

33 Ibid., 43.

34 W. Irwin Gillespie and Richard Kerr, *The Impact of Federal Regional Economic Expansion Policies on the Distribution of Income in Canada,* Discussion Paper no. 85 (Ottawa: Economic Council of Canada, 1977), 99. The point has also been documented in a DREE publication, *Climate for Regional Development* (Ottawa, 1975), 34.

35 Ibid., 100.

36 Ibid., 77.

37 According to a presentation made at Fredericton by André Raynauld while Chairman of the Economic Council of Canada. In this context, see Claude Tessier, "Echec de la politique de développement régional," *Le Soleil* (Oct. 9, 1975).

38 P. Fréchette et al., op. cit., 374–75, our translation.

39 Ibid.

40 Ibid., 375; see also Pierre Fréchette, "Y a-t-il un avenir pour les régions," in D. Latouche (ed.), op. cit., 82. This policy of *saupoudrage* has replaced the "growth pole" approach on which DREE was originally established in 1969; see B. Higgins, F. Martin, and A. Raynauld, *Les orientations du développement économique régional de la province du Québec* (Ottawa: DREE, 1970).

41 Jim Laxer, "Canadian Manufacturing and U.S. Trade Policy," in Robert M. Laxer (ed.), *Canada Ltd.* (Toronto: McClelland and Stewart, 1973), 134.

42 *Bâtir le Québec,* op. cit., 24, our translation.

43 Maxwell and Pestieau, op. cit., 19.

44 Fernand Martin, "Regional Impact of Selected Non-Expenditure Decisions of the Federal Government," in *Proceedings of the Workshop on the Political Economy of Confederation* (Kingston: November 8–10, 1978), 331–56.

45 *Politiques fédérales et économie du Québec,* op. cit., 39.

46 Maxwell and Pestieau, op. cit., 100.

47 As cited in J. Maxwell, C. Pestieau, op. cit., 83, n11.

48 P. Gourevitch, op. cit., 243.

49 R. Gilpin, op. cit., 874.

50 Philippe Garigue, "Le fédéralisme, solution supérieure," *Le Devoir* (May 6, 1980), 7.

A Newfoundland Culture?

JAMES OVERTON

Recent years have seen the growth of radical regionalism in Canada.[1] Against what is seen as a centralist and neo-colonialist federal government, writers such as George Woodcock and George Melnyk have advocated greater autonomy for Canada's regions.[2] In one recent plea for radical regionalism, Arthur Kroker, drawing on the work of Woodcock, has placed culture at the centre of his analysis. He has issued a clarion call for Canadians to become "regional patriots" as part of an effort to recover what he calls the "Canadian cultural imagination." He takes what has been happening in Quebec in recent years as the model for the rest of Canada. In the independence movement he sees signs that Quebec is the "centre of active political consciousness" in North America. While society in the rest of the continent "drifts towards stasis," in Quebec a French-language society is attempting to "recover an authentic public life." This society is, for Kroker, the "centre of the utopian imagination" because it has "initiated a political experiment which is...outside the grim monotony of the technological life-order of North America." Quebec stands out alone against the technological logic of political economy, North American pragmatism, and the myths of progress and accumulation. With its emphasis on democracy, communitarianism, and the preservation of community and culture, Quebec stands in sharp contrast to the "homogeneity of North America."[3]

In Kroker's analysis, the future of Canada lies in encouraging what is happening in Quebec to take place in other regions of the country. He thinks Canada should be reconstituted as "a confederacy of autonomous regional centres," an alliance of "heterogeneous cultures." Accordingly, he calls for an upsurge of "regionalist discourse." This "expression of cultural freedom" will be achieved by "coming home to the popular culture of the regions" and by allowing "indigenous, popular cultures...to speak for themselves," that is, "to articulate their own understanding of the relationship between emotion, locale and expression."[4] At the core of regionalist thinking is the notion that there are distinctive, indigenous, popular regional cultures or ways of life in Canada and that these cultures, each growing in its own appointed soil, should be the basis for the nation's future political and economic organization.[5]

In Newfoundland, a powerful current of regionalist sentiment has developed in the last fifteen years or so—a current which has economic and political dimensions to it, but which is also very much concerned with culture. A number of "intellectual patriots" have been involved in "cultural regeneration," claiming to be "articulators of the collective unconscious of Newfoundland" (to use Kroker's terminology).[6] They have attempted to come home to Newfoundland's distinct culture, searching for it, discovering it, surrendering to it, recording it, defending it, preserving it, promoting it, reviving it, and drawing inspiration from it for their artistic work. This essay investigates the place of culture in regionalist thinking in Newfoundland.

James Overton, "A Newfoundland Culture?" *Journal of Canadian Studies* 23, 1/2 (Spring/Summer 1988): 5–22.
Reprinted by permission of Dr. James Overton.

It will consider what is being said about Newfoundland culture and some of the broad political implications of this thinking.[7]

Culture is on the march in Newfoundland. In the last decade or two it has become one of the most widely used words in the province, particularly, but not exclusively, among what may be called the new middle class. Many lament the loss of a distinctive way of life rooted in the outports. Others complain about the destructive effects of mass culture and North American values on "traditional culture" and attempt to preserve and revive this unique culture. Cultural arguments have been used in defence of the seal hunt and to justify the stand of Brian Peckford's Progressive Conservatives on the control of offshore and other resources. References to tradition, culture, way of life, identity, lifestyle, and heritage liberally sprinkle newspaper columns, the pages of various small magazines, the speeches and slogans of politicians of all stripes, and the lyrics of popular songs. Newspaper adverts attempt to sell cod jiggers using the caption "Nfld. Roots"; Captain Newfoundland, the province's own superhero, spouts a kind of mystical nationalism from the comic cuts of the *Newfoundland Herald;* bumper stickers declare "I believe in Newfoundland"; and 1970s rock 'n' rollers like Bruce Moss have, in the 1980s, become folk-singing patriots.[8]

Academics have begun to write copiously about the Newfoundland soul and character and about cultural survival, and there has been the development of what F.L. Jackson terms "Newfcult in the arts."[9] A local publishing industry has grown up specializing in Newfoundlandia and compulsory courses in Newfoundland culture have been introduced into the high schools of the province.[10] One long-standing newspaper columnist has even begun to tackle the thorny question of "what is a Newfoundlander?"[11] The government, in its promotional literature, has also made much of Newfoundland culture. In one recent tourist advertisement, fiddler Kelly Russell entertains visitors who have found just what they are looking for: "A beautiful blend of history and culture, kept alive by a friendly people who are ready to share...the adventure of living in a unique society" and "a life-style that's unhurried, hospitable and always full of fun." A similar message is presented in *The Newfoundland Adventure,* a promotional pamphlet issued by the Department of Industrial Development. This devotes a large section to "A Way of Life," complete with a picture of an accordion player and excerpts from various folk songs. The potential investor is tempted by the promise of abundant cultural wealth. Newfoundland, it is suggested, has a rare culture which is not contrived or artificial. It is "an oasis of nature and humanity" in a "world of serious ecological and philosophical problems." And much is made of the advantages of locating industry in the land of a "hardy, fun-loving race" with its simple, traditional philosophy and its propensity to "keep working, regardless of...suffering or hardship." Newfoundlanders are a "tender, tough, frivolous, fearless, simple and sophisticated" body of people, and uncomplaining workers into the bargain.[12]

In politics, as anthropologist Robert Paine notes, Brian Peckford "deliberately or not... politicizes Newfoundland ethnicity," finding appeals to the natural cultural community useful in a variety of contexts.[13] He can wax lyrical about the mystical experience of rabbit catching in Green Bay or his roots in the area and link such things to his stance on oil resources and the need to preserve Newfoundland's unique identity. For Peckford, Newfoundlanders have "culture" and "tradition." They even have a "tradition of culture" that must be defended against outside forces.[14] The cultural theme has become so pronounced in recent years in Peckford's political rhetoric that one sociologist has described the province's Premier as the leader of a "psycho-cultural" liberation movement on the part of what is "by and large a distinct ethnic group," reacting against "hand-outs, rip-offs and put-downs."[15] Another sociologist, Douglas House, sees Peckford "as simply the most visible member of a strong Newfoundland social movement that has its roots in the 1960s, and has branches in art, music, drama, education, and many other spheres."[16] According to this view, Peckford is the articulator of "a strong sense of regional identity and grievance among Newfoundlanders."

The cultural revival in Newfoundland is largely a phenomenon of the 1970s and 1980s, even though its roots and antecedents can be traced back to earlier periods. The movement has been, to a large extent, the creation of the intelligentsia that has emerged in Newfoundland in the post-Confederation period, the urban, educated and relatively affluent strata of the population which was a product of what F.W. Rowe calls the province's "cultural revolution."[17] Within this broad movement there are many strands of thinking and activity, and a variety of individuals and institutions have played key roles in both facilitating and shaping the revival and its ideology. Memorial University in St. John's, for example, has perhaps been the most important institution in this respect. By the early 1960s Memorial was well on the way to developing what was called "academic regionalism." The establishment of the Institute of Social and Economic Research at Memorial facilitated the development of the "Newfoundland school" of social science with its emphasis on the province's uniqueness and its attempt to create "an anthropology of locality."[18] In the late 1960s this bloomed into a culturalist critique of modernization. Taking the part of rural dwellers and "small society" against big government and big capital, this populist school of social science promoted a "small is beautiful" approach to development.[19] Another expression of academic regionalism was the introduction of folklore studies in the University in 1962 and the creation of a separate department of folklore in 1968.

Memorial's Extension Service played a key role in the cultural revival. Concerned with community development and also promoting a "small is beautiful" approach to development, the Service became involved in cultural matters, often in connection with efforts to encourage tourism. Assistance to the visual and performing arts was provided, community theatre was encouraged, and craft development programs were introduced in many parts of the province. By the 1970s a host of small entrepreneurs had become involved in the culture industry. Capitalizing on the Newfoundland mystique, they produced a variety of goods for the new body of consumers that had emerged since Confederation in 1949. The "way of life" of rural producers was packaged and commodified for consumption by the new middle class.[20]

The academic regionalism and the going-to-the-people of the community development movement of the 1960s and 1970s was paralleled and connected with what has become known as the counter-cultural movement of the 1960s. Broadly speaking, this movement was an anti-materialist, often romantic, rejection of certain aspects of urban-industrial society with its orientation towards progress, its bureaucratic rationality and its middle-class values. The movement also hinged on the notion that there is "a richer human sensibility to be found on the edges of society."[21] This led to a search for the primitive and a willingness to appreciate other ways of life and states of being. In this context Newfoundland was discovered as an already existing alternate society. According to popular satirist Ray Guy, Newfoundlanders had always been "hippies," waiting for the rest of Canada to catch up.[22] From the late 1950s, but increasingly in the 1960s and early 1970s, many of those searching for an alternative to modern urban life were attracted to the rural parts of Newfoundland. The best-known visitors were Farley Mowat and Franklin Russell. But ex-Newfoundland residents also came home in the period. Artist Gerald Squires again "found his place" and Edyth Goodridge became the Head of Memorial's Art Gallery, making it "the crossroads and command post for Newfoundland's cultural revolution."[23]

This cultural revival rests on certain essential ideological foundations. The key assumption of the revival is that there exists a distinctive Newfoundland culture, way of life, ethos, character, soul, or ethnic identity (older writers tend to use the term "race"). This unique culture, centred on the outports, has been undermined by industrialization, the welfare state, urbanization, and the introduction of North American values in the period since the Second World War. Newfoundland culture is now threatened with extinction, although some artists have attempted to keep the "sleeping, visionary spirit of the soul of Newfoundland" alive even in its "death throes." The cultural movement in Newfoundland, according to Sandra Gwyn, is part "collective tragic muse," a lament for the vanishing way of life of the outport and the small producer.[24] But it is also an attempt to defend this way of life and to build on it in an effort to maintain or recreate a distinct Newfoundland identity.

It is no accident that the policy of resettlement (the movement of small communities to growth centres), which had its roots in the 1930s, but became a much-publicized government development strategy in the 1950s and 1960s, turned into one of the main focuses of concern of the cultural revival in the 1970s. Some of the most bitter and emotional criticism of the government of J.R. Smallwood was over the resettlement issue, by authors such as Farley Mowat, Al Pittman, Gerald Squires, and those who wrote for Memorial University's Institute of Social and Economic Research.[25] But other forces which were regarded as destructive of outport life and folk culture were also the focus of critical attention: inappropriate development schemes, industrialization, consumerism, mass

culture, the media, and even regular employment.[26] In sum, an authentic culture and a rural way of life had been sacrificed to Smallwood's "develop or perish" philosophy. A life with real quality and humanity had been sold for a mess of pottage. The new "plastic Newfoundlander" was busy consuming "junk culture" and "junk food" and was "running around like a headless chicken." Under the influence of "musical Quislings," Newfoundlanders had begun to reject their own culture and become addicted to country music and rock 'n' roll.[27] The golden age of rural Newfoundland was over and a peaceful and pastoral life was vanishing. In short, the *machine* was in the garden.

This is a culturalist critique of modernization. It laments the loss of a traditional way of life and the destruction of a distinct culture. It takes culture and tradition as the point from which to criticize mass civilization and urban-industrial society. It is a pessimistic expression of disenchantment with many of the changes that occurred in Newfoundland during and after the Second World War by people who were in a very real sense the product of those changes.

The point is further emphasized when we examine the notion of Newfoundland culture that is at the centre of the revival. In fact, this culture largely conforms to the picture outlined in an article in *Maclean's* magazine in 1964 and in much of the tourist promotional literature on the province. According to R.J. Needham in *Maclean's,* there is no factory time in Newfoundland, there are only nature's rhythms. The pace of life is slow, people work when they want to and "break into poesy when they feel like it." They have a colourful language and are kind and friendly. They are simple folk who are contented with what they have.[28] A somewhat similar view is given by Richard Gwyn in his biography of J.R. Smallwood. According to Gwyn, the Newfoundland character was "forged...out of heredity and environment." It has Celtic roots. Newfoundlanders are "proud and sentimental, tough and impractical." They are a people who "rejected the dynamism and tyranny of the Protestant ethic for a humanism which placed people above things and the spiritual above the material." This constitutes what Gwyn terms "the Newfoundland mystique." And in these musings on the Newfoundland character we have a theory to explain the country/province's backwardness in economic and political terms. For Gwyn, the hard struggle for survival "exhausted ambition and creativity" and left the people simple but happy. And gentle, spiritual people are ill-suited to politics. "Gentle mystics are poor politicians," according to Gwyn, in a comment which is presumably intended to account for Newfoundland giving up responsible government in 1934.[29] But "the Newfoundland mystique" also proved an obstacle in Smallwood's fight to bring the country into Canada.

One idea which crops up time and time again in writing about the province is that traditional Newfoundland culture was and remains essentially humanistic. According to a 1974 editorial in *Decks Awash,* the magazine of Memorial's Extension Service, "we in Newfoundland still have, if only instinctively, the remnants of a fast disappearing humanism that has its roots in a harsh land and harsher shore."[30] But it is important to note again the orthodox view that this humanism is threatened and is in fact quickly vanishing. For Richard Gwyn, the existence of the "gentle mystic" is being undermined by materialism and industrial development. Other arguments are essentially the same even if the language varies. For example, folklorist Kenneth Peacock, writing in 1965, described Newfoundland as "a distinctive, homogeneous cultural entity," one of a few "rare examples" of a "neo-primitive white culture." This culture he regarded as "tribal" in nature, but in the process of being "softened" by Canada's "semi-socialist technical culture."[31]

Many writers assume, like Peacock, that Newfoundland is a homogeneous cultural entity.

But even those who recognize a number of sub-cultures in the province retain the idea of an over-arching Newfoundland culture. One recent history text for schools put the argument this way:

> In our studies we have seen that Newfoundland and Labrador possess many sub-cultures—regional, ethnic, urban, linguistic, or rural—although some are more prominent than others. Yet over and above the sub-cultures there has arisen a super structure of Newfoundland culture which bridges the sub-cultures and basically reflects the identification of the people with the place and society in which they live. Multiple cultures have been filtered by the experience of living here to form the unique culture of Newfoundland and Labrador which we recognize today.[32]

Yet, when it comes to trying to actually identify this unique culture, the authors of the above text prove to be on slippery ground. Newfoundland culture is a "super structure," but it is also "dynamic and ever-changing." It is the "ties that bind" the inhabitants of the province "together in a common society," but, on the contrary, "one can never say what a culture *is* at any given time—only what it *may have been* in the past."

Nevertheless, these authors do mention some characteristics they think typical of Newfoundland culture and the Newfoundland character. Newfoundlanders are hospitable, self-reliant and religious, and there is evidence they have a strong work ethic. Others also opt for a national character definition of Newfoundland culture. Philosopher F.L. Jackson finds that the distinguishing features of the Newfoundlander are traditional pride, cheerful optimism, puckishness, stoical grit, and spiritual self preservation. They also have a peculiar language, colourful expressions and unique mannerisms. Douglas House sees independence, egalitarianism, personalism, distrust of strangers and a fondness for religion as being typically Newfoundland. Cyril Poole, another academic, suggests that among the significant traits of the Newfoundland "soul" are a "sense of fatalism" which has "seeped into the very marrow of our bones," lack of creativity, passivity in community and social affairs, religiosity and a belief in ghosts. Patrick O'Flaherty even suggests that the need to kill seals is part of the Newfoundland character. Still, others have tried to "develop the concept of the Newfoundland character" by looking for those "qualities" that are more outstanding in Newfoundlanders than in other people.[33] D.W.S. Ryan and T.P. Rossiter argue that a distinctive character emerged in the nineteenth century in pioneering times. Newfoundlanders have distinct mannerisms, attitudes and speech. They are a proud, independent people. They are industrious and innovative, resourceful and hard-working. They are a people of stamina, endurance, wit, honesty, hospitality, bravery and heroism. They are God-fearing, stoical, fatalistic and strongly patriotic.

In all these accounts it is the way of life and the attitudes and experiences of the rural small producer that form the core of a distinctive Newfoundland culture. The outport is the seat of home-grown Newfoundland culture, authentic and popular. It is a culture that has developed organically in isolation and it is the environment (especially the sea) that has been one of the key forces which has moulded the Newfoundland character. Newfoundland culture unites people across social divisions based on class, religion, gender, region, etc. It is something that exists as an observable "fact" for many people, even if there is some disagreement as to the precise nature of this culture. Even those who see Newfoundland culture as a reaction to put-downs and stigma still assume that there is a common culture or character which is being negatively evaluated, usually by outsiders.[34] Thus, whether it is viewed in negative or positive terms, the assumption of most observers is

that there is a single, distinct Newfoundland ethos, character or culture. Newfoundlanders are religious, *not* atheistic. They are peaceful, *not* violent. They are simple, *not* complex. Rather than acknowledge and explore the contradictions and variations in people's actual behaviour, we have instead a simple, idealized character.

Perhaps we should not be surprised at this view of Newfoundland. As anthropologist Margaret Hodgen notes, there has long been a habit of defining distinct nations through their "vices, deficiencies, virtues, and honest properties." And, as Jacques Barzun notes, a "cultural relativism" that saw the world as consisting of distinct peoples each with a culture which was a "unique product of history" and "worth preserving in its integrity" was a particular characteristic of nineteenth-century Romantic thinking.[35] The "differential" concept of culture continues to be central to much social thinking, as Zygmunt Bauman observes, with "the fact" of "plurality or separateness of cultures" seldom being regarded as "something which requires arguing or verifying proofs." According to Bauman, many people assume that "the 'uniqueness' of what they see and describe is an attribute of the phenomenon described" and that the differential concept of culture "reflects the objective truth" that has been "discovered." This view has become "so deeply ingrained in popular thinking" that we now view the world "through the spectacles of the differential concept." It has become a self-evident truth that the world is composed of distinct and separate cultures, that certain events can best be interpreted as clashes between cultures, and that the breaking of the cup of culture (to use Ruth Benedict's metaphor) leads to social disintegration and even violence.[36] Culture explains a great deal according to this view.

The notion of Newfoundland culture and character has provided yeoman service when it comes to explanation. This is certainly true in the political and economic arena. In 1933, for example, following an acute economic and political crisis, the Amulree Commission suggested that Newfoundland surrender responsible government for government by Commission. Part of the Amulree Commission's argument was that the country's problems were of a moral nature.[37] The people had proved incapable of sustaining parliamentary democracy because of their deficiencies. Faced with bankruptcy and a breakdown of social order, the Newfoundland government went along with the recommendations of the Amulree Commission. The political events of the early 1930s, and the findings of the Commission, put Newfoundland's "national character...under a shade," according to J.L. Paton. This led to a great deal of discussion about the peculiarities of the Newfoundland character. Paton, for example, publicized various positive character traits of the country's inhabitants in an effort to make clear that there were "other things besides graft in the Newfoundlander."[38] During the same period J.R. Smallwood, in a soul-searching vein, was led to argue that Newfoundlanders should shoulder some of the "blame" for their "backwardness." He speculated that "the very nature of our struggle, of our methods of wresting a living from Nature" might have "helped unfit us for creative and constructive effort." Perhaps living by *"killing"* everything from cod and seals to birds and trees had developed a "trait of destructiveness" in the Newfoundlander? But in spite of all difficulties and regardless of such dark thoughts, Smallwood was not pessimistic, believing that ultimately the spirit of "The Fighting Newfoundlander" would eventually lead to "greatness."[39]

Others were less optimistic about the country's future. Ellsworth Huntington, the eugenicist, compared Newfoundland with Iceland in the 1940s in an effort to determine why the former country was so backward when compared with the latter. Huntington's explanation built on the observations of Thomas Lodge, made while he was a member of Newfoundland's Commission of Government in 1935. Lodge

suggested that the poor quality of political life in Newfoundland was due to a process of "negative selection."[40] A steady "exodus" of population had deprived the country of the "best individuals of all classes" and this had "lowered the general standard of both ability and character." However, the fact that those who left generally succeeded proved to Lodge that "in a reasonably favourable environment," the Newfoundlander might achieve success. For Huntington, as for Lodge, weakness in political and economic terms was, at least in part, a result of weakness in character. Newfoundlanders were of good stock but they had degenerated. Most of the smart people had emigrated and those left behind had proved incapable of making a go of it in the harsh Newfoundland environment. Put in an easier environment, Newfoundlanders might prove successful, but in the North Atlantic things were just too taxing for their limited abilities.

Nor have such arguments vanished. They remain, although the terminology used is different. As already noted, Richard Gwyn suggests that Newfoundlanders are spiritual Celts who have proved political failures because of this. And more recently Kenneth Westhues has come up with some similar ideas in his "meditation" on Newfoundland's underdevelopment.[41] Measured against his notion of what a good society should be, he finds the province wanting. It is a "sad society" which offers very little to sate this academic tourist's hunger for "some fresh experience." Something is terribly wrong in Newfoundland; Nonia sweaters and Terra Workboots do not compare with the skyscrapers of New York or the Flamenco of Spain. Newfoundland is a bruised and battered "date" for Westhues, a failed romance (as it was for Farley Mowat). Newfoundlanders have nothing to offer Westhues. They are fatalistic and they are the butt of their own jokes. The problem, according to this eminent sociologist, is "one of stunted development, or, to use the local phrase, the condition of being stunned." Newfoundland is a dependent culture, *not* a self grown, independent one. The people have no "economic poise and self-possession." Having been kept in a box for centuries, they have assumed the shape of the box. This is the explanation for the economic, political and cultural malaise of Newfoundland according to Westhues: a pessimistic, bitter, stunted character. But Westhues, like Lodge, believes that Newfoundlanders can succeed and break out of the box if only they escape from the province; for, after all, he has taught the children of Newfoundlanders elsewhere and they show every sign of being normal.

National character and culture are often used as an explanation for economic and political success or failure, as Nigel Harris observes.[42] When the economy grows, it is attributed to the peculiar and wonderful qualities of Canadians or Newfoundlanders or Italians. When it stagnates or declines, its failure (in this "common sense" view) is due to the characteristics of foreigners. Japanese, for instance, are regarded as cunning. And once the concept of a national or regional character exists, it can be used to understand events and to guide action. All kinds of things can be viewed through this particular lens, including voting patterns and the consumption of particular brands of beer. F.L. Jackson, for example, talks easily about "the worst side of the Canadian soul: the flatness, the chronic self-consciousness, the sense of inferiority that causes absurd excesses of self-congratulation."[43] He offers the opinion that it is this character which makes it difficult for Canadians to accept politicians such as John Crosbie and Brian Peckford with their "lively forthrightness, simplicity and freshness of outlook." Such people have something that "gets under the Canadian skin," especially when they "act like Newfoundlanders in public." Jackson assumes that Crosbie's "open, intelligent, frank, honourable and earnest" approach to politics is an expression of his Newfoundland soul and that he is just a little too "ethnic" for central Canadians to accept.

Newfoundland's traditional culture very often has been seen as one explanation for underdevelopment.[44] For modernization theorists like Ian Whitaker, writing in the mid-1960s, it was traditional values and attitudes which were an obstacle to development and, in particular, to the flowering of entrepreneurial spirit which was regarded as essential for economic success.[45] Traditional values and behaviour patterns had, therefore, to be modified or removed by education in order for development to occur. Such ideas are still around, although they are presented rather differently in the 1980s. In Peckford's version of modernization, for example, traditional culture and traditional values are positive.[46] The rugged individualism which is supposedly characteristic of Newfoundlanders can, it is argued, be used by people to become entrepreneurial pioneers in oil-related businesses. Other traits, such as independence and self-reliance, are also recognized as valuable at a time when both federal and provincial governments are cutting social spending. Community spirit, neighbourliness and family responsibility are characteristics of Newfoundlanders that are quickly being rediscovered as governments unload their responsibilities in a number of areas. And this conservative policy direction is currently being endorsed by such documents as the recent Report of the Royal Commission on Employment and Unemployment in Newfoundland, *Building On Our Strengths.*[47] The call is out to educate for entrepreneurship and to build on Newfoundland's outport culture in order to limit dependence on the state.

The assumption of a common culture and character and the argument that this needs to be defended against outside destructive forces has a number of political implications. The search for and the embrace of Newfoundland culture in many cases goes hand in hand with a rejection of all that is held to be alien to the Newfoundland essence. The high priests of

Newfoundland culture do express their concern with alien influences like electric guitars and mindless pop music. Audiences are told by performers to shut up and be quiet because "we're preserving your fucking culture." We are warned that the "mindless, passive acceptance of alien cultural pressures can kill" the Newfoundland "spirit." The Reverend Bob Mills does express concern that the influx of outsiders associated with oil development will "dilute the hardiness of good Newfoundland stock."[48] And the question of who is a Newfoundlander becomes important when the benefits of oil-related development are to be handed out. For after all, according to Wick Collins, charity begins at home and there should be some way to limit the influx of "mainland drifters" who are likely to be attracted to Newfoundland when oil development gets fully underway. Cultural and economic survival are linked here as in the seal hunt campaign.[49] And it is assumed that it is natural and desirable that cultural differences should be maintained. Like wants to be with like and identity comes from being part of a cultural community associated with a particular homeland.

What I want to stress at this point is that our concepts, categories, theories, and "ways of seeing" are, as Sean Sayers suggests, social and historical products, in exactly the same way that our practical relations to the world and our forms of activity in it are. Following Sayers's argument, we can usefully compare the influence of categories and concepts with a lens. And this can be extended to a specific discussion of the differential concept of culture in general and the concept of Newfoundland culture in particular. A concept, like a lens, can be considered to be "a refracting medium" which "both transforms and transmits" and "distorts and reveals" the object.[50] Lenses, however, are not to be viewed merely as the means by which reality is obscured and clouded or distorted. Without lenses we cannot see and it is with lenses that the world is experi-

enced. The lens metaphor is useful, but it should be used with caution. We do not look through our concepts onto reality. As John Berger suggests, our concepts create their own space, "the space of experience."[51] And, of course, all lenses are not equally useful. We live in a world of competing interpretations of reality, a world in which lenses are continually ground anew.

One of the aims of this discussion is to draw attention to the fact that the idea of a Newfoundland culture is a particular lens through which the world is experienced. This essay, in fact, is part of a larger project to document and understand the historical development of the idea of "a Newfoundland culture," and to explore the meaning in social and political terms of this particular "imagined community."[52] Accordingly, we wish to stress that Newfoundland culture can be seen as something which has been invented in much the same way as the "traditions" examined in Eric Hobsbawm and T. Ranger's book, *The Invention of Tradition,* or the "identity" discussed in R. White's book, *Inventing Australia.*[53]

This view of Newfoundland culture as a construct, the emphasis on the process by which this construct was fashioned, and the broad political and social meaning of the construct should all be contrasted with approaches that view Newfoundland culture as an objectively-existing "fact."[54] The aim is not to expose culture as an empty abstraction and to suggest that Newfoundland culture is an illusion. Rather it is to suggest that culture is a particular lens through which the world is "seen" and to raise some questions about how this lens was ground and the nature of the vision that it allows. Concepts express real needs and feelings, they are an effort to grasp something significant and important about experience, they can be a protest against certain conditions or a sigh of oppression. But they are social and historical products and we need to look at the social forces which shape them.[55]

I want to suggest that the small region and the cultural community that the radical regionalists and those concerned with Newfoundland culture make much of are an emblem for a wide range of social values which they regard as desirable. In effect, the region and culture become the standpoint for pointing out the inadequacies of urban-industrial life. In the process, regional life and popular culture are romanticized and idealized. They come to represent all those values which are supposedly threatened and denied by modern mass society. Much regionalist writing is part of a broad upswell of what Leo Marx calls "pastoral idealism" with its fatalistic view of technology and progress.[56] Against the industrial machine a more acceptable life is found to exist on the margins of society. In true Romantic style, culture represents freedom, humanism, spontaneity and naturalness. In the small region the soul can be recaptured from the machine.

This view is supported by Anthony Smith. He suggests that the ethnic movement of recent years (a movement related to radical regionalism) is one of both rejection and quest. It represents those who would turn their backs on the materialism of modern life, on technological advance and commercialism, and on the centralized, regulatory state. They seek an antidote to all these in a more natural existence. The ethnic community and the region are posed as alternatives to the alienation of modern life: "The ethnic renaissance has the power to heal the rift in the alienated consciousness of marginalized men and women, and draw from them its special ideological character."[57]

A similar argument is put forward by Peter Hinton. He notes that from the 1960s liberal cultural pluralism recognized the existence of deeply felt human needs "for attachment to metaphorical 'tribal' groups, to ethnic groups which gave people a greater sense of belonging than the impersonal groupings which industrial or industrialising societies tended to throw up."

He suggests that the "new ethnicists" work with this set of assumptions. They have challenged the melting pot and embraced ethnic diversity:

> Indeed, many see it as being a positive development as alienated man, in an automatised, overcrowded and achievement obsessed society, finds new fulfillment for his deepest needs by renewing his ethnic attachments. It is almost as if middle class, liberal intellectuals are discovering the virtues of tribal life a decade or so after the flower people of Haight-Ashbury and San Francisco.[58]

Against the alienation of modern life and the individualism of mass society, the organic community, whether in the past, present or future, stands as a metaphor for wholeness and humanity. It represents an alternate way of living, an already existing Schumacher world of small-is-beautiful and nonmaterial values. As I have suggested elsewhere, this "golden age vision" is a kind of utopia and, as such, it is "less a description of Newfoundland than an expression of current alienation and a longing for a more satisfying way of life."[59]

The promotion of regionalism and local attachment has long been seen as an important counter to the alienation and antagonism of class society. This is an important theme in the thinking of the founder of geo-politics, Halford Mackinder, the regionalist academics of the southern United States in the 1920s and 1930s, and T.S. Eliot and the Scrutiny Movement in Britain.[60] It is a strong theme in the writing of F.L. Jackson in Newfoundland at the present time. Jackson argues strongly for the corporate community (with a monarch at its head) as a "counterbalance against the kind of tyrannical populism, levelling and destruction of distinctive values, into which a purely unlimited democracy, by its own logic, threatens always to disintegrate." Without a sense of belonging to a community, the individual remains "but one of a faceless multitude, all pursuing isolated, unrelated destinies." Without community, not only is a basic human need denied, but there are distinct dangers from the placeless, roofless, atomized mass of people that is created:

> To be forced out of one's own familiar place, work and personal round of life into the cold, featureless realm of a wider society, where particular interests and demands alone rule, and wherein no clear limits are ever reached or individualistic ambitions satisfied, is to know a spiritual-political alienation that leads people to seek spurious solutions in anarchistic wantonness or totalitarian security.[61]

Like Matthew Arnold, Jackson poses culture against anarchy. The cultural community and local attachment are to provide a cosy cocoon for the alienated, a sense of belonging that will counter the tendency to "anarchistic wantonness" or even worse in modern society. And, as with Matthew Arnold, it is the actions of the working classes that trigger Jackson's concerns about anarchy. In the summer of 1985 Jackson accused Fraser March, the head of the Newfoundland Association of Public Employees (NAPE), of leading his followers into "the wasteland of civil disobedience" by producing a "mini-rebellion against the state."[62]

Coming home to the popular culture of Newfoundland has been a dominant theme in the radical regionalism that has developed in Newfoundland in recent years. The culturalist critique of modernization that has emerged in the province since the late 1960s has, however, proved ambiguous and limited. It represents an intellectual anti-capitalism and contains many deeply conservative assumptions, even if politically it crosses the spectrum. As a critique it has always contained within it the potential for use in non-progressive ways. Since the early 1970s this critique of modernization has been inextricably linked with the resurgence of Conservative politics in Newfoundland and with the condemnation of Liberal politics that is such an important element of the new conservatism. It is because of the fact that much of Newfoundland's radical regionalism has taken on a conservative flavour that it is the focus of attention in this essay. It remains to make a few comments about the politics of coming home to Newfoundland culture to draw this out.

At one level, the promotion of regional cultures along the lines suggested by Arthur Kroker and others may be seen as a way of giving people a sense of identity in an increasingly homogenized and alienating world. For those who do feel uprooted and uncertain, being part of an "imagined community" may be comforting. It provides a sense of belonging. And through this the world is ordered. Good and bad are clearly identified. Devils can actually or symbolically be cast out and a sense of purpose achieved. It may well be that the rise of radical regionalism, in part, provides a compensation for demoralization and frustrated hopes and a means of dealing with anxiety and uncertainty. The quest for region and culture does express great dissatisfaction with the existing state of affairs in society. But it offers a populist and romantic critique of industrialism and development. And its alternative to the lonely crowd is the community of folk tied together by common sentiments, values and interests. And, as we have seen in our discussion of the ideas of F.L. Jackson and others, this promotion of the natural community can have a distinctive reactionary slant. Jackson issues a call for Newfoundlanders to "reclaim a heritage," to save not "the body of the older life, but the spirit" and use this to "move on." They should retain their "living morality, their responsibility to family and society, their artfulness in speculation, their will to community" and their "relation to God," defend it against "encroaching cultures," and use this as the basis for constructing a new Newfoundland society that is "humane, meaningful and self-reliant."[63]

And following the logic of Jackson's argument, this would clearly be a society where alien union radicalism, unlimited democracy, atheism, and junk food would not have a place.

For people such as Jackson it has been no big step from a concern with culture to support for the Peckford Conservatives with their regionalist rhetoric. This has been true even for those who see themselves as socialists. Once the cultural community is accepted as the natural political unit and the leader of this political unit is seen as unproblematically representing the will of the people, then more critical perspectives may get lost. And Peckford has proved quite adept at using the politics of the natural community. He has to a large degree captured the cultural question for the Conservatives. As a "born again" Newfoundlander he is defending a way of life against outside, hostile forces.[64] He is trying to create a new Newfoundland, rich, independent and confident. All that needs to be done is for people to follow his direction.

If Peckford has come home to Newfoundland culture, so have others in recent years. One example of this is the report of the Royal Commission on Employment and Unemployment. In this report an appeal is made for rural Newfoundlanders to return to the ancestral wisdom of the outports in order to become more self-reliant. In the context of continuing high levels of unemployment and with the "dawning realization of the limits of the welfare state," Newfoundlanders are urged to return

"to our own backyards" in order to build on the strengths of "traditional culture."[65] A do-it-yourself approach to job creation is suggested, while production-for-use (through hunting, fishing, gardening, or house repair) is to be used to supplement the low wages that people will earn and the low guaranteed income supplement that the state will provide to replace Unemployment Insurance and income from both federal and provincial make-work schemes. Thus, at a time when the state is retreating from responsibility for both employment creation and the support of the unemployed, the virtues of outport culture have been rediscovered and presented as essential to the construction of a "post-industrial society." This picture of a populace that is less dependent on the state is an attractive one for conservative politicians at the present time. If the suggestions of the Royal Commission on Employment and Unemployment are followed, this will ensure that rural Newfoundlanders in the 1980s conform well to the picture of them presented in the promotional material put out by the Department of Industrial Development in the 1970s (discussed above). They will have no choice but to "keep working, regardless of suffering or hardship." For people trapped in rural poverty, no doubt the traits of stoical grit, cheerfulness, optimism and resourcefulness will quickly be developed if they don't already exist. And if all this does not prove enough to deal with the situation, then a little religion might not be a bad thing.

Notes

1 George Melnyk, *Radical Regionalism* (Edmonton: NeWest Press, 1981). This book is introduced by George Woodcock. Melnyk argues that regionalism is similar to Third World liberation struggles with their emphasis on self-reliance and appropriate development and that "in the hands of the people" it is a progressive force. Writers on Newfoundland have also seen regionalism in these terms. R. Johnstone, "In Praise of Peckford," *This Magazine*, 15 (1981), 8–12, and D. House, "Premier Peckford, Petroleum Policy, and Popular Politics in Newfoundland and Labrador," *Journal of Canadian Studies*, 17, 2 (1982), 12–31 even argue that this is the case when the movement is led by the Progressive Conservatives.

2   George Woodcock, "Introduction," in Melnyk, 10.

3   Arthur Kroker, "The Cultural Imagination and the National Questions," *Canadian Journal of Political and Social Theory*, 6 (1982), 5–11. Kroker's use of the term *patriotism* is significant. As with George Orwell, patriotism is distinguished from nationalism. The former is regarded as a natural expression of local attachment and love for one's way of life. In *Confederation Betrayed!* (Madeira Park, B.C.: Harbrow Pub., 1981), 1–5, George Woodcock argues that patriotism is by nature defensive whereas nationalism is related to the desire for power. This argument is also found in his *The Meeting of Time and Space: Regionalism in Canadian Literature* (Edmonton: NeWest, 1981). David Alexander also distinguishes "nationalism of the ugly sort" from "patriotism that arises like a plant from the traditional culture." For Alexander, people need to feel a sense of attachment to some collectivity. The growth of regionalism in Canada he regards as a result of the lack of a sense of collectivity at the national level. See D. Alexander, "New Notions of Happiness: Nationalism, Regionalism and Atlantic Canada," *Journal of Canadian Studies*, 15, 2 (1980), 31.

4   Kroker, 9–10.

5   The soil metaphor is taken from Jacques Barzun, *Classic, Romantic and Modern* (Boston: Little, Brown, 1961), 91–92. Northrop Frye argues that "culture has something vegetable about it, something that demands a small region and a restricted locale." He likens the creative act in humans to that of bird song in defining territory. Such ideas about culture have always been at the heart of romantic nationalism. See Frye, *Divisions on a Ground* (Toronto: Anansi, 1982), 62.

6   J. Overton, "Towards a Critical Analysis of Neo-Nationalism in Newfoundland," in R.J. Brym and R.J. Sacouman, eds., *Underdevelopment and Social Movements in Atlantic Canada* (Toronto: New Hogtown Press, 1979), 219–49; Kroker, 9–10.

7   This essay is part of an on-going study of culture and development in Newfoundland in the last fifty years.

8   See J. Overton, "Living Patriotism: Songs, Politics and Resources in Newfoundland," *The Canadian Review of Studies in Nationalism*, 12 (1985), 239–59.

9   F.L. Jackson, "Local Communities and the Culture Vultures," *The Newfoundland Quarterly*, 81 (1986), 7–10.

10 See the recent grade 5 text book by F. Cramm and G. Fizzard, *The Atlantic Edge* (St. John's: Breakwater Books, 1985).

11 The question was asked by Wick Collins, *Daily News* (St. John's), July 23, 1983.

12 *The Newfoundland Adventure* (Government of Newfoundland, Department of Development, 1975).

13 Robert Paine, *Ayatollas and Turkey Trots: Political Rhetoric in the New Newfoundland* (St. John's: Breakwater Books, 1981), 4.

14 See B. O'Neill and J. Overton, "Will the Real Brian Peckford Please Stand Up?," *This Magazine*, 15 (1981), 15–19; and J. Overton, "Oil and Gas: The Rhetoric and Reality of Development in Newfoundland," in R. Clark, ed., *Contrary Winds: Essays on Newfoundland Society in Crisis* (St. John's: Breakwater Books, 1986), 150–75; *Evening Telegram* (St. John's), November 2, 1984.

15 Johnstone, "In Praise of Peckford," and R. Johnstone, "Developing Forces in Newfoundland," *This Magazine*, 16 (1982), 36–37. See also his "Bones and Bare Cupboards: Dependency, Class and Crisis in the 'New Newfoundland,' An Overview," in Clark, ed., 176–86.

16 J.D. House, "The Mouse That Roars: New Directions in Canadian Political Economy—The Case of Newfoundland," Department of Sociology, Memorial University of Newfoundland, St. John's, 1983, 4–5.

17 F.W. Rowe, *Education and Culture in Newfoundland* (Toronto: McGraw Hill Ryerson, 1976), xiii.

18 E.R. Seary, "Regional Humanism," *The Newfoundland Quarterly*, 65 (1966), 13–16; A.P. Cohen, "The Anthropology of Proximate Cultures: The Newfoundland School and Scotland," *Scottish Journal of Sociology*, 4 (1980), 213–26.

19 See J. Overton, " 'Small Is Beautiful' in Newfoundland: Critical Comments on Populism in Rural and Regional Development," in C. Leys, B. Fairley and R.J. Sacouman, eds., *Restructuring and Resistance in Atlantic Canada* (forthcoming).

20 J. Overton, "Promoting the 'Real' Newfoundland: Culture as Tourist Commodity," *Studies in Political Economy*, 4 (1980), 115–37.

21 G. Pearson, *The Deviant Imagination* (New York: Homes and Meier, 1975), 144.

22 Cited in the introduction to H. Horwood and J. de Visser, *Historic Newfoundland* (Toronto: Oxford University Press, 1986).

23 Overton, "Promoting the 'Real' Newfoundland"; James Overton, "A Whale for the Killing and the Politics of Culture and Ecology," *Journal of Canadian Studies*, 22, 1 (1987), 84–103. See "'I have found my place!': Interview with Gerry Squires," *The Livyere*, 1

(1981), 9–10; and S. Gwyn, "The Newfoundland Renaissance," *Saturday Night,* 91 (1976), 38–45.

24 Michael Cook, "Culture as Caricature," *Canadian Literature,* 100 (1984), 72; Gwyn, "The Newfoundland Renaissance."

25 The village is a powerful totem in Western thinking. Artists have been mining this rich vein for centuries. The deserted or lost village has been an especially poignant symbol at least since the days of Oliver Goldsmith. In Newfoundland, Farley Mowat emerged as an early critic of resettlement as noted in my "Politics of Culture and Ecology." Poet Al Pittman's "Death of an Outport" is to be found in C. Rose, ed., *Baffles of Wind and Tide* (Portugal Cove: Breakwater, 1973), 48–54. Pittman took up the resettlement issue again in his play *West Moon* (1980). G. Squires's painting *Resettlement* dates from 1977. He claims it as his only political statement. Folksinger Valdy wrote a popular song about the resettlement of people from the islands of Placentia Bay to Arnolds Cove. Many of the early I.S.E.R. studies focused on resettlement. Ralph Matthews continued his work in this area in *"There's No Better Place Than Here"* (Toronto: Peter Martin, 1976).

26 See, for example, *Decks Awash,* 2, 5 (1973).

27 F.L. Jackson, "Can Newfoundland Survive?," *The Newfoundland Quarterly,* 75 (1979), 3–10, and the "Editorial," *Decks Awash,* 2, 5 (1973), 38; David Benson, "Barkin' Kettle: Honest Tradition," *Arts in Formation,* 2 (1983), 18–19.

28 R.J. Needham, "The Happiest Canadians," *Maclean's,* November 2, 1964, 14–17, 35–39.

29 Richard Gwyn, *Smallwood: The Unlikely Revolutionary* (Toronto: McClelland and Stewart, 1970), 62, xi.

30 "Editorial," *Decks Awash,* 3, 5 (1974), 32.

31 Kenneth Peacock, *Songs of the Newfoundland Outports, Volume 1* (Ottawa: National Museum of Canada, 1965), pp. xix, xxv.

32 K. Matthews, E.R. Kearley and P.J. Dwyer, *Our Newfoundland and Labrador Cultural Heritage, Part 2* (Scarborough: Prentice Hall, 1982), pp. 114 and 120.

33 Jackson, "Can Newfoundland Survive?"; J.D. House, *Newfoundland Society and Culture* (St. John's: Memorial University, 1978); Cyril Poole, *In Search of the Newfoundland Soul* (St. John's: Harry Cuff, 1982), 91–101; P. O'Flaherty, "Killing Ground," *Weekend Magazine,* 29 (1979), 22–24; D.W.S. Ryan and T.P. Rossiter, *The Newfoundland Character* (St. John's: Jesperson Press, 1984).

34 Johnstone, "In Praise of Peckford."

35 Margaret T. Hogden, *Early Anthropology in the Sixteenth and Seventeenth Centuries* (Philadelphia: University of Pennsylvania Press, 1946), 179 ff; Barzun, 91–92.

36 Zygmunt Bauman, *Culture as Praxis* (London: Routledge and Kegan Paul, 1973), 33–36.

37 *Newfoundland Royal Commission, 1933, Report* (London: His Majesty's Stationery Office, 1934), 192–97.

38 J.L. Paton, "Newfoundland: Present and Future," *International Affairs,* 13 (1934), 394, 397.

39 J.R. Smallwood, "Newfoundland To-day," in J.R. Smallwood, ed., *The Book of Newfoundland, Volume 1* (St. John's: Newfoundland Book Publishers, 1937), 1, 3.

40 Ellsworth Huntington, *Mainsprings of Civilization* (New York: John Wiley, 1945), 127–48; Thomas Lodge, "Newfoundland To-Day," *International Affairs,* 14 (1935), 637.

41 Kenneth Westhues, "Meditation on Newfoundland," Queen's College Seminar, Memorial University of Newfoundland, February 1983. A copy of this paper is deposited in the Centre for Newfoundland Studies in the Library at Memorial University of Newfoundland.

42 Nigel Harris, *Of Bread and Guns* (Harmondsworth: Penguin Books, 1983), 9–29.

43 *Evening Telegram,* June 27, 1983.

44 Ian McKay, "Historians, Anthropology, and the Concept of Culture," *Labour/Le Travail,* 8–9 (1981/2), 185–241 provides a very good discussion of the problems with using the concept of culture for analysis. He suggests that "culture" has replaced "race" as "a *deus ex machina* of social theory" (218). He also notes that the notion of national culture is an abstraction which is "almost wholly self-confirming."

45 Ian Whitaker, "Sociological Preconditions and Concomitants of Rapid Socio-Economic Development in Newfoundland," Appendix 5, *The Report of the Royal Commission on the Economic State and Prospects of Newfoundland and Labrador* (St. John's: Queen's Printer, 1967), 369–95.

46 J. Overton, "Progressive Conservatism? A Critical Look at Politics, Culture and Development in Newfoundland," in *Ethnicity in Atlantic Canada,* Social Science Monograph Series, University of New Brunswick, No. 5 (1985), 84–102.

47 Government of Newfoundland and Labrador, *Building on Our Strengths: Report of the Royal Commission on Employment and Unemployment* (St. John's: Queen's Printer, 1986).

48 Peter Narvaez, "We're Preserving Your Fuckin' Culture," *This Magazine,* 16 (1982), 9–12; F.L. Jackson, *Surviving Confederation* (St. John's: Harry Cuff, 1986), 15; R. Mills, "Comment," *Outlook,* CBC St. John's, August 19, 1980.

49 Wick Collins, "To Stay or Not to Stay," *Newfoundland Lifestyle,* 1 (1983), 47–48; Overton, "Living Patriotism."

50 Sean Sayers, *Reality and Reason: Dialectic and the Theory of Knowledge* (London: Basil Blackwell, 1985), 133 ff.

51 John Berger, "Credibility and Mystery," *Marxism Today,* 30 (1986), 45–46.

52 Benedict Anderson, *Imagined Communities* (London: Verso, 1983).

53 Eric Hobsbawm and T. Ranger, eds., *The Invention of Tradition* (Cambridge: Cambridge University Press, 1983); R. White, *Inventing Australia: Images and Identity, 1688–1980* (Sydney: Allen and Unwin, 1981).

54 The "fact" of Newfoundland culture is accepted by David Alexander. See "New Notions of Happiness," 31.

55 Raymond Williams, *Keywords* (Glasgow: Fontana, 1981).

56 Leo Marx, "American Literary Culture and the Fatalistic View of Technology," *Alternative Futures,* 3 (1980), 45–70.

57 Anthony Smith, *The Ethnic Revival* (Cambridge: Cambridge University Press, 1981), xiii.

58 Peter Hinton, "Where Have the New Ethnicists Gone Wrong?," *Australian and New Zealand Journal of Sociology,* 17 (1981), 14–19. Along similar lines Susan Crean and Marcel Rioux, *Two Nations* (Toronto: James Lorimer, 1983), 135, suggest that the alienation experienced by industrial workers has more to do with cultural impoverishment than lack of control over production.

59 James Overton, "Coming Home: Nostalgia and Tourism in Newfoundland," *Acadiensis,* 16 (1985), 84–97.

60 Discussed in James Overton, "Plastic People, Concrete Babylons, Frozen Food and Traditional Values: F.L. Jackson and the Politics of the Natural Community," unpublished paper, 1982. The Southern Sociologists are discussed in M. O'Brien, *The Idea of the American South, 1920–1941* (Baltimore: Johns Hopkins University Press, 1979). F. Mulhern, *The Moment of Scrutiny* (London: New Left Books, 1979) provides a good discussion of T.S. Eliot and the Scrutiny Movement.

61 F.L. Jackson, *Newfoundland in Canada: A People in Search of a Polity* (St. John's: Harry Cuff, 1984), 42, 43.

62 *Evening Telegram,* September 20, 1986. See also Matthew Arnold, *Culture and Anarchy* (Cambridge: Cambridge University Press, 1978).

63 Jackson, *Surviving Confederation,* 33.

64 *Evening Telegram,* June 4, 1980.

65 *Building On Our Strengths,* 24, 77, 314. I have offered some critical comments on the Royal Commission's report. See J. Overton, "Building on our Failures: The Newfoundland Commission's small but not-so-beautiful package for industrial poverty," *New Maritimes,* 5 (March 1987), 6–7.

Allegories and Orientations in African-Canadian Historiography
The Spirit of Africville[1]

JAMES W. ST. G. WALKER

In the 1960s the Halifax community of Africville was a symbol of the African-Canadian condition: marginalized, impoverished, dependent. Because it straddled the main trans-Canada railway line, it attracted considerable attention. Nation-wide publicity labelled Africville a "blot" and a "disgrace," an anomaly in a land supposedly free of racial disadvantage. Then it became a positive symbol in the mind of white Canada for slum clearance and urban renewal and racial integration, as the population of about 400 were removed from their homes "for their own good" and the physical community of Africville was bulldozed into the ground. Since 1970, when the last resident was forced out, Africville's symbolic role has shifted again. The community has continued to exist despite its physical destruction, and it is taken now as a symbol of the unconquerable black spirit in Nova Scotia. The relocation itself has been deemed an act *of* racism rather than *against* racism, something to be regretted and reversed.

Africville has been Canada's most highly publicized black community, but it was by no means unique. Every feature and every condition of life in Africville up to the time of its demolition was shared with other African-Canadian communities, with differences only in degree. Indeed, throughout its history, the Africville story serves as allegory for the African-Canadian experience, especially in Nova Scotia, and its refusal to die has forced a reconsideration and ultimately a recognition of the powerful community orientation of black history in Canada.

I

Like every other black settlement in early Canada, Africville owed its origin to fugitive American slaves. In this case they were among the Black Refugees attracted to the British during the War of 1812 and carried to Nova Scotia and New Brunswick on the promise of free land and equal rights. Neither promise was fully honoured. The lands assigned to the Black Refugees were given on "licenses of occupation" rather than grants, which meant that although they had full use of the land they lacked outright ownership and therefore could not sell it or use it for collateral. In any case the land distributed to them came in tiny plots of only eight to ten acres per family, neither large enough nor fertile enough for subsistence agriculture, and they were clustered in segregated tracts on the fringes of larger white towns, sufficiently close to commute as labourers but sufficiently remote to avoid social contact. And so Black Refugee settlements evolved, as had Black Loyalist settlements beginning a generation earlier, in physical

James W. St. G. Walker, "Allegories and Orientations in African-Canadian Historiography: The Spirit of Africville," *The Dalhousie Review* 77 (Summer 1997): 155–172.

circumstances that consigned them to isolation, poverty and economic dependence, but that at the same time encouraged the development of institutions and cultural styles suited to their own specific needs.

In 1842, following requests and petitions from black settlers and their white sympathizers, legal grants were given to those who were qualified. This permitted some to sell their land, if a buyer could be found, to finance a move to a more advantageous location. A few families in this way were enabled to relocate closer to Halifax, purchasing about thirteen acres along the shores of the Bedford Basin. Though no better for farming, the new location was more convenient for Halifax employment, it offered a readier market for produce and crafts, and it provided fishing opportunities in the Bedford Basin. In 1848 the earliest black deeds were registered, and in 1849 a Baptist church was established. The community took the name of Campbell Road, from its thoroughfare, and by 1851 it showed a population of 54. This represented almost exactly one per cent of the African Canadians living in Nova Scotia at that time.

Africville, as Campbell Road came to be known, literally grew in place; houses and outbuildings were added as families expanded or new ones moved in, with no concern for street plans or legal niceties. Separated from the rest of the city by a strip of bushland, it retained a rural atmosphere though it was formally within the Halifax city limits. As Halifax modernized, its sewers and street lights and water system were not extended to Africville. The police did not patrol there, and although the fire brigade responded to emergencies, without road access or water hydrants the firefighters could not provide effective protection. Halifax did offer employment, though only of the type deemed appropriate for black people. Some of the early male residents had skilled trades, but over the generations most were relegated to unskilled labour. They worked on the docks and the coal barges, they

hauled night-soil, a favoured few became railway porters. Equally typically, Africville women became cooks and cleaners in Halifax homes and nearby institutions. Fishing and farming were a modest supplement to irregular employment and extremely low wages. In 1959 the Dalhousie Institute of Public Affairs conducted a study which showed only about 35 per cent of Africville residents with regular employment, and 50 per cent earning less than $1,000 per year.[2]

Physical isolation from the Halifax mainstream therefore carried certain disadvantages, but it did not preserve Africville from encroachments. Scarcely had the settlement been founded than the railway lines cut through it in the 1850s, requiring the first relocation for several families. Another relocation occurred when additional lines were constructed just before World War I. A prison was established adjacent to the community in 1853, night-soil disposal pits in 1858, an infectious diseases hospital in the 1870s. To this concentration of undesirables were added a fertilizer plant, two slaughterhouses, a coal-handling facility, a tar factory, a leather tannery. Some new employment opportunities were created, at the level of general labour, along with a great deal of noise, soot and pollution. The *coup de grâce* came in the 1950s when the Halifax city dump was located within a hundred metres of Africville homes. Frequent petitions to civic authorities were to no avail. A certain undesirable human element encroached as well. In the absence of police surveillance, bootleggers and their customers found a favourable haven, and their drunkenness and debauchery both disturbed the peace of the settlement and at the same time attracted a reputation which the community itself did not deserve. To outsiders, Africville smacked of impermanency and even immorality.

Community insiders had an entirely different perspective. Central to their community experience was the Seaview African United Baptist church. The church and the community were born together in the 1840s and they grew together for a century thereafter. At the request of the Campbell Road residents, the Reverend Richard Preston convened a congregation there and became its first pastor, as he was for several other Halifax-area churches, and when Preston created the African Baptist Association in 1854 there were Campbell Road delegates at the founding convention. As a spiritual institution the church sustained the human dignity of the parishioners, promoted a sharing of burdens and mutual honesty through the Sunday testimony, elevated souls with prayers and praise. The 'communion' of this community derived from the church. But the church was central in many other ways as well. Since they could never afford a full-time resident pastor, it was always people from within the community, people just like everyone else, who led the affairs of the congregation. Other community organizations were church-connected—the women's auxiliary, youth groups, missionary society—and community meetings were held in the church building. The first school was conducted in the church beginning in 1883. The elected elders and deacons were the *de facto* government of the settlement and the negotiators with the society outside. The name 'Seaview'—adopted in 1916, following construction of a new church necessitated by the railway expansion—evoked the peaceful view over the Bedford Basin, scene of public baptisms and of the universally attended Easter Sunrise Service.

The scene was not to last. Modern secularism had its impact on Africville just like everywhere else, undermining the elders' role as leaders and mediators. Church membership declined, particularly after World War II. In that same period Africville lost its second most important institution, the school. While the qualifications of its teachers and hence the quality of its education had often been poor, the Africville school promoted a sense of identity and paralleled the church as a provider of a black perspective upon the world and its mean-

ing for life in Africville. In 1953, just one year before the American Supreme Court ordered school desegregation in the United States, the Africville children were integrated into a neighbouring Halifax school. The community's pillars were being weakened, just when they would be needed the most.

Talk of expropriating Africville and relocating its people began as early as World War I. So often was the subject raised that residents took it as nothing but talk, as an excuse for the city's failure to provide services. However, the talk became serious in the late 1950s as Halifax began a major urban renewal program that resulted in the relocation of thousands of citizens. The 1957 Stephenson Report condemned the "deplorable" conditions in Africville and noted the industrial potential of its location, emphasizing the benefits both to Africville and to Halifax from its removal.[3] But the people themselves called for development of their community right where it was, for running water and paved roads and decent housing and police protection. In 1961 they appealed to Sid Blum of the Canadian Labour Congress, a celebrated community campaigner. Blum asked Alan Borovoy to visit Halifax, to help Africville organize a defence.

Borovoy concluded, during his visit in August 1962, that relocation was inevitable. It was simply not acceptable in the 1960s for Canadian officials to restore and reinforce a black 'ghetto'; integration was socially desirable and politically necessary. He therefore concentrated his efforts upon making the best possible deal for those about to be uprooted. To that end Borovoy formed the Halifax Human Rights Advisory Committee, to arouse public support and to bring political pressure on Africville's behalf. It was this Committee, made up of black and white Haligonians all with experience in human rights causes, which suggested that the city engage Dr. Albert Rose to do a report on Africville conditions and to consider the appropriate solutions. Rose, too, became convinced that relocation was the only viable alternative. Believing that the people were willing to leave if the circumstances were favourable, Rose recommended that the removal should be spread over several years, that compensation be negotiated with each family, that the services of a lawyer and a social worker be provided free of charge, and that a post-relocation package be offered including job training and employment assistance.[4] The Rose Report was discussed at a meeting in Seaview Church in January 1964, and was approved in principle by 37 of the 41 people in attendance. Halifax city council then endorsed a program basically following the Rose recommendations. This involved two types of compensation: payment for expropriated land and buildings, and relocation assistance. The project social worker negotiated specific financial settlements with each of the relocatees and arranged for new housing in Halifax, for welfare and other allowances. The Halifax Human Rights Advisory Committee remained in existence as a watchdog, to ensure fair dealing and to advise the people of Africville. Despite these precautions the relocation experience was a bitter one. Only those who had legal title, 14 families, were eligible to negotiate a land settlement: the others were granted a blanket $500 each in exchange for their squatters' right to their land. As soon as any family moved, their house was immediately demolished, to encourage remaining residents to settle their affairs quickly. The reluctant were expropriated. No serious employment program was developed for them. Adjustment assistance was minimal. Although their housing conditions were improved, they had much higher expenses for rent or mortgages, and since underemployment prevailed this meant debt or welfare, and family stress. Group resources for mutual support were diminished, extended families were disrupted, the community was scattered. An overwhelming majority expressed their dissatisfaction in 1969, convinced that the entire operation had been designed to the advantage of the city, a device to remove them from valuable land. In an effort to confront their disappointments and prevent total discouragement, the Africville relocatees nurtured their old community ties and retained their identity, culminating in 1983 in the foundation of the Africville Genealogical Society dedicated to perpetuating "the spirit of Africville" for themselves and their descendants.

As the bearer of such a negative image—characterized by the city dump and bootleggers and racial segregation—Africville was not mourned by the broader society when the bulldozers did their work. Since it had been defined as a social problem, its removal must be a positive step and a benefit to the inhabitants. This was slum clearance in an era of urban renewal, the elimination of a black ghetto in an era of desegregation. The *Star Weekly* hailed "the slow welcome death of Africville,"[5] and *Time* complimented Halifax for its "determined, if belated, effort...to right an historical injustice."[6] Africville deserved to go, as even most Halifax blacks were ready to concede. If a problem was recognized it was not in the removal itself but in the way it was done, the inadequate compensation, the absence of genuine consultation, the failure to provide post-relocation assistance. It is worth remembering that, at that time, African Americans were insisting upon integration, and the Canadian government even proposed the elimination of native reserves in the 1969 White Paper on Indian policy. Arguments in favour of Africville's continued existence were not considered seriously.

But that moment, too, would pass. Urban renewal and mass relocations would soon be discredited, to be replaced as a development model by the idea of building upon local community traditions to improve economic and social conditions. The African-American movement grew suspicious of integrationism and began to celebrate black pride and distinctiveness. Above all, black people throughout North

America, engaged in a community-based struggle for their collective rights, became increasingly conscious of the communal nature of their history and culture and the foundations to their identity in black institutions. As black history was re-defined as a community story, Africville *as community* could be taken seriously. The sense of loss experienced by the relocatees was respected and shared by others, especially other blacks, as it was recognized that a viable community had been uprooted, a beloved church destroyed, an identity undermined. The arguments put forward by the people of Africville were given retroactive validity, including their interpretation of the city's sinister motives. White society had awakened to the historic pervasiveness of racism in Nova Scotia; the pre-relocation condition of Africville could be recognized as a direct consequence of racial injustice, and the relocation not as a corrective but a continuation of the racist syndrome.

These ideological developments and value shifts were experienced across the continent. Africville did not cause them to happen, but it did become the concrete Nova Scotian example to illustrate the general principle; it entered the discourse, locally, to engage and enhance a different perspective and a different paradigm that would redefine the meaning of black community, culture and identity. The genuine yearning for community lost is apparent in such evocations of the Africville memory as Shelagh Mackenzie's film *Remember Africville,* Joe Sealy's jazz album *Africville Suite,* and George Boyd's play *Consecrated Ground.*[7] Africville came to stand, for the black people of Nova Scotia, as a warning not to accept any more government promises, not to submit to the direction of outsiders. Africville stood too as an inspiration: the black spirit and community identity had demonstrated its strength; that Africville could overcome its physical annihilation revealed a source of power that could generate positive change for all black people. Province-wide organizations were stimulated to utilize black distinctiveness and communal bonds in a renewed confrontation with the racism that had restricted black lives for generations.

II

As Africville's experience was being redefined in this way, the relocation process was being recorded and interpreted by two distinguished scholars, Don Clairmont and Dennis Magill, in one of the few classics to grace the field of African-Canadian studies. Their findings were published first in the *Africville Relocation Report* (1971), then in book form as *Africville: The Life and Death of a Canadian Black Community* (1974), which appeared in a new and slightly revised edition in 1987.[8] They came to their study, in the summer of 1967, convinced that it was a model relocation, an example for other cities to follow. They grew disenchanted as they witnessed the Africville people being ignored by social technocrats, and in fact they became engaged with relocatees in organizing to demand better compensation and re-establishment programs. They had entered their own story, and they had changed it. What they had discovered was that the "liberal welfare model" of planned social change was bureaucratic, dictatorial, undemocratic, and that it was not serving the best interests of the people of Africville.

The interpretation that emerged from the Clairmont and Magill study was that Africville was a "social problem" and its residents were "victims": historically, they were victims of city neglect and encroachment, which produced the unsatisfactory "problem" conditions which in turn justified relocation; then they were victims of the way the relocation was organized, the unfair compensation and the failure to follow through on adjustment assistance. This thematic thrust does not change through the three published versions, but the package of information which carries the theme does undergo some subtle and very interesting shifts. In 1971 there was more discussion of theory and "relocation models," as if the intended audience was sociologists and urban planners, there was more detail on land records and deeds of the early settlers, and a more elaborate description of the century of white encroachments emphasizing a long-standing interest in Africville land by the city of Halifax. In 1974 Africville as "social problem" receives more attention, including analysis of the impact of those past encroachments in terms of poverty, living conditions and social outlook. Although the text was almost identical, this direction was strengthened in the 1987 edition. A section entitled "Citizen Involvement During the Relocation Programme" in 1974, becomes "*Lack of* Citizen Involvement During the Relocation Programme" in 1987:[9] the story is basically the same, but the reader's attention is being directed more powerfully. And in 1987 a paragraph headed "Powerlessness" enshrines the perspective of victimization:

> Africville residents, being black and poor, viewed the world with pessimism and resignation. Political bargaining with the "outside world" had been unsuccessful; the dominant attitude within the community was one of powerlessness and political ineffectiveness....[10]

But while the 1987 edition indicates most clearly the depredations committed upon the body and soul of Africville, there are some clues, really no more than glimmers, that *pre*-relocation Africville may not have been so bad, so incorrigible, so obvious a candidate for destruction. In 1987 the illustrations are sharper, and fewer in number, giving a far less depressing and decrepit impression of historic Africville. A reader would be affected differently. Consider also the subtle difference in impact of the opening sentence of the Introduction. In 1971 it was worded:

> Africville was a Negro "enclave" within the city of Halifax....

In 1974 it became:

> Africville was a black enclave [no quotation marks] within the city of Halifax....

And in 1987:

> Africville was a black community within the city of Halifax....

The community perspective which infused black historical interpretation during the 1970s, and which had gripped the black people of Nova Scotia in the wake of Africville, was reflected in the way the scholarly interpretation was being presented.

The story has been told anew in a book compiled by the Africville Genealogical Society, *The Spirit of Africville*,[11] and the evolving social attitude toward the historic Africville community is given full voice. The first things you notice are the beautiful pictures. Gone are the drab and grainy photos of Clairmont and Magill; these are coffee-table quality, with flowers and bright blue skies, colourful houses and smiling black faces, declaring that this was a place worth saving. A preface by Irvine Carvery, president of the Africville Genealogical Society, announces:

> We, the people of Africville, hope that you will enjoy reading this book and gain a better understanding of what it is like to grow up in a black community in Nova Scotia. (xviii)

The first article is a whimsical and nostalgic stroll through Africville in 1959, setting the tone by emphasizing the positive human aspects of community life. Even the dump was an asset, a source of many valuable things from saleable scrap metal to usable food and clothing.

Some folks say the dump was put here to drive us out. If that's true, things kind of backfired, didn't they? (33)

There follow two articles by Don Clairmont, "An Historical Overview" and "Moving People: Relocation and Urban Renewal," which succinctly capture the scholarship of his earlier publications but with a distinctly different effect: the people of Africville were "wronged" by the century of trespass against them, but they did not become "victims." Clairmont does not disguise the hardships, but neither does he invoke pity. His perspective has shifted from the student of urban renewal to the student of black society. Africville is presented as a viable community; the injustice in the relocation was not in the way it was handled but in the very fact that it happened at all.

Equally effective in presenting this revised history of Africville is a report from a meeting in Halifax in November 1989, entitled "Lessons for the Future." Former residents speak their pride and their pain. Persons involved in the decision to relocate, both black and white, declare that they made a mistake. A black human rights activist and negotiator then on Africville's behalf says: "Would I have acted today as I did then? Of course the response is no."[12] A city councillor from the relocation era admits: "Looked at from today, I have to say that I think we also undervalued the importance of a sense of community."[13] A now-retired provincial official draws the essential lesson:

> I think we have to learn that many such communities, and Africville is a prime example, have a cultural identity, a personality and an emotional place in the hearts and minds of their people which could provide the solid foundation for the future growth and development of that community.[14]

The demand from that meeting, and the current platform of the Africville Genealogical Society, is not simply for compensation but for restoration. The people of Africville want to go home again, to rebuild their community on the shores of the Bedford Basin. To dramatize their demands, one group has launched a physical 'vigil,' camping on the former location of the Seaview Church and claiming it for the community. The Genealogical Society itself filed suit against the city of Halifax in 1995, seeking legal title to the land first settled by their ancestors. Their declared intention is to develop the site both as a historical memorial and as a source of employment and revenue, to enable a reversal of the 1960s dislocation. Negotiations with the city were continuing in early 1999.[15] The perspective of community members and the thematic orientation of the academic observers have come together in *The Spirit of Africville*. As previously noted, Africville serves as allegory for the history of African Canadians; it can be added that it also reflects, in its multiple versions, the variety of interpretations both popular and scholarly which shape the way that history is told. The same event can encode quite different meanings depending on who are deemed to be the principals of the story and whether their goal is legitimated and their attributes respected. In its telling as in its living, Africville history is representative.

III

For the sake of this article I have identified five 'orientations' in African-Canadian historiography. They are 'orientations' rather than 'schools' because they are not deliberate or even conscious groupings of scholars; furthermore several orientations can coexist in the same piece of historical writing. Although my own preferences will be obvious, I do not pretend that there is *one* acceptable interpretation in this field or in any other. The orientation labels are descriptive rather than definitive, and they refer explicitly to one particular feature: what distinguishes one orientation from another is the role assigned to black people in the making of black history. As shall be seen, each has its advantages and its liabilities.

The first orientation I have labelled *Black Clients*. It is readily recognizable to anyone who has watched the C.R. Bronfman Foundation's "heritage moment" on the Underground Railroad, which plays occasionally during commercial breaks on Canadian television. This one-minute historical vignette shows a black woman in great distress, being comforted by a white matron who assures her that "he will arrive safely." The black woman runs outside and meets a farm wagon driven by a white man. Boards are removed, and out of a secret compartment leaps a black man. He and the black woman embrace, while a voice-over announces that "this is part of the Canadian heritage." In this *Black Clients* orientation the focus is on white people; black people enter the story as recipients of white justice and white philanthropy: they are cooperative, loyal and grateful. Almost anything with Underground Railroad in the title shares this *Clients* orientation, incorporating the image of fugitive slaves as 'passengers' being 'transported' to freedom by white agency. Literature of this type may acknowledge the existence of racism in Canadian history, but usually presents it as something that has been overcome by Anglo-Canadian justice or, if it does continue, it is only among certain 'rotten apples.' As a society, in other words, Canada is untainted, and the few rotten apples in our communal barrel can be plucked out. This understanding of the nature of racism was reflected in Canadian public policy until fairly recently.

The *Clients* orientation was more popular a few generations ago—the best examples are to be found in the writings of Fred Landon and W. R. Riddell—but it continues on television and in the popular mind, and it has more recently received credibility from Allen P. Stouffer's *The Light of Nature and the Law of God: Antislavery in Ontario 1833–1877*.[16] Although Stouffer explains that his book is intended to be about white abolitionists, and therefore his exclusive focus on whites is justifiable, still the black actors who do cross his stage are fundamentally seen as recipients rather than participants; from the perspective of white abolitionists, blacks *are* clients. Stouffer is careful to describe white racism, even within antislavery ranks, but the congratulatory imagery of most earlier *Clients* historiography had already provoked a reaction, creating what I shall term the *Black Victims* orientation.

Black Victims began to appear during the development of a new sensitivity to human rights and race relations in Canada, reflecting a *mea culpa* attitude at the discovery that Canadian history shared comparable examples of racism with the United States. Often, in fact, it was *tua culpa*, as American scholars pointed the finger at the racist reality lurking behind the North Star mythology so beloved by Canadians. Jason H. Silverman's *Unwelcome Guests: Canada West's Response to American Fugitive Slaves, 1800–1865*[17] is a good example of this orientation. African Canadians are redefined, from *Clients* to *Victims*, but the focus is still on white actors. Black history becomes the story of what was done *to* black people, rather than what was done *for* them, while the black characters remain do-*ees* instead of do-*ers*. Literature with a *Victims* orientation did make a solid contribution, revealing the deep roots of racism in Canadian history. It was no longer possible to hold seriously the 'rotten apple' view, and to this extent the *Victims* moved us forward, toward an understanding of systemic racism. But the liability was that African Canadians were not responsible for their own history, and a dangerous by-product often was that black culture was presented as 'pathology,' as the result of oppression. As has already been described, versions of *Africville* shared in this liability.

The next orientation I shall call *Black Achievers*. The focus is at last on African-Canadian actors. The racism is there, but certain individuals are able to 'make it' in the white world, and according to the criteria of the white world, by their own talents and diligence. Stephen L. Hubbard's *Against All Odds: The Story of William Peyton Hubbard, Black Leader and Municipal Reformer*[18] can serve as our example. The Hubbard of the title was a prominent Toronto city politician and a champion of public ownership of utilities, but he was never a "Black Leader" if that implies 'leader of black people.' The people Hubbard led were white. His achievement early in this century was remarkable, and his biographer properly treats him as an exception. This characterizes the *Achievers* orientation: African Canadians are central, their individual equality is recognized and their contributions are celebrated, but to be classed as a contribution they had to do something in and for white society. The liability was that these outstanding black people had to stop being black to win historical recognition. This is still a powerful orientation, especially among non-professionals. When I speak at Black History Month events I am most often asked about 'Black Achievers,' and the people posing the question are most often African Canadians themselves.

The early movement for civil and human rights fitted in with a *Victims* imagery, but as 'Black Power' and 'Black Pride' emerged the victim/pathology model was no longer acceptable. Black people were clearly not 'recipients' any longer, if they ever had been, and the focus moved to what they were doing and what they had done. This shift coincided with and participated in the social history movement, the researching and writing of history 'from the bottom up.' The rediscovery of black initiative and culture led to an appreciation of the communal nature of the black identity, and so it is appropriate to style this as the *Black Community* orientation. It produced a recognition of the things that made black people distinct from whites, of the contributions made to that process rather than to mainstream developments, and of the collective nature of the black struggle in North America. The most important by-product of the *Community* orientation was the rehabilitation of black culture, which became not only valid but central to the African experience in the New World. This in turn served to rehabilitate the African connection, the identification with the mother continent, as reflected in the current use of the terms 'African Canadian' and 'African American.' A liability of the *Black Community* orientation is that it may focus exclusively on what black people were doing, ignoring the context in which those developments took place, ignoring even the racism that set so many boundaries around individual and communal activity, and it may tend to idealize the past rather indiscriminately. *The Spirit of Africville* demonstrates both the vitality and the liability of the *Community* orientation.

The *Community* and *Victims* orientations are, or should be, incompatible. When my own *Black Loyalists* first came out in 1976[19] with its *Community* theme, Robin Winks wrote that I had effectively "put an end to the 'victims' school of Canadian Black historiography."[20] Not only was Professor Winks altogether too flattering, he was rather premature, for the *Black Victim* has been revived and multiplied since then. Sometimes this is a straight revival, but increasingly there is a twist upon it, and it is modified by a touch of *Achiever*. For this reason I shall give the 1990s version a distinctive name, and call it the *Black Survivors* orientation. 'Survivor' has a particular cultural meaning in the 1990s; it is not exactly a euphemism for 'victim,' for it has a nuance, and a therapeutic significance. In the *Black Survivors* orientation the focus is on black people but the perspective is back with the oppressor; African-Canadian history becomes the story of 'persons living with discrimination.' An extremely interesting example is Dionne

Brand's *No Burden to Carry: Narratives of Black Working Women in Ontario 1920s to 1950s*,[21] or rather the editor's introduction, for this is a collection of interviews conducted with African-Canadian women. Brand emphasizes exploitation and perseverance under suffering, but the interviews themselves emit a vibrant *Community* orientation. Work and racism are *not* allowed to define their identity as these women proceed beyond the editor's agenda to describe lives contoured by church and school, black organizations and communal activities. The *Survivors* orientation can no doubt have a therapeutic effect, especially for those who lack a community background, and it may even win certain political advantages, in the short run, to make a claim based on sympathy. But the liability is that the African-Canadian story enters the contemporary discourse of power with black people as objects rather than subjects.

IV

These five categories are not, of course, exclusive, and perhaps it is worth repeating that the books mentioned here and the literature in this field generally have innumerable strengths, and weaknesses, which characterize them at least as much as my 'orientations.' Still, as our attention returns to Africville and its current campaign for restoration, I want to emphasize the political significance of historical interpretation and within this context the centrality of the role played by black people in their own history. *History as it is understood* enters a political discourse, it becomes a participant in a power dialectic and it influences power relationships. George Orwell knew this when he gave Big Brother the slogan "Who controls the past controls the future; who controls the present controls the past."[22] Whatever Orwell's cynical intent, we can recognize that people do in fact act on what they believe to have happened in the past. This applies to African-Canadian history as it is understood by both black people and white people. The writing of history is a political act, deliberate or not.

In the past two decades approximately 80 articles, 50 books and 40 graduate theses have been written on African-Canadian history or at least with relevance to African-Canadian history. Besides regional studies, the most popular topics have been slavery and abolition, immigration, discrimination (particularly economic and legal), education, religion, culture, and life stories. Especially in the recent decade, black women have been receiving increasing attention. Thematically the literature ranges over all the orientations identified in this article, but if there is a trend it is toward the *Survivor,* the 'person living with racism,' the individual who perseveres 'in spite of it all.' Although *Community* is not neglected and blacks as historical actors are present, this is still not a prevailing focus in African-Canadian historical interpretation. This is unfortunate, in my view, because a focus on the black community is a key, is *the* key, to understanding African-Canadian history—the *meaning* of the racism, the migrations both in and out, the school and churches, the newspapers, the anti-slavery movement, the individual achievements and the distinct role and position of women—because it all arises from or is profoundly influenced by the dynamics generated within black society and institutions. Oppressors may have dominated the process for much of the time, but they have never controlled it, not even in slavery and certainly not in Africville. To ignore the community dynamic would be to forego a powerful political impulse. It was through the community that black people related with external forces and structures, and as the community changed over time so did that relationship. The endeavour by the people of Africville to go home again is one illuminating example of how this process has always worked. The history lesson and the political strategy coincide.

Notes

1 A shorter version of this article appeared in *The Literary Review of Canada*, July 1993: 3–5.

2 Dalhousie Institute of Public Affairs, *Condition of the Negroes of Halifax City* (Halifax: Dalhousie Institute of Public Affairs, 1962).

3 Gordon Stephenson, *A Redevelopment Study of Halifax, Nova Scotia* (Halifax: City of Halifax, 1957).

4 Albert Rose, "Report of a Visit to Halifax with Particular Respect to Africville" (Nov. 1963), in Donald Clairmont and Dennis Magill, *Africville Relocation Report* (Halifax: Dalhousie Institute of Public Affairs, 1971), Appendix F.

5 *Toronto Star Weekly,* 1 Jan. 1966.

6 *Time* (Canada ed.), 6 April 1970.

7 *Remember Africville*, dir. Shelagh Mackenzie, NFB, 1991; Joe Sealy, *Africville Suite*, Seajam Recordings, 1996; George Boyd, *Consecrated Ground* (Eastern Front Theatre, Halifax, 1999).

8 Donald Clairmont and Dennis Magill, *Africville Relocation Report* (Halifax: Dalhousie Institute of Public Affairs, 1971); *Africville: The Life and Death of a Canadian Black Community* (Toronto: McClelland & Stewart, 1974); revised edition with a preface by Bridglal Pachai (Toronto: Canadian Scholars' Press, 1987).

9 See 1974 ed. (175) and 1987 ed. (159).

10 1987 ed. (160).

11 Africville Genealogical Society, *The Spirit of Africville* (Halifax: Formac, 1992).

12 *Spirit of Africville*, 97.

13 *Spirit of Africville*, 100.

14 *Spirit of Africville*, 101.

15 Conversation with Irvine Carvery, Halifax, 4 Nov. 1997, confirmed in a telephone conversation, 7 Jan. 1999.

16 Allen P. Stouffer, *The Light of Nature and the Law of God: Antislavery in Ontario, 1833–1877* (Montreal: McGill-Queen's UP, 1992).

17 Jason H. Silverman, *Unwelcome Guests: Canada West's Response to American Fugitive Slaves, 1800–1865* (Millwood, NY: Associated Faculty Press, 1985).

18 Stephen L. Hubbard, *Against All Odds: The Story of William Peyton Hubbard, Black Leader and Municipal Reformer* (Toronto: Dundurn Press, 1987).

19 James W. St.G. Walker, *The Black Loyalists: The Search for a Promised Land in Nova Scotia and Sierra Leone, 1783–1870* (London: Longman, 1976).

20 *The Dalhousie Review* 57 (1977–78): 150.

21 Dionne Brand, *No Burden to Carry: Narratives of Black Working Women in Ontario 1920s to 1950s* (Toronto: Women's Press, 1991).

22 George Orwell, *1984,* special ed. (Oxford: Clarendon, 1984), 217.

Chapter 5 of *Lament for a Nation: The Defeat of Canadian Nationalism*

GEORGE GRANT

The confused strivings of politicians, business-men, and civil servants cannot alone account for Canada's collapse. This stems from the very character of the modern era.[1] The aspirations of progress have made Canada redundant. The universal and homogeneous state is the pinnacle of political striving. "Universal" implies a world-wide state, which would eliminate the curse of war among nations; "homogeneous" means that all men would be equal, and war among classes would be eliminated. The masses and the philosophers have both agreed that this univer-sal and egalitarian society is the goal of histori-cal striving. It gives content to the rhetoric of both Communists and capitalists. This state will be achieved by means of modern science—a sci-ence that leads to the conquest of nature. Today scientists master not only non-human nature, but human nature itself. Particularly in America, scientists concern themselves with the control of heredity, the human mind, and soci-ety. Their victories in biochemistry and psychol-ogy will give the politicians a prodigious power to universalize and homogenize. Since 1945, the world-wide and uniform society is no longer a distant dream but a close possibility. Man will conquer man and perfect himself.

Modern civilization makes all local cultures anachronistic. Where modern science has achieved its mastery, there is no place for local cultures. It has often been argued that geogra-phy and language caused Canada's defeat. But behind these there is a necessity that is incom-parably more powerful. Our culture floundered on the aspirations of the age of progress. The argument that Canada, a local culture, must dis-appear can, therefore, be stated in three steps. First, men everywhere move ineluctably toward membership in the universal and homogeneous state. Second, Canadians live next to a society that is the heart of modernity. Third, nearly all Canadians think that modernity is good, so nothing essential distinguishes Canadians from Americans. When they oblate themselves before "the American way of life," they offer them-selves on the altar of the reigning Western god-dess. When Pearson set out on his electoral campaign of 1963, he was photographed read-ing Will Durant's *The Dawning of the Age of Reason*. To Durant, the age of reason is the age of progress. The book was therefore appropriate reading for Pearson, who was about to persuade Canadians to adopt American atomic arms.

There are many who would deny the sec-ond statement in the previous paragraph, that the United States is the spearhead of progress. Strangely enough, the two groups that deny it do so from opposite positions. The Marxists

---

George Grant, Chapter 5 of *Lament for a Nation: The Defeat of Canadian Nationalism*, (McGill-Queen's University Press, 1997).

deny it from progressive assumptions, and American "conservatives" deny it because they consider their country the chief guardian of Western values. These two points of view are sometimes confused and combined by certain Europeans whose jealousy of the United States leads them to accuse Americans of being too reactionary and too modern at one and the same time. To maintain my stand that the United States is the spearhead of progress, these two denials must be refuted. To do so, I must turn away from Canadian history to the more important questions of modern political theory.

Marxists believe that their philosophy leads to the true understanding of history. They insist that the aims of the United States are hostile to the interests of developing humanity. They assert that American corporation capitalism— its system of property relations and consequent world policies—makes the United States an essentially "reactionary" rather than a "progressive" force. The Russian and Chinese leaders may disagree on how to deal with this situation, but they do not disagree about the diagnosis. Canadian Marxists have therefore argued that Canadian nationalism serves the interests of progress because our incorporation in the United States would add to the power of reaction in the world. To be progressive in Canada is to be nationalistic. To see where the Marxists are wrong in detail about Canada, I must discuss where they are wrong about the age of progress in general.

Marx believed that history unfolds as progress, and that when man's control of nature has eliminated scarcity, the objective conditions will be present for a society in which human beings no longer exploit each other. With the end of exploitation, men will not be alienated from their own happiness or from each other. A society will emerge in which the full claim of personal freedom and social order will be reconciled, because the essential cause of conflict between men will have been overcome. This world-wide society will be one in which all human beings can at last realize their happiness in the world without the necessity of lessening that of others. This doctrine implies that there are ways of life in which men are fulfilled and others in which they are not. How else could Marx distinguish between man's alienation and its opposite? Marxism includes therefore a doctrine of human good (call it, if you will, happiness). Technological development is a means by which all men will realize this good. But such a doctrine of good means that Marx is not purely a philosopher of the age of progress; he is rooted in the teleological philosophy that pre-dates the age of progress. It is the very signature of modern man to deny reality to any conception of good that imposes limits on human freedom. To modern political theory, man's essence is his freedom. Nothing must stand in the way of our absolute freedom to create the world as we want it. There must be no conceptions of good that put limitations on human action. This definition of man as freedom constitutes the heart of the age of progress. The doctrine of progress is not, as Marx believed, the perfectibility of man, but an open-ended progression in which men will be endlessly free to make the world as they want it. In Marxism, technology remains an instrument that serves human good. But many technologists speak as if mastery were an end in itself. To conquer space it may be necessary to transcend ordinary humanity, and produce creatures half flesh and half metal.

North-American liberalism expresses the belief in open-ended progress more accurately than Marxism. It understands more fully the implications of man's essence being his freedom. As liberals become more and more aware of the implications of their own doctrine, they recognize that no appeal to human good, now or in the future, must be allowed to limit their freedom to make the world as they choose. Social order is a man-made convenience, and its only purpose is to increase freedom. What matters is that men shall be able to do what they want, when they want. The logic of this liberalism makes the distinction between judgements of fact and judgements of value. "Value judgements" are subjective. In other words, man in his freedom creates the valuable. The human good is what we choose for our good.

In an earlier generation, liberals such as John Dewey claimed that this doctrine improved upon the past because it guaranteed a society in which all could do what they wanted, in which the standards of some would not be imposed upon others. Tastes are different, and we should have a society that caters to the plurality of tastes. How much fairer this would be than the old societies in which standards of virtue were imposed on the masses by pertinacious priests and arrogant philosophers. But this is not what is happening in our state capitalism. In the private spheres, all kinds of tastes are allowed. Nobody minds very much if we prefer women or dogs or boys, as long as we cause no public inconvenience. But in the public sphere, such pluralism of taste is not permitted. The conquest of human and nonhuman nature becomes the only public value. As this planet becomes crowded and even dangerous, our greatest public activity becomes "the exploitation of the solar system." The vaunted freedom of the individual to choose becomes either the necessity of finding one's role in the public engineering or the necessity of retreating into the privacy of pleasure.

Liberalism is the fitting ideology for a society directed toward these ends. It denies unequivocally that there are any given restraints that might hinder pursuit of dynamic dominance. In political terms, liberalism is now an appeal for "the end of ideology." This means that we must experiment in shaping society unhindered by any preconceived notions of good. "The end of ideology" is the perfect slogan for men who want to do what they want. Liberalism is, then, the faith that can understand progress as an extension into the unlimited possibility of the future. It does this much better than Marxism, which still blocks progress by its old-fashioned ideas of the perfectibility of man.

Marxists fail to understand the modern age when they assume that socialism is a more progressive form of organization than state capitalism. Implied in the progressive idea of freedom is the belief that men should emancipate their passions. When men are free to do what they want, all will be well because the liberated desires will be socially creative. This belief lies at the very centre of liberal movements.[2] Marx claimed to be the inheritor of the noblest aspects of liberal thought. He believed that when scientists had eliminated scarcity as the cause of greed and oppression, a society would arise in which the freedom of each to pursue his desires would not conflict with a happy social order. The dictatorship of the proletariat was a passing necessity that would lead into a society of freedom. Under Communism, the passions would be emancipated, but they would be socially useful, not the corrupt passion of greed caused by scarcity. Even those socialists who did not follow Marx in the doctrine of the withering away of the state still generally believed that socialism would create a society of freedom in the sense of the emancipated passions. Socialism was considered an essentially progressive doctrine. It led to freedom.

There is confusion in the minds of those who believe in socialism and the emancipation of the passions. It is surely difficult to deny that greed in some form is a desire that belongs to man *qua* man, and is not simply produced by the society of scarcity. If this is so, to emancipate the passions is to emancipate greed. Yet what is socialism, if it is not the use of the government to restrain greed in the name of social good? In actual practice, socialism has always had to advocate inhibition in this respect. In doing so, was it not appealing to the conservative idea of social order against the liberal idea of freedom? Even if socialists maintain that their policies would lead in the long run to a society of unrestricted freedom, in the short run they have always been advocates of greater control over freedom. This confusion in their thought is the chief reason why socialism has not succeeded in the large technological societies since 1945. Western civilization was committed in its heart to the religion of progress and the emancipated passions. Those who accepted such a doctrine found corporation capitalism was a much more suitable régime than the inhibiting policies of socialism.[3] Since 1945, Marxist socialism has had its triumphs, but these have been in authoritarian régimes, in societies that needed the discipline of authority in order to industrialize quickly. The triumphs have not been in the West.

Early capitalism was full of moral restraints. The Protestant ethic inhibited any passion that did not encourage acquisition. The greed of each would lead to the greatest good for all. But in the age of high technology, the new capitalism can allow all passions to flourish along with greed. *Playboy* illustrates the fact that the young executive is not expected to be Horatio Alger. The titillation of the jaded tastes of the masses serves the purpose of the corporation élites, so long as a sufficient quota of the young is siphoned off as scientists and executives. With automation, the work-ethic of Protestantism disappears. Liberal ideology reconciles the political power of the élites with the private satisfactions of the masses. State capitalism and liberalism are much more advanced manifestations of the age of progress than the Russian system with its official Marxism.

American conservatives also claim that the United States is not the most progressive society on earth. Conservatives maintain that American society retains certain traditional values that have been lost in Communist societies. This claim appeals to history by asserting that the American Revolution was essentially conservative—as distinct from the radical revolution in France. The American Revolution did not appeal to the perfectibility of man but to the traditional rights of Englishmen. At its heart there were the ideals of a constitutional government and the inalienable rights of persons and their property. It is admitted in such arguments that many who supported the revolution were influenced by French revolutionary ideas; but at the centre of the Republic were such men as Washington, Madison, Hamilton, and Adams, rather than such men as Jefferson and Paine. Edmund Burke castigated the revolution in France while he defended the American cause. This indicates the conservatism of the American Revolution. The claim of conservatives is that bourgeois constitutionalism has remained the dominant tradition of the Republic despite the continuing liberal attack.

This argument has at its heart an interpretation of the history of political philosophy with which the present writer would agree. To put that interpretation simply, modern political philosophy may be divided into two main waves.[4] The first wave started with Machiavelli and Hobbes and found its bourgeois expression in such British thinkers as Locke, Smith, and Hume. The chief originator of the second wave was Rousseau, and this wave has spread out into the world through Kant and Hegel. The earlier thinkers criticized the classical view of nature and natural law, but they still maintained some conception of what was natural. While believing that man's essence was his freedom, the later thinkers advocated the progressive mastery through that freedom of human and non-human nature. Man in his freedom was thought to stand outside nature, and therefore to be able to perfect it. We could interfere with nature and make it what we wanted. It is from this doctrine that the continuous revolution of the modern era has proceeded.

In applying this interpretation, the American conservatives claim that the United States was founded on the thought of the first wave, while the Communist empires took their ideology from Rousseau and Marx. Therefore the United States should be called a conservative force. The founders of the American Republic were followers of Locke.[5] The assumptions of Locke and Smith are said to have given English-speaking societies stability of constitutional government and freedom from continuous revolution. They escaped the worst results of totalitarianism (call it, if you will, totalitarian democracy) which swept eastward from the continent of Europe. The capitalism of the English-speaking world was stabilized by being founded on a conception of human nature. The doctrine of human nature of Locke and Smith may be inadequate compared to the classical teachings, but it is less destructive of humanity than the later doctrines, which assert that men are completely malleable to perpetual conditioning. Because of the conservative nature of the United States, as against the revolutionary character of the Communist empires, Christianity and Judaism have been able to survive in North America, while they are persecuted in the modern empires of the East. Whatever the imperfections of American government, it remains at least formally constitutional, while the Marxist societies are tyrannies. The United States must be accepted as the guardian of western values against the perversions of western revolutionary thought as they have spread into the East.

It is important to point out one effect of this argument on Canada and the United Kingdom. This appeal to Lockean liberalism has been the philosophy of those who have believed that English-speaking unity was the hope of the modern world. The basic assumption of Churchill's life was that the British future lay in its alliance with the United States—the unity of the democratic-capitalist nations.[6] In Canada, this appeal to English-speaking unity has also been used as an argument for the destruction of Canadian independence. In the events around which this writing turns, many conservative

Canadians were convinced that Diefenbaker was being false to English-speaking unity in refusing nuclear arms. The Liberal victory was welcomed in the press of the United Kingdom, and Pearson has always appealed to those in England whose hopes lay in the special relation with the United States. Yet it must be pointed out that the argument from English-speaking unity must play an ambiguous role in relation to Canadian nationalism. If Lockean liberalism is the conservatism of the English-speaking peoples, what was there in British conservatism that was not present in the bourgeois thought of Hamilton and Madison? If there was nothing, then the acts of the Loyalists are deprived of all moral significance. Many of the American Tories were Anglicans and knew well that in opposing the revolution they were opposing Locke. They appealed to the older political philosophy of Richard Hooker. They were not, as the liberal Canadian historians have often described them, a mixture of selfish and unfortunate men who chose the wrong side. If there was nothing valuable in the founders of English-speaking Canada, what makes it valuable for Canadians to continue as a nation today?

To return to the general argument, there is some truth in the claim of American conservatives. Their society does preserve constitutional government and respect for the legal rights of individuals in a way that the eastern tyrannies do not. The perpetuation of these depends on the continuing tradition of Lockean liberalism among influential classes. Bourgeois Protestantism, with its Catholic and Jewish imitations, have survived in the United States and give some sense of the eternal to many people. Nevertheless, these traditions—no longer the heart of American civilization—become more residual every year. Sceptical liberalism becomes increasingly the dominant ideology of those who shape society; and, as it was argued earlier, this ideology is the extreme form of progressive modernity. The United States is no longer a society of small property owners, but of massive private and public corporations. Such organizations work with the scientists in their efforts to master nature and reshape humanity. Internationally, the imperial power of these corporations has destroyed indigenous cultures in every corner of the globe. Communist imperialism is more brutally immediate, but American capitalism has shown itself more subtly able to dissolve indigenous societies. This can make it harder to resist than the blatant thrusts of the Russians or the Chinese. The new methods the social sciences use to dissolve the opposition in friendly or enemy societies are welcomed by the government of the United States.[7]

The history of how modern liberalism has replaced the older republican traditions cannot be given in detail. It is not surprising that this should have happened. It was in the West the idea arose that human nature is completely malleable, and this the United States today inherits. American society has also inherited the older aspects of the western tradition: the Church, constitutional government, classical and philosophical studies. But every day these become more like museum pieces, mere survivals on the periphery.

The Americans who call themselves "Conservatives" have the right to the title only in a particular sense. In fact, they are old-fashioned liberals. They stand for the freedom of the individual to use his property as he wishes, and for a limited government which must keep out of the market-place. Their concentration on freedom from governmental interference has more to do with nineteenth-century liberalism than with traditional conservatism, which asserts the right of the community to restrain freedom in the name of the common good. Senator Goldwater appealed directly to the American Constitution and to Locke, its philosophical architect. The Senator's chief economic adviser, Professor Milton Friedman, appeals to the British liberal economists of the nineteenth century. They are "conservatives" only in terms of the short history

of their own country. They claim that the authentic American tradition went off the rails with the mass liberalism of the New Deal and should return to the individualism of the founding fathers. The makers of the Constitution took their philosophy from the first wave of modernity; the spirit of the New Deal belonged to the later waves of liberalism. In this sense, Goldwater is an American conservative. But what he conserves is the liberal philosophy of Locke. The founders of the United States took their thought from the eighteenth-century Enlightenment. Their rallying cry was "freedom." There was no place in their cry for the organic conservatism that pre-dated the age of progress. Indeed, the United States is the only society on earth that has no traditions from before the age of progress. Their "right-wing" and "left-wing" are just different species of liberalism. "Freedom" was the slogan of both Goldwater and President Johnson.[8]

The clobbering of Goldwater at the polls in November of 1964 shows how little the American people cared about the early liberalism of their founders. Johnson's "Great Society" expressed the new American "freedom" far better than Goldwater's talk of limited government and free enterprise. The majority tradition in the United States backs Roosevelt, Kennedy, Johnson, whose liberalism is the most modern. The older liberalism of the Constitution had its swan song in the election of 1964. The classes that had once opposed Roosevelt were spent forces by 1964. The leaders of the new capitalism supported Johnson. Goldwater's cry for limited government seemed as antediluvian to the leaders of the corporations as Diefenbaker's nationalism seemed to the same elements in Canada. Johnson was supported not only by such obvious groups as Negroes and labour but also by the new managerial bourgeoisie of the suburbs. The farmers, who were supposed to be the last bastion of individualism, were not slow in voting for the continuance of subsidies. Four of Goldwater's five states were from the South.

This was the last-ditch stand of a local culture. But it is doomed to disappear as much as an indigenous French Canada. The Goldwater camp was outraged by the sustained attacks of the television networks and newspaper chains. Were they not aware who had become the American establishment since 1932? Corporation capitalism and liberalism go together by the nature of things. The establishment knew how to defend itself when threatened by the outrageous challenge of outsiders from Arizona. The American election of 1964 is sufficient evidence that the United States is not a conservative society. It is a dynamic empire spearheading the age of progress.

The foregoing is platitudinous. But one consequence of the argument is not always made explicit: the impossibility of conservatism as a viable political ideology in our era. The practical men who call themselves conservatives must commit themselves to a science that leads to the conquest of nature. This science produces such a dynamic society that it is impossible to conserve anything for long. In such an environment, all institutions and standards are constantly changing. Conservatives who attempt to be practical face a dilemma. If they are not committed to a dynamic technology, they cannot hope to make any popular appeal. If they are so committed, they cannot hope to be conservatives. For example, the most brilliant conservative of our era has only been able to preserve what he loves (the power and culture of France) by gaining support for nationalism from the most advanced technocrats. De Gaulle has had immediate success, but in the long run he will have helped to build a Europe in which the particularities of France cannot hope to exist. Other examples are legion. These days even the Papacy attempts to liberalize itself.

The impossibility of conservatism in our epoch is seen in the fact that those who adopt that title can be no more than the defenders of whatever structure of power is at any moment necessary to technological change. They provide the external force necessary if the society is to be kept together. They are not conservatives in the sense of being the custodians of something that is not subject to change. They are conservatives, generally, in the sense of advocating a sufficient amount of order so the demands of technology will not carry the society into chaos.[9] Because they are advocates of nothing more than this external order, they have come to be thought of as objects of opprobrium by the generous-hearted.

Notes

1 In what follows I use "modern" to describe the civilization of the age of progress. This civilization arose in Western Europe and is now conquering the whole globe and perhaps other parts of the universe. "Modern" is applied to political philosophy to distinguish the thought of Western Europe from that of the antique world of Greece.

2 This last doctrine reminds one of the vast gulf that separates modern moral philosophy from the central teachings of the antique world.

3 This failure of socialism to recognize itself as an essentially conservative force has nowhere been so patently obvious as in the confusions of the Canadian socialist movement.

4 For this account of political philosophy see Leo Strauss, *Natural Right and History* (Chicago: University of Chicago Press, 1953).

5 A recent Roman Catholic form of the argument from Locke makes an even fuller claim. It identifies the Lockean thoughts of the nation's founders with the political philosophy of Aquinas. Father Courtney Murray has made the same attempt for the United States that Acton made a century ago in England—the identification of the modern belief in political freedom with Catholic Christianity. Suffice it to say that Locke largely accepted Hobbes's account of the state of nature, while Aquinas accepted the Aristotelian account. How then can

their doctrines of natural right be closely identified? Those who make such attempts should surely be asked to read Coleridge's writings on Locke. To find any close identification between Aquinas's and Locke's doctrine of the virtues surely requires a looser reading of both than nationalist prejudice and flattery of the spirit of the age should allow. This branch of Roman Catholic American political philosophy is hardly then to be treated seriously.

6   Many contemporary English Conservative leaders—Churchill, Macmillan, Hogg, and others—have been born of wealthy American mothers.

7   See "Toward a Technology of Human Behaviour for Defence Use" by Charles W. Bray, in *The American Psychologist* (August 1962). This is a synopsis of a report to the American Secretary of Defense.

8   In an earlier day, this was one respect in which Canada could be differentiated from the United States. Canadians had memories of conservative tradition that was more than covert liberalism. At their best, Canadian conservatives never stood on an abstract appeal to free enterprise. They were willing to use the government to protect the common good. They were willing to restrain the individual's freedom in the interests of the community. The recent conservatism of Toronto, as expressed by the *Globe and Mail*, is American, not Canadian conservatism. They call for the protection of property from government interference. Canadian Goldwaterism shows how much Toronto is now in spirit a part of the United States.

9   The next wave of American "conservatism" is not likely to base its appeal on such unsuccessful slogans as the Constitution and free enterprise. Its leader will not be a gentleman who truly cares about his country's past. It will concentrate directly on such questions as "order in the streets" which are likely to become crucial in the years ahead. The battle will be between democratic tyrants and the authoritarians of the right. If the past is a teacher to the present, it surely says that democratic Caesarism is likely to be successful. In the fight between Sulla and Marius, it was the descendants of the latter who established the Julian line of emperors.

Hockey as Canadian Popular Culture

Team Canada 1972, Television and the Canadian Identity

Neil Earle

It is commonplace to assert that ice hockey signifies something about Canadian popular culture, indeed, about Canadian culture as a whole. Yet what it might signify has not been explored at any length by scholars. The 1972 Canada-Soviet series can serve as a useful model to probe certain questions. How does electronic technology impact upon a mass audience? Is there a bardic function for television? Only recently has popular culture theory become advanced enough to attempt an analysis of these questions. In *Canada Learns to Play: The Emergence of Organized Sport, 1807–1914,* Alan Metcalfe tells us that G.M. Trevelyan wrote the social history of 19th-century Great Britain without once mentioning the most famous Englishman of his time, the cricket champion W.G. Grace.[1] If Canada were substituted for England, Donald Creighton for Trevelyan, and Foster Hewitt or Wayne Gretzky for W. G. Grace, we would be going some distance towards framing the theme of this study, namely ice hockey in Canadian culture as perceived through the codes and aesthetics of electronic technology.

Hockey and television still seem inseparably linked in the popular imagination. On 7 October 1992, the Canadian Broadcasting Corporation (CBC) presented a televised documentary of the 1972 international hockey series between Team Canada and the former Union of Soviet Socialist Republics (USSR), a program that explored the lyricism and the menace that suffuses hockey at most levels. Later that winter hockey announcer Danny Gallivan, for years the eloquent and elegant voice of the Montreal Canadiens, died. On 28 February 1993, hockey's dark side was further probed by another CBC "hybrid drama" involving the career of former Toronto Maple Leaf Brian "Spinner" Spencer. The theme was a "life cursed by violence" both on and off the ice.[2] But it is the Canada-Soviet Series of September 1972 that offers an especially useful paradigm for a study of "our game" on two levels: first, the series occasions reflection on the cultural nexus of the great national pastime; and second, electronic technology was sufficiently developed by 1972 to allow a fairly sustained probe into some of its codes and structures. Especially interesting is mass technology's capacity to transform play into a form of collective drama.

Popular culture theory provides the methodological tools to study systematically the game that—for good or for ill—has helped define Canadians.[3] While no irrefutable thesis has yet come to light as to why hockey looms so large in the Canadian popular imagination, Americans

Neil Earle, "Hockey as Canadian Popular Culture: Team Canada 1972, Television and the Canadian Identity," *Journal of Canadian Studies* 30, 2 (Summer 1995): 107–123. Reprinted by permission of Neil Earle.

have long known what we were about. "Canadians value hockey so highly," wrote the authors of *The Social Significance of Sport: An Introduction to the Sociology of Sport,* that "it has been called Canada's culture."[4] If hockey broadcasts and telecasts have long been a recognizable staple of Canadian popular culture, the question about what it signifies is less clear. This article blends the insights of such theorists as Horace Newcomb, John Fiske, and Paul Rutherford with the observations of players and keen followers of the game such as Ken Dryden, Michael Novak, Jack Ludwig and Doug Beardsley. "Technology," taught Martin Heidegger, "is a way of revealing."[5] Remarkably, in September 1972 at least 12 million Canadians gathered around their television sets and radios to hear the animated voice of hockey broadcaster Foster Hewitt exclaim "Henderson has scored for Canada!"[6] The question remains: what did this electronic national drama signify?

For 27 days in September 1972 Canadian television was the matrix for a sports event that has become an enduring folk memory, a cultural text. For once, disparate notions of class, ethnicity and gender were welded into a rare Canadian moment. Millions of adult Canadians reserve hallowed psychic space, not just for Pearl Harbor or the assassination of President John Kennedy, but also for the memory of Paul Henderson's winning goal in Game Eight of the 1972 Canada-Soviet series. Is this hockey as mythos, the arena as locus for a technologically driven actuality drama? One could respond that if hockey is just a game in Canada, then the Rockies are just hills on the prairies. The game, like the mischievous "puck" itself, has the ability to ricochet and career unexpectedly in and out of the Canadian experience. Rick Salutin, in preparing his 1977 play *Les Canadiens,* was astonished to hear a sportswriter for the *Montreal Star* relate how the enduring success of the city's celebrated franchise had been seen by many as a ritualistic act of revenge for the Plains of Abraham. Wayne Gretzky's move to the United States in 1988 during the Prime Ministership of Brian Mulroney was a cultural signpost to an era, as was the refusal of Ontario's Eric Lindros to play for the Québec City *Nordiques* in the aftermath of the Meech Lake constitutional crisis. The transcendence attached to the 1972 series is further attested to by the fact that both President Nikolai Podgorny and Premier Alexi Kosygin were in the audience that September night in the Luzhniki Arena in Moscow when the Soviet team won their hometown opener over Team Canada.[7] Students of sport, especially as it pertains to popular culture, have elaborated upon its myth-making potential. Michael Novak is one of the few analysts willing to penetrate through to hockey's mystical core:

> What is the basic underlying myth dramatized in hockey? One can't help noticing hockey's speed, its teamwork, its formal plays, its violent contact and exceptionally hot temper tantrums... and finally the exhilaration of slapping a tiny rubber puck into a narrow, low net.... The game is played on ice. Its symbolic matrix lies in the lands of snow, blizzards and dark, freezing nights.... One gets suggestions of an Ice Age once again smothering the planet. One senses the sheer celebration of hot blood holding out against the cold, the vitality of the warm human body, of exuberant speed rejoicing in its own heat, of violence and even the sight of red blood on white ice as a sign of animal endurance....[8]

Novak's study of our gender-biased yet pervasive national pastime applies to Canada, even though we are not his prime focus: "Hockey celebrates the heat and passion of survival. Take the worst, accept and conquer. Give as well as get. Take it to them. If hockey is, with chess, the national sport of Russia, let the world recognize the fierce resolve of people toughened by their climate; let them remember Stalingrad."[9]

Doug Beardsley's personalized account of the game, *Country on Ice,* argues that in Canada hockey is played for its own sake, for the fact that almost every Canadian has been touched by its mystery and mystique. It is noteworthy, too, that hockey is a sport played with equal relish on both sides of the Ottawa River. Ice hockey has been called the "common coin" of Canada. Roch Carrier's tender and moving short story *The Hockey Sweater,* for example, touched both solitudes. It is hard to forget the impact of Maurice "the Rocket" Richard on French and English Canadians in the period just after World War II. Hockey as our authentic "national anthem" may indeed weave one of the few imaginative strands in a huge country with a diverse population.[10] Jack Ludwig offers anecdotal evidence for the significance of hockey as a Canadian badge of identity on the international scene. At Munich, where over 300 expatriates gathered to watch Canada lose 7 to 3 in the series opener, an Australian flung out this challenge to a disappointed Canadian: "Aye, mate, isn't this your game.... What's going on losing to the Ruskies?"[11]

Yet at home it was televised hockey that had elevated the game into a national preoccupation. Canadian content is (except during players' strikes) alive and well on prime time each April to June, as the Stanley Cup playoff series skate their seemingly interminable way across the nation's television screens. Broadcast historian Paul Rutherford offers this perspective:

> Hockey on television was an actuality broadcast. The broadcasters adjusted to the rhythms and routines of the game itself.... The experience wasn't all that different from being in the arena.... The camera's role was always to focus on the puck, providing close-ups around the nets or when the action got heavy and personal, say, on the boards or in the corners.... The first producer of hockey was Sydney Newman who hadn't any real experience with the sport. After watching a game he told two old pros that it would be easy to cover—it was really like ballet....[12]

Rutherford argues further that television and hockey seemed to be made for each other: "The audience for hockey grew to about 3.5 million English Canadians and around 2 million French Canadians.... The success of hockey, first on CBC and later on CTV, had no counterpart in the United States, until the birth of ABC's "Monday Night Football" in 1970.... Many people experienced hockey only via the television set or the radio."[13]

Television is suited to the game's strengths. Hockey is a transition game—everyone gets a chance to play, and it is one of the few games where players can change "on the fly." Crucially, the spectators are very much part of the action in the confined, enclosed arena; they are close to the ice surface. This serves to heighten the intensity of crowd reactions, reactions which the cameras and microphones—in that relatively small space—can easily amplify. It is not extravagant to assert a parallel between televised hockey's participatory dynamic and the presentational and affective aspects of Greek and Shakespearean drama, the Odeon and the "wooden O." Add to this the distinctive pacing and "rhythm" of a hockey game, the changing mood and psychological tempo created by the switches in focus from the team to the individual player and back again, and one is offered aesthetic spectacle "par excellence." An excerpt from a game narrated by Danny Gallivan in the early 1960s is illustrative:

> The Hawks regrouping behind their own line coming out over centre. Beliveau STEALS the puck, takes a shot right on the short side and Hall was there to stymie him with a scintillating save...Cournoyer now CUTTING IN on goal, trying to get right IN FRONT... ANOTHER SHOT...the Canadiens really firing the puck around with authority... Lemaire WINDS UP, Beliveau takes a poke at it...COURNOYER A REAL SPINNERAMA... THEY BANG AWAY AT IT, THEY BANG IT IN! and the Montreal Forum crowd goes crazy.[14]

Hockey's speed and intensity played well to the myth of a rough, tough game demanding skill, effort, commitment, endurance. "It was the Canadian game because we had created it.... It suited a land in which the winter always loomed so large," explains Rutherford. "Even more the game fitted an image of Canadian manhood."[15] If there is no Canadian Stalingrad or Marathon, might not the Stanley Cup play-offs and the international Canada Cup competitions form an imaginative substitute? Ward Cornell, a broadcaster from the 1960s, expressed one aspect of hockey's overweening maleness: "We're tough, rugged guys from the North," he expostulated half-jokingly to Rutherford.[16] The element of catharsis encouraged the "juvenile" facets of the game ("Stand your ground, don't back down from a fight!"), the ugly primitivism that led inevitably to the outcries and protests against hockey violence. "Canadian seamen of long professional foul-mouth careers would sound like Little Lord Fauntleroy at any NHL practice session.... To be a man in Canada is to *fight*. The sweetest hero this side of heaven is someone like Derek Sanderson, who isn't really very good at fighting, but fights nevertheless, because getting beaten shows much more macho than skating away."[17]

Yet, hockey reflects another part of the male sensibility that televised hockey magnifies and transmits. This aspect is its most redeeming cultural feature and lies close to the core of the hockey mystique. This was and *is* the game's evocation of a peculiarly Canadian paradisiacal myth, the appeal to "the boy inside the man," a myth that intelligent students and players of the game have captured. Ken Dryden is a former goal-tender in the National Hockey League. One of the photographs in Dryden's *Home Game: Hockey and Life in Canada* is simply and tellingly entitled "Icons." It features a small square photograph of the Montreal Forum scoreboard imposed upon a two-page spread of boys in toques and sweaters playing shinny (the unstructured form of hock-

ey) on a slough in St. Denis, Saskatchewan.[18] The picture brilliantly captures hockey's imaginative hold over millions of Canadian males.[19] The image of the boy with his hockey stick on the outdoor pond evokes something distinctive— "the true north strong and free," a myth that, as we shall see, can be enhanced by technology. What Dryden elsewhere characterized as "the voice in my head" was an electronic imprint. The alchemy of electronic technology thus made possible in televised hockey a synchronization of the mythopaic and the mechanical. A flooded driveway became a locus of myth:

> It was Maple Leaf Gardens filled to wildly cheering capacity, a tie game, seconds remaining. I was Frank Mahovlich or Gordie Howe. I was anyone I wanted to be, and the voice in my head was that of Leafs' broadcaster Foster Hewitt: '...there's ten seconds left, Mahovlich, winding up at his own line, at center, eight seconds, seven, over the blueline, six—he winds up, he shoots, he scores!' It was a glorious fantasy, and I always heard that voice. It was what made my fantasy seem almost real. For to us, who attended hockey games mostly on TV or radio, an NHL game, a Leafs game, was played with a voice. If I wanted to be Mahovlich or Howe, if I moved my body the way I had seen them move theirs and did nothing else, it would never quite work. But if I heard the voice that said their names while I was playing out the fantasy, I could believe it. Foster Hewitt could make me them.[20]

This is the romance of hockey; play as idyll. The mysterious bonding of millions of Canadian males to "the game" traces back to the pond, the slough, the indoor rink; to the iced driveway, to the time when they, in their youthful fantasies, were Gordie Howe or Bobby Orr or Wayne Gretzky. Here is hockey's cultural core, the central explanation for its mystical attraction for prime ministers and pipe-fitters, for Nobel Prize winners and new immigrants. This beguiling innocence mitigates and helps neutralize the inherent sexism and violence of the game.

On 28 September 1972 both Ken Dryden and Foster Hewitt were on hand when 12 million Canadians—not all of them male—heard the most memorable lines in Canadian sports history: "Cournoyer has it on that wing. Here's a shot. Henderson makes a wild stab for it and falls. Here's another shot. Right in front. They score! Henderson has scored for Canada."[21] Televised hockey is superb participatory drama, complete with the requisite heroic, antiheroic, and otherwise transcendently significant leading characters. Keith Cunningham believes that sport resembles sacred time:

> There is a festival time in the soul. We dress ourselves up and jump from profane time, time as linear continuation, 9 to 5, week in week out, into sacred time. In sacred time, as Mircea Eliade has called it, we enter the flight of mythic fantasy. We enter again the old tales, we live again the high adventure of the soul. Everything becomes fluid in a shifting landscape; we are Hercules as much—or as little—as our existential selves. We are here and we are there.[22]

Sacred time is re-emphasized in the ritual aspects of sport, as in, for example, the lighting of the Olympic torch. Cunningham links the mythos of sport to drama:

> Always at issue is man's relation to Being. Is he going to remain a dreamer in the cavern, repeating the round of illusions and pleasure-principle fantasies forever, or is he going to recognize the dynamic patterns behind the scenes which govern his own life…. The drama is itself a symbol, unfolding in time…. The dramatic hero, like the dream ego, acts as our magic double, inhabiting the compressed underworld of the drama, subjected to trials and experiencing incredible delights for our

sake. [Drama] immerses us in the emotional experience of growth through crisis.[23]

Drama, argues Cunningham, is an acting out, a symbolic participation in ritual. As such, ice hockey's values of actuality and involvement provide an experience with the potential to "wound us with knowledge." In September 1972 technology created an electronically centred national drama, a conclusion attested to by recent developments in popular culture theory.

Many theorists of popular culture refuse to ascribe a mere passive or negative role to the television audience. John Fiske, for example, sees culture-making as a social process. Fiske differentiates popular culture from mass culture. In popular culture, he asserts, the people themselves actively engage in shaping social meanings from the products offered by the consumer society. A hockey stick is a product of mass culture, but a hockey stick advertised by Mario Lemieux becomes an artifact of popular culture. People, in effect, invest mass commodities with socio-cultural meanings. In Fiske's term, "meanings meet."[24] The public, as consumers of mass culture, give mass-produced items a meaning that they "decode" from the product. Semioticians speak about "the phenomenon of duplicity," a larger possibility of meanings than is connoted by the obvious, intended meaning.[25] Thus, for an item of mass culture—a three-piece suit, a pair of blue jeans, or a Canadiens sweater—to become a significant item of the popular culture, a process of mediation must take place. In the Fiskean analysis, the consumer is engaged in cultural production, in giving an artifact of mass culture a meaning which will assure it a place in the public imagination.[26] Just as millions of teens had their "favourite Beatle" in the 1960s, so millions of Canadians have been able to identify with Maurice "the Rocket" Richard, Ted "Teeder" Kennedy, Gordie Howe, Bobby Hull, Bobby Orr, Wayne Gretzky, and Doug Gilmour.

One could thus argue that Canadians are involved in a form of collective myth-making when watching hockey telecasts. The mass audience polyvalently "decodes" the game. On one level, there is a fairly straightforward hero-worship dynamic at work. Yet there are hidden duplicities as well. Some enjoy the "we're rough, tough guys from the North" message; hence, hockey's violence has never hurt its ratings. Others more likely enjoy the social segmentation noted by Rutherford. ("Where are all the women?" said one wife to her husband during her first game at Maple Leaf Gardens.) Then, as the wrestling phenomenon illustrates, excess possesses its own appeal. The striking uniforms, the crowd noises, the body checks—these aspects of excess throw into bold relief conventional notions of decorum, propriety and law and order. Hockey's very physicality is part of its appeal. Ice hockey thus represents a multifaceted, rich and duplicitous text, rooted in rural signifiers, the symbolic recall of simpler, more innocent days when life was fresh and bright and bracing and friendship seemed forever. Here are aspects of a northern pastoral that in Canada (at least until fairly recently) was not all myth. Is this hockey's *sanctum sanctorum,* a locus of that elusive intangible, "the true north strong and free"?

In 1972, then, "meanings met." The series with the USSR stirred potent cultural signifiers. Ken Dryden felt it and wrote at the time: "[A]s far as the vast majority of Canadians are concerned, this series was not conceived in a spirit of brotherhood and understanding but as a means of putting down the Russians and asserting our claim to hockey supremacy."[27] The mass audience across Canada functioned as an imaginative sensorium capable of being "wounded with knowledge," of experiencing Aristotelian tragic pity and fear as well as moments of transcendence. In September 1972, the codes and aesthetics of television gave a heightened dramatic spin to a moment of high nationalist tension: an imaginative echoing, metaphorically, of the Greek-Persian wars.[28] In September 1972, Canadian television tapped the latent myth-making inherent in all sport:

Sports (offers) cohesion and identity, the mythic model. Because of the powerful visibility of such a model, it has always been used as far more than either entertainment or cultural unifier. It is quickly transformed into a vehicle for cultural values, and we translate the playing field into an image for "real life." The virtues of practice, hard work, dedication, desire, competitive spirit, fair play, "good sportsmanship," and a host of other commodities are pointed out to generation after generation of young people. The language of the games, the initiations into rituals, the formalities of winning, are transformed into mystical moments. Sport is hallowed as holy text.[29]

Some 15 million Canadians shared in the vicarious climax when Henderson scored for Canada. Many were to watch the last game at home, at work or at school as—in some cases—television sets were brought into classrooms by excited teachers aware that a moment of Canadian history was being made. Scott Young remembered the excitement the series generated in the country: "Nothing to match the excitement of this series had ever happened in Canada; rarely anywhere in any sport. The last time Canada had beaten the Soviets at hockey was in the world championships of 1961.... Nine years of regular beatings later, Canada said to hell with it and withdrew from world competition.... The ultimate...then and now, is for world championships to be decided by the best against the best; the best, in Canada's terms, meaning professionals."[30]

Ken Dryden also caught the embedded nationalist agenda:

The talk all through the summer of 1972 was about the series. And because Canada was the best and sure to win, Canadians couldn't wait for the series to begin. It would be a glorious "coming out" party, a celebration of us. This gave to it a more fundamental dimension. For though much may be special about Canada, surrounded as it is historically and geographically by countries that are bigger, richer, more powerful, whose specialness seems more obvious, we cling to every symbol. A game is a game. But a symbol is not. We had to win this series.[31]

Dryden is right; symbols are important. The team's name—"Team Canada"—was rife with meaning, cast in a form that would be easily translatable into both French and English, thus fitting the bilingual ethos of the times. Little wonder that the 2 September 1972 opening night at the prestigious Montreal Forum resembled, in retrospect, the first act of a national drama. Phil Esposito, the rugged goal-scorer from the Boston Bruins, was almost manic about the need to win the opening event: "It was only a ceremonial face-off, but I had to win that draw.... I mean, I had to win that draw! This guy didn't even try and it really aggravated me.... I remember I drew the puck back and put up my hand like, wow, we won the first face-off!" The tension was contagious: "At that same moment, sounding a little surprised himself, Foster Hewitt, who had in his lifetime described thousands of games, was telling his nation-wide audience, 'I can't recall any game that I've ever been at where you can just feel the tension. And it keeps building up.'"[32]

The opening moments exploded with emotional energy and harbingers. Esposito scored for Canada after the first 30 seconds, Paul Henderson six minutes later. But in the next 53 minutes, recalled Dryden, "Team Canada's players, its fans, Canadians, could feel everything slipping away."[33] After such an explosive start the Soviets doggedly fought back to win 7-3. It was the worst of all possible scenarios: Team Canada humbled in one of the holy of holies of Canadian hockey, the Montreal Forum. The nightmarish spectacle that was to engage the entire nation for the next few days was launched.

As the continued fascination with "horror" movies reveals, popular culture is pleasurable even (perhaps especially) when it takes on nail-biting intensity. After the first game, Canadian coach Harry Sinden commented: "A little piece of all of us died today." Scott Morrison captures perfectly that mingled feeling of exhilaration and apprehension as the second game opened two nights later in Toronto: "The best players the NHL was allowed to assemble playing under the name Team Canada had been soundly beaten, and their pride had been deeply wounded. So, when they stepped on the ice that night for a second game in Toronto, they weren't playing for a doubting nation, but mostly for themselves. As a team."[34]

The nation-wide audience knew that according to the tried and true rhythm of play-off hockey, this second game would be crucial. The feeling in Maple Leaf Gardens was palpable. The cameras framed a bright red maple leaf on the television screens of the millions who watched: "There existed in historic Maple Leaf Gardens that night more stifling pressure than excitement...though the support of the fans was staggering. In conservative Toronto, where the fans are generally quite reserved...on this night they stood as one and chilled the air singing the national anthem. But there also remained a sharp sense of trepidation, of apprehension. This sense no longer pertained to what the opposition would bring, but the home team."[35]

The cameras and commentary were relaying "bardic television," functioning as an electronic stage bringing together viewers from the Atlantic and Pacific coasts. It superbly transmitted tragic pity and fear. Once again the Chorus-like presence of Foster Hewitt accentuated the strained emotion. A hapless Team Canada felt the sting of tragic reversal: after Game One a solid majority of their countrymen condemned them for refusing to shake hands with the Soviets, a convention of international hockey. That night, however, Maple Leaf Gardens was the venue for the spectacle of redemption: Team Canada won 4-1. It was to be their most decisive victory of the series.

Television's superb "theatre of the ether" synergized ice hockey, Team Canada and the electronic aesthetic in a transcendent moment. Peter Mahovlich's shorthanded goal at 6:47 of the third period incarnated Novak's words:

> One imagines that in every human life is cocooned an ideal form, the ideal beauty of which the human race is capable.... Imagine that we walk through our days on hidden tracks, in cycles round and round, and at fore-ordained moments we are lifted out of the ordinary sphere and allowed momentarily in the eternal "time of the heroes".... In the sacred time of sports, the time of the heroes occasionally breaks through. No one dictates the moment. It comes when it comes.... One experiences a complete immersion in the present, absorption in an instantaneous and abundant now...life in a different mode from that of the life we normally lead in time....[36]

Mahovlich scored as the Soviets, with a one-man advantage, were pressing hard. Paul Henderson would never forget it: "I can still see that goal.... He was one-on-one with the defenceman (Evgeny Poladyev), and when he got to the blue line he faked the slapshot, pulled in the puck and froze the defenceman. Then he just barged through and reached around Tretiak to tuck the puck behind him. It was an absolutely incredible goal. That one put the icing on the cake for us. It was short-handed and put us ahead 3-1."[37]

Yet, the redemptive drama that unfolded in Game Two was only a prelude to the theatre of the absurd that would characterize Games Three and Four. Professional hockey's crude commercialism emerged in full force, beginning with the public squabble about the exclusion of superstar Bobby Hull, who had signed with the Winnipeg Jets of the rival World Hockey Association. The National Hockey League, which supplied most of the roster for Team Canada, refused to let him play despite urgent pleas from Prime Minister Trudeau. The internal team squabbles went public and a few of the highly touted stars found that relative newcomers like Bobby Clarke and J.P. Parise were out-playing them and getting more ice time as a result. Thus a fractious Team Canada was forced to endure the irony of superstar Bobby Hull watching his brother Dennis play in Winnipeg. Game Three was a heart-breaking encounter. The Canadians gave up two leads on brilliant shorthanded goals by the Soviets—scoring while Team Canada had the one-man advantage. Team Canada was thankful to skate away with a 4-4 tie. A feeling of impending doom was intensifying as Game Four loomed in Vancouver.

The ambivalence about Team Canada that was building up across the country is best expressed in theatrical terms: the footlights were definitely down; the spectators were very much part of the action, and they were angry. One of the dimensions of popular culture is the pleasurable opportunity sometimes presented to vent feelings of rage or frustration at an object of disapproval. Sneering at politicians or at inane commercial advertisements on television are classic examples. Oppositionality—having it both ways—is an earmark of the popular. The mass audience treasures its freedom to pick and choose, to mediate between alternatives, to have it both ways.

On 8 September 1972, the Vancouver fans chose revenge. The feverish fourth game in British Columbia saw Team Canada crushed 5-2. Worse, it was a loss Team Canada perhaps made inevitable by drawing two rather silly minor penalties in the first 10 minutes. The "home" part of the series had ended with the Soviets holding a commanding 2-1-1 lead. The final four games were to be played in Moscow. Ken Dryden later related: "It seemed as though it had all slipped beyond us." Then came an unusual chain of events. First, the players, seared by the reaction of the Vancouver fans, steeled their determination and decided to "win it for themselves."[38] Second, what Horace Newcomb has called "the aesthetics of television" began to emerge as a factor in its own right. According to Newcomb, "The central symbol of television is the family...a tightly knit circle." The perennially popular situation-comedy format is television's stock in trade: "The smallness of the television screen has always been its most noticeable physical feature. It means something that the art created for television appears on an object that can be part of one's living room, exist as furniture. It is significant that one can walk around the entire apparatus. Such smallness suits television for intimacy; its presence brings people into the viewer's home to act out drama."[39] Television, claims Newcomb, has a bias for intimacy: "Television is at its best when it offers us faces, reactions, explorations of emotions registered by human beings. The importance is not placed on the action, though that is certainly vital as stimulus. Rather, it is on the reaction to the action, to the human response."[40]

Not action but reaction—an interesting thesis. That wild night in Vancouver did not end with Team Canada's loss. Something else happened. Television beamed the spectacle of a totally believable Phil Esposito—his "sad-eyed, washed-out face, bathed with the sweat of the world," in Dryden's words—speaking "heart to heart" with the Canadian public. Esposito, who had emerged as the unofficial leader of Team Canada, had his moment of personal angst captured in close-up by the camera as waves of frustration convulsed his countrymen. Yet, Esposito treated the audience to what television does so effectively, some would say too effectively: the personalizing and humanizing of a complex, mass spectacle: "To the people of Canada, we're trying our best.... The people boo us. We're all disappointed, disenchanted. I can't believe people are booing us. If the Russians boo their players like some of our Canadian fans—not all, just some—then I'll come back and apologize. We're completely disappointed. I can't believe it. We're

trying hard. Let's face facts. They've got a good team. We're all here because we love Canada. It's our home and that's the only reason we came."[41]

The "intimate" medium was about to transform the 30-odd players of Team Canada into "our guys," an embattled little family up against life's bewildering complexities and letdowns. This was what television had been transmitting and celebrating for decades: the surrogate families of *Star Trek* and *The Beachcombers,* of *A Gift to Last* and *Upstairs, Downstairs.* Audiences identified with the tight little worlds of the Plouffes and the Bunkers, the Kings of Kensington and the Waltons.

If there was intimacy there was also *continuity,* the second of Newcomb's televisual aesthetics. Prime time's dynamics helped make Team Canada as familiar as extended family: Clarke and Cournoyer, Henderson and Ratelle, Esposito and the Mahovlich brothers. Heroes are often found in defeat, as the reputations of Winston Churchill, Charles de Gaulle and John Diefenbaker can attest. The shrill voice of Foster Hewitt crackling across the ether from the grim and dour Soviet capital for the last four games thus deepened the element of participatory drama. In Ken Dryden's words, those scratchy transmissions over the pole came embedded with their own dramatic intensity, "momentous with distance...never certain of getting through."[42]

Canadians watching the telecast of 22 September 1972 from Moscow, by now were involved in something deeper than sport. There was an element of heroic daring in the fact of a middle power contending with the largest national land mass in the world, a nuclear-armed superpower at the time, for hockey supremacy. The dénouement would be played in a capital that had refused to yield before Napoleon and Hitler. Who were the Canadians to think they could redeem themselves in such a place?[43] The very audacity of the attempt seemed heroic. The fight had to be played out to the final seconds, according to the prescribed codes of sport. If this was not Newcomb's "mythic model," then what was?

Team Canada lost their first game in Moscow 5-4. Yet the Canadians "were adjusting, adapting, experimenting...now able to break up the Soviets' intricate passing plays." Thus, Game Six was do-or-die for Team Canada, a spiritual *ne plus ultra*. They chose to "do." Game Six produced the first Canadian victory since that seemingly long-ago night in Toronto. It was noted for something else as well; a particular piece of infamy that starkly reflects hockey's darker side. Canada's Bobby Clarke purposely set out to "tap" and thus sabotage the speedy Russian Kharlamov's ankle. Years later Clarke was only mildly repentant: "It's not something I would've done in an NHL game, at least I hope I wouldn't. But that situation...at that stage in the series, with everything that was happening, it was necessary."[44]

"With everything that was happening"—if there was little grace in Clarke's confession there was admittedly some in his candour. For by now these were obviously more than just hockey games; the whole experience had been lifted beyond sport.[45] The series was pointing to something beyond itself, something primal, something of hockey's own elemental origins. The juvenility and sexism, the Odysseus-like cunning and calculated cruelty—hockey's eternal dark side was always present though somehow counterbalanced by a sense of transcendence. The 3,000 plus fans who flew to Moscow to shout "Da, Da Canada; Nyet, Nyet, Soviet" testified to that. So did Bobby Orr's desire to sit behind the bench as a supporter, his bad knees making it impossible for Sinden to play him. Another quiet piece of heroism could be seen when players of the calibre of Stan Mikita and Rod Seiling waited patiently for ice time that hardly ever came.

All added to the drama. The telecasts revealed more and more of the pride as well as the insecurity welling up from deep inside the psyche of a young nation at a "coming out party" with the whole world watching. "They were Russia. We were Canada," Harry Sinden recalled. The attitude was: "I'm playing for... every Canadian in the world who ever put on skates and thought about being the best in the world, if only in his dreams."[46] The emotional intensity of this electronic drama stunned all the participants. "Some of them [the players] after that series were never the same," Tony Esposito related years later.

After Team Canada pulled together for a 4-3 victory in a wild stick-swinging Game Seven to tie the series, the stage was set for the final resolution, the eighth and final game of the series. "The game was broadcast on both CBC and CTV. All other programming came to a stop. Canada's population in 1972 was 21.8 million. On this Thursday afternoon, a work day, 7.5 million watched."[47] Foster Hewitt had been saying "Hello Canada!" for decades, but it never seemed to resonate with such meaning before. For, in an amazing moment of postmodern reflexivity, it was Foster Hewitt "playing" Foster Hewitt that added to the sense of other-worldliness that last night in Moscow. The aura lingers even today. As a sporting phenomenon that ended in an incredible display of the power of the television aesthetic and of the mythos of sport, the Canada-Soviet series is unique. It carried the freight of multiple, embedded meanings.

The last four games no doubt evoked another shared folk memory. There was the weighted sociological meaning of over four decades of small-town families huddled around the radio as Foster Hewitt's voice came crackling from one of the few big cities in Canada at the time. From the 1930s to the 1960s it was Foster Hewitt who had provided, for millions of Canadian boys, the electronic voice in their heads:

How old were we when we first heard the nasal, rasping voice of Foster Hewitt's "He shoots! He scores!" coming at us over the airwaves? [Foster Hewitt]...convinced me that the world of the imagination was where I wanted to be.... Sitting by the fire having supper or doing the dishes. On the farm. In a tiny fishing village. No other game has been such a force in bringing our country together. A Canadian boy's dreams were nurtured by Foster Hewitt.... To steal a famous baseball announcer's axiom: "Nothing happened until he said so."[48]

On 28 September 1972, 12 million Canadians heard that voice say that they were the best in the world at the game of hockey. It was a unique Canadian epiphany. A Soviet coach commented years later: "We do not have the spirit to draw on that these Canadians do." To him, the Canadian players had "a light that cannot be put out.... You defeat them sometimes, but you discourage them never."[49] What was the source of that light? Was it money and commercialism? Was it the male physicality and exclusiveness? Or perhaps it was something much deeper—the intensification and celebration of a collective myth as enhanced by electronic technology.

The national fervour unleashed across the country was unprecedented in modern, peacetime Canada and beyond. "Muscovites saw them everywhere," the *Toronto Sun* reported on the 3,000 Canadians who had travelled to Moscow, "Walking hand in hand through the Gum department store. Singing Da, Da, Canada—Nyet, Nyet, Soviet; waving their little Canadian flags in the lineup which occasionally stretched for a mile outside Lenin's tomb."[50] Back home, Ontario Education Minister Tom Wells intervened to allow half a million elementary and secondary school students in the province to watch or listen to the final game in school auditoriums or cafeterias. A *Toronto Star* survey "failed to find a single school where students would not get the chance to follow the game."[51] On 29 September, the day after the final victory, the *Globe and Mail* led with

"From Russia With Glory." Colin McCullough's report from the USSR interestingly profiled "The fans who discovered their own nationality in Moscow":

> The games have been splendid of course... [b]ut the series produced more than hockey scores. For one thing, a lot of Canadians discovered their nationality. Had any of them ever before stood up and loudly sung O Canada, even the high notes, with tears running down their cheeks? They did it at the Palace of Sports at Lenin Central Stadium, and it was because of Canada, not hockey.... In the hotels and in the streets, the factory worker from Hamilton felt quite comfortable discussing hockey on the Moscow subway with Seagram's president Edward Bronfman of Montreal or any other available Canadian.[52]

The *Halifax Chronicle-Herald* reported that the federal election campaign of 1972 had "ground to a standstill" for the last act of the drama.[53] Frank Moores, then Premier of Newfoundland, invited all members of the victorious Team Canada to spend a week's holiday hunting and fishing at government expense, while at the other end of the country, British Columbia leader Dave Barrett exulted: "The French couldn't do it [i.e. conquer Moscow], the Germans couldn't do it; now Canada has done it and they had better get out of town before it starts snowing."[54] The *Calgary Herald*, whose front page on 28 September pictured a crowd of Calgarians watching the game in a downtown department store, a scene "undoubtedly repeated in stores, offices and living rooms across the country," recorded how actor William Hutt, declaiming King Lear at Stratford, Ontario, paused dramatically during the storm scene, to announce the score to the 2,000 students in his audience.[55]

Hockey, for all its regrettable "male-only" encodements, its violence and occasional juvenility, serves as a primal source of identity-reinforcement for Canadians. It is rooted in a paradisiacal locus of the imagination, drawing upon the game's rural, northern signifiers. Playing hockey on the ponds that dot the frozen landscape for many appears to be nothing less than a Canadian rite of passage, a vital part of the acculturation process. It began in the backyards and on the rivers, continues in the arenas and indoor stadiums, and injects into the growing-up process something Canadians do that is distinctive, something no one else does with quite the same intensity and devotion: "firewagon hockey."[56]

If the 1972 series was a Canadianized form of the Persian-Greek Wars, and Foster Hewitt—to stretch the metaphor—was our electronically relayed Homer with a microphone, then television served as national theatre. The tiny screen became the locus for "the time of heroes." Television's bias for intimacy helped enshrine one of those rare shared moments of collective national myth, an electronically catalyzed national drama.

In 1972 television superbly transmitted the poetry of hockey, its lyricism and its menace. Paul Henderson's game-winning goal in Game Seven is illustrative. With four Soviet players close around him at the centre line, he somehow scooped up the bouncing puck and pulled away with the Russians in hot pursuit. Moving in

over the Soviet line he had one defenseman draped around him as he began to fall. Incredibly, he was able to squeeze away a shot at the Russian goaltender and beat the Soviet goalie from an almost impossible angle. Finally, he and the Soviet defender slid gracefully out of camera range together, a freeze-framed tribute to the poetry of hockey and of television.

To watch that goal is to see incarnated Novak's sense of northern hardiness wresting narrow victory against the primitive elements of ice and snow, a Canadian *corrida* set against the inhospitability and bleakness of the landscape. A game nurtured amid the eternal mountains, lakes and prairie that make up Canada—scenes of both lyricism and menace—does indeed fulfill Novak's celebration of "hot blood holding out against the cold." Through hockey Canadians characteristically celebrate a delight in speed, skill and gracefulness of form in the face of a bleak and often unforgiving environment.

The 1972 series lives on in the popular imagination. It demonstrated as never before or since that televised hockey, perhaps the most characteristic artifact of Canada's popular culture, points to a desire for something essential about Canadians as a northern people. Winter, with its abstract black and white patterns, its long shadows and desolation, has nurtured—perhaps to their surprise—a nation of myth-makers after all.

Notes

1 C.L.R. James quoted in *Canada Learns to Play: The Emergence of Organized Sport, 1807–1914,* by Alan Metcalfe (Toronto: McClelland and Stewart, 1987), 9.

2 Barbara Righton, "Waking up 'The Spin,'" *TV Times: Vancouver Sun* (February 26, 1993), 2.

3 Donald Macintosh and Donna Greenhorn, "Hockey Diplomacy and Canadian Foreign Policy," *Journal of Canadian Studies,* 28, 2 (Summer, 1993), 96–112. The authors construct the thesis that it was concern for Canada's prestige

on the international level that was a prime springboard for the 1972 series.

4 Barry D. McPherson, James E. Curtis and John W. Loy, *The Social Significance of Sport: Introduction to the Sociology of Sport* (Champaign: Human Kinetics Books, 1989), 21–23. Unfortunately the authors do not expand on that statement.

5 Martin Heidegger, *The Question Concerning Technology* (New York: Harper and Row, Publishers, 1977), 12.

6 Scott Morrison, *The Days Canada Stood Still: Canada vs USSR* (Toronto: McGraw Hill, 1989), 14. Morrison, a sports reporter for the *Toronto Sun,* is President of the Professional Hockey Writers' Association. His book is a valuable resource for the series not the least because of the interviews conducted with the help of his colleague Pat Grier. The interviews amount to as thorough a personal retrospective as we presently have from the principals involved with Team Canada 1972.

7 Ibid., 135.

8 Michael Novak, *The Joy of Sports: End Zones, Bases, Baskets, Balls and Consecration of the American Spirit* (New York: Basic Books, Inc., 1976), xii, 94–96.

9 Ibid.

10 Doug Beardsley, *Country on Ice* (Winlaw: Polestar Press, 1987), 26. Morrison, *The Days Canada Stood Still,* 220. A key organizer of the series, Alan Eagleson, shared his reflections on his reception in Montreal upon arrival from Moscow. He was overwhelmed by excited spectators crowding the train station, and "everyone talking about the series, and all of it in French."

11 Jack Ludwig, *Hockey Night in Moscow* (Toronto: McClelland and Stewart, 1972), 46. Ludwig's engaging and frank account is a valuable reference for anyone studying the 1972 series as a cultural signifier. His string of colourful recollections still have a ring of "having been there" over 20 years later.

12 Paul Rutherford, *When Television Was Young: Prime-Time Canada, 1952–1967* (Toronto: University of Toronto Press, 1990), 242–43. Rutherford is an indispensable source for anyone analyzing television's impact upon Canadians in its early years. He is generally fair and objective, both on the issue of "Canadian content" and on the subject of the medium itself.

13 Ibid., 245.

14 Beardsley, *Country on Ice,* 24–25. Perhaps more attention needs to be paid to the aesthetics of hockey announcing as a cultural form. Hewitt and Gallivan's styles are the best places to start.

15 Rutherford, *When Television Was Young,* 248.

16 Ibid., The loquacious Howie Meeker, another of the game's intense analysts and a television commentator of note, opened up all kinds of possibilities for postmodern students of ideology in a personal interview at Maple Leaf Gardens in November 1991. "Boy, it's rough," Meeker told the writer, "We play it hard. I tell you it's free enterprise.... [It] reflects the countries it's played in...it's a reflection of the free market system."

17 Ludwig, *Hockey Night in Moscow,* 41–42. Of course Ludwig happily provides evidence of this Canadian equation of manliness and hockey in his gripping series of vignettes sprinkled through his account of the 1972 series: Wayne Cashman playing with a serious gash in his tongue; Serge Savard likewise afflicted with a hairline fracture; the 6'8" (on skates) Peter Mahovlich charging over the boards, stick at the ready, to rescue a beleaguered Alan Eagleson in the final game.

18 Ken Dryden and Roy MacGregor, *Home Game: Hockey and Life in Canada* (Toronto: McClelland and Stewart, 1989), 4–5.

19 This seems to apply to many women as well. One thing that surprised me at a University of Toronto graduate seminar on hockey was how all the women accepted hockey's "boy inside the man" mythos as more than compensating for its physicality. "Well, it's a rough game played by rough people," was a common response.

20 Ken Dryden, *The Game: A Thoughtful and Provocative Look at a Life in Hockey* (Toronto: Harper and Collins, 1983), 67–68.

21 Morrison, *The Days Canada Stood Still,* 15.

22 Keith Cunningham, "Myths, Dreams and Movies: Exploring the Archetypal Roots of Cinema," *The Quest: A Quarterly Journal of Philosophy, Science, Religion and the Arts* 5, 1 (Spring 1992), 30. The linkage between film and television, though not absolute, is clear enough for our purposes.

23 Ibid., 33, 35.

24 John Fiske, *Reading the Popular* (London: Unwin Hyman, 1990), 2, 84.

25 Terence Hawkes, *Structuralism and Semiotics* (Berkeley: University of California Press, 1977), 68. Roland Marchand, *Advertising the American Dream: Making Way for Modernity, 1920–1940* (Berkeley: University of California Press, 1985), 235–38, 270, 154–55.

26 John Fiske, *Television Culture* (London: Routledge, 1987), 14.

27 Ken Dryden with Mark Mulvoy, *Face-Off at the Summit* (Toronto: Little, Brown, 1973), 65.

28 CBC television production, "Summit on Ice" (7 October 1992). Earnest testimonials to this deduction were not lacking in this telecast: "It wasn't a game, it wasn't a series," Phil Esposito declaimed to an interviewer, "it was our society against their society." Alan Eagleson, a key organizer, stated: "In those days, the Soviet Union was the...home of Communism, the enemy of democracy." Serge

Savard speculated on what a Canadian defeat would mean: "It was like the...Communist country sending the world a message that our system was better than yours."

29 Horace Newcomb, *TV: The Most Popular Art* (New York: Anchor Press, 1974), 193.

30 Scott Young, *Hello Canada! The Life and Times of Foster Hewitt* (Toronto: Seal Books, 1985), 172.

31 Dryden and MacGregor, *Home Game*, 202. Dryden's summation of the series in Chapter Five has a fine postmodern ring in its title, "No Final Victories."

32 Ibid., 204–5.

33 Ibid.

34 Harry Sinden, *Hockey Showdown: The Canada-Russia Hockey Series* (Toronto: Doubleday, 1972), 8. Morrison, *The Days Canada Stood Still*, 65–66.

35 Ibid., 64–65.

36 Novak, *The Joy of Sports*, 130, 131.

37 Morrison, *The Days Canada Stood Still*, 69.

38 Ibid., 94, 97, 102.

39 Newcomb, *TV: The Most Popular Art*, 261, 245.

40 Ibid., 245–46.

41 Morrison, *The Days Canada Stood Still*, 95.

42 Dryden and MacGregor, *Home Game*, 194.

43 The military analogy was also seized upon by Jack Ludwig, as noted in his comments after the game opener: "Not only had the headlines in the Montreal papers been of a size and blackness one associated with a World War, but the metaphors used in the days that followed were frequently derived from World War I and World War II. Ypres was invoked. Dieppe, Dunkirk." (*Hockey Night in Moscow*, 45.)

44 Morrison, *The Days Canada Stood Still*, 151,167.

45 CBC, "Summit on Ice." By now Team Canada was, in a Cunningham phrase, "out of the body and flying." Yvan Cournoyer considered the experience "Better than ten Stanley Cups." Paul Henderson testified "Almost every day of my life a Canadian will come up to me and shake my hand and say, 'Thank you for one of the greatest thrills of my life.'" Ron Ellis ruminated "Folks alive at the time can remember where they were and what they were doing," while Ken Dryden speculated darkly before the last game on the chances of being "the most hated man in Canada" if his team had lost. The Soviet participants were equally enthralled: "It will never again be the same as it was in '72. The series with Canada was an historic affair," said Boris Mikhailov.

46 Harry Sinden, *Hockey Showdown*, 15.

47 Dryden and MacGregor, *Home Game*, 1940.

48 Beardsley, *Country on Ice*, 19–20.

49 Ibid., 36.

50 Douglas Creighton, "Canadian unity at peak in Moscow," *Toronto Sun*, 30 September 1972, 19.

51 "500,000 in Metro Schools may be watching hockey," *Toronto Star*, 28 September 1972, 2.

52 Colin McCullough, "The fans who discovered their own nationality in Moscow," *Globe and Mail*, 29 September 1972, 1.

53 "Feared winter of discontent: Hockey win helped campaign—Trudeau," *Halifax Chronicle-Herald*, 29 September 1972, 3.

54 "Giant Welcome for Team Canada: They'll return as conquering heroes," *Vancouver Sun*, 29 September 1972, I-2.

55 "Canadians flip as Russians slip—WE'RE THE CHAMPS," *Calgary Herald*, 29 September 1972, 1. The article also mentions how Québec Premier Robert Bourassa telegrammed to Team Canada that "[y]our teamwork and your determination to win has earned you the admiration of Quebeckers and all Canadians."

56 Trevor Brown, a Jamaican-born mathematics professor at York University, attests to hockey's significance for today's youth, and immigrant youth in particular. Brown's son enjoys informal league hockey every Saturday night at Chesswood Arena in northern Toronto. The team includes Vietnamese and Trinidadian immigrants and has at times involved both Jewish and Arabians. "Hockey is far more than a puck and a stick to a youngster living in Canada," says Brown. "It is a ceremony, a ritual, an almost mystical rite.... The playing of the game credentials a boy and makes him an authentic Canadian." (Personal communication, 16 November 1993.)

Post-Modern
Canada

Since 1975 Canada has been shaped by a variety of new and often conflicting forces. Technology has changed employment patterns so much that service jobs, whose importance in the overall scheme of the economy rose throughout the twentieth century, easily outdistanced all other forms of employment. Technological innovations and the globalization of capitalism resulted in the relative decline of industrial jobs, as many industrial assembly jobs were transferred to low-wage countries where workers enjoyed few rights.

Globalization has been accompanied by increasing corporate pressure on governments to make their nations' economies attractive to investors by keeping taxes low, and limiting state regulation of companies' practices, including those that affect the environment. In this economic climate, the welfare state came under attack. Particularly after the collapse of Communism in the former Soviet Union and eastern Europe in the late 1980s and early 1990s, governments of capitalist countries focused on reducing government spending.

Canadians have responded ambivalently to the claims of transnational companies that governments no longer have a major role to play in establishing economic rules. On the one hand, a sense that much government money is misappropriated, along with a sense of being overtaxed, has led to some sympathy for "neo-liberal" politicians who call for limitations on government spending and for more reliance on the private sector to deliver services long offered by governments. On the other, Canadians have been reluctant to part with social programs that were wrenched from governments after decades of popular campaigns to establish them. Those seeking social justice for economically disadvantaged provinces and regions, for labour, for women, and for the poor, as well as environmental groups, have particularly denounced the notion that the nation-state no longer has the same responsibilities or capabilities that it did in the early post-war period.

Gerald Friesen's article examines the emerging critique of the direction of federal policies from "the West." As he observes, the notion of a united western region in Canada is something of a new phenomenon, and one that, examined closely, reveals a number of ambiguities. At one time, notes Friesen, the functional regions of Canada, in political and cultural terms, included two regions west of Ontario, the Prairies and British Columbia. The Prairie economy had been defined, particularly before the Second World War, by its reliance on agricultural exports, while British Columbia's economy centred on its natural resources, including lumber, minerals, and fish, with agriculture also important but on an order of much lower importance than on the Prairies. Since 1945, however, the growth of the oil and gas sector in Alberta and the huge growth in population in that province while the populations of Manitoba and Saskatchewan stagnated, weakened the coherence of the Prairies as a political, economic, and cultural region. But the perception in the four western provinces of continued central Canadian control over the federal government led to the creation of a western bloc in federal politics and to cooperation among the four western premiers in dealing with federal policies. To a large degree, right-wing political parties, dominated by Albertans, have led the charge in the creation of "the West" as an imagined community with political and cultural cohesion.

While regional forces have attempted to mobilize people to think of themselves as having common interests in fighting the federal government, Ottawa has tried in various ways to strengthen individuals' support for a strong federal body with the power to overrule provincial governments in a variety of areas. The Canadian Charter of Rights and Freedoms, reprinted in Part 5, is an important example of federal action of this type. A charter was proposed by Prime Minister Trudeau in 1980 as he presented his government's plans for repatriating the Canadian constitution to the provinces. Several provinces resented the idea of a charter since it represented an intrusion of the federal government into areas of "civil rights and property," which the British North America Act of 1867 had reserved for the provinces.

Public pressures in favour of a charter played a role in convincing nine of the ten provincial premiers to agree to a compromise with Trudeau in late 1981 that paved the way for the incorporation of the Charter of Rights and Freedoms into a repatriated constitution that came into effect the following year. Only Quebec refused to endorse the new constitution, which both major provincial parties felt condoned federal intrusion into areas where Quebec, if not other provinces, had a right to maintain its exclusive jurisdiction.

Notably, the ten people who made the deal to allow for repatriation with a charter were all white men. In the weeks that followed the federal–provincial agreement, lobbies by women and Natives forced the federal and provincial governments to incorporate language that recognized the right of both sexes to equality in Canada, and that promised several constitutional conferences with the objective of enshrining Native rights in the constitution. But both women and First Nations people would find that their constitutional victories were somewhat short-lived. While the Canadian Charter of Rights and Freedoms became a means for using the courts to win some victories, it still left basic patterns of economic exploitation of various groups largely intact. Tania Das Gupta's portrait of the working lives of South Asian women in Canada demonstrates vividly how limited the scope of the rights guaranteed under the Charter often proved in practice. South Asian women were generally relegated, she notes, to the least skilled and most poorly paid jobs in the economy. Regardless of their education, skills, or work performance, they were rarely given opportunities for advancement in the firms where they worked.

The federal and provincial governments appeared to do less to help the disadvantaged in the closing decades of the twentieth century than they had done in the three decades following the Second World War. The post-war consensus had favoured concessions on the part of the capitalist system to ward off the threat of socialism: industry would remain largely under private ownership, but state social programs would redistribute wealth sufficiently to ward off social unrest. By the late seventies, however, with the socialist political threat apparently contained, and state spending soaring, industrial leaders promoted a new ideology: neo-liberalism. They wanted a return, as much as possible, to the "free market" conditions that prevailed before the Second World War. While the state would continue to provide social services, it would have to cut the overall costs of these services and leave more and more people to fend for themselves. Otherwise individuals and industries in Canada would be overtaxed, and unable to compete in the new global marketplace in which, increasingly, national tariffs and quotas were being replaced by free trade among countries. Jim Stanford traces the development of this anti-statist ideology, and the efforts of its proponents to blame "welfare state" spending for the large debts that governments had incurred by 1980. According to Stanford, it was cuts in corporate taxes rather than increased social spending that contributed to the state's shortfall in funds.

In the final reading, Jane Jenson provides an example of a successful coalition of the kind Stanford advocates in the daycare movement in Quebec. She traces their successful efforts to convince the Parti Québécois government in the 1990s to ignore neo-liberal arguments and make a commitment to quality, economical, largely state-funded daycare for all Quebec children.

Defining the Prairies

or, Why the Prairies Don't Exist[1]

Gerald Friesen

In a wonderful lecture on Canadian regionalism delivered in 1980, British Columbia geographer Cole Harris employed the image of a nighttime flight from Atlantic to Pacific to suggest that, seen from above, the country "dissolves into an oceanic darkness spotted by occasional islands of light." And therein lay the metaphor that carried the rest of his talk: "Canada is a composition of islands," an archipelago situated "between an implacable north and the United States."[2] Because the geography of settlement is discontinuous, Canadians have been accustomed to thinking about their country in broad "regional" generalizations—regions being the names they apply "to blocks of country where they do not live." Over the decades, such broad terms as the West, Central Canada, the East, the North, labels that have "only fuzzy locational meaning," crystallized into something more: they became "part of our vocabulary of spatial ambition and resentment."

Harris suggested that the regional labels also conveyed interpretations of community identities. They established, he said, notions about the rhythms and realities of some Canadian community experiences against others. Thus, "in the older settlements of the Maritimes, the rhythms of the land, the traditional ways that earned a living, and the people who lived nearby comprised the context of most experience. Even today, genealogical conversation is a Maritime staple, a reflection of communities whose people have

known each other through the generations." The West, by contrast, Harris argued, is not so rooted in history and in the chronicles of identifiable families. He wrote: "In the West such conversation is rarer for the local texture has been different, having less of custom and the generations and more of movement, technology, markets, and memories of other places."

These observations merit closer analysis. Yes, western family stories remain within the family and do not become community or regional conversations except in carefully edited, community historical volumes. But history has borne heavily upon westerners and *has* shaped community self-perception. Moreover, certain historical images are now a source of confusion because westerners utilize inherited concepts in circumstances where such notions no longer apply. And, as Harris emphasizes, region does play an important role in western Canadians' perceptions of the communities in which they live.

My purpose is, first, to outline the ways in which observers have defined the prairies. Second, it is to argue that our inherited regional folk tales have grown stale. And, third, it is to defend the relevance of region as a means of understanding western Canadians' social identities. Westerners define their community or citizenship identities in terms of their provinces, their cities, and their location as residents of the "West" in national conversation. The prairies, as a folk memory, inform their

---

Gerald Friesen, "Defining the Prairies: or Why the Prairies Don't Exist," in Robert Wardhaugh, ed., *Toward Defining the Prairies: Region, Culture, and History* (Winnipeg: University of Manitoba Press, 2001), 13–28. Reprinted by permission of the publisher.

perception of these alternative identities but nothing more. The prairies have ceased to be a dominant citizenship image.

The notion of "region" bedevils analysis of the prairies. There are three main ways of thinking about it: the formal, the functional, and the imagined.[3] The formal region is built upon land forms and climate. It assumes that there are distinctive portions of the earth's surface that are more or less eternal. The prairies, in this approach, simply look different from the surrounding territories—the environment is distinctive—and life here must be different. The fur trader David Thompson, who first labelled "the great Plains," was proposing a formal region with these words.

The functional region is defined by the purpose of one's analysis. One could speak in terms of buffalo regions, or wheat-raising regions, or a region favourable to the Reform (now Canadian Alliance) Party. It discovers coherent patterns in the spatial distribution of certain defined elements and a larger system in which they are located. The two best-known academic discussions of prairie Canada, the frontier thesis and the staples or Laurentian thesis, posited the existence of functional regions. Each frontier zone was complemented by a settled civilization and each staple-producing territory by a metropolis. The frontier and Laurentian schools also sustained the notion of a formal prairie region because they were built upon several implicit economic assumptions: that the new societies would rely on the raising and export of primary products, especially farm goods; and that the distribution of natural resources was a crucial defining element in human history.

The imagined region is an approach much favoured by students of prairie literature. It asserts that a place must be imagined before it can exist. Though originally associated with environmentalism (and thus with the notion of a formal region), it was elevated to a new level of sophistication by the poet and critic Eli Mandel in the 1970s. In a number of papers, Mandel described the prairie region as a "mental construct...a myth." He found a "certain coherence or unity or identity" in prairie literature, which was rooted in a few specific characteristics. These included a local landscape, a child's view of *first* things, a grotesque storyteller, a regional dialect, and stories of the past. Thus, prairie storytellers projected onto the land their chosen images and, in doing so, created a regional pattern within the broader corpus of world literatures.[4]

These three approaches have been employed to define the prairies during the past two centuries. Each has a part to play in the following discussion.

In pre-Contact Aboriginal societies, a definition of physical space would have been a matter of distinguishing resource zones, the homelands of particular cultural groups, and the band's perception of the trails to heaven. As the ice sheets retreated toward the Arctic, and as glacial Lake Agassiz shrank, Aboriginal peoples moved into the prairies. They established patterns of resource harvesting that reflected the distribution of food according to the season. Scholars have reconstructed these seasonal movements, and proposed the existence of several different annual cycles of movement, including plains-parkland and parkland-forest patterns that probably evolved over a period of several thousand years. By the time Europeans arrived in this territory in the seventeenth and eighteenth centuries, Aboriginal rhythms of movement and patterns of alliance and war were long established.

Did these Aboriginal lands in the northwestern interior of North America—the prairies—constitute a formal, functional, or imagined region? The answer lies in a combination of economy (notably food resources), diplomacy (including trade and defence arrangements but also effective sovereignty), and cultural inheritance (including language but also a collective memory). The presence of several different language groups, diplomatic alliances, and food-harvesting patterns in these lands suggests that the Aboriginal communities did not see the world in terms of a formal prairie region. However, one could describe the territory occupied by bands sharing a culture and language as a functional region—*their* homeland. Several such functional regions existed in the Aboriginal universe. Moreover, one could think of this cultural universe—including the stories of creation and of the natural world—as an imagined region, one in which such depictions were repeated by a number of bands or groups, and were handed down over time. Thus, one could speak of imagined and functional regions in this era but, because of the economic and political complexity of this land and because the cultural universe did not conform to geographic landforms, the prairies did not represent a formal region.

Between the mid-seventeenth and mid-nineteenth centuries, Aboriginal movements and the European fur trade reconstituted society in the northwestern interior. For purposes of company administration, this territory did become a unit. Both Nor'West and Hudson's Bay Company officers would have recognized a map that integrated the forests of the north and the plains of the southern interior. Such a zone encompassed the North and South Saskatchewan river basins and extended as far as Hudson Bay. Its boundaries rested in the west at the Rocky Mountains, in the east at the Petit Nord above Lake Superior, in the north at the Divide between Saskatchewan and Churchill River country, and in the south at the Missouri basin.

During this fur trade era, the Cree-Ojibwa-Assiniboine alliance also served to unite the interior. The chief enemies of the alliance included the Siouan-speaking peoples such as the Dakota southwest of Lake Superior, the Dene-speaking peoples north of the Churchill River, and the shifting group of western enemies of their ally, the Blackfoot, such as the Kootenay. On the east, the boundary was more

difficult to define, largely because of the decimation of Aboriginal populations.

More important for a regional perception than Company administration or Aboriginal diplomacy alone was a new and distinctive pattern of European-Aboriginal relations. This pattern was facilitated by an extended period of peace, a great deal of trade, and large numbers of interracial marriages. Eventually, the signing of treaties during the 1870s ensured that the entire territory would recognize, and respond to, a single type of relation between Aboriginal people and the government of Canada. Though one could argue about the scope and location of what historians now describe as a distinctive "fur trade society," I suggest that it found a clear territorial expression in the northwestern interior.

At the heart of this community was the emergence of the Métis as a new people. As working families, as political actors, as founders of several distinct community ways of life, and as creators of a powerful historical tradition, the Métis reinforced the notion of a prairie region. Not that their sphere was limited to the prairies. There were mixed race people from the Atlantic to the Pacific and from the American states to Russian Alaska. Yet, because of the sinews of fur trade administration, the functional and imagined region found resonance in Métis activities associated with Fort Garry, Fort Ellice, and Fort Edmonton, as well as the Touchwood Hills, Cypress Hills, and Batoche. The songs of Pierre Falcon, the stories told about Paulet Paul, and the writings of Louis Riel established the bounds of this imagined region.

To summarize this era of prairie definition: there were functional and imagined regions in pre-Contact Aboriginal society but they did not coincide with a 49th parallel, Great Lakes-Rockies formal region *or* some narrower Great Plains formal region. During the fur trade era, however, formal and functional regions *did* coincide. One could talk about defining the prairies within their boundaries.

After several hundred years, in which European and Aboriginal communities lived together in the northwestern interior, the "technological arsenal" of the mid-nineteenth century enabled far-sighted politicians to create a new nation. The achievement of Confederation and Canada's subsequent annexation of the vast western and northern reaches of the continent reconstructed regional perceptions and realities.[5] One component of the new nation could be labelled "the prairies."

Why did this region take shape?[6] The staples theorists had a ready answer—wheat. A decade after leading the Confederation movement, Sir John A. Macdonald chose to build a national economy. Having just left the shelter of the Second British Empire (with its navigation, sugar, timber, and corn laws, 1784–1849), and having been rejected by the United States after a brief trial of North American free trade (the Reciprocity Treaty of 1854–1866), Canada would now be shaped by protective tariffs, railway subsidies, and land policy.[7] The centre would carry on the manufacturing while the prairies would produce grain for world markets. For a century thereafter, Canadians would think of nation-building as being synonymous with economy-building.

Political and cultural experience reinforced the economic. The election of third-party members in the federal election of 1921 must be part of the explanation for this sharpened image. But so, too, was the emergence of Winnipeg as a genuine regional metropolis. Similarly, the popularity of prairie novelists such as Ralph Connor, Nellie McClung, Robert Stead, F.P. Grove, Douglas Durkin, and Laura Goodman Salverson, and the presence of important institutions that seemed at the time to have a particular connection with prairie society, such as the North-West Mounted Police, the One Big Union, and the United Church, also established aspects of a regional image. The lines on the map, the circulation of civil servants, and the

slow and painful collective decision to accept English as the dominant language of public discourse all played a part in creating this imagined prairie community.

Proof that formal, functional, and imagined perceptions had coalesced can be found in the writing of prairie history. In 1946, W.L. Morton described the prairie experience as one of the "decisive fields of Canadian historical interpretation." Juxtaposed with French survival and Ontario domination, this third decisive sphere was built upon "the subordination of the West."[8] Morton argued that the then-dominant interpretation of Canadian history, the Laurentian school, would mislead generations of western schoolchildren: "Teaching inspired by the historical experience of metropolitan Canada cannot but deceive, and deceive cruelly, children of the outlying sections. Their experience after school will contradict the instruction of the history class, and develop in them that dichotomy which characterizes all hinterland Canadians, a nationalism cut athwart by a sense of regional injustice."[9] Morton believed that, in the prairie case, this sense of injustice had combined with economic and political and cultural factors to create a distinctive way of life. In his view, an identifiable prairie place was home to distinctive prairie people. Moreover, Morton suggested that western experience provoked a sectional political response: "For Confederation was brought about to increase the wealth of Central Canada, and until that original purpose is altered, and the concentration of wealth and population by national policy in Central Canada ceases, Confederation must remain an instrument of injustice."[10] Therein lay a community identity, Morton implied, as profound as Quebec's French nationalism and Ontario's British nationalism.

Morton argued that the West would have to "work out its own identity in terms of its own historical experience. It must realize its latent nationalism, a nationalism neither racial like the

French nor dominant—a 'garrison' nationality—like that of Ontario, but environmental and, because of the diversity of its people, composite."[11] By understanding regional history, the prairie West could "free itself, and find itself."[12] The seventy-five years between 1867 and the 1930s were sufficient to define a new prairie region. This was a space and society in which formal, functional and imagined territories coincided, thus imprinting upon Canadian consciousness the sense that not just group interests but even individual qualities might be different in this distinctive land.

It is so easy to assume that this prairie region still exists. It is even comforting to think that such continuity distinguishes our community life. The historic resentments of a peripheral community still spring immediately to mind when a slight occurs, as in the case of the federal government's allocation of an aircraft overhaul contract in 1986 or of Prime Minister Chrétien's appointment of an Alberta senator in 1998. But such reflex responses are only that—reflexes conditioned by past experience. Canada has moved on. The prairies, as a defined community, are far less relevant than they were in earlier days.

What has changed? Consider, first, some obvious economic differences. Among these, one of the most striking is the decline in rural population. An entire farm society constructed between the 1880s and the 1920s, which embraced several thousand places anchored by as little as a store or elevator or school, each place carrying a name and a meaning, has disappeared. In its stead, there is a new rural network, one that is changing so rapidly year after year, that the eight per cent of prairie Canadians actually engaged in farm production cannot be certain that their economic role will even exist a decade from now.

This small farm population creates far more wealth, measured by volumes of field crops, and dairy, poultry, and animal production, than its predecessor did. Paradoxically, the story of rural decline and decay must be accompanied by a narrative of export growth and individual wealth. This new agricultural economy is based on larger farm units and a much wider range of products. The fact that the Outstanding Young Farmer award for Manitoba now goes to a couple, not a man, and that the winning family must earn one-third of its household income off the farm, suggests the temper of the times.

The rural story is just one of the economic differences in the modern West. More important in terms of dollars earned and societies reconstructed is the resource sector. Oil and natural gas brought prosperity to Alberta after 1947. Potash, uranium and other mines, hydroelectric dams, and forest enterprises have brought jobs and investment to parts of every western province, not to the same degree as in Alberta, but still with sufficient effect that the passage of fifty years has made the Norths of each province unrecognizable to a pre-1940 resident. This is especially noteworthy for the change it has brought to Aboriginal communities.

Another profound economic difference lies in the cities. Much of the work in a service and knowledge economy occurs in urban areas, so cities have grown in relation to—indeed, at the expense of—the countryside. Anyone could cite the new industries, from Global Television and Palliser Furniture in Manitoba to Ballard Power Systems and MacDonald Dettwiler computer applications in British Columbia.

A picture of the contemporary prairies as functional region is thus fragmented and confusing. It features, simultaneously, rural decline and rural prosperity; it adds to this the uneven development of resource industries; it also adds the rapid expansion of city-based enterprises, each provincial pattern being different from the other. The emergence of rural-urban, north-south, Aboriginal-non-Aboriginal tensions in each province mirrors this economic change. This is not enough to account for the end of old regional habits, perhaps, but it is sufficient to sustain a broader challenge to the prairie notion.

After economic factors, the biggest change in the post-1945 West is due to government. Confederation created provinces and the industrial age created cities. The combination of the two, the province with its governmental apparatus and the metropolitan centre with its social power, established two new territorial or spatial identities for Canadians. As bureaucracies and communications technologies grew in influence, these provincial and urban identities became ever more important in daily life.

Following the decade of depression during the 1930s and a world war in which the federal government took the lead in Canadian life, the province has come into its own.[13] The delivery of health care, the establishment of resource policies, and the management of industrial relations, to name just three immense jurisdictions, illustrate the significance of decisions within the provincial sphere.

The provinces are also responsible for much more activity in social and cultural realms, areas formerly reserved for personal and family supervision. It is obvious that Canadians spend more time in classrooms today than they did in the 1930s. Many of these educational moments, from daycare to college and trades training, are now administered and sponsored by the province. Research and development institutes, whether in medicine or farm machinery or social issues, also rely on provincial support. Peter Lougheed's $300 million fund for health research in Alberta may stand out, but there are sufficient other examples of university-related research to make the case convincing. The provinces are also more powerful forces in the conduct of national politics than they were fifty years ago. And they sponsor cultural and heritage programs, and networks of parks, sites, museums, and galleries that were undreamt of in the interwar decades.

The case that is made for provinces can also be made for cities. City-building strategies in Calgary, Vancouver, and Winnipeg differ one from the other, but each has shaped a cultural and political community. And cities have become powerful magnets, attracting newcomers from rural areas and overseas. Cities have become an aspect of citizens' identities. One need only observe the adaptation of a newcomer, the process by which new loyalties are forged and new patterns of life, including political and cultural views, are tested and adopted.

The alterations in economy and government have been the consequence of local initiatives. A third sphere of change, in culture and communications, has been driven entirely by developments in the wider world that have submerged local societies under a wave that could easily be mistaken for a global cultural consensus. Radio served as the dominant public medium on the prairies, the location of community conversation, between the 1930s and the 1950s. Television has been dominant since then. Both have increased the influence of the great entertainment production capitals of the world and diminished local centres. But within peripheral communities such as Western Canada, both have also reinforced the power of the provincial metropolises. Both have elevated the role of the provincial government and established community conversations that adhere to provincial boundaries and yet seem excessively concerned about the experience of the metropolis. This is why Manitobans outside the capital region speak bitterly about Winnipeg's perimeter vision.

I am arguing that economic, governmental, and cultural forces have combined to elevate the provinces and the largest cities in the identities of individual Canadians. To define the prairies in this new circumstance is to say that the old notion of prairie unity has been eclipsed by three provincial societies and at least five—and probably many more—urban societies. These are both functional and imagined regions. The old formal region, and the vision of a common Winnipeg-to-Rockies identity, has outlived its usefulness.

Alberta can serve as a brief illustration. What is the most profound defining moment of Albertans' relations with the rest of Canada in the last three generations? I suggest it is their response to the National Energy Policy during the 1980s. What would Albertans pick out as the most important public policy decision to affect their lives in the last thirty years? I suggest the so-called Klein Revolution of 1993 to 1997. What do Albertans see as a collective birthright? Lower taxes than other Canadians pay? What is the archetypal story encountered by visitors from other parts? How about the "amazing true inspirational testimonial," told by someone who heard it from someone who knew the person, wherein a former gasfield worker or restaurant employee begins knitting toques or moulding fudge in a basement or garage and, before you can turn around, is worth a million, maybe two?

Alberta is the noisiest province in English-speaking Canada. It is the tempestuous—and slightly smaller—brother or sister who is not going to be hushed, thank you very much. It has money in its pockets and it's going to make its opinions heard. If it loses the money, it's probably your fault. And it will get it back, and more, and you'll probably want some when that happens. Significantly, it will share its good fortune. It is headstrong but generous, and it does care about others in the family. And remember, it will pipe up, uninvited and unrepresentative though its message may be, so take with a grain of salt its claim to represent the entire West.[14] That sounds like a cultural identity, an imagined community distinct from its neighbours, and a functional region, too.

What has happened to the prairies? I am arguing that, in the half-century since 1945, it has broken into three component provinces and at least five major cities, and that these units are far more important than any single prairie entity in contemporary Canadian life.

The final step in my argument is that a different Western region has coalesced during the past few decades. The view that there are two regions between Ontario and the Pacific, the Prairies and British Columbia, should be replaced by a new political reality and cultural perception—a single Lake of the Woods-to-Vancouver Island region. The case for a single West rests upon recent studies in psychology, reading, and opinion formation. It also relies upon popular culture and the media. The purpose of such an analysis is to establish the outlines of a new and distinct functional region, a "political West."

Cole Harris's observation, quoted earlier, suggested that regions were the names applied to blocks of land where one did not live—the Atlantic, the North, Central Canada. It is noteworthy how often "Western Canada" figures in public discussion today. One illustration: Diane Ablonczy, a Reform Member of Parliament, explained to a reporter that "in the West there is a can-do attitude. Instead of seeking help from government, it's 'get the government out of my face, I'll look after things.'"[15] David Bercuson and Barry Cooper, like Tom Flanagan, members of the University of Calgary faculty, refer regularly to "the West" in their columns for the *Globe and Mail*.[16] A featured session at a national Social Science and Humanities conference was entitled "Accommodating the New West" and all the panellists adopted the term without qualification.[17] These illustrations could be multiplied many times.

The image has spread from journalism to youth culture. This is not the old square-dance-and-string-tie image of the Stampede and the farm, but a new version featuring baseball caps and snowboards. One hears now of distinctions between a "west style" and an "Ont style" (for Ontario)—meaning that in the West one encounters greater informality in dress and pastime but, also, a superior, outdoors-and-exercise youth culture. The West has come to be defined by Calgary and Vancouver, by the Mountain Equipment Co-op and Kananaskis and Whistler, by Starbucks and Second Cups.

When these stereotypes of the West arise, is a new community taking shape? There is much overlap and confusion when this question arises, some of it intentional. An opinion always seems stronger if it can plausibly be shown to be shared by thirty per cent of Canadians (the West's proportion of Canada's population for most of the twentieth century). But I believe the strength of such images lies less in some imagined social unity than in an imagined political force. Behind these generalizations about "the West" lies a functional region—a Canadian political region—that is much more important than the community labelled "prairies."

Why should a different region, a new West, have coalesced? Recent research on reading and political communications has relevance. An American study of news and the construction of political meaning argues that citizens employ just a few frames to capture and process information. At the broadest level, some of these frames offer capsule narratives that enable a concerned public to follow the drift of ongoing news stories such as a global economic crisis, a community's descent into war, a complex trial, or the like. Such narratives provide frames that involve economic assessment (as in profit-loss, prosperity-poverty), conflict (as in win-lose), the powerful and the powerless, individual emotion (as in concern for self and others), and morality (doing the right thing). Citizens utilize these frames actively as they filter, sort, and reorganize information.[18]

These frames have been likened to static pictures, on the one hand, and to narrative patterns, on the other, each serving to store knowledge in retrievable form and to organize it efficiently. Add to this research the study of short-term memory and background knowledge (labelled schema, or schemata) that scholars have employed to consider the development of cultural systems.[19] Whatever one thinks about E.D. Hirsch's use of these ideas to promote lists of essential names and dates in grade school education, one can be struck by the convergence of his analysis of reading with discussion in the disciplines of political science and communications about opinion formation.

I take from this research the following rough hypothesis. Canadian citizens cannot be expected to balance the interests and outlooks of thirty million compatriots, a hundred ethnic groups, and political districts, the provinces and territories, in all of their thinking about the evolution of the community. I suggest that they develop schemata or frames to deal with this circumstance. They learn a specialized "national language," a series of constructs that represent the whole. This language evolves slowly but it does evolve. It varies in content from one dominant communication system to another: in England's language, class will matter more, and in the United States, race; in Canada, region matters a great deal.

You might protest that the frames or schemata exist because the social phenomena preceded them. And you might also object that, by concentrating on the words rather than on the economic and social conditions, my approach permits rhetoric to supersede reality. I disagree. I prefer to see merit in recent scholarly work in language and communications that places the cultural (interpreted to mean words, ideas, and performance) on a par with the economic and the technological.

In adapting the recent scholarly discussions of frames and schemata, I am proposing that a cultural and political approach to the contemporary West reveals a significant component of Canadian thought, the functional political region. This is not a formal region based on physical geography. Nor is it, as yet, a fully realized, imagined region. It is certainly not united or homogeneous as a social system. The differences in provincial economies demonstrate that there is not a western economic region, though one might contend that the economic patterns, inevitably associated with the export of primary products, are similar in most of the West. Rather, popular perceptions have established the West as one of the "functional" regions in Canadian political life.

In recent years, the functional region, "the West," is said to be Reform/Canadian Alliance in sympathy. There is a rough justice in this label. Reform Members of Parliament held sixty of the West's eighty-eight seats in the House of Commons after the 1995 election, and sixty-six after the 1999 election. Similarly, we describe the Bloc Québécois faction as representative of Quebec. Our country requires greater subtlety in political thought, but it does indeed operate on these rough simplifications. As a consequence, this part of the country is made to stand for all the right wing or conservative responses to the great issues of the modern world. Affirmative action? The West is made to answer, in unison with the Reform/Alliance Party, as an opponent. Alternative sexualities and the family? The West is said to represent opposition to the new and defence of the traditional. The role of the government in dealing with the market's excesses? The West stands for free enterprise. We may approve of or reject these crude labels, but they do serve a purpose in national politics and they do conform to the majoritarian character of the Canadian political system.

Cole Harris concluded his essay on Canadian regions by emphasizing that the scattered islands of settlement belonged to an archipelago. He insisted that Canadianness had, indeed, crystallized, that the nation had congealed around the political state itself: "But there could be, and was, an accumulating national experience.... A political space has been institutionalized across the archipelago, creating a web of experiences that are part of Canadian life...."[20] One of the entities in that political space, I am suggesting, is the contemporary West.

The shibboleths of prairie loyalties are with us still. But they are disappearing quickly. In September 1998, the Prime Minister appointed a senator to a vacant seat for Alberta during a provincially established campaign to elect senators-in-waiting for just such vacancies. Albertans described his action as a slap in the face for two imagined communities, Alberta and the West. Their responses did not mention the prairies.

There was once, in the days of Aboriginal dominance, a number of imagined and functional regions in the northwestern interior of North America. During the fur trade, all three types of region could have been discerned in the patterns of human action and reflection. After Confederation, another prairie region took shape, this one so firm and influential that W.L. Morton could see it as a complete social order. In recent decades, this prairie region has been replaced by two different levels of community, an Ontario-to-the-Pacific West, and one constructed upon four distinct provinces and numerous metropolitan centres.

This is not an attack on the old prairie stories. All Canadians can enjoy *Jake and the Kid*. But it is important to remember that nostalgia is just that, nostalgia—a sentimental evocation of some period of the past.

Robert Fulford, Toronto journalist, recently wrote a column on his first encounter with a spiky Vancouver magazine, *Geist*. Fulford noted a number of articles that had caught his eye, among them one on prairie hockey. This particular story, "a fantasy by Stephen Smith," concerned "a hockey player who chews on a puck to quiet pre-game nerves while reflecting on the suicide ritual an old player in the West performs when his time is over": "He skates out onto the ice of the big bay until he can skate no more, to wait for the final thaw."[21]

When I first read the account, I was delighted. The story smacked of American tall tales, of an Aboriginal folk memory conveyed in school classrooms, and of the current interest in hockey as an expression of Canadian nationhood. Unfortunately, it also rang a note that I eventually recognized as "soft news from the hinter-lands," the sensation aroused when the national television news leaves the important, fast-break-ing, and globe-shattering issues to feature a human-interest piece about a Saskatchewan town or a Newfoundland storm. What's wrong with that?

There is one great shortcoming in such genuflection to the "outlying regions." If this is all the nation is being told about the realities of today's Manitoba, Saskatchewan, or Atlantic community, the story falls short of the ideal. Neither the news story nor Stephen Smith's pic-ture of the dying hockey player are reaching the important long-term matters of contemporary life in this part of the country. Thus, by smiling fondly on the image of an aging man in hockey pads sliding through the ice and into oblivion, I was letting Fulford and Smith get away with another piece of nostalgia. What is more, the larger structure of feeling, of which it forms a part, evaded the more difficult public issues that confront citizens in peripheral economies. One can't build countries on stories that miss the cuts and bruises of the everyday.

It is time to take stock of a new West. It is time to leave behind the imagined prairie region. The new ways of thinking about this part of the country are the result of changes in the western economy, in the structure of gov-ernment, and especially in the cultural and communication contexts of contemporary life.

Notes

1   This essay is based on my book, *The West: Regional Debate, National Ambitions, Global Age* (Toronto: Viking/Penguin, 1999).

2   Cole Harris, "The Emotional Structure of Canadian Regionalism," lecture delivered at McGill University, printed in *The Walter L. Gordon Lecture Series, 1980–81,* vol. 5, *The Challenges of Canada's Regional Diversity* (Toronto: Canada Studies Foundation, 1981).

3   This section summarizes an argument that appears in "The Prairies as Region: The Contemporary Meaning of an Old Idea," in *River Road: Essays on Manitoba and Prairie History* (Winnipeg: University of Manitoba Press, 1996).

4   Eli Mandel, "Images of Prairie Man," in *A Region of the Mind: Interpreting the Western Canadian Plains,* ed. Richard Allen (Regina: Canadian Plains Research Centre/University of Regina, 1973), 203; and Mandel, "Romance and Idealism in Western Canadian Fiction," in *Prairie Perspectives 2: Selected Papers of the Western Canadian Studies Conference, 1970, 1971,* eds. Anthony W. Rasporich and Henry C. Klassen (Toronto: Holt, Rinehart and Winston, Canada, 1973).

5   It also separated European from Aboriginal, thereby introducing the segregation in historical interpreta-tion that is only in recent decades being transcended.

6   I agree wholeheartedly with Cole Harris's view (out-lined in the article on regionalism cited above) of the creation of Canada. This approach asserts that the Industrial Revolution, read broadly to include such globe-changing innovations as steam trans-port, telegraphy, and commodities futures markets, made Canada possible. Harris wrote: "To say that Canadian Confederation requires this technological arsenal is to understate the case. Confederation became conceivable within an industrial technology and, in good part, is one of its by-products." This is, I suggest, why V.C. Fowke included the Confederation pact itself as one of the original "national policies." This view asserts too that changes in the technology of communication underlie the evolution of regional perceptions. (V.C. Fowke, "The National Policy—Old and New," *Canadian Journal of Economics and Political Science* 18, no. 3 [August 1952]: 271–86.)

7   These included some matters of great importance to the prairies, notably railway freight rates, immigra-tion and homestead policy, western surveys, and western policing arrangements. This national framework was extended in later decades to include grain handling, grain marketing, industrial rela-tions, and other important economic institutions.

8   W.L. Morton, "Clio in Canada: The Interpretation of Canadian History," in *Contexts of Canada's Past:*

Selected Essays of W.L. Morton, ed. A.B. McKillop (Toronto: Macmillan, 1980), 105. The essay was first published in 1946. Morton explained that the Atlantic and Pacific provinces had their own importance but were not central to the story that concerned him because they had "destinies alternative to that of incorporation in Canada" whereas, without the other three, "there could have been, in the larger sense of the name, no Canada." All that was on offer in historical interpretations at the time, Morton implied, was the economic determinism of Laurentian scholars who placed metropolitan centres in positions of control and the West in a position of inferiority. This flawed interpretation, as he saw it, drew upon imperial political assumptions: "the historical interpretation follows the pattern of commercial imperialism it undertakes to trace." What was even worse, however, was that the Laurentian interpretation assumed not just metropolitan economic power and political imperialism but "uniformity of the metropolitan culture throughout the hinterlands."

9 Ibid., 108.

10 Ibid., 108.

11 Ibid., 110.

12 Morton held out the hope that Ontario's control might be ended, that Canada's subordinate regions might win equality, and that Lord Acton's prescription for a great nation might become the principle for Canada: "No power can so efficiently resist the tendencies of centralization, of corruption, and of absolutism, as that community which is the vastest that can be included in a State, which imposes on its members a consistent similarity of character, interest, and opinion, and which arrests the action of the sovereign by the influence of a divided patriotism." (Acton, *The History of Freedom and other Essays* [London 1907], cited in "Clio," 111.) Significantly, the prairie region was one of the sources of a "divided patriotism" in Canada. Prairie Canada did not find a comfortable home within the mythology of the newly constructed nation. Though the dominant peoples tried alternative definitions of the country, foremost among which was northernness, none was sufficiently inclusive to be convincing. As Cole Harris concluded: "The fact was that a satisfying national definition would not be found. If some islands could be defined easily enough, the archipelago could not. Definitions that satisfied here, grated there...." (Harris, "Emotional Structure")

13 Legally equal to Ottawa after the Judicial Committee rulings of the late nineteenth century, the provinces have actually become moulders of economic activity and even of cultural expression. This came about in part because of their resource income, but also because their constitutional responsibilities and even their political systems made them increasingly central in public life.

14 For an illustration of the interpretation that the economic downturn of the 1980s was the fault of outsiders, see "Albertans blame NEP for their economic woes," in *Globe and Mail,* 2 June 1987, B6.

15 Peter O'Neil, "Reform MP rejects traditional stereotype," in *Vancouver Sun,* 18 July 1998, B4.

16 David Bercuson and Barry Cooper, "Envoi: how the West was awakened," in *Globe and Mail,* 19 September 1998, D2.

17 The panellists at the University of Ottawa meeting in June 1998 were Doug Owram (University of Alberta), Tom Flanagan (University of Calgary), Gordon Gibson (Vancouver journalist), and Nick Taylor (Alberta senator).

18 W. Russell Newman, Marion R. Just, and Ann N. Crigler, *Common Knowledge: News and the Construction of Political Meaning* (Chicago: University of Chicago Press, 1992); a different approach is described in William L. Miller, Annis May Timpson, and Michael Lessnoff, *Political Culture in Contemporary Britain: People and Politicians, Principles and Practice* (Oxford: Clarendon Press, 1997).

19 "A schema functions as a unified system of background relationships whose visible parts stand for the rest of the schema. Because our narrow windows of attention confine us to just a few elements at a time, the technique of using surface elements to stand for larger wholes is an essential feature of our mental life. Schemata are our necessary instruments for making the surfaces of what we read connect significantly with the background knowledge that is withheld from immediate consciousness by the limits of short-term memory." (From E.D. Hirsch Jr., *Cultural Literacy: What Every American Needs to Know* [New York: Random House, 1988], 54–55.)

20 Harris, "Emotional Structure."

21 Robert Fulford, "*Geist* defies convention in its renderings of mundane culture," in *Globe and Mail,* 29 July 1998, A1.

Canadian Charter of Rights and Freedoms

Whereas Canada is founded upon principles that recognize the supremacy of God and the rule of law:

GUARANTEE OF RIGHTS AND FREEDOMS

Rights and freedoms in Canada

1. The *Canadian Charter of Rights and Freedoms* guarantees the rights and freedoms set out in it subject only to such reasonable limits prescribed by law as can be demonstrably justified in a free and democratic society.

FUNDAMENTAL FREEDOMS

Fundamental freedoms

2. Everyone has the following fundamental freedoms:

(a) freedom of conscience and religion;

(b) freedom of thought, belief, opinion and expression, including freedom of the press and other media of communication;

(c) freedom of peaceful assembly; and

(d) freedom of association.

DEMOCRATIC RIGHTS

Democratic rights of citizens

3. Every citizen of Canada has the right to vote in an election of members of the House of Commons or of a legislative assembly and to be qualified for membership therein.

Maximum duration of legislative bodies

4. (1) No House of Commons and no legislative assembly shall continue for longer than five years from the date fixed for the return of the writs of a general election of its members.

Continuation in special circumstances

(2) In time of real or apprehended war, invasion or insurrection, a House of Commons may be continued by Parliament and a legislative assembly may be continued by the legislature beyond five years if such continuation is not opposed by the votes of more than one-third of the members of the House of Commons or the legislative assembly, as the case may be.

Canadian Charter of Rights and Freedoms, Part I of the Constitution Act, 1982, being Schedule B to the Canada Act 1982 (U.K.), 1982, c. 11.

Annual sitting of legislative bodies	**5.** There shall be a sitting of Parliament and of each legislature at least once every twelve months.

MOBILITY RIGHTS

Mobility of citizens	**6.** (1) Every citizen of Canada has the right to enter, remain in and leave Canada.
Rights to move and gain livelihood	(2) Every citizen of Canada and every person who has the status of a permanent resident of Canada has the right

    (a) to move to and take up residence in any province; and

    (b) to pursue the gaining of a livelihood in any province.

Limitation	(3) The rights specified in subsection (2) are subject to

    (a) any laws or practices of general application in force in a province other than those that discriminate among persons primarily on the basis of province of present or previous residence; and

    (b) any laws providing for reasonable residency requirements as a qualification for the receipt of publicly provided social services.

Affirmative action programs	(4) Subsections (2) and (3) do not preclude any law, program or activity that has as its object the amelioration in a province of conditions of individuals in that province who are socially or economically disadvantaged if the rate of employment in that province is below the rate of employment in Canada.

LEGAL RIGHTS

Life, liberty and security of person	**7.** Everyone has the right to life, liberty and security of the person and the right not to be deprived thereof except in accordance with the principles of fundamental justice.
Search or seizure	**8.** Everyone has the right to be secure against unreasonable search or seizure.
Detention or imprisonment	**9.** Everyone has the right not to be arbitrarily detained or imprisoned.
Arrest or detention	**10.** Everyone has the right on arrest or detention

    (a) to be informed promptly of the reasons therefor;

    (b) to retain and instruct counsel without delay and to be informed of that right; and

    (c) to have the validity of the detention determined by way of *habeas corpus* and to be released if the detention is not lawful.

Proceedings in criminal and penal matters	**11.** Any person charged with an offence has the right

    (a) to be informed without unreasonable delay of the specific offence;

(b) to be tried within a reasonable time;

(c) not to be compelled to be a witness in proceedings against that person in respect of the offence;

(d) to be presumed innocent until proven guilty according to law in a fair and public hearing by an independent and impartial tribunal;

(e) not to be denied reasonable bail without just cause;

(f) except in the case of an offence under military law tried before a military tribunal, to the benefit of trial by jury where the maximum punishment for the offence is imprisonment for five years or a more severe punishment;

(g) not to be found guilty on account of any act or omission unless, at the time of the act or omission, it constituted an offence under Canadian or international law or was criminal according to the general principles of law recognized by the community of nations;

(h) if finally acquitted of the offence, not to be tried for it again and, if finally found guilty and punished for the offence, not to be tried or punished for it again; and

(i) if found guilty of the offence and if the punishment for the offence has been varied between the time of commission and the time of sentencing, to the benefit of the lesser punishment.

Treatment or punishment **12.** Everyone has the right not to be subjected to any cruel and unusual treatment or punishment.

Self-crimination **13.** A witness who testifies in any proceedings has the right not to have any incriminating evidence so given used to incriminate that witness in any other proceedings, except in a prosecution for perjury or for the giving of contradictory evidence.

Interpreter **14.** A party or witness in any proceedings who does not understand or speak the language in which the proceedings are conducted or who is deaf has the right to the assistance of an interpreter.

EQUALITY RIGHTS

Equality before and under law and equal protection and benefit of law **15.** (1) Every individual is equal before and under the law and has the right to the equal protection and equal benefit of the law without discrimination and, in particular, without discrimination based on race, national or ethnic origin, colour, religion, sex, age or mental or physical disability.

Affirmative action programs (2) Subsection (1) does not preclude any law, program or activity that has as its object the amelioration of conditions of disadvantaged individuals or groups including those that are disadvantaged because of race, national or ethnic origin, colour, religion, sex, age or mental or physical disability.

Official languages of Canada	**16.** (1)	English and French are the official languages of Canada and have equality of status and equal rights and privileges as to their use in all institutions of the Parliament and government of Canada.
Official languages of New Brunswick	(2)	English and French are the official languages of New Brunswick and have equality of status and equal rights and privileges as to their use in all institutions of the legislature and government of New Brunswick.
Advancement of status and use	(3)	Nothing in this Charter limits the authority of Parliament or a legislature to advance the equality of status or use of English and French.
English and French linguistic communities in New Brunswick	**16.1.**(1)	The English linguistic community and the French linguistic community in New Brunswick have equality of status and equal rights and privileges, including the right to distinct educational institutions and such distinct cultural institutions as are necessary for the preservation and promotion of those communities.
Role of the legislature and government of New Brunswick	(2)	The role of the legislature and government of New Brunswick to preserve and promote the status, rights and privileges referred to in subsection (1) is affirmed.
Proceedings of Parliament	**17.** (1)	Everyone has the right to use English or French in any debates and other proceedings of Parliament.
Proceedings of New Brunswick legislature	(2)	Everyone has the right to use English or French in any debates and other proceedings of the legislature of New Brunswick.
Parliamentary statutes and records	**18.** (1)	The statutes, records and journals of Parliament shall be printed and published in English and French and both language versions are equally authoritative.
New Brunswick statutes and records	(2)	The statutes, records and journals of the legislature of New Brunswick shall be printed and published in English and French and both language versions are equally authoritative.
Proceedings in courts established by Parliament	**19.** (1)	Either English or French may be used by any person in, or in any pleading in or process issuing from, any court established by Parliament.
Proceedings in New Brunswick courts	(2)	Either English or French may be used by any person in, or in any pleading in or process issuing from, any court of New Brunswick.
Communications by public with federal institutions	**20.** (1)	Any member of the public in Canada has the right to communicate with, and to receive available services from, any head or central office of an institution of the Parliament or government of Canada in English or French, and has the same right with respect to any other office of any such institution where

(a) there is a significant demand for communications with and services from that office in such language; or

(b) due to the nature of the office, it is reasonable that communications with and services from that office be available in both English and French.

Communications by public with New Brunswick institutions

(2) Any member of the public in New Brunswick has the right to communicate with, and to receive available services from, any office of an institution of the legislature or government of New Brunswick in English or French.

Continuation of existing constitutional provisions

21. Nothing in sections 16 to 20 abrogates or derogates from any right, privilege or obligation with respect to the English and French languages, or either of them, that exists or is continued by virtue of any other provision of the Constitution of Canada.

Rights and privileges preserved

22. Nothing in sections 16 to 20 abrogates or derogates from any legal or customary right or privilege acquired or enjoyed either before or after the coming into force of this Charter with respect to any language that is not English or French.

MINORITY LANGUAGE EDUCATIONAL RIGHTS

Language of instruction

23. (1) Citizens of Canada

(a) whose first language learned and still understood is that of the English or French linguistic minority population of the province in which they reside, or

(b) who have received their primary school instruction in Canada in English or French and reside in a province where the language in which they received that instruction is the language of the English or French linguistic minority population of the province, have the right to have their children receive primary and secondary school instruction in that language in that province.

Continuity of language instruction

(2) Citizens of Canada of whom any child has received or is receiving primary or secondary school instruction in English or French in Canada, have the right to have all their children receive primary and secondary school instruction in the same language.

Application where numbers warrant

(3) The right of citizens of Canada under subsections (1) and (2) to have their children receive primary and secondary school instruction in the language of the English or French linguistic minority population of a province

(a) applies wherever in the province the number of children of citizens who have such a right is sufficient to warrant the provision to them out of public funds of minority language instruction; and

(b) includes, where the number of those children so warrants, the right to have them receive that instruction in minority language educational facilities provided out of public funds.

ENFORCEMENT

Enforcement of guaranteed rights and freedoms

24. (1) Anyone whose rights or freedoms, as guaranteed by this Charter, have been infringed or denied may apply to a court of competent jurisdiction to obtain such remedy as the court considers appropriate and just in the circumstances.

Exclusion of evidence bringing administration of justice into disrepute

(2) Where, in proceedings under subsection (1), a court concludes that evidence was obtained in a manner that infringed or denied any rights or freedoms guaranteed by this Charter, the evidence shall be excluded if it is established that, having regard to all the circumstances, the admission of it in the proceedings would bring the administration of justice into disrepute.

GENERAL

Aboriginal rights and freedoms not affected by Charter

25. The guarantee in this Charter of certain rights and freedoms shall not be construed so as to abrogate or derogate from any aboriginal, treaty or other rights or freedoms that pertain to the aboriginal peoples of Canada including

(a) any rights or freedoms that have been recognized by the Royal Proclamation of October 7, 1763; and

(b) any rights or freedoms that now exist by way of land claims agreements or may be so acquired.

Other rights and freedoms not affected by Charter

26. The guarantee in this Charter of certain rights and freedoms shall not be construed as denying the existence of any other rights or freedoms that exist in Canada.

Multicultural heritage

27. This Charter shall be interpreted in a manner consistent with the preservation and enhancement of the multicultural heritage of Canadians.

Rights guaranteed equally to both sexes

28. Notwithstanding anything in this Charter, the rights and freedoms referred to in it are guaranteed equally to male and female persons.

Rights respecting certain schools preserved

29. Nothing in this Charter abrogates or derogates from any rights or privileges guaranteed by or under the Constitution of Canada in respect of denominational, separate or dissentient schools.

Application to territories and territorial authorities

30. A reference in this Charter to a Province or to the legislative assembly or legislature of a province shall be deemed to include a reference to the Yukon Territory and the Northwest Territories, or to the appropriate legislative authority thereof, as the case may be.

Legislative powers not extended **31.** Nothing in this Charter extends the legislative powers of any body or authority.

APPLICATION OF CHARTER

Application of Charter **32.** (1) This Charter applies

    (a) to the Parliament and government of Canada in respect of all matters within the authority of Parliament including all matters relating to the Yukon Territory and Northwest Territories; and

    (b) to the legislature and government of each province in respect of all matters within the authority of the legislature of each province.

Exception (2) Notwithstanding subsection (1), section 15 shall not have effect until three years after this section comes into force.

Exception where express declaration **33.** (1) Parliament or the legislature of a province may expressly declare in an Act of Parliament or of the legislature, as the case may be, that the Act or a provision thereof shall operate notwithstanding a provision included in section 2 or sections 7 to 15 of this Charter.

Operation of exception (2) An Act or a provision of an Act in respect of which a declaration made under this section is in effect shall have such operation as it would have but for the provision of this Charter referred to in the declaration.

Five year limitation (3) A declaration made under subsection (1) shall cease to have effect five years after it comes into force or on such earlier date as may be specified in the declaration.

Re-enactment (4) Parliament or the legislature of a province may re-enact a declaration made under subsection (1).

Five year limitation (5) Subsection (3) applies in respect of a re-enactment made under subsection (4).

CITATION

Citation **34.** This Part may be cited as the *Canadian Charter of Rights and Freedoms*.

Political Economy of Gender, Race, and Class

Looking at South Asian Immigrant Women in Canada

Tania Das Gupta

Introduction

In this article, theoretical discussion will be conducted about the linkages between the variables of class, race, and gender as they operate within the immigrant communities of South Asian women, focusing on Toronto and Vancouver where the population is concentrated. The term "South Asian" refers to women whose origins lie in India, Pakistan, Bangladesh, Sri Lanka and Nepal. Although immigrants from these countries have varied histories, particularly in Canada, their commonalities as women coming from the same region in Asia far outweigh their differences.

This article is by no means exhaustive in terms of theoretical development or field research in the area. It is more a review of available literature on South Asian immigrant women, as well as a linking of the author's experiences in the community in Toronto and its relation to theoretical understandings of concepts such as race, gender and class. This article is a point of departure for future research rather than a final destination point.

Migration History

Before 1920, South Asian women were absent from the Canadian scene, even though their male counterparts have been here since 1904 in small numbers. Thus, early South Asian communities were basically "bachelor societies," although many of the men were married and had left their wives (and children) back in India. Of course, this was not totally by choice, but partially by coercion, enforced by racist and sexist immigration policies.

In order to have economic development, one of the major ingredients is labor power, since only it can produce surplus (Clement, 1988:163). Historically, Canada has been a resource-rich and labor poor country. Therefore, it became crucial for its development to import labor—in selected amounts and varieties. In the beginning of the twentieth century there was an emergence of an Immigration Act. This marked the intervention of the Canadian state in the capitalist production process by regulating labor supply, by regulating markets and by using its coercive forces during strikes.

Tania Das Gupta, "Political Economy of Gender, Race and Class: Looking at South Asian Immigrant Women in Canada," *Canadian Ethnic Studies/Etudes ethniques au Canada* 26, 1 (1994): 59–73.

What is fascinating is that even though those in power were fundamentally motivated by the need for labor power, this desire was satisfied very selectively. There was no open floodgate as such, at least for all countries of the world. Immigration remained restricted to white European and American male populations, even further restricted to northern and western Europe. These restrictions were based on race and gender ideologies, justifying the domination and indeed exclusion of people of color, particularly women. In so doing, the state was able to retain a synthesis between the industrialists' need for labor and the general climate of racism and sexism.

Initially, Indian ex-army officials from the Far East were encouraged to come to Canada by steamship companies, which had been losing revenues, and by B.C. businessmen, who needed an alternate form of cheap labor when a $500 headtax effectively barred the entry of Chinese immigrants (Law Union of Ontario, 1981). No women and children came with the early batch from the Far East because they had no intention of settling outside India permanently. Later on, South Asian immigrants mainly consisted of Sikh peasant men from Punjab.

As the number of South Asians increased from 45 in 1904–05 to 2,623 in 1907–08 (Buchignani & Indra, 1985:7) B.C. society, including its government, unions and people at large, began to be alarmed as it had been in the case of Chinese and Japanese immigrants. Discriminatory restrictions were imposed in order to halt their entry and to restrict their rights. They were denied the right to vote by April 1, 1907. By June 8, 1908, South Asians could land in Canadian (B.C.) ports only by "continuous journey" and they also had to possess $200 each. Moreover, the government persuaded the Canadian Pacific Railway (CPR) not to accept South Asians as passengers from Hong Kong and to stop issuing tickets to them (Law Union of Ontario, 1981).

These rules effectively blocked off further South Asian entry into Canada, including the exclusion of wives and children of those who were already in Canada. Probably the first South Asian women and children entered as family members of Teja Singh, a popular community leader who entered Canada from the U.S. where he had been a visitor and a lecturer (Buchignani & Indra, 1985:26). Despite support from some individuals (e.g. some clergymen), the immigration of South Asian women was decried by Canadians in general, including some white women's groups (e.g. the National Council of Women), for fear of encouraging the permanent settlement of South Asians (Doman, 1984:101).

It is interesting to note that in these early years, the banning of wives and children of South Asian immigrants from reunion with their menfolk provoked the most intense anger and fuel for political organizing in B.C.'s South Asian community. The men realized that without women and children, their community would remain temporary, lacking in stability and stripped of political and social rights in Canada. In this, there was a realization of the reproductive and maintenance role of women in society, which is the essence of gender ideology as it exists today. Women with their child-bearing and child-rearing functions are essential for the generation and daily regeneration of labor power.

Lobbying against immigration restrictions included such actions as sending delegations, signing petitions and writing in community publications as well as holding militant rallies to attract the local press. Despite the fact that there were some individuals within the government who wanted to relax restrictions on the wives and children of South Asian immigrants in Canada, this was not enough to remove the discriminatory bar (Buchignani & Indra, 1985:40).

Nevertheless, in 1912, Balwant Singh and Bhag Singh were able to bring their wives and children. Initially, women and children were refused passage from Calcutta, Rangoon and

Hong Kong due to the "continuous journey" stipulation in effect at the time. When they reached British Columbia, the two men landed but the women and children were first deported, then later released on $2,000 bail. Both Bhag and Balwant Singh were well-known community leaders and priests at the local temple. Authorities wanted to avoid a political crisis in the South Asian community. The Canadian state played its role here of maintaining status quo. Subsequently, the few women and children who entered were negligible in numbers and they did so as a result of pressures from the South Asian community. However, the law remained unchanged (Buchignani & Indra, 1985:42).

It was not until 1919 that women and young children could enter Canada, after an agreement was reached following repeated pressure by British colonial officials at the Imperial War Conferences between 1917–19 (Buchignani & Indra, 1985:66). The British were motivated by a desire to ease conditions in India, partially by migration of Indians out of the country. Nevertheless, even after the ban was removed, few women and children migrated because of formal requirements to be registered as "legitimate" wives and children in India and the lack of any registration procedures until 1924. Between 1921 and 1923, only 11 women and 9 children entered (Doman, 1984:102). Between 1920 and 1930, 144 adult women and 188 children entered Canada (Buchignani, 1985:73). All these women were married to South Asian immigrants in Canada. Older children could not migrate to reunite with their parents.

In the early 1930's, illegal immigration of South Asian men increased in order to beat the discriminatory ban, for example by smuggling men across the U.S.-Canada border or applying for Canadian immigration using false registration documents. The government reacted by denying immigration to the wives and children of such immigrants, a ban which was removed only in 1947 when India achieved independence from British rule (Buchignani & Indra, 1985:105).

In 1951, pressured by the newly independent Indian government and facilitated by diplomatic relations between India and Canada, a policy of immigration quotas was established for countries of South Asia (i.e., 150 Indians, 100 Pakistanis and 50 Sri Lankans per year). These immigrants could later sponsor their wives and young unmarried children under 21. In 1957, the quota from India was raised to 300 a year. Soon afterwards, mothers over 60 and fathers over 65 could be sponsored as well. The South Asian community, which was becoming more heterogeneous in its cultural and religious origins, was also starting to spread out of British Columbia. By the end of 1961, 2,338 immigrant visas had been issued and 2,000 had come to Canada as their dependents (Buchignani & Indra, 1985:106). One can assume that the latter figure included women, young children and elderly parents.

The restricted quota system was removed only in 1967, when the points system emphasizing the skill and educational qualification of applicants was brought in (Green, 1976:17). This replaced the earlier racially motivated immigration policies. With this new emphasis, the immigration of professional South Asians to Canada increased, changing the size and character of the entire community.

Behind the removal of the racial criteria for immigration lay the needs of the post-1960's capitalist economy in Canada. The labor process had become more mechanized, thus displacing unskilled workers. There was a rising need for managerial, technical and clerical workers. Since workers from the "preferred" countries were not interested in coming to Canada as much as they had been earlier due to demographic changes in Europe, Canada had to attract labor from non-traditional sources.

Just as in the 1920's and 1930's, the majority of South Asian women in Canada today entered as wives, mothers and daughters of South Asian men (i.e. as sponsored immigrants). This is fairly typical of most immigrant women, who find it virtually impossible to apply and be accepted as independent immigrants, given the criteria used to assess applicants under the Points System. Such criteria as education, employability in "open occupations," and knowledge of English/French and other similar factors render ineligible most immigrant women, particularly from the working classes and from the so-called Third World countries.

The only other way that women have been able to enter Canada has been through various domestic worker programs (e.g. the Foreign Domestic Movement (FDM) and the Live-in Caregiver Program) or the seasonal farm labor programs, which are special government programs to import low-cost contract labor for specific occupations and for specified periods of time. The Points System is an example of systemic racism and sexism since it adversely affects women of color who apply for immigration into Canada.

The post-1970's slump in the economy again resulted in restrictions of immigration and the scapegoating of immigrants of color for contributing to unemployment, reminiscent of events in British Columbia in earlier years. In 1982, a "Canadians First" program was unveiled (*Toronto Star*, May 1, 1982) which resulted in lowering immigration except for those with "essential skills" designated by the government and for those bringing in capital for investment. This orientation continues to the present time.

By reflecting on the immigration history of South Asians in Canada, we see the state interfering in a very direct way with the capitalist production process. This was done by regulating the labor supply, specifically one which could be super-exploited and kept passive by the denial of political and legal rights rationalized by racist arguments.

FAMILY ORGANIZATION

As can be surmised by the preceding section, the South Asian family structure in Canada has been severely distorted by the direct intervention of the state through its immigration policies. Prior to 1920, the community was predominantly male. Despite this, village and kin relations from the Punjab were utilized and strengthened to establish "family-like" linkages and structures facilitated by the long voyage by ship, usually below deck, away from other passengers in miserably crowded conditions. The men cooked, ate, and developed friendships with each other through the journey, living communally. This pattern continued once they landed and were allowed into Canada. Four to twelve men would live together in a household, creating some semblance of an extended family structure based on the Indian norm (Buchignani & Indra,1985:33). They pooled their money for the necessities of life and shared household duties. It was apparently common for an unemployed member to do the cooking. In this set-up the sick and the unemployed were well-looked after, to the point that these early immigrants developed a reputation of being financially independent and self-sufficient. Living collectively also allowed them to save money in the long run despite the low wages they earned. One wonders if in these early male family units there were power differentials between those who did the wage labor and the ones who did the cooking and the housework. If gender ideology was operative in these contexts, then we could hypothesize that there would indeed be inequalities among the men based on who was doing the waged work and who was doing the domestic work.

When women started coming in small numbers to join their husbands, they lived mainly within the home, occupying themselves with housework, child care and cooking. Their personal relations with women from other Indian households continued the extended family organization they had been familiar with in India, although the British Columbia families were nuclear in themselves. Doman writes that "community life was closely structured to resemble village life in India" (Doman, 1984:102). There was no direct contact of these women with non-Indians. Therefore, there was no need to learn English. Interestingly enough, they adapted to their new environment in other ways, for example, in their dress and in their methods of food preparation. The lack of contact with the larger society, as well as the absence of real extended families and friends, produced considerable social isolation. Annual religious celebrations which were organized with great fanfare became the only recreational activity for many of these women.

Children growing up in this environment faced a dual culture as in the case of most immigrant families. They were encouraged to learn English and adapt to Canadian institutions; however, they were also expected to retain many of their indigenous cultural values and traditions. For instance, the youth who grew up in Canada were still expected to adhere to the arranged marriage system, facilitated by relatives in India. Future marriage partners were selected by family members. Marriages would take place in India and then spouses would be brought back to Canada to settle (Buchignani & Indra, 1985:160).

Men who did not have their wives or other close family members with them continued to live collectively with other male friends. As before, they shared in household tasks. The community continued to be marked by its solidarity and mutual assistance, especially during economically difficult times such as the Depression of the 1930's.

From this author's observation of the South Asian community in Toronto over the last twenty years, it is apparent that the family has developed as a hybrid form, somewhere in-between an extended or joint family and a nuclear family,

where women are primarily responsible for child care and housework. When a family sponsors an elderly parent-in-law, sister or brother, the newly arrived immigrant invariably lives with her/his sponsor until the acquisition of a decent job and some degree of financial independence. In the case of elderly parents, often they never move out because it is expected that their children will look after them. Settled immigrants also extend similar support to close friends and distant relatives from their own village or town.

The burden of housework is made heavier for women by the frequency of such joint family situations. All the chores of housework multiply, particularly in light of the lack of assistance from men. In such situations, women are collectively responsible for domestic tasks. While women may derive some support from female camaraderie, life can also be made more difficult if a woman does not get along with her female relatives. South Asian families are also marked by hierarchies of sex and age, where the elder male and female hold decision-making power. Thus, younger women in the household are usually subordinated not only to males, but also to older females. Similar findings in Britain among South Asian families confirm this reality (Westwood and Hoffman, 1979:27).

Arranged marriages, or some form of it, are still prevalent among South Asian immigrants (Buchignani & Indra, 1985:158; Westwood and Hoffman, 1979:31). Moreover, dowry transactions are becoming more and more prevalent today among Indian immigrants, perhaps in line with similar patterns in India, especially among business families of upper and middle castes (*Free Press Journal,* 1986). The dowry has become a source of new wealth and status for these Indian families where brides frequently have to pay the price of unsatisfactory transactions in the form of abuse and even death.

Women are still expected to pass on cultural traditions in a foreign environment, often of a hostile nature. Thus, women are often prevented from cutting their hair, changing their dress code or learning English. This is partly a result of the concern of the majority of the South Asian community to reproduce their cultures. Westernization is seen as a threat to gender relations at home, i.e. westernized women are often portrayed as being promiscuous. Such a change is seen as a signal of sexual availability to men outside the family. Lesser degrees of pressure towards traditional conformity are experienced by men as well, but women are the main recipients of it, especially young women. When men experience this pressure to conform to traditional ways, the overriding motivation is to resist the forces of assimilation from the dominant Canadian culture, which is often expressed as an overemphasis on cultural lifestyles.

Research shows that most South Asian women experience mixed emotions when it comes to choosing between traditional South Asian versus dominant Canadian values and practices (Naidoo, 1980:193; Asianadian, 1978:9; Westwood and Hoffman, 1979:29; Littman, 1981). For instance, women may wish to choose their own marriage partners, but do not do so in reality, or they may want their children to feel completely comfortable in a Canadian environment and at the same time want them to retain their indigenous dress and language and to opt for arranged marriages.

One of the reasons for this ambivalence in women is the fact that after immigrating to a new country, the "family" becomes a source of strength despite its many oppressive features. It provides the networks for socializing and for surviving the struggles of settling in an environment with new values and systems. It provides a support group in which members can share and deal with experiences of failure and discrimination. It is a safe haven where men and women can continue to live a life similar to their pre-immigration days.

The ambivalence described here *vis-à-vis* women is also felt by men. Westwood and Hoffman (1979) discuss how the latter want their wives to learn English and become "modern" women yet fear their loss of control in the process. The author's own work within the community in Toronto has revealed that men are supportive of their wives' having a source of earning because it is essential for the family's economic survival; yet when women are compelled to stand up for their rights as workers, they often have to do so on their husbands' terms (Das Gupta, 1988).

These mixed reactions to integration with the dominant Canadian culture on the part of both men and women also indicate that the "overseas" South Asian family is in transition and that old and new values clash, especially with regard to gender relations. Separations and divorces have increased as a result (*Asianadian,* 1978; Cranney, 1988:9). The age hierarchy has also become less significant socially. Previously, elderly parents (including women) held a great deal of decision-making power within the family, however today they are often marginalized and isolated, lacking in socially recognized skills (including the ability to speak English) and hence lacking in economic and social influence (Hoffman and Westwood, 1979:30). Adolescent women who are expected to comply with arranged marriages are rebelling against South Asian sexual mores. A survey in Toronto (*Diva,* 1988:3) indicated that they are dating young men, a practice held to be taboo in the community. Usually this is being done without the knowledge of or against the will of their parents. A considerable amount of tension, depression, even suicidal feelings was expressed by those questioned in the above-mentioned survey owing to the fact that they could not practice dating openly like other adolescents and with their parents' support.

Despite the rise of dating, young men and women often have to resort to arranged marriages in their final selection of a life partner. One interesting practice which seems to be thriving in some quarters is that of matrimonial ads in newspapers, a practice also popular in South Asian countries (*Milan Introductions,* May, 1988). All this goes to show that ethnic roots run deep in the community. These roots are also strengthened by the boundary which exists between the community and white Canada. The experience of racism has helped to insulate and make more secure the indigenous cultural practices, values and norms as a shield against the forces of assimilation.

Recently, the practice of utilizing amniocentesis to abort female foetuses (a practice arising in some parts of India today) has reared its head among South Asians in British Columbia. A sample of the pregnant woman's amniotic fluid can be drawn from the womb and tested to determine the sex of the unborn baby. In cultures where there is an overwhelming preference for male over female children, this procedure is being used by some to abort female foetuses around the sixteenth week of pregnancy. Apart from the blatant sex bias evident in this practice, the procedure is also considered unsafe at this stage of the pregnancy (Bhayana, 1988:11). Culture, ethnicity and gender oppression are all manifested in this phenomenon. Although the practice has been condemned and made a political issue by activist, feminist groups in India (it has been banned by one Indian province at least), it remains to be seen what the future holds for South Asian women here.

Wage Labor

The fact that South Asian women have almost always come as sponsored immigrants holds true today. From the limited literature available in this area, it appears that women in wage labor are a post-1960 phenomenon in this community. Up to the 1960's, they were by and large unpaid family workers and housewives. Perhaps this was a reflection of the class of immigrants who came at

each period. From the 1920's to the 1950's, most of the immigrants came from rural peasant backgrounds, skilled in household production which required women to work in and around the house, to complement men's work in farms and small businesses later on. More middle class, professional and urban families came in the post-1960's period. Women in this class were better-educated and more westernized, familiar with commercial relations and therefore more open to engaging in wage labor. Moreover, the Canadian economy in the post-1960's had a need for managerial and clerical workers on the one hand and unskilled factory workers on the other.

Women have maintained a relatively high rate of labor-force participation in recent times compared to non-South Asian women. For instance in 1981, 64.1 per cent of them were in the labor force in Ontario, compared to 55.2 per cent of all women combined. Their participation was behind only to black and Philippino women (*Census Canada,* 1981). In 1986, South Asian women's participation rate across Canada was 64.1 per cent compared to 61.6 per cent for women of northern European origins (*Census Canada,* 1986). In 1986, 21.7 per cent of South Asian women in the labor force were in managerial and professional jobs, while 39.1 per cent were in clerical and sales occupations. Product fabricating, assembling and repairing and construction jobs occupied 10.6 per cent of the women (*Census Canada,* 1986).

Different provinces will provide different occupational statistics depending on the overall nature of its economy. A study of Canadian economy reveals uneven development (Carroll, 1988:144; Drache & Clement, 1985:111). There are regions marked predominantly by manufacturing industries (e.g. Ontario), while others are more agricultural (e.g. the Prairies) or are experiencing depression and high unemployment (e.g. the Maritimes).

It is clear that this reality is significant in the determination of where South Asian women work for a wage. For example, in B.C. a sizable proportion work as farm workers. In Atlantic Canada, according to the 1986 Census data, 41 per cent of South Asian women are in managerial and professional (especially teaching and health) work; 31 per cent are in clerical and sales work and none or very few in manufacturing and construction work. Ontario statistics from 1981 reveal that compared to the total population of women, the proportion of South Asian women in managerial and professional sectors is higher, the proportion in clerical, service, and sales is lower and the proportion in manufacturing and construction is slightly higher. The relatively significant proportion in managerial and professional sectors can be explained by the fact that many of these women arrived in Canada with higher levels of education, reflecting the improvement of accessibility to education of middle-class women in South Asian countries. Among all immigrant women in Ontario, the ones from South Asia have the highest levels of education (Estable and Meyer, 1989:24), while they also receive the lowest income among all university-educated immigrant women ($12,210) (Estable & Meyer, 1989:22).

Not much specific research has been done on the occupations of South Asian women. Among the professional group, they are lawyers, nurses, doctors, teachers, social workers, librarians and so on. Among the clerical workers, they do such work as keypunch operating, bookkeeping, secretarial duties, bank-telling, word processing and related work. Service work includes such jobs as cafeteria and kitchen help, and janitorial work and cleaning. Among manufacturing workers, they are concentrated in unskilled factory work, such as in garment, plastic, paper, rubber, textiles and food-processing plants (Khosla, 1983/84:13). These plants are often non-unionized with the result that workers have to work with dangerous health and safety conditions, low wages, and virtually no opportunities for upward mobility (Aggarwal, 1987:42; Das

Gupta, 1988). One common managerial practice with South Asian women workers is to ghettoize them in the worst and least-paid tasks and in specific shifts or areas of the shop floor. This physically and socially separates them from women of other ethnic backgrounds. Frequently, they are paid less than white workers doing the same job (Das Gupta, 1988).

As mentioned before, the majority of farm workers in British Columbia are South Asians. The largest proportion among these are non-English speaking women and girls (Khosla, 1983/84:14). Farm work does not even appear in official labor statistics, thus illustrating the status of this sector of work. The work is seasonal and workers are paid by piece wages (e.g. by the number of flats filled with produce). Moreover, farm workers have to pay a portion of their wages to contractors who recruit them to work in particular farms.

As in factory work, health and safety conditions are of least concern to employers, causing illnesses and even death in workers. Pesticides are sprayed on crops which are later picked by farm workers without any protective masks or clothing. A number of children have drowned on farms in the absence of proper child care facilities for farm worker parents. Since the farms are located far away from the residences of farm workers, they are transported and housed in converted sheds and barns for each season. These makeshift houses have no toilet facilities, no electricity and no windows. They are also overcrowded and generally not fit for human habitation (Khosla, 1983/84:13).

Like some other immigrant groups, South Asian women are concentrated in the professions in small numbers while a large group is concentrated in manual and service occupations (Estable & Meyer, 1989:22). Research has to be conducted in specific occupations to gain a complete picture of South Asian women's experience in waged work. As Estable & Meyer (1989) pointed out, it would be misleading to simply focus on the "average" since gross exploitation in the lower level occupations can easily be missed with that approach.

Politics

In this section, discussion will be restricted to the involvement of women in community as opposed to electoral politics. The political experience of women in the South Asian community is an area for future research as a preliminary literature review conducted by the author indicates a lack of readily available literature. While the community as a whole historically has been very involved in activities related to the anti-colonial struggle in India in the pre-1947 period, women are not portrayed as participating in human rights campaigns and anti-racism movements in the post-1960's period. Whether women have really been absent or whether they have been rendered invisible by sexist historians and writers remains to be identified.

It is important to recognize that women are involved on various community fronts currently. However, they are relatively few in number and often operate as individuals (i.e. they are not members of community organizations of South Asian women). Since the popular movements in South Asian countries are fairly well-organized and active and also include large numbers of women, it is interesting to contrast that reality with the seeming absence of South Asian immigrant women in Canadian politics. In the following analysis of this reality, discussion will be restricted to those women coming from India, as the author is most familiar with this community.

The majority of women in that community are from *petite bourgeoisie* families, whether from small business or professional/technical fields, or from rich peasant backgrounds. The bulk of the women's movement in India is made up of landless, agricultural laboring women in rural areas (Omvedt, 1987), the working poor,

and westernized intellectuals (i.e. teachers, researchers, journalists, etc.) in urban areas. Therefore, the majority of women who have migrated to Canada have not been involved at any level of the women's movement in India, or with any social movement for that matter. Lacking this experience, they have stayed away from community-level politics in Canada.

Having said that, I hasten to add that in the history of working-class struggles in Canada, there have been at least three instances in the 1970's and 1980's when working women have engaged in militant action for their rights. They are the farm workers in British Columbia who organized the Canadian Farmworkers Union (A Time to Rise, National Film Board, 1980); the pizza workers in Toronto who fought and won a human rights case for being fired unjustly (Das Gupta, 1988), and the women from Superplastics Ltd. (Aggarwal, 1987:42) in Mississauga who engaged in a strike to defend their rights as workers.

It is interesting to note that in all these examples, women were not fighting strictly for gender-related issues, but rather on human rights and working class issues. This trend is in keeping with the women's movement in India, particularly in the period before 1975.

The reality for most immigrants, or "economic refugees" as they are sometimes called by community advocates, is a search for a better life or upward mobility. Most South Asian families (apart from those who are political refugees) have come here to earn money, accumulate property, and have better educational opportunities, the latter being a key to lucrative employment in their eyes. Women in these families constitute an important factor in facilitating the process of upward mobility. They provide an additional income in most cases, thus adding to family finances. On the basis of this, a family may save up just enough to buy a new house. Next comes the struggle to make the mortgage payments. Moreover, given the large families, as described earlier, women have their hands full in terms of housework and child care. This does not allow them any additional time to engage in political work outside the home.

Within the South Asian community, men often participate in political work through religious institutions, such as temples and churches, or through cultural organizations. In most cases these institutions are male-dominated with almost all official positions being held by men. A high level of segregation exists between men and women members, thus upholding gender divisions. For women to initiate or participate actively in any political action in such a context is a difficult undertaking.

Community activities or any form of political activity for women have to be introduced through the men. Even the most non-threatening activity like inviting women to attend an English class often has to pass the approval of their husbands and fathers. During the struggle of the pizza workers in Toronto (Das Gupta, 1988), some of the male relatives of the women involved persuaded their wives or daughters to "drop out" as it did not promise any immediate gain. These women were subsequently prevented from attending any meetings or giving any input into the community action. On the other hand, some of the strongest women workers were those who had the full support of their male relatives.

In this context the larger women's movement, which is predominantly white and English-speaking, is rendered ineffective. Due to language barriers, feminist activists would not be able to involve themselves directly in the South Asian community. Moreover, the women's movement, having by and large excluded men, is perceived as being staunchly anti-male. In a community where males are still the go-betweens with the outside world, channels of communication can most effectively be opened by female activists from within the immigrant community itself.

On the other hand, the strike by Superplastics workers was greatly strengthened by weekly solidarity pickets organized by International Women's Day Committee and Women Working with Immigrant Women. This is an example of indirect intervention by the larger women's movement which made a strong contribution to the Superplastics workers' action, despite language and race barriers. In contrast to the pizza workers' case, some of the Superplastics workers could speak English; men were involved in the strike, and it was a unionized group. A greater involvement by feminist organizations in the case of the Superplastics workers indicated rising maturity in feminist practice (i.e. increasing awareness of race, gender, and class) as these relations operate in the workplace. It also indicated that individual South Asian women, however few in number, had integrated into the larger women's movement and had made an impact on the latter's overall perspective of extending solidarity to women of color.

Another development within this community of South Asian women is the network of community-based self-help and service organizations that have sprouted up in major Canadian cities. Examples include the South Asian Women's Group (now known as South Asian Women's Centre) in Toronto, South Asian Women's Community Centre in Montreal and Indian Mahila Association in British Columbia. Toronto has an inter-agency network of South Asian programs and organizations, named Coalition of Agencies Serving South Asians (CASSA), as well as a women's magazine called *Diva*.

All of these illustrate a rich experience of community organizing around gender, class, ethnic and race issues. These are examples of "communities of resistance," to use a phrase from anti-racist writer Sivanandan (Sivanandan, 1990:51). They are alternative organizations created by women in the community themselves, based on their self-identified needs and the reality of their lack of access to the so-called "mainstream" institutions. This lack of access is the result of a series of systemic barriers, such as the absence of cross-cultural and anti-racist approaches to service delivery and the lack of outreach into the communities, as well as financial barriers, legal exclusion of certain categories of immigrants and refugees from services or programs, such as sponsored groups and the lack of people of color among the service or program deliverers. All these together amount to systemic racist and/or sexist practices which have historically excluded South Asian women (and other immigrant women and women of color for that matter) from making full use of them (Das Gupta, 1986; Estable and Meyer, 1989).

Summary

In this paper, the history of South Asian women mainly in Ontario and B.C. has been focused on, with reference to the family and to paid workplaces. The following theoretical notions emerge from the historical survey:

1. The experience of South Asian women must be seen within the political economy of Canada.

2. Gender relations were reproduced by the aid of the Canadian state via its immigration policies as well as by the institution of the family, most importantly by older male members.

3. Their experience in paid workplaces illustrates the reproduction of both gender and race relations, aided once again by the Canadian state.

4. Their political history illustrates organized resistance against exploitation as members of the working class, as well as of an oppressed racial minority group.

Brief explication of these assertions follow.

Immigration, Race, and the Canadian State

Whether South Asians, in particular women, have come to Canada or not, when they came and what socio-economic grouping came, are all determined by the immigration policy as developed by the needs in the economy, specifically the needs of a capitalist system. Immigration statistics clearly show that the immigration flow has been turned on and off depending on the specific need for cheap labor, whether it was for building of railways or for logging in earlier years, or for factory and farm labor in post-war years.

Racism as an ideology which subordinates a people on the basis of skin color, ethnicity or religion proved to be very effective in maximizing the capitalist drive for profits. Economically speaking, racism rationalizes the super-exploitation of South Asian men and women by perpetuating dangerous working conditions and inhuman labor processes. Racist ideology includes the labelling of such laborers as "unskilled," "uneducated," or "inferior" and therefore "cheap." On the other hand, politically, racism encourages the reproduction of a dual labor market, based on a division between white, male, "skilled," unionized workers and female, "unskilled," unorganized workers of color who can be exploited at different rates. This keeps the working class divided and disempowered to challenge the common exploiters. Racist hostility reproduces the silence and intimidation of workers who fear being fired or deported, the latter threat being enforced through immigration and refugee policies.

The Canadian state has been an interventionist one since historically it has taken part in the process of capital accumulation and profit-making by ensuring a steady stream of immigrants, through its immigration and refugee policies. Also, it has played its coercive function through these same policies in the form of deportation clauses, exclusionary measures, the denial of family reunification and the imposition of head taxes (as in the case of Chinese immigrants) and the use of police and military forces.

The state's ideological role by imposing control through consensus, by the preservation of hegemony, is also worth noting, although this role was not fully explored in the paper. However, it is noteworthy that the government was able to practice covert racism, such as implementing the "continuous journey" stipulation, voting rights and excluding women, all due to popular racist sentiments among white Canadians in general. These actions provided a ready climate in which to deny basic human rights to South Asian men and women immigrants.

Gender and State

Gender relations are also socially organized in the South Asian community, particularly in the early years. The exclusion of female immigrants from South Asia meant that South Asian families in Canada were destined to be "bachelor," male-oriented families. Racism is implied here as well, since the exclusion of females ensured the non-permanence of the immigrant communities from South Asian countries. They were the predecessors to the guest-workers in Europe today.

In the post-1967 period, the points system reinforced the male-dominated, nuclear-family form. Females could come primarily as "sponsored" immigrants and therefore as "legally dependent" immigrants, since their second-class status in the home countries prevented their qualification as "independents" in most cases. Their past status continues after immigration. This reinforces patriarchal family norms and practices within South Asian families, with certain cultural peculiarities (e.g. the significance of age hierarchies). In contradiction, the family was also a safe haven in the settlement period, an oasis in the stressful journey towards survival.

Even though the family as an institution has been less than egalitarian to most South Asian women, the principle of family reunification has been one of the most important political demands from the community, predominantly voiced by men.

Labor Process, Race, and Gender

In the labor sectors where South Asian women predominate—farm work, office work, secondary manufacturing (to name a few sectors)—working conditions are less than acceptable. Work is by and large casual, part-time, piece, contractual, marked by low wages and insecurity—guided by the dictum "last hired, first fired." Those South Asian women who are in professional and managerial sectors are often underemployed and underpaid.

South Asian women experience the phenomena of ghettoization and segmentation, which achieve both a divided work force and a cheap, captive labor pool. Those women professionals (e.g. teachers, doctors) often complain of working in contract jobs, where their prior educational and professional qualifications are not recognized.

Gender, Race, and Politics

South Asian women have made major contributions in the history of human rights, labor and community-based service organizations in Canada. These efforts all relate to who most South Asian women are (i.e. working class women of color with a variety of cultural/linguistic heritages). As unorganized workers in the secondary-labor market, they have fought back against dehumanizing working conditions, lobbying for safer work environments and protesting the contracting system, which ensures them wages which are not even enough to reproduce their labor power. Middle-class, professional women have mostly restricted themselves to traditional cultural and recreational organizations, which could be placed under the rubric of "multiculturalism." These were not reviewed in this paper.

As people of color, they have resisted blatant and systemic racism, as in cases of differential treatment vis-à-vis white workers and name calling on the shop floor. They also have a rich history of organizing community programs for self education, self-help and greater independence (e.g. English as a Second Language classes, support groups, employment counselling and socio-recreational activities). It is useful to reiterate the validity of linking the "personal" to the "political," an approach which is one of the most important contributions of the feminist movement as a whole. In order to participate effectively in larger political movements, women of color and working-class

women have to be personally empowered. Learning English or French is a very concrete way of achieving that goal.

To emphasize an introductory comment, this article is "a point of departure rather than a destination." Throughout the article, various areas have been indicated in which research is seriously lacking. Firstly, in the area of "migration history," a gap exists in information from the 1930's to the present time. Secondly, in the area of "family organization," research on dowry and the abuse of reproductive technology would definitely be a contribution. Thirdly, in the area of "paid labor," knowledge of labor market conditions and experiences in specific occupations and also in different provinces would be extremely valuable in terms of advancing our understanding of how race, gender, and class intersect in the paid workplace. Finally, further research waits to be conducted in specific cases of South Asian women organizing throughout their existence in Canada.

References

Aggarwal, Pramila, 1987, Business As Usual in the Factory. *Resources for Feminist Research* 16(1):42.

Bhayana, Bhooma, 1988, A Female Physician's Perspective. *Diva* 2(2).

Buchignani, Norman, Doreen Indra and Ram Srivastava, 1985, *Continuous Journey: A Social History of South Asians in Canada.* Toronto: McClelland & Stewart Ltd.

Cranney, Brenda, 1988, Profile of South Asian Community. *Diva* 1(1).

Census Canada, 1981.

Carroll, William K., 1988, The Political Economy of Canada. *Understanding Canadian Society*, eds. James Curtis & Lorne Tepperman. Toronto: McGraw-Hill Ryerson Ltd.

Clement, Wallace, 1988, The Labor Process. *Understanding Canadian Society*, eds. James Curtis & Lorne Tepperman. Toronto: McGraw-Hill Ryerson Ltd.

Das Gupta, Tania, 1988, Working Together: Toronto's South Asian Community. *Diva* 1(2), July.

Das Gupta, Tania, 1986, *Learning from Our History: Community Development by Immigrant Women in Ontario 1958–86.* Toronto: Cross Cultural Communication Centre.

Diva, 1988, Dating: The South Asian Experience. 1(2), October–December.

Doman, Mahinder, 1984, A Note on Asian Indian Women in British Columbia 1900–1935. *Not Just Pin Money*, eds. Barbara K. Latham and Roberta J. Pazdro. BC: Camosun College.

Drache, Daniel & Wallace Clement, 1985, *The New Practical Guide to Canadian Political Economy.* Toronto: James Lorimer & Co. Pub.

Estable, Alma & Mechthild Meyer, 1989, *A Discussion Paper on Settlement Needs of Immigrant Women in Ontario.* Canada: Immigrant Settlement & Adaptation Program, Canada Employment & Immigration Commission, March.

Green, Alan G., 1976, *Immigration and the Post-war Canadian Economy.* Toronto: Maclean Hunter Press.

Khosla, Prabha, 1983/84, Profiles of Working Class East Indian Women. *Currents,* Winter.

Law Union of Ontario, 1981, *The Immigrant's Handbook: A Critical Guide.* Ontario: Black Rose Books.

Littman, Sol, 1981, New Freedom Pits Muslim Women Against Old Ways. *Toronto Star,* June 4.

Milan Introductions, 1988, 1(4), May.

Naidoo, Josephine, 1980, East Indian Women in the Canadian Context: A Study in Social Psychology. *Visible Minorities and Multiculturalism: Asians in Canada,* eds. Gordon Hirabayashi and K. Victor Ujimoto. Toronto: Butterworths.

National Film Board, 1980, A Time to Rise.

Omvedt, Gail, 1987, We Shall Smash This Prison Someday. *The Illustrated Weekly of India,* April 18.

Sivanandan, A., 1990, *Communities of Resistance: Writings on Black Struggles for Socialism.* London: Verso.

The Asianadian, 1978, From Chapathies To Hamburgers 1(3), Fall/Winter.

Toronto Star, 1982, Canadians First, May 1.

Westwood, Sallie and Dallah Hoffman, 1979, *Asian Women: Education and Social Change.* England: University of Leicester.

The Economics of Debt and the Remaking of Canada[*]

JIM STANFORD

Introduction

Few would disagree with the proposition that public sector debts and deficits have been the dominant public policy issue of the 1990s in Canada, and in most other industrialized economies as well. Business leaders and most of the mass media have focused great attention on the debt and its real or imagined consequences. Governments at all levels, and of all political stripes, have used the growing debt to justify increasingly harsh cutbacks in financial support for the entire range of public and social programming. And the public at large seems to have agreed that the public debt is a huge, and perhaps the preeminent, problem of our times. Now, in contrast to conventional political wisdom, program-slashing politicians—from Ralph Klein to Paul Martin—tend to become *more* popular with each cutback.

On the face of it, this marked shift in political culture would seem to signify a huge defeat for the Left. An increasingly widespread concern with the fiscal bottom line has been a key weapon—both financial and ideological—in the ongoing dismantling of many of the most progressive programs and services of the welfare state. Indeed, many on the Left attempted to defend those services by unsuccessfully opposing the growing obsession with debts and deficits. The most common left responses to deficit-mania have relied on several arguments that, in various largely unconvincing ways, attempt to downplay the importance of the public debt. For instance:

- *Corporations also have debt, so why shouldn't the government?* Yet any corporation that accumulated large negative cash flow for 20 consecutive years, as has our federal government, would be long since bankrupt.

- *It is a lie that we have hit the "debt wall"; Canadian governments can still borrow abroad.* Yes, but for how long do we *want* to borrow abroad? When *will* we encounter the limit to debt accumulation? And will we like what happens when we get there?

- *The deficit was artificially created, via tax breaks for corporations and the rich, to give right-wing governments an excuse to cut valued programs.* In 1993, governments could have collected all of the after-tax profits of

Jim Stanford, "The Economics of Debt and the Remaking of Canada," *Studies in Political Economy*, 48 (Autumn 1995): 113–35. Reprinted by permission of Jim Stanford.

[*] Views expressed are those of the author, and should not be attributed to the CAW. Non-incriminating thanks to Sam Gindin, Leo Panitch, Greg Albo and John Loxley for comments on an earlier draft.

all corporations in Canada, and still only offset 53 per cent of their combined deficits—not considering, of course, the catastrophic impact that a 100 per cent corporate tax rate would have on economic activity in the country.

- *Public-sector debt was also large following World War II.* Interest rates at that time were 2 or 3 per cent, and the rate of economic growth often exceeded 10 per cent per year. Moreover, the *cause* of the debt—war spending—had been suddenly and permanently eliminated.

- *The deficit may be important, but social programs are more important.* Presumably, therefore, we should simply accept ongoing deficits and a perpetual rise in the public debt. Will our lenders be so placid?

These arguments, not surprisingly in retrospect, have proven to be manifestly ineffective. Canadians do not buy the argument that deficits and debts do not matter, and it is condescending to presume that this is solely because they have been brainwashed by right-wing propaganda. Only one *interpretation* of Canada's debt spiral has been aired with much vigour—namely the view that the debt was caused by excessive spending on public programs, and therefore cutting those programs is the only way to solve the debt—and thus it is the "slash-and-burn" approach to deficit-reduction that is now winning the day.

One can hardly blame hard-pressed labour or community groups for grasping whatever arguments were available, in their desperate struggle to defend programs and services that are of crucial importance to the real living standards of millions of Canadians. But it is nevertheless surprising and unfortunate that Canada's Left found itself in the position of implicitly or explicitly *defending* government deficits. In fact, the growing fiscal crisis of the state over the past two decades is evidence of a profound weakness in the economic underpinnings of welfare-state capitalism. A critical analysis of the institutions of the welfare state, and a focus on the inadequacy and impermanence of the post-Keynesian social contract, used to be hallmarks of radical political and economic analysis. More recently, however, this critical approach has taken a back seat to a more defensive strategy, aimed at preserving whatever is possible from that "kinder, gentler" post-war regime. Instead of defending deficits because they are preferable to cutbacks, it is time to turn a more critical and radical eye on the question of why Canada's governments no longer seem capable of financing programs that were implemented (and paid for) in decades gone by.

Indeed, by developing an alternative, radical analysis of the causes of Canada's debt crisis, we can simultaneously advance a more far-reaching agenda of possible solutions to chronic deficits and escalating debts. This would help to provide the Left with a stronger and less defensive platform from which to address fiscal issues. Rather than trying to dodge public concern about Canada's growing public debt, we can go on the offensive, arguing that the debt is a fundamental problem of our entire economic and social system, one that demands radical measures.

The rest of this article is divided into three parts. The following section describes the growth of Canada's public debt, and argues that—even from a left perspective—it is a serious problem with major negative consequences. The next part summarizes an alternative analysis of the causes of the debt crisis, focusing on the importance of long-run changes in macroeconomic strategy that were first introduced fifteen years ago. The concluding section sketches some possible policy conclusions that are suggested by this alternative analysis of deficits and debt.

The Scope and Consequences of Canada's Debt Crisis

Canada's federal government began to experience large and chronic annual deficits beginning in the late 1970s; these became noticeably worse in the early 1980s. The federal deficit has exceeded 4 per cent of Canada's GDP virtually every year since 1982.[1] Large deficits also began to be incurred at about the same time by most provincial governments; these accounted for another 3.5 per cent of GDP in 1992, although they have shrunk rapidly since then.

It is interesting to note that Canada's public sector ran essentially balanced budgets, on average, until the late 1970s. Occasional deficits were largely offset by subsequent surpluses. The average federal deficit from 1950 to 1980 was an insignificant 0.3 per cent of GDP.[2] During this time, the federal government introduced virtually all of the major policy innovations that make up today's system of social programs: Canada-wide medicare, universal pensions, the modern Unemployment Insurance system, and cost-sharing with the provinces for higher education and welfare. (These programs were all introduced during the 1960s and early 1970s, yet budgets remained roughly balanced.) During the 1980s and 1990s, there have been very few new public programs introduced; the clearly dominant trend has been toward cutbacks and privatization. Indeed, the public sector has already been downsized markedly since the zenith of the "just society" of the mid-1970s. For example, federal program spending (excluding interest payments) declined as a share of GDP from 18 per cent in 1975 to just over 15 per cent in the first half of 1995—*before* the large cutbacks announced in the 1995 federal budget. Immediately one must be suspicious of the claim that social programs have "caused" our deficit.

A deficit, of course, is a one-year shortfall of revenues below expenditures. The bigger, longer-run problem of accumulating debt is encountered when annual deficits are added to one another, without intervening years of budgetary surplus. [...] The federal government's net debt now approaches 70 per cent of Canadian GDP. [...] Total net public sector debt in Canada now exceeds 100 per cent of GDP, ranking us with the handful of most heavily indebted countries in the world.

It is the long-run accumulation of debt, more than a deficit experienced in any particular year, that makes the fiscal situation of the state especially difficult, because of the large and continuing interest expenditures that are required to service that debt. In 1995 the federal government will dedicate some $44 billion (over 30 per cent of its total tax collections) to interest payments. These interest payments are larger than the deficit itself. They are also more expensive than any single social program. Indeed, the government's interest payments are larger than the *total* cost of all of the social programs that were examined in the grandiose (and ultimately irrelevant) review undertaken by Human Resources Minister Lloyd Axworthy. Needless to say, these interest payments are the only major item on the government's expenditure side that is *growing*: despite his commitment to "fiscal restraint," Paul Martin allows interest charges to rise to $51 billion in 1996–97; by then they will consume 37 per cent of the government's total revenue.

It is interesting to note that there is no correlation between the relative "generosity" of a nation's social welfare apparatus and its level of indebtedness. In other words, there is nothing "left-wing" about deficits and debts. There are relatively progressive welfare states (such as Belgium) which have large accumulated debt loads, and there are others (such as the Scandinavian countries) which have very small accumulated debts. Indeed, the four Scandinavian countries have had among the most balanced budgets in the industrialized world, with an accumulated public debt equal to less than 10 per cent of GDP in 1994, and hence interest payments on that debt that accounted for only 1 per cent of all public spending.[3] Because these countries (until recently, at least) have maintained roughly balanced books (in part thanks to their more energetic commitment to full-employment macroeconomic strategies, as will be argued below), they are not hamstrung by the continuing drain of huge interest payments, making it more feasible to continue to fund public programs. In this light, the proposal to tolerate chronic deficits because they are somehow "less important" than the preservation of public programs seems especially shortsighted.

Are there real consequences resulting from Canada's large accumulated public debt? Much of the right-wing hysteria about the deficit is clearly exaggerated. The claims of some business groups, for example, that real investment in Canada is held back by business uncertainty about the size of our debt is clearly ludicrous: businesses are much more concerned about what they can produce and sell than about the government's fiscal health. Contractionary solutions to the deficit (such as huge spending cutbacks) will have a much more negative impact on business investment, by virtue of their negative macroeconomic consequences, than will the debt itself.

Nevertheless, it is also clear that the huge public debt does have widespread and regressive real consequences, as well. First, the payment of huge sums of interest out of the public purse to largely well-off bond-holders and other financial investors clearly has a significant regressive impact on the distribution of income: the government collects taxes from average Canadians and pays a rising share of that revenue (40 per cent or more by the end of the century) directly to the wealthy. One US study has estimated that

for each dollar of interest paid on the federal debt, barely one cent ends up in the pockets of the poorest 30 per cent of households.[4]

The large interest payments associated with the accumulated debt require, of course, that government not dedicate an equivalent amount of money to other, more deserving goals, with a variety of economic and political consequences. Apart from squeezing out government funding for actual public programs and services, the debt-servicing burden also robs government of much of its stimulative or counter-cyclical capacity. With less fiscal leeway in recessionary times, government is hard-pressed to maintain existing programs, let alone to introduce new spending to offset a slowdown in the private economy. Unlike direct spending on programs, or transfer payments to low-income households, payments of interest to investors have very little positive macroeconomic spin-off effect, since a large share of these payments are simply added to the savings of these investors (rather than being recirculated in the form of subsequent re-spending).

In order to come even close to balancing its budget in the face of large interest expenditures, government must run an "operating surplus": that is, its tax revenues must greatly exceed the day-to-day cost of the concrete services that it provides to its constituents. The forecast operating surplus of the federal government will reach $30 billion by fiscal 1996/97, and yet the government will still experience a large deficit. This imbalance between the revenues and actual program spending of government cannot but contribute to public cynicism about the usefulness of government and taxes: when federal taxpayers receive on average perhaps 75 cents of actual public services back for each dollar of taxes they pay, they will inevitably come to question the value of their public sector transactions.

Moreover, since an increasing share of the public debt is foreign-owned, the accumulation of public debt has contributed mightily to a growing foreign indebtedness that dwarfs the importance of foreign direct investment—long an obsession of the Canadian Left. By the end of 1993, direct investment accounted for less than 10 per cent of Canada's huge $300 billion net foreign indebtedness. Our total foreign debt has grown by 10 times since the nationalist heyday of the early 1970s, yet the Left has paid scarce attention to the rise of this far more serious form of foreign control over Canadian economic developments. Today approximately one-third of Canada's federal debt is foreign-owned; this obligation is some seven times as large as is our net liability in foreign direct investment. Net payments of investment income to foreigners (most of it interest on bonds) will exceed $30 billion in 1995, overwhelming what will probably be an all-time record surplus in our merchandise trade. Astoundingly, in 1993 (most recent data available), less than *one per cent* of our total deficit in cross-border interest and dividend payments was due to foreign direct investment in Canada.

The large public debt, and the internationalization of its ownership, has also been a major factor in the loss of domestic control over monetary policy and interest rates. When the federal government is constantly selling huge volumes of public bonds—not just those required to finance new deficits, but also renewing the much larger stock of bonds that finances the existing debt load—then the need to keep Canadian rates of return "competitive" (after adjusting for expected inflation and changes in exchange rates) with those in other jurisdictions becomes all the more pressing. A fear by investors that their profits from Canadian bonds may fall (due to lower interest rates, higher inflation, or a weak Canadian dollar) will result in a large sell-off in the secondary market for Canadian-dollar bonds and other investment instruments.[5] This produces strong immediate downward pressure on the Canadian dollar and makes it very difficult for the government to sell further bonds.

Incidentally, the solution to this problem cannot be solely to "repatriate" the debt, as many commentators have suggested. Commercial Canadian investors (such as Canadian banks and financial institutions) are *at least* as aware of the potential impacts of macroeconomic policy and exchange rate fluctuations on their asset holdings as are foreign investors, and they have access to somewhat more complete and timely information about Canadian economic developments. Hence they are likely to sell off their own Canadian-denominated assets (thus profiting from an expected fall in the dollar) even faster than foreign investors, actually helping to start a run on Canadian financial markets. What is required is not simply to repatriate the debt, but to place more of it in *nonspeculative* instruments (such as Canada Savings Bonds and other types of bonds where the investor is concerned primarily with the ultimate interest paid, not with profiting from speculative price changes in resale markets).

What are the limits to public debt accumulation in Canada? There is no "debt wall," of course, contrary to the panic-stricken warnings of the business media. Most Canadian governments, including the federal government, are still able to borrow funds on commercial financial markets at "reasonable" interest rates (where "reasonable" is defined in relationship to the structure of relative rates charged to various types of borrowers, rather than in terms of the overall *level* of interest rates—which is clearly not "reasonable"). But it is equally naive to assume that Canadian governments could continue to borrow *ad infinitum*. For example, those provincial governments which are relatively more heavily indebted (especially the Atlantic provinces) already face higher interest rate penalties in their borrowing, and hence have been forced to balance their provincial budgets more quickly than other provinces. Other governments will similarly face a rising interest rate premium on future loans as their debt loads increase.[6] To presume otherwise is to assume that lenders do not care about the ability of their debtors to repay their loans, and there is no evidence of such a happy-go-lucky attitude on the part of the world's financial elite.

Bond rating agencies, of course, receive a lot of bad press, since their evaluations carry an immediate and usually painful impact on governments' fiscal bottom-line. Yet these agencies are merely performing a rational and systematic service on behalf of their clients—financial investors—who are quite naturally interested in the risks they face of not having their loans repaid (either through outright default, in the worst case, or through the adoption of high-inflation or low-currency strategies which would reduce the ultimate real value of loan repayments). The more indebted are the debtors, the more likely is the perceived risk of non-repayment, and lenders are quite naturally interested in this information. To blame the bond-rating agents is to hope that without them indebted governments could somehow keep lenders in the dark forever about their rising indebtedness.

It is convenient to blame the *agents* of a financial system for the pain that is encountered as a result of becoming indentured to that system: the bond raters who publicize the borrower's financial difficulties, the red-suspendered foreign exchange traders who facilitate their clients' efforts to reduce their exposure to weak currencies. The real problem, however, is deeper. It is the very existence of an institutional environment in which the owners of financial wealth are able to demand such high returns, and are able to enforce those demands through their geographic mobility and their ability to impose swift and painful punishment on renegade clients.

The Historical Causes of Deficits and Debt

The dramatic rise in Canada's public-sector indebtedness since the early 1980s was not caused by an undue expansion of public programs (since, for the most part, Canada's existing network of public programs was already in place by the mid-1970s, and has been steadily *eroded* since then). Rather, the historical data clearly suggest that the marked and permanent decline in economic growth and employment over the past fifteen years has been the dominant factor in the deterioration of public finance. Since the advent of monetarist, anti-inflation macroeconomic strategy in Canada, beginning in about 1981, the Canadian economy has been mired in a state of more-or-less "permanent recession." Strictly speaking, the economy continues to experience alternating periods of expansion and contraction. But in the present era, even the periods of expansion are strictly controlled to maintain a permanent degree of slackness and desperation in labour markets—with the result that even periods of recovery still "feel" like tough times for most members of society. Thus in contrast to the stated commitment of earlier post-war governments to the maintenance of full employment (or something resembling it), elected and unelected economic institutions have since embarked on a policy that deliberately fostered a state of controlled economic stagnation. Permanent unemployment was reestablished in order to repair the "damage" done to the profit system by 30 years of full employment, rising wages, growing unions, and an increasingly interventionist public sector.

The primary goal of this "permanent recession" was to discipline labour: undermining both wage demands and worker resistance to speed-up and other productivity-enhancing practices in the workplace. Indeed, even in the heyday of Keynesian policies, Michal Kalecki expressed his scepticism about the market system's ability to tolerate full employment over long periods of time, by virtue of the negative implications of labour's stronger economic bargaining position on wage demands and labour effort.[7] Full employment, in short, is ultimately bad for business. But unemployment alone does not sufficiently discipline labour if social programs provide unemployed workers with some degree of economic security, independent of their status as sellers of a commodity (namely labour services).[8] Thus the strategy of permanent recession must also involve a radical downsizing of the protections offered by the welfare state;[9] conveniently, the impact of the permanent recession on public finance provided ample *fiscal* motives for this downsizing, in addition to the underlying *political-economic* motives.

In this strategy of deliberate stagnation, no instrument has proved more powerful than the very high real interest rates[10] that have been implemented almost universally across the developed market economies. Indeed, the onset of high real interest rates provides the best indicator of the timing of this sea-change in macroeconomic management. [...] The impact of this dramatic change in monetary policy on real economic activity has been dramatic: the average real rate of economic growth has been cut in half (despite the acceleration of technological change and productivity growth, which should allow for *faster* real growth), while the average rate of unemployment has doubled, and the average annual change in real wages has fallen from over 2 per cent per year between 1950 and 1980, to a small annual *decline* since 1981 (again contrasting sharply with the growth in the real productivity of labour during these same fifteen years).[11] High rates of return on financial investments are a blunt, destructive, but effective way of both slowing down the entire economy (cutting deeply into both consumption and investment spending), while simultaneously shifting the structure of income distribution back in favour of capital.

No better example of the strategy of permanent recession can be found than the economic events that transpired in Canada in 1994 and 1995. In 1994, the Canadian economy experienced its first year of reasonably strong growth since the free-trade recession which began in 1990: the economy grew by 5 per cent, and the official unemployment rate fell to 9.4 per cent. This pace of growth was entirely unremarkable, by the standards of the earlier postwar era (when 5 per cent growth was merely *average,* and unemployment above 5 per cent was generally considered unacceptable). Nevertheless, alarm bells began ringing in corporate boardrooms and the Bank of Canada, and economic policy elites began warning of the "unsustainability" of such a rapid growth rate. Their real concern, of course, was that unemployment might actually fall low enough that workers could begin winning some small share (in the form of higher wages) of the fantastic productivity growth that the Canadian economy has experienced in the last five years. Similar concerns were expressed in the US, interest rates were cranked up, and the Canadian economy stalled in its tracks.

Investors and financial pundits have become well aware of the link between continued corporate profitability and permanent slackness in the economy; in the 1990s stock markets have tended to *decline* on news that unemployment has fallen, and vice versa, giving rise to ironic headlines such as the one printed in the July 20, 1995 *Toronto Star:* "Good news puts stocks in tailspin." Stock markets in both the US and Canada reached all-time record highs later in 1995 when economic data suggested that the "soft landing" pilots at the central banks may have created the perfect conditions for a continued but profitable permanent recession: never before in Canadian postwar history has business enjoyed such a combination of healthy capacity utilization and hence high profits, simultaneous with such profound weakness in labour markets. In the wake of the recent globalization of their markets, most Canadian corporations seem unconcerned about the chronic stagnation of the domestic market: since many producers of tradable commodities sell most of their output into foreign markets, the continued stagnation of domestic consumption that is a consequence of the permanent recession poses less of a constraint on demand (although from a *global* perspective, of course, this stagnation if experienced widely must ultimately limit overall demand).

A fringe benefit of the permanent recession has been the creation of large, structural deficits in public finance. Generally, government deficits are *counter-cyclical:* they automatically increase when the economy is weak, since tax revenues (from both income taxes and sales taxes) decline with economic activity, but expenses for unemployment insurance and other social programs automatically increase. Making matters worse, of course, is the fact that high interest rates have dramatically increased the government's own debt-servicing expenses. Thus, the shift from a full-employment regime to the permanent recession will naturally wreak havoc on the government's balance sheet. This problem has not been solved by repeated rounds of program cuts over the past fifteen years, since the resulting savings have been insufficient (until now, at least) to offset the fiscal drag resulting from chronic economic stagnation. Indeed, addressing the fiscal crisis through cutbacks requires government to swim against the tide, since the cutbacks themselves contribute significantly to the underlying macroeconomic weakness which caused the deficit in the first place.

In short, the combination of high real interest rates with permanently slow economic growth—both of which have been deliberate components of post-1980 economic strategy—ensured that the previous activities of the Canadian state became fiscally unsustainable. A simple mathematical formula contained in Paul Martin's 1994 pre-budget public discussion paper summarized this quandary admirably.[12] Suppose that a government becomes initially indebted due, say, to a one-year recession. If the real interest rate that must be paid on that debt is higher

than the subsequent real growth rate of the economy, then that initial debt will grow *exponentially* as a share of the economy (that is, in relation to the country's ability to service the debt).

This is a "knife-edge" problem: under super-high interest rates, anytime a country falls off a balanced-budget path, an initial deficit will blossom, as interest on the debt grows faster than the economy's ability to pay that interest, into a full-blown debt crisis. The only way to stop this process is for the government to generate an ongoing operating surplus large enough to offset most of the interest charges on the initial deficit, so that the initial debt is stabilized as a share of GDP. The required size of the operating surplus depends on the size of the initial debt, and on the gap between real interest rates and the real growth rate. For Canadians in 1995, with a $550 billion net federal debt, and a huge gap between real long-run interest rates (currently about 6 per cent) and virtually nonexistent economic growth, the operating surplus required just to stabilize the debt as a share of GDP (let alone to ever pay off any of that debt) reaches an astounding $35 billion. It is hard to imagine that Canadians will be willing to tolerate for very long such a huge and ongoing transfer of public wealth into generally well-off private hands. On the other hand, anytime the real interest rate is *less* than the pace of ongoing economic growth (as has not been the case since 1980), then an economy can grow out of an initial debt without requiring massive cutbacks.

Within a full-employment regime, it is possible to fund a high-quality network of public programs and income security, at a relatively affordable cost to taxpayers. The number of employed taxpayers earning income from which to pay taxes is high, and the number of needy citizens who must draw on those programs is small. The cost per employed worker of exactly the same programs grows by several times as the economy shifts from full employment to permanent high unemployment. Therefore, unemployment and deficits have tended to be positively correlated in the post-war era; the last time the federal government balanced its books was in 1974, and the last time the unemployment rate was less than 7 per cent was in 1975. It is possible to eliminate the deficit in a high unemployment context, but the result will not look pretty in terms of social security and public programs. The current crisis in Canada's public programs represents an effort by the state to forcibly harmonize these programs into line with the bitter new fiscal realities implied by the implementation of the permanent recession fifteen years ago.

Conclusion: Alternative Policy Directions

The preceding analysis of the causes and consequences of Canada's public debt casts doubt on the traditional view that supporters of public services should tolerate or indeed defend government deficits—presumably in the hope that current programs might thus be spared, and that brighter economic times in coming years would allow the resulting debt to be serviced. Brighter economic times are not on their way; the chronic stagnation of the past fifteen years has been deliberate, and will only be reversed with a far-reaching and radical change in macroeconomic direction. Canada's huge accumulated debt represents the legacy of the intervening lag period, during which governments have gradually been forced (by an increasingly binding budget constraint) to downsize their services into line with the fiscal implications of the permanent recession. Continuing to fund existing programs through deficits, while failing to challenge the fundamental direction of economic strategy, at best delays the inevitable, and merely increases the extent of bankers' control over the economy when restructuring ultimately occurs.

It is better for progressives to challenge the underlying political-economic assumptions that permanent unemployment, slow growth, high interest rates, and "lean-and-mean" production practices are the key prerequisites for modern economic success. Deficits should be eliminated, the sooner the better. The only way to accomplish this, while preserving an extensive and affordable network of social services and public programs, is to create an economic regime in which more Canadians work. A *minimum program,* therefore, would be to undo the great U-turn in economic policy which occurred fifteen years ago: abandon the strategy of permanent recession, use existing monetary policy instruments (and especially the market-making power of the Bank of Canada) to bring real interest rates down to 3 per cent or less (a level at which they can be feasibly exceeded by the rate of economic growth, thus allowing the economy to grow its way out of debt), and foster vibrant and sustained economic growth.

The implementation of such a program, however, would immediately spark a crisis of confidence on the part of capital—both financial capital (fearing the impact of higher inflation and a lower currency on the real returns to financial investments) and industrial capital (considering the longer-run impacts of vibrant growth and high employment on the micro-level conditions of production and employment). Both the financial and the real sides of the economy would experience a flight of capital, as investors sought out safer havens (low-inflation, high-interest monetary regimes for the financial investors, and more profitable and stable business environments for the real investors), with consequently negative side-effects felt throughout the macro-economy. That is why a full-employment strategy must also be supported by a *maximum program* of institutional changes in the structure of capital markets which could help to reduce the vulnerability of the economy to a loss of investor confidence.

A wide range of such institutional measures has been proposed, with varying degrees of detail and credibility. They could include some types of controls over international capital movements (such as the elimination of the 20 per cent foreign investment exemption currently allowed for registered pension plans), to forcibly keep more capital in Canada.[13] Given the difficulty of forcing capital to do things it would rather not, however, a supplementary and important long-run direction will involve the development over time of alternative institutions participating in the realm of both financial capital and real capital accumulation—institutions that are insulated from the profit-seeking imperative that currently drives financial market behaviour and real investment.[14] For example, publicly-controlled pools of capital (such as those associated with public auto insurance programs, credit unions, or pension funds) could in essence be directed to withdraw from the ever-more-flexible search for maximum rates of return, and instead be managed in a fashion which offered acceptable negotiated returns in a fashion more consistent with the need for a healthy macroeconomy. Alternative investment mechanisms (such as social investment funds, a public investment bank, and other proposals) could be established to inject capital directly into strategic Canadian industries, bypassing the extremely high hurdle rates of return that are currently erected by commercial lending institutions.[15] Monetary institutions (including the Bank of Canada) must also be reformed to reflect a better balance of the needs of the whole macroeconomy, rather than (as at present) just the interests of the owners of financial wealth.

It is a massive understatement, of course, to suggest that the progressive movement in Canada needs to work on fleshing out these proposals considerably. For example, a coalition of labour unions and popular movements came together in 1995 to prepare an "Alternative Federal Budget," under the leadership of the Canadian Centre for Policy Alternatives and the Winnipeg-based CHO!CES coalition. This project demonstrated that a low-interest, high-growth deficit-reduction strategy was more effective (not to mention more socially beneficial) than the "slash-and-burn" approach of Paul Martin. While our report recognized that fundamental institutional and monetary reforms would ultimately be required in order to implement such a strategy within a globalized financial system, our description of the extent and direction of these reforms was incomplete and unconvincing—a shortcoming that future versions of this project will attempt to redress.

Some of the foregoing policy measures would require coordination on an international level, enlisting the cooperation of like-minded governments to reform financial institutions on an international level; others offer the possibility of substantial unilateral implementation even within the borders of a single country. But given the underdevelopment and lack of democracy characteristic of present-day international institutions, the determined action of individual national states will be required in order to advance the agenda of beginning to control capital markets.

These are far-reaching and long-run institutional changes that would require a very fundamental reorientation of the structure of economic and political power in our economy. They probably seem far-fetched to most observers, given the current pessimistic trends in Canadian political culture. They represent first steps towards putting the ultimate socialization of capital back onto the political agenda of the Left. Hence it is not surprising that many of those who want to preserve what remains of the welfare state would lean toward more "reasonable" proposals, those that seem to hold out more hope of being immediately achievable—proposals such as simply tolerating the deficit, or perhaps raising additional taxes to partly off-set revenues lost because of the permanent recession. The economics of the public sector have been changed too fundamentally and permanently by the permanent recession, however, and these marginal measures fail to address the root problem. In short, even to preserve what remains of the welfare state, let alone to extend its protections, there are no non-radical solutions left.

Notes

1 Throughout this paper, deficit and debt figures are stated in "national accounts" terms (generally somewhat smaller than alternative "public accounts" measures, which include pension liabilities and other factors). Statistics are taken from the *Canadian Economic Observer* and other standard Statistics Canada sources; detailed sources are available on request from the author.

2 Indeed, when deficits are this small, the public debt will not grow as a share of GDP, since the economy is generally growing at a faster rate than the debt. It is thus quite possible for a growing economy to regularly experience *small* deficits without encountering a debt problem. The *large* deficits of the last fifteen years, however, cannot be perpetually managed.

3 Norway, Finland, Sweden, and Denmark (Iceland excluded). Data are arithmetic (unweighted) averages. This evidence is presented not to support the claim that existing social-democratic economies are somehow able to completely avoid the economic difficulties that have beset Canada and other welfare states; it is only intended to demonstrate that there is no correlation between existing debt accumulations and the progressiveness of social policies. Sweden's government, for example, has begun to encounter very large annual deficits in the 1990s (exceeding over 10 per cent of GDP), so its presently low debt burden is growing rapidly; in Sweden, as in Canada, the explosion of government deficits corresponded almost exactly with the demise of full-employment industrial and macroeconomic strategies.

4 See Thomas R. Michl, "Debt, deficits, and the distribution of income," *Journal of Post-Keynesian Economics* 13/3 (Spring 1991), 351–365. Incidentally, this result casts doubt on another reformist argument that the "debt doesn't matter"; some have suggested that as long as the debt is domestically owned, "we are simply lending money to ourselves," but this clearly depends on how "we" is defined.

5 The secondary market is where investors sell already-issued bonds to each other, in order to adjust the asset mix of their holdings, or to profit from changes in the re-sale price of those bonds.

6 Note, however, that the size of this interest rate *premium* is often overstated, relative to changes in the overall *level* of interest rates. Contrary to right-wing arguments, there is no evidence that Canada would enjoy *low* interest rates if we cut our debt. Yes, we do pay a small premium because of our high debt load, but the size of this premium is insignificant in comparison to the general rise in *all* interest rates (including those paid in countries with small accumulated debts) over the past fifteen years.

7 See "Class struggle and the distribution of income," *Kyklos* 24/1 (1971), 1–9. Subsequent economic research in the Kaleckian or "structuralist" tradition has further explored the central role of unemployment in maintaining a profitable balance of power between employers and employees, and the macroeconomic dimensions of the subsequent "profit-squeeze equilibrium." See, for example, Samuel Bowles, David M. Gordon, and Thomas E. Weisskopf, "Business ascendancy and economic impasse: a structuralist retrospective on conservative economics," *Journal of Economic Perspectives*, 3/1 (1989), 107–134; and Peter Skott, *Conflict and Effective Demand in Economic Growth* (Cambridge: Cambridge University Press, 1989).

8 In this sense, Gösta Esping-Anderson suggests that post-war income security programs provided labour with some prospect of "decommodification"; see "The three political-economies of the welfare state," *Canadian Review of Sociology and Anthropology* 26/1 (1989), 10–35.

9 An attack on trade union rights and other determinants of labour's institutional power in the employment relationship is also likely to form part of this strategy: less unemployment will be needed to sufficiently discipline labour, if worker's institutional and organizational power is already relatively weak.

10 The real interest rate equals the nominal interest rate less the rate of inflation. The real rate is the more accurate indicator of the concrete importance of interest payments. Interestingly, the real interest

rate in the first quarter of 1995 (8.5 per cent interest less 1.5 per cent inflation) was just as high as in 1981 (18 per cent interest, on average, less 11 per cent inflation), when thousands of Canadians lost their homes and high interest rates were a front-page controversy.

11 Real total labour costs, when the cost of fringe benefits is considered, have risen more rapidly than wages during this time, but have still lagged far behind productivity growth.

12 See *A New Framework for Economic Policy* (Ottawa: Department of Finance Canada, October 1994), 82–83.

13 It is worth noting that the so-called Tobin Tax, which would collect a small tax on each foreign exchange transaction, could not make a significant contribution to this goal: when investors fear that the adoption of a full-employment economic strategy is likely to cut significantly into the real profitability of their investments, it will take far more than a Tobin Tax to encourage them to keep their money in Canada.

14 The gradual development of alternative structures governing the accumulation of both financial and real capital might be thought of as a "Gramscian" approach to challenging the current power of capitalist finance and investment relationships. While this approach, to some extent, may "sidestep" an initial confrontation with financial interests over the overall direction of financial regulation and economic policy (by building up alternative institutions which gradually expand their operations while continuing to let existing capital markets operate), this confrontation is still likely to eventually occur—when a progressive government enacts measures which favour these alternative institutions, or when private financial interests find their scope of operations unacceptably curtailed.

15 The initial seed capital for such ventures could come from investments by government or by the Bank of Canada, or from community deposits from such existing vehicles as pension funds or mutual funds. The public funds could then recycle this initial capital into repeated loans in exactly the same multiplied fashion as do current commercial investment banks.

Family Policy, Child Care and Social Solidarity

The Case of Quebec

JANE JENSON

Quebec's Summit on the Economy and Employment, held in October 1996, brought together employers, unions and a broad selection of popular sector groups to reflect upon plans for the medium-term future of the province.[1] At the summit's end, Premier Bouchard announced a major revision of family policy. Eventually, the process launched at the summit would create a system of Early Childhood Centres to provide centre-based care and oversee family daycare providers while delivering services that cost parents no more than five dollars per day. Maligned by students for his refusal to freeze tuition fees, pressured by anti-poverty activists and socially marginal groups to embrace the goal of *appauvrissement zéro* (zero poverty) rather than striving to achieve a "zero deficit," Lucien Bouchard might simply be accused of searching for a theme that would unite rather than divide.[2] But the decision to announce a major reform of family policy, with universal and affordable child care at its centre, was much more than an effort to get out of a sticky political situation. It represented the victory of a coalition of activists and officials seeking to address the needs of families and children within Quebec's societal strategy (projet de société).

Indeed, the summit was only one moment, albeit a crucial one, in a long discussion about family policy in Quebec. Child care and family policy have been subjects of explicit debate for over two decades. By the mid-1990s positions were aligned, in part, with reference to the government's Third Family Action Plan (1995–1997). Elaborated after broad public consultations in the 1995 International Year of the Family, the action plan was multi-faceted: its focus on prevention addressed preventing spousal abuse and inducing greater participation of fathers in child rearing; its focus on balancing work and family addressed the needs for greater child care and adolescent education about the importance of both parents sharing family responsibilities; its focus on financial support for parents and family environments addressed improving housing, valuing solidarity across families and emphasizing the family dimension in all services.[3] This list, while not exhaustive, represents responses to the demands of a wide range of actors and interests involved with family policy: feminists, the family movement, anti-poverty activists, social workers and experts on development and early childhood education, as well as government bureaucrats. While some of these actors are located in the private sector and involved in policy development through consultations, others are located inside the state's "structure of representation" in particular parts of the public-service sector and para-public bodies.

Jane Jenson, "Family Policy, Child Care and Social Solidarity: The Case of Quebec," in Susan Prentice, ed., *Changing Child Care: Five Decades of Child Care Advocacy and Policy in Canada* (Halifax: Fernwood Publishing, 2001), 39–62. Reprinted with permission of Fernwood Publishing Co. Ltd.

Family policy is a key element in a broader process of social reform, as is social assistance and labour-market policy. This multidimensional reform sought (1) to improve parents' capacity to balance work and family life; (2) to provide both financially accessible and developmentally sound child care services that facilitated school readiness; and (3) to induce parents with low-incomes or on social assistance to find either employment or better jobs.[4] Given this strategic location in the process of modernizing social policy, it is not surprising that the announcement of the new family policy garnered a huge amount of attention. Nor did this abate over the following months. In January 1997, the government published the White Paper, *Les enfants au coeur de nos choix* (Children at the Heart of our Choices) and legislated the following July.

Who were the major actors involved in debating family policy in Quebec? What was at issue in their disputes over the new policy, including the child care initiatives? The story begins with an overview of the history of such controversies—both to set the context and because Quebec is the only province which has had a self-identified family policy for several decades. In Quebec, the more European-style language of "family policy" describes the range of services and benefits available to children and their parents. In the name of social solidarity, Quebec has designed a number of benefits to redistribute income from the childless to those responsible for raising children. However, all these actions have provoked debate about how to achieve this redistribution and express this solidarity. In addition, child care policy and family policy have been, in recent years, increasingly integrated with other policy domains, so that an even wider range of actors is involved in disputing goals, forms and definitions of fairness. Advocates share a view of child care as one part of a larger whole and engage points of access as numerous as they are.

The resulting family policies can set a number of priorities. They may seek, for example, to promote child development, to maximize equality of opportunity and condition among all types of families, or to advance gender equality.[5] Quebec's family policy over the last decades has always had a range of goals, as the Third Action Plan described above well indicates. Nonetheless, promoting parental employment has recently emerged as the top priority. For example, in June 2000, in a speech vaunting the "Quebec way," the Deputy Minister of Child and Family Welfare, Maurice Boisvert,[6] described the 1997 reforms as follows: "We decided that we had to increase our support to families.... As a result we put in place a number of structural measures for the society of the year 2000, the harmonious functioning of which centres on employment." Nor is this statement surprising. The institution responsible for family policy, the ministère de la Famille et de l'Enfance[7] was created in 1997 by amalgamating the Family Secretariat—the Office des services de garde à l'enfance (OSGE) responsible for regulating child care—and the Ministry of Income Security. This new ministry quietly sought advocates' input and approval, creating an advisory board in the spring of 1999.

Child Care After the Quiet Revolution: From Social Development to Family Policy

As Yves Vaillancourt[8] has stated, Quebec is the province that had the most privatized social services (before 1970) and then created the most public ones (after 1970):

> In the 1970s, the social service system which had so recently depended to a great extent on the commercial or nonprofit private sector, very quickly became one in which the public

sector clearly formed the main component, thus relegating the various private agencies and services to a complementary—indeed residual—role.[9]

This pattern remains true today, in the child care field at least, as the province moves against the current, putting most of its money into universal and inexpensive public services.

Quebec's social services were altered fundamentally by the wave of reforms initiated by the Quiet Revolution of 1960. Previously, services had been provided either by the Catholic Church (to Catholic Quebecers), or via a network of charitable and non-profit agencies (to non-Catholic communities). This changed dramatically as a new team of reformers, based in both the Quebec Liberal Party and the Parti Québécois, took the reins of power in the next decades. Modernizing politicians, bureaucrats and other experts have had a major influence over the shape of policy since 1960, but they have also had to contend with a mobilized civil society that has sometimes had different assessments of the best direction for change. The 1960s reform thrust also intersected with initiatives from Ottawa that were setting all the provinces down some new paths.

During this period in Quebec, the combination of internal and external forces for change was dramatic. The *Social Assistance Act* of 1969 was Quebec's response to the Canada Assistance Plan (CAP), while the *Health and Social Services Act* (1971) established Quebec's universal healthcare system. Both pieces of legislation followed in the tracks of the Castonguay-Nepveu Commission, a major investigatory body that framed the terms of debate about health and social services for several decades. The commission consulted most of the province's key specialists on social policy, both conservative and reformist, and heard from almost every sector of Quebec society.[10]

Despite a new non-categorical social assistance regime that adopted an individualized approach to social security,[11] there was a con-comitant concern about families. One result was a provincial family allowance regime, elaborated in 1969, that did not share with Ottawa the distrust of large families that had shaped federal family allowances since 1946.[12] These family allowances, altered at each moment of reform over the last decades, remain a key pillar of Quebec's family policy.

The Castonguay-Nepveu Commission was very critical of private services, whether non-profit or commercial; it clearly put the accent on public services.[13] Nonetheless, opposition to non-profit provision was somewhat tempered because of the non-statist approach of Quebec's highly mobilized civil society. In the 1960s and continuing today, this movement was traversed by a dense network of community groups, agencies, projects and popular initiatives whose *political project* was and remains to provide services "differently." From the early 1960s, citizens' committees were actively intervening in the social policy domain. They were equally critical of the individualistic "case work" approach of social workers and the charity-based models of religious organizations. They sought instead to provide collective solutions and services that would build local leadership and develop community capacity. While they turned to local governments, as well as to Quebec and Ottawa, for funding and support, their take on social services, as mentioned earlier, was never statist. By the late 1960s these popular-sector groups' *(groupes populaires)* political project was quite explicit. Rather than lobbying for public services, they mobilized self-help groups and community action, creating infrastructure such as legal aid, literacy training and family budgeting programs, child care centres and people's clinics.[14] Unions were also active participants, backing local self-help groups that promoted financial independence among low-income communities by setting up food, child care or other co-ops.

This mobilization, both in cities and rural areas, might have gone the way of contemporaneous collective action throughout North America—that is, towards obscurity—had it not been institutionalized in important locales, two of which are of central importance to this chapter. A central action of the popular-sector movement was establishing daycare centres (garderies). These centres were incorporated as non-profit organizations and run by councils of parents and staff that embraced both democratic and child development goals.

The establishment of such services had also been a major goal of the second wave of the women's movement, since the movement's appearance in the mid-1960s. The Fédération des femmes du Québec (FFQ) at its founding in 1965 included state-provided child care on its list of six demands and continued to agitate for child care, for example, in its brief to the Royal Commission on the Status of Women (RCSW).[15] The Confédération des syndicats nationaux (CSN) also presented a brief to the RCSW centred on child care. Taking things in their own hands, women's and other popular-sector groups used funds from the federal Local Initiative Programme (LIP) to set up non-profit, democratically run, parent-managed centres in disadvantaged areas and other neighbourhoods.[16] These first politicized child care centres have been reclaimed as the model for today's central institution for child care and development, the Early Childhood Centres,[17] created by the 1997 reform.

A second important institution created at this time was the Centre local de services communautaires (CLSC). Modeled on the people's clinics, the CLSC serves as a point of entry to the healthcare system—providing home care (including postpartum care for multiple births), perinatal care, parenting support, and so forth—and is intended to be a pivotal actor in community development projects.[18] The CLSC is in many ways an institutionalized expression of the community-based, progressive approach to health and social services—an approach suspicious of "medical" solutions, professionals, centralization

and commercialization. Employing social animators as well as social workers and healthcare professionals, the CLSC has official responsibility to liaise with the voluntary sector and the community.[19] The CLSC remains a key partner in virtually all programs for children and families, with local CLSCs becoming a crucial link in the family policy chain, working closely with Early Childhood Centres in their catchment area.

In contrast to the popular-sector movement, the government of Quebec was not quick onto the child care field.[20] Its first formal involvement was in 1974, when the temptation of CAP dollars led to subsidies for low-income parents using regulated child care. New legislation in 1979 continued subsidies to low-income parents, established direct subsidies to centres, and created an allowance for the care of children with disabilities. At the same time, the regulatory and licensing body, the Office des services de garde à l'enfance, was created.

Over these same years, despite the philosophy and rhetoric privileging non-profit and community groups, the commercial private sector was not at a standstill, in part because of governmental foot dragging. When the supply of public and non-profit services could not keep up with demand, commercial providers rushed to expand.[21] The mix was always an uneasy one, however, with ministers frequently expressing an aversion to commercial expansion and even seeking to halt it.[22]

Setting Family Policy: Juggling a Variety of Purposes and Multiple Instruments

There has never been consensus on family policy in Quebec. Opinions vary over the most desirable types of services, to be sure. Some vaunt non-profit while others argue for a level playing field for commercial services. Some claim public financing is sufficient, while others believe services must also be publicly delivered. Beyond these controversies, there is always the issue of the birth rate, and whether public policy should be natalist in its goals.

We have already described the positions of the late 1960s and emphasized their continuity with those underpinning the 1997 reform. However, before those community-, child- and democracy-centred positions could become sufficiently strong to launch a new regime, Quebec passed through a controversial period when other ideals triumphed and alternative goals were promoted. In these debates the actors remained the same, but the balance of forces was different. Thus, by the 1970s the women's movement was an important force supported by "femocrats" (feminist bureaucrats and other civil servants) within several ministries as well as the Conseil du statut de la femme. But demographers and the family movement also were influential actors, as were outside experts and bureaucrats from a range of social and economic ministries.

Three years into its first term in office, the Parti Québécois (PQ) government launched what would become a long and vibrant debate about family policy: one that continued through the terms of the succeeding Liberal government, culminating in 1987–88 in a new family policy and two new institutions—the Conseil de la famille (a para-public body responsible for advising the minister) and the Secrétariat à la famille.[23] While it began as a focused discussion of economic growth, including the population size needed to sustain development,[24] the discussion, prompted by the PQ government's economic strategy statement, *Bâtir le Québec* (1979), soon became a wholesale public debate about families, equality and social equity.[25]

Before going any further, it is important to understand the policy context of the mid-1980s, particularly surrounding the 1984 Green Paper, *Pour les familles québécoises,* that framed

the debate and positions later adopted by major provincial actors. In 1984 the PQ government was already actively considering tax reform and strategies for protecting the French language and Quebec culture in the face of a declining birth rate. The tax reform process was tending in the direction of favouring two-parent and working families, while a parliamentary commission, headed by Richard French and reporting in 1985, had a mandate to analyze the demographic situation in the context of cultural policy. The commission proposed a dualistic approach of increasing immigration and fostering a higher birth rate.[26]

Seeing both these policy developments emerging, women's groups were anxious. Despite guaranteeing gender equality in Quebec's 1975 Charter of Rights and Liberties and despite a progressive program to advance equality between the sexes put into place in 1978, in an attempt to deal with cultural challenges the province appeared to be moving back towards traditionalism, via the tax treatment of families.[27] In response, in 1985–86, feminists coming from both the FFQ and the more traditionalist Association féminine d'éducation et d'action sociale (AFEAS) actively intervened in provincewide consultations organized by the touring three-person Consultative Committee on the Green Paper. Women were optimistic that their voices would be heard, because one member of the committee, Nicole Boily, was a feminist who had worked with the FFQ, and another member, Christiane Bérubé, had just ended her term as president of AFEAS.

In addition to tax reformers, natalists and feminists, the debate engaged professionals who had a stake in establishing clear, new norms and gaining additional resources for social work, psychology, health and other social fields.[28] Last but never least, the family movement too was actively involved. This movement of individuals and groups promoting healthy families and family life, has been an important actor for decades.

Renée B. Dandurand describes its two wings:[29] "There is a conservative and Catholic one, very close to the Church. But there is also a liberal wing, which looks to the state to support families, in their diverse needs and their diverse situations." It was with this second, progressive branch of the family movement that the third member of the consultative committee, author Maurice Champagne-Gilbert, was associated.

The consultative committee's reports[30] came down strongly in favour of the principle of shared responsibility between parents and the community. They recognized the variety of situations in which families live, and they downplayed natalism. More generally, the committee argued that there was no crisis of the family. The real challenge, they proposed, was instituting new forms of solidarity between the sexes. In its recommendations, the committee sought to avoid supporting natalist policy, proposing higher levels of spending and more coherent support for families, as well as improved parental leaves, conditions of part-time employment and family allowances. It was strangely silent on the matter of child care, only recommending that (1) the current regime be better organized and that everyone, including employers, do their part and (2) the existing subsidy for low-income families using services be retained.

With the Liberals in government by the time the second report was issued, some adjustments to expectations were inevitable. However, the change from one party to another did not mark a major policy reorientation. The 1987 statement on family policy issued by the ministère de la Santé et des Services sociaux stood on four principles, most of which reflected the general thinking of the consultative committee. The fourth principle was, of course, the exception to the above generalization. The four principles were: (1) providing public support for the costs of child-rearing; (2) fighting poverty; (3) encouraging parents to seek employment; and (4) supporting a higher birth rate.[31]

The second and third principles provided the rationale for needs-based subsidies for child care; tax credits; recurring funding to child care centres; generous maternity and parental leave packages; as well as allowances for young children and income support for working parents. Thus, 1988 also saw the creation of the Parental Wage Assistance program, known as APPORT in French. This program sought to draw both parents into the labour force by providing a wage supplement to families with even a tiny amount (now $100 per month) of earned income and offering extra support for child care expenses.[32]

Principles one and four generated four types of family allowances. One was universal. Others addressed the particular needs of young children and the disabled. Perhaps best known was the birth allowance, whose amount increased to very generous levels for the third child and subsequent children.[33] Birth allowances favouring "the third child" never gained unanimous support, and controversy surrounding them touched all the central issues of Quebec politics. Sustained from the 1980s, these issues ranged from economic development to the role of the state, from immigration to linguistic protection; conservative demographers debated feminist demographers; proponents of social spending confronted neo-liberals; natalists verbally sparred with familialists and feminists. The controversy shook all the major players: the National Assembly; government agencies, such as the Secrétariat à la famille; para-public bodies (including the Conseil du statut de la femme and the Conseil de la famille); the press; and intellectuals.

The post-1987 system was coherent, in the sense that it stood on the four principles listed above, but it was complicated, with a wide variety of different programs. Moreover, while coherent in themselves, as an expression of the goals of family policy, the design did not always mesh well with other governmental goals. There were still problems of linking it to employability measures; there was mounting concern about the "poverty trap" and intergenerational reliance on social assistance.

After its election in 1995, the PQ government, as did its Liberal predecessor, undertook to reform social assistance programs, eventually tabling the very controversial Bill 186 (only passed in June 1998). In one decade, Quebec transformed its social assistance regime into one based on both income support and its own notion of "employability."[34] Because of the limited results rendered from training and other programs and due to rising rates of unemployment and welfare, another large debate on the subject of social assistance was opened. From the beginning, due to policy makers' concerns for single mothers and poor families, child benefits were part of this discussion as was the idea of expanding child care.

In preparation for reforming social assistance, the government asked a group of experts to make proposals for redesigning the system. Eventually, when the experts failed to agree, two disparate reports were published: one by the majority (headed by psychologist Camil Bouchard and hence coined the *Bouchard Report*) and one by the minority (headed by economist Pierre Fournier).[35] Nonetheless, despite their disagreements on a range of other matters, both groups agreed that "children should be removed from social assistance" and both recommended the creation of an integrated family allowance.[36]

Also, the estates-general of Education, after months of touring the province for consultations, in their 1996 report recommended increased and more accessible child care for young children and extended preschool education services. Such services were deemed imperative to combat high drop-out rates and curb school failure in general. The Conseil supérieur de l'éducation made similar recommendations, as did the majority *Bouchard Report*. The experts reminded Quebecers that these proposals were by no means new, citing the *Parent Report* (the Quiet Revolution blueprint for secularizing and modernizing education) that decades earlier recommended kindergarten for four- and five-year-old children.

During this time, the women's movement had also mobilized and the 1995 march for *Pain et Roses* (Bread and Roses) identified child care as a key goal, as did the later interventions of the FFRQ during the Quebec summits of 1996.

The claims and proposals of these expert studies, consultations and groups addressing poverty and promoting gender equality all fed into the major reform of family policy announced at the Summit on the Economy and Employment in 1996. Also, they particularly influenced the White Paper released the following January. That wide-ranging document became the basis for the redesign of family policy and the creation of several new benefits and institutions: unified family allowance, reorganized child care sector, new parental leave and insurance schemes, housing subsidies for low-income families and insurance for prescription drugs.[37] Hence, several decades of engaging debate culminated in one comprehensive document.

Towards a Family Policy with "Children at the Heart of Our Choices"

As we have seen, changes to child care programs in Quebec have always been located in a broader set of family policies. The 1997 reform, perhaps best known for its five dollars-per-day spaces, is no exception here. This shift in funding arrangements, as well as the emphasis on universality and a developmentally appropriate curriculum, is part of a much broader effort to reform social assistance, develop broad-based support for the PQ's political vision, promote gender equality and demonstrate Ottawa's recalcitrance with respect to the federal principle. With such an all-encompassing agenda, it is not surprising that a number of actors considered the reform to be of consequence to their interests.

The first of these actors were the fiscal conservatives, who wanted to achieve a zero deficit and deemed universal family allowances and generous birth allowances a "waste" of state funds. Provided as they were to families whether they "needed" them or not, these allowances prompted those who shared Finance Minister Bernard Landry's overwhelming fear of deficit spending (at least on social programs) to look for a change.

Next on the list of actors was the women's movement. The 1995 March for Bread and Roses mobilization had visited increasing prominence on the movement, and FFQ president, Françoise David, was an important player at the Summit on the Economy and Employment. Movement women now also had ties to women within the state; feminists and social democrats, such as Pauline Marois and Louise Harel, had risen to high cabinet responsibility, and femocrats were scattered throughout the bureaucracy, but perhaps of equal influence was the PQ's desire to assure that no gender gap would interfere with its support in the next referendum.

Other crucial actors in this policy network, often providing the glue that allowed all the parts to hold together, were child development experts. Camil Bouchard, for example, had published a formative document in 1991, *Un Québec fou de ses enfants (Quebec, Mad about its Children)*[38] that it made the case, well before Fraser Mustard had arrived on the scene, that early childhood education was crucial to proper development. Moreover, it argued that poverty and disadvantage were the factors most likely to place children at risk of negative developmental outcomes. In the preparations of the 1997 White Paper, Bouchard helped link domains such as social assistance (recall, he had signed

the majority report of the 1996 expert consultation on social assistance reform), early childhood education and social solidarity.

The White Paper was not preceded by any formal public consultation. It was written by the secretariat of the Committee of Priorities of the Executive Council and signed by one of its members, Pauline Marois, minister of education.[39] The government had judged it important to keep the drafting process under firm control for a number of reasons. First, the major lines of the reform had already been announced at the summit; the government knew what it wanted to do. Second, the direction of reform was not universally popular. The natalist wing of the family movement was not happy with the threat to the birth allowances that the paper posed. Commercial child care operators were also opposed to the reform. Indeed, Minister Marois' concern about the rising importance of commercial child care providers in the system and her decision immediately after the 1995 election to place a moratorium on new licences, both informed the paper. It was, therefore, obvious to the commercial sector that its future was on the line. Third, the government was facing resistance to its parallel reform of social assistance and did not want to open up another line of attack. Finally, the government, as well as the bureaucrats and experts who supported the reform, understood that it made sense only as a package. None of the parts in and of itself was a compelling reform, but together they created a momentum for positive change. Therefore, the whole had to hold together and be held together.

The White Paper made an argument for coherence, presenting a strong case for "integration" across social, educational and employment domains. As a result, family policy is now described as having four main objectives: (1) to ensure fairness by offering universal support to families; (2) to give more assistance to low income families; (3) to facilitate the balancing of parental and work responsibilities; and (4) to foster children's development and equal opportunity.[40]

In the White Paper there was a somewhat great emphasis on promoting employment and equal opportunity. Despite such differences, however, the policy has a number of clear principles; some continue past practices while others break with the past.[41] Family policy pursues its objectives through the following programs: an integrated family allowance, targeted to low-income parents, covering the estimated costs of raising a child from birth to age 18; universality in the tax regime, including a tax exemption for dependent children's basic needs and a non-refundable tax credit for dependent children; parental insurance providing paid parental leaves to virtually all employed new parents; educational and developmental child care services organized by Early Childhood Centres; accessible child care services, via fees of five dollars per day and reduced-cost child care for low-income working parents and 23.5 hours per week free child care for social assistance recipients, in order to ensure that children at-risk use the developmental service; full-day kindergarten for five-year-old children; half-day kindergarten coupled with child care for four-year-olds living in Montreal's disadvantaged neighbourhoods.

The focus on equal opportunity, equity and solidarity across classes is expressed in the integrated family allowance, available to all low-income families with dependent children under eighteen years. It replaces three family allowances[42] and those parts of the social assistance regime that had been paid with respect to children. The amount varies according to the birth order of the child and the number of parents living with the child as well as according to family income. The Family Allowance supplements the Canada Child Tax Benefit (CCTB) that Revenue Canada pays to Quebec families. In other words, if necessary, it tops the CCTB up to Quebec's preferred supplement level. Until 2000 at least, Quebec was among the eight provinces taxing back the CCTB going to families on social assistance. When the federal government increased the amount paid out in the CCTB and its supplement in the 2000 budget, Quebec decided not to tax back all the increase. According to some, the province extended this generosity in an attempt to maintain its financial involvement—that is, visibility—with many families.

The overall assessment of this unification of programs suggests that they keep low-income parents more or less where they were in terms of benefits, as long as these parents stay on social assistance.[43] However, because the benefits are neutral as to employment, there is a gain made by those who are working in a low-paying job. Therefore, reflecting the link to employability goals, the policy offers an incentive to seek employment.

The major losers in this shift to a single, targeted family allowance are middle-income families with more than two children. They no longer could count, for example, on a birth allowance injecting up to $8000 into the family treasury. While middle-income parents lost the previously universal family allowance, they acquired less costly child care. This was a gain for those who used the services, but families who cared for their own children or used informal care received no benefit. Therefore, there has been some dispute about the fairness of the new system, and about whether it recognizes the diversity of family needs.[44]

In contrast to the targeted Family Allowance, an emphasis on universality is evident in several programs maintained by the 1997 reform: the tax exemption for dependent children, the non-refundable credit for the first child of single-parent families and the non-refundable tax credit to all families.[45] This third credit is the only universal tax credit in the country for families with children[46] and it is worth $598 for the first child ($897 for a single-parent family) and $552 for subsequent children. These tax advantages are a key expression of solidarity in the form of universality; the same principle underpins the child care programs.

The 1997 family policy announcement continued Quebec's established tradition of providing the most generous programs of paid maternity leave and unpaid parental leave in Canada.[47] The White Paper also announced that the government would institute a new program of Parental Insurance. This idea of redesigning parental leave, to extend coverage and cleave it from eligibility for Unemployment Insurance, had been promoted by the PQ for almost a decade. It was part of the 1981 election campaign, promoted primarily by Lise Payette, and in 1996 Louise Harel took up the idea once again. The Conseil du statut de la femme had also been pushing for such a change since 1988, when it published a detailed analysis of the gaps in coverage.

Ottawa's 1971 decision to link eligibility for both maternity and parental leave to Unemployment Insurance and the ongoing restructuring of the labour force were of grave consequence to many Quebec women. According to the estimate of the Conseil du statut de la femme (CSF), fully 50 per cent of women who gave birth in Quebec in 1988 were not eligible for paid leave, despite the fact that 72 per cent of Quebec women between ages twenty and thirty-five were employed. This gap resulted from many workers' failure to meet the eligibility requirements of the federal regime. Still, this problem has not been solved by the shift to Employment Insurance, which has further reduced eligibility in some cases, while increasing it in others (such as for part-time employees).[48]

It was in response to this family policy that the White Paper proposed to completely break the link to employment. A new regime, based on earned income rather than duration of work, would make leaves available to any parent who earned at least $2,000 in the year prior to birth.

Management of the program would be transferred to the Régie des rentes, with the funding rate set at 75 per cent of the previous year's income.[49] It also proposed a paternity leave of five weeks, with the rate calculated on the father's income. There would also be an adoption leave of twelve weeks.[50]

In addition to a paternity leave of five weeks, the draft bill sets out two options for parents: forty weeks at 75 per cent replacement of the previous year's earnings or fifty weeks at 70 per cent for the first eighteen weeks and 55 per cent replacement for the remaining thirty-two weeks.[51]

Parental Insurance has not been implemented but it is on its way. Intergovernmental negotiations broke down in March 1997 when Quebec asked Ottawa to transfer a portion of the Employment Insurance funds to the province, while noting that Quebec parents using five-dollar-per-day child care would no longer claim the Child Care Expense Deduction (CCED); thus saving federal dollars. In the face of this failure (and a number of others in the following years), Quebec began to mobilize support. The PQ twice promised a new regime—in the 1998 election campaign and at the March, 1999 National Assembly opening. In May 1999, consultations with employers, unions, and family organizations began on a go-it-alone strategy, and in fall 1999, ministry-led consultations with employers brought agreement in principle.[52] The February 2000 Youth Summit endorsed a "made in Quebec" plan; included in the consensus were not only youth groups but also employers, unions, women's groups and so on. In the face of continued rejection by Ottawa and a growing mobilization in Quebec, Minister of State, Pauline Marois, tabled Bill 140 on June 6, 2000. In presenting the bill, the minister cited as her impetus the "historic demand of women's groups" and other socioeconomic groups, as well as the consensus expressed at the summits of 1996 and 2000.

Getting to Five-Dollar-per-Day Child Care and the Early Childhood Centres

Of course the White Paper did not only address parental leave; a major dimension of the family policy reform of 1997 was the redesign of child care delivery. Until 1997, Quebec shared with most other provinces a mixed-bag approach to child care services, providing regulated daycare centres *(garderies)* and family daycare *(garde au milieu familial),* as well as unregulated nursery schools, drop-in centres *(haltes garderies)* and school-based child care all under the jurisdiction of the Ministry of Education.[53] In 1995, the licensing body (the Office des services de garde à l'enfance—OSGE) imposed a moratorium on new licences because department officials and the minister responsible were concerned about the commercial sector's increasing role in the overall system. The 1997 reform ended that moratorium but, more importantly, it created a new institution, the Early Childhood Centre *(Centre de la petite enfance).*[54]

Once up and running as intended throughout the province, these centres will mark a major shift from established thinking about young children, about work and family and about the transition to school. The centres are governed as a non-profit corporation, with parents a majority on the governing council. Offering different kinds of child care, they incorporate under a single roof both the traditional centre-based *garderies* (for at least seven children) and the supervisory responsibility of family daycare.[55] The family daycare option tends to be selected for infants (almost half of all children under twelve months old are in a family daycare) and older children who are in kindergarten part of the day. Centre-based care predominates among two- to four-year-old children,[56] and centres may also take school-age children who do not have access to an after-school facility. Efforts have been made to make Early Childhood Centres widely available. There are twenty centres operating in Aboriginal communities, and an agreement is being developed to transfer administrative responsibility for governing these services to the Kativik Regional Government. Services are also available in the far north, including in Inuktitut.[57]

Other family daycare providers have access to the resources and educational programs of the neighbourhood Early Childhood Centre. The centres, in collaboration with other agencies, offer a variety of programs to the broader community. Most often these collaborations include that other important Quebec institution, the CLSC (Centre local des services communautaires).

Probably the best known result of the child care reform is the provision of truly affordable child care, set at a standard rate—paid by all parents regardless of their income—of five dollars per day, or twenty-five dollars per week for full-time daycare, up to ten hours a day. The province fills the gap between fees and operating costs with direct grants to the centres. The money for financing the program was found, among other places, in the cancellation of the tax deduction for child care expenses. As sufficient low-cost spaces become available, parents can no longer deduct child care expenses from their provincial income taxes. Nor can they claim the federal CCED, as providers do not issue receipts.

Beginning in 1997, four-year-olds were offered low-cost spaces, with care for three-year-olds and after-school care covered in September 1998. The program aimed to reach newborns by the year 2001, but the schedule was sped up, so that, as of September 2000 the five dollar-per-day rate was universally available to parents of any child in a centre, family daycare or after-school care.[58]

Parents on social assistance, with preschool children over age two or children with a medical certificate prescribing attendance, have access to free child care for twenty-three and a half hours a week in a centre or in family daycare. Clearly, the goal here is to prevent parents' exclusion from the labour force from hindering their child's development. The Ministry of Social Solidarity will pay for child care hours in excess of twenty-three and a half for parents on social assistance participating in employability programs. Finally, parents eligible for the income supplement program (the Parental Wage Assistance Program) receive a three dollar-per-day subsidy that reduces their fees to only ten dollars a week per child.

Such encouragement, by means of free or very low-cost care, illustrates child care policy's direct and unabashed basis on the principle of enabling all parents, even those with low earning capacity to enter the labour force. All parents on social assistance with children aged two and older are now classified as "employable." But there are also inducements—and significant assistance—for these parents to use not only regulated child care but care with a strong educational content.

Early childhood education and development is clearly a focus of this reform, promoting school readiness for all children and seeking to overcome the learning disadvantages often associated with low income and poverty. Early childhood education is defined as the key program for successfully integrating children into society, for school readiness, and for preventing problems later in life. Thus, Early Childhood Centres have a strong educational mandate, based on a new, provincewide program. Tailored to different age groups, the program is based on techniques of learning through play.[59]

Developmental priorities also underpin the extension of kindergarten in September 1997 to a full day for five-year-olds. While compulsory schooling is begun at age six and kindergarten attendance is optional, over 98 per cent of five-year-old children do attend full-day programs.

In addition, four-year-olds living on the island of Montreal in areas designated as "disadvantaged" have access to half-day junior kindergarten and educational child care. This differential treatment of certain four-year-olds is the only part of the program which is not universal.

This new educational emphasis demanded some serious attention be paid to improving the credentials of child care workers and raising their wages. The former is long overdue; Quebec's regulations for staff ratios and training are among the least demanding in the country. Indeed, in 1999, 23 per cent of Early Childhood Centres did not meet the licensing requirements for trained workers.[60] In response, new training programs are being developed. For example, managers of child care facilities may enroll in a program developed by the Université de Québec à Montréal (UQAM), while family daycare providers can now be trained in a provincewide distance learning program through Quebec's Télé-Université.

Wages have been paid some attention—they were raised after workers threatened to strike in the spring of 1999. Seeking to avoid the disruption such a strike would provoke, the government settled with the union, affiliated to the CSN, after a series of short stoppages and well-publicized threats. Wages have been improved by an average of 38 per cent, and the ministry has allowed Early Childhood Centres to increase the income of family daycare providers.[61] Despite the hoopla, the starting salary of a child care worker with a junior college (CEGEP) diploma will be only a modest $25,000 (currently it is $20,293). Nevertheless, the ministry reports a 56 per cent enrolment increase in such programs.[62]

Critics and Responses

The new family policy, along with the child care component, has many supporters, not least of which are its designers and promoters inside the state. However, there is also a good deal of popular support. During the 1998 election campaign, Jean Charest criticized the five-dollar-per-day program as "not meeting the needs of all parents." In less than thirty-six hours the item had disappeared from the campaign agenda, as negative reactions and objections swamped the Liberal leader.

This said, there are still critics. First are those parents who cannot get a space for their child. While any parent may use child care, centres still ration access, via waiting lists and so on, as there are not enough spaces to meet demand. In 1998–99, for example, the number of spaces increased by 17 per cent overall. There were major differences across regions, however, with rural and peripheral regions benefiting particularly. For example, spaces in Montreal increased by 6 per cent, while those in the region Nord du Québec rose from 356 in 1996–97 to 712 in 1998–99. Spaces in Nord du Québec rose again by 68 per cent in 1999–2000, and that same year spaces in the Côte Nord increased by 35 per cent.[63]

Often parents with "atypical needs" still do not have their needs met, and they must resort to all the usual forms of unregulated care, including drop-in centres or unlicensed kindergartens. However, several pilot projects announced in 2000 sought to provide services twenty-four hours a day for shift workers. This promise had been included in the 1997 White Paper but was previously left aside.

The constant pressure to create new spaces remains. Waiting lists continue to grow, despite the increase of spaces. Indeed, the auditor general reported a shortfall of 135,213 places in March 1999; of the 229,323 children needing a space, only 94,110 had one.[64] In response, the government claimed, in June 2000, to have added 34,000 spaces over the previous two years, or 300 a week for the years 1999–2000.[65] The government's future target is 12,000 new early childhood educator jobs by 2005.

This juggling of numbers and targets represents, in part, the difficulty of predicting demand. The initial calculations that informed the White Paper were based on a survey done under the old regime, in 1993–94.[66] Many more parents than anticipated appeared at the doors of Early Childhood Centres seeking to transfer their children into educationally focused programs from the informal care or other arrangements they were currently using.

Among critical parents are those who have lost ground under this new program. And they have not hesitated to make their voices heard. One such group is those who saw their tax deductions disappear; parents employing nannies and in-home babysitters or using unregulated but receipted care could no longer deduct those expenses from their Quebec taxes (of course they retained the federal deduction). Parents also complain that, in this competitive market for spaces, centres are charging additional fees (registration fees are an example) or hiding higher costs in "program fees." Therefore, parents charge, the promise of fixed costs may in some cases be illusory.

A second important critic has been the auditor general, who issued a damning report in 1999. The report criticized the ministry for general mismanagement, as well as for its lack of evaluation criteria of the central goals, that is, child development and school readiness. Beyond these somewhat accountantlike criticisms were others going to the heart of the matter. The auditor general found an increased use of family daycare—from 26 per cent of spaces in 1996 to 34 per cent in 1999.[67] Yet, the oversight, with respect to educational content, sometimes appeared more "virtual" than real. The report also pointed out that Quebec still lacked the administrative capacity to issue licences to drop-in centres and private kindergartens. Yet this type of service was still providing a fair amount of child care, filling the above-described gap between supply and demand.

The ministry has responded to the criticisms about training and has established a task force to investigate the "contribution" of drop-in centres.[68] Nonetheless, there are still gaps in the capacity to regulate and to manage the system.

A third, vociferous and long-standing critic is composed of the other major losers under the new regime; many commercial operators, with their limited access to grants, have difficulty making ends meet. These actors, whom the minister made no bones about preferring to see play a more diminished role, have been hard hit. The original White Paper had suggested that commercial providers would be phased out, but after a major mobilization and the sobering recognition that without them there would not be enough available spaces, a compromise was eventually struck. Existing commercial operators now receive public funds, but at a lower rate than public facilities, via an agreement in which the government rents spaces. Since 1997, there has been a five-year moratorium on new licences. Owners have also been offered the possibility of transforming their businesses into centres, by selling to a non-profit association of parents that would form the governing body. The mishandling of these transformations forms another of the auditor general's criticisms. The process is cumbersome and slow, and in the meantime the ministry is closing its eyes to illegal operators, as it can not afford to lose spaces.[69]

A fourth set of critics comes from within the family movement. These opponents of the 1997 design do support state spending on children and families. However, they would prefer to see the generosity that Quebec directs toward child care diverted to a universal family allowance, recognizing the contributions to society of all parents. Thus, in a dramatic winter 2000 re-release of a study originally published during the 1998 ice storm, the Institute for Research on Public Policy[70] reported that three-quarters of families received less money under the new regime than under the previous one.

The authors were critical of the government's actions in abandoning universal family allowances and substituting allowances targeted at low-income parents. They recommended, as in the traditional French system, generous and universal family allowances for *all* parents, in the name of horizontal redistribution across families, rather than vertical redistribution from better-off to low-income families.

However, this group's recommendation with respect to child care was an about-face. The authors claimed that child care should be universal instead of market driven, allowing parents to choose whether to pay for care or provide it themselves, as well as to select the type they preferred.

These two positions exactly oppose those adopted by the government in 1996–97. The government policy sought to build solidarity via universality and to invest in children's development in the realm of child care, while it expressed a commitment to equity with its targeted family allowances. In part, the divergence comes from differing assessments of two elements of the family policy mix. One is clearly the educational component of child care. The authors of the IRPP study[71] insist that "parents know best" about the quality of care and that governments should not be in the business of establishing standards for credentials or programs.[72] Thus, the editor's note, signed by Carole Vincent of the IRPP, makes a plea not only for greater choice but for re-valuing parental care. She summarily writes, "Indeed it is difficult to argue that the benefits generated by daycare services exceed those generated by parental care."[73]

The government, in contrast, inspired by the literature on child psychology and early childhood development, takes another position. It attributes value added to quality child care services, not only for disadvantaged children but for all children. Thus, the program seeks to overcome the threat to some children posed by their parents' circumstances, such as living in poverty, or from the failure to diagnose and intervene early enough when a child exhibits developmental and other delays. In addition, the government sees the educational content of the program as greatly promoting school readiness for all children.

A second difference between the positions of the IRPP and the government is evident in the attention to matters of equality, especially gender equality. Even if there has been a discernible decline in the rhetoric of gender equality in the post-1997 family policy, as compared to its predecessors, the argument is still present. Therefore, the design of parental insurance, child care and family allowances reflects, *inter alia*, attention to gender inequalities in the labour market, for all

women, whether low-income single mothers or professionals living in two-parent families. The IRPP report, in contrast, is virtually silent on matters of gender equality—never the strong suit of the family movement.

This last comparison takes us back to the fundamental issues raised for decades by women's movements and experts in child development. From this somewhat lengthy comparison of two positions promoted in the ongoing and lively debate about child care and family policy in Quebec, we can appreciate the fact that these issues are not settled. While the new regime has widespread support, its critics both inside the state and in civil society are not without influence. Childcare in Quebec, as elsewhere, remains a work in progress.

Notes

1 This chapter is part of a larger project supported by a SSHRC research entitled Citizenship Regimes and New Social Unions: Learning from Caring.

2 The press at the time made such arguments. See, for example, Cloutier 1996 and Charette 1996.

3 "Family Policy History." Available at www.famille-enfance.gouv.qc.ca.

4 See the press at the time. For a recent review of the Summit declarations, see the Auditor General's 1999 report (Vérificateur Général 1999: para 4.16), available at www.vgq.gouv.qc.ca.

5 Jenson and Stroick 1999a: 2–3 provide one such list.

6 Boisvert 2000: 3.

7 In its own documentation in English, the ministry translates its name as Ministry of Child and Family Welfare. We will use this translation as well.

8 Vaillancourt 1988: 144.

9 Vaillancourt 1988: 151.

10 Lesemann 1981.

11 Boychuk 1998: 84.

12 Bergeron 1997: 261–68.

13 Vaillancourt 1988: 147–49; 151.

14 Bélanger and Lévesque 1992: 715–24.

15 Collectif Clio 1992: 464.

16 Desjardins 1991: Ch 3; Lamoureux 1992: 699.

17 See Boisvert 2000: 5, who says of the new ECC: "I would be remiss if I failed to mention the beginnings of these child care centres. The current network was created out of parent-run day care centres and home day care providers who formed agencies responsible for their management. The collaborative spirit between educators and parents has been maintained, protected—I would even say made a priority."

18 The CLSCs resemble the "people's clinics" in many ways, especially in the emphasis on empowerment of communities through mobilization and action. Nonetheless, several of the groups running "people's clinics" (which were staffed by a mix of medically-trained personnel, social animators and volunteers) opposed Bill 65 which established the CLSCs because they saw them as excessively statist (Bélanger and Lévesque 1992: 721–22).

19 Roy 1987.

20 Baillargeon 1996.

21 Vaillancourt 1988: 161.

22 Jenson and Phillips 2000.

23 A Secrétariat à la politique familiale was set up in 1984, but reorganized and renamed in 1988.

24 The emergence of concerns about the birth rate is hardly surprising, given the fact that in the single

decade from 1961 to 1971, the average Quebec family fell from four to two children, while in the mid-1980s the birth rate dropped to 1.4 (Dandurand 1992: 368).

25 Jenson 1998.

26 Academic demographers, always important actors in this policy network in Quebec, had been writing of the demographic crisis for years. The Parliamentary Commission, reporting in September 1985, had a mandate to "study the cultural, social, and economic impact of current demographic tendencies for the future of Quebec as a distinct society" (Dandurand 1987: 354).

27 Dandurand 1987: 353.

28 Ibid: 355.

29 1987: 355–56.

30 These were *Le soutien collectif réclamé pour les familles québécoises. Rapport de la consultation sur la politique familiale* (1985) and *Le soutien collectif recommandé pour les parents québécois. Rapport de la consultation sur la politique familiale* (1986). The move from "families" to "parents" signals the shift in perspective that the Committee was trying to provoke.

31 Lefebvre 1998: 221.

32 Beauvais and Jenson 2001: Appendix A, Table 8.

33 The *prime à la naissance* was profoundly natalist in design: $500 for the first and second births (which in 1989 became $1,000 for the second birth). In 1988, third births brought $3,000, in 1989 $4,500 and, until 1997, $8,000 spread over five years. Prior to the 1997 reform, the basic family allowances and young child allowance also rose with the number of children.

34 Noël 1996.

35 Ibid 1996.

36 Lefebvre 1998: 215–16.

37 Rose 1998.

38 MSSS 1991.

39 Her executive assistant and the chief negotiator throughout this process was Nicole Boily, who had been a member of the 1984–86 Consultative Committee and who would subsequently be named President of the Conseil de la famille et de l'enfance.

40 These three goals are constantly reiterated in a range of documents. This English version is from Boisvert 2000: 4. Sometimes, however, the first and second are merged, to generate three main objectives (see, for example, "Family Policy History," available at www.famille-enfance.gouv.qc.ca).

41 Current information about the programs can be obtained from "Family Policy History." Available at www.famille-enfance.gouv.qc.ca.

42 A separate allowance for children with disabilities is still available.

43 Rose 1998.

44 IRPP 2000; Vérificateur Général 1999.

45 There are also a range of other tax benefits for families with children. For the details and comparisons to other provinces, see Beauvais and Jenson 2001: Appendix A, Tables 10, 12.

46 Clarke 1998: 13.

47 In 1978, Quebec created a Maternity Allowance. This benefit provides coverage for the first two weeks of maternity leave not covered by federal Unemployment Insurance (now Employment Insurance). Quebec also has the most generous unpaid parental leave in Canada. In 1990, new parents, both birth and adopting, could access 34 weeks of unpaid parental leave; the unpaid leave was extended to 52 weeks in 1997. For a comparison with the other provinces, see Beauvais and Jenson 2001: Appendix A, Table 4.

48 This estimate of eligibility is also made by the Canadian Labour Congress. It reports that between 1988 and 2000, the percentage of new mothers eligible for UI or EI parental benefits remained at just under 50 per cent, despite the extension of EI to part-time workers (Beauvais and Jenson, 2001: 9).

49 This idea of a separate *caisse* for parental leave, as well as extended coverage, had been promoted by the PQ for a number of years. See *La Gazette des femmes* 1996.

50 Lepage and Moisan 1998.

51 See Ministère de la Famille et de l'Enfance 2000.

52 Québec 2000: Vol. III, 133.

53 Childcare Resource and Research Unit 1997: 25.

54 The Ministry's documentation in English calls these "child care centres" but I believe "early childhood centre" is a better translation, both because it makes a distinction between what has become the term in many places for *any* daycare centre and because it makes the link to "early childhood development" which is a major part of their mission.

55 Family day care providers can care for up to six children, or nine if they have an adult assistant. For details about the Early Childhood Centres, see *Les centres de la petite enfance* or the overview in "Family Policy—Educational and Childcare Services," both available at www.famille-enfance.gouv.qc.ca.

56 Québec 1999: 130.

57 Boisvert 2000: 7.

58 Québec 2000: Vol. III, 132.

59 One of the major criticisms launched against Quebec's program is its failure to truly live up to this promise. With most attention paid to creating enough spaces, including at a high rate in family daycare, the spotlight has not been kept consistently on supervising the implementation of the educational program. This is one of the criticisms of the Auditor General, for example (for an overview, see Lacroix 2001).

60 Vérificateur Général 1999: para 4. 65.

61 Québec 2000: Vol. III, 132.

62 See Ministère de la Famille et de l'Enfance 2000.

63 Lacroix 2001: 90.

64 Vérificateur Général 1999: para 4.45.

65 The first figure is from Boisvert 2000: 7 and the second from Ministère de la Famille et de l'Enfance 2000.

66 Vérificateur Général 1999: para 4.48.

67 Vérificateur Général 1999: para 4.53.

68 Ministry, communiqué de presse, June 22, 2000.

69 Vérificateur Général 1999: para 4.77 ff.

70 IRPP 2000.

71 IRPP 2000: 28–29.

72 They concede a role for regulation of health and safety, however.

73 IRPP 2000: 3.

Index

debt and deficit

alternative policy directions, 496–498

alternative radical analysis of causes of crisis, 489, 493–496

arguments for debt, 488–489

balanced budgets, 490

bond rating agencies, 493

challenge to political-economic assumptions, 496

counter-cyclical deficits, 495

"debt wall," non-existence of, 493

foreign-owned share of, 492

full-employment strategy, 496–498

growth of, 490

historical causes of, 493–496

institutional changes, maximum program of, 496–498

interest payments, 491

minimum employment program, 496–498

operating surplus, 491

"permanent recession" strategy, 493–496

political culture, shift in, 488

postwar debt, 489

"repatriation" as solution, 492

scope and consequences of debt crisis, 490–493

slash-and-burn approach to deficit-reduction, 488, 489

social welfare programs, lack of correlation with, 491

structural deficits, creation of, 495

Delaney, John, 29

Delaney, Theresa, 30

Delisle, Esther, 221

demographic revolution in 1900s, 188

Dempsey, Hugh, 23

Department of Fisheries
Atlantic salmon fishery. *See* Atlantic salmon fishery

Department of Indian Affairs, establishment of, 25

Department of Marine and Fisheries, patronage in, 41–42

Department of Regional Economic Expansion (DREE), 398–399, 400

dependants' relief legislation, 143

The Descent of Man (Darwin), 175

L

Le Devoir, 311, 312

D

Dewart, E.H., 176–177, 179, 180, 181

Dewdney, Edgar, 27

Diefenbaker, John, 435
and economic nationalism, 56

Dion, Joe, 31

Dippie, Brian W., 277

Diva, 483

Domestic Workers' Union, 110

Dominion Coal Company, 226–227

Dominion Steel Corporation, 227, 228–229, 235

Dorion, Noël and Frédéric, 311

dower, 139

Dower Act (Alta.), 144

Dower Act (Man.), 146

dower legislation, 140–148

Dreyfus, Alfred, 163

Drouin, Oscar, 308

Drummond, Henry, 176

Dryden, Ken, 442, 443, 444, 445, 447

Duncan, Sara Jeanette, 79

Duplessis, Maurice, 306, 312, 313, 331

E

Earle, Neil, 331

East Indian immigrants
exclusion within labour movement, 100–115
women. *See* South Asian women

economic nationalism, 55–64

the economy
Canadian commercial exchanges, 393

capitalist as hero, 61

deliberate stagnation strategy, 494

distribution of persons working, by sectors, 395

economic nationalism, 55–64

free-trade recession, 494

industrial and manufacturing sector, 48

Klondike gold rush, 65–75

manufacturing industries, index of concentration, 396

mercantilism, 61

and patronage system, 48

peripheral nature of, 392–396

"permanent recession," 493–496

protectionism, 55–64

public debt and deficit. *See* debt and deficit

slow development of industry, 48

Edwards, Henrietta, 143

Eisendrath, Maurice, 213

Eldorado (creek), 69

élite theory, 63

Emerson, Ralph Waldo, 198–199